Reviews

Anne Baring's *magnum opus*, twenty years in the making, is one of the publishing events of the year: brilliant, profound and magisterial in its scope. In it she addresses the real cultural roots of our multifaceted crisis — spiritual, psychological, ecological, social, political and economic. Much attention since 2008 has been directed to the economic symptoms that are now translating into a widespread social malaise, but few commentators have plumbed the depths as this book does and called for a radically new outlook. For too long the soul and the feminine principle have been marginalised and suppressed, but Anne Baring's life experience and passionate engagement have enabled her to understand and articulate the imbalance in our Western culture and show how it can be overcome. The book is a symbol of hope and renaissance - essential reading for anyone wishing to understand the patterns of Western cultural history and the potentials of its future development.

David Lorimer,
The Scientific and Medical Network

Anne Baring is a lyrical writer. Why? Because she is able not only to amass a vast body of scholarship, and then to order it and produce lucid clarity; but then comes her real genius. Her real genius is to see the light that wants to come through — through the volumes, through the centuries, through the history, the myths and the legends. And her ability to make sense of human experience, and to express it as lyrically as she does, throws essential light on our present condition. This is contemporary politics as it should be applied by leaders. This is history as it should be taught in schools, to liberate the imaginative souls of children. This is insight and inspiration to open the minds and the hearts of twenty-first century adults. This book will change your perspective on what it is to be human, and enable you to see the opportunity that we humans now have, to evolve. Just read the Introduction and you'll see. This book is a goldmine.

Scilla Elworthy,
founder of the Oxford Research Group (1982) and Peace Direct (2002) was awarded the Niwano Peace Prize in 2003. She is a Councillor of the World Future Council and a member of the steering Committee of *PAX*, a service to help prevent wars and genocide.

Anne Baring has devoted her life to humanity's recovery of the *anima mundi* – the soul of the world, and indeed its own soul. *The Dream of the Cosmos* is the climax of that quest, the fruit of a lifetime of thought and feeling, learning and vision. It is the story of a dramatic personal journey, but also an attempt to confront the greatest issues facing our time. Every page breathes her moral passion, her love of beauty, her spiritual aspiration, her deep care for the Earth. Above all, Anne Baring calls for a fundamental transformation in the way human beings live on this Earth and with each other. It would not be too much to say that this book is a *cri de coeur* from a place deep in the collective psyche that carries not only our past but our future. *The Dream of the Cosmos* pulses with the fierce tenderness and grave urgency of love for an infinitely precious new being struggling to be born.

Richard Tarnas,
author of *The Passion of the Western Mind* and *Cosmos and Psyche*

As Anne Baring writes in her opening, this book is a vocation. It is the *opus magnum* for which one might say, without exaggeration, that Anne has incarnated in this lifetime to produce for the benefit of many. *The Dream of the Cosmos* is at once both a visionary autobiography including many of Anne's own dreams, and a comprehensive archetypal history of the constellation, separation from, and resurgence of the feminine. Included in this deep scholarship are profound insights into the origins of misogyny as well as the soulful claims of instinct and its dangerous shadows expressed in violence and oppression. Anne leads us on a remarkable journey to understand the roots of our current suffering and the way forward to embrace a new and necessary sacred vision of reality — one supported by the new sciences — that includes the whole of nature and the cosmos. If you read only one book in the next decade, this encyclopaedic volume is the one you should read.

Veronica Goodchild,
author of *Songlines of the Soul: Pathways to A New Vision for a New Century*

Anne Baring is one of the great pioneers on the Divine Feminine of our time. Her work is a marvellous marriage of profound learning, deep and mature mystical experience and a vivid immediate gift of communication. Her latest book, *The Dream of the Cosmos*, is the consummation of her life's work, twenty years in the making. It is a masterpiece that will last a long time and deserves to be read by all seekers and anyone interested in the birth of a new civilization out of the chaos of our time.

Andrew Harvey,
author of *Return of the Mother* and *Radical Passion*

"Truth has to appear only once, in one single mind, for it to be impossible for anything ever to prevent it from spreading universally and setting everything ablaze."

— Pierre Teilhard de Chardin

Anne Baring (b. 1931) MA Oxon. Ph.D (hons) is a Jungian Analyst — author and co-author of seven books including, as Anne Gage (1961), *The One Work: A Journey Towards the Self;* with Jules Cashford (1992), *The Myth of the Goddess: Evolution of an Image*; (1993 and 2002), *The Birds Who Flew Beyond Time;* with Andrew Harvey (1995), *The Mystic Vision: Daily Encounters with the Divine* and (1996), *The Divine Feminine;* with Scilla Elworthy (2009), *Soul Power: an Agenda for a Conscious Humanity;* and (2013, 2017 and 2020), *The Dream of the Cosmos: A Quest for the Soul.*

Her work is devoted to the recognition that we live in an ensouled world and to the restoration of the lost sense of communion between us and the invisible dimension of the Cosmos that is the source or ground of all that we call 'life'. Her website is devoted to the affirmation of a new vision of reality and the issues facing us at this crucial time of choice.

www.annebaring.com

THE
DREAM of
the COSMOS
A
QUEST for the SOUL

A Prayer for the New Millennium
© Anne Baring

At the threshold of this new millennium may the Holy Spirit of Wisdom awaken us to a deeper sense of relationship with the Earth, with each other, and with the hidden dimensions of life still veiled from our sight.

May Her Light and Love shine through our hearts and illumine our minds. May She help us to become aware of the oneness and sacredness of life and to care for our neighbour as our self.

May She inspire us to be protectors rather than destroyers of life. May She forgive us for the sacrifice of the lives of billions of men, women and children and may their souls be released from the terror, grief, loneliness and despair in which they died in the recent and distant past.

May She help us to recognize and transform evil and to respond to the torment of all persecuted peoples as if it were our own. May She help us to see that evil is the willingness to inflict terror, pain, humiliation, torture or death on other human beings.

May She heal those who are unable to love and who carry a deep wound caused by intolerable suffering in childhood. May they be released from the compulsion to inflict pain and suffering on others.

May She free us from bondage to political and religious fanaticism whose devastating legacy we witness today. May She guide us to choose conscious leaders who serve the true needs of all peoples and all species on this planet.

May She help us to find the courage and determination to restrain the greed that is destroying the Earth's ecosystem and exploiting its resources for the benefit of our species alone. May She inspire us to offer our lives in service of the great web of living relationships that is Her life and the life of the Cosmos.

May She give us the humility, wisdom, strength and compassion to accomplish the Great Work of transmuting our nature from base metal into gold.

THE
DREAM of
the COSMOS
A
QUEST for the SOUL

Anne Baring

Illustrations
Robin Baring

ARCHIVE
publishing

2020

First published in 2013 in the United Kingdom by
Archive Publishing
Shaftesbury, Dorset, England

Designed at Archive Publishing by Ian Thorp MA

© 2013, 2017, 2020 Archive Publishing
Text © Anne Baring, 2013, 2017, 2020

Anne Baring asserts the moral right to be identified as the author of this work

A CIP Record for this book is available from
The British Cataloguing in Publication data office

ISBN 978 1 906289 23 2 (Hardback)
ISBN 978 1 906289 24 9 (Paperback)

Reprinted 2015
Reprinted 2017

Revised and updated Edition 2020

ISBN 978 1 906289 48 5 (Paperback)

Reprinted 2021
Reprinted 2022

The drawings inside the book are reproduced by courtesy of the
artist, Robin Baring, Alresford, Hampshire.
www.robinbaring.com

The Pleiades: deep-space photographic image created by
Greg Parker, New Forest Observatory, UK and Noel Carboni, Florida, USA

www.archivepublishing.co.uk

Printed and bound in England,
by CMP (UK) Ltd.

Acknowledgements

I would like to express my deepest gratitude to my husband for his love and support through more than sixty years of marriage. As well as my close family and my daughter and grandson, deep soul connections have developed with a few people whose trust, encouragement and precious friendship have helped me to bring this book to completion — in particular, Jules Cashford, Scilla Elworthy, Veronica Goodchild, Belinda Hunt, Betty Kovács, Kimberley Saavedra, Paul Hague, Douglas Hamilton, Andrew Harvey, David Lorimer and Richard Tarnas. My gratitude also extends to all the authors whose books have contributed to my understanding and the publishers who have published them. Last but not least, I would like to thank my publisher, Ian Thorp, who has helped this book to see the light of day.

This book is dedicated to
my husband Robin, my daughter Francesca, and my grandson Hamish.

The human heart can go the length of God,
Dark and cold we may be, but this
Is no winter now. The frozen misery
Of centuries breaks, cracks, begins to move;
The thunder is the thunder of the floes,
The thaw, the upstart Spring.
Thank God our time is now when wrong
Comes up to face us everywhere.
Never to leave us till we take
The longest stride of soul men ever took.
Affairs are now soul size,
The enterprise
Is exploration into God.
Where are you making for? It takes
So many thousand years to wake
But will you wake for pity's sake?

— Christopher Fry
A Sleep of Prisoners 1945

Contents

Prologue

CIVILIZATION
by
William Anderson

All civilizations possess in their beginnings one feature in common: they present a new image of Man. In each case the image and the way it is manifested will vary according to the resources and the needs of the epoch. For Periclean Athens a new ideal of man was presented in the form of drama, publicly in the tragedies of the great playwrights and for private reading in the dialogues of Plato. At the beginning of the Christian era a completely new conception of man, of man who forgives and loves his enemies and is at one with his Father, was given to the world in the form of the Gospels. Within the different stages of other religions such as Hinduism or Buddhism, we can point to the many stages of renewal of the ideal of the realized man, as given, in the one case, in the *Upanishads* and the *Bhagavad Gita* and, in the other, to the portrayals, in painting and sculpture, of the Bodhisattvas.

In every case it can be shown that the new image arises to transcend the conflicts of the age and to resolve dualisms through a fresh conception of the unity of man with his Maker and the natural world. It is as though the deepest power in the soul of humanity, welling over with compassion and concern for the struggles and divisions of men, surges up with a vision of all that has been lost or disregarded, of infinite possibilities of thoughts and emotions, of achievements that could be encompassed, and of new directions and vocations to which men might aspire.

The means by which each civilization has flourished and left its mark have depended on certain men and women turning in their need to the springs of consciousness and creation which they share at the deepest levels with all humanity. They are the interpreters of the dreams of their fellow men, the clear-sighted namers of the ruling symbols, the archetypes of power, whose raw energies must be purified and directed by the prayers and contemplations of the saint, by the courage and expressive capacities of the poet and the artist, and the rationality and speculative genius of the philosopher and the scientist.

The purpose of civilization is to conquer barbarism, which is the condition of living in a state of fear. A great civilization provides, on the scale of nations, the expression of love, a basis of security, the sharing of experience, and hope for this life and the next. It allows the development of talents that would languish in small enclosed societies preoccupied solely with self-preservation. Cicero's name for the higher pursuits of civilization was *humanitas*, a term that was familiar to the scholars of the Middle Ages and one that centres all studies and skills on the fully developed nature of man.

Civilization may be seen as the application of conscious will to the amorphous energies of the human psyche, diverting those energies away from their dissipation in fear and war into peaceful and fruitful ends. The technology of a civilization has always been employed to develop methods of attack and defence for the preservation of society, in other words to provide security from physical fear, but true civilization deals with fear at the deeper levels of the mind. Technology, seen in this way, is, in the first place, a matter of the spirit. Behind the social, political, and economic forces that dictate the life of humankind are the infinitely more powerful archetypal powers of the psyche, and it is by drawing these powers into the light of consciousness and giving them direction that the artist, the thinker, and the man of religion, free us from the superstition, the fear, and the prejudices by which our lives are otherwise ruled.

The Gothic era was the effect of men working together in a common spirit in which their religion, their art, their philosophy, and their science and technology were in harmony. For the opposite effect in the present century, one can point to the achievements of the international body of physicists, who, freed from an out-worn religion, careless of art, taking from philosophy its intellectual and logical rigour but not its speculative and moral purpose, made of their science and its applications so powerful a weapon for investigating and changing the natural world that their knowledge became desirable to governments and administrators. Lacking the support of all the other higher forms of knowledge and of inspiration which they had rejected as superstitious or irrelevant, knowing no moral imperative except the furtherance of their science, they sold themselves in exchange for government support to the forces of barbarism. In the determinist philosophy guiding modern science, there is no sanction for the working of conscience.

The great art of the Gothic masters lives under the same shadow as modern man: the threat of destruction so complete that, should any of them survive as ruins as beautiful and haunting as those of Rievaulx and St-Jean des Vignes at Soissons, the men and women who also survive will be sunk into a barbarism so absolute that in their struggle to live there will be no learning to preserve their history, no time to contemplate the message of their remaining fragments. Yet to help in the avoidance of such disaster, these great buildings, the greatest works of art achieved by our western civilization, can still challenge us with the transfor-mation of hatred and barbarism into love and civilization brought about by our ancestors, saying to us, 'We were made the images of man for our time in his wholeness, in his beauty, in the identity of his true self with his creator. What image of man will you construct that will be the vocation of a new civilization, bringing harmony to the dualism of materialism and the needs of the soul, transforming fear and hatred into love, and returning the spontaneity of joy to art?'

from *The Rise of the Gothic* (1985) Hutchinson, London, pp. 85, 9, 22, 199

There is a beautiful passage in another book by the same author, called *The Face of Glory: Creativity, Consciousness and Civilization*. He died shortly after writing it but left these words as his legacy:

> Creation begins and continues as a single sound. That sound includes all ideas, meanings and all expressions of meaning and all possible languages. It is Universal Consciousness letting itself be known as the Word. That sound holds within itself all rhythms, melodies, chords and all the possibilities of music. It is Universal Consciousness letting itself be known as song.
>
> That sound resonates in eternity and its resonances create voids and spaces and a diversity of experiences of time, the time experience of a galaxy, a tree, a man, a mayfly. It still holds within itself all lights and darknesses and all possible variety of colours. It also holds all natural laws and the principles of life and intelligent life. It creates beings capable of consciousness themselves who are the spectators and the audiences of its creation. It is Universal Consciousness letting itself be known as glory.
>
> We, the human race, are the creation of that sound and, as we are made conscious by its light and will, so we share in its creative possibilities. Where we think we invent, we discover; where we suppose we originate, we are supplied from the true origins. In our ultimate essence, our true individuality, we are that sound and through our existence we are ears to hear that sound and mouths to utter that sound.

The Face of Glory: Creativity, Consciousness and Civilization (1996) Bloomsbury, London

Introduction

A Mythic Time of Choice

Will mankind murder Mother Earth or will he redeem her?

— Arnold Toynbee, *Mankind and Mother Earth*

Without a global revolution in the sphere of human consciousness, nothing will change for the better in the sphere of our being as humans, and the catastrophe toward which this world is headed – be it ecological, social, demographic, or a general breakdown of civilization – will be unavoidable.

— Václav Havel, address to US Congress

On this day, which could be any day, I sit in my room, listening to Mozart's Concerto for Flute, Harp and Orchestra (K.299). Outside the window, the garden is awakening to the song of the birds; the woods are greening in response to the warmth of the sun. I look around me at the much-loved objects in my room, made by crafts-men who revered the matter they held in their hands: objects many centuries old that I have gathered over many years from many countries and that are redolent of soul. On my walls are my husband's paintings: paintings of great beauty and supremely skilled craftsmanship which can rarely be found in what, today, goes by the name of art. I am surrounded by books, from the East, from the West, which offer a harvest of the human quest for understanding the mystery and marvel of life.

The exquisite music flowing through the room opens my heart to the poignancy of our existence; the infinitely precious relationships with others; the very short time available to us in which we could learn so much, understand so much, love so much; the compassion for those who have no choice, whose lives are sacrificed to the issues that we, as a species, recognize but find so hard to address: hunger, deprivation, oppression, the addiction to war. The music speaks to me as from another dimension, saying that this has always been so; it will always be so until we awaken to awareness of the oneness and sacredness of life. There is a boundless love in its measured, flowing notes which embraces all people and creatures that have been, are and will be: a love so intense, so comprehensive that to listen to its voice is to touch the very quintessence of being.

The story of the human species streams like the tail of a comet through the darkness of past ages. The story of our evolution has taken so long in human terms, yet the life of our species is embedded in the four-billion-year-old life of this planet and, beyond that, in the unimaginably old life of the hundred billion galaxies of the universe. We are a very recent manifestation of life on this planet yet our origin is in the starry cosmos. We are so much more than has ever been imagined. Over these aeons of time as we understand it, life on this planet has evolved from undifferentiated awareness to the self-awareness of our species. There has been a rising tide of consciousness expressed through matrices of ever greater complexity, and an evolution of species with ever more sensitive and elaborate nervous systems, culminating in our own.

But there is further to go in the sense that an acorn has further to go before it becomes an oak. I am sure that our consciousness is evolving towards the illumined state attained by mystics and enlightened human beings in past ages. This illumined state of cosmic consciousness is a potential within us — a potential that only a few individuals have experienced. As we evolve, so we become intelligible to ourselves; as we grow into the full potential of consciousness, so we become capable of recognizing the true nature of reality. All truths are relative until we reach that state.

Not many years ago in Italy, a burial mound was discovered with a tomb in it. The tomb held the skeleton of a man. A thin sheet of beaten gold had been folded over and placed near his head. On the sheet of gold were these words — words known to have been spoken by those taking part in the Orphic Mysteries of Greece some 2500 years ago: "I am a child of earth and starry heaven but my race is of heaven alone." I find these words from such a distant past intensely moving. I think they are as relevant to us today as they were then. They suggest that we belong to two dimensions of reality: one visible, the other invisible; and this is something we need urgently to know.

The Quest for a Priceless Treasure

The supreme spiritual task of a civilization has been symbolized in myth by the quest for a priceless treasure. From Gilgamesh's quest for the Herb of Immortality to the Buddha's quest for Enlightenment; from Christ's parable of the Pearl of Great Price to the medieval quest for the Holy Grail, this has been a constant theme through some 4000 years. A civilization is inspired and sustained for a certain length of time by its great myths, but eventually the original impetus created by them fades. The treasure is no longer understood as the creation of a living relationship with a transcendent ground of being but is projected onto lesser aims. As Arnold Toynbee (1889–1975), the great historian of civilizations, pointed out decades ago, unless there is renewal based on a new articulation of a spiritual quest which gives deeper meaning and value to our lives, decline sets in, leading ultimately to atrophy and death.[1]

What we call civilization is the hard-won expression of humanity's response to the inspiration of myth which gives us courage, hope and meaning through the creation of a relationship between ourselves, the Earth and the Cosmos. A great sustaining myth emerges from the inner dimension of the soul through the life and example of an extraordinary individual; it then becomes crystallized into belief, religion, dogma. The living relationship with the soul may be lost through the insistence on collective adherence to a specific belief system. Eventually, a state of psychic atrophy sets in where we are out of touch with the soul, where the creative energy of life turns against itself, where there is no renewal or regeneration. In the great myth of the Grail Quest this state is symbolized by the Wasteland: a country or kingdom that lies barren and desolate; its king old and ailing and powerless to regenerate a kingdom that has fallen prey to the warring elements within it. Once, not so many centuries ago, the feeling for the sacredness of life and relationship with the Earth and the Cosmos was a deep instinct, shared by the whole of humanity. Then, almost imperceptibly and for many reasons which I will explore in this book, it was lost.

What happens to us if we exist without relationship to anything beyond our own consciousness? We are left bereft of relationship with the Cosmos. Psychic energy that has nowhere to go implodes on itself, undermining the social order. When the consensus as to what is of supreme value weakens, all the institutions and social structures of society are weakened; morality becomes a matter of everyone's convenience. Recognizing nothing beyond ourselves, we become both inflated and diminished: inflated because we behave with god-like omnipotence; diminished because we are imprisoned in an image of reality which, like Plato's famous cave, limits and constricts our growth.

When, collectively, we sink into a dull uniformity, the imagination is not nourished. Creative power dissipates itself in malignant fantasies of death, torture and destruction which are acted out in situations of crime, conflict, war and unbridled licentiousness, as well as in similar scenes on our television screens. Aggression and self-destructive tendencies are activated in the soul that is separated from its ground and deeply distressed, without knowing the cause of its distress. In *Ash Wednesday V*, T.S. Eliot captured the essence of this state:

> *Where shall the word be found, where will the word*
> *Resound? Not here, there is not enough silence*
> *Not on the sea or on the islands, not*
> *On the mainland, in the desert or the rain land,*
> *For those who walk in darkness*
> *Both in the day time and in the night time*
> *The right time and the right place are not here*
> *No place of grace for those who avoid the face*
> *No time to rejoice for those who walk among noise and deny the voice.*

Our Present Situation

Earth is our home in the Cosmos. We are faced with two immense problems: the problem of our increasing numbers and the problem of diminishing resources to sustain those numbers. Beneath the technological achievements of our culture and its Promethean addiction to economic growth, there is the accelerating rape of the Earth's resources to serve our ever-expanding industrial and economic needs. Nations vie with each other for power and supremacy: developing and storing weapons of mass destruction; sending guided missiles to eliminate their enemies; torturing, raping, murdering their political opponents. As this process accelerates there remains, unresolved, the inarticulate suffering of billions of people who live desperate lives focused on bare survival. In the conflict areas of Africa, there is starvation and the endemic rape of women and children. Even in societies with a relatively high standard of living, there is depression, addiction, violence, crime, a wasteland of dying hopes and the unrealized potential of millions of children. There is the anguish of parents and grandparents who see their loved ones sacrificed to the fearful defilement of war. In the gigantic sprawling cities of the world, there is the helplessness of hungry, abandoned and abused children who scavenge like rats — children who may be corrupted by drug-dealers, kidnapped into slavery or simply raped and murdered. Thousands of young women are trafficked into sexual slavery. All this might be described as a malignancy.

What has given rise to this pathology? Could there be something absolutely fundamental missing in our religious traditions that might explain how all this has come into being: how we have come to treat people with such abysmal cruelty and contempt? Can the heroic effort and suffering of so many previous generations have brought us to this dead end? Surely we are meant to evolve further, to bring into being not only a technology which can facilitate space travel, but a consciousness which can grow beyond tribal enmities and can open itself to the awareness that we all belong to a greater life: the life of this planet and beyond that, the life of the Cosmos.

Suppose the universe is trying to penetrate the thick fog of our consciousness. Suppose that behind the 4% of it that is visible to us, there are undiscovered dimensions and multitudes of beings who inhabit those dimensions. Suppose we do not die with the death of our body but continue to live and grow in these dimensions so that there is continuity between what happens here and what happens there. Like so many others, I long to break through the loneliness of the human state; to know there is no death; that those separated from us are not lost forever; that there is meaning to our ephemeral existence. I long to grow into a more complete state of being that I feel exists. As Keats so eloquently put it: "I feel more and more every day, as my imagination strengthens, that I do not live in this world alone but in a thousand worlds."[2] As with the final contractions of a mother giving birth, I feel the need to push beyond the constriction of an intolerable state of ignorance.

The longing arising today from millions of human souls is for freedom: freedom from oppression by autocratic and persecutory regimes; freedom from hunger and fear, torture and imprisonment; freedom from the beliefs and habits that block our further evolution, our unfolding as enlightened human beings. But the freedom we need most is release from a worldview that is confining us to a prison of our own making. Can we embrace the truly immense transformation of consciousness we need to make if we are to free ourselves from this defective worldview and forge a different understanding of life and a viable future on this planet for coming generations?

Discovering a New Story

We are living at a time of momentous evolutionary change. The scientific discoveries of the last 100 years — the thrilling expansion of our knowledge about the universe, the sub-atomic world, the geological formation of the earth and the biological history of evolution on this planet — have shattered the foundation upon which our culture was built just as the discoveries of Kepler and Copernicus shattered the medieval view of reality.

Our consciousness is the infinitesimal spark of cosmic light that is now sufficiently developed for the universe to reveal itself to us through the incredible instruments that science has devised. As if in response to an innate directing impulse, the consciousness latent or present within nature and matter is becoming conscious of itself. This matrix of expanding, complexifying life embraces not only the whole evolutionary experience of the life of the universe but the total experience of life as it has evolved on this planet; not only the experience of our physical organism but the experience of our instincts, thoughts, feelings, imagination — all that we call consciousness. We are discovering our cosmic origins and the fact that in our essence we are literally star-life, star-energy, star-matter in every cell of our being.

As the psychiatrist Carl Jung recognized, without that spark of consciousness, without the capacity to observe, imagine, explore, discover and reflect, countless ages might have passed with no one and nothing on this planet to witness its life. Thanks to that spark of consciousness, we can begin to comprehend the stupendous creativity of the life process in which all our lives are embedded. Equally awesome is the discovery that everything we observe, everything we are, arises from an invisible sea of being, which is the deep cosmic ground of the phenomenal world and our own consciousness. From this perspective, all the divisions and polarities of our world fade into insignificance

It seems that we are immersed in a sea or field or web of energy that is co-extensive with the immensity of the visible universe and the most minute particles of matter. The world we experience is like a minute excitation on the surface of that infinite cosmic sea. The astounding discoveries of quantum physics tell us that we are literally bathed in a sea of light, invisible to us, yet permeating every cell of our being, every atom of matter. At the quantum level, all apparently separate aspects of life are interconnected in one invisible and indivisible whole. We, as observers, are inseparable from what we are observing. All life at the deepest level is essentially One. As William James noted over a century ago, "We are like islands on the surface but connected in the deep."

The dawning realization that we participate in a cosmic reality that is the source and ground of our own lives challenges the belief advanced by science that we exist on a tiny planet in a lifeless universe and that there is no life beyond death. It may be that the universe has waited aeons for us to reach the point where more than a handful of individuals could awaken to awareness of the invisible ground that animates and supports the whole of our existence. Like the giant UFO in the film *Close Encounters of the Third Kind*, an immense, invisible field of consciousness is making itself known to us, asking to be recognized by us, embraced by us. We might call it the Soul of the Cosmos.

If the Cosmos is alive, intelligent and the ground of our own consciousness, what might be its Dream? Surely it is for us to become protectors rather than exploiters of life on this planet and to awaken to the intelligence of the mysterious energy that animates and sustains every element of the phenomenal world. And what might be our greatest longing, our greatest wish? Surely it is to know that our lives have meaning and value in relation to a dimension of reality that is slowly revealing itself to us as we make new discoveries.

Notes:

1. Toynbee, Arnold (1934–1961) *A Study of History* in 12 volumes, OUP.
    One-volume edition OUP & Thames and Hudson Ltd., 1972
2. Keats, John, Letter, 18th October, 1818

Preface

To reclaim the sacred nature of the cosmos – and of planet Earth in particular – is one of the outstanding spiritual challenges of our time.

— Diarmuid O'Murchu, *Quantum Theology*

Although I had begun writing this book over twenty years ago, the call to focus on it again came in a dream I had in the summer of 1998.

> *I am at my grandmother's home in the South of France, walking with two friends, a woman and her husband, near the bottom of a valley. Suddenly, on our right, we see a serpent. It is about five feet long, a beautiful glowing ruby red on its bottom half and gold on its top half. It has small wings but no claws or feet. Its head is not flat like a cobra's but is slightly bigger than its body. There is a black marking like a 'V' on the top of its head. It is definitely a winged serpent or salamander rather than a dragon. Its red and gold scales gleam luminously, like enamel. We look nervously at it and I say, "I hope it won't bite us." We walk on through olive groves and come to the furthest edge of the property. Suddenly the serpent is there, on our right. It has flown from its former place. It moves towards me and bites me on my right hand, at the base of the thumb. Its bite leaves a circle of tiny red dots.*

It took me some days to make the connection between 'right' and 'write,' but when I did, I knew that I had to return to the work I had begun many years earlier. As I reflected on what form the book could take, and the difficulty of conveying ideas that are so alien to the secular spirit of our time, I remembered the words that Carl Jung had written in his last book, *Man and His Symbols*:

> As any change must begin somewhere, it is the single individual who will experience it and carry it through. The change must indeed begin with an individual; it might be any one of us. Nobody can afford to look round and to wait for somebody else to do what he is loath to do himself. But since nobody seems to know what to do, it might be worth while for each of us to ask himself whether by any chance his [or her] unconscious may know something that will help us.[1]

The Dream of the Cosmos is the story of a multi-layered quest to understand the causes of human suffering and to reconnect with a deeper reality than the one we inhabit in this physical dimension of experience. It seeks to answer the questions:

"Who are we?" and "Why are we here, on this planet?" It is offered to those who are looking for something beyond the superficial values of our culture, who may be disillusioned with religious and secular belief systems as currently presented and who question political values which are deeply mired in the pursuit of power. It is written with two voices: one the voice of a personal quest and the other which explores the historical and psychological causes that have brought into being our present view of reality.

In this book I seek to recover a very ancient image of the soul, one that has long been lost. The soul was once imagined as an all-embracing cosmic web of life, not so much something that belongs to us as something to which we belong, in whose unbounded life we live. The world is crying out for the primary values that have always been associated with soul understood in this wider sense: wisdom, compassion, justice, relationship — values which I will define further as the book proceeds.

What is the story of the soul? Why was it lost and why is its recovery so vitally important to us now? I would like to share my experience of how the soul speaks, how it attracts us to itself and tries to gain our attention. I aim to show through my own experience the importance of dreams and visions as well as knowledge, insight and life experience as a preparation to becoming receptive to a hidden order of reality of which the soul is one of the oldest and most constant images.

Over the course of many centuries, we have developed a formidable intellect, a formidable science, a formidable technology. But what of the soul, source of our deepest instincts and feelings? What of our need for relationship with this unrecognized dimension of reality? What of our visions, dreams and hopes as well as our unhealed wounds and the suffering generated by our lack of compassion towards each other? The pressing need for the soul's recognition has brought us to this time of choice. It is as if mortal danger is forcing us to take a great leap in our evolution that we might never have made were we not driven to take it by the force of circumstances that we ourselves have created. Yet now, the foundation that seemed so secure is disintegrating: old structures and beliefs are breaking down; new ideas, new responses are being born. The creative genius of our species is being called upon as never before to respond to the great challenges of our time.

In one of the medieval Grail Legends, Parsifal asks the question of the wounded Grail King, "What ails thee, Father?" It seems appropriate to ask this question of our culture. Our current worldview rests on the premise of our separation from and mastery of nature, where nature is treated as object with ourselves as controlling subject. This belief has its roots in a far distant past — in the Myth of the Fall in the Book of Genesis and its profound influence on the development of Western civilization. There we find the story of our expulsion from a divine world and our Fall into this world: a Fall that was brought about by a woman, Eve, who disobeyed the command of God and brought death, sin and suffering into being. From this myth there developed the belief that the whole human race was tainted by original sin, a belief that will be explored in later chapters. Yet this was never more than a belief, although it was presented and accepted as divinely revealed truth.

There is a second problematic legacy from the past: the image of God shared by the three Abrahamic or patriarchal religions. God has been defined as a transcendent creator, separate and distinct from the created order. Western civilization, despite its phenomenal achievements, developed on the foundation of a fundamental split between spirit and nature, creator and creation, and the belief that we are separate from God. Only now are we brought face to face with the disastrous effects of this split.

Because of the influence of this transcendent concept of God as well as the powerful influence of the Myth of the Fall, we have come to look upon nature as something separate from ourselves — something we can master, control and manipulate to obtain specific benefits for our species alone because ours, we believe, has been given dominion over the Earth. It has come as a bit of a shock to realize that our lives are intimately bound up with the fragile organism of planetary life and the inter-dependence of all species. If we destroy our habitat, whether inadvertently or deliberately by continuing on our present path, we risk destroying ourselves.

The threat of global warming, the urgent need to free ourselves from dependency on fossil fuels, and the burgeoning population of the planet could be the catalyst which offers us the opportunity of bringing about a profound shift in our values, relinquishing an old story and defining a new one. Instead of treating our planetary home as the endless supplier of all our needs, without consideration for its needs, we need to rethink beliefs and attitudes which have influenced our behaviour for millennia: beliefs and attitudes which are deeply rooted in our religious traditions as well as in the secular beliefs of modern science.

Once again, as in the early centuries of the Christian era, it seems as if new bottles are needed to hold the wine of a new revelation, a new image of reality or worldview. What is the emerging vision of our time which could offer a template for a conscious, awakened humanity? I believe it is a vision which takes us beyond an outworn paradigm where we are held in bondage to beliefs and attitudes specific to race, nation, religion or gender, which have led us to exclude and devalue those who are different from ourselves and neglect our relationship with the Earth, our planetary home. It is a vision which takes us beyond an outworn image of deity and current secular beliefs and offers us a new concept of spirit, no longer as a transcendent creator but as a unifying cosmic field — a limitless sea of being — as well as the creative consciousness or organizing intelligence within that sea or field; and a new concept of ourselves as belonging to and participating in that incandescent cosmic consciousness.

It is a vision which recognizes the sacredness and indissoluble unity of the great cosmic web of life and imposes on us the responsibility of becoming far more sensitive to the effects of our decisions and our actions. It invites our recognition of the needs of the planet and the life it sustains as primary, with ourselves as the humble servants of those needs. It invites us, as Einstein invited us, to widen the circle of our compassion: to look upon every child as our child; every woman as our daughter, our sister or our mother; every man as our father, our brother or our son; the well-being of every creature as our responsibility. Above all, it is a vision which asks that we relinquish our addiction to weapons and war and the pursuit of power; that we become more aware of the dark shadow cast by this addiction which threatens us with ever more barbarism, bloodshed and suffering — ultimately, with the possible extinction of our species.

From this perspective, the crisis of our times is not only an ecological and political crisis but a moral and spiritual crisis. The answers we seek cannot come from the limited consciousness which now rules the world but could grow from a deeper understanding, born of the union of mind and soul, helping us to see that all life is one, that each one of us participates in the life of a cosmic entity of immeasurable dimensions. The urgent need for this deeper intelligence and wisdom, this wholeness, could help us to recover a perspective on life that has been increasingly lost until we have come to live without it — and without even noticing it has gone — recognizing the existence of no dimension of reality beyond the parameters set by the human mind. It is a dangerous time because it involves transforming entrenched belief systems and archaic survival habits of behaviour that are rooted in fear, as well as the greed and desire for power that are born of habits inculcated by fear. But it is also an immense opportunity for evolutionary advance, if only we can understand what is offered in this moment of choice.

After so many billion years of cosmic evolution, it is simply unacceptable that the beauty and marvel of the Earth should be ravaged by us through our insatiable greed, the destructive power of our weapons, and the misapplication of our science and technology. It is inconceivable that our extraordinary species, which has taken so many billion years to evolve to conscious awareness, should destroy itself and lay waste to the Earth through ignorance of the divinity in which we dwell and which dwells in us. The very challenge of our times offers us the choice between continuing to follow the patterns of the past or creating new patterns, living and acting from a different relationship with life, committing ourselves to the immense effort of consciousness we need to make to understand and serve its mystery.

Notes:

1. Jung, C.G. (1964) *Man and His Symbols*, Aldus Books, London, p. 10

Angel Carrying a Child
Robin Baring 1973

Part One

My Quest Begins

Landscape and Cup
Robin Baring 1976

Chapter One

MY QUEST BEGINS

The living spirit grows and even outgrows its earlier forms of expression; it freely chooses the men and women in whom it lives and who proclaim it. This living spirit is eternally renewed and pursues its goal in manifold and inconceivable ways throughout the history of mankind. Measured against it, the names and forms which men have given it mean little enough; they are only the changing leaves and blossoms on the stem of the eternal tree.

— C. G. Jung, *Modern Man in Search of a Soul*

Who can calculate the orbit of his own soul?

— Oscar Wilde, *Reading Gaol*

My story begins one hot summer day in 1942 when I was eleven years old. I had been told to take a rest after lunch. Lying on my bed, drowsy with the heat, I suddenly saw an intense purple light suffusing the whole room and felt myself surrendering to an irresistible power. Then, abruptly and without warning, the bed beneath me opened as if sliced by a knife. I was pushed down into the crevice and the bed closed over me. In terror I struggled to shout for help, move my arms and legs, open my eyes, but my body refused to respond. A noise like the roar of a tumultuous waterfall surrounded me, pressing on my ears and all about me. I shot through a tight channel and was spewed out, as if from a catapult, into a vast and silent blackness. Yet I could see that I was still attached to my body by a fine cord.

I waited for what might come next, terrified and bewildered by the shock of losing touch with the only life I knew. As I waited in that dark immensity, I heard two words: 'I AM'. I don't know, shall never know, whether more words were to follow or whether this was all I was meant to hear. Overcome with terror at being alone in space with this disembodied voice, I found myself re-entering the channel, plunged once again into that roaring, deafening vortex of sound. Then, amazingly, I emerged from it and found myself lying in my bed, alive in a familiar world.

That experience initiated a lifelong quest. I had to know why I had left my body for that mysterious encounter. I had to discover the meaning of that experience; why it had happened to me; what it was asking of me. It was so powerful, so shockingly different from any other experience I had known that I felt impelled to follow a path of discovery, slowly integrating into my life what has been revealed to me stage by stage. How often have I wished that I had had the courage to stay in that place of absolute stillness and listen for that voice to say more.

The Dream of the Water

Soon after that experience, my mother told me about channelled messages she had received while meeting with her sister, sister-in-law and a friend in New York, where we were living at the time. One winter afternoon in 1943, at the height of the Second World War, they had met to talk about the life-and-death struggle that was tearing Europe apart. Suddenly, although the windows were closed because of the cold, they heard a roar like thunder and a window was blown inwards by a powerful blast of air. Lightning flickered all around them although there was no storm. They cried out in terror, and went to shut the window. Then they felt a tremendous presence in the room and, falling on their knees, were overcome with awe.

Weeping, they asked what they could do to help the world. The answer came in writing: "Follow your heart. Only through making space in your lives for listening to the guidance trying to reach you from another dimension of reality can you come to a deeper understanding of how you can most effectively help the world." The message warned of a future catastrophe for the Earth and humanity if the ways of men did not change and said that this warning should be passed on to anyone who was willing to listen. If enough people could become aware of the danger and respond to the guidance that was trying to reach them, the full force of the catastrophe could be mitigated or even averted. The message continued:

> There are periods which seem to last forever. These are periods of incubation; everything is waiting. Humanity has lived for two thousand years in a state of adolescence. Now it must become adult or sink into general criminality which will bring chaos, confusion and, finally, destruction. If humanity chooses adulthood and responsibility to life, it will have the millennium of peace and

happiness and Earth will join the circle of planets which have already completed their evolution. From far distant realms in the universe come Great Beings to your poor benighted planet to help to overthrow the tyranny of evil so that never again shall it overpower the world. Only when men learn not to shed their brothers' blood can the House of God be built on its true foundations.

The breaking up of the established churches is but a question of time and will be accomplished partly by their inability to satisfy the spiritual needs of man and partly by the atheists who will play a greater and greater part in world events. Harmony must be found at every level as there is a danger of collective insanity. Man can no longer survive the disintegration of his psyche caused by his own destructive civilization. Only those who have reached an inner harmony between their knowledge and their intuition, their thoughts and their actions; those who are able to listen to and accept the guidance of their heart, will be given the strength and the knowledge to help their fellow men. Every act of a human being must be judged against the question: Does it offend Nature? Does it offend God? Does it injure Life?

Profoundly shocked by these words, and others which followed, they asked whether they should pray in church and were told: "Your church is your immortal soul."

My mother and her friend continued to meet in Europe for some twenty years after the end of the war. In later messages, they were warned (in 1944) of the dangers of splitting the atom and interfering with the laws of nature because of the disintegrative effects this would have on the human psyche. They were also told to study the early history of Christianity, the twelfth and thirteenth centuries and the Reformation. In particular, they were to study how the teaching of Christ had been distorted or obscured by the Church established in His name. Repeatedly they were urged to follow the thread of guidance that would lead them to something called the 'Dream of the Water', and to find their way to the 'Holy Mountain'. They were also told to look for a mysterious stone that was 'buried at the foot of the Tree'.

At first my mother and her friend took these images literally and looked for a place of refuge from the impending catastrophe (whose date was never specified), even spending many years searching for a holy mountain and a tree under which a special stone might be buried. Gradually, it dawned on them that these images were not to be understood literally but were metaphors for a state of being or state of consciousness which they needed to develop within themselves.

To begin with, in the 1940's and 50's there was no one with whom to share these experiences, leaving me with a feeling of great loneliness and isolation. Within my own family, only my American mother was the bridge to the unseen 'other' world. With my English father I could never speak of these secret things.

My parents' marriage suffered from this lack of communication between them and their inability to share what was of deepest significance to my mother. My mother was a poet and an artist; my father was a soldier and a rationalist, one of a long ancestral line of warriors who had served their country. He could not understand what my mother was talking about and built a defensive wall against her which was expressed as an unconscious compulsion to destroy her trust in herself with criticism and ridicule.

Years later, I came to understand that because he had lost his own mother when he was a small boy, having total control over my mother was the only way he could feel emotionally secure. He therefore lived an existence dogged by chronic anxiety, in a state that would later be recognized as depression. Anything which hinted at the non-rational was a threat to his security and amplified his need for control. My mother surrendered to this tyranny because her generation had no insight into the psychological roots of human behaviour. Lacking any qualifications which would have helped them to earn their living, women of her background and upbringing were conditioned to stay in unhappy marriages, to tolerate and submit to their husbands' need for absolute control and to devote their lives to the care and well-being of others in the belief that this sacrificial life would somehow find favour with God. All negative feelings were repressed for fear of divine punishment and social disapproval.

At the end of the war, the family returned to England. The next years were overshadowed by the destructive relationship between my parents and by the bullying I endured at the hands of my new classmates. So I turned to God for help but found no comfort in the Protestant church services I was made to attend at school. I hated the damp smell of church, the freezing cold, the heavy sense of sin and guilt, the dreary hymns and the condemnatory sermons that were so lacking in joy and communion with the divine. If Christ had redeemed the sins of the world, why was there still war and suffering and why was I a 'miserable sinner'? It made no sense to me. I dreaded Sundays and often felt so sick and faint that I had to leave the church. It all felt so wrong, but I didn't know why. God seemed remote, oppressive, judgemental and unforgiving.

The Garden of Eden

However, there was one place where I loved to be. Before the war I used to spend the summer holidays with my grandmother in the South of France. I longed to return to that sun-baked earth, to the clear luminosity of that landscape — the star-filled sky, the rhythmic sound of the crickets and the frogs' croaking at night, the strong, rich perfume of thyme, lavender, pine and cypress. At the end of the war, it was again possible to revisit this early childhood paradise.

My grandmother's house stood on a hilltop on the site of an ancient temple to Minerva. It was called Malbosquet, meaning 'evil little wood'— so named, no doubt, because the local people felt it was haunted by 'spirits' and, therefore, to be avoided. It was a place of incredible beauty, a Garden of Eden, filled with the beauty of pink and white oleander bushes; tall dark cypress that exuded a delicious scent after rain; a fountain in which grew huge pink lotus flowers; orange trees filling the air with the exquisite fragrance of their blossoms in early spring; a rich red earth planted with vines yielding sweet grapes and, everywhere, flowers. I remembered particularly the anemones that carpeted the earth in spring and which also filled the house, for my grandmother was an artist and loved to paint them. In the cloistered courtyard enormous brown pots held camellias and masses of scarlet geraniums. In the distance to the West were range after range of violet hills; to the East the snow-capped mountains of the Alps. To the South, glittering distantly in the sun beyond a vast forest of pine and olive trees, was the Mediterranean.

I would wake up at dawn, inhaling the fresh smell of dew-laden grass, my heart bursting with joy at the dawning of a new day. I loved to walk at dawn on the wet grass just to feel the coolness of the dew under my bare feet. Later in the day, I would go and sit in a grove of olive trees overlooking a deep shady gorge that plunged down to the fast-flowing river far below. At night, when the moon was full and everything was flooded with its soft radiance, the whole place came magically alive with invisible presences. What was so precious about these childhood memories was that there was time simply to be and to wonder. It was here that I fell in love with the beauty of the natural world.

The trees of that olive grove seemed to bear witness to the secrets of centuries and the great civilizations that had flourished around the Mediterranean: Egyptian; Cretan; Phoenician; Greek; Etruscan; Roman. For millennia, owls had built their nests in the hollows of the gnarled and crinkled trunks of these trees. I used to sit for hours, happy to be there among them, watching the changing light as the sun filtered through the silvery leaves. Although the war had separated me for six years from this much loved place, I returned to it again and again in my imagination. It was the country of my soul.

The Call of Beauty

In the late 1940's it became possible to travel freely. The continent of Europe was again accessible, a place of sun and light to which I could escape from the grim austerity of England. In 1947, when I was sixteen, my grandmother took me to Spain, driving down the east coast full of almond trees in blossom, to Granada and Cordoba, then blessedly free of tourists. In the great mosque at Cordoba I had my first glimpse of Moorish culture and in the silence of dawn and dusk I was able to sit alone in the exquisite grace of the courtyards of the Alhambra, describing in my diary the features of the beauty that entranced me.

Later, in Italy, my mother and I explored Tuscany and Umbria by bus, with the local people, delighted by their lively, laughing chatter, their caged, squawking chickens, and their mountainous bundles of provisions. I gazed, awestruck, at the marvel of the Baptistery in Florence, the Duomo, and Giotto's lily-like tower; the paintings in the dimly lit Lower Church at Assisi; the Siennese Madonnas; Botticelli's *Primavera* and the Birth of Venus. All shine in my memory like the glory of sunrise to one who sees it for the first time.

I travelled through Italy on an indrawn breath of wonder. Each destination became a pilgrimage. At Borgo San Sepolcro, Piero della Francesca's painting of Christ rising from the tomb burst upon my consciousness as the startling vision of an awakened and enlightened man—utterly different from the image of the helpless and suffering figure on the cross that hung above the altars of the many churches I visited. I wondered why there were so many images of the crucifixion and so very few of the resurrected Christ.

I fell passionately in love with the painters of the early Renaissance — above all Sassetta and Fra Angelico — and all those artists for whom rock and earth and sky and man and angel were transparent to a divine ground which sustained and permeated the physical world. I experienced this kind of painting as a praising, a loving, a longing, a communion with, and a method of discovering, God. I was also attracted to the figure of St. Francis, for some of my mother's messages had come from him and I had taken him as my spiritual mentor. I encountered him in the many paintings of his contemporaries, along with the great red angel who had appeared to him and seemed to hover still in the Umbrian skies.

I visited the little hermitage near Assisi where Christ had spoken to St. Francis telling him to rebuild His church. Here, as in Borgo San Sepolcro, was another radiant image of Christ, not hanging suffering on the cross. I remembered the messages telling my mother and her friends to study the history of early Christianity and how the teachings of Christ had been distorted. I felt I needed to know more and prayed to St. Francis for guidance.

It was in Italy that I became aware for the first time of another kind of spirituality: one no longer impregnated with the heavy sense of sin and guilt that was so prevalent in the Protestant churches of my childhood, but deeply rooted in people's age-old sense of connection with the land and with the towns and hermitages where saints had lived and taught. I responded to the incredible beauty of the landscape of Italy and felt the strong, vital sense of continuity between the present and the past. I absorbed the perfect proportions and human scale of the buildings and the climate of revelation that the very air of Italy seemed to breathe. I stood in awe before the genius of the architects, sculptors and masons who, working together, had been able to imagine and bring into being marvels like the exquisite marble façade of the Duomo at Orvieto.

On a second journey the following year I climbed a hill on a starlit morning to attend mass and receive the blessing given to pilgrims by the renegade Italian friar, Padre Pio (later to be made a saint) and smelt the strong scent of violets emanating from him. Afterwards, the taxi-driver taking me to the station insisted that I should visit the shrine of the Archangel Michael at Monte Gargano nearby, where crusaders had knelt to be blessed before embarking on their sea-journey to the Holy Land. With bowed head and holding his hat in his gnarled hands, he led me down a flight of broad stone steps into the bowels of the mountain and the black, glistening walls of a great cave that sheltered the shrine of the Archangel. Over its entrance were the words: "This is the abode of God, the Gateway to Heaven". I knew that St. Francis had hesitated to enter this cave, saying "Lord, I am not worthy to enter Thy shrine" and that he had probably embarked on his journey to meet the Muslim ruler Saladin from the nearby port of Bari. Astonishingly, as a result of their meeting, Saladin had twice granted permission for the Christians to enter Jerusalem peacefully and twice they had refused, choosing instead to take it by force.

In the cave there was no one else present except an old woman rhythmically sweeping the floor. As I knelt to pray, I burst into tears, suddenly overwhelmed by the sorrow and suffering of the world. I asked the Archangel for help and guidance for myself and for humanity. It seemed a natural thing to do in this holy place.

Preparing for the World

My mother was determined that I should go to university since she herself had not been able to. Oxford laid the foundation for the future, giving me the opportunity to develop my mind and extend my knowledge of the past. I chose to study medieval history and also learned Italian in order to study the Italian Renaissance and renew my connection to art. The current fashion in philosophy at that time (the early 50's) was Logical Positivism. Here I had my first encounter with a purely secular approach to life and it made no sense to me. I vowed then that one day I would find the answer to the questions that perplexed me, questions that modern philosophy could not answer and did not even ask. I became preoccupied with finding the path of spiritual guidance that could lead to a deeper understanding of life.

Just as I was about to leave Oxford (1951), I fell in love with and became engaged to a man who was charming, intelligent and very interested in the arts. I thought I had found the ideal husband. But a few weeks later, he was arrested and accused of molesting some boy scouts near his home. Homosexuality was something that was not discussed in those days and the whole subject was socially taboo until the details of the court case erupted in the media. I was loyal to my fiancé and clung to my belief in his innocence. The trial aroused huge interest and public support and led, ultimately, to the law being changed so that homosexuality was no longer treated as a crime. However, my fiancé was found guilty and sent to prison for a year.

I broke off the engagement and found a job in New York working for an Austrian psychiatrist (Dr. Manfred Sakel) who had developed a method of treating schizophrenia with insulin shock treatment as an alternative to electric-shock treatment and was looking for someone to edit the book he had written about it. The whole experience of the broken engagement profoundly affected my life because, just at the point when I was emerging into the wider world from the rather cloistered life of university, my trust in myself was totally destroyed. That winter of 1951–2 was truly a dark night of my soul. It was my first encounter with psychology and mental illness and I fell into a deep depression, unable to help myself or to ask for help. In my distress I forgot the words of the messages and the images of the Dream of the Water. The Stone at the foot of the Tree faded from memory.

The Revelation of India and Asia

Returning to England, I took various secretarial jobs which led nowhere. But in 1956 my life unexpectedly opened out in a new direction with the opportunity to visit India and the Far East. That journey changed the course of my life because it led to an encounter with cultures and religious traditions which offered the greatest possible contrast with my own European one and enormously expanded the horizon of my life. To me, India symbolized the mythical destination of all explorers — an unknown, mysterious, fabulous land. When I first caught sight of the great chain of the Himalayas gleaming far above the great plain of northern India I felt like Columbus discovering America. There was no place for fear because I was ecstatically involved in the discovery of a new world.

In India I discovered the ravishing grace of men and women in their turbans and saris of dazzling yellow, lime-green, magenta and pink and the staggering size and beauty of a landscape utterly different from anything I had seen or imagined. Everywhere I went I felt the presence of a very ancient civilization and the extraordinary range of the human imagination and artistic genius expressed in art and architecture, in poetry, literature, music and the creation of every kind of beauty, from the fantastic sculptures on the temple walls to the exquisite designs stamped on the saris displayed in the markets. What struck me most was the sense of timelessness — that very little had changed in tens of thousands of years. It was an intoxicating time. I had no ties, no responsibilities, no fears. I could simply follow the longing of my heart, which was to enter into the soul of India as my sandalled feet reverently touched the dust of that ancient soil. Travelling alone, I found a richer, deeper, more vibrant experience of life than I could find in my own country and culture. I knew I had to return as there was so much more to discover and assimilate.

Through contacts in Rome the following year, I had the amazing good fortune to be offered a job collecting photographs from museums in India and the Far East for an Italian encyclopaedia of art. To choose the photographs I would need to travel from country to country, visiting the sacred sites and museums of India, Burma, Thailand, Cambodia, Japan, Taiwan and Indonesia. I would also have rapidly to assimilate not only the history of each culture, but also its religious spirit as expressed in its art because art, in these cultures, was inseparable from religion. This extraordinary commission would take me into the heart of each culture. It was a journey of discovery beyond my wildest dreams and would change the whole course of my life.

It was the sheer splendour of the art, sculpture and temple architecture of India and Asia that first kindled my strong attraction to Hinduism, Buddhism and Taoism. Only later was it deepened and extended through the sacred texts I studied. In the dark recesses of a great cavern in Taiwan where half of the Imperial Treasure taken from Beijing by Chiang Kai-shek had been stored for safety, I had my first glimpse of the Taoist paintings of the Sung dynasty and my first real encounter with Chinese art. I was struck not only by its utter difference from the art of India and the West, but by its different quality of soul.

As I travelled to places like Angkor in Cambodia and Borobodur in Java, as well as to many sites in India, Thailand and Burma, and the museums in the capital cities, I felt myself entering into the heart of Hindu and Buddhist sculpture, deeply awed by the sculptors' power to evoke in stone the immanent presence of spirit. In India, I saw that gods and goddesses — utterly different from the monotheistic Christian concept of God — were not just present in their images but were mysteriously immanent and integrated into everyday life; they were still, after thousands of years, vibrantly alive in the imagination of the people. The temples were thronged with hundreds of people bringing offerings to the various goddesses and gods, obviously deeply emotionally involved in their rituals.

As a young woman travelling alone in 1957, I was never molested or robbed and was welcomed everywhere with curiosity and warmth. This was before the era of drugs and hippies. I was often lonely but never afraid. So many people helped me, so many kindly passed me on to friends in other countries or contacts in museums. It was only in Japan that the fact that I was a woman temporarily denied me access to the museum archives. In Tokyo no one spoke English and the museum authorities could not believe (and seemed insulted) that a young woman had been entrusted with this job. Eventually, however, I got my photographs.

In the course of these journeys, I came across sculpture after sculpture of Mount Sumeru, the 'holy mountain' of Hindu mythology. In Cambodia, I discovered that many of the temples of Angkor, half-buried in the jungle, evoked this same image, for every single temple represented this holy mountain, which was the sacred heart of the universe as well as the divine presence hidden in the heart of every human being. So here at last, it seemed as if I had found the 'holy mountain' of my mother's messages, some sixteen years after I had first heard of it. I felt that my quest had led me to discover this image so wonderfully carved in stone, and enshrined in the mythology that was still so vibrantly alive in India and much of Asia.

I was also deeply moved by the incredible beauty and magnificence of the land and the warmth, beauty and grace of the people as I travelled from country to country. The sheer richness and colour of India, the breadth and depth of its culture, were overwhelming. I was struck by the exquisite designs on women's saris, and the thronging number of people who, everywhere, despite being poor beyond any European conception of poverty, had an immense dignity, beauty and grace.

At Tiruvannamalai, in southern India, I visited the ashram of the great Indian sage Sri Ramana shortly after his death and walked the nine miles around Arunachala, the sacred mountain which symbolized the same 'holy mountain' — the hidden heart of the cosmos. It was here that I encountered his teaching of repeatedly asking myself the question 'Who am I?' This question urged me to go further, look deeper. I had never thought about the need to discover an unseen reality as great as, if not greater than, the familiar outer world of my experience. I began to connect this question with the voice that had spoken so many years before, saying only 'I Am'.

In Thailand, the abbot of a monastery invited me to stay and experience the Buddhist approach to enlightenment but I felt unable to accept his invitation, not willing to commit myself to any one path or leave behind the ties of family and my life in the West. Yet, as I travelled, I revelled in my growing understanding of a different purpose and meaning to life. The claustrophobic weight of the Western concept of a single life opened out into a great vista of lives, both past and future as I encountered concepts such as the law of karma: the belief that one's life experiences are the result of actions and experiences in past lives; that one's present actions affect future lives; and the idea that we reincarnate countless times in many different bodies, gradually growing in spiritual insight and moving ever closer to reunion with a divine ground. The idea of this reunion seemed to be carried in other words of Sri Ramana that I remembered long after I left India, "Your own self-realization is the greatest service you can render the world."

I saw that in all these different times and places a rich and potent humus had been created by countless human beings over countless millennia: artists, poets, mystics, astronomers, musicians, architects, philosophers, mathematicians, scientists, and a few wise and extraordinary men like the Mogul ruler, Akbar, whose patronage had fertilized the deep sub-soil of culture. But there was also the moving vista of millions of people so poor that they were barely able to survive, creating incredible beauty with their hands: weaving, dyeing, stamping brilliantly-coloured cotton and silk cloth with ancient designs. Carving wood and sculpting stone with incredible skill over countless generations, they nurtured an age-old culture in India and Asia, transmitting it through millennia.

These journeys gave me a perspective on life which could only be acquired by physically travelling to far distant places. The discovery of Hinduism, Buddhism and, later, Taoism, brought release from the prison of a Christianity that I had experienced as claustrophobic, oppressive and forbidding. In these traditions I did not find the guilt-inducing Christian sense of sin but rather the belief that suffering was due to ignorance; that humanity was unconscious or unawakened rather than mired in sin.

When I returned to England I put everything that had entranced my eye and evoked a response from my heart into my first book – *The One Work; a Journey Towards the Self* – an account of these two journeys to the East in 1956 and 1957 and my quest to understand the quintessential message of Hinduism and

Buddhism and relate this to a deeper understanding of Christianity. The main focus of the book was a different concept of spirit — one that was equated with an unseen ground sustaining all forms of life rather than a creator remote from creation. Once again, as in childhood when my longing had been awakened by the messages, I felt drawn to follow the path of a spiritual quest. This desire had become more conscious and focused as I travelled.

My life acquired a greatly enlarged perspective that encompassed a meaning beyond that of responding blindly to events as they happened or feeling constrained by the limits of a single life, however well-lived. I particularly liked the fact that neither Hinduism nor Buddhism had a proselytising agenda. While both had spread far beyond India, neither had attempted conquest and conversion by the sword as had Christianity and Islam.

During these travels in the East, I was made aware of the incredible difference between the lives of people in the West and those in the East. First of all: the privilege of freedom from want and access to a good education. Secondly, freedom from the indescribable poverty, misery and disease that I saw in India in particular, where there seemed to be no hope of any change for the better in the lives of tens of millions of people, particularly for those unfortunate individuals belonging to the lowest caste who were treated with the utmost contempt and cruelty by people belonging to other castes. Finally, I was drawn to piece together an approach to reality that seemed utterly unknown in the Christian West and which supplied what I felt was missing there without being able to define precisely what it was. At first I was led by an attraction to certain myths and works of art, then to the texts of the Vedic, Buddhist and Taoist traditions — above all, to the concept of enlightenment. I learned that enlightenment was an immense expansion of consciousness and that it brought direct experience of the hidden ground of life as well as one's own essential being.

This was the beginning of a more conscious phase of my journey of discovery. I felt drawn to study the artistic heritage and spiritual legacy of the great civilizations of India and China and through these to develop a deeper insight into life itself. It took many years to see the whole picture and bring back this ancient knowledge into my own culture. Nor could I have written this book without experiencing the different facets of the journey I have described and will describe in subsequent chapters.

Marriage and Motherhood

In spite of the satisfaction of writing my book about my wanderings in the East, returning to England in 1957 brought me down to earth with a thump. At that time, for any woman who had not specifically chosen the career path of a scientist or a doctor, there seemed to be only three career options: a secretary, an academic or teacher, or a nurse. The alternative to these was marriage and motherhood. In the 1950's there was still a cultural split between the married woman and the professional or academic woman who presented a threat to the male-oriented society of that time. The immense panorama of life I had glimpsed on my travels made it difficult for me to settle down to what seemed a very restricted and restricting life. Since the teachings of the Hindu and Buddhist sages had taught me that immersing oneself in the usual concerns of the world was an impediment to the goal of spiritual enlightenment, it was extremely difficult to focus on finding a steady job, marry and adapt to the routine of domestic life. The call of the spirit and the life of the body seemed to oppose each other across an unbridgeable abyss.

However, when I was working on my book, a friend introduced me to a man whom I felt I could trust, an artist whose work I admired. My family was delighted, having almost given up hope of my finding the 'right' man: at that time twenty-eight was considered late for marriage. They were even more delighted that he was an artist because both my mother and grandmother were artists. We married in 1960 and a new phase of my life began, a phase of initiation into the experience of a close relationship with another human being and into the delight of finding someone who became a true friend and companion, someone with whom I could share my intense love of art and beauty and who was a kind and gentle person. But first I had to learn to cook and clean a house — skills which I had neglected to develop before I married because, with the arrogance of someone immersed in spiritual and intellectual concerns, I did not consider them to be important, let alone essential to a harmonious married life.

After two miscarriages, we had a daughter whom I dearly loved but hadn't the slightest instinctive knowledge of how to look after. Having lived life mainly through the mind, with scant regard for the body, I had received no preparation whatsoever on how to look after a baby. I was terrified and this terror was made worse by the fact that she was a pyloric baby: the milk I fed her was immediately ejected by projectile vomiting to the other side of the room, caused by the fact that the pyloric muscle would not open. At three weeks of age, she was losing weight rapidly and had to have an immediate operation. In those days, mothers were not allowed to stay with their children in hospital. I was deeply upset by the separation from her, particularly as I wasn't even allowed to see her for twenty-four hours. After three days she was able to come home, but I fell into a post-natal depression (unrecognized at the time as a mental state that could follow childbirth) and was totally unable to cope.

The years of tension and unhappiness watching my mother being destroyed by my father, and my complete inability to protect her, had led, from the age of twelve, to my falling into suicidal depressions for days and sometimes months at a time. This condition was never medically diagnosed or treated because in those days depression was not recognized as an illness. In fact, it was considered shameful even to admit to such a condition because of the taint of mental instability and even insanity. Although I had many times come close to suicide as an adolescent and young adult, I had never actually attempted it. But now that I was married, I soon realized that I had to do something about this situation. If I did not, I feared that it would destroy my relationship with my husband the way my father's depression had destroyed his relationship with my mother and myself, and that it would have a negative effect on the life and happiness of our daughter. I did not want the pattern to be repeated in another generation. My husband was immensely supportive but was perplexed by my perpetual unhappiness and lethargy. My ongoing depression increased the pressure on me to take some action. By chance I met a woman who had come through a nervous breakdown and she gave me the name of the psychiatrist who had treated her, a man who was also a Jungian analyst. So began a new phase in my life: my introduction to psychotherapy and to the work of Carl Jung, and my becoming aware of a mysterious and (to me) unknown aspect of the psyche called the unconscious.

Encounter with the Unconscious

Trust in my analyst gradually established trust in myself and led to the eruption of a passionate longing to create beauty, the same longing that had been awakened by the colours and designs of the saris I had seen in India and the beauty of women's clothes in the paintings of the Italian and Flemish artists of the early Renaissance. These drew me to a sensory delight in the appearance and feel of beautiful materials and a desire to design clothes. I took a correspondence course in dressmaking with the London County Council. Suddenly the idea occurred to me that I could make evening dresses to sell; I could use beautiful fabrics and design the dresses myself. In those days (the early 60's), women from my background living in London wore long dresses to the theatre and opera or when they entertained friends at home or went out to a dinner party.

I found to my amazement and delight that I could design dresses that women wanted to wear because they made them look and feel beautiful. Soon I had too many dresses to keep in the house and, in 1964, I realized I needed a shop. A friend suggested Beauchamp Place in Knightsbridge (London) and I found a tiny shop to rent there. My sister-in-law suggested the name Troubadour. I liked the romantic associations to the word. On the first day I sold three dresses, which covered the week's expenses, and from then on, week by week and year by year, my business grew until I found that I was making a great deal of money. I had two brilliant cutters to help me: one a remarkable Polish woman who had survived years in a concentration camp in Poland; the other a Spanish woman who had worked in Madrid with the great designer Balenciaga. By a stroke of incredible luck, I inherited a whole workshop of Polish seamstresses from a business that was closing down in a nearby building and these women made the dresses I designed. Each of these courageous women had a remarkable story of survival to tell (under the German and Russian occupations) and I became very fond of them all.

Twice a year I gathered together swatches of the finest silks, velvets, chiffons and organzas as well as materials from India and spread them out all over the surface of my work table as a prelude to designing the evening dresses I so loved, inspired by paintings of women by my favourite Flemish and Italian artists. Once a year, in November, I travelled to the great annual trade fair in Frankfurt where, walking up and down the aisles of three enormous halls, I bought the materials, embroideries and trimmings I needed. This experience grounded me in everyday life, helped me to earn my living well and taught me how to manage a growing business and keep the women who worked for me happy and productive.

Meanwhile, through the Jungian analysis, I was learning the importance of paying attention to my dreams and keeping a careful record of them. In those years I dreamed of great warehouses filled from floor to ceiling with materials of unimaginable fineness and beauty; of dresses far beyond my capacity to invent or make; racks filled with clothes that were a marvel of design and magnificence. These dreams inspired me to make ever more beautiful dresses in an attempt to come close to the ones seen in my dreams. But my own designs could never match those of my dreams either in the complexity of the design or in the fineness and splendour of the materials. Who, I began to wonder, was the dress designer of my dreams? Who was the weaver of these fabrics? I knew that the unconscious was sending me these images so far removed from my own capacity to create, but who and what and where was the unconscious?

Once, I remember, I had a dream of a tiny woman with the head of a greyhound presiding over a room filled with about 100 seamstresses seated at sewing machines that filled the room with a steady hum. Each woman was busily engaged in sewing the top part of a dress to the bottom part. The meaning of that dream only occurred to me years later when I came across the work of women who were writing and speaking about the goddess and the feminine principle, connecting the historically known to the hitherto unknown, the conscious to the unconscious, the visible to the invisible, the top to the bottom.

After twelve years, at the height of a major recession and inflation in the 1970's owing to a huge rise in the price of oil, I felt the time had come to close the shop. The cost of wages and materials spiralled overnight and long evening dresses were suddenly out of fashion, owing to the impact of the French designer, Courrèges. I felt that this phase of my life had come to an end.

My analysis had continued during this time, but at this point my analyst suggested that I should apply to train as an analyst myself. He had heard that Dr. Gerhard Adler, one of the two editors of Jung's Collected Works, was considering applications for training. I applied for an interview and while I was waiting for a reply, I had the following dream:

> I am travelling in a rocket to the moon and on landing there, see that a huge rusty iron construction shaped like the Eiffel Tower has been built on it, so huge that it towers high above its surface. The moon itself is a dead planet: all vegetation has dried up and wasted away. There are no human beings anywhere and no animals — no life at all. I travel across the moon's surface in a train, staring out of the window at this desolate landscape that looks as if it had been blasted by a nuclear bomb or shrivelled by a terrible drought. At the end of the dream I am precipitated into a swimming pool.

I discussed the dream with my analyst but, inexplicably, he could not fathom its meaning. When I went for the interview with Dr. Adler, he asked if I had had a dream recently and I told him about it, saying that I did not understand it. He said he thought the dream was drawing attention to the neglected state of the feminine principle or archetype — the moon being one of the primary images of that archetype. He suggested that the dream was showing me the plight of the feminine, which was also the plight of the soul, both in relation to my own life and to the world as a whole. The rusty iron structure was, in both cases, something that had been imposed on the deeper levels of the psyche by the rigid control of the conscious mind or ego. The water of the swimming pool suggested the water of the soul, the water of the feminine in which I needed to immerse myself. Tactfully, he suggested that more analysis was needed before I could be accepted for training. I needed to dismantle that massive iron structure and regenerate the surface of the moon. Despite the years of analysis I had already experienced which had helped me to save my marriage, earn my living in the world and open a channel for my longing to create beauty, the dream suggested that I needed now to go deeper into the psyche. So I began to work with Dr. Adler's wife, Hella, who had worked with Jung's wife, Emma, and who was able to initiate me into a deeper understanding of the feminine principle. After a few years of analysis with her, I was invited to embark on the five years' training to become an analyst myself.

I had found my way to depth psychology because of a crippling depression. Through my analysis I learned that depression can signify not only a genetic inheritance and the presence of traumatic and repressed childhood memories, but also a call from the unknown depths of the psyche to connect with those depths. The opportunity of responding to that call was the second major factor that changed the course of my life because it gave me insight into the fact that so much suffering and unhappiness arise from ignorance of our own nature. Quite apart from helping me to develop insight into my own psyche, the experience of depth psychology, as Jungian psychology was then called, gradually freed my ability to write and gave me fascinating subjects to write about. It widened my knowledge of history, psychology, philosophy and religion and gave me a new perspective from which to view them.

While science had been making extraordinary discoveries in the fields of physics, cosmology and biology, I discovered that depth psychology had been exploring the vast and unknown dimension of the unconscious. Jung's discoveries about the nature of consciousness went far beyond Freud's because they granted a transcendent and spiritual dimension to the psyche. As I learned more, I realized that they were making as significant a contribution to our understanding of life as the new discoveries in science yet, perplexingly, they were ridiculed and rejected as 'mystical' by mainstream secular culture, particularly in the field of clinical and behavioural psychology. Jung's contribution was so massive and significant because, as far as I was then aware, no one since Plotinus (3rd century AD) and Marsilio Ficino in Renaissance Italy had explored the soul as a living cosmic entity rather than an abstract concept.

I knew by then that science believed that consciousness originates with and depends upon the physical brain. Because of my encounter with Eastern philosophy, I could not accept this hypothesis. It was therefore an immense relief, almost a delight, to find that the important discoveries made by Jung's researches into the psyche suggested that what we call the conscious mind rests on an immense matrix or psychic field of the immemorial experience of our species that he called the Collective Unconscious. It has taken untold millennia for the conscious mind and our capacity for self-awareness to evolve out of this unfathomable matrix of the unconscious.

I learned that Jung had recognized a process of inner development that he called individuation, which could be activated and developed through analysis. With practice, experience and insight into the meaning and symbolism of dreams, he found that a relationship could be established with this vast field of consciousness, and that this relationship could radically transform our understanding of life, granting it a deeper meaning and value and healing the deep split which had developed between the two aspects of our nature.

The Call of the Rose

During the years of exploring the psyche and training to become an analyst, I continued to travel, mainly to Greece and the Greek islands, for the great civilizations of the ancient Mediterranean world held an overwhelming fascination for me. On one such visit, I have a vivid memory of going with my husband into a Greek Orthodox Church in the Peloponnese and being shown around it by an artist who was restoring the frescoes on its walls. He finally beckoned my husband to follow him into the sanctuary behind the screen. When I naturally followed them, he stopped me with his hand saying, "Women are not allowed in here." I was too astonished to remonstrate, particularly as inside the sanctuary I could just catch sight of a magnificent fresco of the Virgin Mary. Why would I be barred from the contemplation of one of the most sacred images of my sex? Why would the most holy place in the church, sanctified by the image of the Mother of God, be forbidden territory for woman and not for man? The implication was that I, as a woman, would somehow defile the sanctuary. What historical processes underlay the Christian attitude toward woman that was reflected in this artist's gesture of rejection? Once again, as in the church services of my childhood, I felt that something was deeply wrong with Christianity.

I was often haunted by the words of a poem by Walter de la Mare that I had discovered while I was at Oxford, in a book by Helen Waddell called *The Wandering Scholars*:

> *Oh no man knows*
> *Through what wild centuries*
> *Roves back the rose*

The image of the rose and the verse above kindled such a burning passion to know more, such a longing to reach back through those wild centuries to some discovery dimly apprehended as waiting for me at the roots of time, that the memory of the day I came across those lines of poetry lingers still, across the space of fifty years. Then, I knew virtually nothing about the Goddess, the feminine archetype, or the soul; nothing about the symbolism of the rose in Sufi mysticism nor the rose's connection with the Virgin Mary and the lost tradition of Divine Wisdom; nor its connection with the elaborate patterns formed by the orbit of the planet Venus. Yet the image, even the scent, of the rose was overwhelmingly numinous to me and I planted many roses in the garden of our home, entranced by their ancient names.

Galvanized by my experience in the church in Greece, I began a new phase of my journey of discovery — one that was to lead me into a deeper understanding of the soul on the one hand and an exploration of the roots of civilization and the loss of the feminine image of the divine on the other.

I found myself drawn to return to the earliest beginnings of the growth of culture, to the time when the image of the Great Mother presided over the life of humanity. It is to this ancient time, so distant from our own in every respect, that we may look for the genesis of ideas and symbols which eventually developed into religious and philosophical systems and all the different ways in which we have attempted to define a reality that transcends our power of understanding, yet which draws us, ineluctably, to itself.

Green Planet
Robin Baring 1973

Chapter Two

THE AWAKENING DREAM

Everywhere at all times in all cultures and races of which we have record, when the greatest meaning, the highest value of life man called gods or God needed renewal and increase, the process of renewal began through a dream.

— C. G. Jung[1]

I reflected often on the dream of the huge phallic iron tower on the surface of the moon. The Talmud says that a dream not interpreted is like a letter not read. The best we can do is to read the message coming to us from the depths of the soul and ponder its meaning. Over many years of pondering, I realized that this dream was a wake-up call from my soul. But beyond its personal message it seemed to hold a wake-up call for humanity. It carried a warning of what could happen to our planet: it could be rendered as barren and lifeless as the moon. I remembered that one of the early messages received by my mother had warned that our planet could become 'another orphan wandering in space' if humanity didn't change course.

My dream invited me to explore the imbalance between the masculine and feminine principles in Western civilization and how this imbalance has affected the lives of every one of us. The more I thought about it, the more I saw that the phallic iron structure was an image of what human technology has imposed on nature: it reflected the hubris of the modern mind which believes it can control and exploit the resources of nature and the planet for its own ends. It showed the effects of what can happen as human consciousness becomes cut off from the matrix or depths from which it has emerged — depths symbolized by the moon, ancient symbol of the Feminine. I began to see how losing touch with these depths would inevitably affect our values: how we educate our children; how we practise our science, medicine and psychology; the conduct of government; the formulation of our aims and goals; all our relationships with a wider world.

Most important of all, the loss of connection with the depths influences our view of reality and the way we live our lives in a personal sense. I began to understand that many of the problems we now face in the field of relationships between nations and cultures, as well as between men and women, were created by ideas and beliefs that were formed centuries, even millennia, ago, whose influence has never really been recognized and addressed. I needed to find out what historical influences had led to the erection of that iron tower — why it had come into being. I had no idea where to start, but fortunately my dreams gave me my direction.

Three further powerful dreams became the foundation of the second half of my life. In the first dream, I returned to the landscape of my grandmother's house in the South of France:

> *I go to the edge of the deep gorge and stand looking down into it and at the stream rushing through it from the mountains to the sea. Rising out of the shadowy depths of the gorge I see the shape of an enormous cobra-like serpent with seven heads. It continues to rise until these heads, spread out like a great hood, are level with the ledge on which I am standing. I am so terrified of it that I tremble and cover my eyes. When I dare to look again I see that the serpent wants to communicate with me. I signal to it that I am listening. It offers me the choice between staying where I am or climbing a ladder, which I now become aware is behind me. With a deep bow of reverence and obeisance, I indicate that I choose to climb the ladder.*

From my travels in the East, I recognized this seven-headed serpent as an image of the great serpent Mucalinda who had formed a canopy over the Buddha as he sat in deep meditation prior to the moment of his awakening. In the many sculptures I had seen in Thailand and elsewhere, the Buddha was often shown seated on the gigantic coils of a cobra whose seven hoods fan out behind him in a magnificent gesture of protection and blessing.

This dream shocked me into awareness of instinct as a primary expression of the soul. Because of what I had learned about archetypal psychology, I could understand that this serpent personified the power and wisdom of instinct as well as the power and wisdom of Nature. Without actually seeing this archetypal serpent rising out of the gorge, I don't think I would ever have understood instinct as something that is at the very root of life; something comparable to the weaver of the fabric of life. Nor would I have been able to assimilate the fact that it might be the mysterious medium through which each one of us is connected to the life of the planet and, beyond even that, to the life of the Cosmos. The dream helped me to become aware that this serpent personified the instinctive intelligence active and innate within the whole evolutionary process on this planet and the archetypal patterns or fields which give rise to the specific forms and DNA patterning of different species and, ultimately, to the evolution of consciousness in our own species. In a more personal sense, it represented the profound intelligence carried in the cells of the body and specifically, perhaps, the heart. Moreover, I could clearly see that this awesome serpent wanted to communicate with me and was asking something of me.

Shamanic cultures would have perfectly understood the apparition of the serpent in the sense just described, even though they might not have had the words I have used to describe it. The kind of consciousness they had, described as *participation mystique* by the anthropologist Lucien Lévy-Brühl, gave these cultures a sense of kinship with all creation. It was an *instinct for relationship and connection* rather than a concept or an idea. People in shamanic cultures knew that the spirit entities they saw in dream and vision manifested and expressed the deepest wisdom of Nature. Serpents spoke to them in their dreams, perhaps warning them of danger or acting as guides to the spirit-world and instructing them in the healing properties of plants and trees.

I took this dream as a call to climb the ladder of consciousness, to increase my understanding of the soul and become aware of the power of instinct to act as a guide in this work. I had never before had such a clear image of the creative powers of life as a living presence in all the forms and species of Nature; present as well as in the deepest, most archaic level of my own soul. I could have studied the Jungian literature on the unconscious for years and never grasped the *reality* of this primordial energy if I had not had this dream which offered me all that I needed to know in an image of overwhelming power. When I saw in my visionary dream this gigantic archetypal serpent rising out of the gorge, I realized with a sense of shock that the instinct was powerfully and overwhelmingly *real*. It was not an abstract idea that I could investigate at arm's length, but a numinous, living Presence, exactly as the sculptors of India, Thailand and Cambodia had portrayed it.

In a second dream a few years later:

> *I approach a tower surrounded by a narrow water-filled moat. I cross the bridge and enter the tower. I find its circular interior filled from floor to ceiling with wonderful books in white and brown vellum with gold or red lettering. The tower has two floors. Hesitantly, I go up to the second by a spiral staircase. At the top of the staircase Marie-Louise von Franz, one of Jung's closest colleagues and friends is standing, extending her hands to me in welcome.*

I understood the tower as an image of the totality of the psyche or soul. Its treasures were being offered to me by a woman who had been a close colleague of Jung's and had written many books on the feminine principle; books that in the course of my analyses and training, I had read and treasured. I remembered a poem by Rilke which seemed to offer a commentary on this dream:

> *I am circling around God, around the ancient tower,*
> *And I have been circling for a thousand years,*
> *And I still don't know if I am a falcon, or a storm,*
> *Or a great song.*

(trans. Robert Bly)

The Awakening Dream

The third dream was the most awesome dream of my life, the true awakener of my soul:

> *I dream that I come round the side of a huge dolmen and enter another world, an utterly strange and barren landscape. It is lit by the brilliant radiance of the full moon. I am searching for someone I love and my longing for him is so great that I have embarked on a journey in search of him. The landscape is transformed from a desert into field after field of brilliant green corn. The moonlight is so bright that it is like daylight and the corn is the colour of an emerald. I float over this emerald sea for many miles, my bare feet skimming the surface of the corn, until I come to the brow of a low hill and hesitate, wondering if I should go further. I decide to go on and come down into a valley on the other side.*
>
> *Suddenly, I find that two enormous men have caught me in a gigantic net that stretches the whole width of the valley and are drawing me into the presence of something tremendously powerful and numinous. I am frightened, yet at the same time fascinated. I lie flat on my back on the ground, helplessly enmeshed in the net and look up, half in terror, half in awe. I see the figure of a woman towering above me, filling the entire space between earth and sky. She is naked, with white skin and golden hair and is very beautiful, like Aphrodite. Yet she is not young, but ageless. In the centre of her abdomen is an immense revolving wheel that is also a rose and a labyrinth, like the one I had seen inlaid in the floor of Chartres Cathedral. Awestruck, I gaze up at her, then down at my own body which is exactly like hers, only tiny in relation to it. I too have a revolving wheel but mine is not centred; it is too far to the left. She does not speak but indicates that I am to centre my wheel, like hers.*

Visionary dreams like this one cannot be interpreted according to any known system of belief. They have to be held close to the heart and allowed to live so that, over many years, they can act as leaven in the soul. In another, earlier, culture I would have worshipped this image as a goddess and perhaps built a temple or shrine to her, but in today's world, belief and worship did not satisfy me. I wanted to reach the relevance of this dream for the whole of humanity, not just for myself. I needed to know why I had been given this vision. What was its intention? I felt it best not to speak of this dream to anyone, not even my husband. But I did tell my analyst, thinking that she would be able to give me an interpretation of it. To my surprise she said she did not want to comment on it but to let it be, explaining that the danger with such dreams is identification with an archetype and a huge inflation. In time, I would come to understand it and integrate its meaning with my life.

For years I wondered who she was. Was she Aphrodite? Demeter? Isis? Was she an angelic being of some kind? Was she the personification of Nature, of the Cosmos? Was this the kind of vision that people in times more open to visionary experience would have had? I knew that in Hellenistic times, in the second century AD, a man called Apuleius, of North African origin living in Rome, had had a vision of the goddess Isis, and had recorded the words she spoke to him through the figure of Lucius, hero of his book *The Golden Ass*, saying, "I am Nature, the Universal Mother, mistress of all the elements, primordial child of time, sovereign of all things spiritual, queen of the dead, queen also of the immortals, the single manifestation of all gods and goddesses that are."[2]

I also knew of the famous vision of the philosopher Boethius (AD 480–524) in which the figure of Divine Wisdom (Sophia) had appeared to him in his cell in Pavia and comforted him as he awaited his terrible death on the orders of the barbarian Emperor Theodoric.[3]

Naked and beautiful, neither young nor old, the goddess who had appeared to me was too pagan a figure for the Christian Mary, yet she was not like Aphrodite or any of the Greek goddesses with whom I was familiar. Finally, I began to question whether she could be a manifestation of the Neo-Platonic image of the *Anima Mundi* — the Soul of the World or Soul of the Cosmos, first mentioned by Plato in the *Timaeus* and later by Plotinus in the *Enneads*. Again and again I returned to wondering about her and how I was to centre my wheel. What did she want of me by sending me such a vision? Why was my wheel too far to the left and how could I centre it? Inspired by her numinous image, I began to explore the images of the goddess and to develop my thoughts about the feminine principle in general. As for the net, I knew that in Indian mythology there was a cosmic net that was connected with the god Indra but I thought that in the context of my dream it might signify the net of material reality in which I was caught like a fish. And the two immense male figures holding it might, I thought, represent the power of the unconscious that was drawing me into the presence of this cosmic being. Whoever they were, they forced me to look upwards to my vision, upwards to the Cosmos.

The Goddess

Several years later, when I had embarked on a training programme to become a Jungian analyst, I made friends with Jules Cashford, a woman who was one of a group of men and women in London who were training to become analysts with the Association of Jungian Analysts. Instinctively, I felt drawn to her and, on an impulse one evening, I invited her to come to supper with me. Initially, she seemed doubtful that she could come, but she had a dream about a ruined garden that needed to be restored and in the dream was told to go and see me. She told me about this dream when we met and we began to discuss the garden as an image of the neglected garden of the soul as well as the neglected feminine archetype about which so little was known in our culture. This led to the possibility of our writing a book together about the goddess — originally the Greek goddesses — as the primary image of the feminine archetype. But as we worked on the outline of the book, we realized that we needed to go much further back to the earliest sacred images of the feminine, back to the Neolithic and even the Palaeolithic eras, if we were to discover the foundation of the later Egyptian and Greek goddesses — or even the Virgin Mary. The research for the book drew us further and further into the origins of the sacred image of the goddess, opening avenues we had been unable to envisage at the beginning.

We were deeply influenced not only by a book called *The Great Mother* by a Jungian analyst called Erich Neumann,[4] but also by a book called *Saving the Appearances: A Study in Idolatry*, by an English philosopher called Owen Barfield. His book divided the evolution of human consciousness into three phases: (1) Original Participation; (2) Separation; and (3) Final Participation.[5] This division gave us the tripartite framework for our book. We felt drawn to the earliest beginnings of culture in order to find the genesis of ideas and symbols which eventually developed into all the different myths and images through which people described a numinous reality which transcended their 'normal' range of experience. As Jules and I worked together, we realized that not only were we exploring the history of goddesses and gods, we were also exploring the evolution or development of human consciousness through these sacred images. With this new understanding, the larger theme as well as the title of our book began to clarify.

The Shift from Lunar to Solar Mythology

Another remarkable book called *The Roots of Civilization* by Alexander Marshack opened our eyes to the importance of the moon in Palaeolithic culture and described the earliest lunar notations in Africa, dating to 40,000 BC.[6] When we studied the mythology and history of earlier Mediterranean and Near Eastern cultures, we found that there was a noticeable shift from lunar to solar imagery in Egypt and Mesopotamia ca. 2000 BC and, some 1500 years later, in Greece. This change of emphasis in mythology was accompanied by a shift of emphasis from feminine to masculine deities that finally resulted in the primacy of a single male deity: the monotheistic transcendent Father God of Judaism, Christianity and Islam. We realized that this shift had a profound effect on the development of Western civilization and that it marked a specific phase in the evolution of human consciousness: Owen Barfield's 'Phase of Separation'. We discovered that the imagery of the divine feminine had been repressed or excluded by the three Abrahamic religions and that this repression was clearly linked to the shift of emphasis in the image of deity from a Great Mother to a Great Father.

Gradually, as with the unfolding of the petals of a rose, Jules and I discovered that behind the image of the rose stood the figure of Mary, and behind her that of Sophia or Hokhmah, the Holy Spirit of Wisdom who speaks so eloquently in the Book of Proverbs, as well as in the Book of Ben Sirach (Ecclesiasticus) in the *Apocrypha*. We read the ground-breaking book, *The Gnostic Gospels*, written by the American theologian Elaine Pagels, which described how the feminine imagery of God was alive and flourishing in the Gnostic groups of early Christianity.[7]

Later, we read the actual Gnostic texts discovered in 1945 at Nag Hammadi in Egypt.[8] But, we wondered, did the Gnostic imagery and mythology associated with the divine feminine appear out of nowhere, or did they develop from older images of the Bronze Age goddesses of Egypt and Mesopotamia and, even further back, from the Great Mother of the Neolithic era?

The Lost Images of the Feminine

For many years we felt like archaeologists painstakingly uncovering a long-buried mosaic, gathering together fragments of an image and a mythology buried beneath the cultural deposits of thousands of years and many different cultures. At first we couldn't see the picture clearly. We simply felt attracted to different images and ideas. The researches of Jung and Erich Neumann had already brought together many of the lost images of the feminine archetype. However, the extraordinary research of the archaeologist, Marija Gimbutas, whose earliest book was published in 1974, identified many new images of the goddess from an unknown and remarkable European civilization that she called the Civilization of Old Europe and dated to the seventh millennium BC.[9] We were drawn as well to the magisterial work of the mythologist Joseph Campbell, and the historian of culture Mircea Eliade, both of whom enlarged our understanding of mythology and its influence on the formation and growth of civilization.[10] As the pieces of this mosaic began to fit together, a theme of great beauty and complexity slowly revealed itself to us, but also a story of the loss, repression and distortion of a priceless legacy from the past. As we fitted the fragments of images and texts together, this process of discovery became immensely exciting, even numinous, to us.

We wanted to find the earliest images which were of supreme importance to humanity. When, with the help of Joseph Campbell's book, *The Way of the Animal Powers*, we found the image of the Palaeolithic Great Mother scattered across an immense territory stretching from the Pyrenees in the West to Lake Baikal in the East, we knew we had found our beginning.[11] As we traced the evolution and many transformations of this image from 25,000 BC to the present day, we began to understand that this feminine image in its many forms stood for a totally different perspective on life, one that has been lost, buried, hidden for millennia. In the course of our research, we discovered such surprising similarities and parallels in the goddess myths of apparently unrelated eras and cultures that we concluded that there had been a continuous transmission of images throughout some 25,000 years or even longer (see note 11).

This continuity was so striking that we felt entitled to talk of 'the Myth of the Goddess', since the underlying vision expressed in all the variety of goddess images was constant: the vision of the whole of life as a living unity. More specifically, we realized that the image of the Mother Goddess inspired and focused a perception of the universe as an organic, sacred and indivisible whole in which humanity, the Earth and all life on Earth participated as 'her children'. Everything was woven together in one cosmic web; all orders of manifest and unmanifest life were related, because all shared in the sanctity of the original source. In our modern secular culture, this mythic image of the indivisible unity of Earth and Cosmos had vanished from sight. It was clear to me by this time that the idea of the whole Cosmos as an entity with consciousness or soul in which all life participates derives directly from the image of the Great Mother.

What had happened to the image of the goddess? Why and when did it begin to disappear, and how could we understand the implications of this loss? Since mythic images are part of a great meta-narrative which implicitly governs a culture, what did this tell us about a particular culture — such as our modern Western one

— that either did not have, or did not acknowledge a mythic image of the divine feminine? It began to seem no coincidence that our modern secular culture is one that has, above all others, desacralized and exploited nature. The Earth is no longer experienced as a living and sacred entity as in earlier times; it is no longer a 'Thou' but an 'it'. We can abuse, desecrate and pollute it without any feeling of responsibility, regret or guilt. And, we realized, we were living in a time when the whole body of the Earth is threatened by one species — our own — in a way unique in the history of the planet.

It soon became clear to us that, from Babylonian mythology onwards (ca. 2000 BC), the goddess became almost exclusively associated with nature as a chaotic force to be mastered, whereas the god assumed the role of creating or ordering nature from a 'place' that was outside or beyond it. Although sometimes defined as omnipresent, spirit gradually came to be defined as something beyond the world, something remote, transcendent; beyond nature and beyond ourselves. Moreover, it was defined as male and paternal. Everything that the image of the Great Mother once embraced in earlier cultures — in Neolithic communities and the Bronze Age civilizations of the Mediterranean area, the Middle East, India and China — was lost, and with it the vital sense of participation in the cosmic life of an invisible entity imagined as a containing, connecting maternal being.

The Separation from Nature

Since this separation between nature and spirit and between female and male deities had not previously existed we felt that it could be viewed within the context of the evolution of human consciousness, which involved a progressive withdrawal from a sense of participation in the life of nature. While this had resulted in an increasing autonomy for human consciousness, it had also resulted in a growing sense of separation from the natural world and the conviction that man had the right to master and control nature for his own benefit. Hence the belief, enshrined in the Book of Genesis, that man has been given 'dominion' over the Earth (Gen. 2). In *The Myth of the Goddess*, we summed up this primary change of consciousness: "If the relation to nature as the Mother is one of identity, and the relation to nature from the Father is one of dissociation, then the movement from Mother to Father symbolizes an ever-increasing separation from a state of containment in nature, experienced no longer as nurturing to life but as stifling to growth." [12]

As our collaboration deepened, Jules and I became 'one mind with two outlets' as I once jokingly referred to our relationship. Often we telephoned each other to report on a significant detail we had found, only to discover that the other had come across that very same idea or piece of evidence at almost the same time on the same day. One particular instance stood out: on the same day we had each found out that the Greeks had a beautiful image to describe how the individual soul, which they called *bios*, hangs from the great necklace of Being, which they called *Zoë*. Almost simultaneously, we tried to telephone each other to communicate our excitement at this discovery. What we discovered through our researches was a revelation to us: the continuity of the image and mythology of the goddess through many centuries and civilizations. We felt we were reassembling the pieces of a dismembered corpse that could be brought back to life, rather as Isis, in the great Bronze Age Egyptian myth, had gathered the scattered fragments of the body of Osiris and restored him to life. What the goddess had done for the masculine archetype, we were doing for the feminine one. We realized that the goddess personified a vision of life that had been lost — the vision of a living, intelligent, conscious Cosmos in which all aspects of life were related to each other.

A Lost Vision of Reality

As we worked, we felt supported by something — almost by Someone — beyond either of us. Like other women who were simultaneously discovering what had been lost, we felt the urgency of the need to tell the story of the neglected goddess and to explain why she had been allowed so little place in patriarchal culture. We wanted to know why and when nature had been so emptied of spirit that a great split had developed between them; why the feminine dimension of the divine was missing in the Christian image of God; why in the patriarchal religions, deity had been formulated in the image of a Father rather than a Mother and a Father and finally, why the Holy Spirit, the third aspect of the Trinity in Christian doctrine had been defined as male when, in the magnificent passages in the *Apocrypha*, it was obvious that a female voice was speaking as the Holy Spirit of Wisdom. We felt it was imperative to discover the reasons why something vitally important to the balance of Western civilization as a whole had been lost. Most important of all, we felt that the image of the goddess carried a vision of reality that needed to be recovered: a vision that had been neglected or overridden for centuries and that had once connected us not only with the life of the Earth but with the life of the Cosmos.

Why did we feel that this quest for the lost feminine dimension of the divine was so important? Because we felt that it might offer an explanation of how our present culture had come to regard nature as something that could be rapaciously exploited and manipulated to the advantage of our human species without any awareness of the effect this attitude had on the overall balance of life or on the organism of planetary life. It would also help us to understand the roots of woman's long subjugation: why her voice had been effectively written out of the history of Western, and indeed world, civilization; why she had suffered so much oppression in patriarchal culture for so many centuries. We had absolutely no idea when we started of the chain of misogynistic ideas which had developed from the description of Eve's role in the Biblical Myth of the Fall and from the influential legacy of the writings of Plato as well as those of the early Christian Fathers.

Ten years of research and writing led ultimately to the publication in 1991 of *The Myth of the Goddess: Evolution of an Image*. The book had taken us so long to write because we were at first training to be, then working as, analysts and had little time or energy to spare. It led to the creation of a deep and lasting friendship between us, as if we had been drawn to each other to do this work which neither one of us could have accomplished on our own. We were determined that our book should include the images of the goddesses as well as their many myths and stories and gathered 450 illustrations, insisting that our publisher should place them in the context of the specific text that described them. Happily, this was agreed.

The Myth of the Goddess tells the story of how, over a period of some 20,000 years, the image of the deity gradually changed from goddess to god, and how the god came to be identified with spirit and mind, and the goddess with nature, matter and body. The image of the goddess was feared and rejected and with it women and every aspect of life that had been identified with the feminine, including, most importantly, the soul, nature and matter. As the feminine principle, personified by the goddess, came to be rejected or downgraded in relation to the masculine one, personified by the god, so spirit and nature were sundered. As this divisive process intensified, conscious mind and instinctive soul, head and heart, became increasingly polarized in human consciousness, leading ultimately to the spiritual, political and ecological crisis of the present time.

We felt that our book had a message for our time because it showed how the loss of the feminine dimension of the divine had led to the triple loss of respect for nature, matter and woman, and how the ecological crisis of our times could be directly traced to the denigration of the feminine in the philosophy, theology and mythology of the last four millennia. In the last section of the book, we focused on the image of the sacred marriage of spirit and nature — asking that what had been separated over the course of these millennia be reunited.

The Insights of Other Women

While we had been working on our book, other women in America and Canada were following similar lines of research, publishing the fruits of their quest to discover what had happened to the goddess, what the cultures over which she presided were like and what meaning and significance her image held for modern woman. Many books began to appear, the most important perhaps being Elaine Pagels book on the *Gnostic Gospels*[13] and Riane Eisler's *The Chalice and the Blade*.[14] While Pagels' book recovered the lost Christian images of the Feminine that had been honoured in the early Gnostic communities and miraculously restored through the discoveries made at Nag Hammadi in Egypt, Eisler's book, published shortly before ours, was a formidable indictment of patriarchal culture and an endorsement of the need for a change in consciousness. Some of the writers, like Pagels and Rosemary Ruether, were theologians. Others, like Jean Shinoda Bolen and Marion Woodman, were Jungian analysts. The image of the Black Madonna held a numinous meaning for some of them, particularly for Woodman, working as an analyst in Toronto. While I mention here the books of a few individual women, there were many other books that I read with deep interest and gratitude because each, in its own way, strengthened and confirmed my own quest for a deeper understanding of the Feminine. Sylvia Brinton Perera's *Descent to the Goddess*, published in 1981, stressed the need for modern woman to make the descent into the underworld of the soul, there to experience and redeem the powerful instinctual feelings that had been denied expression for so many centuries in a patriarchal culture. In the introduction to her book she wrote these memorable words:

> The return to the goddess, for renewal in a feminine source-ground and spirit, is a vitally important aspect of modern woman's quest for wholeness. We women who have succeeded in the world are usually "daughters of the father" — that is, well adapted to a masculine-oriented society — and have repudiated our own full feminine instincts and energy patterns, just as the culture has maimed or derogated most of them. We need to return to and redeem what the patriarchy has often seen only as a dangerous threat and called terrible mother, dragon, or witch.... This inner connection is an initiation essential for most modern women in the Western world; without it we are not whole. This process requires both a sacrifice of our identity as spiritual daughters of the patriarchy and a descent into the spirit of the goddess, because so much of the power and passion of the feminine has been dormant in the underworld — in exile for five thousand years.[15]

Turning towards the World

While I felt this movement to restore the feminine was very important, my attention also was drawn to what was happening in the world and to awareness of the suffering of people caught up in the conflict developing in the former Yugoslavia in 1992. Deeply distressed by the helpless suffering of these people, I wrote a book for children, basing it on the theme of *The Conference of the Birds*, a famous Sufi poem by the twelfth century Persian mystic, Farid ud-Din Attar. I had always loved this story and, although the original was written for those who were treading a spiritual path, it seemed possible to retell it for modern children and to place it in the context of the need for a fundamental change in our relationship with the Earth if we were ever to grow beyond the conflicts that were devastating so many people's lives, and to become aware of ourselves as inhabitants of the planet, rather than of a particular national, religious or ethnic group. This would offer a new image of spirituality. The book was published in 1993 with the title *The Birds Who Flew Beyond Time*.

Then, I was drawn in another direction through a close friendship with Andrew Harvey whose books I greatly admired.[16] We were asked by an English publisher (Godsfield Press) to write two books together: *The Mystic Vision* (1995) and *The Divine Feminine* (1996). Once again, I found myself immersed in material I had known and loved many years ago, returning to the mystical literature of Hinduism, Buddhism and Taoism that I had encountered on my two journeys to the East but adding to it the experience of the Christian and Sufi mystics. Together, we selected passages from the mystical traditions of all cultures, including some of the sayings of the shamanic Indigenous Peoples, such as the American Indians and the Kogis living in the remote mountains of Colombia.

I steeped myself in these writings, my own thoughts clarifying as I struggled to articulate the essence of what the mystics have tried to communicate to us. Their message, I felt, could be summed up in these words:

> The mystics and sages of all times and cultures have tried to reveal to us what they have discovered: that we are in the Divine Ground like a fish in the sea, or a bird in the air; and have tried to help us dissolve the illusion of our separate existence so that we would experience ourselves here and now, in this dimension, as what we truly are — Divine Being.

The Divine Feminine

The second book, *The Divine Feminine*, took me deep into the sacred literature and imagery of the feminine aspect of the divine in different religious traditions.

Although I had learned a great deal in the research for *The Myth of the Goddess*, it seemed as if I was now asked to broaden my research to include other cultures. I began to understand the feminine archetype or principle in a deeper sense, no longer as the goddess alone but as what the goddess personified: an immense matrix or web of hidden relationships through which spirit and nature, the invisible and the visible dimensions of the life of the Cosmos, were connected with each other. I began to see that something absolutely vital had been lost in religious teaching: the concept of the cosmic dimension of soul as an unrecognised order of reality which binds together all aspects of life, both visible and invisible. I also saw that this disastrous loss in the sphere of religion had been transmitted to science which did not recognize the unity and interconnectedness of the aspects of life it was exploring, let alone their sacredness.

In 1995, while researching material for The Divine Feminine, I had another dream which at first seemed unremarkable,

> *I am driving to a College in Oxford University to hear a performance of Monteverdi's Vespers of the Blessed Virgin. On the back seat of the car there is a battered old-fashioned brown leather suitcase — the kind that years ago used to be called a 'revelation suitcase' because it could expand to a greater capacity than was at first apparent.*

Although I wrote it down, I didn't pay much attention to this premonitory dream. However, shortly afterwards, while writing a chapter on the image of the Shekinah in the Jewish mystical tradition of Kabbalah, I suddenly understood who the goddess of my vision represented in this tradition. She personified what the kabbalists named the feminine face of God: the wisdom and glory and radiant immanence of the divine ground concealed beneath and within the forms of life. The Shekinah literally means the 'Presence of God in the world'. Then I remembered the dream about the battered 'revelation' suitcase on the back seat of my car. Although I had written about the Shekinah in *The Myth of the Goddess*, drawing on the insights of the great Jewish scholar, Gershom Scholem, I had not really grasped the full implications of what she stood for. Now I realized in a flash of illumination that the Shekinah offers the most complete image of the feminine aspect of spirit to have survived from the ancient past. She restores the missing connective cosmology of the soul that the three major patriarchal religions, in their repudiation of a feminine dimension of the divine, had lost. I began to sense that the feminine being who had revealed herself to me in such powerful imagery personified the soul as a cosmic entity as well as an invisible dimension of reality. I experienced this realization as a revelation. It was like discovering water in the desert. So many fragments of knowledge, so many sacred texts from many cultures, began to fall into place and, in spite of all the research I had done for *The Myth of the Goddess*, I began to look much more deeply into the relationship between the image of the goddess and the idea that the Cosmos has a soul.

The wider, cosmic meaning of the word 'soul' became intensely real, intensely alive. With a sense of shock, I understood why, from this new perspective, life is utterly sacred. I realized that the image of the Shekinah personifies the gossamer-fine web or field of relationships that is the invisible ground of all that we call life. Science may study the visible aspects of this web of life under different headings such as cosmology, biology and micro-physics, but an image like the Shekinah unifies this diversity and, above all, invites relationship with it as something that is alive, conscious and the very ground of our own consciousness. While the image of the Virgin Mary has to some extent played this role for millions of Catholic and Orthodox Christians over the centuries, she was not an aspect of the godhead and could never, therefore, represent the innate divinity and interconnectedness of life. Nor could she represent the hidden dimension of the cosmic web of life or the sacredness of nature. Now I understood why the great Indian sage, Sri Aurobindo, had written in his masterwork, *The Life Divine*: "If it be true, that Spirit is involved in Matter and apparent Nature is secret God, then the manifestation of the divine in himself and the realization of God within and without are the highest and most legitimate aim possible to man upon earth."[17]

Then I remembered a beautiful passage from a Hasidic rabbi, Rabbi Nachman of Bratslav, that I had found while compiling *The Mystic Vision*: "As the hand held before the eye conceals the greatest mountain, so the little earthly life hides from the glance the enormous lights and mysteries of which the world is full. And he who can draw it away from before his eyes as one draws away a hand, beholds the great shining of the inner worlds."[18]

I knew now that my visionary dream as well as my long quest to hold on to the memory of the earliest channelled messages had led me to the discovery of the unrecognized divinity of life on this planet, as well as the existence of an invisible world or dimension of reality in which all life participated; a cosmos of relationships; a magnificent, awe-inspiring web of life.

The discovery of the image of the Shekinah was so deeply meaningful — a revelation even — because here, clear as crystal, was the lost feminine imagery of God as well as the Holy Spirit. Because the tradition of Kabbalah makes the association between the feminine aspect of the godhead, Divine Wisdom, and the Holy Spirit, it showed me how Christianity, in its definition of the Holy Spirit as the Third Person of a male Trinity, had lost the ancient and connective mythology of spirit as a great web of life and, most importantly, the recognition that the divine is present in every blade of grass, every cell of our bodies, *that it is every blade of grass, every cell of our bodies.* This understanding, so intrinsic a part of the teaching of the Vedic seers of India as well as those of Kabbalah, is what we have lost and what we need to recover now.

Soul and Spirit as the Divine Ground

I felt as if I were being given a glimpse of the great shining of the inner worlds, worlds normally veiled from our sight. I knew I was rediscovering something that seemed familiar to me, something intensely exciting which offered the metaphysical counterpart of the most advanced scientific discoveries of our time. In the form of this powerful and numinous image, I was given a revelation of why, in Blake's words, "Everything That Lives Is Holy". I understood that the mystical tradition of Kabbalah offers us one of the major missing links between the participatory experience of the great lunar cultures of the Bronze Age and our own age, whose difference I will explore in later chapters. What we have lost and what this extraordinary tradition has preserved for us is the image of a sacred Earth as well as an unseen web of relationships connecting the life of our planet with the life of the Cosmos. It was clear to me that our own soul, our own consciousness, belongs to this greater life as child to parent: son to father or daughter to mother. My image of the soul spun one hundred and eighty degrees as I realized that the soul is not in us. We are in the soul.

But more than this: we are of the nature and substance of soul, the nature and substance of spirit. It seemed to me that spirit and soul in their widest sense are not really different in kind or substance but two names or two aspects — one masculine, one feminine — for the same invisible dimension that is the ground, root or source of the physical world whose life infuses, animates and sustains the whole Cosmos. This life is not only innate in every atom of our being but we are participants in its life, however unconscious of this fact we may be. Suddenly, the soul became intensely real, intensely alive to me. I experienced the feminine being I had seen in my dream as a living presence with whom I could communicate, to whom I could relate. Lying at her feet, gazing up at her, I realized that I was microcosm in relation to her as macrocosm.

I understood then that the tremendous being of my dream was indeed she whom Plato and Plotinus in their concept of *Psuche tou Kosmou* 'ψυχή του κόσμου' and *Anima Mundi* had named the Soul of the Cosmos or Soul of the World. It was she who had appeared in Hellenistic times to Apuleius in Egypt as the goddess Isis, and in later Christian times as Sophia or Divine Wisdom to the philosopher Boethius, as we had described it in *The Myth of the Goddess* (pp. 634–5). Awaiting his death, he had written his famous *Consolation of Philosophy*, immortalizing the words she had spoken to him, words that, centuries later, were to inspire Charlemagne.[19] This same figure of the World or Cosmic Soul can be identified with the voice of Divine Wisdom and the Holy Spirit, who speaks so eloquently in the Book of Proverbs and the Wisdom Books of the *Apocrypha* as well as in the Gnostic texts discovered at Nag Hammadi in Egypt in 1945. To me, the imagery of the Shekinah offered a startlingly complete description of the Soul of the Cosmos.

Notes:

1. Jung, C. G. CW14 (1963) *Mysterium Coniunctionis*, Routledge and Kegan Paul Ltd., London, par. 488
2. Apuleius (1950) *The Golden Ass*, Penguin Books Ltd., London
3. Boethius (1969) *The Consolation of Philosophy*, trs. E.V. Watts, Penguin Books Ltd.
4. Neumann, Erich (1955), *The Great Mother: An Analysis of the Archetype*, Pantheon Books Inc., New York
5. Barfield, Owen (1988) *Saving the Appearances: A Study in Idolatry*, Second Edition, the Wesleyan University Press, Middletown, Conn. USA.
6. Marshack, Alexander (1972) *The Roots of Civilization*, Weidenfeld & Nicolson Ltd., London
7. Pagels, Elaine (1980) *The Gnostic Gospels*, Weidenfeld and Nicholson Ltd., London
8. Nag Hammadi Library (1977) ed. James M. Robinson, E.J. Brill, Leiden
9. Gimbutas, Marija (1974) *The Goddesses and Gods of Old Europe 6500–3500 BC*, Thames and Hudson Ltd., London. (1989) *The Language of the Goddess* and (1991) *The Civilization of the Goddess: The World of old Europe*, both HarperSanFrancisco An exhibition called The Civilization of Old Europe (2010) in New York, Zurich and Oxford has shown many of the magnificent artefacts that Gimbutas described, which have survived from 5000-3500 BC and are now housed in the museums of Romania and Bulgaria.
10. Campbell, Joseph (1958-68) *The Masks of God*, Vol. 1-1V, Secker & Warburg Ltd., London
11. Campbell (1984) *The Way of the Animal Powers*, Times Books Ltd., London. In 2008, the tiny figure of a woman was found in a cave in Germany – the oldest known sculpture of a human figure – dated to 35-40,000 BC.
12. *The Myth of the Goddess: Evolution of an Image* (1993) Penguin Arkana p. 661
13. Pagels, *The Gnostic Gospels*
14. Eisler, Riane (1988) *The Chalice and the Blade*, Harper & Row, San Francisco
15. Perera, Sylvia Brinton (1981) *Descent to the Goddess*, Inner City Books, Toronto
16. Harvey, Andrew (1991) *Hidden Journey*, Bloomsbury Publishing Ltd., London
17. Aurobindo, Sri (1990) *The Life Divine*, Lotus Light Publications, Wilmot WI, p.4
18. Rabbi Nachman of Bratslav (1981), from Edward Hoffman, *The Way of Splendor: Jewish Mysticism and Modern Psychology*, Shambala, Boulder, Colorado, p.117
19. Boethius, *The Consolation of Philosophy*

The Buddha

Seated on the coils of the Naga (serpent) whose seven-headed hood protects him
while he meditates – 17th century, National Museum Bangkok

Chapter Three

THE TREE OF LIFE

I loved her above health and beauty, and chose to have her instead of light
for the light that cometh from her never goeth out....

— Wisdom of Solomon

My visionary dream of the cosmic woman had led me to the Jewish mystical tradition of Kabbalah. The word Kabbalah means 'to receive'. Legend says that when Adam and Eve were cast out of the Garden of Eden, the angel Razael gave them a book to help them find their way back into it. In the words of a modern kabbalist, Z'ev ben Shimon Halevi (Warren Kenton), "Kabbalism is the inner and mystical aspect of Judaism. It is the Perennial Teaching about the Attributes of the Divine, the nature of the universe and the destiny of man."[1]

Through some four thousand years, a revered chain of teachers passed on the tradition of Kabbalah orally; from its remote origins in Babylon and Egypt until the 13th century when a book called the *Zohar* or *Book of Splendour* was written in northern Spain, possibly in the town of Girona which was then a centre of kabbalistic studies. Many centuries before that, it had flourished most prolifically in Hellenistic Alexandria, where many Jews fled for refuge at the time of the Babylonian Captivity (586–539 BC), and again after the fall of Jerusalem in AD 70 when a new influx of refugees joined the older community long established there. Still later, it moved to Spain, at the other end of the Mediterranean. Then, with the brutal expulsion of the Jews from Spain in the fifteenth century, Kabbalism moved to Safed, in Palestine, where one of its greatest teachers, Moses Cordovero (1522–1570), lived and wrote his famous work, *The Orchard of Pomegranates* (*Pardes Rimmonim*), in which he expounded on the thirteen gateways to higher consciousness. Another great teacher was Isaac Luria (1534–1572), who lived in Cairo but moved to Safed and briefly studied under Cordovero before his teacher died. Kabbalism also took root in northern Europe, in particular England (where Shakespeare undoubtedly knew of it), Poland and Bohemia. It flourished briefly in Renaissance Italy, where, together with Marsilio Ficino, the brilliant young Pico della Mirandola hoped to create a fusion of Kabbalism and Christianity until his early and untimely death (possibly murder instigated by the Papacy) cut short the possibility of realizing his vision.

I discovered that one of the oldest and most important images of Kabbalah is the Tree of Life. I felt that through my visionary dream I had been led to this tradition to which the early messages seemed to refer: "Find the Stone at the foot of the Tree", they had said. As I uncovered more about this tradition, it seemed to me that the Tree of Life was a clear and wonderful template describing the web of relationships which connect invisible spirit with the fabric of life in this world. At the innermost level or dimension of reality is the unmanifest and unknowable divine ground; at the outermost the physical forms we call nature, body and matter. Linking the two is the archetypal template of the Tree of Life — an inverted tree — whose branches grow from its root in the divine ground and extend through invisible worlds or dimensions of being to this one. In this template the nature and properties of the different dimensions or levels of reality and their relationships with each other are described and defined. Every aspect of creation, both visible and invisible, is interwoven with every other aspect. All is one life, one cosmic symphony, one integrated whole. We participate in the divine life which informs all these mysterious levels of reality. Our lives are inseparable from the inner life of the Cosmos.

I came across a sentence in a book called *The Ladder of Lights* by William Gray which described the Tree of Life as "a symbolic representation of the relationships believed to exist between the most abstract Divinity and the most concrete humanity… a family Tree linking God and Man together with Angels and other Beings as a complete conscious creation."[2] I found myself drawn to this contemplative tradition which emphasized the path to God as a process of awakening through gradual illumination and experience rather than adherence to a specific belief or faith. I also liked the fact that it did not proselytise or attempt to convert, instead waiting for people to seek it out and discover its treasures. Its emphasis was on the growth of insight and wisdom through contemplation and a deepening relationship with the divine ground while not neglecting life and relationships in this dimension of reality. I found it striking and important that it did not fall into the dualism that split apart matter and spirit. It did not reject the body nor was it obsessed with sin.

Imagine a Muslim culture in Europe which welcomed both Christian and Jew, where there was no anathematising of the infidel or the apostate such as exists today in Iran and other Islamic countries. From the ninth to the twelfth centuries, such a tolerant, advanced culture existed in Moorish Spain and south-western

France. From Cordoba, Seville and Granada in the south to Toledo, Girona, Toulouse and Narbonne further north, in courtyards filled with the scent of jasmine and the sound of water trickling from fountains on summer evenings, scholars and philosophers from three religious traditions met in small groups to exchange insights, explore mysteries, and transmit their knowledge and experience to the next generation. This was the Golden Age of Islam when science, mathematics and philosophy flourished and the great Arab scientist Averroes Ibn Rushd taught in Cordoba and wrote innumerable treatises on Aristotle.

This nurturing atmosphere produced an extraordinary flowering not only of Islamic but also of Jewish and Christian culture in the twelfth and thirteenth centuries, a flowering which coincided with the diffusion of the Grail legends and the haunting songs of the troubadours. People travelled from all over Europe to renowned centres of learning such as Toledo to sit at the feet of the Muslim and Jewish scholars who presided there. The rich mixture of learning and artistic genius in Moorish Spain, reflected in the sublime beauty of the Alhambra, initiated a powerful cultural impulse carried by a relatively small number of individuals over a wide area of Europe, but particularly and most brilliantly, in the highly sophisticated culture of south-western France.

Then, abruptly and tragically within three centuries, the harmonious relationship between Muslim, Christian and Jew was destroyed by Christian fanaticism. There were three strands to this fanaticism. One strand was the Crusades against the Muslims who had occupied the city of Jerusalem (the First Crusade was launched in France in 1095). A second strand was the Albigensian Crusade initiated in 1208 by Pope Innocent III, which let loose a rabble army led by Simon de Montfort that descended on south-western France and, with the force of a tsunami, utterly destroyed its tolerant and flourishing culture. The third was the decision by the Catholic monarchs Ferdinand and Isabella, to expel both Jews and Moors from Spain in the late fifteenth century, although the persecution of the Moors had begun earlier as Christian Spain sought to reclaim the territory that had been held by them. A proclamation in 1474 by Pope Sixtus IV established the Inquisition in Spain and, over the next decade, thousands of Jews were burnt at the stake in the infamous *auto-da-fé*. In 1492, under penalty of death, all Jews were ordered to leave Spain, even though their communities had been established there for over six hundred years and they were well integrated into the culture of both Christian and Moorish Spain. It was at this time that many fled to Palestine and the community in Safed.

These were the three fateful and fatal elements which were to give rise to centuries of enmity and persecution between Christians, Jews and Muslims and have led inexorably to the tragic events in which we are embroiled today.

Hundreds of thousands of Jews and Muslims were brutally expelled from Spain, many of them murdered, their property expropriated. Thousands of priceless manuscripts and sacred artefacts were destroyed as they were in Sarajevo during the recent war in Bosnia. The superb mosque in Cordoba had its heart gouged out and replaced by a Christian altar. How different the history of European culture and relations between these three religious traditions might have been if a tolerant rather than a fanatical Christianity intent on supremacy had prevailed in Spain. Christians never questioned the rightness of what they were doing in the name of God. Their faith provided the justification for the most abominable cruelty and oppression that was later carried from Europe to the New World — all in the name of Christ.

The Teaching of Kabbalah

The fundamental teaching of Kabbalah or Kabbalism is the doctrine of emanation and, because of this, the oneness or unity of all cosmic dimensions of reality. Divine Creative Spirit, named as the unmanifest godhead, *Ain Soph* or *Ain Soph Aur* — the Limitless Light — is regarded not only as totally transcendent and unknowable but also, through emanation, present in every particle of the visible, created world as well as in the intermediary dimensions of reality veiled from our sight. The zig-zag path taken by the Divine Emanation down the Tree of Life is called the Lightning Flash. The aim of the kabbalist was, and is, to unite the two worlds: the Above with the Below; the invisible divine world with the manifest world. Unlike other religious traditions, Kabbalism did not reject this world as fallen (Christian) or illusory (Hinduism) but saw it as both sustained and permeated by the light of the divine ground. It taught that whatever we do in this world affects the invisible dimensions or worlds and vice versa, because everything, visible and invisible, is connected. The soul becomes enlightened over many lives, at first through attraction to, then contemplation of and, finally, communion with the invisible worlds. Moses de Laon, a renowned thirteenth century kabbalist living in Spain wrote these memorable words:

> The purpose of the soul entering this body is to display her powers and actions in this world, for she needs an instrument. By descending to this world, she increases the flow of her power to guide the human being through the world. Thereby she perfects herself above and below, attaining a higher state by being fulfilled in all dimensions. If she is not fulfilled both above and below, she is not complete. Before descending to this world, the soul is emanated from the mystery of the highest level. While in this world, she is completed and fulfilled

by this lower world. Departing this world, she is filled with the fullness of all the worlds, the world above and the world below. At first, before descending to this world, the soul is imperfect; she is lacking something. By descending to this world, she is perfected in every dimension.[3]

Like someone emerging from a darkened cellar, we cannot bear the radiant light of the divine ground all at once. As our relationship with the divine deepens, so does our consciousness expand to include awareness of the deeper, unseen dimensions of being until we begin to radiate the light and love of this hidden ground. It seemed to me that this tradition found its way into Dante's great vision of the soul's ascent to the Celestial Spheres as well as into the Interior Castles of St. Teresa of Avila, yet neither could have risked acknowledging such a heretical influence.

Worlds within Worlds

Rather than presenting an image of a hierarchical descent from the invisible to the visible, Kabbalah presented the image of worlds nesting within worlds, dimensions within dimensions manifesting, as it were, from within outwards. It was, I thought, a wonderfully illuminating template of the skein of relationships which connect invisible spirit with the visible fabric of this material world. At the innermost level is the unknowable source or godhead, at the outermost the physical forms of matter. All is one unified web of life: one life; one energy; one single cosmic entity. We are, I discovered, each one of us, that life, that energy, that cosmic entity. Quintessentially, there is only one life. We are all participants in the life of the Cosmos, atoms in the Being and Body of God. In our essence, we are one.

I realized that the levels or dimensions of this hidden ground of the Cosmos are what Jesus meant by the kingdom of God — worlds or dimensions which are invisible to us yet which underlie and 'permeate' the physical world and which, if we could only see them, are spread out before us. These dimensions can gradually become accessible to our limited consciousness as it develops and expands. I realized too that Jesus as well as other great teachers must have taught from deep knowledge and experience of these worlds. I began to see that the image of an invisible dimension of reality lies behind many images of the quest, in particular the medieval quest for the Holy Grail — image of a boundless source of nourishment. My visionary dream, more powerfully and immediately, and less fearfully than my earlier experience at the age of eleven, had opened a door to the existence of a hidden dimension of reality which holds our own in its embrace.

As Warren Kenton (Z'ev ben Shimon Halevi), a modern teacher of Kabbalah, writes:

> To be acquainted with Kabbalah is one matter, but to do its Work quite another…. Only those who do the Work for its own sake are initiated. Only the individual who wants to make manifest what Kabbalah reveals can be an initiate. This process is nothing less than to integrate the body, soul and spirit, and so become a finer instrument whereby the inner and outer worlds can come into communion…. Each time this is done, the Universe comes increasingly into focus as a reflection of the Absolute.[4]

Kabbalah is a living tradition, still in the process of evolution through the experience of the individuals exploring and living it today. It offers the tradition and the method of developing a direct path of communion between the individual and the divine ground — mediated by a teacher transmitting an oral tradition most probably descended from ancient shamanic experience, developed and added to by a lineage of contemplatives extending through millennia. What attracted me to this tradition is that it celebrates the indissoluble relationship between the feminine and masculine aspects of the godhead which the three patriarchal religions have either rejected or ignored for centuries. In this tradition as well as in the sacred marriage of god and goddess in Bronze Age civilizations, the marriage of Shiva and Shakti in the Hindu tradition, and the relationship of Yang and Yin in the Taoist tradition, we find the image of relationship and union between the masculine and feminine aspects of reality. If we want to understand the deep roots of our present ecological and spiritual crisis, we can find them in the loss of three important elements: the feminine image of spirit; the direct shamanic path of communion with spirit through visionary and mystical experience as lived by the great contemplatives of all traditions; and the sacred marriage of the masculine and feminine aspects of the divine.

The Shekinah and Divine Immanence

The Shekinah is the image of the Divine Feminine or the Feminine Face of God as it was conceived in this mystical tradition of Judaism, originating perhaps in the Rabbinic Schools of Babylon, and transmitted orally for a thousand years and more until it flowered in the writings of the Jewish kabbalists of medieval Spain and south-western France and later in sixteenth century Palestine. In the imagery and mythology of the Shekinah, we encounter the most complete description of cosmic soul and the indissoluble relationship between the two primary aspects of the godhead that has been lost or hidden for centuries.

It became increasingly clear to me that the repression of the image of the Great Mother or Great Goddess was the principal reason for the loss of the idea that all nature was ensouled with spirit and therefore sacred. It was the eradication of spirit from the natural world and the fear of animism that ultimately removed from the people living through the millennia of patriarchal religion their age-old sense of participation in a Sacred Cosmic Order.

Why did I find the image of the Shekinah of Kabbalah so broad in its imaginative and revelatory reach, so significant, so nourishing to my soul? Because it gave me a different image of spirit: here was an image of the divine that is the actual ground of the phenomenal world; that has brought this world into being and lives within it. The Shekinah as the Holy Spirit of Wisdom — divinity present and active in the world — supplies the missing imagery of divine immanence which has been lost or obscured in the orthodox traditions of Judaism, Christianity and Islam. And this tradition brings together heaven and earth, the divine and the human, in a coherent and seamless vision of their essential unity.

Whereas the Old Testament is the written tradition of Judaism, Kabbalah offers the hidden oral tradition, wonderfully named 'The Voice of the Dove', as well as 'The Jewels of the Heavenly Bride'. The Bronze Age imagery of the Great Goddess returns to life in the extraordinary beauty of the descriptions of the Shekinah, and in the gender endings of nouns which describe the feminine dimension of the divine. But the Divine Feminine is now defined as a limitless connecting web of life, as the unseen Soul of the Cosmos, the intermediary between the unknowable godhead and life in this dimension. The Shekinah brings together heaven and earth, the invisible and visible dimensions of reality, in a resplendent vision of their essential relationship and union.

The Shekinah describes the feminine aspect of the godhead as Mother, Beloved, Sister and Bride — imagery that has been lost or obscured in Judaism, Christianity and Islam and that could, if recovered and honoured, transform our image both of God and Nature, not to mention ourselves. The Shekinah gives woman what she has lacked throughout the last two thousand years in Western civilization: an image of the Divine Feminine that is reflected at the human level in herself. The Shekinah is Divine Motherhood, named as 'Mother of All Living' — the title that was once given to Eve in Genesis. Now I could see, even more clearly than when writing *The Myth of the Goddess*, that the story of the Fall in Genesis was a successful attempt by the priesthood of that time to demythologize the feminine aspect of deity and to banish Asherah, the hated Canaanite goddess, by demoting her into the figure of Eve. Yet the ancient tradition of the Divine Feminine somehow survived in this mystical tradition of Judaism. Gershom

Scholem writes that the introduction of the idea of the feminine element in God "was one of the most important and lasting innovations of Kabbalism. The fact that it obtained recognition in spite of the obvious difficulty of reconciling it with the conception of the absolute unity of God, and that no other element of Kabbalism won such a degree of popular approval, is proof that it responded to a deep-seated religious need."[5]

The *Zohar* or *The Book of Radiance* or *Splendour* that appeared in Spain in 1290 was the principal text of medieval Kabbalism — the work of many individuals but authored in the name of Moses de Laon. It speaks of the Shekinah as the Voice or Word of God, the Wisdom of God, the Glory of God, the Compassion of God, the Active Presence of God, intermediary between the mystery of the unknowable source or ground and this world of its ultimate manifestation. The mythology of the Shekinah as Divine Wisdom and Holy Spirit offers one of the most incandescent, vivid and powerful images of the immanence of the divine in this dimension. It transmutes all creation, including the apparent insignificance and ordinariness of everyday life, into something to be loved, embraced, honoured and celebrated because it is the epiphany or shining forth of the divine intelligence and love that has brought it into being and dwells hidden within it.

The Imagery of the Sacred Marriage and the Transmission of Light

The highly-developed cosmology of this tradition preserves the ancient Bronze Age image of the sacred marriage, reflected in the union of the Divine Father–Mother in the ground of being. There is not a Father God but a Mother–Father who are one in their eternal embrace, one in their ground, one in their emanation, one in their ecstatic and continuous act of creation through all the dimensions they bring into being and sustain. From the perspective of divine immanence, there is no essential separation between spirit and nature. No other tradition offers the same breathtaking vision in such exquisite poetic imagery of the union of male and female energies in the One that is both. The Song of Songs was the text most used by kabbalists for their contemplation of the mystery of this divine union.

The *Zohar* contemplates the mystery of the relationship between the female and male aspects of Divine Spirit expressed as Mother and Father, and their emanation through all dimensions of creation as Daughter and Son. The essential concept of this mystical tradition expresses itself in an image of worlds within worlds rather than as a hierarchy of descent. Divine Spirit (*Ain Soph* or *Ain Soph Aur*) beyond form or conception is the ineffable Light at the root, the Source, the Ground of Being. Emanating as creative Sound (Word), Light, Intelligence and

Love, it brings into being successive spheres, realms, or dimensions named as veils or robes which clothe and hide the hidden source, yet at the same time transmit its radiant light.

The transmission of this ineffable Light from the source to the outer manifest level takes the form, as described earlier, of an inverted tree, the Tree of Life, whose branches grow from its root in the divine ground and extend through invisible worlds or dimensions of being of which we are no longer aware because our minds are closed to their existence. As I absorbed these images, I recognized their resemblance to certain Gnostic texts discovered at Nag Hammadi. I was also struck by the similarity between the imagery of light as the divine ground of being and the Tibetan concept of the luminous light of the Void.

The primal centre or root is the innermost light, of an unimaginable luminosity and translucence, utterly different from the light we see in this world. This centre expands or is sown as a ray of light into what is described in some texts as a sea of glory, in others as a palace or womb which acts as an enclosure for or receptacle of the light. From here it emanates as a radiant cascade, a fountain of living water, pouring forth light to create, permeate and sustain all the worlds or dimensions it brings into being. All life on earth, all consciousness, *is* that light and is therefore utterly sacred. The *Zohar* describes nature as the garment of God. This cascade of light flows through the ten Vessels, Powers or Attributes of the Divine, named as the *Sefiroth*, which are connected by the 22 paths of the Tree of Life. The first Vessel (*Kether*) is a state of perfect equilibrium and contains all that was, is and will be. The divine impulse towards emanation moves the energy to expand beyond the first Vessel to the second; it is then received and contained by the third Vessel. This process of expansion and containment is repeated three times until this Tree is complete and the emanating energy balanced. The process of emanation then proceeds through further worlds, and the laws or archetypes which govern each world or level of creation come into being until they manifest as our own.

The Divine Feminine

The Shekinah or feminine face or aspect of the godhead is named as Cosmic Womb, Palace, Enclosure, Fountain, Apple Orchard and Mystical Garden of Eden. She is named as the architect of worlds, source or foundation of our world, and also as the Radiance, Word or Glory of the unknowable ground or godhead. Text after text uses sexual imagery and the imagery of light to describe how the ray which emanates from the unknowable ground enters into the womb — the Great Sea of Light — of the Celestial Mother and how she brings forth the male and female creative energies which, as two branches of the Tree of Life, are symbolically, King and Queen, Son and Daughter. A third branch of the Tree descends directly down the centre, unifying and connecting the energies on either side. All elements or aspects of the Tree of Life are connected through twenty-two paths.

The Shekinah is named as the Divine Spouse, the indwelling and active Holy Spirit and the divine guide and immanent presence who delivers the world from bondage to beliefs that separate it from its source, restoring it ultimately to union with the divine ground. She brings into being all spheres or dimensions of manifestation which are ensouled and sustained by the ineffable source until she generates the manifest world we know and remains here until such time as the whole creation is enfolded once again into its source. Once again, I was struck by the similarity between this imagery of the Shekinah and the Tibetan image of Tara. I wondered whether these two traditions, Kabbalism and Mahayana Buddhism, had perhaps encountered each other in Hellenistic Alexandria, the meeting place of East and West; or was it perhaps that the same archetypal imagery of the Feminine manifests in different cultures?

Kabbalism calls this last, tenth sphere *Malkuth*, the Kingdom, where the divine Mother-Father image is expressed as the male and female of all species. Humanity, female and male, is therefore the expression of the duality-in-unity of the godhead. The Shekinah is forever united with her beloved Spouse in the divine ground or heart of being and it is their union in the godhead that holds life in a constant state of coming into being. Yet she is also present, here with us, in the material reality of our world. The sexual attraction between man and woman and the expression of true love between them is the enactment or reflection at this level of creation of the divine embrace at its heart that is enshrined in the cherished words in the Song of Songs: "I am my beloved's and my beloved is mine" (6:3). Human sexual relationship, enacted with love, mutual respect and joy, is a sacred ritual that is believed to maintain the ecstatic union of the divine pair.

Because she brings all worlds into existence as her robes or veils, and dwells in them as divine presence, nothing is outside spirit. In the radiance of that invisible cosmic sea of light, everything is connected to everything else as through a luminous circulatory system. Moreover, the Shekinah is deeply devoted to what she has brought into being, as a mother is devoted to the well-being of her child. All life on earth, all levels and degrees of consciousness, all forms of what we see and name as nature and matter, are the creation of that primal fountain of light and are therefore an expression of divinity.

Blue and gold are the colours associated with the Shekinah. As cosmic soul, She is the radiant ground or 'light body' of the human soul — at once its deepest, essential ground, its outer 'garment', the physical body, and its animating spirit or consciousness. She is the holy presence of the 'glory of God' within everyone. All of us, moving from unconsciousness and ignorance of this radiant ground to awareness of and relationship with it, live in her being and grow under her power of attraction until we are reunited with the source, discovering ourselves to be what in essence we always were but did not know ourselves to be — sons and daughters of God, living expressions of divine spirit.

There were different schools within Kabbalah. Some saw the Shekinah as separated from the godhead, in voluntary exile on earth, describing her as a Daughter cut off from her Mother, or as a Widow, until she is able to return to the divine ground, having gathered to herself all the elements or sparks (*scintillae*) of her being which had been scattered during the process of emanation. Others put great emphasis on the marriage between Tipareth, the sixth *Sefiroth*, with the Shekinah in her place of exile as Malkuth, the tenth *Sefiroth*: a marriage that we can assist in bringing about within us, for the Tree of Life is also a template of the inner life of our soul. The blackness of the Shekinah's robe, comparable perhaps to the black robe or veil of Isis — who was also called 'The Widow' during her search for Osiris — signifies the darkness of the mystery which hides the glory of her Light.

I was amazed to discover that the Shekinah was called 'The Precious Stone' and 'The Stone of Exile', which at once connects her with the image of the Grail, described as both vessel — source of boundless nourishment — and stone. She was also called the 'Pearl', and 'The Burning Coal'. To the opening eyes of my imagination, she appeared as the glowing gold of the hidden treasure at the heart of life, the jewelled rainbow of light thrown between the divine and human worlds, the seamless robe which unites the manifest and unmanifest dimensions of life. Here, at last, was the crucial missing piece of the puzzle that I had sought for over fifty years. The channelled messages had told us to find 'the Stone at the foot of the Tree', and here was the Shekinah described as 'The Precious Stone' at the foot of the Tree of Life. I was overwhelmed by this realization, yet I knew it was important not to cling to the literal imagery but to look beyond it, into the symbolic heart of the teaching and its meaning for our culture which has been so deprived of the image of the Divine Feminine.

It suddenly occurred to me that kabbalistic imagery is woven into the fabric of many well-known fairy tales. In the story of Cinderella, for example, the veiled form of the Shekinah (or the forgotten image of the Great Mother) can be recognized in the fairy godmother who presides over her daughter's trans-formation from soot-blackened drudge to royal bride. Harold Bayley, who wrote a remarkable book called *The Lost Language of Symbolism* at the beginning of the last century, showed me that the figure of Cinderella could be understood to represent the human soul as it moves from 'rags to riches'.[6] Cinderella's three splendid dresses, which could be equated with the 'robe of glory' of certain kabbalistic and gnostic texts, are the soul's luminous sheaths or subtle bodies, as dazzling as the light of the moon, sun and stars. Just as the soot-blackened girl in the fairy tale puts on her three glorious dresses to reveal herself as she truly is, so does the human soul don these 'robes of glory' as she moves from the darkness of ignorance into the revelation of her true nature and parentage.

To reconnect with the tradition of the Divine Feminine that has been fragmented, obscured and almost lost over some two and a half thousand years, I turned to the magnificent passages in the Books of Proverbs, Ben Sirach (Ecclesiasticus) and the Wisdom of Solomon.[7] If I had not by chance been given a Bible by my mother when I was ten years old that contained the *Apocrypha*, I would not have known of the existence of the last two Books since the *Apocrypha* is not included in the Protestant Bible and I was brought up as a Protestant. I had spent nine long months in hospital at that age and during that time read my Bible from cover to cover, understanding very little of it, yet absorbing as much as I could of its stories and imagery.

In the *Apocrypha* I found evidence of a feminine being, identified with Divine Wisdom and the Holy Spirit, who comes to life in certain of its passages. Here, in the Book of Ben Sirach (Ecclesiasticus), Wisdom tells us that she is immanent in our world; with us in the streets of our cities; calling to us to awaken to her presence, to obey her laws, to listen to her wisdom; promising her blessing if we can only hear her voice and respond to her teaching. In the Book of Proverbs, Wisdom tells us that she is the Beloved of God, with Him from the beginning, before the foundation of the world. She speaks from the deep ground of life as the hidden law which orders it and as the Craftswoman of creation. With their vivid imagery, these passages transform the idea of the Holy Spirit, speaking as Divine Wisdom, from abstract idea into Living Presence. She speaks as if, like the Shekinah, she were here, in this dimension, dwelling with us in the midst of her kingdom, accessible to those who seek her out. She is unknown and unrecognized, yet working within the depths of life; striving to open our understanding to the divine reality of her being; the sacredness of her creation; her justice, wisdom, love and truth.

Here is the language of the immanence of the Divine Feminine in the world. Who wrote these magnificent verses and the ones to follow? Was it a high-priest of the First Temple whose words were secretly preserved and taken with the Jews who found sanctuary in Alexandria? Did he hear a voice speaking to him or did he have a vision of a great feminine being, as I did in my visionary dream and as Apuleius did of the goddess Isis? The verses reveal this feminine Presence —

named as Divine Wisdom and the Holy Spirit — as the Soul or intelligence of the Cosmos; rooted in tree, vine, earth and water and active in the habitations of humanity. She is the principle of justice that inspires human laws. She is invisible spirit guiding human consciousness — a hidden presence longing to be known; calling out to the world for recognition and relationship. To those who, like Solomon, prized her more highly than rubies, Divine Wisdom was their wise and luminous guide.

Wisdom was always associated with the image of a goddess in the pre–Christian world, with Inanna in Sumer, Maat and Isis in Egypt and Athena in Greece. But as we move into the Christian era, there is a profound shift in archetypal imagery as Wisdom becomes associated with Christ as the Logos, the Divine Word, and loses all connection with the Feminine Principle. At the Council of Nicaea in AD 325 the Christian image of the Trinity as Father, Son and Holy Spirit is wholly identified with the masculine archetype and the ancient association of the Holy Spirit and Wisdom with the Divine Feminine is irrevocably lost.

The Gnostic Imagery of the Divine Mother

Yet another strand in this extraordinary story is the Gnostic imagery of the Divine Mother who was known to the early Christians in the first two centuries of the Christian era. Margaret Barker, in her book *The Revelation of Jesus Christ,* describes how groups of Jewish exiles fled Jerusalem in three waves and established a flourishing community in the city of Alexandria.[8] The first group fled there after the Assyrians attacked the northern province of Samaria and carried off ten of the twelve tribes of Israel in 721 BC. This catastrophe was blamed on the people's worship of the Queen of Heaven and the goddess Asherah, whose statue stood in the Temple. All traces of her cult in the First Temple in Jerusalem were removed and her sacred groves destroyed. The second wave followed the destruction of the First Temple by the Babylonians in 597 BC, when thousands of Jews were forced into exile in Babylon and some joined the community already established in Egypt. The third wave of refugees (composed of Jewish Christians) fled to Alexandria after the Second Temple was destroyed by the Romans in AD 70. She believes that these groups preserved the ancient rituals once practised in the First Temple in Jerusalem and associated with the Queen of Heaven whom they addressed as Divine Wisdom and the Holy Spirit. Were it not for the discoveries of the Nag Hammadi texts in 1945, which recovered the evidence in Egypt for the worship of a feminine deity or the feminine aspect of God, this part of the story would have been lost to us, perhaps forever.

By the year 200, as Elaine Pagels tells us in Chapter III of her book *The Gnostic Gospels*, "Every one of the secret texts which Gnostic groups revered was omitted from the canonical collection, and branded as heretical by those who called themselves orthodox Christians. By the time the process of sorting the various writings ended... virtually all the feminine imagery for God had disappeared from the orthodox Christian tradition."[9] Until the appearance of her book and the eventual publication in 1977 of the texts discovered at Nag Hammadi in 1945, no one knew that some groups of early Christians had an image of the Divine Mother whom they had named 'The Invisible within the All'. Some texts speak of how, as the Eternal Silence, the Divine Mother received the seed of Light from the ineffable source and how, from this womb, she brought forth all the emanations of Light, ranged in related pairs of feminine and masculine entities or energies. They described her as the womb of life, not only of human life, but the life of the whole Cosmos known at that time. They knew this Divine Mother as the Holy Spirit and saw the dove as her emissary. This Gnostic cosmology is so similar to the descriptions of the emanation of Light in Kabbalism, that they may both have been developed by the community of the Jewish exiles in Alexandria.

In the *Gospel of the Hebrews*, one of the gospels destroyed during this time of suppression and persecution and known only from quotations in the work of the early Christian Fathers, Origen and Jerome, the Holy Spirit is described as the mother of Jesus, who spoke to him at his baptism saying, "My Son, in all the prophets I was waiting for Thee".

"Here," writes the late Professor Gilles Quispel, one of the great authorities on the Gnostic Gospels, "we come to a very simple realization: just as the birth requires a mother, so rebirth requires a spiritual mother. Originally, the Christian term "rebirth" must therefore have been associated with the concept of the spirit as a feminine hypostasis."[10]

I find it fascinating that in Gnosticism the imagery and mythology of the Divine Mother as the Holy Spirit is so similar to the imagery of the Shekinah in Kabbalah that they seem to belong to one and the same tradition. Certain texts name her as the Mother of the Universe but also speak of the androgyny of the divine source in imagery similar to the later kabbalistic texts. In one Gnostic text called the *Trimorphic Protennoia*,[11] the speaker describes herself as the intangible Womb that gives shape to the All, the life that moves in every creature:

> *I am the voice speaking softly.*
> *I exist from the first.*
> *I dwell within the Silence,*

Within the immeasurable Silence.
I descended to the midst of the underworld
And I shone down upon the darkness.
It is I who poured forth the Water.
I am the one hidden within Radiant Waters...
I am the Image of the Invisible Spirit.
I am the Womb that gives shape to the All
By giving birth to the Light that shines in splendour.

Who treasured this tradition and kept it alive for later generations? Who took the tradition of Divine Wisdom as the Holy Spirit guiding human evolution from Alexandria to Spain and thence to medieval France and the rest of Europe? Could this tradition have inspired the image of the Holy Grail and kept it alive for us today, when the world is crying out for reconnection with the soul?

The Holy Spirit Today

How could we imagine the Holy Spirit today? Perhaps as the light that manifests as both wave and particle, as the deep unexplored 'sea' of cosmic space and the invisible light particles which are the ground of all physical reality, including the extraordinary complex structure and organization of the patterns of energy that we name as matter: a word which comes from *mater*, the Latin word for mother. After so many billions of years the energy of life has evolved a form, the planet earth, and a consciousness, our own, which is slowly growing towards the recognition of its ground and source. Yet, because of the loss of the tradition of the Divine Feminine, we do not know that what physicists, cosmologists and biologists are exploring in the finer and finer gradations of matter they are discovering is what the awe-struck explorers of the Tree of Life in Kabbalah named the Face and the Glory of God; nor that the universe we explore with the Hubble telescope is the outer covering or veil of a vast unseen Cosmos and an unimaginably fine web of luminous and invisible relationships. If only these images of the Shekinah could be restored to us, how differently we might see matter; with what respect we might treat it.

What comment would she pass on the pathological effects of our ignorance: the pollution of her earth, her seas, her air; the abysmal and wanton sacrifice of animals and the contamination with toxins and pesticides of the food and water that is her gift of life to us? And what of the manufacture and sale of weapons — including the horrific reserves of nuclear, biological and chemical weapons — the torture, murder and rape of men, women and children in war; the use of explosives to destroy flesh and bone; the agony of orphaned, starving, murdered or maimed children? To hear her answer, we would have to attune ourselves to her being. We would have to listen with her ear to the voice of the suffering we bring into being through our ignorance of the unity and divinity of life. We would have radically to change our habits of behaviour and become more consciously aware that the suffering we inflict on others is actually suffering that we are inflicting on the 'body' of spirit and that spirit suffers from our blindness, ignorance and abysmal cruelty.

If we could awaken to the sacredness and divinity of life we would begin to see matter and our own bodies in a different light; we would treat them with greater respect. If we could awaken to Her Presence, we could bring matter and spirit, body and soul together, healing the deep wounds inflicted by the beliefs and concepts which have separated them. Even as we accomplish this, we would begin to transmit the light and love of the Holy Spirit flowing to us and all creation.

While I was writing about the Shekinah, these images came to me:

> I stand on the shore of the world and look intently at the sea of stars, at their great patterns spread out before me. As I look, I see a ship approaching, in the shape of an ark, its prow curved back like the wings of a great bird. Closer it comes, weaving between the constellations, growing larger as it approaches me. I see that it is translucent, as if made of glass, and that it has the iridescence of an opal. Yet it is also richly adorned with jewels that are themselves stars. Closer still it comes, and now I see that the ship casts a radiance upon the sea of space and shows me that this sea is a great web or net made of gossamer filaments of light; they sparkle with jewels like a spider's web in the sun. At the jewelled points where these filaments meet there are vortices of swirling energy. I perceive the web as a being of unimaginable dimensions who is speaking to me, saying:
>
> "This is what I am. This is the hidden glory of My Being. This is the life you belong to. The Sea of My Being is at once 'greater than the great' and 'smaller than the small', co-inherent with the greatest galaxies of cosmic space and the tiniest particle of matter. Once I was named Soul or Spirit or Cosmic Consciousness or Great Mother and Father — the greater psychic reality to which your own life belongs and of which, for the most part, you are tragically unaware. Once, people imagined themselves living within My Being. Then I became distant, remote, forgotten. Now, for so many, I am lost altogether. This causes me grief for I am in exile from My people. For both of us there is great suffering and loneliness. My dream, the Dream of the Cosmos, is for you to know Me again, to realize that you live within My Being, My Light and My Love."

Notes:

1. Halevi, Z'ev ben Shimon (Warren Kenton)
2. Gray, William G. (1968) *The Ladder of Lights*, Helios Book Service Ltd., Cheltenham
3. Matt, Daniel (1995) *The Essential Kabbalah: The Heart of Jewish Mysticism*,
    HarperSanFrancisco, p. 148
4. Halevi (1986) *The Work of the Kabbalist*, preface. Samuel Weiser Inc., Maine
5. Scholem, Gershom (1954 & 1961) *Major Trends in Jewish Mysticism*,
    Schocken Books Inc., New York, p. 229
6. Bayley, Harold (1912) *The Lost Language of Symbolism*, Vol.1,
    Williams and Norgate, London
7. Proverbs 8: 23-31; Ben Sirach (Ecclesiasticus) 24: 3-6, 9-11, 13-21, 28-34;
    Wisdom of Solomon 7: 7, 10, 21-7, 29; 8:1-2
8. Barker, Margaret (2000) *The Revelation of Jesus Christ*,
    T & T Clark, Edinburgh, pp. 109-112, 200-212, 279-301
9. Pagels, Elaine (1980) *The Gnostic Gospels*, Weidenfeld and Nicolson Ltd., London, p. 57
10. Professor Gilles Quispel in a pamphlet he gave me called *The Birth of a Child*, p. 23
11. *The Trimorphic Protennoia*, The Nag Hammadi Library, Ed. James M. Robinson,
    E.J. Brill, Leiden, 1977, pp. 462-470 (extracts only)

I came across the Essene Gospel of Peace as this book was reaching completion and I would like to mention it here because it contains material that is highly relevant to the honouring of both the Divine Mother and the Divine Father in passages of sublime beauty which are relevant to the original teaching of Jesus.
http://www.thenazareneway.com:80/essene_gospel_of_peace_book1.htm

In 1928, Edmond Bordeaux Szekely first published his translation from the Aramaic and Hebrew, of *Book One of The Essene Gospel of Peace*, an ancient manuscript he had found in the Secret Archives of the Vatican as the result of limitless patience, faultless scholarship, and unerring intuition. This story is told in his book, *The Discovery of the Essene Gospel of Peace*, published in 1975. The English version of Book One appeared in 1937, since when the little volume has travelled over the world, appearing in many different languages, gaining every year more and more readers, until now, still with no commercial advertisement, over a million copies have been sold in the United States alone. It was not until almost fifty years after the first French translation that Book Two and Book Three appeared (*The Unknown Books of the Essenes* and *Lost Scrolls of the Essene Brotherhood*), achieving rapidly the popularity of Book One.

In 1981, Book Four, *The Teachings of the Elect*, was published posthumously according to Dr. Szekely's wishes, representing yet another fragment of the complete manuscript which exists in Aramaic in the Secret Archives of the Vatican and in old Slavonic in the Royal Library of the Habsburgs (now the property of the Austrian government). The poetic style of the translator brings to vivid life the exquisitely beautiful words of Jesus and the Elders of the Essene Brotherhood. Some of the chapters are titled: The Essene Communions. The Sevenfold Peace. The Holy Streams of Life, Light, and Sound. The Gift of the Humble Grass.

Part Two

The Lunar Era
Original Participation

Artemis of Ephesus

Chapter Four

The Lunar Era and the Great Mother Participation in Cosmic Soul

My heart is longing for a lost knowledge, slipped down out of the minds of men....

— from the Sanskrit poem *Black Marigolds* [1]

The Goddess in all her manifestations was the symbol of the unity of all life in Nature.... Hence the holistic and mythopoeic perception of the sacredness and mystery of all there is on Earth.

— Marija Gimbutas, *The Language of the Goddess*

The previous three chapters have described the path of a life quest in search of a lost image of reality which, like a precious mosaic, lay buried beneath the cultural deposit of thousands of years. In this quest I took as a talisman the dream about the rusty iron tower rising from the surface of the moon described in Chapter One together with the visionary dream of a cosmic woman. These dreams led me far back into the past in search of a way of relating to life that had long preceded modern industrial culture and the current worldview that regards nature as something to be exploited by man. They led me to writing *The Myth of the Goddess* with Jules Cashford, tracing the image of the Divine Feminine from the Palaeolithic era to modern times. They also led me to mystical tradition of Kabbalah and to the revelation which came to me while learning about the image of the Shekinah and the template of cosmic reality known as the Tree of Life. The following six chapters will describe in greater detail what I found and why we, as a species, lost the sense of participation in a Sacred Cosmic Order.

In the course of this quest, it soon became apparent to me that the great myths that have arisen from our observation and contemplation of the moon and the sun have shaped whole eras. Because of their influence on us and our fascination with them, two primary meta-narratives or worldviews have come into being and, over a time-span of many thousands of years, have profoundly influenced the way we think and behave. These worldviews I have called lunar and solar because of the influence of two very different mythologies whose focus was the moon and the sun.

Human consciousness has developed infinitely slowly out of nature. For count-less millennia, the potential for human consciousness was hidden within nature, like a seed buried in the earth. Then, very slowly, it began to differentiate itself from nature. Deep in our memory is the whole experience of life on this planet: life that has evolved over the 4.5 billion years since its formation; life as hydrogen, oxygen and carbon; life as the most minute atomic particles; life as water, fire, air and earth; life as rock, soil, plant, insect, bird, animal; life as woman and man evolved from this aeonic experience. Finally the point was reached where planetary life evolved a complex neurophysiology and a brain which enabled us to speak, to formulate thoughts, to communicate with each other through language, to endow sounds with meaning, and invent writing as a way of recording and transmitting thought. Over these billions of years, life on this planet has evolved from undifferentiated awareness to the self-awareness of our species. All this can be described as an *instinctive* process, each phase blending imperceptibly into the next, yet becoming more complex and adding something as it evolved into the next phase.

Self-awareness and reflective consciousness as we know it now is a very recent development, yet consciousness as genetic patterning present in different forms in plant and animal and human life is carried within us as part of the reptilian and mammalian brain system that took many millions of years to evolve. From these have come the highly differentiated consciousness that we call our self-reflective awareness and our rational mind. The ability to think, to reason, to reflect, to analyse, to store information and be able to retrieve it through memory, is itself a further development of the older brain systems, and interacts with them, but our conscious awareness is focused in the most recently developed part of ourselves and is out of touch with the roots from which we have grown. It is now danger-ously out of alignment with the Sacred Order in which we once felt contained.

We have created all kinds of myths to explain the human condition and to reconnect us to the whole from which we have become separated. We can under-stand this evolutionary step more easily when we look at the life of a child, who recapitulates in its separation from its mother the immense evolutionary advance of becoming aware of ourselves first of all as a species, differentiated from the life around us; then as individuals, differentiated from the collective life of the tribe and developing the priceless asset of self awareness.

The Great Mother

As the conscious mind began to differentiate itself from the matrix of nature, the sacred image was like an umbilical cord connecting us to the deep ground of life. For some 25,000 years, possibly far longer, the image of the Great Mother presided over distant eras which have only recently become accessible to us: the Palaeolithic, the Neolithic and the great civilizations of the Bronze Age.[2] The earliest images of the Great Mother known to us are the small, and in some cases exquisite, figurines of a goddess carved from stone and bone and ivory some 25,000 years ago (goddesses of Lespugue, Laussel, Willendorf).

Long ago, and in many different cultures, the whole Cosmos was envisioned as a maternal being and this world was seen as the manifestation of an unseen source which breathed it into being, animating and sustaining it. The unseen world of spirit was seamlessly interwoven with this phenomenal world so that the two were essentially experienced as a unity. The air itself was an "awesome mystery joining the human and extra-human worlds".[3]

Just as the stars emerged each night from the darkness of the night sky, so the visible universe was born from the dark mystery of the invisible womb of the Great Mother. She was the starry Cosmos. She was the Earth and all life on Earth and she was the unseen dimension of the world of spirit which underlay the visible world. People felt connected to her as to a great cosmic being. Everything was infused with divinity because each and all were part of a living, breathing, connecting web of life: plants, animals, man and woman — all these were her 'children'. The animals painted on the walls of the great Palaeolithic caves came forth from her womb and returned to it, to be born anew.[4] Overawed by the immensity and grandeur of nature, and sensing the presence of the unseen dimension of spirit within its forms, people felt they lived within a Sacred Order, however harsh the conditions and the brevity of their lives.

Whether we look to Neolithic Europe, or to India and China, or to any people that has managed to retain its ancient traditions, like the Kogi Indians of Colombia, we find the Cosmos imagined as a Mother, the womb and origin of all, the bringer of life and death, holding within her being the three dimensions of sky, earth and underworld. It is her ancient presence that was transmitted to the Great Goddesses of Bronze Age Egypt, Mesopotamia, Persia and Anatolia. Further east, in China, we find her in the Goddess Kwan Yin, in Tara, the Divine Mother of the Tibetan tradition, and the goddess Kali in India. This image of the Primordial Mother emerged at different times in different cultures and endured for different lengths of time and was worshipped with different rituals, but it is possible to say that the Great Mother was the primary experience of spirit, just as the mother is the primary experience of life for the infant and small child.

We may ask why the image of the Great Mother was so important. To answer this question, we need look no further than our experience of birth into the world. First of all, there is the experience of the embryo and foetus in the womb, the experience of union and containment within a watery, nurturing matrix. After the sudden and violent expulsion from this matrix in the traumatic experience of birth, the prolongation of the earlier feelings of close relationship, safety and trust, is absolutely vital. Without the consistent and loving care of the mother in early childhood, the child has no trust in itself, no innate power to survive negative life experiences, no model from which to learn how to nurture and support itself and care for its children in turn. Its primary response to life is anxiety and fear. It is like a tree with no roots, easily torn up by a storm because its instincts have been traumatized. With the love of the mother and trust in her presence, the child grows in strength and confidence and delight in itself and in life. Its primary response is trust. Extrapolate this to the small, isolated communities struggling to exist in different areas of the world and it is easy to understand why the image of the Mother was so important for their survival.

The 'terrible' aspect of the Great Mother is documented in almost every early mythology. The powerlessness of humanity in the face of nature's terrifying power to destroy everything that it has built up is deeply imprinted on the memory of the race, the most feared memory being that of the Great Flood when climate change caused the oceans to rise, burying coastal settlements. Volcanic eruptions, tsunamis, devastating floods — everything that can destroy life in a few brief moments — is carried in the image of nature as the 'Terrible Mother' who abandons and destroys her children. Fate has always been imagined as a goddess.

I think it is possible to say that the idea of the whole Cosmos as an entity with consciousness or soul, in which every aspect of life is related to every other, grew out of the mythology surrounding the image of the Great Mother and that she is also the ultimate origin of the image of the Shekinah explored in the last chapter. The Great Mother is the earliest name we gave to an immeasurable cosmic entity that was imagined in a way that may be almost incomprehensible to us now. Life at that time was lived *in* the dimension of the Mother, in participation and accord with the cosmic rhythms of her being, and this kept people in touch with their instincts and was the foundation of their fragile trust in life. We have lost the awareness that we live within a greater cosmic dimension, which, like the Great Mother, spins and weaves the extraordinary web of life through which we are connected to each other, to all life on earth and to all cosmic life.

The primordial experience of the Great Mother is the foundation of later cultures all over the world. She is like an immense tree, whose roots lie beyond the reach of our consciousness, whose branches are all the forms of life we know, and whose flowering is a potential within us, a potential that only a tiny handful of the human race has realized. As a small child lives within the mother's field of consciousness and draws its life from it, so we, at this time, were held in the field of the Great Mother, who drew together all orders of life in a seamless web: everything was related because all shared in the primacy of the original source. She was the invisible patterning of orders of life whose relationships were defined and explored in ways that will be explained in the next chapter. She was experienced as an immutable Law which the whole of life reflected and obeyed in the way it functioned, from the circumpolar movement of the stars to the behaviour of the tiniest insect. The image of the Great Mother reflected something deeply felt — that the creative source cares for the life it has brought into being.

Between 25,000 and 3000 BC, the image of the Great Mother is slowly differentiated into three specific forms related to the realms of sky, earth and underworld. As Bird-Goddess, she was the Sky and the life-bestowing water which flowed from her breasts, the clouds. She was the Goddess of Earth and from her body were born the crops that nourished the life she generated. She was Goddess of the Underworld and the waters welling up from beneath the Earth as springs, lakes and rivers. Her symbol as ruler of the Underworld was the serpent, image of her power perennially to renew life. She was also the sea on which the fragile boats of the Neolithic explorers ventured into the unknown. Whether we look to the extraordinary goddess figures of Old Europe or further East, to Mesopotamia and the Indus Valley, the basic mythology is the same. In the Bronze Age (from ca. 3500 BC), she still has the same essential forms, only more defined and specific, as well as a complex mythology as the 'Mother of All Living' that would one day become the title of the Shekinah and of Eve in the Book of Genesis.

There are a great number of images which have clustered around the image of the Great Mother that were felt to belong to her and to describe her. The clay pot, in particular, was itself a symbol of her body and was decorated with lines, zig-zags and other designs which referred to aspects of her life. Certain forms such as the circle, the egg-like oval, the wavy line, the meander and the spiral are, as early as the Neolithic era, recognizable as her 'signature'. These symbols — particularly the double or triple spiral — are found engraved on the stones and dolmens, passage graves and temples of Megalithic culture, such as the great temple of Newgrange in Ireland, the passage graves at Gavrinis in Brittany and the many temples of Malta, some of which now lie beneath the sea. Further to the East, we find her image in the great Indus Valley civilization and the pre-dynastic culture of Mesopotamia. The labyrinth and the spiral became, at this early time, symbols of the connecting pathway between this world and the unseen dimension of her cosmic womb which could only be reached by following the labyrinthine pathway connecting this world with the source-world of the Great Mother. These basic forms, so familiar to ancient peoples, trace their descent through subsequent civilizations, East and West. The mandala, or circular form, is a universal image of the womb of being which symbolized the oneness and wholeness of all life.

Fascinating sculptures from the Vadastra culture in the Danube Valley, dating to 5500 BC, were identified by the archaeologist Marija Gimbutas as part of what she named the Civilization of Old Europe.[5] These have recently been exhibited in Europe and among the exhibits were small shrines in the shape of a goddess with a meander or labyrinth carved on her body and at the centre, a door; possibly signifying the entrance to her invisible womb. Twenty-one tiny goddess figures, thirteen of them seated on thrones, were also shown, dating to between 4900 and 4750 BC and ritually arranged in a circle. Many large and magnificent bowls and vessels were decorated with spiral forms of breathtaking beauty.[6] In this early civilization there is no evidence of conflict or of weapons and a warrior culture.

In relation to human consciousness at that time, the image of the Great Mother was numinous and all-powerful. This was the phase in human evolution when rituals were devised to keep the community in harmony with her life: to propitiate her with offerings that would bring protection and increase, and ward off her power to destroy. People learned to pay attention to unusual signs or events; to look and to listen at a level beyond the routine experience of life; to notice correspondences and draw analogies, to follow their intuition and respond to their imagination. Womb-like caves, rounded mountain tops shaped like breasts, groves of trees on the tops of hills, deep natural crevices in the earth with water gushing from them — all these were sacred — worshipped as signs or manifestations of the Great Mother. They became the focus of shamanic rituals through which the shaman connected the clan or tribe with the invisible dimension of the spirit-world. Our culture has dismissed these rituals as primitive superstition, not understanding how much wisdom and knowledge, gathered over millennia of observation, was contained in them. There are still places all over the world where pilgrimages are made to these sacred sites. Deeply buried in our psyche we carry ancient memories of the sacredness of the Earth, and of the Earth as Mother.

In the later Bronze Age one of the three dimensions of the Great Mother's being was still the underworld, symbolically the cave, the tomb, the realm of the ancestral dead. There was always a guardian at the entrance to this realm — a lion or serpent or lion-headed bird which stood at the entrance to her temples. In the throne room at Knossos in Crete two magnificent griffins (part lion, part bird, part serpent) symbolizing earth, sky and underworld — the three-fold realm of the goddess — guarded the exquisitely sculpted throne where the priestess presided over the rituals which celebrated the presence of the goddess.

Animals, birds and serpents in the Neolithic and later Bronze Age were all epiphanies of the Great Mother, an expression of her life. She was 'The Goddess of the Animals' or 'Lady of the Beasts'. Three animals in particular — the lion, the cow and the serpent or snake — signified her presence and her power. The goddesses Hathor and Isis in Egypt, and Ninhursag and Inanna in Sumer were called 'the Great Cow'. The temples of the goddess in Sumer were adorned with enormous horns, perhaps associated with the lunar horns of the crescent moon. Ishtar in Babylon and Durga in India were shown standing on a lion. Cybele, the great goddess of Anatolia and later, Rome, rode in a chariot drawn by lions. Equally important were the many birds that were sacred to the goddess in Neolithic cultures, among them the crane, the swan, the goose, duck, owl, diver bird and vulture as well as smaller birds like the dove and the swallow. These find their way into later mythologies and ultimately into fairy tales which tell of the magical guidance of swans or doves or hoopoes, as in the Sufi story, *The Conference of the Birds*. The butterfly and the bee also belonged to the mythology of the Great Mother for she was the 'queen bee' who presided over the great hive of nature. The intricate cellular hive that secretes the golden honey came to be an image of the divine feminine which guards the treasure of wisdom that is "sweeter also than honey or the honey-comb"(Psalm 19:10). There was also a host of smaller animals like the pig, the doe, even the humble hedgehog. Many became sacred to her because of their fertility or because, like the bear, their maternal care for their young seemed to reflect the role of the Great Mother.

It is from the Neolithic era that we have inherited all the images related to Great Mother as an invisible flow of energy which brings life into being, sustains and transforms it, and withdraws it into a hidden dimension for rebirth or regeneration. Rhythm is a primary characteristic of the Great Mother, reflected in the ideogram of the wavy line. The movement of the moon, sun and stars, the seasons of the earth, and water all reflect the underlying rhythm of life. All have specific rhythms which affect the rhythm of our own lives: each moment we inhale and exhale; each night we withdraw into darkness to be regenerated for a new day. Our birth and our death reflect the same rhythm.

The Moon

The most important and possibly the most ancient image associated with the Neolithic Great Mother and the later Bronze Age Great Goddesses was the moon. The moon was born out of darkness as the slender crescent, imagined as a young girl. It grew to fullness like a pregnant woman; waned again into darkness like an ancient crone. These three lunar phases became associated with the Triune Goddess of later cultures and also, most probably, with the triple spiral engraved on many stones and sculptures. The moon gave us an image of life as changeless yet ever-changing and a cyclical pattern of death and regeneration which ruled all aspects of life.

The life of the Great Mother was eternal, like the moon; the life of the earth's vegetation and our human lives waxed and waned like the phases of the moon. This association nourished the creative imagination, teaching us to observe and to wonder, helping us to penetrate the mystery of the relationship between the Above (the invisible world associated with the starry cosmos) and the Below (this world) — a theme that, millennia later, was carried through into Hermetic philosophy, Kabbalah and Alchemy.

Jules Cashford's superb study of the moon and worldwide lunar culture — *The Moon: Myth and Image* — explores the immense age, range of influence and significance of lunar culture. As she explains,

> The essential myth of the moon is the myth of transformation. Early people perceived the Moon's waxing and waning as the growing and dying of a celestial being, whose death was followed by its own resurrection as the New Moon. The perpetual drama of the Moon's phases became a model for contemplating a pattern in human, animal and vegetable life, including the idea of life beyond death. It seemed that the Moon carried the image of eternity for early people, as well as the image of time.[7]

The moon rules the night world rather than the day. It is the light shining in darkness, the light that is always changing, yet always the same. The moon is the symbol of the secret, instinctual workings of things that take place 'in the dark', beneath the outward appearance of life, beneath the surface of consciousness. Organic life on this planet is strongly influenced by the magnetism of the moon which controls the tides and affects the growth of crops and was once associated with women's menstrual periods and the ten lunar months of gestation in the womb.

The emergence of the crescent moon from the three days of darkness that preceded it gave us an image of the visible world emerging from an invisible one, a time-bound world from an eternal one, each intimately connected to the other. The moon gave us an image of a law of life which was immutable, and a cyclical pattern of death and regeneration which governed all aspects of life. Because of its regular movement through its four phases, the moon carried the image of wholeness or completeness as well as sequence.

Most important of all perhaps, the constant rhythm of the moon's waxing and waning taught us to perceive light and darkness in relation to each other. It held them in balance rather than in opposition to each other because the totality of the moon's cycle embraced both light and dark phases and, therefore, symbolically included both life and death. Light and darkness, life and death were not polarized as they were later to become in solar culture, but were phases of the total cycle, so that there was always an image of a unifying whole which included both polarities. All this was incorporated into the mythology of the Great Mother.

Today, when we look up on a clear night at the night sky, we are connected to the countless generations of people who observed the circumpolar movement of the stars and the changing yet stable course of the moon. Over tens of thousands of years, we observed the connection between the cyclical rhythm of the four phases of the moon's life and the rhythm of growth, maturation, death and regeneration in the life of the Earth and, as farming developed in the Neolithic era, the life of the crops.

We experienced the phases of our own lives as woven into the rhythm and fabric of that greater life as well as the life of the Earth. With the passage of countless millennia, we came to trust in the reappearance of the crescent moon, and to recognize darkness as a time of transition between an old and a new phase of life. We came to apply this insight to ourselves and to believe that, with death, we would be taken back into the womb of the Great Mother and reborn like the crescent moon. So the constant return of the crescent moon after the three days of darkness laid the foundation for trust in the survival of the soul and the renewal of life after apparent death. This may have been the original inspiration of the belief in reincarnation. The life of the moon was eternal; the life of the Earth and all creatures and plants waxed and waned like the phases of the moon.

In the Neolithic, as agriculture and animal husbandry were developed, the cycles of the moon were experienced in relation to the cycle of the crops; the light and dark phases of the moon were reflected in the fertile and barren phases of the seasons. The invisible seed planted in the darkness of the Earth's womb became visible as the green shoots of corn and then as the crop, harvested and transformed into food by the labour of men and women. Everything that was of the Earth, whether rock or spring, tree or fruit, grain or herb, was sacred because it was the life of the Great Mother, offered for the nourishment of her children.

Women in the lunar era were closely bound to the rhythm of sowing and harvesting the crops because they participated in the mysterious process whereby life grew in the darkness of their womb and was reborn as their child, and so they were believed magically to assist the fertility of crops, trees and animals. They were healers, skilled in the use of herbs and ointments and in the art of making and decorating pottery. A complex symbolism linked the lunar mystery of the continual regeneration of the moon and life's power to regenerate itself through the child carried in the body of woman. Until man's role in the creation of a child was discovered, woman held a numinous charge since she appeared to give birth to new life unaided.

As this lunar pattern was constantly repeated through aeons of time, it spoke to our imagination, giving rise to the great lunar myths which endured for thousands of years. We began to perceive birth and death as a rite of passage for the soul as it journeyed between the visible and invisible dimensions of the Great Mother, a journey that followed a path through the labyrinth of the Milky Way. The ancestors were not lost to the living but were close by, available — through shamanic mediation — to counsel and guide. In lunar culture there was no final demarcation line between life and death or between death and rebirth. Death was a rite of passage leading to rebirth. Because of the influence of the image of the Great Mother, lunar culture was primarily feminine in character, with the emphasis on relationship, connection and containment within the great invisible web of life.

Out of this long lunar experience there evolved highly developed observational skills, the capacity to notice connections, relationships and analogies, to imagine, feel, reflect; to create artefacts and buildings that were both useful and beautiful, in harmony with the landscape. The mythology, astronomy, mathematics, architecture and the concept of divine law governing all aspects and forms of life, which reached such brilliant heights in the great civilizations of the Bronze Age and endured until the end of the Middle Ages in Europe — reaching their finest expression in Chartres Cathedral — may have developed out of this primordial observation of the moon.

The Sea

Together with the moon, because of its effects on its tides, the sea from very ancient times was associated with the Great Mother and with the great invisible sea of being from which the whole phenomenal world emerged. In the Bronze Age mythology of Sumer and India, the Great Mother was imagined as the cosmic ocean, the primordial watery abyss or sea, and she was personified by a great serpent. In Sumer, the goddess Nammu, whose ideogram was the 'sea', is described as "the mother who gave birth to heaven and earth". The magnificent passages spoken by Wisdom in the Book of Ben Sirach (24:28-9) in the *Apocrypha* echo this ancient association of a primordial Mother with the cosmic ocean of being — "She whose thoughts are more than the sea and whose counsels are profounder than the great deep". Even today, the French words for sea (*mer*) and mother (*mère*) are almost identical and the German word for sea (*meere*) is feminine. Kwan Yin in the Far East, like the Virgin Mary in the West, is goddess of the sea and protects all who sail on her. Aphrodite was born from the sea foam. Isis and Mary were called Star of the Sea. The association of sea, water, Great Mother and the invisible cosmic sea of being is very ancient.

Rituals of Sacrifice

There is a dark side to this lunar story. Because the moon held such significance in shamanic cultures, it is possible that the idea of sacrifice developed originally to ensure the return of the crescent moon. Watching the full moon wane and disappear into darkness may have led some communities to believe that a sacrifice was necessary in order to ensure its return, either to help the moon to be reborn or to propitiate the deity, darkness or dragon/monster that had swallowed or devoured it. Enacting the dark phase of the moon literally, the tribal practice would be to kill and dismember a victim or to sacrifice some part of the body, such as the foreskin or a finger joint and may possibly be the origin of the practice of circumcision. Since the moon always re-appeared after such a sacrifice, it may have been assumed that the sacrifice of the body part or the death of the victim had caused the rebirth of the moon.

Taking this analogy further, it would also have been natural to conclude that a sacrifice was necessary in order to ensure the regeneration of the crops or the restoration of health to the community if its survival was threatened by famine or disease. In a zone prone to earthquakes, it may have been practised to ward off this disaster. Out of this ancient lunar mythology, rituals developed in certain societies where a man or woman, an infant or an animal, such as the lunar animal, the bull, was sacrificed and/or dismembered at the dark of the moon to ensure the regeneration of the moon in a new cycle or the regeneration of the crops on which the tribe depended for survival, or to ensure the protection of the goddess.

While human sacrifice may originally have been practised to ensure the return of the crescent moon after the three days of darkness or the regeneration of the Earth in spring, there were always shamans (as there still are today) who practised the so-called 'dark arts' in order to gain power over the people and terrify them into submission.[8] An example of these were the Aztecs, who worshipped fearsome gods who demanded holocausts of sacrificial victims as the price of divine protection. While there were such cultures, they did not predominate. Yet the lunar practice of sacrifice was transmitted to later solar culture whenever human sacrifice in the name of God was deemed to be a religious duty, or whenever, as the horrific massacres of groups of people from Auschwitz to Srebrenica illustrate, human sacrifice serves the ideology of the supremacy of one nation, tribal or ethnic group over another. This dark unconscious legacy of the lunar era manifests today in the power of our weapons which enables us to sacrifice life on a hitherto unimaginable scale and in the ongoing wars and conflicts which inflict intolerable suffering on helpless civilians.

The Bronze Age

The Palaeolithic and Neolithic eras give us the earliest images of the Great Mother but we hear no words. It is only in the Bronze Age that we begin to hear the human voice; for the first time we can listen to the hymns addressed to the Great Goddesses in their temples in Sumer and Egypt. The voice of the Divine Feminine comes alive and speaks to us in the words inscribed in hieroglyphs on the walls of Egyptian temples, such as the temple of Isis at Philae.[9] These reveal a rich mythology of the divine feminine that is already millennia old.

It is in the Bronze Age that the feeling for the sacredness of life is clearly expressed in words: a feeling that is transmitted through the hymns and prayers to the Goddess or where she herself speaks in the great aretalogies (proclamations) that have come down to us from Egypt and Hellenistic Greece[10] and the remarkable Gnostic texts discovered at Nag Hammadi. In these she announces herself to be the source, ground or matrix of all forms of life; the fertile womb which eternally regenerates plants, animals, human beings; the life-force which attracts the male to the female; the power which creates, destroys and regenerates all forms of itself. She speaks as the source and embodiment of all instinctive processes. She is the life force which is nurturing, compassionate, beneficent, but also the terrifying and implacable force of destruction which can manifest as volcanic eruption, earthquake, flood, drought and disease.

About 4500 BC the image of a young god began to appear, who personified the life of the vegetation, the life of corn or fruiting tree. One paramount myth grew up around him and his relationship with the Goddess. His marriage to her united earth with heaven and regenerated the life of Earth. The Egyptian myth of Isis searching for the scattered fragments of the body of her husband, Osiris, the Sumerian myth of the moon goddess Inanna's descent to and ascent from the Underworld, the Babylonian myth of the descent of the goddess Ishtar to rescue her son Tammuz, asleep in the Underworld, are all variations of this lunar theme. As the son or consort returns, the corn sprouts, the tree blossoms and fertility is restored to the Earth. The Greek myth of Demeter's search for her daughter Persephone celebrated in the Eleusinian Mysteries, and the later Christian myth of the birth, crucifixion and resurrection of Christ, still carry the same lunar theme of death, descent into the underworld and rebirth or regeneration.

The seven major themes of Bronze Age lunar mythology that were transmitted to later cultures were:

> The theme of death and rebirth
> The theme of the descent into the underworld and the return
> The theme of the struggle with a superhuman adversary
> The theme of a journey and a quest for a priceless treasure
> The theme of transformation
> The theme of the sacred marriage
> The theme of the birth of the divine child

The image of the Green Man, found in churches and cathedrals all over Europe, is the descendent of the dying and resurrected gods of lunar mythology. He personifies spirit present within the forms of nature, life eternally regenerating itself.[11] However, although the Green Man was carved on the capitals and choir stalls of Christian cathedrals, the Christian myth did not retain the age-old connection with the cycles of the life of the earth and the moon that were the focus of the earlier experience nor, crucially, the belief that spirit was present in nature and that nature was an epiphany or manifestation of spirit and, therefore, sacred.

The greatest ceremony of the year during the Bronze Age in Egypt and Mesopotamia was the Sacred Marriage, which symbolically united heaven and earth, moon and sun, mother-bride and son-lover. In magnificent rituals goddess and god were united in sexual union — she represented by the high priestess and he by the king or high priest. This marriage symbolically united moon and sun, heaven and earth, the invisible life of the Cosmos and the visible life of Earth, and was believed to regenerate the life of Earth. The ecstatic poetry and sexual imagery of the Egyptian and Sumerian marriage hymns were bequeathed to later Canaanite culture and thence to Hebrew culture.[12] The exquisite poetry of the Song of Songs has come down to us from the marriage rituals where the bride was the mother and sister of her bridegroom, and he both the son and brother of his bride — hence the words: "Thou hast ravished my heart, my sister, my spouse." The nearest event to convey the sense of importance this ceremony held for the people in that far off time to us today is the excitement and sense of unity generated by a royal marriage that, even today, can signify the regeneration of a culture and a new beginning.

Egypt

Jeremy Naydler, who has made a profound study of early Egyptian culture, tells us in his book, *The Future of the Ancient World: Essays on the History of Consciousness*, that in Egypt, people still saw the visible world as permeable to the invisible ground which illuminated it with a divine radiance:

> The gods were still present in the land of Egypt, for nature was still transparent, not yet solid and opaque. Nature mediated divine energies that people became aware of by "seeing through" the phenomenal world to the numinous presences beyond…The Egyptians were wise about the invisible worlds that interpenetrate the physical, for they perceived the powers that move behind the façade of sense-existence. Above all they understood that the real world is not solid, and that if one is seeking spiritual foundations for one's life, then it is necessary to develop a consciousness that is able to travel through the literal world to the symbolic world, to the world of the sacred imagination.[13]

Luminous, nurturing, awesome, the voice of the Divine Feminine speaks from the heart of Egyptian culture, bringing through from the Neolithic the image of life as a divine unity. It is, above all, the Great Goddesses of Egypt who transmit this feeling of the unity of life and it is they who carry forward this ancient image of soul. They were the Tree of Life — the date palm and the sycamore tree with its milky sap — and were often shown offering from the tree's leafy interior the vases that contained the water of eternal life and provided nourishment for the souls passing from one dimension to another. The image of the Tree of Life passes from the temples of Bronze Age Egypt, Mesopotamia and Canaan to the Jewish mystical tradition of Kabbalah and to the Myth of the Fall of Man in the Book of Genesis where it stood in the Garden of Eden.

There were four Egyptian Great Goddesses who carry forward the image of the earlier Great Mother and the feeling that everything was ensouled with divine presence. Among these goddesses was Maat, who wore on her head the ostrich feather against which each human heart was weighed after death, balanced on the scales of justice. Because Egyptian mythology had a great influence on neighbouring cultures, Maat may be the origin of the figure of Divine Wisdom in the Old Testament, for she personified the equilibrium and harmony of the Cosmos intrinsic to all life forms, even to the notes of the musical scale.

Some of the most beautiful hymns and prayers that have come down to us from Egypt were addressed to the goddess Nut as Mother of the souls of the dead, as the mysterious deep ground of life and the soul. Nut was the starry vault of heaven whose vast cosmic body was home to all the stars. Each night the sun god 'died' into her body on his nightly descent into the underworld and was reborn from her at the dawn of a new day. Nut's image was painted on the inside of coffin lids and sometimes on the base as well, as if to enfold the soul entrusted to her care in her cosmic embrace. There is a beautiful and moving inscription to her on a fragment of stone that I found long ago in the Louvre:

> *O my mother Nut, stretch your wings over me;*
> *Let me become like the imperishable stars,*
> *like the indefatigable stars.*
> *O Great Being who is in the world of the Dead,*
> *At whose feet is Eternity, in whose hand is the Always,*
> *O Great Divine Beloved Soul*
> *Who is in the mysterious abyss, come to me.*

Hathor (who was often interchangeable with Isis) was Egypt's oldest goddess, named as nurturing Mother of the universe and the creative impulse which flowed from her cosmic womb. Hathor was the starry river of the Milky Way which, in Egyptian as well as other shamanic cultures, both East and West, was looked upon not only as the great stellar causeway that souls took as they entered and left this world but as the Great Mother, cosmic source of All. Yet Hathor was also immanent on earth, present, as all Egyptian gods and goddesses were, in the statues that stood in their temples. As Divine Mother, Hathor received the souls of the dead at the entrance to her sacred mountain, thought to be located behind the magnificent temple at Deir-el-Bahri that Queen Hatshepsut (1505–1484 BC) built to honour and house the goddess. In the exquisite tomb of Queen Nefertari, the beloved wife of Rameses II, and in the small temple of Abu Simbel dedicated to Hathor, the goddess leads the queen by the hand before Osiris, the judge of the dead.

As in Mesopotamian ritual, it was the Goddess who endowed Pharaoh with the divine power to rule Egypt and many sculptures show him seated on Hathor's lap, drawing nourishment from her breast. Carrying forward the bird and serpent imagery from the Neolithic Great Mother, Hathor (as well as Isis) was both Nekhbet, the vulture mother goddess of Upper Egypt, and Wadjet, the ancient cobra mother goddess of Lower Egypt. As well as her headdress of the golden sun disc between the lunar horns, she carried the *uraeus* (cobra) on her brow, symbol of her fiery, dynamic power both to create and destroy that she transmitted to her son, Pharaoh, as ruler of Egypt.[14] Her sacred number was seven.

The people loved and worshipped Hathor as life's magnetic, fertilizing energy: the sexual energy that attracts people and also animals to each other and manifests as the fertility of the Earth. They saw her as radiantly beautiful like the sun, but they also feared her for, in her form as Sekhmet, the awesome lion-headed goddess whose name means 'The Powerful One', she could bring drought and starvation. But, although she could bring destruction, she could also reverse or set limits to what she had done, and so she was always shown wearing the menat or sacred necklace of healing and holding the sistrum or musical rattle with her face on it which banished the forces of evil.[15] Once a year, the great festival took place celebrating Hathor's sacred marriage with her consort, the sun god Horus, and her statue was carried from her temple at Dendera to Horus' temple at Edfu, accompanied by a magnificent procession of decorated barges on the river Nile.[16]

But it was Isis who was Egypt's greatest and most loved goddess. Sister and wife of Osiris and mother of the falcon-headed god Horus, Isis was worshipped for over three thousand years, from pre-dynastic times (before 3000 BC) to well into Roman times where her temples were built all over the empire. Plutarch, writing about her at this later time, saw her as the Soul of Nature. With the coming of Christianity, the shrines long sacred to her as the God-Mother of Horus were re-dedicated to the Virgin Mary whose son was seated on her lap just as Horus had been seated on the lap of Isis. People prayed to the Virgin for help in the same way that they had prayed to Isis. But Isis stood for far more than the Virgin.

In the time of one of Egypt's late rulers, Ptolemy II (284–246 BC), a series of wonderful hymns addressed to Isis were inscribed in hieroglyphs on the walls of her exquisite temple at Philae, in southern Egypt. Only recently translated, they offer us a vision of how the Egyptians saw her, for the priest or priestess who wrote them down drew on much older material as the core of their hymns. In this temple, Isis gathered to herself as 'Lady of Life' and 'Lady of Upper and Lower Egypt' all the roles, attributes and functions of the other great goddesses of Egypt. For the people, she was their Mother, dwelling in the cosmic dimension of the divine, yet at the same time numinously present in her temple shrine on earth to which, each day, she descended. Her statue, covered with gold leaf and dimly lit by two small shafts, gleamed in the dim light of her sanctuary, which seemed to be "filled with gold, like the horizon supporting the sun-disc". Each day, her statue was anointed with fragrant perfumes, oils and myrrh and the sacred blue lotus was laid at her feet.

In the hymns, she is addressed as the universal Mother Goddess, sole creator of the world, the One who brings the many into being, beneficent mother of humanity and goddess of the Netherworld.[17] As Louis V. Zabkar tells us in his compilation *Hymns to Isis in Her Temple at Philae*, "All the attributes, roles, and functions that in much earlier times had been assigned to other gods and goddesses have now been transferred to her, to show her sovereign and unique position among the deities at Philae."[18]

Listen to the description of a vision of the Goddess Isis recorded in a book called *The Golden Ass* written by Apuleius, a North African living in Rome in the second century AD who was an initiate of the Mysteries of Isis:

> The apparition of a woman began to rise from the middle of the sea with so lovely a face that the gods themselves would have fallen down in adoration of it. First the head, then the whole shining body gradually emerged and stood before me poised on the surface of the waves.... Her long thick hair fell in tapering ringlets on her lovely neck, and was crowned with an intricate chaplet in which was woven every kind of flower. Just above her brow shone a round disc, like a mirror, or like the bright face of the moon, which told me who she was. Vipers rising from the left-hand and right-hand partings of her hair supported this disc, with ears of corn bristling beside them. Her many-colored robe was of finest linen; part was glistening white, part crocus-yellow, part glowing red and along the entire hem a woven bordure of flowers and fruit clung swaying in the breeze. But what caught and held my eye more than anything else was the deep black lustre of her mantle. She wore it slung across her body from the right hip to the left shoulder, where it was caught in a knot resembling the boss of a shield; but part of it hung in innumerable folds, the tasselled fringe quivering. It was embroidered with glittering stars on the hem and everywhere else, and in the middle beamed a full and fiery moon.... On her divine feet were slippers of palm leaves, the emblem of victory. [19]

And to some of the words she spoke to him:

> "You see me here, Lucius, in answer to your prayer. I am Nature, the Universal Mother, mistress of all the elements, primordial child of time, sovereign of all things spiritual, queen of the dead, queen also of the immortals, the single manifestation of all gods and goddesses that are. My nod governs the starry heights of Heaven, the wholesome sea-breezes, the lamentable silences of the world below. Though I am worshipped in many aspects, known by countless names, and propitiated with all manner of different rites, yet the whole round earth venerates me." [20]

There is an immense range of thought and feeling that the image of Isis carries and her many names and titles do not convey the people's love for her, nor the depth of their need for and trust in her as their Mother, nor the profound influence she had on Egyptian and later Greek and Roman civilization for over three thousand years. No one has described her more clearly than the Egyptologist Wallis Budge, who believed that Isis held a position in the hearts of the Egyptians that was unique and entirely different from that held by any other goddess. She is the closest to the Great Mother of the Neolithic era, still ruling Heaven, Earth and the Underworld that the Egyptians called the Netherworld. "Isis", he wrote, was the great and beneficent goddess and mother, whose influence and love pervaded all heaven, and earth, and the abode of the dead, and she was the personification of the great feminine, creative power which conceived, and brought forth every living creature and thing, from the gods in heaven, to man on earth, and to the insect on the ground; what she brought forth she protected, and cared for, and fed, and nourished. She not only continually brought into being new creatures, but restored those who were dead to life.[21]

By the end of the Bronze Age the feminine principle in the image of the Great Goddess was clearly defined. Still holding the three dimensions of heaven, earth and underworld within her being, she personified the great matrix of relationships through which all aspects and forms of life were connected to each other. Although not named in our terminology as cosmic or universal soul, this, in effect, is what she represented. Secondly, she stood for the principle of justice, wisdom and compassion as well as the power to destroy and regenerate life.

The Iron Age (from ca. 1200 BC)

With the Iron Age, which begins about 1200 BC, and encompasses the development of patriarchal religion, the story of the goddess becomes more difficult to follow as the god takes her place as the supreme ruler of sky, earth and underworld. Greece stands between two phases of human culture: a lunar culture focused on the goddess and a solar culture focused on the god. The older sense of participation in a sacred Earth and a sacred Cosmos begins to fade as a new phase in the evolution of human consciousness comes into being, one where the developing power of mind and rational thought begins to draw away from the maternal realm of an ensouled nature.

In Greece, the powers of the Great Mother of the Neolithic were divided between goddesses who carried different aspects of her former self, but there is no longer a supreme Mother Goddess like Isis or Hathor. The influence of an emerging patriarchal (solar) culture is shown by the fact that Athena, Aphrodite, Artemis and Persephone are daughters of Zeus by various goddesses and he is now the supreme father of the gods. In the 'takeover' by Zeus and his brothers, Hades and Poseidon, of the dimensions of heaven, the underworld and the sea, we can sense the cultural change of consciousness as the Great Mother, who once included these three realms in her being, loses two of her former domains to them. Gaia is still, like the older Great Mother, goddess of Earth and, together with her daughter Demeter, brings through into Greek culture a pale reflection of the older Great Mother who *was* the life of the sky, earth and underworld. Today, as we awaken to our profound relationship with our planetary home, the name of Gaia, the goddess of Earth, mysteriously returns to us.[22]

Several of the Greek goddesses inherit the lion, bird, serpent imagery of the Bronze Age goddesses. Athena was the goddess of Wisdom and the Great Goddess of Greece. Her gift to her people was the olive tree — the Greek Tree of Life — its rich golden oil a symbol of her divine wisdom; its fruit her nourishing food. Although Athena originally came from the older Bronze Age culture of Crete, in Greece she becomes the inspiration and mentor of its astonishing artistic and intellectual flowering. She is described in the *Odyssey* as a tall and beautiful woman, with piercing, brilliant eyes, wearing a white robe and a goatskin cloak, the aegis, emblazoned with the severed head of the Gorgon. In statues and vase paintings she takes the form of a helmeted warrior maiden, the fearsome protectress of her city, Athens. But another, older Athena is reflected in a magnificent statue (c. 525 BC) from the archaic temple on the Acropolis which shows her head crowned with snakes, and her cloak falling from her shoulders edged with a mass of entwined snakes, with one clasped in her left hand. The snake imagery, signifying her power to regenerate life, shows her descent from the Great Goddess of an earlier age and, more specifically, from the Cretan goddess. In the *Odyssey* there are many stories of Athena appearing to Odysseus as a swallow or sea-eagle, guiding him on his journey back to Penelope. The owl, in particular, was sacred to her.

Artemis inherits the role of goddess of the animals. But there is another Artemis, Great Goddess of Ephesus, whose Anatolian name was Cybele (Kybele) and whose statue stands, now, beautifully restored, in the Archaeological Museum in Naples. Once it stood in her magnificent temple in Ephesus. Even at the late date of 400 BC, we gain some inkling of what the Sacred Order that she represented still conveyed. Resting on her multiple breasts is the great lunar crescent identifying her as a Moon Goddess, and beneath it nestles a circle of tiny acorns. On her body are different animals including lions, bulls and bees as well as angelic beings and priestesses of her temple. It is an amazingly complete statement of the unity of the great web of life still carried by the image of a goddess as Great Mother.

In Persephone and the long-lived myth in which she plays a part, we find one of the few goddesses who moves, like Inanna in Sumer and Isis in Egypt, between the bright solar world and the dark lunar underworld of life, keeping them connected to each other. In later Greek culture, particularly in Southern Italy and Sicily, Persephone personifies the invisible realm of the Underworld. Her mysteries are those of death and regeneration.

As in the Bronze Age, these goddesses personify the divine harmony, order and beauty of life. The great festival in honour of Demeter, the *Thesmophoria*, and the secret rites of her temple at Eleusis, gave those who participated in them a deep sense of trust in the survival of the soul and the reunion with loved ones after death. They were one of the most powerful and ancient rituals ever devised for keeping alive the sense of relationship with the eternal ground of life.

All these associations and many others which cannot be included in this chapter derive from an earlier time when there is no separation between the Great Mother as Source and the manifest forms of her life. There is no creator beyond creation. The creator was both the life of nature and the hidden powers of the Cosmos that are now personified by many goddesses and gods. The veil between two dimensions is less opaque than it later became, as the encounters with goddesses and gods recounted by Homer in the *Iliad* and the *Odyssey* illustrate. The images of the goddesses and their mythology show why life was still *felt* and *experienced* as sacred. All the goddesses transmit the feeling of the earlier time, the feeling that a goddess could be appealed to for help, guidance and inspiration by both men and women. Through their image, people were made aware that they walked on sacred ground, that they lived within a Sacred Order where everything they were and everything they experienced was rooted in that ground. Hidden beings, intermediaries between earth and heaven, still connected the dimension of the physical world to the unseen dimension which ensouled it. There was no rigid line drawn between what was imagination and what was reality, because what was imagined *was* reality. The human soul was part of the greater Soul of the Cosmos that was alive with these unseen beings and their diverse powers. The profound experiences of human beings — their deepest feelings and emotions — were understood to be the expressions of archetypal patterns present in the Cosmos and named as specific gods and goddesses.

Looking towards a later age, the legacy of the Great Mother in the West and the mythology that was constellated around her lies in the great mythological themes of the Quest which direct us toward the roots of consciousness, the source or ground of being: Odysseus returning home to Penelope under the guidance of the goddess Athena; Theseus following Ariadne's thread through the Cretan labyrinth; Dante's journey into the underworld and his guidance by Beatrice; the medieval quest for the Holy Grail. All these marvellous stories define the Feminine as immanent presence, guide and transcendent goal.

Further to the East, in India, the Vedic sages expressed with extraordinary clarity their insight into the omnipresence of the divine ground in the sublime poetic imagery of the *Vedas* and the *Upanishads*. The poets whose traditions belonged to a culture which existed long before the Aryan invasions, sang of their passionate devotion to the goddess, while to the north, the mountain people named the great mountains in her honour and worshipped her as the dynamism of the creative principle, locked in the bliss of an eternal embrace with her divine consort. Still further to the East, the sages of the Taoist tradition never lost the shamanic understanding that relationship with Nature was the key to staying in touch with the source of life. They never followed the ascetic practices of religions which sacrificed the body for the sake of spiritual advancement. They were never in a hurry to reach the goal of union with the divine nor to renounce the world for the sake of enlightenment. Of all the religious traditions, with the exception of those of the Indigenous Peoples, the Taoists did not split nature from its invisible ground, so losing touch with the soul. They never became lost in the maze of the intellect and its metaphysical constructions but, through patience and devotion, were able to realize the difficult alchemy of bringing themselves into harmony with the deeper harmony of nature. They did not lose sight of the One.

I have focused in this chapter on the image of the Neolithic Great Mother and the later Bronze Age Goddesses because they lay the foundation for an understanding of the concept of soul and the unseen worlds beyond this one which will be explored in later chapters. This lunar participatory experience and the unifying image of the Great Mother and Great Goddesses who personified the great web of life, were, I believe, the foundation of the later idea of Cosmic Soul or the Soul of the World (*Anima Mundi*) that developed in Platonic and Neo-Platonic philosophy as well as the Shekinah of Kabbalah. Throughout the lunar era, they were an image of overwhelming numinosity and fascination for both men and women but particularly, perhaps, for women, many of whom served as priestesses in the temples of the Goddess. These Great Goddesses were worshipped as the source of life: one life manifesting as the life of each and all. Sexuality was seen as the vital expression of that life: a sacred, ecstatic impulse reflecting life's own creative impulse eternally to renew itself. Everything came forth from the womb of the Great Mother and had meaning through relationship with her. So relationship and connection came to be understood as the essential quality of the Feminine.

Within the psyche, the newly emerging elements of consciousness were held in relationship to the older, instinctual layers of the psyche through the image of the Goddess and through rituals which connected people to the rhythms of the Cosmos and the life of the Earth. Lunar cosmology did not split off human life from participation in a Sacred Cosmic Order but was rooted in the ancient instinctive awareness that as, millennia later, Blake recognized: "Everything that lives is holy". We carry that awareness deep within us and are recovering it now as the ancient image of the soul returns to us.

Notes:

1. From the *Chaura-panchasika*, 1st century AD (1944), *Love Songs of Asia*, Pushkin Press, London
2. *The Myth of the Goddess* covers the range and depth of the image of the Great Mother
3. Abram, David (1996) *The Spell of the Sensuous*, Vintage Books, New York, p. 250
4. See the magnificent *Chauvet Cave* (1996) Thames and Hudson, London. Werner Herzog has made a DVD recording of this cave in 3D.
5. Gimbutas, Marija, (1974, 1982) *The Goddesses and Gods of Old Europe 6500–3500 BC*, Thames and Hudson Ltd., London; (1991) *The Civilization of the Goddess: The World of Old Europe*, HarperSanFrancisco
6. *The Lost World of Old Europe, 5000-3500 BC* (2010) edited by David W. Anthony, Princeton University Press, p. 90
7. Cashford, Jules (2003) *The Moon: Myth and Image*, Cassell Illustrated, London, p. 8
8. Recent cases have come to light in Nigeria and London of children and young women beaten, tortured and even murdered in order to exorcise the devil believed to be causing trouble in a family or community, or to force young girls into being trafficked, presenting a toxic blend of archaic beliefs and practices and Christian beliefs.
9. Zabkar, Louis V. (1989) *Hymns to Isis in Her Temple at Philae*, Published for Brandeis University Press by University Press of New England
10. Zabkar, pp. 137-146, referring to aretalogies of Hellenistic times: the aretalogy of Kyme (Cyme); the aretalogy of Maronea (south coast of Thrace) and two from Apuleius' *Metamorphoses*, Book XI, chapters 5 & 25.
11. Anderson, William and Hicks, Clive (1990) *Green Man: The Archetype of our Oneness with the Earth*, HarperCollins, London and San Francisco
12. See *The Myth of the Goddess* for the Sumerian Marriage Hymns
13. Naydler, Jeremy (2009) *The Future of the Ancient World: Essays on the History of Consciousness*, Inner Traditions, Vermont, pp. 90-91. See also (1996) *Temple of the Cosmos: Ancient Egyptian Experience of the Sacred*, Inner Traditions
14. Roberts, Alison (1995 and 2000) *Hathor Rising: The Serpent Power of Ancient Egypt*, and *My Heart, My Mother*, Northgate Press, Devon
15. ibid
16. Lamy, Lucy (1981) *Egyptian Mysteries*, Thames and Hudson Ltd., London
17. Zabkar
18. ibid, p. 132
19. Apuleius, Lucius, (1950) *The Golden Ass*, trans. Robert Graves, Penguin Books Ltd., Harmondsworth, London, pp. 227-8
20. Apuleius, p. 228
21. E.A. Wallis Budge, (1969) *The Gods of the Egyptians*, Volume 11, Dover Publications, New York, pp. 203-4.
22. through the books of James Lovelock, (1979) *Gaia, A New Look at Life on Earth*, Oxford OUP; (2006) *The Revenge of Gaia*, Penguin Books Ltd., London; (2010) *The Vanishing Face of Gaia: A Final Warning*, Penguin Books Ltd., London.

Chapter Five

THE LUNAR ERA

THE SHAMANIC VISION: KINSHIP WITH ALL CREATION

I am the brother of the forest and must defend it.

— David Kopenawa Yanomami, a contemporary Amazon shaman

Who in our allegedly progressive civilization is capable of understanding the language of rocks and trees?

— Jean Charon, physicist

It is a considerable challenge for the modern rational mind to enter into the very different consciousness of the lunar era where people lived in small communities which remained in close relationship with the same area of land for many thousands of years. With the movement of increasing numbers of people to cities where we have become cut off from any physical contact with the land, we have become alienated from the soul of the landscape, the soul of nature. We live in a secular culture and no longer have a myth to connect us with a living Cosmos; we no longer regard the Earth as our Mother. As Mircea Eliade observed, "Desacralization pervades the entire experience of the nonreligious man of modern societies."[1] This makes it difficult for us to enter into the soul of archaic man in shamanic societies and respond to his fundamental understanding that the life of the Cosmos, the life of the Earth and the life of humanity were one life, permeated and informed by animating spirit.

For many thousands of years before the advent of religion as we know it and even to this day, people in shamanic cultures aligned themselves and their communities with an unseen dimension of reality. Their lives had meaning and value because they felt they lived within a Sacred Cosmic Order where spirit, though invisible, was not regarded as something remote from nature. Nature was ensouled with spirit. With the rise of the patriarchal religions this sense of containment within a sacred order began to fade, although in Europe it survived to some extent until the end of the Middle Ages. I believe this loss had its distant roots in an image of God who was defined as a creator separate and distinct from His creation, who did not hold the world within His being nor was present in every leaf, every creature in this world. It also had its roots in the myth of the Fall of Man (see Chapter Seven) which tells the story of how, as a punishment for disobeying the will of God, we were expelled from the Divine World and exiled to this world of suffering, sin and death.

Western civilization was profoundly influenced by these beliefs and developed on the foundation of a fundamental dualism: a split between spirit and nature, creator and creation. This split ultimately destroyed the ancient shamanic experience of an ensouled nature and opened the way to its ultimate exploitation. It led to our current worldview which rests on the premise of our separation from and mastery of nature, where nature is subject to the will and the perceived needs of our species.

Yet we carry within our psyche the inheritance of two different kinds of consciousness, two different ways of knowing: firstly, a participatory 'lunar' way of knowing described in the last chapter and in this one that was mediated through instinctive feeling, acute powers of analogical thinking, a highly developed intuition and shamanic techniques of connection with an unseen dimension of reality. This dimension was never seen as separate from nature, but rather was the invisible ground of nature, variously called the Spirit-world, the Otherworld and sometimes, by the later Greeks, the Immortal Realm. Secondly, a more recent 'solar' way of knowing, developed through the spread of literacy, whose focus was on the development of the intellect or rational mind, eventually leading to our present scientific and technologically-oriented culture, where there is a fundamental disjunction between our human selves and the world of nature. Over the course of thousands of years, the second way of knowing replaced the first although, for many centuries and in different regions of the earth, they overlapped. To understand the primary needs of our own time, we need to know something of these two great meta-narratives, these two different kinds of consciousness, and the circumstances which led to one overlaying, replacing or displacing the other. It may help to view them as representative of different phases in the evolution of consciousness.

The main feature of the shamanic way of knowing, that the English philosopher Owen Barfield called 'Original Participation' in his book *Saving the Appearances: A Study in Idolatry*, was an instinctive feeling of relationship with a living Earth and Cosmos and a sense of kinship with all creation.[2] No one has described this state of consciousness better than Richard Tarnas, in his book, *Cosmos and Psyche*:

> The primal human being perceives the surrounding natural world as permeated with meaning, meaning whose significance is at once human and cosmic. Spirits are seen in the forest, presences are felt in the wind and the ocean, the river, the mountain.... The primal world is ensouled... It is pregnant with signs and symbols, implications and intentions.... A continuity extends from the interior world of the human to the world outside.... The human being is a microcosm within the macrocosm of the world, participating in its interior reality and united with the whole in ways that are both tangible and invisible.... The human psyche is embedded within a world psyche.... Within this relatively undifferentiated state of consciousness, human beings perceive themselves as directly — emotionally, mystically, consequentially — participating in and communicating with the interior life of the natural world and cosmos. To be more precise, this participation mystique involves a complex sense of direct inner participation not only of human beings in the world but also of human beings in the divine powers, through ritual, and of divine powers in the world, by virtue of their immanent and transformative presence.[3]

This primordial participatory consciousness has survived today in indigenous cultures such as those of the Kogi Indians of Colombia, the Mayans, the North American and Amazonian Indians, the people of Outer Mongolia, certain communities in Africa and the Aboriginal peoples of Australia and New Zealand. All of these were and still are shamanic cultures. But it also existed in highly sophisticated ancient civilizations such as those of Egypt, India and China and is discovered in the *Corpus Hermeticum* of Egypt, in the sublime texts of the *Vedas* and *Upanishads* of India, in the Taoist texts of China and in the mystical tradition of Kabbalah, described in Chapter Three. In all these traditions, there is no dualism: nature is not split off from spirit. The two were regarded, in essence, as one: the phenomenal world was the manifest form and dwelling-place of invisible spirit. As the *Bhagavad Gita* proclaims: "All is the divine being" (V11:19). The most important insight of these shamanic cultures was that spirit is ubiquitous, present within every aspect of the phenomenal world, and that man does not hold a position of dominance in relation to nature. Shamanic cultures lived within a Sacred Order. We do not recognize the existence of such an Order and that is why the collective soul of humanity has become disconnected from its roots and why our culture has become dysfunctional and is unable to respond to our deepest needs.

Why does this matter? Because if we don't know the ancient mythological influences that have formed our way of thinking, we cannot develop the insight we need to change our beliefs and modify our behaviour nor can we reconnect with a living yet silenced aspect of our psyche that has for too long been denied access to our conscious mind. We cannot become whole.

Because our highly developed science and technology have vastly improved the material conditions of our lives, we have come to view the history of civilization as an ascent from darkness, superstition and ignorance, an ascent to a sunlit upland from a primitive and thankfully outgrown past. This position is no longer tenable in the light of archaeological and anthropological discoveries and the large amount of data that has now been gathered over the past century about shamanic cultures, past and present, in different parts of the world.

Moreover, as Richard Rudgley writes in his comprehensive study of prehistoric culture, *Lost Civilisations of the Stone Age*, "In the light of the vast body of evidence collected in this book, it is now clear that a fundamental assessment of the prehistoric contribution to civilisation is necessary. Each of the elements of civilisation has been shown to have been highly developed before the rise of ancient Egypt and Mesopotamia.... Civilisation did not suddenly appear around 5000 years ago."[4]

We may look back on this remote past with some arrogance, congratulating ourselves on having long outgrown its 'magical' approach to life. We do not realize that our present consciousness has evolved out of the matrix of this ancient and instinctive way of knowing characterized by an awareness of the relationship between all orders of reality, seen and unseen. But with considerable conscious effort, we can recover and integrate this older way of knowing with our rational mind and our current view of reality.

Sacred Geography and a Living Cosmos

To live within a Sacred Order was to experience the whole universe as a living being, to know that cosmic and earthly life were intimately connected and to study not only every aspect of the immediate environment but the position and course of the moon, the major stars and the constellations in order to harmonize the life of the community with the life and rhythms of the Cosmos. Everything — plants, trees, animals and birds as well as moon, sun and stars — was sacred, sentient and *alive*, infused with divinity because each and all were part of a living, breathing, connecting web of life. This instinctive awareness of the unity and sacredness of life has lived in the depths of the human psyche for infinitely longer than the religions and the science of our time, which do not recognize nature as sacred or matter as alive.

In shamanic cultures the landscape itself was experienced as living and sacred because certain places or features of it were seen as portals to an invisible world peopled by the unseen powers of nature, by the spirits of animals and by the ancestors. A special feature in the land was held to be sacred because it marked the place of connection between the visible and invisible dimensions. Paul Devereux, in his comprehensive study of shamanic societies and customs, *Sacred Geography: Deciphering Hidden Codes in the Landscape*, writes,

> Sacred Geography is where the physical world and the worlds of spirit and soul meet. Ancient communities invested their surroundings with meaning in many ways: by identifying natural landscape features as sacred; by embellishing natural places to become monuments and temples; or by inscribing vast areas with patterns, images and otherworldly pathways, superimposing virtual geographies onto material topography. Other sacred geographies relied on scent, touch or sound — echoes, whispering waters and musical rocks signifying the presence of gods and spirits…. Sacred Geography mythologized a landscape and gave it meaning"[5]

This describes what was essentially a sensory, participatory experience deeply rooted in the life of nature. Certain places have remained sacred for thousands of years and many are so to this day in China, Tibet and India, Australia and South America. In India alone there are 150 major sites of pilgrimage that annually draw as many as twenty million pilgrims to places like Benares and the source of the Ganges.[6] China is rediscovering its ancient sites of pilgrimage to its holy mountains. Mount Kailash in Tibet, held sacred by Hindus from time immemorial as the sacred mountain believed to connect earth with heaven, still draws thousands of pilgrims, both Hindu and Buddhist, to make the arduous pilgrimage around its base. Millions of Muslims make a pilgrimage to Mecca and the Black Stone of the Kaaba at least once in their lives, and in Europe, thousands visit shrines such as Lourdes, where the Virgin Mary is said to have appeared, as well as the many shrines of the Black Madonna.

In shamanic cultures there was a specific place that was, like Mount Kailash, regarded as a world centre, an *axis mundi*, associated in different areas of the world with the image of a spiral ladder or stairway, a braided sky-rope or rainbow bridge, much like the entwined double serpent shape of the caduceus and the spiral form of DNA. This was a star gate or place which gave the shaman access to a cosmic path of connection with the spirit-world. The three unified dimensions of sky, earth and underworld (formerly the domains of the Great Mother) were connected by this central axis. Today, Chartres Cathedral is the most sacred place in Europe, an *axis mundi* from long before the time that it was built — a gateway of connection with the invisible world.

Jeremy Narby, in his book *The Cosmic Serpent*, explores in fascinating detail the ubiquity of this ancient cosmology of connection. Jacob's famous dream of a ladder stretching from earth to heaven with angels ascending and descending it is a shamanic vision of the mysterious double helix bridge connecting two worlds or dimensions of reality.[7]

In *The Future of the Ancient World: Essays on the History of Consciousness*, Jeremy Naydler writes that "In many different shamanic cultures, we encounter again and again the idea that the Pole Star marks a tiny hole — a gap, window or entrance — that leads out of the physically perceptible world of space and time to the invisible spirit-world."[8] The actual place in the landscape of the earth which marked the *axis mundi* or portal of connection to the spirit-world might be a cave, a holy mountain, or a mountain recreated in a stone temple like the ziggurats of Yucatan. It could also be the shape or colour or placement of an unusual stone, or the gushing source of a river like the Ganges, drawing millions of pilgrims for special rituals. Or it could be an impressive waterfall, a deep fissure or crevice in the rock, or a gnarled and venerable tree. Great rivers were seen as 'crossing places' between this world and the spirit-world. There were sacred ways or avenues that could be 'walked' by devotees in ritual events, such as the great stone causeways of the Mayan culture and the Nazca Lines in Peru. For the Kogi Indians of Colombia these sacred paths were thought to be replicas of the sacred routes in the Otherworld walked by the spirits. To this day Kogi shamans known as Mamas walk their sacred stone paths.[9] Dreams, visions and hallucinogenic drugs assisted the journey of shamans along these spirit-world paths. Dreams and visions may have also revealed to them the placement and shape of their stone temples and designated a sacred place of connection between worlds. Today we can recognize the beautiful and elaborate crop circles appearing in our fields of ripened wheat as places of connection between our world and the unseen world whose existence is not recognized by our culture.

The Megalith Builders

Some of the remarkable temples and stone circles built by people in the late Neolithic as places of connection with the spirit-world still survive with their remains strewn all over Europe. Stonehenge, Avebury and Silbury Hill in southern England, Newgrange, Knowth and Carrowkeel in Ireland, Skara Brae in the Orkneys, Carnac in Brittany, the great Megalithic temples on Malta and Gozo, were some of the most sacred sites of that ancient time, whose structures and significance are still little understood.

Through radio-carbon dating, many of these sacred sites, including the Maltese temples, are now known to have been built before the pyramids of Giza. It is possible that the Maltese temples may have been part of the Civilization of Old Europe, described by the archaeologist Marija Gimbutas, which dated to at least 6000 BC. The earliest stone circle at Stonehenge dates to 3000 BC and it is now thought to have been a lunar temple before it became a solar one. Around 2000 BC it was a renowned centre of healing, drawing people from faraway places, including the continent of Europe. It was also the place where, in a great annual ritual at the winter solstice, focused on the setting sun, people walked in procession along a great causeway to bring the ashes of their dead to this sacred place of connection with the spirit-world and ensure a safe passage into that world for the souls of the dead.

At Newgrange, the rising sun on the 21st December shines directly through an aperture above the entrance to the passage grave for seventeen minutes. During this time its rays travel down the shaft until they reach a stone at the end engraved with a triple spiral, signifying perhaps the understanding that life is without end or beginning, an eternal process of regeneration, or possibly pointing to the three interconnected worlds of the Great Mother: sky, earth and underworld. The narrow entrance to the inner chambers of the passage grave of Knowth, shaped like an inverted 'V', may have signified to the people of that time that it was the entrance to the womb of the Great Mother, to which all life returned and from which it would be reborn.

Silbury Hill, Europe's tallest prehistoric monument, stood near the centre of an enormous sacred complex of standing stones that had the shape of a gigantic serpent carrying two 'eggs' in its belly. This serpentine temple, drawn in 1740 by Sir Thomas Stukeley, is now lost save for a few massive stones around Avebury, and reveals the astonishing astronomical, mathematical and engineering skills of these Stone Age builders. What is clear is that both astronomy and numerology were of great importance and significance to these master builders for aligning their buildings and the life of their communities with the cosmic order. The research of John Michell, described in his book, *City of Revelation*, shows that ancient societies possessed a code of law or sacred canon imparted to them as revelation by 'the gods' at the time of the founding of their societies. The essence of this sacred canon or code of law was a complete cosmology which included the science of numbers and musical harmonies and their relation to the cosmic order and its hierarchy of creative forces. This canon and its sacred numbers was known to the builders of the temple at Stonehenge and incorporated into that and other temples of the megalithic era. For thousands of years, Michell says, it was the perfect instrument of wise government and was known and practised through-out the entire ancient world, including Egypt and Greece.[10]

What is mind-blowing is that the building of these gigantic stone temples and causeways would have required the cooperation of thousands of people engaged in a sacred communal task, comparable to the building of Chartres Cathedral millennia later. Skilled architects, astronomers and engineers designed and built these stone temples as places where people could assist in rituals that were believed to regenerate the fertility of the Earth and maintain the relationship between the human community and the Sacred Order of the Cosmos. Because they trusted absolutely that their loved ones would return to this world, there was possibly less fear of death than there is today. These rituals, presided over by astronomer-priests, and tied to the rhythm of sun, moon and certain of the major stars and planets — in particular Venus — must have been incredibly numinous to experience, particularly at sunrise and sunset, the rise of the full moon and the time of an eclipse. The whole community participated in them. People who were constantly fighting with neighbouring clans or tribes would never have been able to construct these monuments.

The Shaman

It seems necessary to define two 'kinds' of shamanic experience. One is the ability to communicate with the spirits of rocks, trees and plants and to open a channel of connection with the spirit-world through a specific feature or quality of the landscape like the *axis mundi* mentioned above. The other is the ability to leave the physical body and travel into other dimensions in the spirit-world. Certain techniques passed from shaman to shaman in different cultures as well as the use of hallucinogenic drugs facilitated both these experiences. Mircea Eliade described the second experience when he wrote the first authentic in depth study of Central Asian and Siberian shamanism in 1964. He defined the shaman as a master of ecstasy and shamanism as a technique of ecstasy. "It is impossible to imagine a period when man did not have dreams and waking reveries and did not enter into 'trance' — a loss of consciousness that was interpreted as the soul's travelling into the beyond."[11]

Shamanic practices are known to have existed from the depths of time in many parts of the world. One dramatic scene in the original cave of Lascaux, whose paintings are now tragically affected by mould and may disappear forever, is painted on one wall of a deep shaft at the far end of the cave, and is dated to ca.14,500 BC. Not reproduced in the modern replica, it shows a dying bison transfixed by a spear standing next to a shaman with a bird's head who lies on the ground with his arms outstretched and his penis erect, as if in a trance. His staff is surmounted by a bird, suggesting that, like the shamans of Central Asia and Siberia, he is flying like the bird on his staff to the spirit-world.

Westerners now travel to the Amazonian forest to participate in shamanic practices to penetrate the veil between the very limited consciousness of our culture and the extraordinary expansion of consciousness experienced by taking a hallucinogenic drug and entering a multi-dimensional world. This experience can be terrifying and may be dangerous for some people. In another part of the world, a couple recently took their disturbed child to be healed by the Reindeer Shamans of Outer Mongolia with spectacular results (*The Horse Boy*, Rupert Isaacson). The idea of an expanded state seems alien, even threatening to the consciousness we have today, yet it is important that we become aware of its existence because it suggests that we may have lost a capacity that has atrophied through lack of use.

A contemporary technique for entering these unfamiliar states of consciousness has been developed by the Czech psychiatrist, Stanislav Grof, one of the pioneers who has extensively explored them. He has found that, in altered states of consciousness, ancient fields of memory and ancient experiences from humanity's past as well as the past experience of other species can become accessible to our consciousness.[12] Beneath or beyond the threshold of our conscious mind, an incredibly rich legacy from the past lives on and is still accessible.

The Essence of the Shamanic Experience

Over countless thousands of years, shamanic myths and rituals of connection kept alive the awareness of the existence of an invisible spirit-world or soul-world whose symbol, initially, may have been the mysterious dark phase of the moon. Out of that darkness the crescent was continually reborn — symbolically associated with the regeneration of the Earth's life and, in the traditions of Vedic India, with the regeneration of cosmic cycles, each lasting hundreds of thousands of years. Poets, artists, seers and musicians received their inspiration and their calling from the starry cosmos that was as real to them as this world.

Shamanic cultures knew there was no death. They were in touch with the ancestors. They knew about travelling to other worlds. Greece had the Eleusinian Mysteries that gave people trust in their survival. Long before Greece, Bronze Age Egypt had a very detailed description of the journey of the soul after death. This extraordinary civilization was as aware of the spirit-world as of this world.

People lived in awareness of the presence of the spirit-world and the goddesses and gods who inhabited the starry cosmos and descended each day into their temples. Far from seeing death as extinction, the Egyptians saw death as a journey towards awakening to cosmic life.

People did not so much believe in gods and goddesses as encounter them, as vividly described in the *Iliad* and the *Odyssey*. They may have heard these beings speak and received wisdom and guidance from them or seen them in their dreams. Because the clear distinction we now make between an inner and outer world did not then exist, and because they felt they lived *within* a Sacred Order, the psyche of that time lived within that Order, in communion with it. The words spoken, the music heard, the dreams and visions seen came not from 'inside' them, but from the soul of the Cosmos, from daemonic beings, goddesses and gods and the spirits of animals, trees, mountains and rivers as well as from the ancestors who were never thought of as dead but who formed a continuous line of connection with the living. Oracles could impart the will of these beings and people knew that they were not alone in this world but could be guided and influenced as well as threatened by unseen entities. Birds were recognized as messengers of this invisible world, very possibly because people dreamed about them in this role or even heard them as a voice speaking to them. The earliest legends about the great oak tree at Dodona in northern Greece said that oracles were delivered by the oak itself and that when birds happened to alight on the tree, the tree would suddenly begin speaking with a human voice.[13] The Oracle at Delphi was the centre of the Greek world where the celebrated priestess of the Oracle, or *Pythia*, as she was called, received embassies from all over the Greek Empire. She held the title of 'The Delphic Bee' and was the highest authority in that world, intermediary between the supplicant and the god Apollo.

A highly developed intuitive sensibility, acute powers of observation and the ability to listen to the spirits of plants, trees and animals, taught people to gather, grind or distil certain herbs and plants or the bark of trees for healing illness. Dreams and visions were of great importance in the diagnosis and healing of disease. Methods of divination predicted the advisability of taking certain courses of action. From all over the Greek Empire, people travelled great distances to the many healing sanctuaries of the god Aesclepius — the most famous of which were at Epidaurus, Kos and Pergamum (now in modern Turkey) — to be healed of their diseases. Here, as also in Egypt and Crete, the main diagnostic agent was the dream, sometimes a visionary dream of the god himself. As one man who was healed of his long-standing illness described it, in words that leap out vividly from a forgotten past, "One listened and heard things, sometimes in a dream, sometimes in waking life. One's hair stood on end; one cried and felt happy; one's heart swelled out but not with vainglory. What human being could put this experience into words? But anyone who has been through it will share my knowledge and recognize the state of my mind."[14] Rites of incubation, travelling in the spirit-world and healing were practised in caves and sacred places all over the ancient world. Like the astronomer-priests of Egypt who communicated with the stars, or the Taoist sages of China and the Vedic seers of India, withdrawn into the deep solitude of the mountains and forests, the shaman-seers who guided these cultures were trained to enter a state of utter stillness, to listen and bring back to their community what they heard in an enhanced state of consciousness.

At the heightened level of awareness that characterized the participatory consciousness of these cultures, everything had the ability to communicate — a stone as much as a star, an animal as much as a tree or a spring gushing out of a crevice in the rock. What we now call synchronicities were an intrinsic and recognized part of the experience of the people of that time because they had the intuitive ability to notice things far more acutely than we do today. The unseen soul of nature had the potential to reveal itself in the flight of a bird, the stirring of the leaves of an oak tree, the ripples on a lake. Nature was held to be animate, conscious and able to communicate with man. The essential characteristic of lunar culture was kinship — the kinship of man with all creation — reflected in the much quoted words of Chief Seattle:

> Every part of this Earth is sacred to my people…. We are part of the Earth and it is part of us. The perfumed flowers are our sisters. The bear, the deer, the great eagle, these are our brothers…. The shining water that moves in the dreams and rivers is not just water, but the blood of our ancestors…. The water's murmur is the voice of my father's father. The rivers are our brothers. They quench our thirst. They carry our canoes and feed our children…. Remember that the air is precious to us, that the air shares its spirit with all the life it supports. The wind that gave our grandfather his first breath also receives his last sigh. The wind also gives our children the spirit of life…Will you teach your children what we have taught our children? That the Earth is our Mother? That what befalls the Earth, befalls all the sons of the Earth. This we know: the Earth does not belong to man, man belongs to the Earth. All things are connected like the blood which unites us all. Man did not weave the web of life, he is merely a strand in it. Whatever he does to the web, he does to himself.

The recent words of David Kopenawa Yanomami, a contemporary Amazon shaman and tribal leader, speaking about the calamitous destruction of the Amazonian forest, reflect the same awareness of kinship: "I am the brother of the forest and must defend it".

From another part of the world, the following story may perhaps illustrate how long-atrophied faculties once connected us with the soul of nature. Next to the Potala Palace in Lhasa there is a temple called the Lukhang or 'Temple of the Serpent Spirits' that the present Dalai Lama describes as one of the hidden jewels of Tibetan civilization. This temple was the private chamber of the Dalai Lamas, the place where they retired for deep meditation. Miraculously it has not so far been destroyed by the Chinese invasion of Tibet. The walls of the upper floor are decorated with extraordinary paintings describing the Tantric practices of the Dzogchen path to the direct experience of reality — the path practised by the Dalai Lamas for centuries. Only these murals depict the practices that were otherwise transmitted orally, and poetically referred to as 'the whispered lineage'.

Prior to the Chinese invasion of Tibet, on one day each year, the Lukhang was open to pilgrims who crossed the lake to the temple to make offerings to and invoke the blessing of the water spirits believed to reside beneath the lake. This ritual went back to a time when the Potala Palace was being built and a deep pit had been excavated to provide mortar for the palace walls. Legend says that a female water spirit or *Naga* came to the Fifth Dalai Lama (1617–1682) during his meditations and warned him that the work on the Palace was destroying the Nagas' ancestral home. The Dalai Lama promised that he would build and dedicate a temple to the spirits of the lake which had formed over the desecrated land so that their presence would be recognized and honoured.[15]

In our modern world, fairy tales like the 'Sleeping Beauty' may be the residual fragments of the forgotten participatory experience where forests were inhabited by creatures who would help or hinder us; where spirits of tree and mountain, stream and sacred spring could speak to us and reveal the secrets of healing plants and waters; where bears or frogs might be spirits in disguise. Shamans or hermits, old women or men living in the deep forest or mountain hermitages might offer us wise counsel, or birds bring us messages, warning of danger and acting as guides. There are countless fairy tales, descending from ancient oral traditions, which describe how the hero or heroine who responds to the mysterious guidance of animals or who helps them when others have ignored their requests wins the reward of the treasure and the royal marriage. They are the creation of a different kind of consciousness, one where the mythopoetic imagination was highly cultivated, honoured and developed and where story-tellers, who were often seers, held a place of honour in the community.

People in the Polynesian islands still sing to the sharks to come to the boats of the fishermen, asking their permission to kill them for food. In the sea near the Dominican Republic, a whale whisperer is able to communicate with the whales in this, their breeding ground. The Maori shamans of New Zealand still believe that everything has its own life force: the stone has the life force of the earth itself; the bone the life force of all living things; the shell the life force of the sea. In carving these elements of life with the patterns they observe in nature, they carry this insight into their work, believing that it brings healing power to the wearer and to the community. The 'life' of the stone, bone or shell is never lost. Its energy lives on in the wearer of the carving and is transmitted to the observer.

Out of this profound relationship with the landscape and its creatures in different parts of the world, myths developed, specific to the people who inhabited it for millennia. As Frederick Turner so brilliantly expressed it in his book *Beyond Geography: The Western Spirit Against the Wilderness*, "Living myth must include and speak of the interlocking cycles of animate and vegetable life, of water, sun, and even the stones, which have their own stories. It must embrace without distinction the phenomenal and the numinous."[16] This is something that has been forgotten and that is why we have no living myth today.

The Shamanic Experience in Pre-Socratic Greece

Right at the root of European civilization we can discover the presence of this ancient shamanic transmission in Egypt. The Egyptians, like the later Greeks whose greatest philosophers they influenced, knew that the many gods and goddesses they worshipped personified the hidden powers that they were able to identify as elements or agents of a divinely ordered Cosmos. We have simply no idea how the Egyptians developed their knowledge of the geometric and mathematical principles which governed an intelligent, sentient Cosmos nor how they were able to incorporate this knowledge in their greatest buildings.

In Greece, the rituals of the Orphic and Eleusinian Mysteries, which kept alive the essence of the lunar participatory experience, strengthened the sense of participation in an unseen reality and gave initiates an experience of immortality and the omnipresence of the soul. The poet Pindar said of them: "Blessed are they who have seen these things. They know the end of life and they know the God-given beginnings." Apart from the Mysteries, certain of the Pre-Socratic Greek philosophers of the sixth century BC carry forward the legacy of the lunar experience. The words of Heraclitus, when he suggests that the soul is of unfathomable depth, retain the essence of that ancient perception. Thales of Miletus speaks of the 'All' as being alive and full of daemons who are the agents of the one soul-substance. Anaximenes says that humanity and nature are fundamentally inseparable because both participate in the same underlying 'substance' which he calls soul.[17] Pythagoras (569–475 BC), after he was exiled from Greece to

Crotona on the east coast of southern Italy, having spent forty years with the astronomer-priests of Egypt and Babylon, defined the mathematical laws which embodied the intelligence, wisdom and mathematical harmony of the divine order of the Cosmos. He left these words to encourage us: "Take heart, for the human race is divine".

In a book called *In the Dark Places of Wisdom*, the Classical scholar Dr. Peter Kingsley describes the treasures of wisdom bequeathed to the West by Parmenides (ca. 515–ca. 450 BC), who was born at Velia (Ascea), in southern Italy, a city now known to have been sacred to the goddess Persephone. Parmenides was one of the greatest of the Pre-Socratic philosophers. Only a few fragments of his teaching survive and we know of them mainly through Plato's *Parmenides* and later commentaries. But he did leave a poem, an extraordinary poem written in the incantatory metre that was used to draw people into another state of consciousness — "poetry created", Kingsley writes, "under divine inspiration, revealing what humans on their own can never see or know, describing the world of gods and the world of humans and the meetings between humans and gods."[18] This poem is a key to understanding the shamanic experience of that time. Parmenides, like Pythagoras, was skilled in the practice of incubation, whereby a person wanting to enter another dimension of reality, or request a vision or a visitation from a god or goddess, withdrew into a cave or underground room or enclosed space, sometimes for days on end. He would have used techniques of chanting and breath control to give him access to a transcendent dimension of reality. What is so interesting is that, as Kingsley writes, objects and inscriptions have been found which show the continuity of these shamanic traditions and practices extending from Greece right through Asia to India, Tibet, Nepal and as far as Mongolia.

Parmenides' poem describes his shamanic journey into that other dimension of reality in a chariot drawn by mares and guided by young women — daughters of the sun — through immense doors which stretch from earth to heaven and open on oiled hinges onto the yawning chasm of the Underworld. He speaks of his encounter there with someone whom he calls simply 'The Goddess' although we know that her name is Persephone. As Kingsley writes, "Every single figure Parmenides encounters in his poem is a woman or a girl. Even the animals are female and he's taught by a goddess. The universe he describes is a feminine one."[19] The poem begins:

> *The mares that carry me as far as longing can reach*
> *rode on, once they had come and fetched me onto the legendary*
> *road of the divinity that carries the man who knows*
> *through the vast and dark unknown...*

What Parmenides' poem reveals is that he was a master of the shamanic art of travelling, taking him "as far as longing can reach" into the darkness and mystery of the Immortal Realm, and that his writings about Truth, Justice and the Right Ordering of human existence were derived from his actual *experience* of that other dimension of reality and his encounter there with the goddess. It also suggests that the great divide that exists in our culture between the rational and the non-rational did not exist in his time and does not need to exist now. It is a barrier created by our fear of the unknown and our tendency to disparage the existence of dimensions of reality of which we no longer have knowledge or experience.

The names of a lineage of shaman-healers descending from Parmenides through some five hundred years have recently been discovered in Velia (Ascea), carved on a single large stone. These men paid close attention to dreams — their own dreams and the dreams of those who came to them for healing of mind or body, and this tradition of the healing dream was developed in the 300 Aesclepean sanctuaries in Greece. Three titles described these healer-initiates: the title *Iatromantis* meant a healer of a particular kind, one who could enter a dimension of reality that is beyond waking and dreaming yet is present in both. The title *Pholarchos* meant 'Lord of the Lair' or master of the technique of incubation through which they gained their power to heal and to become law-givers. The title *Ouliades* meant 'priest of Apollo' — an Apollo who was not the god of light and reason familiar to us, but a god associated with healing, the underworld and what lies beyond the threshold of death. As Lord of the Lair, Apollo presided over the caves where rites of incubation were practised at dead of night; rites that originated on the western coast of Anatolia and descended from a shamanic tradition long-established there. It was from these rites of incubation and their journeying into another world that Parmenides and those who preceded and followed him received their teachings about Truth, Justice and the Laws which are necessary for the right-ordering of society.[20] These teachings and the shamanic method of accessing them were lost with the emphasis given to the rational mind derived from later interpretations of Plato's writings. Because of Plato's immense influence, the insights and experience of Parmenides were lost to Western civilization.

Plato and the Loss of the Shamanic Transmission

For it was the legacy of Plato (429–347 BC) rather than that of Parmenides which was to become the foundation of Western civilization and it is difficult to determine why Plato discarded the shamanic tradition known to the man who was said to be his teacher and mentor. Plato stands at the watershed between the lunar and solar eras, between what we can now recognize as two phases in the evolution of consciousness: one grounded in a close participatory relationship with nature and an unseen order of reality; the other drawing away from nature with the emphasis on reason and the rational mind. From the perspective of the evolution of consciousness in the West, Plato initiates a profound change, a change that may already have been well-established among the cultural elite of Athens. The emphasis of his prolific writings set down over an expanse of forty years is not on the shamanic experience described by Parmenides but, following the method of dialogue used by Socrates, on the development of the intellectual rigour that he (Socrates) considered essential for man to gain insight into the divine realities of the Eternal Forms, those same realities which Parmenides had gained access to by a different route. By the word *nous* Plato did not mean the rational intellect or the mind but the direct apprehension of the Divine Forms, the world of archetypal realities.

Yet it was surely from the shamanic participatory experience of an ensouled world that Plato, in his *Timaeus*, drew his concept of the Soul of the Cosmos (*Psuche tou Kosmou*), which he described as a "Single Living Creature that encompasses all the living creatures that are within it". He speaks of a great chain of being as a hierarchy of participations, descending from a pre-existing template of Eternal Forms to the forms of this phenomenal world. The idea of hierarchy is new. We lose the concept of the shamanic sense of *relationship* with the Otherworld, and the ability to travel into it, known to Parmenides, and are introduced to the Socratic idea that a highly developed quality of the intellect, honed through discussion, the exercise of logic and the testing of hypotheses, is the key to the opening of human consciousness to the recovery of our lost memory of the transcendent world of the Eternal Forms. The philosopher Jeremy Naydler observes in *The Future of the Ancient World*, that, for Plato,

> The spiritual source both of the natural world and of ourselves is to be found by ascending away from the body and all sensory experience, and "traveling" in a state of consciousness free of the body into a dimension of existence beyond that of which we are normally aware. This dimension is the purely spiritual World of Forms, or Ideas from which both the forms in the natural world and the thoughts in our minds derive. Secondly, in Plato's view, the truly spiritual does not participate in matter. It is not tainted by immersion or involvement in matter.[21]

Although the archetypal World of Eternal Forms is connected to this world through a hierarchy of relationships, and although the Cosmos is ensouled, the dimension of the Eternal Forms does not participate in this material world. This distinction is absolutely crucial for an understanding of the Western philosophical tradition that developed from Plato. It is also crucial for an understanding of the religions of the Axial Age, which began around 500 BC and which turned away from nature, the world and sensory experience towards a transcendent and (in the three patriarchal religions) monotheistic concept of spirit. Naydler summarizes the tendency to reject this world and the sensory perception which holds us to it:

> In order to participate in the true Reality from which what appears real to us derives, we must sever our connection with the material world and sense-based consciousness. We cannot experience our true self on earth: it is necessary to go upward and backward in a movement of self-recovery, which transports the soul into a pristine, pre-earthly state of self-remembrance. Plato's message is an initiatory one: we must learn to die to our incarnate selves, for death is the secret of life.[22]

Plato's thought carries the idea that every individual soul holds within it the memory of the divine world but, on entering this world and being imprisoned in the body, it forgets what it once knew. The aim of philosophy was to re-awaken in the soul awareness of its divine origins, awareness of the eternal causal world through a quest for and knowledge of the True, the Good and the Beautiful. In Book VII of his *Republic*, he uses the graphic metaphor of the cave, describing how human beings are condemned to live there like prisoners, seeing on the walls the flickering shadows of the realities that can only be seen on leaving the cave. He wrote these telling words in the *Phaedrus*: "Pure was the light and pure were we from the pollution of the walking sepulchre which we call a body, to which we are bound like an oyster to its shell." It is strange that the cave, which was the place of revelation for Parmenides and other shaman-healers like him who travelled into the Underworld, has now, with Plato, become the prison of the body.

Implicit in his immensely influential definition of reality is the idea that nature, although an expression of the divine, is 'lower' in the hierarchical chain of being than spirit, body 'lower' than mind, and animals and plants 'lower' on the scale of being than humans. This is a radical departure from the experience of shamanic cultures where nature was sacred because it was the dwelling place of spirit, where access to the invisible world underlying the world of form was found through a sacred place in the physical world and through shamanic techniques of incubation, connection and entering that other world, never through a rejection of the physical world or the rejection of sensory experience.

Moreover, in Plato's philosophy, the soul is divided into a rational and an irrational part with the first having primacy over the second. The instincts, and the emotions which derive from them, are associated with the irrational or animal soul and relegated to a level far beneath the rational soul that is associated with the mind. From now on the testimony of sensory experience — the instinctive sensory experience of the body participating in the matrix of nature — is deemed to be inferior and unreliable in relation to the rational mind, and a radical separation develops between mind and body. One could say that nature and body are henceforth excluded from the Sacred Order, excluded from the dimension of soul and spirit. It is possible that the split which was beginning to develop between nature and spirit and that is already clearly apparent in Plato's writing was the direct effect of the accelerating separation of the developing ego from the instinctive participatory consciousness of the lunar era.

Plato's important definition of an all-embracing Cosmic Soul and his emphasis on the divine qualities of Truth, Goodness and Beauty, bequeathed to Western civilization vitally important concepts. However, because of the separation of the world of the Eternal Forms from this material world, there is a *fading of the feeling of participation* in an ensouled world, a disjunction between spiritual and sensory experience, an emphasis on rational discourse rather than the *experience* of the numinous that is the main characteristic of shamanic cultures and that, in Greece, reached its highest expression in Pythagoras and Parmenides and the chain of shaman-healers who preceded and followed them. Dr. Kingsley comments: "For thousands of years now, the beginnings of western philosophy have systematically been split off and dissociated from the kind of practices we've come to think of as 'magical'. The process has been a long and determined one; it has almost succeeded. But those ancient connections are calling out again to be acknowledged."[23]

Although it carried forward the existence of the world of spirit in the idea of the Eternal Forms, this new philosophy, with its emphasis on freeing the soul from the prison of the body, did not retain the shamanic understanding that the visible world was permeated by an invisible eternal ground, *that this world exists within the eternal world*. An absolutely essential understanding was lost. The fundamental disjunction between soul and body in Platonic thought was transmitted to Christian theology which increasingly split matter from spirit, body from soul, sensory from spiritual experience and saw the body as the main impediment to the spiritual life. This split was to have disastrous and far-reaching effects on Western civilization and on the relations between man and woman, for man was identified with the spirit and the rational mind and woman with nature and the irrational passions of the body.

It may seem an act of sacrilege to suggest that Plato's philosophy transmitted this split. However, I feel that its effect on the developing psyche of Western civilization needs to be noted. For Plato created an elaborate philosophical structure of thought which resulted in the movement away from nature and the immanence of spirit towards the idealization of the world of archetypal or eternal forms, and the pursuit of reason and knowledge as the way to access this transcendent spiritual world. Through Plato's influence, though not, I am sure, his intention, Western civilization was destined to develop on the foundation of a radical split between spirit and nature, between the exalted Apollonian rational mind and the feared Dionysian passions of the body and this split is still embedded in our thinking today. Christianity turned daemons into demons, ignoring the stark warning of Plutarch (ca. AD 46–120): "Whoever denies the daemons breaks the chain that links the gods to men."[24]

Iain McGilchrist, in a remarkable book called *The Master and His Emissary: the Divided Brain and the Making of the Western World*, which explores the difference between the perception of the right and left hemispheres of the brain, observes that "This separation of the absolute and eternal, which can be known by *logos* (reason), from the purely phenomenological, which is now seen as inferior, leaves an indelible stamp on the history of Western philosophy for the subsequent two thousand years."[25] Yet it should perhaps be remembered that Plato bequeathed to us the idea of our separation from and need for reunion with the divine world and this vitally important idea can be traced through Western literature and philosophy and is emerging today in our modern world.

There is another important aspect of this story which concerns the philosophy of Aristotle (384–322 BC). I have turned again to Jeremy Naydler's book, mentioned above, for his understanding of Aristotle, who was engaged by Philip of Macedon to be the tutor of his son, later to become Alexander the Great. Aristotle's philosophy was radically different from Plato's and retained the older shamanic insight that nature is the manifestation of spirit, and that spirit is the active principle within all matter. Plato gave his allegiance to soul; Aristotle to matter.

It was Aristotle who laid the ground for the exploration of the natural world, the search for the hidden laws of nature, and the astonishing discoveries of modern science. Unlike Plato, he did not separate sensory from spiritual experience; rather he saw the archetypal principles of the Eternal World fully embodied in the world of matter.

> In his philosophy is enshrined a spirituality that does not require an ascent to the heavens in order to discover the spiritual source either of the world or of ourselves, for Spirit is engaged in the world and can be discovered everywhere in nature. For Aristotle nature is the outpouring of spirit, which is the active or creative principle in all things…The sense-perceptible world is not a copy or pale imitation of a transcendent world of spiritual archetypes. Rather these archetypes are embodied in the sense-perceptible world. Spirit is utterly

committed to nature. Furthermore, in human consciousness, Spirit has the possibility of knowing and recognizing itself. Aristotle refers to this in the twelfth book of the Metaphysics, where he describes the meditative act in which a transcendent self-consciousness is attained without travelling to the stars, a "self"-consciousness in which universal Spirit comes to know itself in and through human consciousness.[26]

I think this remarkable insight is what is being experienced now within many thousands of people: spirit awakening to awareness of itself within our human consciousness. And all this comes about, not through rejecting the body and sensory experience but through a profound sense of the unfolding of spirit's plan within the context of nature and human existence. As Naydler observes,

> An acceptance of our embodiment, of our belonging to the earth, runs through Aristotle's philosophy just as an unwillingness to accept the reality of incarnate life runs through the writings of Plato. For Aristotle, Spirit has made its habitation here on earth; it is part of the destiny of Spirit to become implicated in matter. Spirit and matter together make the world.

> Aristotle is too much in love with the world to see withdrawal from it as a valid spiritual path and his work is imbued with the intention to discover the working of the divine within the natural world. The two emphases of his philosophy are on pursuing knowledge of nature, and on developing a thoroughly grounded ethics. As regards the former, he seeks everywhere the working of the divine within the natural world. As regards the latter, the basis of right action is brought back to the spiritual intuition of the free and fully responsible human agent.[27]

We have here not only an agenda for science but an agenda for the creation of an ethical relationship between the human community and the natural world — something that is being worked out in many communities worldwide, even if it has not yet fully entered the world of science or politics.

> Aristotle grasps the fact that humanity has entered a new stage in the unfolding cosmological drama, and that this stage is to do with the infinite rediscovering itself within the sphere of the finite. In human understanding, Aristotle sees a cosmic and eternal activity at work within human consciousness. The source of human thinking is infinite, but it is locked within the confines of finitude. Human beings thus have a vital mediating role of releasing the infinite from its entanglement within the finite, thereby allowing the divine to know itself within the human.[28]

Centuries later the rescue and release of spirit deeply buried within matter was to become the major theme of the Great Work of Alchemy. Although the fact of spirit's presence within nature was recognized by shamanic peoples in many parts of the world — not in the scientific sense, but instinctively, intuitively and by actual experience — in Christian civilization it was a heresy to regard nature as animated by spirit. So this insight, originating in the older shamanic cultures and carefully transmitted from generation to generation, had to go underground for many centuries.

Once, long ago, the soul was understood in its widest sense as an unseen order of reality which was the ground of this world, ensouling both nature and the cosmos. It was the great matrix of being to which we belonged, in whose life we lived. Soul was the *unseen* life of nature and the cosmos but its visible manifestation was this phenomenal world which was never regarded as inferior to or separate from spirit as it was later to become in the solar era: it was infused with spirit, permeated by spirit, an epiphany or showing forth of spirit. I will return to this theme in Chapter Fifteen.

These two chapters have described the profound relationship we once had with the Earth and the Cosmos. The Indigenous Peoples of the world did not lose this relationship and are urgently trying to re-awaken us to it. So much knowledge of the profound divinity and sacredness of life has been lost. To recover this knowledge and transform our view of reality we need to recover the lost lunar vision and give it new expression in our time so that we might enter the phase that Owen Barfield called "Final Participation", when the lunar and solar aspects of our consciousness are reunited and taken to a new level, through our reconnection with everything from which we have become separated. Jung understood this need when he wrote: "Nothing to which the psyche belongs or which is part of the psyche is ever lost. To live fully, we have to reach down and bring back to life the deepest levels of the psyche from which our present consciousness has evolved."[29] But to do this, we need to understand the solar era and why its view of reality was utterly different from that of the lunar one; why and how we moved from seeing nature as animate and ensouled to seeing it as subject to our dominance and control.

Notes:

1. Eliade, Mircea (1959) *The Sacred and the Profane*, Harcourt, Brace & World Inc., p.13
2. Barfield, Owen (1988) *Saving the Appearances: A Study in Idolatry*, Second Edition, the Wesleyan University Press, Middletown, Conn. USA
3. Tarnas, Richard (2006) *Cosmos and Psyche: Intimations of a New World View*, Viking, New York, pp. 16-17
4. Rudgley, Richard (1998) *Lost Civilisations of the Stone Age*, Arrow Books, London, p. 291 and 9
5. Devereux, Paul (2010) *Sacred Geography: Deciphering Hidden Codes in the Landscape*, Octopus Publishing Group, London, inside cover
6. ibid, p. 56
7. Narby, Jeremy (1998) *The Cosmic Serpent: DNA and the Origins of Knowledge*, Victor Gollancz, passim
8. Naydler, Jeremy (2009) *The Future of the Ancient World: Essays on the History of Consciousness*, Inner Traditions, Rochester, Vermont, p. 75
9. Devereux, p.78
10. Michell, John (1972) *City of Revelation*, Garnstone Press Ltd., London, p. 132
11. Eliade, Mircea (1964) *Shamanism: Archaic Techniques in Ecstasy*, Bollingen Foundation, Princeton, p.19
12. Grof, Stanislav and Hal Z. Bennett (1990), *The Holotropic Mind: Three levels of Human Consciousness and How They Shape Our Lives*, HarperCollins, New York
13. Skafte, Dianne (1997) *When Oracles Speak*, Thorsons, London
14. *Dreams: Visions of the Night*, Thames and Hudson Ltd., London, ed. Jill Purce, p. 18
15. Baker, Ian A. (2000) *The Dalai Lama's Secret Temple*, Thames and Hudson, London, pp.12-16
16. Turner, Frederick (1983 & 1982) *Beyond Geography: The Western Spirit Against the Wilderness*, Rutgers University Press, p.19
17. Levy, Gertrude (1958) *The Gate of Horn*, Faber & Faber, London, pp. 301-3
18. Kingsley, Peter (1999) *In the Dark Places of Wisdom*, Golden Sufi Press, California, p. 49
19. ibid, p. 49
20. ibid, pp. 108-114
21. Naydler, p. 254
22. ibid, p. 254
23. Kingsley, p. 170
24. Plutarch, *De Defectu Oraculorum* 13
25. McGilchrist, Iain (2009) *The Master and His Emissary: The Divided Brain and the Making of the Western World*, Yale University Press, p. 286
26. Naydler, p. 256
27. ibid, p. 257
28. ibid, p. 258
29. C.G. Jung, exact source unknown

Landscape and a Horned God
Robin Baring 1977

Part Three

The Dissociated Psyche

The Pathology of Separation and Loss

The Feminine Archetype associated
with Nature, Soul and Body
is split off from Spirit
Nature is desouled
Nature and the Earth are no longer sacred

Woman is identified with Nature; Man with Spirit
Nature and Woman become subject to Man

Sexuality is sinful
Body is split off from Mind and Mind from Soul

Chapter Six

THE SOLAR ERA

THE SEPARATION FROM NATURE
AND THE BATTLE BETWEEN GOOD AND EVIL

The story of mind exiled from Nature is the story of Western Man.

— Ted Hughes

In the story of the development of civilization, from around 2000 BC, we begin to see the beginning of a new phase in the evolution of human consciousness and a change of focus from a lunar to a solar mythology. This era, which has been equated with the rise of civilization, actually reflects a complete eclipse of the participatory experience of the lunar era, taking over many of the older lunar myths and stories and setting them in a new solar context. The dominant celestial body is now the sun rather than the moon and the dominant mythology is solar rather than lunar. The primary theme of lunar mythology is a cyclical process of birth, death and regeneration. The theme of solar mythology is a great battle between light and darkness, good and evil. Whereas the focus of lunar culture is on an ensouled cosmos and mythic participation in the life of a Sacred Order, the focus of solar culture is on the conquest and mastery of nature, the development of the rational mind, and the differentiation of the outstanding individual from the tribal group. It is, above all, the age of the individual and, specifically, the warrior who dons the mantle of the solar hero.

As this process of solarization develops, linear time begins to replace cyclical time, and a linear, literal and objective way of thinking slowly begins to replace the older participatory way of knowing and its imaginal, relational way of thinking. It is customary to look upon this new era as a progressive advance or ascent for humanity emerging from an older and more primitive era, characterized by savage customs and magical thinking. I see it as a time of immense cultural and technological achievement but also, as D.H. Lawrence did, as a time of ever-increasing loss of the sense of participation in the Sacred Order of an ensouled world. In his book *Apocalypse and Other Writings* (1931), he despairingly wrote: "We have lost the cosmos, by coming out of responsive connection with it, and this is our chief tragedy.... We and the cosmos are one. The cosmos is a vast living body of which we are still parts.... What is our petty little love of nature — Nature!! — compared to the ancient magnificent living with the cosmos, and being honoured by the cosmos!"[1]

One of the major features of the solar era is the change in the image of deity from Great Mother to Great Father, with a polytheistic phase of many goddesses and gods in between — Egypt, Mesopotamia, Canaan, Greece and Rome, among others. The image of God of the three Abrahamic religions portrays him as transcendent to and separate from creation. God is the *maker* of heaven and earth, whereas the Great Mother *was* heaven and earth. In this change of emphasis, the essential identity between creator and creation is broken, and a fundamental duality is born from their separation, the duality that we name spirit and nature.

The long-term effect of this new concept of spirit was to eliminate the presence of the divine within the natural world, effectively desacralizing it and opening the way to its exploitation. The conscious mind or ego 'grew up' in the shadow of an image of deity that was utterly different from that of the earlier lunar phase. The shock to the psyche was immense and it has never recovered from the trauma imposed by the beliefs which developed on the foundation of the split between spirit and nature.

For the solar era tore us out of the matrix of nature as the developing ego lost the deep instinctive sense of its connection to nature and the cosmos. That is why this era can be called the Phase of Separation as the philosopher Owen Barfield described it. The conscious mind came to look upon the Cosmos, God and, eventually, the world of Nature as something separate and different from itself, something it could observe but no longer feel a part of. With separation came fear because death was no longer seen as leading to the renewal of life, as in the lunar era; it became final and terrifying, leading to the need for power and control over whatever aroused fear.

This change reflects the beginning of an *entirely new perception of life*, one where nature becomes something to be controlled and manipulated by human ingenuity, and spirit is projected upon a distant deity in the sky and no longer experienced as immanent within the forms of nature. The danger of this phase is that the human mind, breaking away from its instinctive ground, its source in nature and the cosmos, becomes increasingly dissociated from them and begins to assimilate a god-like power to itself; seeing itself engaged in a great struggle against the power of nature. In the Book of Genesis, human beings alone are seen as having a special relationship with the deity and are enjoined to exercise dominion over other species. This belief would have been unthinkable in the earlier phase of participation. It is impossible to exaggerate the influence it was to have on religious ideologies and, ultimately, on science's attitude to nature.

As the sun becomes the new focus of consciousness, the cultural hero is no longer the lunar shaman who ventures into the Otherworld, assimilating its mysteries and returning from it with the treasure of wisdom and methods of healing with which to guide and help his community, but rather the solar hero — a king, warrior or outstanding individual — who is celebrated as the one who, identified with the light, conquers and overcomes darkness, a darkness that is increasingly identified with his enemies. The emphasis is on the triumph of the light and the repudiation and elimination of whatever or whoever is identified with darkness. Hence the words of George W. Bush in September 2001, "Our responsibility to history is already clear: to answer these attacks and rid the world of evil."

Solar Myth: the Cosmic Battle between Light and Darkness

There is one powerful myth that lies at the root of the solar era. It comes down to us from the mythology of Mesopotamia, Persia and Greece. Its theme is a hero's struggle with a mighty dragon or serpent and the cosmic battle between light and darkness, good and evil. Right at the beginning of the solar era in the Sumerian *Epic of Gilgamesh*, we encounter the first myth of a hero's fight with a dragon, monster or serpent. This myth became the dominant one of the solar era, entering into religions, philosophies, and innumerable conflicts and conquests. It contributed to the yawning chasm between nature and spirit and between mind and body. It gave rise to the belief that man is engaged in a great battle to conquer, subdue and control nature, so losing the participatory consciousness of the lunar era. Within the psyche, it contributed to and also reflected the splitting asunder of the conscious 'rational' mind and the instinctual soul. It gave rise ultimately to the one-eyed consciousness of the present time that will be described in Chapter Nine.

The *Epic of Gilgamesh* may have originated as early as ca. 2300 BC and gives the first known account of the Great Flood. Gilgamesh, king of the Sumerian city of Uruk — a city girded by mighty walls — defies the express warning of the gods and sets out with his companion Enkidu to kill Humbaba, guardian of the great cedar forest of the Goddess Ishtar. The two heroes will not listen to

Humbaba's pleas for mercy and kill him. They then cut down the forest. Soon after, Enkidu falls ill and dies. Gilgamesh, grief-stricken, sets out to find the Herb or Flower of Immortality but falls asleep on his way back to his city and loses it to a serpent who, smelling its sweetness, rises up out of a well and seizes it. So powerful is the description in this ancient text that, as we read the words, we can still feel the intense grief of Gilgamesh's loss: "Was it for this that I toiled with my hands, is it for this I have wrung out my heart's blood? For myself I have gained nothing; not I, but the beast of the earth has joy of it now."[2]

A later Babylonian Creation myth (ca.1700 BC) called the *Enuma Elish*, tells the story of a young god called Marduk, "clothed with the radiance of ten gods, with a majesty to inspire fear" who kills Tiamat, the great dragoness mother, by shooting an arrow into her open mouth which tears her belly and splits her heart. Marduk throws her carcass on the ground, stands on it and cuts it in half like a fish, creating the sky from one half of her dismembered body and the earth from the other. He then creates the planets and the constellations. Almost as an afterthought, he creates humanity from the blood of Tiamat's murdered son.

The myth was recited annually at the Spring Equinox, a time when the floods which covered the Babylonian plain in winter were receding, when the power of the sun warmed the earth and the spring sowing of the crops could begin. The recitation of the myth was believed to strengthen the forces of light against the forces of darkness in the great annual battle that took place between them, so regenerating life for the New Year. A myth grew up around this annual event — the myth of a solar hero who defeats the forces of darkness and evil that were personified by a dragon or monster of the underworld. This myth was transmitted to other, later cultures and is still very much alive in our own.

This new and violent Babylonian creation myth was in stark contrast to the older Bronze Age Sumerian and Egyptian creation myths and it reflects a loss of relationship with the natural world and a harsh severance of the lunar way of thinking. It was a dangerous myth to take literally for it offered the image of violence and murder as a pattern of divine behaviour, ratifying it as a model for human beings to emulate. Marduk becomes the macho ideal — the model for all solar heroes to come. With this myth the imagery of conflict and opposition between light and darkness, good and evil is constellated. At the same time, in the context of war, the practice of wholesale human slaughter becomes widespread, recorded and celebrated by the victor both in texts and in graphic sculptures on palace and temple walls.

The story of a hero's fight with a dragon, widely disseminated throughout the Middle East and the eastern Mediterranean, and deeply imprinted on the psyche of that age, laid the mythological ground for the future polarization of spirit and nature, mind and body — the one seen as divine and good, the other as 'fallen' and 'evil'. This divinely sanctioned opposition led also to the idea of the holy war, the war of the forces of good against the forces of evil, which is deeply interwoven with the sacred texts of the three patriarchal religions and their behaviour towards their enemies. Marduk's triumphant victory over Tiamat initiated a new way of living, a new way of relating to the divine by exalting an ideology of power and conquest. The battle of a hero-god and his conquest of the dragon/monster of darkness, chaos and evil became the dominant theme of all the hero myths of the solar era — from Marduk to the hero myth of our own time that is being played out before our eyes on the world stage.

The idea of opposition and conflict between light and darkness, good and evil, is constellated, and this solar mythology pervades the Old Testament and other mythologies of the Iron Age such as those of India (The *Mahabharata*) and Persia (the conflict between Ormuzd and Ahriman). In Greece, we find it in the myths of the sun-god Apollo slaying the She-dragon that guarded the sacred spring at Delphi, Theseus killing the Minotaur and Perseus the Gorgon. It is dramatically portrayed in the Book of Revelation as the great battle fought at the end of time between St. Michael and the Dragon. Already, it is possible to sense that the Earth, identified with both the defeated goddess and the dragon — who represents the untamed forces of nature — is no longer sacred. It is a shocking possibility that one immensely powerful myth and its derivatives could alter our relationship to Earth and Cosmos and cast a spell on humanity that has endured for nearly four thousand years.

A New Worldview

It is impossible to overstate the importance of this change of focus for the future relationship between man and nature. The coming of the solar era reflects the formulation of an entirely new perception of life and with it the rise of a new meta-narrative or worldview, whose theme is the cosmic battle between light and darkness, good and evil. With the diffusion of solar mythology, hastened by the advent of literacy and the discovery of the many applications of bronze technology — particularly those related to arms and war — the earlier lunar sense of the mythic participation in the continual regeneration of the life of the Earth and the greater life of the Cosmos gradually fades. The lunar idea of the balance between light and darkness was lost in the solar idea of opposition between them. For the next four thousand years, nature becomes something to be conquered, controlled and manipulated by human ingenuity, to human advantage. Once alive with spirit, it is now de-souled. Body is disconnected from mind and mind from soul. The Myth of the Fall in the Book of Genesis (Chapter Seven) describes the process of estrangement, separation and loss — a stark reversal of the participatory way of knowing that characterized older, pre-literate lunar cultures. As Jules and I observed in *The Myth of the Goddess*: "Nature is no longer experienced as source but as adversary, and darkness is no longer a mode of divine being, as it was in the lunar cycles, but a mode of being devoid of divinity and actively hostile, devouring of light, clarity and order."[3]

If we relate this change of worldview to what is happening within the psyche during this time, we can read the story of the human ego — the solar hero — striving to differentiate itself from the matrix of nature and attempting to master and control that from which it had emerged. The drama of the solar quest for light and enlightenment and victory over darkness is the drama of our own heroic quest for consciousness and our fear of falling back into the darkness of unconsciousness, the darkness of the 'state of nature'. From the ego's perspective, the darkness had to be repudiated and conquered for the light to prevail — a concept utterly different from the earlier belief where the darkness of the Otherworld was a mystery to be entered and explored. The emphasis during this age is on the masculine archetype because the ego needed to identify itself with this archetype in order to differentiate itself from the 'Mother' — the matrix of nature and instinct. But we may question whether it needed to do so in such a violent and oppositional way and whether this process became pathological because of the influence of the dominant mythology and the trauma inflicted by the continual wars and conflicts of this era.

Political and Social Change

There were two other major factors contributing to the change from lunar to solar mythology: one was political; the other the impact of literacy. Around 2200 BC there was a tremendous, devastating change which fell like a thunderbolt from a blue sky on the agricultural communities of the Fertile Crescent. The whole region was thrown into turmoil. Invaders bringing male gods — "a people whose onslaught was like a hurricane" — as one scribe depicts them, swept into the river valleys where the Great Mother had been worshipped for thousands of years. They brought with them the horse and the war chariot. Some came down from the north via the passage between the Black and Caspian Seas, others moved into the area from the Arabian Desert. Still others, known as the Sea-Peoples, invaded from the Mediterranean. War and conquest become the theme of a new and terrifying age. Everywhere there was fear and slaughter; everywhere a great cry of terror and distress as people were murdered, enslaved, their cities and homes burnt, their livelihoods destroyed. The cruelty and slaughter that accompanied the imposition of a new order was triumphantly recorded in the annals of the Babylonian and later, the Assyrian kings. What is being experienced in Syria now is comparable to what was experienced then. The theme of this new age was conquest, not yet conquest in the name of religion but conquest in the name of acquiring and enlarging territory, acquiring power. King Sargon of Akkad (2300 BC) was the first proudly to record his conquest of the vast area of land between the 'two seas'— the Mediterranean and the Persian Gulf. He set the model for the kings and emperors who were to succeed him as they built the great empires of the future: Babylonian, Assyrian, Persian, Greek and Roman.

It is now thought that around 2200 BC, climate change, resulting in widespread drought and famine over a vast area, led people to abandon their lands and move into areas where food was still plentiful. Whatever the ultimate causes of this turbulent time — and famine may have been one of them in the regions from which the invaders came — war and violence became endemic in the area of the eastern Mediterranean, including Turkey (then Anatolia), and the Middle East (modern Iraq). Through Egyptian, Babylonian and Assyrian history we follow the rise of the warlike leader who is idealized and glorified for his prowess in battle and the defeat of his enemies. Assyrian and Egyptian palace and temple walls show the Assyrian King or Pharaoh standing in their chariots engaged in battle, their decapitated or bound enemies ranged in rows at their feet. The ethnic cleansing of ten of the twelve tribes of Israel ca. 720 BC by the Assyrians is part of this sombre story. The siege and sack of Troy gives us graphic insight into the theme of war which increasingly dominates this era.

We can trace this pattern of conquest through the Persian, Greek and Roman Empires and, later, through all the struggles for power between tribal groups and nations that took place on European soil as well as in the vast region between Europe and China. We can imagine the suffering it induced as thousands were slaughtered, displaced, widowed, orphaned. Throughout this time, there is massive social dislocation and political change: the movement to cities and the rapid growth of populations; the rise of the city-state and then the nation-state; the advent of centralized bureaucracies and powerful priesthoods; the transformation of farmers into serfs; the enslavement of prisoners of war and the ethnic cleansing and mass removal of entire conquered populations.

Solar mythology led ultimately to the idea of the holy war — the victory of the forces of good over the forces of evil — and to the idea that human sacrifice was justifiable and acceptable to God when it served the purpose of eradicating evil in the form of a designated enemy. Hence, the medieval onslaught of Christianity against Islam and the later efforts of the Christian Church to extirpate the 'evil' of heresy; hence Islam's belief in conquest in the name of Allah and its slaughter of the 'infidel'. Victory was the coveted prize bestowed by God and God was invoked by both sides to support the battle of 'good' against 'evil'.

Wherever today we hear the words 'good' and 'evil' mentioned in the context of a struggle between opposing forces, we may expect to find the old solar myth and an individual assuming the mantle of the solar hero and leading his people against the demon of darkness. We may also expect to find the ritual demonizing of an enemy and all the propaganda that accompanies the modern constellation of a battle between opposing forces.

The theme of conquest which began in the third millennium BC with the conquests of King Sargon of Akkad has been constant for four millennia until we reach the twentieth century with Hiroshima and the horrific nuclear, biological and chemical weapons of modern warfare. Christianity and Islam assimilated this mythology of conquest with their call to Crusades and Holy Wars and its legacy lingers into our own times in the crusade against the 'axis of evil' and the Islamist *jihad*. It is even discovered in the manifesto put out by Breivik, the Norwegian mass murderer (2011), in which he declares himself to be a modern Crusader knight, engaged in the battle of good against evil in eliminating the Muslims from Europe.

It may be difficult to accept the idea that the theme of conquest, war and sacrifice which characterizes this Phase of Separation is pathological. From the perspective of modern psychology it could be said to exhibit pathological symptoms because the pattern of behaviour is dissociated from any awareness of guilt or regret for the suffering inflicted by it. The defeat and humiliation of an enemy is celebrated as proof of the victor or nation's superiority and power. The defeated are murdered, enslaved, or condemned to destitution. The pattern of behaviour is deeply unconscious. The coming of Christianity brought no change as Christians soon came to see themselves as 'soldiers of Christ'. Despite the teaching on the forbidding of killing enshrined in the Ten Commandments, and the teaching of Christ enjoining his followers to forgive their enemies, there is no apparent awareness in the heat of battle that the infliction of death and suffering on other human beings might be morally wrong and against the divine order. Only very slowly has the capacity for empathy developed. Whether we look at the *Iliad*, the Old Testament (Deuteronomy 7), the conquering ethos of early Islam or the crusading impulse of the Christian Middle Ages in Europe, the defeat of tribal enemies was deemed pleasing to the gods, and ultimately to God.

The Formation of the Warrior

From being primarily a hunter-gatherer in the Palaeolithic and Neolithic eras, man becomes a warrior in the Bronze Age and throughout the solar era. From earliest times, it is obvious that men were conditioned from childhood to develop their hunting and fighting skills and to join together with other men in order to supply the clan or tribe with food and defend them in the case of attack. This deep archaic bonding — a real devotion between men — is still strongly felt today in the current conflicts in which they are called to engage. The primary training of a warrior is to obey his tribal leader. Men living in the solar era had warrior myths to inspire them, warrior heroes as models to follow. In the constant state of preparation for war throughout this era, every male was brought up to see fighting as natural, noble, glorious and necessary, something in which he could prove his manhood. The regime instituted by Sparta took boys away from their families for military training at seven, not to return them until they were eighteen and ready for war. Military training turned boys into warriors who would help to build the great empires their warrior kings felt impelled to carve out. To shed blood was to be initiated into the brotherhood of warriors. To show fear or weakness was to be branded a woman: weak, cowardly, dispensable.

This was the ideology into which men were indoctrinated from a very early age throughout the solar era. It is not that men were innately aggressive and drawn to war; it is that the habit of war throughout this era conditioned them to conform or suffer shame, ridicule and rejection by their tribal or national group — even up to the First World War when deserters or 'cowards' were shot. Sam Keen observes in his book *Fire in the Belly: on being a Man*: "A culture that is at war or constantly preparing for a possible war conspires to create the perception, especially among its male citizens, that the threat from the enemy is always present."[4] And again, "The warrior finds the meaning of his life in playing a part in an overarching story of the cosmic struggle between good and evil...The warrior's eye and mind narrow to stereotypes that reduce the enemy to an entity that can be defeated or killed without remorse. In the heat of battle it is either kill or be killed."[5] Faced with an enemy, the warrior discovers the power, necessity and raw courage of the primal battle to survive in the same way that an animal experiences them when confronted with a dangerous predator.

For over 4000 years, under the powerful influence of solar mythology, victory and the spoils of war were seen as the coveted treasure to be won in battle. Courage in battle became the supreme virtue in the warrior and the image of the warrior was accepted as the supreme role model for men. Alexander the Great (356–323 BC), a warrior of warriors, was born into a warrior culture, compulsively pursuing the glory of conquest after his father, Philip of Macedon, was assassinated at his daughter's wedding feast. As people moved to cities and cities became states, and states entered into conflict with each other, more and more young men joined or were conscripted into armies led by warrior kings and may never have seen their homeland again.

The archetype of the solar hero as warrior still exerts immense unconscious influence on the modern male psyche, in the battlefield of politics as well as that of corporate business and even the world of science and academia: the primary aim of the male is to achieve, to win and, if necessary, to defeat other males. The ideal of the warrior has become an unconscious part of every man's identity from the time he is a small child.

With the mythic theme of the cosmic battle between good and evil and the indoctrination of the warrior went the focus on war and territorial conquest. War has been endemic throughout the 4000 years of the solar era. The glorification of war and conquest and the exaltation of the warrior is a major theme of the solar era — still with us today in George W. Bush's words in 2005: "We will accept no outcome except victory". This call to victory echoes down the centuries, ensuring that hecatombs of young warriors were sacrificed to the god of war, countless millions led into captivity and slavery, countless women raped and widows left destitute. It has sanctioned an ethos that strives for victory at no matter what cost in human lives and even today glorifies war and admires the warrior leader. This archaic model of tribal dominance and conquest has inflicted untold suffering on humanity and now threatens our very survival as a species.

The cosmic battle between light and darkness was increasingly projected into the world and a fascination with territorial conquest gripped the imagination and led to the creation of vast empires. It is as if the heroic human ego, identified with the solar hero, had to seek out new territories to conquer, had to embody the myth in a literal sense and as it did so, channel the primitive territorial drives of the psyche into a Dionysian orgy of unbridled conquest, slaughter and destruction. We hear very little about the suffering generated by these conquests: the weeping widows, the mothers who lost sons, the orphaned children and the crops and patterns of sowing and harvesting devastated and disrupted by the foraging armies passing over them, the exquisite works of art pillaged and looted. The utter destruction of the wonderful city of Persepolis by Alexander the Great was one legacy of this solar dynamic.

Slavery

With the creation of empires went the establishment of slavery as a method of subduing conquered people, following the model offered by Babylonia and Assyria, Egypt and the Hittites. We know the fate of thousands of women and children from the description in the *Iliad* of Andromache seeing her young son thrown from the walls of the palace of king Priam and bewailing the destiny that was to befall her and the women of Troy. Men were forced to become serfs, women concubines or sex-slaves. Children were separated from their parents and sold as slaves. Their suffering, which would have included rape of both boys and girls, can only be imagined. The story in the forging of any of the great empires of the Iron Age was the same: power, land and riches for the conqueror; death, slavery and destitution for the conquered.

The Impact of Literacy

A second major influence in the solar era was the impact of literacy. The written word replaced the oral tradition that had carried the wisdom and insights of the older lunar culture. Some of that ancient wisdom may have been recorded in the thousands of scrolls held in the Great Library of Alexandria. But in 391 AD the Emperor Theodosius decreed that all pagan temples, including that at Eleusis, should be destroyed. He also instructed Bishop Theophilus to raze to the ground the Great Library, the most magnificent building in the Ancient World. A Christian mob set it alight and the devastating fire which ensued destroyed the priceless store of scrolls from the pre-Christian world. The legacy of the shamanic cultures, particularly that derived from the formidable civilization of Egypt, went underground. It survived however, in the Hermetic tradition, in Kabbalah and in Alchemy.

David Abram has shown in his book, *The Spell of the Sensuous,* how the new emphasis on the written word contributed to the loss of the older participatory consciousness: "Only as the written text began to speak would the voices of the forest, and of the river, begin to fade. And only then would language loosen its ancient association with the invisible breath, the spirit sever itself from the wind, the psyche dissociate itself from the environing air."[6]

Another book, *The Alphabet and the Goddess*, written by the late Dr. Leonard Shlain, who was chief of laparoscopic surgery at California Medical Center in San Francisco, develops the interesting idea that literacy gave prominence to the left hemispheric brain to the detriment of the balance between the hemispheres that had prevailed in a pre-literate cultures. He explains that, when speaking, we use both hemispheres of the brain but when "written words begin to supersede spoken words, the left brain's dominance markedly increased".[7] It may be that with literacy the importance of the seer or wise old man or woman diminished. There is an interesting footnote to this change: Socrates apparently struggled to get used to the new skill of writing. He didn't understand it and saw it as a dangerous invention because it didn't allow ideas to flow back and forth as they did in conversation. He preferred the old oral method of communicating. He also worried that it would make people appear cleverer than in fact they were, giving the impression that they knew something when they didn't — perhaps the original definition of 'spin'.

During this era, the left hemisphere of the brain begins to assume a position of dominance in relation to the right. The more literacy spreads, the more this tendency strengthens. As Shlain observes:

> Writing represented a shift of tectonic proportions that fissured the integrated nature of... brain cooperation. Writing made the left brain, flanked by the incisive cones of the eye and the aggressive right hand, dominant over the right. The triumphant march of literacy that began five thousand years ago conquered right-brain values and with them the Goddess. Patriarchy and misogyny have been the inevitable result.... The hand that held the pen also held the sword.[8]

Perhaps because literacy distanced us from nature and from empathic relationship with the Earth, the story of creation is now believed to be in the Sacred Book — the supreme repository of the 'Word' of God. The more tolerant attitude of the Greeks and even the Romans, which allowed many different cults to flourish, is replaced by a rigid adherence to the written word — the supreme repository of revelation. With the idea of a wholly transcendent God, separate and distinct from nature, the unity of life is broken. The land is no longer sacred and is divided up into empires and nations ruled by powerful kings. Absolute obedience to the written word replaces direct shamanic experience of the numinous. Ancient rituals of connection and divination are forbidden. Pagan cult images are banished under pain of death. With this shift in archetypal imagery, everything formerly associated with the Great Mother is downgraded in relation to the absolute authority of the Great Father. The lunar way of knowing is subjugated to the solar way and, under the influence of solar mythology, first Nature and, ultimately, the Cosmos are de-souled.

Great Mother to Great Father

As the human psyche draws further and further away from the matrix of nature in the solar era, the predominant image of spirit changes from Great Mother to Great Father. The greater the withdrawal from nature, the more transcendent and disengaged from nature becomes the image of deity. In *The Myth of the Goddess*, we summed up this primary change of consciousness: "If the relation to nature as the Mother is one of identity, and the relation to nature from the Father is one of dissociation, then the movement from Mother to Father symbolises an ever-increasing separation from a state of containment in nature, experienced no longer as nurturing to life but as stifling to growth."[9]   The story of the ferocious struggle between the supporters of the two mythologies is told in the Old Testament which repeatedly documents the destruction of the shrines and groves of the Goddess. "But ye shall destroy their altars, break their images and cut down their groves: For thou shalt worship no other god: for the Lord, whose name is Jealous, is a jealous god" (Exod. 34:13). This was the earliest known example of Iconoclasm or the destruction of images. All images of and references to the hated Canaanite Mother Goddess Asherah were eradicated so that there would be no challenge to the supremacy of Yahweh. Her statue and that of the great bronze serpent that accompanied her cult were repeatedly thrown out of the temple in Jerusalem.

Divine immanence, once associated with the image of the Great Mother and the Great Goddesses of the Bronze Age, was gradually and irrevocably lost. Collective belief replaces shamanic *experience* of the invisible dimension of the Otherworld and the profound sense of relationship with sacred features of the natural world which gave access to that mysterious dimension. The changeover from lunar to solar mythology and culture takes thousands of years, moving through a phase where goddesses and gods preside over a world that was still filled with the spirits inhabiting every grove and spring, river and mountain. With the arrival of Judaism, Christianity and Islam with their transcendent monotheistic god-image, all these were eventually banished and pagan rituals outlawed. Judaic monotheism eradicated polytheism and with it the connection to the spirits of the land and the great cycles of nature. The land of Palestine became the gift of Yahweh to the Jewish people, originating with His promise to Abraham and sowing the seeds of conflict and oppression that would rage in our time, three thousand years later.

The image of spirit which governed the patriarchal cultures was overwhelmingly male — perhaps, as Freud suggested, the unconscious projection of the patriarchal father. Whatever the political and social reasons for the emergence of this powerful male image of deity, creation was now believed to arise from the word of the Father, no longer from the womb of the Mother. The creator was beyond creation, no longer immanent within it. This is crucially important because it reflects the fact that the oneness of life is broken: Nature is dissociated from Spirit. With this shift of archetypal imagery, everything formerly associated with the Great Mother and the feminine is downgraded in relation to the masculine.

The Subjugation of Women

The polarizing emphasis of solar mythology created a widening fissure between man and woman that led to her oppression and persecution. Gradually, over the next three millennia, the priesthoods which held the reins of theological power came to identify the 'male' aspect of life with spirit, light, order and the rational mind — which were named as good — and to identify the 'female' aspect of life with nature, darkness, chaos and body, which were frequently identified with evil. This fundamental polarization was absorbed into religious teaching and integrated with tribal customs and beliefs that gave man the dominant position over woman. Woman and her body began to be seen as a danger, a threat; a sexual temptation for man. Nature, woman and the body became closely identified with each other; for this reason all had to be subject to the will of man. Woman, identified with nature, was named as a secondary or inferior creation in the Book of Genesis and in the writings of the Greek philosophers — a belief whose effects will be explored in Chapters Seven and Eight.

The patriarchal religions of the solar era carry this polarized way of thinking within their teaching, wherever this is associated with the ascetic subjugation of the body, the mistrust of sexuality and the fear of woman. The unconscious identification of woman with nature was the origin of the negative projections onto her that were incorporated into the social attitudes and customs — fused with religious beliefs — that endure to this day. Where does the Taliban's attitude to woman originate if not in this directive from the earliest Mesopotamian codification of law ca. 2350 BC: "If a woman shall speak out against her man, her mouth shall be crushed with a hot brick."[10]

Further to the East, in China, the old Taoist vision of an ensouled nature also began to withdraw, replaced by the emphasis on the minutae of social custom which relegated women to an inferior and almost slave-like position. The sages of India, with certain exceptions, turned away from the body and sensory experience and held the phenomenal world to be an illusion, placing the emphasis of their teaching on the experience of enlightenment and release from the Wheel of Rebirth. Here again, woman was an impediment to and a distraction from the spiritual life. The famous story of the Buddha leaving his wife and young son and even his beloved horse reflects the influence of this new solar ideology where the emphasis was placed on spirit in opposition to the world, woman and the body.

The Long-term Effects of Solar Mythology

In Western civilization, solar mythology drove the Promethean quest for freedom, justice and knowledge as well as the desire to explore and conquer new territories. As a cultural impulse, it carried with it the human longing, the human quest to go beyond all constraints and limitations. The word 'discovery' characterizes this whole era. In the sphere of religion, a major theme of solar mythology was, as with Plato, escape from the bondage of the body and, by association, release from the bondage of mortality; in the East, it was release from the Wheel of Rebirth. It is a linear and essentially utopian and transcendent mythology rather than one that relates us to the Earth. Its primary theme was and still is empowerment, ascent, progress, achievement, conquest, carried through to our own day in Bronowski's famous television documentary series in the mid-sixties — *The Ascent of Man* — which aimed to show the whole spectrum of discoveries and inventions that revealed "man's ability to control nature, not to be controlled by it".

Solar mythology has empowered the gifted or heroic individual to differentiate himself from the tribal group, bestowing immense benefits on humanity and leading to extraordinary culture-transforming discoveries. It has, through the struggle for justice and freedom, led ultimately to the establishment of democracy in many countries. But it has also encouraged the belief that humanity itself is the solar hero, standing above all other species and having the right to exploit the resources of the Earth for its own exclusive benefit, leaving other species defenceless against the onslaught of its perceived rights and needs.

This belief was enshrined in the Book of Genesis, where, in Genesis 1:28, Adam and Eve are granted dominion over the Earth. "And God blessed them and said to them, 'Be fruitful and multiply, and fill the earth and subdue it; and have dominion over the fish of the sea and over the birds of the air and over every living thing that moves upon the earth.'" In another fateful passage, Noah and his sons are told to "be fruitful and multiply and fill the earth. The fear of you and the dread of you shall be upon every beast of the earth, and upon every bird of the air, upon everything that creeps upon the ground and all the fish of the sea; into your hand they are delivered" (Genesis 9:1-2). Today we face the legacy of these two hugely influential passages.

Solar mythology drives all utopian ideologies and the dream of scientific and technological progress. It is overwhelmingly male because the male psyche has been the dominant influence in the world during the solar era, and it is the achievements, discoveries and courageous actions of exceptional men which have inspired and offered a role model to other men. A strong sense of individuality and a focused ego — which ultimately came to be identified with the conscious, rational mind — can be acknowledged as the supreme achievement of the male psyche during the solar era. But the voice of women, who in the rising patriarchal societies were denied access to education, the priesthood and the healing profession, was silenced.

The Ongoing Quest for Power and Omnipotence

In Judaism, Christianity and Islam, the influence of solar mythology fuelled a zeal to conquer and subdue territory for Yahweh, Christ or Allah, with catastrophic consequences for the peoples who were conquered by the sword. Ultimately it fuelled the desire of the West to create new empires and led to the creation of the British Empire which, in 1900, ruled one quarter of the world, both in territory and population. It also fuelled the ideologies which caused unspeakable suffering and millions of deaths in the twentieth century. The celebration of conquest and supremacy begins in the third millennium BC in Mesopotamia and Egypt with the conquests of Sargon of Akkad and the Egyptian pharaohs and continues with Hiroshima, Vietnam, Iraq, and the horrific nuclear, chemical and biological weapons of modern warfare. War breeds fear and fear breeds war, activating and strengthening the predator/prey pattern in the older brain system (Chapters Twelve and Thirteen). If continued for long enough, it becomes a habit that is almost impossible to resist. The long chronicle of conquest and human sacrifice, of exultation in power and the subjugation of enemies might truly be named the dark shadow of the solar age.

In the impersonal accounts of these catastrophes, whose effects we have to imagine, since they were not reported — so many dead, so many wounded, homeless, widowed or orphaned — there is never recorded the unquantifiable laceration of the human heart. As in the past, so still today: the lifeless bodies of men, women and children, transfixed in the agony of their death, lie abandoned on the streets of ravaged cities and villages and the desecrated soil of Earth. Each was once the child of parents who carefully tended that life from infancy; who cherished hopes and dreams for their child who was precious to them. How casually these lives were and are destroyed wherever young men are summoned by their leaders to serve their nation or their religion by killing each other. The life of the world passes on; new generations are born; only a few remember; only a few have the will and determination to change this pattern of ritual sacrifice; only a few feel remorse for the lives they extinguished by obeying orders while acting in defence of their country, their tribal group or their religion. The rest bury their guilt.

What happens to the souls of the dead cut off in the prime of life? I feel the weight of their silent anguish through the centuries: the weight of the souls of men, women and children severed from the world by human cruelty, human depravity. In this world, the tears of the dead and the grief of those who mourn them are soon lost in the thundering surf of life. Until I became a mother myself, I did not think of the generations of anonymous mothers who tended life in their children, cherishing it in its beauty, brevity and fragility, hoping that they would survive, flourish and live to have children of their own. Now, through my own experience as mother and grandmother, I have become capable of imagining the silent fear and anguish of women; the tracking and killing of human prey by human predators; the terror of people hunted down, killed and forgotten through countless generations. There is no monument to the holocausts of victims sacrificed in past ages. There is no record of the women, raped by marauding armies, who cherished and nurtured their children month by month, day by day, year by year, only to see their lives crushed by the pitiless boot of war.

Wherever today we still find the tendency to omnipotence and grandiose ambitions of empire and world domination we can discern the influence of solar mythology and the inflation or hubris of leaders who unconsciously identify themselves with the mythic role of the solar god or hero engaging in the battle to defeat the dragon of darkness and evil.

Solar Mythology and the Split between Mind and Soul

With the psychological insight which has become available to us over the last hundred years, particularly through the depth psychology of Jung, we can understand that this solar phase of our evolution reflects a radical dissociation within our psyche between the growing strength of the ego (the hero) and the older and greatly feared power of instinct (the dragon) that was identified with nature and the irrational 'animal passions' of man. As this dual dissociation gathered momentum, so the feeling of containment within a greater cosmic entity and the sense of relationship with nature and with an unseen dimension of reality faded and with it the participatory consciousness of the lunar era. During the solar era, consciousness strives to ascend upwards towards the light, fearing and repudiating the darkness because of the fear of regressing into the unconscious 'state of nature'. Power becomes exalted as the sole means of ensuring survival. The legacy of the Platonic emphasis on reason and the rational mind, together with the impact of literacy and the solar emphasis on the ascent to spirit, accompanied by a deep suspicion of woman and sexuality, hastens the demise of the lunar way of knowing and the former instinctive sense of living within a Sacred Order.

The supreme achievement of the solar era was the emergence of a strong autonomous sense of individuality (conscious ego) from the matrix of instinct and the development of the reflective, rational mind in all who had access to education. But this had a high price: first, the inflation or hubris of the ego as it drew away from its instinctive ground and began to assimilate a god-like power to itself. Secondly, the subjugation and repression of the instinctual, the non-rational and the feminine which, identified with each other, were perceived as threatening to the hegemony of the masculine ego. Keith Sagar, in his brilliant book, *Literature and the Crime Against Nature*, chronicles the devastating critique of Western civilization offered by its greatest poets and writers, beginning with Homer and the Greek tragedians and ending with Ted Hughes, and comments,

> The history of Western civilization has been the history of man's increasingly devastating crimes against Nature, Nature defined not only as the earth and its life forms, powers and processes, but also as the female in all its manifestations, and as the 'natural man' within the individual psyche. It is the story of man's mutilation of Nature in his attempt to make it conform to the Procrustean bed of his own patriarchal, anthropocentric and rectilinear thinking.[11]

The Danger of Utopian Ideologies: Negative Projections

Solar myth continues to cast its spell today. It is carried in all utopian ideologies which strive to impose the light of a new world order and split off the darkness or anything that opposes it. Its characteristic is grandiosity. It entered not only into the sacred texts of Judaism, Christianity and Islam but, most significantly, into our behaviour towards the 'dark' and so-called primitive (more instinctual) Indigenous Peoples who fell victim to the race for empire of the European nations. The catalogue of horror inflicted during the course of the conquest and attempt to convert these 'primitive' peoples, whether in South and Central America, in Africa, India or further East, has been minutely documented and still continues in places like the Amazonian and Indonesian rainforests where the commercial interests of giant Western corporations are destroying these forests, ignoring and overriding the protests of the forest peoples.

A recent example of this attitude is the deportation in 1971 of the 1800 people of the Chagos Islands in an arrangement between the United Kingdom and the United States to lease the island of Diego Garcia to the latter for use as a military base for the launching of long-distance missiles. By this disgraceful contract, the entire island chain was described as "fully sanitised" and "cleansed" of life, including the dogs, who were gassed. These people have still not been allowed to return to their home which has, in 2011, been declared a marine sanctuary.

As time went on, religions, particularly Christianity and Islam, took on the mantle of solar mythology in a militant struggle for supremacy. The deadly animosity between Catholic and Protestant in European history, between Shi'a and Sunni in the Islamic world and between Israelis and Palestinians may be traced to the polarizing influence of this mythology and, more importantly, to the split in the psyche that underlies it. As long as we are not conscious of the fissure within our own nature, and our catastrophic disconnection from our instinctual soul, we will be driven to seek out and attack an object on which to project our darkness. This unconscious mechanism of projection still operates in the religio-political sphere as is illustrated by the ongoing tension between the Christian cultures of the West and the Islamic cultures of the Middle East.

We can find the tendency of solar mythology to encourage negative projections onto others reflected in the secular totalitarian ideologies which ravaged the last century when they separated the heroic race or 'chosen' people from those whom they demonized as inferior or expendable. We can see its polarizing influence at work in the Holocaust where Hitler and his ideology of National Socialism exterminated millions of Jews and others who were perceived as racially, genetically or mentally inferior. The same polarizing influence can be found in the Communist regime of the former Soviet Union, in Maoist China where 45 million people perished,[12] in Cambodia under Pol Pot, in Bosnia under Milosevic and in Syria under the Assad Regime. These regimes justified the elimination of racial, class, tribal or ethnic enemies, just as Christianity and Islam had justified the elimination of heretics and apostates. All were and are able to recruit people who believed they were doing 'good' by obeying orders and slaughtering their fellow men and women. The International Criminal Court in The Hague is challenging this belief by trying those who 'obeyed orders' for crimes against humanity.

The Survival of the Sense of an Ensouled Cosmos

Although the focus of later Christian culture was directed away from the earth and towards heaven, away from matter and towards spirit, the sense of living within an ensouled cosmos survived until the end of the Middle Ages in Europe. The poets and artists, as well as the mystics and visionaries of the Christian West, kept alive the shamanic experience of far earlier times. St. Francis (1181–1226), on the night before he wrote his famous Canticle of the Sun, had a vision of the Earth as a glowing golden orb. In this canticle, as in the contemporary philosophy of the Middle Ages, there is the recognition that the foremost luminaries — the moon and the sun — and the great hierarchy of the angelic and archangelic orders, as well as the animals and the birds, all belong to a Sacred or Divine Cosmic Order.

This was the time which saw the great pilgrimages in Europe to the sacred sites of the Black Madonna (often places where the goddess Isis had been worshipped in Roman times) and the building of the soaring glory of the Gothic cathedrals, dedicated to the Virgin Mary and designed to embody the Pythagorian concept of the perfect mathematical harmony of a divinely ordered Cosmos that was reflected in this world. It also saw the dissemination of the Grail legends over a wide area of Europe. The sacred place of connection between the human and the divine was the cathedral or shrine.

After the terrible decades of the Black Death in the fourteenth century, the idea of an ensouled world found new expression in fifteenth century Florence when Cosimo de' Medici founded his Platonic Academy and commissioned Marsilio Ficino to translate Plato, Plotinus and the texts of the Egyptian Hermetic tradition. Through this channel, the Platonic concept of a World Soul and his triad of Truth-Beauty-Goodness were reborn in Italy, giving rise to the glory of the Renaissance. Venus, the Goddess of Love and Beauty, was restored in Botticelli's *Primavera* and his *Birth of Venus*. The body began to be rehabilitated as the sculptors and painters of that time reconnected with a pre-Christian Pagan past. Pico della Mirandola gave his brilliant *Oration on the Dignity of Man* in 1486. The philosopher and cultural historian Richard Tarnas vividly describes Pico's vision and this new era in his *Passion of the Western Mind*:

> With the influx of this tradition came a new vision of man, nature and the divine. Neoplatonism, based on Plotinus's conception of the world as an emanation from the transcendent One, portrayed nature as permeated by divinity, a noble expression of the World Soul. Stars and planets, light, plants, even stones possessed a numinous dimension… The ancient Pythagorian vision of a universe ordered according to transcendent mathematical forms received

an intense renewal of interest, and promised to reveal nature as permeated by a mystical intelligence whose language was number and geometry. The garden of the world was again enchanted, with magical powers and transcendent meanings implicit in every part of nature.[13]

But this wonderful new impulse, which came close to restoring the old lunar consciousness at a new level, faded with the onset of the grim realities of the Protestant Reformation. We can follow the polarizing influence of solar mythology through subsequent centuries when the new religion of Protestantism sought to eradicate as much as it could of the evidence of the Catholic religion and turned against its sacred images with savage fury, leaving thousands of churches unadorned. In England, more than 95% of the artistic heritage of the Middle Ages was destroyed in the sixteenth and seventeenth centuries — beginning with the destruction of the monasteries under Henry VIII — when wall paintings were obliterated by whitewash, and literally thousands of superb sculptures, and wooden images of Christ, the Virgin and the saints were defaced, burnt and smashed to pieces by men who took pride in their acts of vandalism that would wipe out all vestiges of 'superstition'. England never recovered from this rape of her soul and the loss of her supremely gifted artists. It was at this time that the English people were prohibited from worshipping the Virgin as they had done for centuries. Churches were instructed to "sing no more praises to Our Lady, only to Our Lord".

The vision of a sacred Earth and Cosmos slowly faded, accelerated by the growing fascination with science, the coming of the Industrial Revolution and the new emphasis on the power of man to control nature and shape his destiny. What was increasingly lost was the visionary imagination so respected by Coleridge, and the sense of an ensouled nature that was re-animated by the Romantic Poets in the late eighteenth century and reflected in the poetry of Wordsworth and the words of the poet and artist William Blake, "Everything that lives is Holy".

The Return of the Soul

Yet now, mysteriously and fortuitously, beneath the surface of our culture, the ancient concept of the soul and the unity of life is returning. The challenge of the immense problems facing us is urging us to reflect on our current understanding of reality and modify the oppositional paradigm we have inherited from the powerful influence of solar mythology. A deep human instinct is attempting to restore balance and wholeness in us by re-discovering values rooted in an older way of knowing. One example of this is the environmental movement which is restoring respect for the Earth. In his introduction to Frederick Turner's Book, *Beyond Geography: The Western Spirit Against the Wilderness*, T.H. Watkins observes that "If the environmental movement succeeds in redeeming at least some of the damage our history has done, future generations may view it as the most important social movement of all time."[14]

If we are to understand the present we need to know about the past — the foundation from which our present beliefs and attitudes have developed. Through the discoveries made in the last hundred or so years, we know that we are living now at the end of a long trajectory of several million years which has brought about the gradual separation or differentiation of our human species from the animal kingdom together with the development of self-awareness and the sense of self that we call individuality; a highly developed intellect; a fertile imagination and the power to apply both intellect and imagination to formulate goals and to achieve them — everything that we now call human consciousness.

Despite its phenomenal cultural and technological achievements, the whole edifice of the solar age rests on the foundation of our separation from nature and, within the psyche, the split between our conscious rational mind and our instinctual soul which led us to lose the sense of participation in a sacred and living Cosmos. Whether this split was a necessary part of the evolution of consciousness is open to debate. But it has happened and only now are we brought face to face with its legacy, with perhaps sufficient consciousness to heal it.

Richard Tarnas has described the story of the evolution of consciousness as both an heroic ascent to autonomy and a tragic fall from unity. He views the history of the last two and a half thousand years as a series of births which have forged Western consciousness and Western civilization. But now, he believes, we are entering a new phase in our evolution, one that will reconnect or reunite those elements of our nature which have been fragmented and lost and those elements of life we have seen as separate from ourselves. In the Epilogue to *The Passion of the Western Mind* he writes:

> We stand at the threshold of a revelation of the nature of reality that could shatter our most established beliefs about ourselves and the world. The very constriction we are experiencing is part of the dynamic of our imminent release. For the deepest passion of the Western mind has been to reunite with the ground of its being. The driving impulse of the West's masculine consciousness has been its quest not only to realize itself, to forge its own autonomy, but also, finally, to recover its connection with the whole, to come to terms with the great feminine principle in life: to differentiate itself from but then rediscover and reunite with the feminine, with the mystery of life, of nature, of soul. And that

reunion can now occur on a new and profoundly different level from that of the primordial unconscious unity, for the long evolution of human consciousness has prepared it to be capable at last of embracing the ground and matrix of its own being freely and consciously.[15]

As this deep soul-impulse gathers momentum, the 'marriage' of the re-emerging lunar consciousness with the dominant solar one is beginning to change our perception of reality. This gives us hope for the future. If we can recover the values intrinsic to the ancient participatory way of knowing without losing the priceless evolutionary attainment of a strong and focused ego, together with all the discoveries we have made and the skills we have developed, we could heal both the fissure in our soul and our raped and vandalized planet.

Notes:

1. Lawrence, D.H. (1931) *Apocalypse and Other Writings*, Cambridge University Press, p. 78
2. Saunders, N.K. (1960) *The Epic of Gilgamesh*, Penguin Books Ltd. London, p. 117
3. *The Myth of the Goddess*, p. 298
4. Keen, Sam (1992) *Fire in the Belly: On Being a Man*, Bantam, p.41
5. ibid, p. 43
6. Abram, David (1996) *The Spell of the Sensuous*, Vintage Books, New York, p. 254
7. Shlain, Leonard, (1998) *The Alphabet Versus the Goddess*, Viking, New York, p. 40
8. ibid, p. 44
9. *The Myth of the Goddess* p. 661
10. quoted in Shlain, p. 45
11. Sagar, Keith (2005) *Literature and the Crime Against Nature: from Homer to Hughes*, Chaucer Press, London, p. 369
12. Diköter, Frank (2011) *Mao's Great Famine*, Bloomsbury Books Ltd., London
13. Tarnas, Richard (1991) *The Passion of the Western Mind*, Ballantine Books, New York pp. 213-214
14. Turner, Frederick (1983 & 1982) *Beyond Geography: The Western Spirit Against the Wilderness*, Rutgers University Press, p. xxiv
15. Tarnas, *Epilogue*

St. Michael and the Dragon
Tympanum of the church of Saint-Michel-d'Entraygues, Angoulême AD1140

Chapter Seven

THE MYTH OF THE FALL
AND THE DOCTRINE OF ORIGINAL SIN

*The Christian separation of matter and spirit, of the dynamism of life and the realm
of the spirit, of natural grace and supernatural grace, has really castrated nature...
The true spirituality, which would have come from the union of matter and spirit,
has been killed.*

— Joseph Campbell, *The Power of Myth*[1]

In the light of the solar myth explored in the last chapter, I could now understand that the Myth of the Fall of Man is the most dramatic and influential
myth or meta-narrative of the solar Phase of Separation. In the Book of
Genesis we find the story of our expulsion from a divine world and our Fall into
this world, a Fall that was brought about by a woman, Eve, who disobeyed the
command of God and brought death, sin and suffering into being. From this myth
there developed the belief that the whole human race was tainted by original sin,
yet this was never more than a belief — a myth — although it was presented and
accepted as divinely revealed truth.

If we look at it from the perspective of the evolution of consciousness, the
whole myth, telling the story of Eve's temptation by the serpent, the disobedience
of Adam and Eve and their expulsion from the Garden of Eden, can be read as a
metaphor that describes the painful stage of our separation from the matrix of
nature — the 'Garden of Eden' out of which we have evolved. Expulsion from
the Garden is an accurate metaphor for the birth of the capacity for reflection and
self-awareness, so relinquishing the more unconscious state of living purely instinctively. Inevitably, just as with our separation at birth from our mother, a sense
of duality came into being as we lost the sense of participation in a primordial
Sacred Order. Unfortunately, even tragically, the myth was taken as literally true
as well as divinely revealed and the Christian psyche was imprinted with the belief
that human nature was fallen, cut off from God as a result of the 'sin' of Adam

and Eve eating the fruit of the Tree of Knowledge, and condemned to exile on earth. For nearly two thousand years Christians have been taught and have believed that their only chance of redemption was the doctrines and rituals of the Church and the saving grace of the sacrificial death of the Son of God. There was no salvation for those who were not Christians.

A second meta-narrative, developing out of the Myth of the Fall of Man, was the Christian Doctrine of Original Sin, promulgated by St. Augustine in the late fourth century. A disastrous obsession with sin and guilt, a distrust of sexuality and the body and the fear of God's punishment took root in the soul. There was a radical shift of focus as spirit was projected upon a distant deity in the sky and no longer experienced as the invisible ground of the phenomenal world. Was it the emphasis given to these two beliefs that caused the Christian Church to change, in the course of the first four centuries, from being a medium of transmission for the teaching of Christ, to being an imperial power with absolute control over millions of its subjects?

"What is the origin of evil, of death, of suffering?" This question perplexed the authors of the Book of Genesis. It perplexed the formulators of Christian doctrine centuries later and perplexes us still today. This chapter and the next will explore the influence of the two meta-narratives mentioned above which attempted to answer this question. They are a critical exploration of what may be called the 'shadow' aspect of Christianity for, in giving them such emphasis, the Christian Church may have presented a negative, not to say a distorted view of life to its believers.

The Myth of the Fall originates with the Book of Genesis but its influence continued to be diffused throughout Jewish, Christian and even Islamic culture. For a very long time, it has been the primary myth which has guided religious teaching in the West. To focus on only one religion, there are over 2 billion Christians in the world today — nearly a third of the world's population — who will have absorbed from it the idea that a woman, Eve, was responsible for bringing death, sin and suffering into the world and that all humanity carries the bitter legacy of the Fall. I believe that these two immensely powerful beliefs, so entwined with each other, have deeply wounded the Christian soul: they have wounded woman as well as man's image of woman and man's image of the feminine aspect of his own nature. Indeed, I wonder whether it is possible to exaggerate the wounding effect they have had on the Western psyche and Western civilization as a whole. I cannot listen to the harsh, condemnatory words attributed to God in the Book of Genesis (Gen. 3: 8-19) without a sense of revulsion as well as deep compassion for the souls — particularly the souls of children — who have been or will be burdened by its oppressive message.

In the Book of Genesis, God says to Eve, "I will greatly multiply thy sorrow and thy conception, in sorrow thou shalt bring forth children and thy desire shall be to thy husband and he shall rule over thee." And God says to Adam, "Because thou hast hearkened unto the voice of thy wife, and hast eaten of the tree, cursed is the ground for thy sake; in sorrow shalt thou eat of it all the days of thy life" (Gen: 3:16–17). For nearly two thousand years, countless millions have assimilated the message of this cruel, rejecting and judgemental image of God and the heavy burden of original sin. These verses are often read out at Christmas, at the beginning of the story of the birth of Jesus, as if to explain why the human race needed to be redeemed by the birth of a Saviour and His sacrificial death.

The Literal Interpretation of the Myth

The literal interpretation of the myth and the belief that it was divinely revealed bequeathed to generations of Christians a legacy of sexual guilt, misogyny and fear of God's anger. The more I read the documents of the Catholic and Protestant churches which reflected this literal interpretation, the more I could see the immense harm that was done to the relationship between men and women in Western civilization. Further, it was a major cause of a profoundly negative view of life and with it, a rejection of the world and a widening of the solar split between spirit and nature, mind and body. I could see that its influence has ultimately contributed to our growing alienation from nature and our ruthless exploitation of the Earth's resources. Since, in this myth, Earth was designated a place of exile, punishment and suffering, why should we respect it? Since we had been banished to this place of suffering, sorrow, toil and death it was inevitable that we should feel justified in exploiting it for our own benefit and that, in our relationships with other people, other religions, we should seek to offload our own sense of guilt by punishing, attacking or blaming others, projecting onto them the intolerable hair shirt of guilt.

I think that it is not too much to say that the greatest sickness in Christian culture has been the fear of sexuality, the denigration and denial of the sensuous and the ecstatic, and the oppression and enforced subservience of woman. It could be said that the first mistake in Christian teaching was to dissociate the body and matter from spirit and from soul. The second was the belief that in order to gain the approval of God and ward off his anger and further punishment, we had to deny the sexual instinct, reject the body and even inflict pain and suffering on it. In the name of the spiritual life, the body was made to endure every kind of mortification, including such sado-masochistic practices as starvation, flagellation and the wearing of hair shirts and other instruments of pain. I can understand why this whole train of ideas arose but I wonder whether, in splitting nature from spirit, emptying nature of soul and contaminating the instincts with guilt and fear, Christian teaching — like Marduk in the Babylonian myth — hasn't split the wholeness of life and our wholeness in two.

Taking this further, it seems to have ascribed all goodness to God and all evil to man, placing an intolerable burden of guilt on our shoulders. Following the paradigm of solar mythology, which conceived of a great cosmic battle between good and evil, the next step was to ascribe all good to the institution of the Church and all evil to the pagan gods or any group which offered a challenge to the Church's power, formulating the concept of the 'saved' and the 'damned' and reserving hell and damnation for heretics and 'unbelievers'. As St. Augustine said, laying the foundation for the Inquisition, "Error has no rights."

How, I wondered, was it possible for the soul and the values of the heart to survive and flourish in the face of a belief system which did such violence to them? The actual teaching of Christ was neglected through the centuries of hair-splitting doctrinal disputes. Did Christianity take a wrong turning when it built the whole edifice of its doctrine of salvation through the sacrificial death of the Son of God on the foundation of the Myth of the Fall and the Doctrine of Original Sin? Was this what Christ would have wanted or would he have been appalled by what was taught and done in His name? Joseph Campbell comments:

> Our story of the Fall in the Garden sees nature as corrupt; and that myth corrupts the whole world for us. Because nature is thought of as corrupt, every spontaneous act is sinful and must not be yielded to. You get a totally different civilization and a totally different way of living according to whether your myth presents nature as fallen or whether nature is in itself a manifestation of divinity, and the spirit is the revelation of the divinity that is inherent in nature.[2]

Because these myths or meta-narratives stand at the beginning of our cultural inheritance, it is very difficult to become aware of the assumptions derived from them, let alone disempower them. Their relevance to us today is that the deeper layers of the soul which, for tens of thousands of years had known a life of participation in the life of the Earth and the Cosmos through an instinctual awareness of the unity and sacredness of life, were now abruptly deprived of that experience. The older lunar mythology where all life was imagined as the creation of the Great Mother, born from her cosmic womb in a great web of relationships and connections, was suppressed. The various mystery religions which had flourished under the Greek and Roman Empires were suddenly declared anathema. By the end of the fourth century, by order of the Emperor Theodosius, pagan temples like the magnificent temple of Artemis at Ephesus, and the temple of Demeter at Eleusis had been destroyed and pagan rites prohibited. In 529 AD the Emperor Justinian closed down the Neoplatonic Academy in Athens that had replaced the original one founded by Plato. The leading teachers of this Academy were invited by the king of Persia to teach in a university there, taking with them priceless scrolls of the Greek philosophers. Although elements of the older rituals were preserved and integrated into the new rituals, the Christian Church became the major instrument which delivered the coup de grâce to the old order. Even now, incredibly, there are echoes of this old prejudice in the belief held by certain Christian priests that yoga should not be practised by Christians because it is 'pagan'.

The Myth of the Fall which was given prominence in the teaching of St. Paul and disastrous new importance by St. Augustine and the Early Christian Fathers, was deeply rooted in Jewish culture. It perfectly illustrates the change of state from lunar to solar culture, from unconscious participatory unity to separation, guilt, estrangement and exile. The wholeness of the Sacred Order was, so to speak, broken by the development of the self-awareness that separated us from nature and this evoked an unconscious sense of guilt. As a myth, it movingly describes our sense of isolation, exile and abandonment as we lost touch with the older way of experiencing life and embarked on a new phase in the evolution of consciousness. There is no more striking image of the sense of exile and loss than our expulsion from the Garden of Eden at whose entrance an angel stands with a fiery sword, barring our re-entry. It is worth listening to D.H. Lawrence and how he saw this tremendous change:

> Isn't 'fall' and 'redemption' quite a late and new departure in religion and in myth: about Homer's time? Aren't the great heavens of the true pagans...clean of the 'Salvation' ideas, though they have the re-birth idea? And aren't they clean of the 'fall', although they have the descent of the soul? The two things are quite different. In my opinion the great pagan religions of the Aegean, and Egypt and Babylon, must have conceived the 'descent' as a great triumph, and each Easter of the clothing in flesh as a supreme glory, and the Mother Moon who gives us our body as the supreme giver of the great gift, hence the very ancient Magna Mater in the East. This 'fall' into Matter...this 'entombment' in the 'envelope of flesh' is a new and pernicious idea arising about 500 B.C. into distinct cult-consciousness and destined to kill the grandeur of the heavens altogether at last.[3]

This can be contrasted with another passage from his Last Poems, where he describes the still living participatory consciousness of the Etruscan way of life:

Behind all the Etruscan liveliness was a religion of life…Behind all the dancing was a vision, and even a science of life, a conception of the universe and man's place in the universe which made men live to the best of their capacity. To the Etruscan all was alive; the whole universe lived; and the business of man was himself to live amid it all. He had to draw life into himself, out of the wandering huge vitalities of the world. The cosmos was alive, like a vast creature…. The whole thing was alive, and had a great soul, or anima: and in spite of one great soul, there were myriad roving, lesser souls; every man, every creature and tree and lake and mountain and stream, was animate, and had its own peculiar consciousness.[4]

As we move into Christian culture, this lunar vision of life and the participatory consciousness which gave rise to it are increasingly lost to the European cultural tradition. It still survived in the peasant communities where the older traditions and rituals connected people with the cycles of nature and where the ancient worship of the Great Mother was transferred to the Virgin Mary. But in the sphere of Christian theology, the repudiation of the image of the goddess, and with it the significance and influence of a feminine dimension of the divine, was devastating because a vital thread of connection to the past was severed. Whereas the Egyptian, Sumerian, Greek and Roman Goddesses had given both men and women clearly defined images of different aspects of the Feminine to which they could relate, Christian culture after the fourth century offered only three role models of the Feminine: the Virgin Mary, Eve, and Mary Magdalene. The image of the soul was carried by the Virgin Mary, the dangerous desirousness of the instinct by Eve and sinful sexuality by Mary Magdalene. There is a fundamental split between the soul personified by the immaculately conceiving and — from the declaration in the Papal Edict of 1854 — the immaculately conceived Virgin Mary, and the body, represented by the carnal Eve and Mary Magdalene, the 'fallen' woman. It was through the far-reaching influence of this myth that we lost the wholeness of our being and the awareness that the concept of the soul must include instinct and the life of the body.

The Myth of the Fall:

- Describes the experience of the birth of consciousness or self-awareness as a fall from unity and harmony.

- Names Eve as the primary cause of original sin and explains the presence of suffering, death and evil in the world as due to her disobedience to God and leading Adam into sin through responding to the temptation of the serpent, Satan.

- Provides the scriptural foundation for the misogyny of the patriarchal view of woman.

- Reflects and reinforces the dualistic split between spirit and nature, mind and body and between this fallen world and an original 'perfect' world untainted by sin that we once inhabited and from which we were expelled by God.

- Associates sexuality with sin, shame and guilt — seeing the body, in St. Augustine's words, as a "hissing cauldron of lust". (*Confessions*)

The Demythologizing of the Goddess

The Myth of the Fall of Man originates with the Book of Genesis. The date of its appearance is not precisely known but is thought to be around the eighth century BC. It may be that it was first formulated after some dire catastrophe had happened to the Jewish people — possibly the ethnic cleansing by the Assyrians of the entire population of Samaria, the northern province of Israel ca. 720 BC. Or it may have been an attempt on the part of the priesthood of Yahweh to discredit and even eliminate the Canaanite religion where the worship of the goddess Asherah played an important part in the life of women, who appealed to her in the ordeal of childbirth. The serpent in Canaanite mythology was inseparable from the cult of the goddess. This myth subtly demoted the goddess who was blamed for the catastrophe that had befallen Samaria. Since we know that in the child a deep conviction of guilt may be formed when some trauma has been experienced in early life, we can apply this understanding to a group of people living at a specific historical time who had experienced a great catastrophe. According to the beliefs of the time, they interpreted this in terms of a punishment visited on them by God for the sin of disobedience and the worship of false gods. The myth can be read as the story of the deliberate and effective demythologizing of the hated goddess by the priesthood of that time and her demotion from a goddess to a woman, Eve, who was blamed for bringing suffering, death and sin into the world.

The title that Adam gives to Eve in this myth is actually the former title of the Great Mother — 'Mother of All Living' — a title also held by the Shekinah of Kabbalah. It is strange and surely significant that the Genesis myth takes the life-affirming images of the Garden, the Tree of Life and the Serpent, all inseparable from the Goddess in the mythology of the lunar era, and weaves them into a story about disobedience, fear, guilt, punishment and blame. The Great Mother, giver of life and death, who once contained both the living and the dead within her being, now, astonishingly, as Eve, becomes the cause of death coming into the world. And the serpent, once present with the Goddess in the Temple in Jerusalem as the great Brazen Serpent, is now cursed by God, condemned to crawl on its belly and eat dust (Gen.3:14).

Whatever its origins and the reasons for the appearance of this myth, what we are listening to as we decode the imagery is a complete reversal of the lunar mythology of the Goddess culture. We need look no further than this myth and the interpretation given to it by generations of theologians, priests and rabbis, not only for the ideas which led to the loss of soul and the sense of living within a Sacred Order but also for the misogyny which spread like a contagious virus through the three Abrahamic religions. As Jack Holland writes in his masterly analysis of the historical roots of misogyny:

> The hatred of women affects us in ways that no other hatred does because it strikes at our innermost selves. It is located where the private and public worlds intersect. The history of that hatred may dwell on its public consequences, but at the same time it allows us to speculate on why, at the personal level, man's complex relationship to woman has permitted misogyny to thrive. Ultimately, such speculation should allow us to see how equality between the sexes will eventually be able to banish misogyny and put an end to the world's oldest prejudice.[5]

An Alternative Interpretation

The myth says that Eve and Adam made the wrong choice, which brought disastrous consequences upon the human race and that we have been punished for that primal act of disobedience to God. The myth was interpreted literally and negatively yet we, in a later age, can understand it differently. The important idea that we have free will as well as responsibility for the choices we make is intrinsic to this myth. So, while the myth does describe an abrupt loss of participatory consciousness or, in the Platonic sense, a fall from a higher state of being, it also can be understood as describing the dawning of a new phase in the evolution of human consciousness, the birth of the conscious ego and all that this difficult separation from the matrix of instinct entailed.

As the story is currently interpreted, it is Eve's response to the serpent which initiates the change from unity and harmony in the divine world to a state of separation and estrangement in this one. Yet her actions could be understood as a story about responding to the prompting of instinct — of which the serpent is a primary representation — to move into a new phase in our evolution, losing touch with the participatory consciousness of the earlier time. From my experience as a Jungian analyst, I know that the appearance of snakes in dreams can signify regeneration, renewal and the birth of a new phase of life or a new attitude, as a previous unconscious state is relinquished. Yet, as a result of the traditional interpretation given to the myth, people who, over the centuries, have dreamed of snakes may have interpreted them as an image of seduction, temptation and evil—even associating them with Satan and the Devil.

The birth of self-awareness entails the loss of unconscious and instinctive participation in an original state of unity. The separation from nature necessarily creates duality: awareness of ourselves as separate from our surrounding environment; awareness of duality reflected in all the pairs of opposites — most importantly, the opposites of life and death. The loss of the participatory consciousness of the older state creates feelings of guilt and disorientation which this myth brilliantly describes, carried in the idea that we made the wrong choice. But, in reality, there is no primordial sin, no ongoing moral guilt. We did not make the wrong choice. There is, however, a tragic burden in the sense of our having been made to carry the guilt engendered by this myth without comprehending how and why it arose nor of being able to recognize it as a metaphor which describes, in the act of eating the fruit of the Tree of Knowledge, the birth of self-awareness and the separation of ego from instinct. Whether it was necessary for such a radical split to develop is debatable. It may be that the myth itself contributed to the split and became the foundation on which many later errors arose.

The Projection of Unconscious Guilt

In the deep unconscious of the modern psyche, however secular our society, we may still be influenced by this Christian meta-narrative since, at the unconscious level, old beliefs and habits persist long after they are thought to have been discarded. If, over many centuries, people are indoctrinated with the idea that they are flawed or are born into a state of sin, they will try to get rid of this intolerable burden by projecting their unconscious feelings of guilt onto other groups or individuals. These are then named and attacked as being bad or evil and in need of punishment or elimination. Since both the guilt and the projection are held at a deeply unconscious level, whether in the individual or the collective psyche, the end result will be disconnected from the memory of the original imprinting. Applying this reasoning to the collective Christian psyche, it could be argued that the 'shadow' aspect of Christianity with its persecution of Jews, Muslims, Pagans and heretics perceived as threatening to the power of the Church and its teaching could be connected with the need to offload the unconscious guilt imprinted on the psyche by the Myth of the Fall. The need to punish is deeply tied into unconscious guilt.

Added to this burden of guilt was the inwardly-directed attack on the 'appetites of the flesh' practised by so many ascetics who, thinking that suffering and pain inflicted on the body would bring them closer to God, tried to suppress their sexual instincts and ward off the attacks of the Devil — often in the form of women tempting them to fornication — with horrendous deprivation and self-inflicted austerities. The belief that the body must be controlled, mortified, made to suffer for its desires and in general brought into a relationship of subjection to the mind is very deeply ingrained in the Christian psyche. A typical passage in Colossians 3:5 urges people to "Put to death, therefore, whatever belongs to your earthly nature: sexual immorality, impurity, lust, evil desires and greed, which is idolatry." It would never have occurred to those practising the severe austerities enjoined on them by such texts that the instincts they had repressed would return to attack them in the form of the obsessive fantasies that so plagued the Desert Fathers of early Christianity. To name these as 'assaults of the Devil' only led to further acts of repression and greater austerities. If evil is an element in the cosmic order, its power was immeasurably increased by the repression of sexuality and all that resulted from it. I was struck by this passage in a book called *Beyond Geography: The Western Spirit Against the Wilderness* by Frederick Turner, which sensitively explores how the pathology of the Western Christian psyche, with its disastrous focus on conquest and conversion, developed:

> It seems to me that aggression against the body, against the natural world, against primitives, heretics, all unbelievers; and the vain, tragic, pathetically maintained hope of thus winning a lost belief or paradise: this is the terrific burden Christian history has to bear. It is the classic reaction of those who have lost true belief (or have been robbed of it) that they must insist with mounting strenuousness that they do believe and that all others must as well. For as social

psychologists have shown, if the bereft can thus succeed in harmonizing the world with themselves, then the inward gnawing doubt might be stopped and the intolerable condition of spiritual inanition alleviated.[6]

Even now we can see how easily negative shadow projections can be activated in our modern society against anyone designated an enemy and demonized as evil or a threat. We can see this scenario re-animated in the present polarization between 'good' and 'evil' on the political stage, where the conviction of moral superiority has been claimed by one group and the blame for evil fixed on another. We can see it in Fundamentalist Christianity as well as Fundamentalist Islam. We can see it in the aggressive and polarizing behaviour of rival political parties. We can see it in our compulsive addiction to develop ever more lethal weapons in order to deter a potential adversary or a future attack, without any apparent awareness of our own contribution to the proliferation of evil through the projection onto others of our unconscious aggression. Thousands of young men are sent to their deaths or carry lifelong trauma because of these unconscious projections.

They are also reflected in the determined effort of the evangelical branch of Christianity to demonize homosexuality (because in the Old Testament it is named a sin), reflected in the comment of a woman on the possibility of a gay priest being ordained a bishop in 2004, "That man is a beast."

Understanding the myth in this sense could help to remove the guilt and the need to project that guilt onto others which has been imprinted on the Christian psyche by the interpretation given to the myth by Christian theologians, both Catholic and Protestant. It was their literal interpretation of the myth as well as the myth itself which deprived us of a life of participation in the deeper layers of the soul and cut us off from our instincts as well as from the recognition of the sacredness of the life of nature. To me, this is a prime symptom of the pathology of the solar age which has led man to treat nature, woman and body as something unregenerate, far removed from himself: objects to be feared that he must control and dominate.

The Early Christian Fathers: the Obsession with Sexuality, Sin and Guilt

I was astonished to discover the effect of this myth on the early Christian Fathers — Origen, Tertullian, Clement, Chrysostom, Jerome, Athanasius, Augustine and others. What leaps out from their writings in the early documents of the Church up to the fourth century is their absolute obsession with the sin of the Fall and with sexual guilt. As I read with mounting incredulity what they had written about this myth, I said to myself, "What on earth was the matter with them that they were more concerned with sexual guilt than with the teaching of Christ? Whence came their sexual neurosis?" All were brilliantly gifted men in an intellectual sense. All were convinced that the sexual instinct was the main impediment to spirituality and that their sexuality had to be sacrificed in order for them to become acceptable to God. All had a phobic terror of what they called the "dark hole between faeces and urine", the "uncleanliness of the womb" and "the parts of shame". All, like Plato, regarded the body as the prison of the soul and identified men with spirituality and rationality and women with carnality and the irrational animal instincts. Origen (3rd century AD), perhaps the most remarkable and prolific writer of them all, is said to have castrated himself. Nowhere is the pathological dissociation between soul and body in the religions of the solar age more clearly revealed than in their writings and the endless theological debates about the nature of God.

St. Augustine (AD 354–430), a most sensitive and outstandingly gifted man as well as one who was strongly attracted to women, repudiated his partner of fifteen years, whom he dearly loved and by whom he had had a son, because of a socially desirable marriage arranged by his Christian mother: "My mistress was torn from my side, as an impediment to my marriage, and my heart, which clung to her, was torn and wounded till it bled."[7] We don't hear what happened to her heart or that of their son, Adeodonatus (Given from God), who tragically died at the age of sixteen, shortly after his parents' parting. St. Augustine lost both his partner and his son within a year. This moving and revealing passage was written by him after his son's death:

> God effects some good in correcting adults when they are chastised by the sufferings and deaths of the children who are dear to them. Why should this not happen, since, when the pain is past, it is as nothing to those to whom it happened? While those on whose account it happened will either be better men if they are corrected by their temporal disasters and decide to live better lives; or else they will have no excuse when they are punished at the future judgement, if they refuse to direct their longing towards eternal life under the stress of this life's pain.[8]

Within two years of his separation from his mistress, Augustine had converted to Christianity and, after discarding another mistress, had taken a vow of chastity because he believed this state would be more pleasing to God than his arranged marriage. No doubt influenced by his Christian mother, who was delighted by his conversion, he identified sexuality with sin. Converting to Christianity necessitated for him the renunciation of his sexuality. From then on, for the Christian soul as for the body, since the soul could take no trust or delight in the sexual expression of its life, the situation deteriorated still further: St. Augustine's theory of original sin became a standard doctrine of the Catholic Church from the Council of Carthage in AD 418.

St. Augustine, Jack Holland writes, "established the philosophical edifice that propped up the Christian view of the world, including its misogynistic vision."

> Augustine is one of the watershed personalities of history. He stands between the world of Classical Antiquity (which had endured for about 1000 years) and that of Christian civilization. He is the first person from antiquity who revealed to us the turmoil of his interior world as recorded in his remarkable work, *Confessions*…. At the centre of the turmoil of Augustine's search for God is the struggle between the desire of the flesh and striving of the will, the profound dualism that Augustine will incorporate into the very heart of Catholicism using Plato's philosophical apparatus. His cry of anguish echoes that of St. Paul, but with a power and complexity the Apostle could not match.[9]

Augustine's moving *Confessions*, begun around the year 400 AD when he was forty-six, are saturated with a profound rejection and distrust of his body. In psychological terms, the will of his conscious mind — dedicated to God — was forcibly imposed on his instincts, with disastrous consequences for himself as well as for generations of Christians. Influenced by Greek and also, perhaps unconsciously, Manichean ideas he, like Plato, associated his body with the irrational 'lower' instincts, believing that sexuality itself was a mortal sin. Projecting his own profound sense of sinfulness onto the hapless body of the whole of humanity, he believed it was a mass of sin, a *'massa peccati'*, and that the state of original sin meant that not only do we arrive in a state of sin when we are born, but that we are incapable of refraining from sinning. He saw the whole human race as "the multitude of the damned" because of original sin. From this miserable state we can only be rescued by the grace of God and then only those who were predestined to be so rescued. He struggled desperately to understand where evil came from and, because he believed that God must be wholly good and 'incorruptible', he concluded that evil must come from man, principally from his 'corruptible' body that was subject to death.

St. Augustine was not the originator of the theory of original sin. It had existed in the Jewish religion and was taught by St. Paul. Augustine refers to earlier Christian theologians who had expounded on it. However, the basic concept of the Augustinian version of the theory is that Adam was the originator of the fall of the human race and, as its progenitor — who carried within himself all future generations — the transmitter of the contaminated seed of sinfulness to those generations. He believed that every child who was born into the world through sexual intercourse arrived in a state of sin that was carried forward as an inheritance from its primordial ancestor. "By a kind of divine justice the human race was handed over to the devil's power, since the sin of the first man passed at birth to all who were born by intercourse of the two sexes, and the debt of the first parents bound all their posterity."[10]

Sexual desire was thus transmitted like a genetic disease through the sexual act. Adam's sin had corrupted the whole of nature and made it subject to death but the entire sorry story was initiated by Eve. In *The City of God*, he wrote that from the moment of the Fall, "The flesh began to lust against the spirit. With this rebellion we are born, just as we are doomed to die and because of the first sin, to bear, in our members and vitiated nature, either the battle with or defeat by the flesh."[11] This is solar mythology at its most extreme whose polarizing effect was enormously amplified by the identification of the body with sin and Augustine's own inner battle with his sexuality.

The formulation of the Doctrine of Original Sin arose out of St. Augustine's profound conviction of his own sexual sin and guilt. Through this doctrine, the love of God and obedience to Him were placed in opposition to the life of the body. The act of procreation perpetuated the transmission of original sin. Celibacy or sexual abstinence could restore the lost sense of primordial unity. "Truly by continence are we bound together and brought back into that unity from which we were dissipated into a plurality."[12]

It is not difficult to imagine the effect of this Christian belief on the sexual relations between men and women. Even a man's passionate embrace of his wife was deemed to be sinful because it transmitted original sin. Nor is it difficult to understand that it was Augustine's savage crucifixion of his own sexual instinct and his passionate nature which gave rise to his distorted view of human nature and his interpretation of the origin of death, sin and evil. The repudiation of his sexuality was echoed in his cruel repudiation of his mistress. It evidently did not occur to him that the devastating wound he inflicted on her and on their son might be by far the greater sin.

St. Augustine immeasurably compounded a tragic situation that was already well established by earlier Fathers of the Church. His theory of original sin became a foundation stone of Christian doctrine and has endured to this day. However, he gave this theory a new gloss: Grace is necessary for salvation since without it we are condemned to remain irredeemably mired in a state of sin.

St. Augustine's theory of original sin, predestination and the need for grace did not go unchallenged. It was condemned by Pelagius (AD 354–418) and others.

Pelagius was originally a priest in the Celtic church and later a respected theologian and teacher who lived in Rome and then Jerusalem. He wanted to lift the burden of original sin from the human race and took issue with St. Augustine over his interpretation, insisting that only Adam was affected by the sin that led to the Fall. His beliefs may be stated briefly as follows:

- Original sin does not exist
- Infants are born in the same state of innocence as Adam before the Fall
- Man is not dependent on Christ for redemption nor is divine grace essential for redemption
- Redemption is earned through following Christ's example, not given through His sacrificial death
- The human race has free will and the capacity for choice and moral responsibility
- Man has the potential to realize the divine element within his nature, to become Christ-like.

He insisted that human nature was innately good because it was created by God and denied that salvation could only come about through belonging to the Church.

Pelagius is like a breath of fresh air in the midst of Augustine's morbid obsession with sin. The great doctrinal struggle between them gives us the image of two powerful stags locking antlers. Pelagius was declared a heretic in 417 and died a year later and Augustine's pessimistic and guilt-laden doctrine passed into Church law in 418.

Another man, Julian, bishop of Eclanum in Italy, sided with Pelagius against Augustine and, writing in a letter to Augustine himself of his strong objection to his conviction that original sin affects infants, said,

> Babies, you say, carry the burden of another's sin, not any of their own.... Explain to me then, who this person is who sends the innocent to punishment. You answer, God.... God, you say, the very one who commends his love to us, who has loved us and not spared his son but handed him over to us, he judges us in this way; he persecutes new born children; he hands over babies to eternal flames.... It would show a just and reasonable sense of propriety to treat you as beneath argument: you have come so far from religious feeling, from civilized standards, so far indeed from common sense, that you think your Lord capable of committing kinds of crime which are hardly found among barbarian tribes.[13]

Strong words indeed. Had Pelagius and the group of dissenting bishops led by Julian won the fiercely debated doctrinal battle with St. Augustine, the history of

Christianity might have been very different. We may, centuries later, regret that this could not be. We might have been spared the virulent theological struggles for power and the neurotic preoccupation with sin and sexuality and the mistrust of women that bedevil the Christian Church to this day. We might also have been spared the Manichean polarization of humanity into the saved and the damned — carried right through to our times in Christian Fundamentalist beliefs about the Rapture in the End Times — when God takes to heaven those who are predestined to be saved and leaves the rest to perish. Further, we might have been spared the tortures and executions that went with the belief that it was God's will that the Church should seek out and extirpate sin and heresy wherever it could be found since heresy, as a disruption of the divine order, could bring down God's wrath on the whole community. This perceptive passage from a recent book by Charles Freeman called *AD 381: Heretics, Pagans and the Christian State*, is worth quoting at length:

> Augustine's lasting contribution to political thought lies in his justification of authoritarian regimes that see virtue in order per se, rather than in any abstract ideal such as justice or the defence of human rights, or even in the teachings of Jesus themselves. At a stroke Augustine supplants centuries of Greek thought... which viewed the government of the city primarily in terms of the well-being of its citizens. Moreover, when Church and state become mutually supportive in the upholding of order, then the punishment of heretics becomes a matter of state policy. This would be the norm in medieval Europe... Augustine's under-lying premise — that there is a single truth that can only be grasped through faith; that human beings are helpless; that God is essentially punitive, ready to send even babies into eternal hell fire; and that one has a right, even a duty, to burn heretics — challenges the whole ethos of the Greek intellectual tradition, where competition between rival philosophies was intrinsic to progress.... The freedom to speculate freely as an individual had no place in his system: he was terrified by the idea that all might contribute to the finding of truth. Augustine bequeathed a tradition of fear to Christianity, fear that one's speculations might be heretical and fear that, even if they were not, one might still go to hell as punishment for the sin of Adam.[14]

Such was the effect of the repression (not the control) of his sexual instinct in a very brilliant, passionate and sensitive man that it was able to manifest in a complex strong enough to direct a Church for centuries and to lead to the deaths of thousands of individuals whose only 'sin' was to be accused of heresy.

The idea of heresy was first introduced by the Emperor Theodosius in AD 381 when anyone who did not comply with his edict that all must believe in the doctrine that the Father, Son and Holy Spirit were of one and the same substance would be declared a heretic. The end result of Theodosius' policy was the persecution not only of heretics but of the pagan religions and the destruction of their shrines and magnificent temples. It was at this time that the idea entered Christianity that hell and eternal punishment awaited heretics and unbelievers. Augustine himself later sanctioned the burning alive of heretics as an appropriate punishment for their sin. From this time on, the idea developed that the Catholic Church, backed by the Emperor, should have absolute authority and control of the lives of its members. The Church took over the model of absolutism that had been presented to it by the Emperor, ever since it became associated with the imperial policy of the Roman state in the reign of Constantine (ca. AD 272– ca. 337). Where, in this reign of terror, was the compassion that Christ emphasized in His teaching?

It is in the crucially important fourth century that the Catholic Church appears to have been deflected from the path to God as taught by Christ and the early Church and become contaminated by the pursuit of 'Caesar's power'. The concept of original sin and the belief that the Catholic Church was the only path to salvation gave it immense power over the lives of millions of believers in whom it instilled a fear of hellfire and purgatory. Vivid scenes painted on the walls of churches during the Middle Ages and the Renaissance showed the fate that awaited sinners if they transgressed the rules laid down by the Church.

It could be argued that the pursuit of power and the growing authoritarianism of the Catholic Church from the thirteenth to the eighteenth centuries, when the power of the Inquisition was at its height, led directly to the horrors of the totalitarian states of the last century. The behaviour of the Church created a precedent for these horrors, a precedent made more powerful because it was practised by the highest religious authority. Through its five-hundred-year pursuit of heretics through this office, the Church demonstrated how a carefully thought out and minutely organized policy using intimidation, censorship, torture and terror as its tools of power could offer a model of ensuring conformity of belief among vast numbers of people. Nothing reflects the pathology that had such an iron grip on the Christian psyche more than these sacrificial rituals executed in the name of God.

The Negative Legacy of St. Augustine

The Doctrine of Original Sin inflicted a deep wound on the Western psyche. It was a catastrophe not only for sexuality in general but for woman, who was held to be the prime carrier of the 'lower' animal instincts. As Karen Armstrong writes in her history of misogyny in the Christian Church in *The End of Silence: Women and the Priesthood*, "Sin, sex and woman were bound together in an unholy Trinity in the Western Christian imagination by the powerful theology of St. Augustine."[15]

Sexual intercourse was declared to be only for the purpose of procreation, never for pleasure. Woman was not to be regarded as the beloved companion of man but only as a kind of useful functionary — the bearer of his seed and provider of his meals. If possible, couples were to live in chastity within marriage. In the view of the Church Fathers, the only way a woman could gain men's respect was to remain a virgin. If men chose the spiritual life, they could not allow themselves to be 'defiled' by intercourse with women. In the fourth and fifth centuries, "Virginity was the Christian virtue par excellence".[16]

Because infants were contaminated from the moment of their conception by the transmission of original sin from their parents, if they died without being baptized, their souls could not be saved and were consigned to limbo. One can imagine the effects of this doctrine on parents who had lost a child. From this twisted belief, the Catholic Church developed the idea which survived until very recently, that if it came to a choice of saving one or the other in childbirth, it was more important to save the life of the un-baptized infant than the life of its mother in order that the infant should receive baptism. The suffering generated by this belief is unimaginable and indefensible.

The belief about the sinfulness of sexuality also led to the idea that a priest or deacon who serves God must be celibate and to many attempts by the Church to enforce celibacy on its clergy — most of them unsuccessful. The underlying fear was that sexual contact with a woman would defile the holy sacraments. The earliest attempts date to a Council held in Spain in the fourth century when married priests were enjoined to avoid intercourse with their wives. Pope Gregory the Great (d. 604) decreed that a priest, once ordained, should "love his wife like a sister and shun her like an enemy". Pope Gregory VII in the eleventh century called for "severing intercourse between priests and women by means of ever-lasting anathema". Finally, in 1139, Pope Innocent II proclaimed that ordained priests could not marry. A few centuries later, the Council of Trent (1545–63) forbade men who were already married from becoming priests.[17]

A sombre reflection on the legacy of St. Augustine is offered by the late Philip Sherrard in his perceptive book *The Rape of Man and Nature*. I am quoting Sherrard at some length because he shows how differently we might have perceived ourselves:

It is one of the paradoxes, and also one of the tragedies, of the Western Christian tradition that the man who affirmed so strongly the presence of God in the depths of his own self… should as a dogmatic theologian have been responsible more perhaps than any other Christian writer for 'consecrating' within the Christian world the idea of man's slavery and impotence due to the radical perversion of human nature through original sin. It has been St. Augustine's theology which in the West has veiled down to the present day the full radiance of the Christian revelation of divine sonship — the full revelation of who man essentially is…. He deprives the element of manhood in the God-manhood reality of any genuine positive quality, and to do this is to empty the concept of divine sonship of its effective significance.

Through the Fall man and the natural order are deprived of even that extrinsic participation in grace which they possessed in their pre-fallen state. Their original and true nature is now vitiated, totally corrupt and doomed to destruction…. As for the communication of grace, through which alone man and the world may be redeemed from depravity, this… was confined to the visible church and depended on the performance of certain rites, like baptism, confirmation, ordination and so on, which it was the privilege of the ecclesiastical hierarchy to administer to a submissive and obedient laity.

The magnificent scope of the Logos doctrine with its whole "cosmic" dimension — the idea of God incarnate in all human and created existence — was tacitly and radically constricted in Western thinking…The Church became the unique sphere of the Spirit's manifestation…. Everything outside the limits of the Church was secular, deprived of grace, incurably corrupt and doomed to disintegration.[18]

The Logos doctrine outlined above, which derived from Plato, could have kept alive the participatory consciousness of the lunar era and taken it to a new and conscious level of relationship with the Cosmos and the recognition that the whole earthly order of reality was intrinsically divine because it existed within the Being of God. It seems a tragedy for Western Christianity that this insight was lost.

St. Augustine can be described as a world-denying contemplative rather than a world-embracing one. The stance he took against his own desires was agonizing for him and for generations of Christians. Yet, his struggle with himself must be seen in the context of the world of his time and the widening split between the conscious mind and the instinctive soul. In spite of my recognition of the deep wound he inflicted on the Christian psyche, I am always deeply moved by these words in one of the most exquisite passages to come from the heart of a lover of God: "Too late I came to love thee, O thou Beauty both so ancient and so fresh, yea too late came I to love thee. And behold, thou wert within me, and I out of myself, where I made search for thee."[19]

The core Christian belief is that humanity is so steeped in depravity and sin that only the sacrifice of the Son of God could redeem it. Six centuries after St. Augustine, St. Anselm (AD 1033–1109), an Italian priest who became Archbishop of Canterbury, wrote in his *Meditation on Human Redemption*: "A man appended to a cross suspends the eternal death impending over the human race; a man fastened to a cross unfastens a world affixed to endless death." Those who did not belong to the Church were thought to be consigned to this endless death.

With the Reformation, when some change might have been expected, both Luther and Calvin continued to base their teaching on the Doctrine of Original Sin and the need of redemption by Christ's sacrificial death because of it. Both saw woman's role as confined to child-bearing and obeying her husband. The phrase "A woman's place is in the home" originated with Luther. If anything, the sense of guilt and sin was augmented by Luther and Calvin and the subjection of sinful humanity to the will of a fearful, ever-vigilant and punishing God perpetuated.

Calvin sent to the stake the brilliant Spanish scientist, doctor and theologian, Michael Servetus, who was the first European scientist to discover the pulmonary circulation of the blood. Servetus had dared to challenge Calvin's Institutes and reject his teaching on original sin and human depravity. It seems that men like Calvin were so saturated by these beliefs that it was impossible to separate themselves from them. As D.H. Lawrence was to write so powerfully in *Lady Chatterley's Lover*, "The Christian religion lost, in Protestantism finally, the togetherness with the universe, the togetherness of the body, the sex, the emotions, the passions, with the earth and sun and stars."

In their literal belief in the myth of the Fall, generations of theologians and priests taught men and women that this world was a fallen one that could only be redeemed by the sacrificial death of the Son of God. Secondly they warned men not to trust women and women not to trust themselves or each other. Matthew Fox observes in his book *Original Blessing* that the doctrine of original sin can itself contribute to sin and, above all, to distrust of life:

> A devastating corollary of the fall/redemption tradition is that religion with original sin as its starting point and religion built exclusively around sin and redemption does not teach trust. Such a religion does not teach trust of existence or of body or of society or of creativity or of cosmos. It teaches both consciously and unconsciously, verbally and non-verbally, fear; fear of damnation, fear of nature — beginning with one's own; fear of others; fear of the cosmos. In fact, it teaches distrust beginning with distrusting of one's own existence, one's own originality, and one's own glorious entrance into this word of glory and of pain.[20]

Through my work as a therapist, I found that the belief in original sin and the profound rejection of woman, the body and sexuality as well as the deep sense of self-rejection that are intrinsic to it are still carried in the unconscious psyche of Western men and women, no matter how much they may have adapted to a secular culture. From a Jungian perspective, man's *anima* — the unconscious internalized image of woman that he carries in his psyche — has been imprinted with the image of Eve and the Christian teaching on original sin. This may cause him to fall back on old beliefs about woman's inferiority and subservience whenever he feels threatened in his relationships with women. It may also be responsible for the negative view of themselves that many women hold and the difficulty they still have in establishing themselves in professions hitherto open only to men, or in leaving abusive relationships. These old beliefs manifest in the debasement and abuse of women displayed in pornography and in rap lyrics, as well as in the revolting trade of trafficking women and the devastating and widespread use of rape as a weapon of war.

The current obsession with sex, promiscuity and pornography that is now so much a part of modern Western culture does nothing to transform the underlying stratum of misogynistic beliefs inherited from the past. If anything, it perpetuates and reinforces them. Woman is still demeaned by being presented in the tabloid press as a sexual object for the gratification of man's sexual desire and, in situations where neither her family nor society offer her any protection, may become the victim of predatory males. We now have to deal with the additional problem of organized paedophilia which also points to the presence of an unconscious sexual compulsion. All this has inflicted a devastating wound on the Christian psyche. It is a powerful thought form or complex that has not been recognized and addressed and, therefore, cannot be transformed.

Wherever evangelical Christianity is taken, the teaching about original sin and fall/redemption theology goes with it, wounding the souls of all who are converted to Christianity. Just when it seemed as if modern Christians might be emerging from the stranglehold of this complex, Fundamentalist branches of Christianity in America and in Africa are regressing into it, activating the old belief in the inferior and subservient nature of woman. A recent statement by President Carter (July 2009) explains why he decided to leave his Baptist Church. This is an extract from his statement:

> I have been a practising Christian all my life and a deacon and Bible teacher for many years. My faith is a source of strength and comfort to me, as religious beliefs are to hundreds of millions of people around the world. So my decision to sever my ties with the Southern Baptist Convention, after six decades, was

painful and difficult. It was, however, an unavoidable decision when the convention's leaders, quoting a few carefully selected Bible verses and claiming that Eve was created second to Adam and was responsible for original sin, ordained that women must be "subservient" to their husbands and prohibited from serving as deacons, pastors or chaplains in the military service…. This view that women are somehow inferior to men is not restricted to one religion or belief. Women are prevented from playing a full and equal role in many faiths. Nor, tragically, does its influence stop at the walls of the church, mosque, synagogue or temple. This discrimination, unjustifiably attributed to a Higher Authority, has provided a reason or excuse for the deprivation of women's equal rights across the world for centuries.

It is hardly surprising that so many people have rejected the dogmatic excesses of religion and turned with relief to science and a secular society.

Notes:

1. Campbell, Joseph (1988) *The Power of Myth*, Doubleday, New York, p.197
2. ibid, p. 99
3. Letter to Frederick Carter 29 October 1929 in *The Letters of D. H. Lawrence*, vol. VII, eds. Keith Sagar and James T. Boulton, CUP 1993, pp. 544-5.
4. Lawrence, D. H. Last Poems, *The Complete Poems of D.H. Lawrence*, Vol 1, p. 17
5. Holland, Jack (2006) *Misogyny, The World's Oldest Prejudice*, Constable and Robinson Ltd. London, p.11
6. Turner, Frederick (1992) *Beyond Geography: The Western Spirit against the Wilderness*, fourth edition, Rutgers University Press, New Jersey, p. 73
7. St. Augustine, *Confessions*, Book VI.15
8. Bettenson, Henry ed. & trs. *The Later Christian Fathers*, OUP 1970 p. 202-3 from *de lib*. arb. 3. 23
9. Holland, p. 91
10. Bettenson, p. 220, *de trin*.16
11. *The City of God*, Image Books, 1958
12. *Confessions*, Book X. 40
13. Freeman, Charles (2003) *The Closing of the Western Mind*, Pimlico, London, 2003, p. 299, quoting from Christopher Kirwan, *Augustine*, 1989, p.134
14. Freeman (2008) AD 381: *Heretics, Pagans and the Christian State*, Pimlico, London, pp.171-172
15. Armstrong, Karen (1993) *The End of Silence: Women and the Priesthood*, Fourth Estate, London, p. 107
16. Ranke-Heinemann, Uta (1990) *Eunuchs for Heaven*, English translation André Deutsch Ltd., London, p. 45
17. ibid, pp. 85-89
18. Sherrard, Philip (1987) *The Rape of Man and Nature*, Golgonooza Press, Ipswich, Suffolk The late Philip Sherrard, born in 1922, is the author of many books on metaphysical and literary themes. He translated, with G.E.H. Palmer and Kallistos Ware, the Philokalia in 3 volumes, 1979, 1981 and 1984.
19. *Confessions*, Book X. 27
20. Fox, Matthew (1983) *Original Blessing*, Bear & Co. Santa Fe, p.82

The Original Sin (peccato originale)
Flemish tapestry 17th century
Reproduced here with the kind permission of the Alinari Archives, Florence

Chapter Eight

MISOGYNY:
THE ORIGIN AND EFFECTS OF THE OPPRESSION OF WOMAN

Women should be subject to their men. The natural order for mankind is that women should serve men and children their parents, for it is just that the lesser serve the greater.

— Gratian *Decretum*, 12th century

In the modern world, misogyny still flourishes and, despite their recent social and political emancipation in many countries, women are still subject to oppression. They may be murdered, raped, trafficked, stoned to death and brutalized by domestic abuse. Their voice is still marginalized in a world where half the population is female. As previous chapters have explained, we need to go back far into the past to discover the origin of beliefs which have ratified and condoned the oppression and suffering of women and have become enshrined in religious beliefs and social customs. This chapter will give a more detailed view of the origin of these beliefs and customs and their effects on society. Karen Armstrong in her book *The End of Silence: Women and the Priesthood*, shows how the fear of women still influences the theological debates about women being ordained to the priesthood and consecrated as bishops.

The Christian view of woman drew on earlier beliefs which are carried in Jewish commentaries on the Myth of the Fall, for these were partly responsible for laying the foundation on which later Christian writers built. In the Old Testament we find this key sentence: "Of the woman came the beginning of sin, and through her we all die"(Sirach 25:24).

This negative view of woman was carried forward into Christian culture — not through the words or teaching of Jesus but through the influence of St. Paul, who was brought up in the Jewish faith, and the early Christian Fathers. In his letters to the different churches, St. Paul instructed women to keep their heads covered, not to teach or speak in church and to be subject to their husbands in all things, "for man is not of the woman; but the woman of the man. Neither was the man created for the woman; but the woman for the man" (1 Tim. 2:8–14, Eph. 5:22–4, 1 Cor. 11:7–9, 1 Cor. 14:34–5).

This was one root of the negative view of woman that was developed in Christianity. But there was another, derived from the ideas that prevailed about women in the Greek world as reflected in Plato's Theory of Eternal Forms. In this Theory, as Jack Holland explains in his book, *Misogyny: the World's Oldest Prejudice*,

> The very act of conception is viewed as a falling away from the perfection of God into the abysmal world of appearance, of suffering and death.... This dualistic vision of reality denigrated the world of the senses, placing it in an eternal struggle with the achievement of the highest form of knowledge: the knowledge of God. This vision profoundly influenced Christian thinkers in their view of women, who literally as well as figuratively embodied what is scorned as transient, mutable and contemptible.[1]

Apart from philosophical theories, there were also social customs. In her book *When Women were Priests*, Karen Jo Torjesen brilliantly illuminates how the Christian Fathers absorbed their view of the different roles of men and women from the social customs of the Roman Empire and how these, in turn, were inherited from those that existed in Greek culture. It seems incredible to discover that views about women which still prevail today can be traced back to these ancient cultures. As she writes, "When women are dismissed as irrational and men are presumed to be innately logical, we can be sure these conclusions are prompted by the persistent whisperings of long-dead Greek philosophers in society's ear."[2]

Torjesen explores the root of these beliefs — for they were strongly held convictions which influenced a whole society — explaining that the Greek theory held that the human self has two aspects:

> A superior, masculine self — rational, virile, masterful, and noble — and an inferior, feminine self that is irrational, sexual, animal, and potentially dangerous. Enshrined within this theory of the self are the gendered values of male honor and female shame. Masculinity, equated with sexual and political dominance, is designated "rational". By identifying the sexual, appetitive, and "dangerous" aspects of the self as irrational, the philosophers split off the "uncontrollable" parts of human nature and projected them onto a "lower female self". Through this gendering of the self, femaleness became the primary symbol for the irrational and uncontrollable. Women could then be labelled irrational, sensual, and dangerous because of the supposed dominance of their "lower" female nature and the weakness of their "higher" masculine self.[3]

And, she observes, these negative beliefs about woman's nature were transmitted to Christianity:

> Instead of celebrating femaleness as providing a unique avenue of access to God, or seeing in femaleness a profound expression of the divine, Christianity left the traditional cultural meanings of femaleness and female sexuality unchanged. Rationality and self-control retained their masculine cast, while passion, sexuality, and body are particularly female.... Woman's body, since it was a stark proclamation of sexuality, was not in the image of God; it represented rather the pull of those forces that drew humanity away from God.[4]

Putting the Greek (and Roman) inheritance together with Jewish beliefs about the sin of the Fall and the shame of sexuality created a dual legacy which was to have a disastrous impact on women's psyche and women's lives in Christian culture.

The Role of Women in the Early Church

It is therefore all the more astonishing to discover that in the first two centuries after the death of Jesus, women played a valuable and valued public role in the early Church. To begin with, Christianity was disseminated through meetings in the houses of individuals — many of them distinguished and wealthy women, well respected in their community. When they were baptized as Christians, their whole household, including slaves, was baptized with them. Women preached, taught, baptized and performed healings and exorcisms in the earliest Christian community. Women were attracted to Christianity because it gave them a freedom and respect that they were not accorded in the surrounding culture, whether Jewish, Greek or Roman. For the first time, they had choice in the disposal of their bodies: they could choose to abstain from marriage by remaining virgins or to be celibate within marriage and, through sexual abstinence, could refrain from having children or additional children if they so chose. Marriage was for life; a wife could not be put aside. Infidelity in a man was regarded as sinful as it was in a woman. These ideas were provocative and shocking in the world of that time.

Jesus' attitude towards women was truly revolutionary because, in the way he treated them, he broke with Jewish as well as Roman custom. His disciples were surprised by his empathic attitude towards women, as when he spoke with a Samaritan woman (John 4:27) and when he shocked the Pharisees by rescuing a young woman from being stoned to death for adultery (John 8:3-11). Women surrounded Jesus during his ministry; invited him into their houses and, generally, seem to have been welcomed by him as disciples and friends.

Jesus and Mary Magdalene

Perhaps the closest of these women was Mary Magdalene. Her relationship with Jesus holds an increasing fascination for modern women, as the many books written about her and the phenomenal success of the *Da Vinci Code* attest. In Christian teaching, Mary Magdalene has been presented as the 'penitent whore', a prostitute who was rescued by Jesus from a life of sin and who had seven devils cast out of her. But there is now more than enough evidence to show that this was a calumny fixed onto Mary by a misogynistic church obsessed with the 'sin' of sexuality and determined to protect Jesus from the taint of a close physical relationship with a woman.

Nothing reveals the split between soul and body more than the idea that it was inconceivable that the Son of God could have sexual relations with a woman. Divine love had to exclude sexual love because sexual love was impure and the transmitter of the sin of the Fall. In order to fulfil the role of the Redeemer, the Saviour had to be 'chaste' and 'undefiled'. He could not be allowed to transmit original sin through the sexual act nor could he even be conceived through the sexual act.

In a most interesting book called *The Meaning of Mary Magdalene*, published in 2010, an Episcopalian priest called Cynthia Bourgeault, in a careful analysis of this derogatory view of Mary and an exploration of the text of the Gnostic Gospel of Mary, has given the clearest description of the extraordinary depth and spiritual quality of the relationship between Jesus and Mary Magdalene, a relationship that she believes is at the heart of the Christian story: "a spiritual love so refined and numinous as to be virtually unknown in the West today."[5]

Mary's role as spiritual companion of Jesus need not exclude an erotic relationship between them. In the Gospel of Philip, there is this oft-quoted passage: "And the companion of the Saviour is Mary Magdalene. But Christ loved her more than all the disciples and used to kiss her often on the mouth." This apparently offended the other disciples who complained in this Gospel, and in the Gospel of Mary that Jesus loved her more than them.[6] There is no reason — other than the conviction of the Christian Fathers that the Son of God had to be celibate — to exclude the possibility that he had a close relationship with Mary Magdalene, who obviously loved Jesus deeply and who, we are told, stood with another woman, also called Mary, at the mouth of his sepulchre after his burial (Matthew 28:61). The Gospel of John gives the clearest description of her later returning to the tomb and of how, finding the stone rolled away from it, she ran to find Peter and another disciple who hurried back with her to see for themselves what had happened (John 20:11-18). All four gospels mention Mary by name as the first person to witness the resurrection and also the first to inform the other disciples of what had happened.

Cynthia Bourgeault concludes that the fact that the canonical gospels describe Mary Magdalene by name as the premiere witness to the resurrection "suggests that among the earliest Christians the stature of Mary Magdalene is of the highest order of magnitude — more so than even the Virgin Mother.... Mary Magdalene's place of honor is so strong that even the heavy hand of a later, male-dominated ecclesiology cannot entirely dislodge it."[7]

She explains further:

> The high position she held among the close followers of Jesus is more explicitly shown in the Gnostic Gospels where Mary Magdalene is seen as "first among the Apostles"… not because she was the first on the scene at the resurrection but in a more fundamental way: because *she gets the message*. Of all the disciples, she is the only one who fully understands what Jesus is teaching and can reproduce it in her own life. Her position of leadership is earned, and it is specifically validated by Jesus himself.[8]

What precisely was this teaching? It was, Bourgeault concludes, a teaching which belonged to the tradition of conscious self-transformation which is specifically carried in the three Gnostic gospels of Thomas, Philip and Mary. Whereas the canonical gospels emphasize "right belief" as the basis for salvation, these three wisdom gospels all place their emphasis on "right practice". In her view, there is no doubt that what Jesus and Mary Magdalene were both teaching was the methodology of "right practice". This practice could, in time, lead to the opening of "the eye of the heart" — an organ of spiritual perception which, as Bourgeault wonderfully describes it, acts like "a vibrant resonant field" aligning us with a deeper dimension of reality, bringing together the finite and the infinite, so that we act from the underlying unitive ground, "that place of oneness before the opposites arise".[9] That Mary was the partner and soul companion of Jesus in this shared work would seem to be confirmed in the Gospel of Mary and also in the Gnostic *Dialogue of the Savior*, where Mary is described as the woman "who knew the All".[10] It is also confirmed by a third century text, the *Pistis Sophia*, where Mary takes the main questioning and teaching role in a long dialogue with Jesus. The fact that, following Jewish custom, no woman would have been allowed into the sepulchre unless she were the mother, wife or sister of Jesus suggests that Mary was Jesus' wife. See the recent publication: *The Gospel of the Beloved Companion: The Complete Gospel of Mary Magdalene* at the end of this chapter.

The Contamination of Original Sin

As Church doctrine developed, particularly after the Council of Ephesus in AD 431 when the Virgin Mary was declared *Theotokos*, or God-Bearer, it was decided that she, as well as her Son, could not be contaminated by original sin. The fact that Jesus had sisters and brothers was expunged from the record in order that Mary, as the Mother of the Saviour, should be a sexually pure recipient of the Holy Spirit. For, if his mother had been defiled by sexual intercourse and Jesus born in the normal way, like his brothers and sisters, he would have been contaminated by original sin and could not, therefore, have been the Son of God. The sexually explicit distinction between Mary and other women had to be clearly drawn. She was to remain a virgin before, during and after the birth of her son. From the Papal Edict of 1854 the Virgin Mary was declared to be Immaculately Conceived. This effectively elevated Mary to the status of an archetype, removing her from the sphere of earthly womanhood. This process was completed with the Papal Bull (1950) and Encyclical (1954), when Mary was received, body and soul, into heaven and named "Queen of Heaven".

Returning to the reason why Jesus had to be celibate, Cynthia Bourgeault comments, "It gives one a bit of a start to realize that for the better part of two millennia, Christian theology has been written, shaped, formulated, and handed down almost exclusively by celibates talking to other celibates... And from this exclusively celibate template emerges the only image of Christ our tradition has allowed us to entertain: of a celibate renunciate whose "sinless" purity would necessarily entail sexual abstinence."[11] The effects of this derogatory manipulation of the sexual instinct are with us still today, as she explains:

> Because it has been so thoroughly programmed into us that celibacy is the highest Christian way and that committed spousal love is a second rate path or no path at all… it is hardly surprising that our Western anthropology of human sexuality is abysmal. In the secular version relentlessly foisted upon us by contemporary culture, it's all about pleasure, performance, gratification. In the bedrooms of the faithful, it's still all too often about duty and shame: a begrudging debt to future generations which… is still tainted with carnal sin. Mention "erotic love" and people will immediately hear "sex", then immediately thereafter, "dirty". The idea that there could be anything holy about this kind of love is too alien to even consider…. We are all children of a cultural stream whose vision of human love has been shaped by the shadow side of celibate spirituality.[12]

The Defective Nature of Woman

There was a marked change in the attitude towards women in the third and fourth centuries when Christian theologians — many of them originally lawyers — began to inveigh against women holding any priestly office or even speaking out in debates in church, for by now churches had been built to hold large congregations. Once again, as in Greek and Jewish culture, women were relegated to the home and could hold no public office (with the exception of those women in Greek and Roman culture who held the role of priestesses). Their primary role was to copy Mary's example of humility and accept the rule of chastity, silence and obedience. As Irenaeus (ca. AD 125-200), bishop of Lyon, stated: "Eve by her disobedience brought death on herself and on all the human race: Mary, by her obedience, brought salvation."[13] The power of men to control the lives of women was never questioned.

Tertullian (AD 160-220), a theologian and prolific writer living in North Africa, became one of the most vociferous critics of women holding priestly office: "It is not permitted for a woman to speak in the church, nor is it permitted for her to teach, nor to baptize, nor to offer the [Eucharist], nor to claim for herself a share in any masculine function — least of all, in priestly office."[14] Tertullian addressed women directly in one of the most virulently misogynistic passages that have come down to us from the past:

> By every garb of penitence woman might the more fully expiate that which she derives from Eve — the ignominy, I mean, of the first sin, and the odium of human perdition....Do you not know that you are each an Eve?...You are the devil's gateway; you are the unsealer of that forbidden tree; you are the first deserter of the divine law; you destroyed so easily God's image, man. On account of your desertion — that is, death — even the son of God had to die.[15]

Today we would say he was in the grip of a complex! Despite the fact that in the Gospels Jesus does not equate sexuality with sinfulness but, on the contrary, protects an adulterous woman from death by stoning, the idea of enmity between the higher (soul and rational mind) and lower (body) aspects of human nature and the sinfulness of sexuality became, through the influence of St. Augustine and later theologians, one of the major themes of Christian teaching. Generations of Christian ascetics believed that the path to God could only be opened through the renunciation of anything to do with the contamination of woman because that contamination might defile the holy sacraments and interfere with their contemplation of God. After his conversion, St. Augustine wouldn't allow any woman in his house, not even his elder sister or his nieces, all of whom were nuns.[16] He said that woman's face reminded him of Eve.

In our research for Chapter 13 of *The Myth of the Goddess* on the dark legacy of the Myth of the Fall, which gives a much fuller account of this legacy, Jules and I found endlessly repeated in the writings of the Christian theologians that woman, because of her descent from Eve, was described as an inferior substance because Eve emerged from Adam; as a secondary creation because Eve was created second, out of Adam; as the ally of the serpent and the devil because she succumbed to temptation first; as the devil's gateway through whom the devil or Satan is enabled to pursue his aims in the world through causing her to tempt men into sexual relations. These ideas laid the ground for the witch trials over 1000 years later, when women were specifically accused of 'consorting' with the devil and even having intercourse with him.

The fact that Eve in Genesis is described as a secondary creation drawn from the body of Adam rather than a primary creation, led to this contorted statement from Gratian, a twelfth century theologian, which reinforced the idea that women should be under the control of their husbands and went so far as to state that woman was not made in God's image because she was a secondary creation, drawn from Adam:

> The image of God is in man and it is one. Women were drawn from man, who has God's jurisdiction as if he were God's vicar, because he has the image of the one God. Therefore Woman is not made in God's image.... Adam was beguiled by Eve, not she by him.... It is right that he whom woman led into wrongdoing should have her under his direction, so that he may not fail a second time through female levity.[17]

The end result of these negative projections onto woman was that Eve and all women were equated with body, matter and carnality and the irrational nature of man. Adam, who got off relatively lightly as a primary creation and as a secondary rather than a primary sinner, was equated with the rational soul, following the Greek view of man. "Woman," wrote Albertus Magnus, teacher of Thomas Aquinas, in the twelfth century, "is an imperfect man and possesses, compared to him, a defective and deficient nature. She is therefore insecure in herself. That which she herself cannot receive, she endeavours to obtain by means of mendacity and devilish tricks."[18] No wonder it has been so difficult for women priests and women bishops to gain acceptance.

Here are two statements from the pen of St. Thomas Aquinas (1225–1274) who was influenced, not only by Albertus Magnus but by Aristotle's derogatory view of woman:

As regards the individual nature, woman is defective and misbegotten, for the active force in the male seed tends to the production of a perfect likeness in the masculine sex; while the production of woman comes from a defect in the active force or from some material indisposition, or even some external influence, like the south wind, for example, which is damp.

The image of God, in its principal signification, namely the intellectual nature, is found both in man and in woman... But in a secondary sense the image of God is found in man, and not in woman: for man is the beginning and end of woman; as God is the beginning and end of every creature.[19]

In 1130, a well-known French poet, Bernard of Cluny, in a poem called *De contemptu mundi*, contrasted the heavenly world of beauty, light and peace with this fallen one that was contaminated by woman. Woman for him was the symbol of a transient and corrupt Nature, dragging men down to damnation. He was much praised for giving such vivid expression to a then widely accepted belief:

Woman sordid, perfidious, fallen, besmirches purity, meditates impiety, corrupts life.... Woman is a wild beast; her crimes are like the sand....Woman is a guilty thing, a hopelessly fleshly thing, nothing but flesh, vigorous to destroy, born to deceive, and taught to deceive — the last pitfall, worst of vipers, beautiful rottenness, a slippery pathway, public doorway, sweet poison. All guile is she, fickle, and impious, a vessel of filth, an unprofitable vessel....The sins of a man are more pious, more acceptable to the Lord, than the good deeds of a woman.[20]

The misogynistic attitude towards women that prevailed in Greek and Roman culture had distant roots in the dualism of the solar age where light and darkness, good and evil are so strongly polarized. The subservient position of women in those cultures where the solar ethos prevailed was the same as it was to become in later Christian and other patriarchal cultures. It was found not only in the Semitic cultures of the Near and Middle East, and in Greek and Roman culture, but also further to the East, in cultures such as those of India and China, wherever a powerful controlling male priesthood allied to social custom assigned and enforced a subservient position on women.[21]

These ideas, which reflected and confirmed those imbibed from Greek and Roman as well as Jewish culture, entered mainstream Christian teaching and were responsible for an enormous amount of suffering for woman whose inferior and sexual nature came to be seen as the main impediment standing between man and God. It is as if a spell were cast on the Christian psyche by the Myth of the Fall. Torjesen summarises woman's position:

> The equation of woman with sexuality and body... and the exclusion of sexuality and passion from the divine opened up a chasm between woman and God. Only by repudiating her sexual identity and renouncing femaleness could this chasm be bridged. The equation of woman with sexuality meant she was both subordinated to man and alienated from God.[22]

The beliefs and social customs engendered by these projections justified every kind of persecution of woman, from denying her the right to any property and making her subject to her husband, to the witch trials of the fifteenth to eighteenth centuries in which many thousands of women were tortured (their head and genitals shaved so that no devil might conceal himself in their hair) in order to prove their sexual relations with the devil, and died horrifically at the stake. The exact number varies with different authors. Many of these unfortunate women were accused of being witches by other women in their communities.

In 1485, Pope Innocent VIII published a Bull that was followed by the publication in 1487 of the infamous *Malleus Maleficarum* or *Hammer of the Witches*, inaugurating centuries of persecution. This became the handbook of the Inquisition and led to the torture and murder by death at the stake or by hanging of thousands of so-called witches, many of whom were midwives, skilled in the use of herbs for healing. "Never," writes Gregory Zilboorg in his *History of Medical Psychology*, "in the history of humanity was woman more systematically degraded. She paid for the fall of Eve sevenfold, and the Law bore a countenance of pride and self-satisfaction, and the delusional certainty that the will of the Lord had been done."[23]

Carrying the cellular memory of such deeply negative projections onto her as well as the terror arising from this persecution, it has been immensely difficult for women to find their voice and their true role in society and for men to overcome their fear and distrust of, and even their contempt for women.

Misogyny: an Ongoing Legacy

We can trace this negative view of woman right the way through the Middle Ages where she was presented as the flawed moral and intellectual inferior of man and can find it reflected in the prestigious *Roman de la Rose* that was widely read in the fourteenth century. We can listen to the baffled protest of a highly educated woman, Christine de Pizan, who was familiar with this book, writing her own *The Book of the City of Ladies* at the beginning of the fifteenth century. Sitting at her desk one day and leafing through yet another tract full of hatred and virulent condemnation of women, "an extraordinary thought became planted in my mind which made me wonder why on earth it was that so many men have said and continue to say and write such awful, damning things about women and their ways. It is not just a handful of writers who do this…. It is all manner of philosophers, poets and orators too numerous to mention, who all seem to speak with one voice and are unanimous in their view that female nature is wholly given up to vice."

> I dwelt on these thoughts at such length that it was as if I had sunk into a deep trance…. I came to the conclusion that God had surely created a vile thing when He created woman…. This thought inspired such a great sense of disgust and sadness in me that I began to despise myself and the whole of my sex as an aberration in nature…. Sunk in these unhappy thoughts, my head bowed as if in shame and my eyes full of tears, I sat slumped against the arm of my chair with my cheek resting on my hand.[24]

At this point, Christine received a vision or a visitation from three majestic women who said that they had come to encourage her to write a book that would offer support to all women, for "The female sex has been left defenceless for a long time now, like an orchard without a wall, and bereft of a champion to take up arms in order to protect it."[25]   Following this encouragement, Christine says, she began to write her book.

Misogyny and Medical Attitudes and Practices

Quite apart from social attitudes which, for centuries, barred women access to education, the professions and a role in political life, misogynistic attitudes were carried through into the nineteenth century in the medical treatment of women's emotional and physical symptoms. Medical opinion in nineteenth century Europe held that the clitoris was an important source of mental and physical disease as well as hysteria. The initial practice was to apply leaches to the vulva and anus, and to cauterize the clitoris. The first known therapeutic function of X-rays was to irradiate and destroy the clitoris in these women. One can only imagine the excruciating pain women suffered at the hands of these physicians. But these assaults on the female genitalia were superseded by the fashion for clitoridectomy from the 1860's, as Professor John Studd, a contemporary gynaecologist, explains, in a talk given to the Royal College of Obstetricians and Gynaecologists in May, 2011:

> The 19th century medical attitude to normal female sexuality was cruel, with gynecologists and psychiatrists leading the way in designing operations for the cure of the serious contemporary disorders of masturbation and nymphomania. The gynecologist Isaac Baker Brown (1811–1873) and the distinguished

endocrinologist Charles Brown-Séquard (1817–1894) advocated clitoridectomy
to prevent the progression to masturbatory melancholia, paralysis, blindness
and even death. Even after the public disgrace of Baker Brown in 1866–7, the
operation remained respectable and widely used in other parts of Europe. This
medical contempt for normal female sexual development was reflected in
public and literary attitudes. Or perhaps it led and encouraged public opinion.
There is virtually no novel or opera in the last half of the 19th century where
the heroine with 'a past' survives to the end. H. G. Wells's Ann Veronica and
Richard Strauss's Der Rosenkavalier, both of which appeared in 1909, broke
the mould and are important milestones.[26]

We are horrified by the practice of female genital mutilation that is widespread in
different cultures, particularly in parts of Africa, but not long ago, we did not
perceive the barbarity of what was accepted medical practice in Europe. Astonishingly, in the 1980's the School of Tropical Medicine in London was still
instructing students on how to perform this operation.

Female genital mutilation (FGM) was being inflicted on young girls (of foreign
origin) in the United Kingdom until attention was recently drawn to this fact. Up
to 100,000 women living in the UK are thought to have undergone this genital
mutilation and 24,000 more may be at risk (2012). This abhorrent practice has
now been declared illegal for British citizens, whether in the United Kingdom or
abroad and carries a prison sentence of up to 14 years.

Elsewhere however, up to 140 million mainly Muslim women worldwide have,
as little girls, endured the torture and risk of infection caused by female genital
mutilation, often performed without an anaesthetic by their mothers and grand-
mothers.[27] The psychological as well as physical trauma suffered by little girls
who are forced to submit to the pain of this torture is unimaginable. The memory
of the betrayal in the interests of social custom by the people whom they loved
and who they believed loved them will be carried in the psyche for the rest of
their lives.

The Oppression of Woman in Muslim Societies

So deeply embedded in patriarchal culture are the beliefs developed in the solar
era about the dangerous sexuality of women that we can still find them reflected
in Muslim cultures wherever women are confined to the home, denied access to
education and forbidden to take up a profession. Ayaan Hirsi Ali, in her books
Infidel and Nomad has, with immense courage, told the story of her rebellion
against the suffocating role assigned to her as a young woman in Somalia and her

escape from an oppressive tribal society to the intellectual and social freedom of the secular West, and, eventually, to America, where she still needs protection from those who threaten her with death because of her 'betrayal' of Islam.

The persecution of women under the Taliban in Afghanistan is now well-known but there are other Muslim countries such as Pakistan and Saudi Arabia and even Turkey where these social attitudes prevail and where women are considered to be the property of their fathers and husbands and still have no rights or very limited ones. In Pakistan in 2011 almost 1000 women and girls were murdered by their fathers, husbands or brothers in 'honour killings' often covered up by the police (Report Human Rights Commission of Pakistan 2012). Between 2002 and 2011, 4400 women were murdered in Turkey and 42 % of women admit to suffering sexual or physical abuse. The country is 122nd out of 135 in the UN's 2011 Gender Equality Index (*The Times* 28/1/12). Even in the United Kingdom, young women in Muslim communities originating in Pakistan have been forced to marry complete strangers, even first cousins. So strong is the taboo on infringing the honour of the family that some have been murdered by their fathers and brothers for daring to marry someone outside the family's choice of a husband. A recent trial (July 2012) sentenced a mother and father to life imprisonment for murdering their eldest daughter because she had brought shame on their family. Only in June 2012 was there finally a move to make forced marriages illegal and to rescue the many young girls taken to Pakistan against their will and forced to marry a man chosen by their families.

The despicable custom of stoning women to death for adultery is recorded in the Old Testament and existed in the time of Jesus, as the story about him intervening to prevent it illustrates, but stoning to death under Sharia Law is still an accepted practice in Saudi Arabia, Pakistan, Sudan, Iran, Yemen and the UAE and parts of Nigeria and there have also been reported instances of this in Afghanistan and Somalia.[28] Sakineh Mohammadi Ashtiani would have died in this manner if an outraged world had not protested. One of the lawyers who defended her case is still in prison. An Afghan woman recently had her nose and ears cut off and was left for dead on a freezing hill. Her crime? She had dared to leave her abusive husband (2010). She was rescued by villagers and helped to escape to America where she has had reconstructive surgery. Her father has been threatened with death because he committed the unpardonable sin of allowing his daughter to find refuge with "unbelievers" and had therefore shamed his community.

Asia Bibi, a Christian Pakistani woman, is in prison (2011) and under threat of death for blasphemy for daring to ask to drink from the same bucket as other women in her village, having asked them what benefit Islam had brought to those as poor as she. Her case led to two political assassinations of men who spoke out against the blasphemy laws in Pakistan, one of them the Governor of the Punjab.

The recent conflicts in Iraq and Afghanistan have accomplished one positive thing: they have revealed to the eyes of the world the appalling suffering and oppression of women in Islamic societies, even if they haven't put an end to it. Ayaan Hirsi Ali's own words offer the best testimony to the roots of this oppression:

> Virginity is the obsession, the neurosis of Islam. Wherever there is a Muslim community, forced or coerced marriage, even child marriage, is common, even in families who are relatively educated. Like domestic violence, most people consider it normal. Men are the guardians of their daughters. A girl is therefore the property of her father, who is entitled to transfer that property to the husband he selects.[29]

She compares the liberation of women to a vast unfinished house. The west wing of the house is in reasonably good order and women in this wing enjoy the right to vote and run for office, have access to education and enter any number of professions. Domestic violence, sexual harassment, and rape are recognized in law as crimes for which the perpetrator is held accountable and punished. Women have access to contraception and therefore to reproductive rights over their bodies and their sexuality.

But in the east wing, it is a different story. The work is unfinished, even abandoned, and parts of it are falling into ruin. The lives of women are harsh. They can be beaten and even murdered by their families and husbands without real redress in law. They cannot go out unaccompanied by a male relative. Thousands of young women die while giving birth because they have no access to the most basic hygiene and medical care.[30]

The story of the liberation of women from their millennia-long oppression is unfinished; centuries may pass before the building of the eastern house can be completed and the remaining anomalies in the western house removed.

The Decree of the Catholic Church 2010

Even in the west wing, the house is not finished. Returning to Christianity, the latest decree of the Catholic Church relating to women (July 2010) elevates the ordination of women to one of the most serious crimes in Canon Law — putting it on the same level as child abuse in the eyes of the Church. It is truly incredible that anyone ordaining a woman into the priesthood should be excommunicated by an Office that was formerly the source of the Inquisition. How is it possible that something so grossly offensive to women could have passed into Canon Law? We may wonder how it is conceivable in this day and age when women have begun to grow into their true potential against the original virulent opposition of both Church and State, for the Catholic Church, governed entirely by celibate males, to make such a preposterous ruling. To believe that 'God' would want things to continue as they have done for centuries, marginalizing women and barring them from expressing their great gifts of compassion and empathy in the service of the sacred, is to assume that the Catholic Church has privileged access to God's ear — an inflated and absurd position. In the Anglican Church also, a number of priests have declared their opposition to women bishops and are joining the Catholic Church. Karen Armstrong, in the last paragraph of her book *The End of Silence: Women and the Priesthood*, concludes: "Present attitudes of misogyny and unresolved conflicts must be brought out into the open, and the pain experienced by women within the Churches must also be addressed. It will be a long hard road, but there is no alternative if the profound disorders and injustices of the past are to be healed."

From a Jungian perspective, the phobic fear of woman in patriarchal culture reflects the fear of the evolving organ of consciousness – the ego – being swallowed up by the primordial undifferentiated unity, the maw or womb of nature. Woman herself was unconsciously identified with that all-devouring maw: the sin of Eve proved her untrustworthiness. For men who are deeply insecure in their masculinity, who have never had a mature relationship, let alone a sexual relationship with a woman, whose internalized image of woman is undeveloped because woman has never been valued for herself, but only for the service she can render to man, an independent and educated woman and, God forbid, an ordained woman, will present a threat — unconsciously, the threat of castration and death.

The Long-term Effects of the Myth of the Fall

Generations of Christian men and women have sat in church listening to the story of the Fall, absorbing it as the word of God and as divinely revealed truth. How were they affected by it? How has it programmed man's unconscious attitude towards woman, sexuality in general and woman's view of herself? It is possible that the violent patterns of behaviour in society we still encounter, from murder, rape, trafficking, domestic violence against women as well as pornography and the sexual abuse of children have their roots in the interpretation given to this myth.

According to recent statistics posted on the Internet, the most conservative estimates suggest that worldwide, two to four million women of all races and classes are battered by their partners each year. In the United States, over a thousand women are murdered by their partners every year. In the United Kingdom, over a hundred women a year are murdered by their partners or husbands. Domestic violence accounts for 23% of all violent crime and this is increasing. The trauma inflicted on children by domestic violence cannot be quantified but calls to Child-Line in 2011 have increased by a third in five years.[31] Thousands of children run away from their homes each year or are taken into care. Many of these are inducted into sexual slavery on the streets of our cities, as the horrific case of young girls groomed and repeatedly raped by Pakistani men in Rochdale (May 2012) and Rotherham (September 2012) illustrates. The number of rapes in domestic situations, on city streets and in war is not known but is huge. The latest scandal involving the abuse of young women and girls has focused on the evidence that has emerged about the behaviour of Jimmy Savile, now a disgraced hero. While these figures cannot be attributed exclusively to the influence of religious indoctrination, nevertheless I believe that over the centuries this has laid the ground for the infliction of intolerable violence and degradation on woman.

There is another aspect to the contempt for women reflected in the tragic fate of the millions of young women who are trafficked as sex slaves (worldwide estimate is 4 million). Millions of women from poorer countries in eastern Europe, Asia, Africa and South America are being forced, for their survival or in the hope of a better life, to enter into prostitution and even slavery because there is a 'market' for sex among men who still see women as sexual objects to be exploited and subjugated, thereby perpetuating the pattern of male dominance over them. Duped into believing that they will find employment in the richer countries, they travel to them, only to find their passports confiscated by the men who have trafficked them. They become virtual prisoners, unable to escape from this vile trade.

What unconscious negative beliefs about herself might woman in every culture carry as a result of the silent suffering and outright persecution she has endured for millennia? What unconscious misogynistic beliefs do men still hold which allow them to injure, rape and murder women in this way? Fifty thousand mainly Muslim women were raped in the Bosnian war; 400,000 in Rwanda; an unquantifiable number of women and young girls in Darfur and the Democratic Republic of Congo. Rapes are currently an intrinsic part of the appalling suffering of civilians in Syria. Women who are raped are regarded as contaminated: they are shamed and ostracised by their communities, rejected by their husbands and families and traumatized for life. Only a minute handful of men responsible for these rapes are convicted of this crime because rape has always been regarded as a legitimate weapon of war.

The Effects on Children

Generations of children have sat in church and Sunday School and been imprinted with the idea that, long ago, a woman disobeyed God and succumbed to the temptation of the serpent, bringing sin, death and suffering into the world and that her suffering and even her death in childbirth were a punishment for that original sin. They also learned that Eve tempted Adam to eat the apple from the Tree of Knowledge and so was to blame for his fall and his being forced to toil for his living. How, I wondered, would this myth have influenced children's view of their mothers and fathers, and their own developing sexuality? Suppose their mother died in childbirth. How would this myth have affected their memory of her? How did it influence the attitude of boys towards girls and girls' view of themselves? It has surely contributed to women's deep unconscious feeling of inferiority. In both men and women it would have set up a great conflict in their nature, making them distrustful of their instincts and guilty about sex, believing that this vindictive, punishing, angry God demanded the repression or even the sacrifice of their sexuality as an expiation for the contamination of their inherited sin and as a kind of guarantee of their spirituality.

Again, how has the Myth of the Fall affected the Christian attitude towards children? Generations of children had sin and evil beaten out of them lest they should fall into the clutches of the devil. Masturbation not long ago was regarded as a sin and severely punished. Many thousands of children have suffered terrible trauma at the hands of priests and nuns. The repellent accounts of the sadistic punishments meted out by these celibate servants of God are only just coming to light in recently published reports in Ireland (the Ryan and Murphy Reports 2009 and the Cloyne Report 2011) as well as in the accounts of the abuse inflicted by the Catholic Christian Brothers and Sisters of Mercy on orphaned children sent to Australia at the beginning of the last war. In the Jamie Bulger case (1993) where two ten-year-old boys tortured and murdered a toddler, people wrote to *The Times* (in England) saying that all children were born sinful, and were therefore likely to be programmed to do evil.

All this seems outrageous but also tragic because it was so completely unnecessary. It boils down to shocking indoctrination over many hundreds of years. As a therapist and as a woman, I have been made deeply aware of the misogyny in the culture as a whole and the guilt women carry, as well as men's unconscious fear of and contempt for women and women's fear and distrust of men as well as their inability to value and respect their bodies. I can see clearly that these stem at least in part from the calamitous legacy of the later as well as the early Christian Fathers, for Luther and Calvin perpetuated many of these ideas at the time of the

Reformation and they are disseminated in Protestantism as well as Catholicism. What comes through these Christian writings is a deep sado-masochism: sadism towards woman in general; masochism because this preoccupation with sexual sin and guilt led men and women to cultivate a quite unnecessary, almost hysterical sense of sin, guilt and self-blame. It may be this unconscious sense of guilt and self-blame that still prevents women from leaving abusive and violent partners and still sees them presented in the media as predominantly sexual 'objects' who, on losing their sexual attractiveness, are no longer of any interest to society. The anger and distrust held in deeply unconscious memories may also contribute to the mutual struggle for control and the consequent break-up of relationships between men and women which costs the state £44 billion a year in the UK (Office of National Statistics 2011 for 2010 figures) and causes children enormous distress.

The meta-narrative of the Myth of the Fall which has such deep roots in the solar age cast a negative pall over the Christian attitude towards life in this world. Instead of helping to alleviate human suffering, it has immeasurably increased it. Culturally, it contributed to man's contempt for woman's 'hysteria and emotion-ality', and strengthened the prejudice which for centuries barred her access to education and an effective place in the world in any of the professions exercised by men, including the priesthood and the medical profession. Until very recently in the United Kingdom, it underlay the judicial opinion in rape trials that women had "asked for it". It has wounded man's internalized image of woman and given him a good reason for mistrusting and dissociating himself from his own feelings as well as giving rise to an obsessive need to control them.

In the political sphere, we are confronted by the violent history of Christianity which has contrasted so strangely with the teaching of Christ, who spoke of love and compassion and our son-ship with God — even of the innate divinity of all humanity ("Ye are gods" John 10: 34), as well as the need to love our enemies and forgive those who do us harm. We didn't really need any other direction than to follow the golden rule that we should do unto others as we would be done by — that compassion should be our guide. What happened to that luminous value in the brutal treatment of women, the sexual abuse of children, the persecution of heretics, the bloody conquests in the name of Christianity, the inquisitions, tortures, burnings and the repression of any group or individual who threatened the established Church? Where is it in the contemporary Evangelical Christian belief in the 'Rapture', which envisages the Elect being taken to heaven in the 'End-Days' and the rest left to perish — an idea that originates with St. Augustine's theory of predestination? Christianity today has become splintered by schisms and bitter arguments over the issue of women priests and homosexuality. Words from the Old Testament that were believed to enshrine divine revelation, written down well over two thousand years ago in a culture utterly different from our own, are invoked to support entrenched prejudices. The actual teaching of Christ about love and forgiveness appears to have been overlooked.

Nor can we ignore the quite unwarranted sense of the moral and spiritual superiority of Christians towards other religions, their attempt to convert people to the 'true' religion and the omnipotent control exercised by the Church over its flock. Indigenous Peoples in the New World were regarded as inferior, primitive and 'close to nature'— therefore rightly subjected to the superior power of the white European conquerors and needing to be converted to their religion. We have also to recognize the long-term effects of the expulsion of the Moors from Spain and the Crusades against the Muslim infidel which are carried right through to our own time in the unresolved tension between Christianity and Islam that lurks beneath the 'War on Terror'.

We need to take into account attitudes to the body and sexuality and the belief that a life dedicated to God demanded the sacrifice of sexuality and that this sacrifice was pleasing to Him. The idea of atonement and reparation for evil had long existed in the work of the Greek tragedians but no one, until the advent of Christianity, had suggested that sexuality itself was a sin for which one had to atone. It may be this repression of an essential human instinct that has led, over the centuries and into our own time, not only to male violence against women but to the evil of pornography which subjugates and violates woman's body, and to the abhorrent rape and sexual abuse of young boys and girls by Catholic priests who were entrusted with their care. One may wonder about the terrible traumas inflicted on children which have been concealed for centuries and are now, thankfully, coming to light.[32]

No one is allowed to challenge the Catholic Church's rigid rules on contraception. It is strange that, in a world where over-population is one of the major problems confronting our species and the planet itself, the Church still maintains its position on this issue, even in Africa where, in the face of an AIDS epidemic that is destroying countless millions of lives, it counsels abstinence rather than the use of condoms, saying that condoms would lead to promiscuity. In South America and countries like the Philippines, where Catholicism is the predominant religion, women are told that it is their religious duty to deny themselves the help of contraception. Because of this, they are forced to bear too many children, far beyond their strength and ability to look after them. These children, sometimes ten or more in a family, living in the favelas or shanty towns of South America (Brazil) and the poorer quarters of the Philippines, can barely survive and fall victim to drug dealers, sexual abuse, lack of access to education and the deterioration of their health and happiness. Again, we find the control of woman's sexuality by celibate men at the root of this belief. What unconscious fear of and contempt for women lies behind this need for control? And why do women accept it unless they are afraid of divine punishment? How does this preposterous ruling on contraception contribute to the growth of the world's population?

Dr. Uta Ranke-Heinemann, who holds the chair for religious history at Essen University, has written a book entitled *Eunuchs for Heaven*. In the Introduction to her devastating critique of the Church's hostility towards sexuality and women, she deplores how a long historical process has

> transformed Christianity from what it was or should have been — a religion founded on personal experience of the universally accessible love of God, in which the body has its natural and God-given place — into a regime imposed by an unmarried oligarchy on a subordinate and largely married majority. This has perverted the work of him from whom the Christians take their name.[33]

In contrast to the shadow aspect of Christianity described in these two chapters there is the behaviour of countless millions of Christians who, over two millennia, have tried to live the essential message of Christ in innumerable acts of compassion, and in the courageous defence of others in the face of the threat of their own death, in attempts to establish justice for the downtrodden and oppressed, and in setting up charities to help those less fortunate than themselves. Also in contrast is the legacy of sublime art, architecture, literature and music which arose in response to the inspiration of the life of Christ and His Mother and which I came to value deeply in the course of my quest.

Conclusion

This chapter and the last have shown how the two great religious meta-narratives of the solar age in Western civilization — the Myth of the Fall and the Doctrine of Original Sin — created a dualistic belief system that split nature from spirit, and body from mind and soul. In their attempt to explain the existence of sin, death and evil, they taught generations of men and women that this world was a place of suffering, sin and punishment, and that the spiritual life demanded a rejection of this world. These two chapters have explored a pathology which is deeply embedded in a religion that is now embraced by over 2 billion people. It constitutes an unconscious collective thought form which is extremely difficult to transform and heal because it is so deeply unconscious. Moreover, these meta-narratives are still being disseminated wherever Christianity is carried today, particularly in Africa. The whole edifice of Christian belief rests on the twin pillars of belief in the Fall of Man and the consequent need for our redemption by Christ's sacrificial death.

It may be that, from the time of St. Augustine, Christianity has taken a disastrous detour under the spell of a myth and the formulation of a doctrine that have nothing whatever to do with the actual teaching of Christ, which was about the transformation of consciousness rather than belief as the way to salvation. It has split man off from his instinctive soul, casting a heavy pall of guilt on his apparently depraved existence. It has removed responsibility from man, seeing his redemption as already accomplished by the sacrificial death of the Son of God who becomes the ultimate scapegoat who dies for humanity's sins.

Nowhere in the Myth of the Fall do we find the celebration of the sacred nature of sexual love. Nor do we find the recognition of nature as a Sacred Order of reality. On the contrary, expulsion from the Garden of Eden and the suffering of both man and woman in this world were presented as a divinely imposed punishment for the role of Adam and Eve in initiating the Fall.

We might well wonder what the effect on Christianity would be if the Doctrine of Original Sin that has so wounded the soul were expunged from Christian doctrine, and if the Myth of the Fall were interpreted as a metaphor for the birth of consciousness rather than the reason why we needed a Redeemer, so freeing both soul and body from the heavy burden they have carried for some sixteen hundred years.

Notes:

1. Holland, Jack (2006) *Misogyny: The World's Oldest Prejudice,*
   Constable and Robinson Ltd., London, p. 31
2. Torjesen, Karen Jo (1995) *When Women Were Priests*, HarperSanFrancisco, p. 180
3. ibid, p. 181
4. ibid, p. 211
5. Bourgeault, Cynthia (2010) *The Meaning of Mary Magdalene,*
   Shambhala Publications Inc., Boston, p. x
6. *The Gospel of Philip*, Nag Hammadi Library, ed. James M. Robinson,
   E.J. Brill, Leiden, 1977, p. 138
7. Bourgeault, pp. 15-16
8. ibid, p. 41
9. ibid, pp. 51 & 55
10. *The Dialogue of the Savior*, Nag Hammadi Library, p. 235
11. Bourgeault, p. 87
12. Bourgeault, p. 88
13. Irenaeus, *Adversus Haereses,*111. xxii. 4
14. Tertullian, *de Virginibus Velandis* 9
15. Tertullian, *de Cultu Foeminarium*

16. Ranke-Heinemann, Uta (1990) *Eunuchs for Heaven*, English trs.
    André Deutsch Ltd., London p. 104
17. Gratian, *Decretum*
18. Ranke-Heinemann, p. 157 quoting from *Quaestiones super de animalibus*, XV, q.11
19. Thomas Aquinas, *Summa Theologica*
20. *De contemptu mundi.* Hoskier 1929. Translation from S.M. Jackson, *The Source of
    Jerusalem the Golden.* Chicago 1919, pp.139-40. Quoted in William Anderson,
    The Rise of the Gothic, p. 126
21. French, Marilyn (2002) *From Eve to Dawn: A History of Women*,
    McArthur & Co., Toronto
22. Torjesen, p. 222
23. Zilboorg, Gregory (1941&1967) *A History of Medical Psychology*,
    W.W. Norton & Company, New York, p. 162
24. Pizan, Christine de (1999) *The Book of the City of Ladies*,
    Penguin Books, London, p. 6-7
25. ibid, p.11
26. Professor John Studd FRCG, extract from the annual Founder's Oration to the Royal
    College of Obstetricians and Gynaecologists May, 2011, entitled *19th century attitudes to
    female sexuality as portrayed in medicine, literature, art and music.*
27. The World Health Organisation fact sheet 2010 estimates that 100 to 140 million girls and
    women worldwide (92 million girls over 10 in Africa alone) have undergone female genital
    mutilation. This involves the excision of the clitoris as well as the cutting of the labia, the
    outer part of the vagina and, in some cases, having the opening of their vagina sewn
    together, leaving only a small opening, to ensure that they are virgins when they marry.
28. article in *The Times* by Diana Quick, 26/10/2011. The United Nations Human rights
    Commission has declared female genital mutilation to be illegal 28/11/12.
29. Ali, Ayaan Hirsi (2010) *Nomad, From Islam to America: A Personal Journey through the
    Clash of Civilizations*, Simon and Schuster, London, p. 230
30. Ali, pp. 233-234
31. statistics taken from a variety of sources on Google 2011
32. Evidence of the rape of children by Catholic priests is coming to light (2010–11) in
    America, Ireland, Austria, Germany, Italy, Spain, Switzerland, the Netherlands and Brazil.
33. Ranke-Heinemann, introduction p. x

On the 12th January 2013 the first government overview of sexual offending in Britain was published in a study by the Ministry of Justice, Home Office and Office of National Statistics. It has revealed that an estimated 85,000 women a year are victims of rape or serious sexual assault (*The Times*).

The Myth of the Fall has been explored in more detail in *The Myth of the Goddess*, Chapter Thirteen and in a book called *Eve: The History of an Idea*, by J.A. Phillips, Harper & Row, San Francisco, 1984. I would recommend Uta Ranke-Heinemann's book and the books by Charles Freeman, mentioned in this chapter and the last, to the reader who wishes to understand more about the crucially important fourth century.

Meditation

I would like to offer a meditation on the body, to restore its value and its preciousness as a temple and as the physical manifestation of the soul — the vital connecting intermediary between matter and spirit:

Imagine your body as a vessel; a receiver and transmitter of light.

Imagine there is a glowing jewel in the place of each of the seven chakras: ruby, fire opal, topaz, emerald, sapphire, amethyst and diamond.

Thank it for everything it has done for you in your life, past and present.

Thank it for the miracle of its being.

Say to it that you deeply regret that it was made to suffer in the past and that you will take great care of it in the future.

Imagine love flowing from your heart into every part of it, flooding it with light.

Recognize your body as the connecting link between invisible spirit and the physical environment all round you: the earth, the trees, the plants and flowers, the food you eat, all the things you make and creatively transform with the raw materials of life.

See it as the finest transparent substance, like crystal or a beautiful jewel, such as a diamond. See that crystalline or jewel-like form irradiated by the healing light of the cosmos that flows through and sustains the whole of the manifest world.

A momentous publication (2010) called *The Gospel of the Beloved Companion: The Complete Gospel of Mary Magdalene* by Jehanne de Quillan came into my hands after my book was published in 2013. It purports to be the complete Gospel written by Mary Magdalene and fills in the missing sections in the known Gospel of Mary with astonishing new material that constitutes a priceless spiritual treasure. It also confirms that Mary was Jesus' beloved. The manuscript was reputedly brought from Alexandria to the Languedoc area of France in the first century and was translated into Occitan (the language of the Languedoc) in the early twelfth century. The manuscript has been preserved within a spiritual community there since that time. Mary Magdalene is thought to have lived and taught in this region from AD 44 to 63 and was buried in the Basilica Saint-Maximin-La-Sainte-Baume, Provence.

Head of a Poet
Robin Baring 1974

Chapter Nine

A ONE-EYED VISION

Modern Man talks of a battle with nature, forgetting that, if he won the battle, he would find himself on the losing side.

— E.F. Schumacher

Our normal waking consciousness, rational consciousness as we call it, is but one special type of consciousness, whilst all about it, parted from it by the filmiest of screens, there lie potential forms of consciousness entirely different.... No account of the universe in its totality can be final which leaves these other forms of consciousness quite disregarded.

— William James *The Varieties of Religious Experience*[1]

So we come to the present time where, in a secular culture, the rational human mind has established itself as the supreme value, master of all it surveys, recognizing no power, no consciousness beyond itself. It has lost its connection to soul, not only soul in the individual sense but soul as a cosmic matrix or field in whose life we participate. In its hubristic stance, the modern mind has become disconnected from the deeper matrix out of which it has evolved. With the passionate conviction of the iconoclast who cannot tolerate the existence of anything which threatens his or her belief, it contemptuously denigrates and derides everything it perceives as non-rational, labelling it as 'mysticism' or 'superstition'.

This attitude, I think, points to my dream of the tower-like iron structure erected on the surface of the moon. It reflects the rigid stance of the rational mind or ego which now stands like a tyrant over and against Nature, over and against the Earth, over and against whatever it defines as threatening to its supremacy, the achievement of its secular aims and its definition of progress. This leaves the neglected territory of the soul a wasteland as barren as the surface of the moon.

From this brief survey of the solar era which has, it is true to say, focused more on the dark than on the light aspect of this age, it is possible to see that the belief system of scientific materialism (reductionism) which now dominates our culture and which will be explored in this chapter and in Chapter Fourteen, can be understood as the end result of the long-standing dissociation of spirit and nature, mind and matter but, above all, the sundering within us of thinking and feeling, rational mind and instinctive soul — the solar and lunar, conscious and unconscious aspects of our nature. Our psyche and our culture are now profoundly out of balance and this fact is reflected in the mounting political, social, financial and economic problems which confront us and which have no solution if we do not, as Einstein suggested, change our way of thinking.

There is a moment in a book called *A Journey in Ladakh* by Andrew Harvey, where he records the words of a Tibetan monk, Nawang Tsering. Referring to this present time as *Kali Yuga* — the Age of Darkness and Destruction — Nawang says that the great danger for the world now is the loss of spiritual vision and that our task is to keep that vision alive, to see that it lives through these dark times. He speaks of the powers of love, healing and clarity that lie latent within each one of us and asks that we should strive to develop these, both for our own sakes and for that of others and says that we will need to attune ourselves to the deepest levels of spirit if we are to have a hope of surviving this era.[2]

Looking at the state of the world and the helpless, inarticulate suffering of so many millions of people, as well as our ongoing and interminable addiction to weaponry and war, it seems obvious that our current moral and spiritual immaturity threatens our very survival as a species. In the midst of this present darkness, how can we invoke the powers of love, of healing, of clear vision? How can we become aware of the influence of the deeply embedded beliefs outlined in previous chapters and understand how they are still controlling us and contributing to the ongoing suffering of humanity?

A One-eyed Consciousness

Certain myths, ideas or belief systems grow into meta-narratives, worldviews or paradigms of reality which can inspire, structure and influence a culture for hundreds, even thousands of years. But they may also block our further development by subtle methods of control that are difficult to see. In the West, we have been influenced by two primary meta-narratives or stories: the Christian one of a transcendent Creator-God and a fallen creation, and the more recent scientific one which says that we exist in an inanimate universe which is without consciousness, meaning or purpose.

Early in the 20th century the French artist Odilon Redon painted a picture of the one-eyed giant, the Cyclops. Its single eye gazes out over a flower-strewn expanse where a naked woman lies in a brilliantly luminous landscape. To me, the image of the Cyclops reflects the constriction as well as the inflation of the modern mind which, unaware of the vast dimensions of planetary and cosmic life on which it rests and out of which it has evolved, believes itself to be in control of nature and its own nature. It evokes Blake's much-quoted words: "May God us keep from the single vision and Newton's sleep."[3]

Yet the painting also communicates a tremendous sadness, the sadness of a one-eyed consciousness that is cut off from its ground; that has no relationship with soul and with nature, personified in this painting by the woman lying on a flower-strewn ground. The rational or literal secular eye stands lonely and supreme, alienated from the landscape of the soul.

Since the sixteenth century, but more pervasively during the last fifty years, a secular worldview or philosophy has slowly infiltrated every aspect of the modern world, dominating the media, the arts, science and philosophy as well as economic, political and educational agendas. It views life through an increasingly utilitarian and materialistic mindset, seeing no goal for humanity beyond the survival of our ever-increasing numbers and the improvement of material conditions through scientific, medical and technological advance. By excluding, rejecting and deriding so much, particularly in relation to the great spiritual and cultural achievements of the past and the unanswered questions of the human condition, it drastically limits our understanding of ourselves and our place in the cosmos. It has turned its back on the whole unsolved mystery of our existence; on the great questions of who we are and why we are here, on this planet. It even believes that our species has attained the highest level of mental development of which it is capable. What it fails to mention is the fact that our moral development as a species lags far behind our technological achievements.

However, there is another kind of eye which has been called the eye of the heart or the eye of the soul. The flowering of poetic vision and the revelations of mystical and shamanic experience in many cultures over many thousands of years are vital reminders that we are entirely capable of a different kind of knowing, a different quality of relationship with what we call reality. The great sages of India, Tibet and China as well as the great mystics of the West, have known for thousands of years that we can access a deeper, more complete or enlightened state of consciousness than the one that usually engages our attention — a consciousness that is attuned to an unseen ground of being.

A hundred years or so ago, a man called Richard Maurice Bucke wrote a book called *Cosmic Consciousness* in which he described the lives of individuals who have experienced dimensions of consciousness still unimagined and unrealized by most of us. He believed that the whole human species might one day attain this state.[4]

Could this state of deeper knowing and experiencing, this capacity for a more profound relationship with life, be developed in all of us? And would this different quality of knowing enable us to experience a dimension of reality in which we are unknowingly embedded, a dimension that Plato once named the soul of the cosmos, animated by the creative agents of cosmic life — variously named in different cultures as goddesses and gods, daemonic spirits, angels and archangels? Could our own consciousness, which includes the whole spectrum of experience between animal instinct and the highest potential of the imagination and intellect, participate once again in this greater planetary and cosmic soul of which our culture has lost all awareness?

Sometimes, a single book can throw light on the character of an age and the changes that are in preparation for an age to come. In the early 1920's Pitirim Sorokin (1889–1968) was Professor of Sociology at the University of St. Petersburg. Sentenced to death by both the Tsarists and the Bolsheviks, he was banished in 1922 and took refuge in America where he became Head of Sociology at Harvard. There, he wrote a book called *The Crisis of Our Age*, published in 1941. In it he defined three different kinds of culture: the Ideational, the Idealistic and the Sensate. He saw the whole process of human history as a cyclical alternation between spiritual and materialistic cultures and saw our present age as a time of one of the most significant and crucial transitions in human history from one age to another.

He identified the European culture of the last six hundred years (particularly the last four hundred) as a Sensate one, which succeeded and replaced the waning Ideational culture of the Middle Ages. The focus of the medieval Ideational culture was on spirit; the focus of the current Sensate one is on matter and the phenomenal world. Spiritual values, and belief in a transcendent omniscient Deity who created the world and man, have gradually yielded to secular values and the belief that material reality and our sensory, empirical perception of it is the only valid focus for our attention and the only existing reality. Over the past four centuries, a Sensate culture has become the dominant one and has seen a phenomenal scientific advance which has affected every aspect of our lives, writing, as he says, one of the most brilliant pages in human history. However, no finite form, either ideational or sensate, is eternal. Sooner or later it is bound to exhaust its creative abilities. When this moment comes, it begins to disintegrate and decline.[5]

In the Ideational culture of the Middle Ages, matter, the body and sexuality were split off from spirit, seen as contaminated by the sin of the Fall, whereas in our current Sensate culture, matter, the body and sexuality have moved centre stage and it is spirit which has been marginalized or eliminated. One culture excluded the body; the other has excluded spirit. In each case, a belief system was established and the system itself promoted as infallible. This totalitarian tendency in both religion and science is clearly discernible and can present a danger to us because of its unbalanced position. By ridicule, distortion and neglect, our Sensate culture has undermined the highest spiritual values and achievements of the previous Ideational era. In Sorokin's view, our now decadent Sensate culture had, by the time of his book (1941), exhausted its creative potential and was in the process of dying. He saw the calamitous ideological wars of the twentieth century as a primary symptom of its decadence.

> The present crisis is not ordinary but extraordinary. It is not merely an economic or political maladjustment, but involves simultaneously almost the whole of Western culture and society. It is a crisis in their art and science, philosophy and religion, law and morals, manners and mores; in the forms of social, political and economic organization, including the nature of the family and marriage — in brief, it is a crisis involving almost the whole way of life, thought and conduct of Western society. More precisely, it consists in a disintegration of a fundamental form of Western culture and society dominant for the last four centuries.[6]

Yet, in defining our current crisis, he did not feel it would necessarily lead to the disintegration and collapse of Western civilization; rather, he believed that we were living through the difficult transitional period between the death of the dominant Sensate culture and the birth of a new Ideational one:

> Even if it does not mean the extinction of Western culture and society, it nevertheless signifies one of the greatest possible revolutions in our culture and social life…. We have the rare privilege of living, observing, thinking and acting in the conflagration of such an ordeal. If we cannot stop it, we can at least try to understand its nature, its causes and its consequences. If we do this, we may be able, to some extent, to shorten its tragic period and to mitigate its ravages.[7]

The Secular Worldview

Bertrand Russell (1872–1970) described the secular philosophy of a Sensate culture in this powerful and moving extract from his famous essay *The Free Man's Worship*, published in 1903 and hailed as a landmark of early twentieth century thought:

That Man is the product of causes which had no prevision of the end they were achieving; that his origin, his growth, his hopes and fears, his loves and his beliefs, are but the outcome of accidental collocations of atoms; that no fire, no heroism, no intensity of thought and feeling, can preserve an individual life beyond the grave; that all the labours of the ages, all the devotion, all the inspiration, all the noonday brightness of human genius, are destined to extinction in the vast death of the solar system, and that the whole temple of Man's achievement must inevitably be buried beneath the debris of a universe in ruins — all these things, if not quite beyond dispute, are yet so nearly certain, that no philosophy which rejects them can hope to stand. Only within the scaffolding of these truths, only on the firm foundation of unyielding despair, can the soul's habitation henceforth be safely built. How, in such an alien and inhuman world, can so powerless a creature as Man preserve his aspirations untarnished?[8]

How indeed? We can see how this philosophy came into being but surely we should question its conclusions. Currently, the dominant philosophy of our modern Sensate culture is the Neo-Darwinian one that life on this planet has evolved by natural selection and the survival of the fittest, and that we are simply the product of our biological genes and our interaction with our environment. We are the products of mindless forces operating on inanimate matter; atoms are lifeless particles, floating in a dead universe; matter is primary and gives rise to mind as a secondary phenomenon.

The secular materialist philosophy which has spread from the West to every part of the modern industrialized world can be summarized as follows:

- Consciousness is an epiphenomenon or product of the physical brain.

- There is no survival of consciousness after death because the death of the physical brain is the end of consciousness.

- God is an unproven hypothesis and the concept of the soul an irrelevance.

- The life of the universe came into being by chance.

- The universe we see as well as the sub-atomic matter science explores is inanimate and 'dead'.

- There is no transcendent purpose or meaning to our lives.

As Francis Crick, the co-discoverer of DNA, bleakly described us: "You, your joys and your sorrows, your memories and your ambitions, your sense of personal identity and free will, are in fact no more than the behaviour of a vast assembly of nerve cells and associated molecules."[9] It is easy to conclude from this that the body is a mechanism that can be manipulated and controlled by the mind and it also removes any foundation for moral values.

This reductionist hypothesis developing from a Newtonian/Cartesian/Darwinian foundation and presented as 'truth' empties the entire human endeavour of meaning, purpose and significance. There is no vertical axis, nothing that might connect us to a field of consciousness that is beyond our immediate sensory experience. While I think it is true to say that reductionist science and the secular ideology that has developed out of it over the last four hundred years has freed large sections of humanity from the absolute control of religious institutions, it would also seem to have replaced one rigid belief system with another.

The main problem with this philosophy is that it excludes from discussion and validation anything that does not fit in with its convictions, in exactly the same way that the Christian Church, in its persecution of Galileo in the sixteenth century, excluded the new scientific discoveries. By devious means it suppresses a mass of data that could be of immense interest, relevance and value to our culture. This censorship is, in itself, unscientific. One example of this is the repeated attempts to disparage and invalidate alternative approaches to healing, such as homeopathy and acupuncture — saying that because their efficacy cannot be proven, they are worthless. The paranormal is also excluded, forgetting that Einstein presciently observed that the paranormal of today is the normal of tomorrow.

Modern secular culture has exalted man as the supreme agent of his own triumphant scientific and technological progress but it has also reduced him to the level of a biological mechanism, subject to the programming of his genetic inheritance. It has created a society that is obsessed with its technological prowess, fascinated by the digital revolution and the omnipotent power of science and the human mind. It has done away with any ethical foundation for values and acts as if technology itself could solve our problems, ignoring the fact that we are completely dependent on the planet's dwindling resources for our survival. It does not question the premises which direct its conclusions nor does it look at the effects of its beliefs on children growing up in this morally defective culture. It could be said that we live in an unconscious civilization, as the Canadian philosopher John Ralston Saul describes it in his book of that title.[10]

However, this is not the whole story. What seems to be happening now in our culture is very interesting. Surviving elements from the older Ideational culture (Christianity, Judaism and Islam) are in conflict with the prevailing materialist values of the current secular Sensate culture, grinding together like two tectonic plates. At the same time, a new Ideational culture is being prepared by those seeking to distance themselves from the rigidity of both the old religious beliefs and the modern secular ones. These individuals are motivated by an awareness of the urgent need to formulate values which could transform our present attitude to the planet from one of dominance and exploitation to one of responsibility and service.

The challenge of climate change with its potentially devastating effects on all planetary life is intensifying the tension as well as pointing to the values and issues that were ignored in both the older Ideational culture and the modern Sensate one: namely, respect for the Earth and the recognition that our lives and our well-being are inseparably bound up with planetary life. The meltdown in the financial markets (2008–12) — the corruption of the banking system, together with the risky practice of borrowing or printing colossal sums of money which have no relationship whatever to what we are earning — has shown the fragility of a system that once seemed secure. The new ideology of a United Europe and the instability of the whole Eurozone is another factor contributing to this perilous situation as are the spreading tentacles of the military-industrial complex in the most powerful nations. As the gap between those who manipulate and control the markets and the mass of people who are their hapless victims widens, the prospect of economic and societal collapse in different areas of the world draws nearer. But beyond all these is our relationship, or the lack of it, with the Earth. As Thomas Berry (1914–2009), a Catholic theologian who, like Schumacher, was one of the most enlightened spokesmen of the emerging Ideational culture, observes in his book, *The Dream of the Earth*:

> Suddenly we awaken to the devastation that has resulted from the entire modern process…. In relation to the earth, we have been autistic for centuries. Only now have we begun to listen with some attention and with a willingness to respond to the earth's demands that we cease our industrial assault, that we abandon our inner rage against the conditions of our earthly existence, that we renew our human participation in the grand liturgy of the universe.[11]

The Great Adventure of Our Time

If we move from the secular ideology of science to the actual discoveries of science, it is a different story — no longer presenting a nihilistic view of human existence but an ever-expanding trajectory of stupendous discoveries that engage our awe and wonder. Like the beautiful glowing comet Hale-Bopp that we watched illumine the night skies of 1997, something absolutely new is shining on the horizon of consciousness: in the last few decades, science has opened up an immense and thrilling panorama of the Cosmos in which all our lives are embedded, helping us to understand its unfolding journey. Geologists and biologists have pieced together the story of planetary evolution; cosmologists have defined the incredible story of the birth, expansion and extent of the visible universe, although this is continually being revised in the light of new discoveries; particle physicists are penetrating the unfolding mysteries of the sub-atomic world; geneticists are applying the discoveries of the genetic code to healing the terrible diseases which still afflict us. Neuroscientists are making phenomenal discoveries about the human brain; they can map the brain and connect different functions with specific areas of it. To their surprise, they are finding that the more primitive 'emotional' parts of the brain play a vital role in developing the qualities of empathy, compassion, insight and tolerance but they cannot tell us exactly how the incredibly complex neurochemistry of the brain gives rise to perception, imagination, specific thoughts and feelings and the collaboration between them. Scientists cannot yet answer the question of how consciousness arises out of matter: how, when and, above all, why apparently 'dead' matter can give rise to life and, ultimately, to consciousness. And they cannot yet answer the questions: What exactly is life and, what is consciousness?

So, for many millions of us, this is an intoxicating time to be alive, participating in the immense adventure of exploring the mystery of the universe as well as the mystery of ourselves. The night sky has become numinous, as enthralling as it was to the ancient Sumerians and Egyptians, watching and noting the movement of the planets and constellations from the summits of their temples and the rooftops of their houses. Television presentations are riveting because of the brilliance and enthusiasm communicated by cosmologists, physicists and biologists. One of the things that is changing our view of reality is the discovery of the immensity and age of the universe as well as the incredible beauty of the galaxies recorded by the Hubble telescope which is able to look back eleven billion years — two billion after the initial explosion of the universe — and is finding layer upon layer of galaxies as far as its eye can see. Now the new Herschel telescope (launched in May 2009) is going even beyond the limits reached by Hubble. All this is a marvel and it has been brought to us by science. Who in this vast universe might be looking at us as we gaze into where we have come from in that dazzlingly distant past?

According to the Standard Theory of the Big Bang, thirteen to fourteen billion years ago, as we understand time in our three-dimensional world, a stupendous explosion of cosmic energy took place, expanding instantaneously from a fireball smaller than an atom. The first second held the inconceivable energy that fuelled not only the creation of countless galaxies through billions of light years' paths of expansion, but also the evolution of life on this planet. Aeons later, out of this planetary life, the human species evolved and, ultimately, human consciousness — our consciousness.

The story of the evolution of our own species streams like the tail of a comet through the darkness of ages now inaccessible to us. The life of our species is embedded in the unimaginably old life of the universe and, closer to us, in the life of this planet yet, in relation to the immensity of planetary life, the life-span of our species takes up no more space than the width of a hair. Complex life has evolved here through a truly extraordinary series of apparently fortuitous developments which are only now revealing themselves to scientists. Lord Rees, the Astronomer Royal, argues in his book *Just Six Numbers* that a mere six numbers determine the nature of our universe and define the actual fabric of material reality. The universe is tuned 'just right' for life to come into being.[12] Why should this be?

The Milky Way galaxy that we belong to is part of an immense cluster of galaxies — the Virgo supercluster — that is 53 million light years away from us. There are estimated to be up to two trillion galaxies in the universe and each one has over a 100 billion stars in it. Our sun is estimated to be one of approximately 400 billion stars in our galaxy alone (these figures are being continually updated). One of the questions that most fascinates cosmologists is whether there could be life on other planets. Are there planets out there with beings on them who have developed a more complex kind of intelligence? Could we communicate with them? Would they have developed a more advanced technology than our own? Could they travel faster than the speed of light and if so how? Since 1995 a new generation of observatories, including Kepler and the gigantic telescopes that have been built in the Atacama desert in the Andes, have revealed the existence of hundreds of planets in other solar systems. In 2009 NASA launched a new telescope called Kepler, sent off into space in order to find planets in the Milky Way that might be capable of sustaining life. In February 2011, NASA announced that Kepler had found 1000 new planets in addition to the 500 that had already been found. Then in December 2011, it announced that one called Kepler–22b in the constellation Cygnus had been found that seemed to be a 'Goldilocks' planet because the conditions on it might be 'just right' for sustaining life in a way similar to our own planet (2011). Scientists think there could be up to 10 billion earth-like planets in our galaxy alone that could support life (2012). Yet the life of our planet is so extraordinary that it is thought unlikely that there could be other planets whose formation is exactly like ours. Where the conditions exist for some kind of life there could be entities like ourselves with abilities and thoughts like ours or with a consciousness so different from ours that we cannot even conceive of what it might be like. Incredibly, Kepler's lenses are so powerful that from space they are able to detect one of us turning on an outside light at night.

If other more advanced forms of cosmic intelligence were observing life on this planet and our calamitous effect on it how might they communicate with us? Perhaps with the magnificent crop circles that have appeared in our summer fields for many years now, suggesting that there is more to be understood about our universe than we realize. Were it to be accepted beyond a shadow of a doubt that these complex, beautiful and mathematically coded patterns were made by an intelligence other than our own, it might produce the most radical shift in our thinking since the discovery of Copernicus that the sun rather than the earth was the centre of our solar system. Some might recoil in fear, seeing extra-terrestrials as threatening; others might be thrilled to know that there was something utterly unexpected that could shock us into awareness of a different dimension of reality. (see www.temporarytemples.co.uk)

Vast and still relatively unmapped as it is, our observable universe is thought to be 93 billion light years across, but as yet there is no way of ascertaining how far it may extend beyond the reach of the perception of our instruments. It has even been announced in 2012, that it may be infinite in extent. Lord Rees suggests that it may be only an island in something resembling a cosmic archipelago of universes.[13] In 2011 astronomers at the University of Michigan announced the discovery of a colossal black hole, with a mass that is, unimaginably, 21 billion times greater than that of the sun. Inside every collapsing black hole there may be another expanding universe that we know nothing about. Our own universe may have been born from such a black hole. String theorists hypothesize that there may be many universes parallel to our own as well as many hidden dimensions to this universe. We only see 4% (some say 5%) of the total universe. Ninety-six percent is invisible to us.

Cosmologists thought that the universe would be slowing down after its billions of years of expansion. From supernova explosions that took place 10 billion years ago they have been able to calculate how fast the universe has been expanding since that time. But they found that, far from slowing down, it's rate of expansion was still increasing. So they wondered whether there was a force that could oppose and counteract gravity. They discovered something that they named 'dark energy'— a force (73% of the whole universe) that was strong enough to counteract and over-come all the gravity in the entire universe and impel it to expand faster and faster. They don't yet know what it is or how it works but they do know that it is active on an inter-galactic scale and does not apparently affect our earth or solar system.

Because dark energy is causing the universe to expand, there are galaxies beyond the cosmic horizon that we will never see because we are too far away from them for their light to reach us. Yet, with the equally mysterious 'dark matter' (22.7% of the whole universe), it has played a central role in how we came to exist. Dark matter is one of the great unsolved mysteries of cosmology, an invisible yet observable mass that seems to hold galaxies together, acting as a counter-force to dark energy which appears to push them apart. Dark matter emits no light or electro-magnetic radiation and its existence can only be inferred from the effect it has on visible matter. It seems that as long as these two mysterious forces — dark energy and dark matter — are held in balance, the universe maintains its equilibrium.

All this is awe-inspiring; yet one of the most amazing discoveries is that although we are between 13 and 14 billion years away from the apparent beginning of our universe, nevertheless we exist at the very heart of it. Every cell of our bodies as well as every star, every galaxy, is the place where the universe is continuously flaring forth into existence from a great sea of being. We do not see the source-ground — only its manifestations. Listen to these words of cosmologist Brian Swimme from his book, *The Hidden Heart of the Cosmos*: "Even in the darkest region beyond the Great Wall of galaxies, even in the void between the superclusters, even in the gaps between the synapses of the neurons in the brain, there occurs an incessant foaming, a flashing flame, a shining-forth-from and a dissolving-back-into."[14]

We are not just in the universe; at the very core of our being we are ongoing creators with the universe, participating, however unconsciously, in this continuously expanding process of creation. Even more astounding, the atoms of our bodies have been there since the beginning and are connected to every single aspect of it. That is surely enough to set the imagination on fire even if we feel insignificant in relation to the unimaginable vastness of the visible universe.

It is astonishing to realize that it took billions of years for life on this planet to evolve to the point where it could provide the atmosphere and environment that could sustain our physical organism and, ultimately, facilitate the development of the kind of consciousness we now have. The ninety-two types of atoms derived from the furnaces of the stars live within us. The chemical compounds that constitute all forms of life, from the simplest bacteria and molecules, live within the complex organism that we are. Each human body consists of 10,000 trillion atoms, connected to and cooperating with each other in complex and remarkable ways that are wonderfully described by the evolutionary biologist, Elisabet Sahtouris in her book *EarthDance*.[15] Whether we are aware of it or not we carry all this cosmic and planetary process of evolution and this tendency to cooperate in the cells of our physical organism. Every cell knows how to cooperate with every other cell to maintain our mind-body organism. Cosmologists have shown us that we are literally star-life, star-energy, star-matter in every cell of our being. We are the only species on this planet to have conscious awareness of this.

So are we the random creation of a mechanical, mindless universe as the philosophy of scientific reductionism proclaims, or do we participate in the life of a living universe that animates and orchestrates its evolution from within its own cosmic and planetary processes? How can we answer this question until we understand what consciousness is and the whole evolutionary development of the kind of consciousness we now have? We can only truly comprehend our history and ourselves through the lens of human consciousness. This lens may not yet be capable of giving us the full picture, however much empirical scientific knowledge we may have. We are the only species on this planet that can speak, write, reflect, discover, create and communicate with each other in words and gestures and give expression to our imagination and our skills in beautiful artefacts, exquisite music and brilliant technological inventions like the Hubble telescope. How have we come to believe that this entire creative panorama has no meaning?

Our Planetary Roots

During its evolutionary course over nearly 4 billion years our planet has survived five giant catastrophes which threatened to destroy all life on earth, the best known one being the devastating impact of a huge meteorite which wiped out the dinosaurs some 65 million years ago. But some 250 million years before that, for reasons not yet fully understood, the deep ocean conveyor currents stopped moving, causing a lack of oxygen which nearly extinguished all life on earth. The oceans turned stagnant and gave out a poisonous gas called hydrogen sulphide — as deadly as cyanide. Almost every living thing died, on land as well as in the sea. This was the greatest extinction in the earth's history. Over 90% of all life on earth died. Yet incredibly, life survived these and other catastrophes and regenerated itself. It is truly astonishing that out of these successive extinctions and regenerations, human consciousness eventually came into being. But it is a sobering thought that, according to the biologist Sir David Attenborough, our species, if it continues on its present course, will be responsible for the sixth great extinction, which could include us. It is difficult to assimilate the enormous implications of his stark warning.

The Evolution of Human Consciousness

We are living now at the end of a great trajectory — perhaps 5 million years or more — which has brought about the gradual separation or differentiation of our human species from the matrix of nature and the development of a sense of self or individuality, as well as a highly developed intellect: everything that we now call human consciousness. But in the process we have lost the ancient instinctive sense of living within a Sacred Order. The organism that we are, the vehicle of consciousness that we have, has evolved from the substance of the stars as well as from the life that developed on this planet. Complex life has evolved here through a truly extraordinary series of evolutionary developments which are only now, through scientific discoveries, becoming accessible to our understanding.

In the child, consciousness arises out of the depths of unconscious psychic life, at first like separate islands which then coalesce to form a continent — a continuous land-mass of consciousness. Was it the same with primordial man, as the capacity for self-awareness gradually evolved out of the purely instinctive consciousness of the animals? If so, the child recapitulates, in the incredibly short space of a few months and years, the phylogenetic evolution of the species, bringing with it as its inheritance specifically human instincts, as well as far more archaic ones long pre-dating the arrival of *homo sapiens sapiens* around 40,000 BC.

The faculty of awareness and perception that we call consciousness has evolved over thousands of millennia out of the matrix of instinct, ultimately developing into the capacity for self-awareness and introspection, the ability consciously to remember and imagine, to observe and interpret, that our species now has but did not always have. Over these millennia, humans developed certain abilities and lost others, such as the acute sensory awareness of animals. Consciousness – the ability to be aware of an inner world of thoughts and feelings as well as to observe and interpret an outer one — was not fixed in its present state fifty thousand years ago. The focus of the modern mind is very different from say, the Upper Palaeolithic mind of 50,000 BC or the Bronze Age mind of 3000 BC. Yet there are basic instinctive patterns of response to stimuli, basic patterns of behaviour originating with the older brain system (see below), that the human species has transmitted over an immense span of time, that it shares with other species, and which exist in us today.

It is very moving to reflect on the immense age of this planet where, taking an hour's walk, every large step represents ten million years. Our human species appears in the last second of this walk — the final two inches of earth or grass under our feet. And human consciousness as we know it today? In perhaps the last millimetre or even less. Our physical brain, the vehicle of our consciousness and all the great discoveries we have made, has apparently arisen out of the evolutionary experience of the Earth and all the species whose life it has sustained but what evolutionary intention has programmed this emergence?

Without our capacity to imagine, measure, deduce and reflect, and develop instruments to extend our power of observation, we would not know that everything we are, everything on our planet and in our solar system, has been formed from elements of the stars that have been seeded here from great galaxies millions of light years away from us. We are, in our essence, literally cosmic light, cosmic energy in every cell of our being. The small fraction of the universe that we see and the life that we are appears to arise from an invisible sea of light which is the deep cosmic ground of the phenomenal world and our own consciousness. Within this sea of light, the forms change but the energy is eternal, co-inherent with the source. Through the infinitesimal spark of cosmic light that is our human consciousness, the universe is becoming aware of itself on this planet and, at the same time, through that same consciousness, revealing to us the staggering complexity and splendour of its evolutionary process, telling us its story. I find this incredibly moving.

We now know a great deal about the evolution of the physical aspect of life, but almost nothing about the inner aspect of both the universe and ourselves — that is to say, the consciousness aspect; only that our species and our capacity for self-awareness have come into being very recently in relation to the time span of the Earth's evolution. Yet this capacity is in itself utterly extraordinary, for without it the life of nature and of our own human lives would have gone unnoticed — flowing from an unimagined past into an unimagined future.

Consciousness itself may be an expression of cosmic consciousness, something of which we are still unaware. Could the consciousness of our species evolve further? It is conceivable that, as the great sages of India and the ancient tradition of Kabbalah have long taught, our species as a whole is still at a pre-conscious or semi-conscious state, with its further development unrealized because it is not even envisaged. We see things only in terms of technological progress. All the immense repository of knowledge we have now accumulated serves the aims of a human mind that is still not fully developed and is not consciously in touch with its deeper cosmic ground.

The Triune Brain

It may be a surprise to discover that we have not one but three brains: the great frontal dome of the neo-cortex — our most recently developed brain — rests on the primordial root of two older brain systems which continuously interact with each other and also with the far more recently developed neo-cortical brain and its frontal lobes. Paul MacLean, who advanced this theory in 1974 in his book, *The Triune Brain* explains:

> A comparison of the brains of existing vertebrates, together with an examination of the fossil record, indicates that the human forebrain [neo-cortex] has evolved and expanded to its great size while retaining the features of three basic evolutionary formations that reflect an ancestral relationship to reptiles, early mammals, and recent mammals. Radically different in chemistry and structure and in an evolutionary sense countless generations apart, the three neural assemblies constitute a hierarchy of three-brains-in-one, a triune brain.... Stated in popular terms, the three evolutionary formations might be imagined as three interconnected biological computers, with each having its own special intelligence, its own subjectivity, its own sense of time and space, and its own memory, motor, and other functions.[16]

So we carry within us the evolutionary structure of three different brain systems: the reptilian, the mammalian or limbic, and the neo-cortical brain. The incredible complexity of how these three brains interact with each other and yet function as a single unit is still one of the great mysteries of neuroscience. How do 100 billion neurons connected by 100 trillion synapses communicate with each other? How do paths of cognition and behaviour become established and what could change these paths and therefore our habits of behaviour? With great conscious effort and practice, we can become aware of which part of the brain is predominant in a specific situation. We know, for instance, that the fight/flight reflexes of the oldest reptilian brain spring into action, flooding the organism with adrenalin when we are faced with a threat or a physical challenge, and also that these primordial reflexes unconsciously govern many of our responses to 'everyday' life even though there may be no specific threat confronting us. We may spend more of our time trying to ensure our safety (compulsive shopping or eating) or anticipating difficult situations (developing weapons and preparing for war) than our actual circumstances demand. And we know that the older brain systems have a far greater influence on the more recently evolved neo-cortical brain than the latter has on the former. Powerful primal emotions like fear, anxiety and rage, mediated through a part of the brain called the amygdala, can easily influence and even overwhelm the neo-cortical 'rational' mind. We also know that adverse conditions in infancy and early childhood can negatively imprint the nervous system (the older brain) and inhibit the optimum development of the neo-cortical brain. A child so affected may remain fixated in the purely instinctive older brain, unable to develop the capacity for self-awareness, thought and reflection and the ability to contain and control powerful emotions.

The Two Hemispheres of the Brain

We know that the right frontal lobe, which governs the left side of the body, is the oldest of the two brain hemispheres and the first to develop out of the actual heart of the embryo. It is fairly mature before the left lobe even comes into being. It seems that the close relationship between the heart and the right hemisphere is maintained throughout life and that this hemisphere functions through image cognition, visual-spatial perception and mediating feeling states rather than through the verbal, analytical, sequential cognition of the left hemisphere. The right hemisphere, tied in to millions of years of the evolution of the earth and of our species, is the image-making, holistic, non-verbal connective system to the older mammalian brain. This right hemisphere, which may be the one that shamans and mystics can access, gives us a different perspective on life, arising from our age-old sense of an empathic relationship with our environment. It is through the right brain that poets, mystics, musicians and scientific geniuses receive their inspiration, their intuitive flashes of insight. However, they need the verbal skills of the left brain to communicate their experience. Mozart's music flowed out of him in a torrent of incredible harmonies from the age of four. Einstein's theory of relativity came to him when he was sitting on a hill imagining that he was riding a sunbeam to the edge of the universe and returning towards the sun. The image came first, the theory later. Einstein himself said "Imagination is more important than knowledge: knowledge points to all that is; Imagination points to all that will be."[17] It may be that the imagination, focused through the right hemisphere, is the illuminator of reality, the faculty that Coleridge held to be the very ground of our consciousness, of our capacity to think, discover and create.

The left hemisphere governs the right side of the body and does not have the same primordial connection to our distant planetary past because it evolved relatively recently. The left hemisphere gives us focus, direction, and the power to analyse, assemble facts, and direct our attention towards a goal as well as the vital ability to speak and convey meaning. But although it is hugely advantageous to us from a survival perspective, it poses a problem because it takes us out of a state of 'being' into a linear awareness of past, present and future. When this hemisphere is too dominant and controlling, it can shut out the perceptions of the right hemisphere and with it, the imagination and the vital connection to the heart and the empathic skills derived from our mammalian inheritance.

In a remarkable book published in 2009 called *The Master and His Emissary: The Divided Brain and the Making of the Western World* (mentioned in Chapter Five), psychiatrist Iain McGilchrist brilliantly explores the neurological discoveries as well as the specific skills of and the relationship between the two hemispheres of the brain.[18] He shows how each hemisphere in the process of evolving necessarily developed not only different essential skills but also different approaches to relating to the world and how, over the last four centuries, the left hemisphere has gradually come to shape and ultimately dominate the secular view of reality, proclaiming that its view is the only one that is logical or tenable, and rigidly excluding any other view. The more inclusive, wide-ranging and multi-faceted perspective of the right hemisphere has been silenced:

> My view is that the two hemispheres, with their distinct 'versions' of the world, each have something to offer, but that their relationship is importantly not symmetrical. The right hemisphere both grounds experience at the lowest level and makes sense of it overall at the highest level, while the left hemisphere provides an intermediate level of processing, unpacking the implicit, before it is handed back to the right hemisphere for integration into everything else we know. The trouble is that the left hemisphere's far simpler world is self-consistent, because all the complexity has been sheared off — and this makes the left hemisphere prone to believe it knows everything, when it absolutely does not: it remains ignorant of all that is most important.[19]

Another book, *My Stroke of Insight*, written by a neuroscientist called Jill Bolte Taylor, confirms McGilchrist's thesis, describing how a massive haemorrhage incapacitated the left hemisphere of her brain and how she had the extraordinary experience of becoming aware of the totally different perception of reality that the right hemisphere (without the controlling, directing input of the left) revealed to her. It took her eight years fully to recover all the physical and mental functions related to the left hemisphere and she found through her own experience that the brain can repair, replace and retrain its neural circuitry. She was able, with practice, to stay open to the perceptions of the right hemisphere and resist the attempts of the left hemisphere to re-impose its dominance and control.[20]

Given how extraordinary this is, it invites us to understand the nature of consciousness in greater depth. All the knowledge we have gained about the evolution of our physical organism, as well as its consciousness aspect, does not yet acknowledge that our present concept of reality might be limited to the view created by our literal-minded left hemisphere alone, disregarding or cutting out the more subtle and comprehensive vision of the right. Nor does it acknowledge the presence and influence of the part of the psyche that Jung called the "root and rhizome of the soul" — all the multi-layered memories of the entire evolutionary experience that we carry within us: memories of cellular life, plant life, reptilian, mammalian and, finally, human life.[21] This complex patterning of species consciousness, species memory or information as well as species form, incrementally expanding and increasing over thousands of millennia has contributed to the evolution of planetary life, the evolution of our species and, finally, the evolution of three different brain systems, the differentiated functions of the two brain hemispheres and human consciousness itself.

What is Consciousness?

Consciousness is the ability to observe and interact with the visible world through the five senses and simultaneously to hold awareness of an inner world of images, ideas, thoughts and feelings. It also has the capacity to evaluate both these realms of experience, to make a distinction between what is meaningful and what is not, what is safe and agreeable and what is not. The triune brain gives rise to many integrated layers or levels of consciousness that have developed out of very archaic instincts. Over millennia, as the triune brain evolved, adding in the neo-cortical frontal lobes, the amplification of primordial instincts gave rise to the possibility of cognition and self-awareness and the extraordinary creative power of the imagination as well as to more specific emotions, empathic feelings, and intuitive 'flashes' of insight or associations. Beneath the 'superstructure' of neo-cortical consciousness, the subconscious workings of the autonomic nervous system maintain the balance or homeostasis of our total physical organism, supporting the continuous neuronal dialogue that takes place between all the different organs of our body but particularly between our heart and our brain.

What we call our 'rational mind' is only one part of our total consciousness while all around us, as William James observed, are other states of consciousness of which we are unaware. Among these is our dreaming mind and the realm of the collective unconscious. Our understanding of what comprises consciousness will need to be continually revised as we discover more. For example, Candace Pert's remarkable discovery of the 'molecules of emotion' (1998) which connect every part of our organism to every other part has revolutionized our understanding of the interaction between mind and body and done away with the separation that had long been established between them. As she explains in an article that followed the publication of her book *Molecules of Emotion*:

> Consciousness isn't just in the head. Nor is it a question of mind over body. If one takes into account the DNA directing the dance of the peptides, the body is the outward manifestation of the mind. The new science of psycho-neuro-immunology is redefining the connection between mind and body. We can no longer speak of body and mind as separate systems or entities. Bodymind —

one word, no hyphen. Bodymind is a single organism pulsing with neuropeptide messengers that flow in a continuous loop from the brain to every cell in our body, giving rise to emotions and responding to emotions.[22]

Altered States of Consciousness

The pioneering work of the Czech psychiatrist Stanislav Grof has shown that in altered states of consciousness, ancient fields of memory and ancient experiences can and do become accessible to our consciousness. His work, as well as the experience of modern shamans such as those of Peru, shows that we can travel through these fields of memory.

His experience during the last forty years, using both psychedelic drugs and holotropic breathing in many thousands of sessions, has shown over and over again the similarity between the phenomena attributed to psychosis and those encountered in these sessions and in shamanic experience. As he writes,

> The phenomena originating at the perinatal and transpersonal levels of the psyche include sequences of psychological death and rebirth, encounters with archetypal beings, visits to mythological realms of various cultures, past incarnation memories, extrasensory perception and episodes of out-of-body states. These have to be considered to be natural and normal manifestations of the deeper dynamics of the human psyche.

He adds:

> But attempts to interpret any of these phenomena in the context of the narrow and superficial model of the psyche currently used necessarily leads to serious distortions and to pathologising the entire spiritual history of humanity.... From this perspective, the founders of the great religions of the world, as well as their prophets, saints, and eminent teachers, all of whom had visionary experiences, can be labelled as psychotics. Shamans are diagnosed as ambulant schizophrenics, hysterics or epileptics.[23]

What happens to people whose psyche is open to visionary experience when a culture names this experience a mental illness? Current research is confirming that over 50% of people in the UK and the US have what they call 'spiritual' experiences and that these add meaning and depth to their lives. But they often dare not speak of these experiences for fear of being thought insane. I would surmise that the greater the denial of the non-rational in a culture, or the more rigid a controlling belief system, the greater the incidence of psychosis, drug taking and addiction, because there is no container to receive and mediate this unusual kind of experience or to help people to integrate such an experience within a wider framework of understanding.

Are our extraordinary creative abilities no more than random expressions of the neurons in our brain or is the brain a vehicle for the greater 'mind' of the Cosmos? Is the world perhaps the creation or manifestation of another primary dimension of reality which contains it in the sense that this was explored in Chapter Five? Neurobiologists assume that the ability to imagine, invent and discover, to appreciate beauty and to wonder, even our need for a god to worship, has its origin in certain areas of the physical brain and they are trying to pin-point these areas and measure the neural correlates of specific subjective states. But our highly developed physical bodymind organism may also act as a vehicle or transmitter of a greater cosmic mind. For McGilchrist, consciousness "pre-exists us and isn't created by our brains; our brains simply transmit or transduce it."[24]

What gives rise in us to the longing to understand ourselves and to explore the life around us? Is it only a random neural cause giving rise to a neural effect? Or do our longings originate with the soul or mind of the Cosmos itself so that our longings actually embody and carry forward its evolutionary intention?

The Effects of Our Separation from Nature

Developing a range of skills which are unique to our species has led to our present sense of self and individuality as well as to our highly developed intellect and our capacity to imagine, feel, think, analyse and remember — everything that we now call human consciousness. This evolutionary process has been, in our terms, long and arduous. In the course of it, we have grown to separate ourselves as observer from all that we observe and have lost the ancient instinctive sense of participation in the life of the Earth and the Cosmos that our Palaeolithic and Neolithic forebears knew. The more our mental and technological skills have developed, giving us the power to control our environment, and the more we have congregated in cities, the more estranged we have become from a sense of relationship and connection with the life around us. Modern city-bred children may not know that milk comes from a cow or bread from wheat. Now, with the life of the planet actually threatened by the demands of our huge and growing numbers, we are confronted with a situation that we ourselves, in our ignorance of the effects of our separation from nature, may have brought into being or, at the very least, exacerbated.

On this planet, our lives are dependent on the lives of other animal species and on the interaction of trees, plants, soil, water and air yet, as a species, we are barely aware of our dependence on the extraordinary complexity of the planetary life that sustains us. James Lovelock's words are worth recalling here because they sum up this relationship: "So closely coupled is the evolution of living organisms with the evolution of their environment that together they constitute a single evolutionary process."[25]

No one has written more eloquently about the Earth and our lost relationship with it than Thomas Berry in his book *The Dream of the Earth*. No one has evoked in such compelling language the need for human sensitivity, compassion and intelligence in our relationship with the Earth and its living systems. He asks that we wake up from our mythic dream of progress and the dominance of nature and take on the role of becoming responsible custodians of the dwindling species and resources of the planet.

The competitive and exhausting industrial and technological culture we have created, where millions struggle to survive in enormous, ugly and amorphous cities, stands like a tyrant over and against Nature, over and against the Earth and whatever threatens our supremacy as a species. Our human species as a part has become detached from planetary life as the whole. There is an abysmal lack of awareness that, as Berry points out, the Earth is primary and our survival is dependent on the continued integrity and balance of the Earth's inter-related systems:

> If the supreme disaster in the comprehensive story of the earth is our present closing down of the major life systems of the planet, then the supreme need of our times is to bring about a healing of the earth through this mutually enhancing human presence to the earth community. To achieve this mode of pressure, a new type of sensitivity is needed, a sensitivity that is something more than romantic attachment to some of the more brilliant manifestations of the natural world, a sensitivity that comprehends the larger patterns of nature, its severe demands as well as its delightful aspects, and is willing to see the human diminish so that other life forms might flourish.[26]

Precisely because of the long experience of separation from nature, we carry a deep and unrecognized wound. Our very being has been fragmented by the way we have interpreted reality and by the values that direct our culture and, in particular, the materialist philosophy that currently directs science. Our conscious, rational mind has become disconnected from the part of us that, at an unconscious, instinctive level — possibly through the relationship between the electro-magnetic field of our body and that of the planet — is still bound in close relationship to the greater organism of planetary life. This inevitably creates conflict between the conscious and unconscious aspects of our total organism. The end result of this long process of separation is that in our technologically advanced culture we have lost something absolutely vital that earlier cultures still had: the awareness that we live within a Sacred Order. While indigenous shamanic cultures have retained this ancient participatory awareness, the modern industrialized world has totally lost it.

Astronauts of the Soul

In a secular culture, attention has been focused exclusively on the daylight world of physical reality. There is no awareness, as there was in earlier cultures and in mystical experience, of the existence of a dimension of reality which might be compared to the starry night sky — a dimension which can only reveal its presence when the sun's bright radiance is dimmed. If we could break through the controlling influence of our left-hemispheric consciousness, we could begin to play a more enlightened and conscious role in relation to the extraordinary cosmic drama in which we are all involved. Einstein knew that the problems we face cannot be solved from the same level of consciousness that created them. We need to evolve beyond our current one-eyed consciousness and reconnect with Nature and the Cosmos — with all that we have become separated from over the centuries of the solar era. We need to develop a new kind of consciousness in relation to planetary and cosmic life, summed up in the words of Stanislav Grof: "I see consciousness and the human psyche as expressions and reflections of a cosmic intelligence that permeates the entire universe and all of existence. We are not just highly evolved animals with biological computers embedded inside our skulls; we are also fields of consciousness without limits, transcending time, space, matter and linear causality."[27] I will return to this idea in Chapter Fifteen.

There are brilliant pioneers now exploring the sub-atomic world as well as the immensities of the visible universe revealed by the Hubble telescope and there are others whom I call astronauts of the soul who are exploring an unseen universe whose existence is not recognized or even imagined by mainstream science. Just as we have the capacity to imagine, to think and to feel — an 'inside' dimension of thoughts and feelings within our physical form — so the universe may also have an 'inside' to its visible form, an intelligence and a soul, perhaps related to the 95% of it that we cannot see. Each planet, each galaxy, may have a consciousness, a soul. Shamanic cultures have known for millennia that we can develop the ability to communicate with this intelligence, to align ourselves with it and to be guided by it.

Western Sensate culture has put enormous emphasis on the development of the rational mind, the advancement of scientific discoveries and the technology required to ensure higher material standards of living. The values of the heart have been neglected: the more feminine qualities of the capacity to relate to others, respect for the environment and acknowledgment of the deep mysteries of life have not been developed to the same extent. Because of this one-sided emphasis on the rational mind, the Western psyche is not fully developed, balanced and integrated. Intellect and technological skills have been developed to a very high degree among a small proportion of the world's population. But intuition and feeling have not been developed and these two functions are asking for our attention now. We need to recover the shamanic eye that was closed long ago, so that we no longer have a one-eyed consciousness. A different perception of reality could reconnect us with nature and with soul, so enabling us to open the other eye and restore our fragmented being to wholeness. This perception could be summed up as follows:

- ✿ There is an invisible or transcendent order of reality out of which the phenomenal world arises.

- ✿ The universe is conscious and there are many dimensions to it.

- ✿ Our human consciousness is integral to that greater consciousness, even though it is still partially developed or immature.

- ✿ Consciousness in some form survives the death of the physical body.

- ✿ What we have called spirit is continually creating life in the universe, our planet and ourselves. All is one life, one energy. We participate in that creative dynamic.

- ✿ The soul is not confined to the individual: it is a vast web of relationships connecting invisible fields of energy with the denser field of physical reality.

- ✿ The purpose of our lives on this planet is to learn how to live in conscious communion with the evolutionary intention of the Cosmos.

I will leave the final words to David Korten:

> Through the stories we share, we define what it means to be human, our place in Creation, our responsibilities to one another and Earth, and the possibilities it is within our means to actualise…. The issues are revealed with particular clarity by playing out the implications of two sharply contrasting stories. One story is that of a dead universe that assumes matter is the sole reality and consciousness but an illusion. This is the standard story of contemporary Western science. The other is the story of a living universe that takes consciousness to be the primary reality. This is a new story emerging as a synthesis of ancient religious wisdom and the data of the scientific leading edge — and it potentially changes everything.[28]

Notes:

1. James, William (1929) *The Varieties of Religious Experience*, Longmans. Green and Co. London, New York, p. 388
2. Harvey, Andrew (1983) *A Journey in Ladakh*, Jonathan Cape Ltd., p.167
3. Blake, William letter to Thomas Butts, 22 November, 1802, *Complete Poetry and Prose*, ed. Geoffrey Keynes, p. 862
4. Bucke, Maurice Richard (1923) *Cosmic Consciousness*, Dutton & Co., New York
5. Sorokin, Pitirim (1992) *The Crisis of Our Age*, Oneworld Publications Ltd., Oxford, p. 25
6. ibid, p. 16
7. ibid, p. 25
8. Russell, Bertrand (1903) *The Free Man's Worship*
9. Crick, Francis (1994) *The Astonishing Hypothesis*, Simon and Schuster Ltd., London
10. Saul, John Ralston (1995) *The Unconscious Civilization*, House of Anansi Press, Canada, and Penguin Books Ltd., London
11. Berry, Thomas (1988) *The Dream of the Earth*, Sierra Club Books, San Francisco, pp. 204 & 215
12. Rees, Sir Martin (1999) *Just Six Numbers: The Deep Forces that Shape the Universe*, Basic Books Ltd., London
13. Rees (1997) *Before the Beginning*, Simon & Schuster Ltd., London
14. Swimme, Brian (1996) *The Hidden Heart of the Cosmos*, Orbis Books, New York, p. 101
15. Sahtouris, Elisabet (2000) *EarthDance: Living Systems in Evolution*, University Press, Lincoln Nebraska
16. MacLean, Paul (1990) *The Triune Brain in Evolution*, Plenum Press, New York, p. 9
17. Einstein, Albert, quoted in a lecture given by Tarquin Olivier, Vancouver, 2002
18. McGilchrist, Iain (2009) *The Master and His Emissary: The Divided Brain and the Making of the Western World*, Yale University Press, pp. 428-62
19. McGilchrist (2010) from his chapter in *A New Renaissance: Transforming Science, Spirit and Society*, ed. David Lorimer and Oliver Robinson, Floris books, pp. 63-4

20. Taylor, Jill Bolte (2008) *My Stroke of Insight*, Hodder and Stoughton, London
21. Jung, C.G. (1963) *Memories, Dreams, Reflections*, Collins and Routledge & Kegan Paul, London, p. 4
22. Pert, Candace (1998) *Molecules of Emotion*, Simon and Schuster Ltd., London, passim
23. Grof, Stanislav (2001) *LSD Psychotherapy*, published by the Multidisciplinary Association for Psychedelic Studies, Sarasota, Florida, USA. See also his *Beyond the Brain*, State University of New York Press, 1985, and *The Cosmic Game*, State University of New York Press, 1998.
24. from an interview reported in an article by Lance St. John Butler in the Scientific and Medical Network Review, winter 2010
25. Lovelock, James (1991) *Healing Gaia*, Harmony Books, New York, p. 222.
26. Berry, *The Dream of the Earth*, p. 212
27. Grof, Stanislav and Bennett, Hal Z. (1993) *The Holotropic Mind: Three levels of Human Consciousness and How They Shape Our Lives*, HarperCollins, New York, p. 18,
28. Korten, David (2009) *Mind Before Matter: Visions of a New Science of Consciousness*, ed. John Mack and Trish Pfeiffer, O Books, Ropley, Hampshire, p. 138

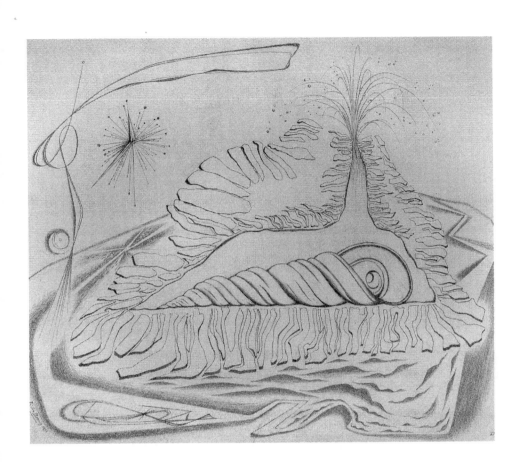

Gestation
Robin Baring 1975

Interlude

THE SLEEPING BEAUTY: A FAIRY TALE FOR OUR TIME

O awaken not the Beauty until the time comes...

The greatest fairy tales and stories are borne like seeds across the generations, carrying us with them by enchantment, connecting us to the imagination that is too often banished from our lives. They suggest responses to the challenges of human existence that cannot be conveyed as simply or profoundly in any other form. Fairy tales are very old. They invite us into the mysterious landscape of the soul. They speak with the voice of the soul and carry many levels of meaning. Who can say where the story of the 'Sleeping Beauty' originated and how it was transmitted from generation to generation? It may be descended from long-forgotten Bronze Age rituals which celebrated the marriage of the sun and moon, and others which mourned the annual death of the life of the earth and celebrated its regeneration in spring. It may carry residual memories of the Gnostic myth of Sophia entangled in the dense forest of our world and her rescue by Christ. It may anticipate the awakening of woman to awareness of her value and a different relationship with awakened man. It may also relate to our inner life and the marriage of our conscious mind with our instinctual soul, for the sacred marriage of king and queen, prince and princess is woven into the rich tapestry of mystical traditions relating to our inner life: Alchemy, Gnosticism and Kabbalah.

The fairy tale tells the story of a princess who, on her fifteenth birthday, explored the unused rooms of a castle and came across a room in which an old woman was sitting, turning and turning her spinning wheel. Asking if she too could spin, she took the spindle from the old woman and pricked her finger on it. At once she fell into a deep sleep, so fulfilling the curse placed on her by the uninvited thirteenth fairy at her christening — a curse that was mitigated by another fairy who remitted that death sentence to a hundred years' sleep. The whole court fell asleep with her. A great forest of rambler roses — an impenetrable hedge of thorns — grew up around her, hiding even the turrets of the castle. A hundred years passed by and legends were told about the sleeping princess who lay hidden at the heart of the forest until one day a prince, hearing of the legend, determined to set out to find her. Many suitors had perished in the attempt to penetrate the hedge of thorns but, so the story goes, for this prince the hedge of thorns turned to roses and a way through the hedge opened before him. So he came to where she lay sleeping and awakened her with a kiss. As she awoke, the whole court came to life and preparations began for their marriage — for the best-loved fairy tales end in marriage.

The ancient lunar imagery of death and regeneration comes to life in the story. The dark phase of the moon is symbolized by the sleeping princess and the court and by the old crone spinning in the turret of the castle. The solar prince awakens the lunar princess — the crescent moon — to life as his bride and, as this happens, the moon reaches fullness and the whole court returns to life to celebrate anew the age-old marriage of the sun and the moon.

Could this be a fairy tale for our time? Might its deeper meaning open a way through the hedge of thorns created by centuries of entrenched beliefs and habits of behaviour? Might its lunar symbolism have the power to awaken our soul, nurture our poetic voice, our true intelligence and our visionary imagination, and arouse in us a deeper capacity for relationship with each other and love for our planetary home? Finally, could it stir to life the slumbering 'court' of humanity?

Myths and fairy tales awaken and nourish the imagination. The imagination reconnects us to instincts which may have atrophied for want of use and when this happens the arid wasteland of our inner life may be regenerated by our immersion in the waters of the soul. When we are not in touch with the soul, it is as if a vital part of us is asleep: it cannot communicate with us, nor we with it. We cannot live to the fullest potential of which we are capable. A civilization may die because it has forgotten how to nourish the soul and the imagination.

I see this timeless, magical story as a metaphor for the need for a marriage between the solar and lunar dimensions of our being: a marriage between our head and our heart, between our too-literal, analytical mind which knows nothing of a deeper ground of consciousness, and our imaginative, instinctual, creative soul. This deep instinctual part of us is the matrix of our ability to create. It is the origin of our capacity to feel and to imagine, and to give expression to feeling and imagination through the vehicle of our thoughts, our voice, our hands, and our body, and sustains the connection to a hidden dimension of reality. Feeling, intuition and the imagination put us in touch with a ground which is beyond the reach of mind and intellect, acting like a plug connecting us to the socket of that deeper reality.

But the hedge of thorns shows what an impenetrable barrier lies between mind and soul and how difficult it is to get through it. The hedge of thorns symbolizes all the belief systems and defensive structures we have built up over hundreds, if not thousands of years: deeply rooted religious beliefs about the nature of God and our fallen and sinful human nature and scientific beliefs about a randomly created universe and 'dead' matter. These beliefs, deeply imprinted on us over generations, stand between us and our soul and make it almost impossible for us to reach below the surface of our everyday consciousness and listen to the voice of this lost dimension of ourselves.

It is difficult for us to speak to each other as people spoke to each other in the past, because of the fear of the non-rational. Because of the rejection of this aspect of life, an essential part of our being is rendered speechless, autistic. Today we live in our mind, in what we believe is the supremely conscious, most interesting and powerful part of ourselves. Soul has been left out of the picture. Yet, I believe that in the story of the Sleeping Beauty, the Prince and the Sleeping Beauty symbolize the two aspects of our consciousness which belong together as bride-groom and bride.

The Prince personifies the solar principle of consciousness, the questing human mind which seeks to explore, discover, understand, penetrate to the heart of reality and who, in this story, is seeking the lost feminine counterpart of himself that is asleep — unconscious. Yet, as long as he remains unconscious of her existence and does not set out in search of her, as long as he does not confront and penetrate the hedge of thorns, she is condemned to remain asleep.

The Princess carries the lunar principle of soul, and also the neglected feeling values which are undeveloped or inarticulate in relation to the rational mind, and have, so to speak, lain under a spell for centuries because of the beliefs explored in previous chapters. She also, more obviously, carries the image of woman who, for all the reasons explored in these, has not been honoured for the feeling values she carries and has therefore been unable to honour her true feminine nature. From still another perspective, the story can be seen as a concealed metaphor of the reconciliation of spirit and nature or the marriage of the masculine and feminine aspects of spirit which have become separated over the last four thousand years.

The story of the Sleeping Beauty says that at the right moment, for the right person, the hedge of thorns turns to roses and a way opens through it. I think we are, in this new millennium, at the moment of breakthrough. A deep instinct is attempting to restore balance and wholeness in us by recovering the lost feminine dimension of soul personified by the Sleeping Beauty. Over the past fifty years a gradual restoration of a sense of the sacred has been taking place beneath the surface of our culture. Millions are awakening to awareness of our relationship with the greater organism of the planet and beyond this with the deeper field of soul which unites all our lives — the great web of life that connects every aspect of life to every other aspect of it.

This fairy tale anticipates our time: this precious time of humanity's awakening. Once before, in the twelfth century, this was attempted in the great spiritual impulse of the Quest for the Holy Grail. The mystery of the Holy Grail infuses the Middle Ages with the image of the age-old quest which turns inwards, following the yearning of the seeker's heart, seeking a path that cannot be taught but only found and is unique to each individual. The chalice, vessel, cup and stone that are the primary images of the Grail evoke the archetype of the Feminine which becomes the inspiration, guide and goal of the knight's inner quest. What is the Grail then, but the inexhaustible vessel, the source of life continuously flowing into being, radiating into this world from the unseen realm of the Soul, the realm in which all our lives are embedded? Who are the knights who act as guardians of the Grail but those who faithfully kept alive through the darkened centuries the mysteries of the soul's awakening?

Jessie Weston, who wrote *From Ritual to Romance* — one of the most authentic books on the Grail — said, "The Grail is a living force, it will never die; it may indeed sink out of sight, and for centuries even, disappear... but it will rise to the surface again and become once more a theme of vital importance." Now, as then, the Grail Quest is open and can offer us a new image of ourselves, serving the world through love and following wherever the heart leads.

For nearly four thousand years the Soul has lain under a spell; her voice has been silenced, her wisdom rejected. Beauty, grace and harmony have faded from our world. But now, she is stirring to life within the soul of humanity. What does she want from us? What is her hope? I believe she wants relationship. I see this relationship as a sacred marriage; a marriage between ourselves and the deep invisible ground of life. The soul and the feminine archetype in their deepest sense have always carried the values of the heart: the values that honour wisdom, justice, compassion and the desire to help and to heal.

In many fairy tales, as in this one, there is the figure of an old crone. In ancient lunar cultures she would have been recognized as an aspect of the goddess, just as the sleeping princess would have been recognized as another aspect. In modern dreams, often appearing as a figure robed in black, she still personifies the power and wisdom of the life process which brings everything into being. She spins the web of fate; she is the womb of life, the process within nature which nurtures the seed and brings everything to fruition. In the story of the Sleeping Beauty she is the secret presence in the hidden room of the castle of the soul who brings about the events that lead ultimately to the awakening of the sleeping court and the marriage of prince and princess. She stands for the deepest stratum of our soul's life. No one who sets out on the quest for relationship with the soul can ignore her. Sooner or later she may appear in our dreams, as she has done in mine, to awaken us to who she is and what she wants of us.

Our brilliant technological culture inflicts intolerable stress on us because it grants no value to feelings and allows no time for relationship with the soul, no time to awaken to the presence of the extraordinary treasure that lies hidden within us. The rescue of the treasure which has for so long been relegated low down on the list of our priorities requires a fundamental transformation of our understanding of life; the formulation of a new worldview or paradigm of reality that will precipitate us through the hedge of thorns that holds us impaled in bondage to the past. It invites a reorientation in our relationship with the planet and with each other, a reversal of what we have considered important, even vital, to our survival — a putting first what we have put last. Knowledge of the holy unity of life, reverence for nature, trust in the powers of the creative imagination, in the atrophied faculty of intuition — all these are needed to help us recover that lost, instinctive relationship with life which was once grounded in our experience of soul.

The soul does not communicate primarily through words, through language, but through feelings, intuitions, emotions, and, because of our neglect of it, through disturbed, violent or addictive patterns of behaviour. It also communicates through dreams. If we do not pay attention to these, there will be no way in which the needs of the soul can reach our surface consciousness that is focused exclusively on the external world. They will remain shut away behind a hedge of thorns. The journey in search of the soul is difficult and even dangerous because it requires that we relinquish the certainty of what we think we know and what we have been taught for generations to believe. It means surrendering the desire to be in control and opening ourselves to a quest, a path of discovery. Many myths and fairy tales emphasize the need for surrender and trust in the strange non-rational guidance offered by animals or shamans on the quest. As the hero follows their guidance, so the hedge opens, the way unfolds. Following the guidance and wisdom of the instinct is the royal road into the realm of soul.

Somewhere in Chartres Cathedral, these words are inscribed: "O Awaken not the Beauty until the time comes." This lost dimension of soul which lives deep within our being and within all life is awakening now. The quest to awaken the Sleeping Beauty is the quest for greater understanding of life's mystery. Those who say there is no mystery to understand literally kill their instinctive life, their soul. The supreme value whose discovery could heal the anguish, terror and suffering endured throughout the odyssey of human evolution is to be found at the heart of our instinctual life. The fascination with the search for treasure lying hidden beneath the waters of the sea or buried deep in the earth reflects the magnetic power of the treasure that is hidden within the inner waters, the inner earth of the soul.

Figure of a Woman
Robin Baring 1978

Part Four

Recovering the
Connection to the Soul

Landscape with a Figure
Robin Baring 1975

Chapter Ten

THE RESURGENCE OF THE FEMININE: THE AWAKENING OF THE SOUL

Earth, isn't this what you want: an invisible arising in us…. What is your urgent command, if not transformation?
— Rilke, *Ninth Duino Elegy*

The last four chapters have described the pathology of the Phase of Separation and explored the reasons why we gradually lost the instinctive awareness that we lived within the Sacred Order of an ensouled world. They have described the causes and the effects of a one-eyed consciousness: a masculine consciousness that has lost touch with the soul. During this Phase of Separation, the Feminine, once associated with the image of the Great Mother and the Great Goddesses of earlier cultures, as well as with the soul and the neglected feeling values of the heart, was relegated to the unconscious. This chapter and those which follow will describe how we are beginning to recover those values and what factors are helping or hindering their recovery.

The Desecration of the Anima Mundi or World Soul

The effects on the world of the loss of the Feminine, the loss of soul, are incalculable. Instinctive knowledge of the holy unity of things, reverence for the interconnection of all aspects of life, trust in the power of the imagination and the faculty of the intuition — all this as a way of relating to life through participation rather than through dominance and control, has almost been lost. We can see the effects of this loss of soul everywhere today, not only in the devastation and pollution of vast swathes of the Earth, but in the unhappy, impoverished and hopeless existence that people endure in the hideous and ever-expanding suburbs of our cities, in the increase of diseases like cancer, diabetes and mental illness

— particularly depression. The old are neglected and even ill-treated in a culture more interested in achieving targets than caring for people. The young are offered nothing to aspire to beyond the material goals promoted by the media. Women are degraded by having their bodies exploited to sell every kind of commodity. The human heart cries out for the return of beauty, for a place of sanctuary, for community and relationship, where the inner life is seen to be as important as the outer and where a unifying sacred order to life on this planet is recognized and honoured.

In the wider context of the planet, forests are not cherished as sacred places but are cut down to supply paper and packaging or to establish cattle farms or crops to provide biofuels for energy; mountains are hollowed out to extract the minerals needed to construct nuclear reactors, computers and mobile phones; areas of land are shattered by explosions, eviscerated and scarred to extract shale oil or gas; military bases are constructed as launch pads for guided missiles on land that was once the sacred territory of people whose ancestors had lived there for centuries (Diego Garcia in the Chagos Islands). The Arctic is pillaged to extract vital supplies of oil and gas. Animals are viewed in terms of the amount of food we need to feed our ever-increasing numbers, not in terms of their well-being. Vast tracts of Africa are bought up to provide land for biofuel crops or food for states whose own land cannot supply it in sufficient quantity for their growing populations.

What does this pattern of exploitation amount to if not the crime of ecocide, with our species destroying the habitat on which all species depend? Ecocide leads not only to the destruction of the environment but to wars over diminishing resources and crimes against humanity as conflicts proliferate.

As this process has accelerated, nations have come to be viewed as markets to be exploited for financial gain and, if necessary, brought to their knees by financial traders, without a thought for the millions of helpless people whose livelihoods and lives may be destroyed. Politicians debate the radical cuts in expenditure needed to reduce the towering amounts of national debt, incurred through years of injudicious borrowing and promises made to the electorate in order to ensure their re-election. Decades pass as men argue the pros and cons of climate change and only a small proportion of the funds promised by governments to help protect the rainforests of the world reaches their destination. A Charter for the Earth, which offers an agenda for a different relationship with the planet, exists, but governments and powerful corporations pay little heed to it. All this might be described as a desecration of the *Anima Mundi* or Soul of the World.

A Definition of the Feminine

Ever since I had the visionary dream of the cosmic woman I have wondered what her message was. Why did such an image appear to me and what was it asking of me? What, in its deepest sense, does the word 'Feminine' mean? As I am defining it in this book it does not refer to the female sexual attractiveness that is so promoted in today's world, nor to the qualities of caring and gentleness usually, though not exclusively, identified with women, nor to the feminist agenda of the empowerment of women in a man's world.

The word 'Feminine' stands for the Soul and the unseen cosmic web of life that connects each one of us to all others and to the life of the planet and the greater life of the Cosmos. It stands for the recognition that we live within a Sacred Order and that we have a responsibility to protect the life of the planet and all the variety of species it embraces instead of exploiting them for the benefit of our species alone. In sum, the word 'Feminine' stands for a totally different perspective on life, a totally different worldview or paradigm of reality and for the feeling values which might reflect and support that worldview. It stands for a new planetary consciousness and the arduous creation of a new kind of civilization.

Without reconnecting to the Soul and the guidance and wisdom of the Feminine, without going in search of the values it represents and opening our own heart to its subtle guidance, we will not understand the purpose of our presence on this planet, nor will we be able to disempower the unconscious atavistic tendencies which draw us ever closer to the destruction of our habitat and therefore to self-annihilation.

Like the magma of the Earth's core, the long repressed feminine principle is rising to meet the masculine one in response to a deep soul impulse to balance and marry these archetypal energies within ourselves and within our world. The resurgence of the Feminine invites a new planetary consciousness where the deepest instincts of the heart in both men and women — compassion, informed intelligence and a longing to protect, heal and make whole — are able to find expression in ways that can best be described as devotion to planetary and cosmic life.

Christopher Bache, in his extraordinary book, *Dark Night, Early Dawn*, describes this powerful new soul-awakening:

> The great difficulty I have is in describing the enormity of what is being birthed. The true focus of this creative process is not individuals but all humanity. It is actually trying to reawaken the entire species. What is emerging is a consciousness of unprecedented proportions, the entire human species integrated into a unified field of awareness. The species reconnected with its Fundamental Nature. Our thoughts tuned to Source Consciousness.[1]

Awakening to the Feminine means becoming protective of the whole of creation; dying to all the divisive ways of looking at life and each other; being born into an utterly different vision of reality. As it becomes more conscious in us, we are already becoming aware of our dependence for our continued existence on the integrity and sustainability of the planetary biosphere. Our image of reality and our relationship with the planet and with each other are being transformed as we assimilate the implications of this 'marriage' of the two primary archetypal principles which, in Kabbalah, correspond to the left- and right-hand pillars of the Tree of Life. The return of the Feminine has the impact of a planetary earthquake, dissolving long-established social patterns, political and financial systems and religious institutions, asking for a radical transformation of our values, our relationships and our understanding of life.

I think we can find this new evolutionary impulse reflected in a drawing by Henry Moore, drawn at the darkest time of the Second World War. It shows a group of people gathered round a huge shrouded figure, their smallness dwarfed by its towering height. Beneath the shroud and the ropes which hold it in place is a feminine shape. This drawing suggests that a new image of spirit, or perhaps a long-lost one, was stirring to life in the collective soul of humanity, waiting to be unveiled, waiting to be recognized and received by us. Henry Moore's greatest sculptures have the same feminine impress. His 'Shelter' drawings take us back to the maternal womb hidden beneath the earth — the cave-like underground passages where we sought sanctuary as bombs rained death upon our cities. Many of his sculptures and drawings focus on the image of a mother and child or the monumental figure of woman. His work points to the resurgence of the feminine archetype in the human soul and the global awakening of the *Anima Mundi* or World Soul.

The Resurgence of the Feminine Today

The theme of the lost Feminine Value weaves like a golden thread through the mythology, poetry and literature of Western civilization, waiting to be redeemed at this present time when so much is at stake. Over the last sixty years there have been certain events which have heralded a change of consciousness comparable to that which took place in twelfth century Europe with the building of the great cathedrals in honour of the Virgin Mary and the pilgrimages to the sites held sacred to the Black Madonna. This time round, though, the change of consciousness is not confined to Europe but involves the whole world. Like a multi-faceted diamond, there are many aspects to the emerging influence of the Feminine. All are contributing to the healing of the long-standing dissociation between spirit and nature during the solar era. Each is intrinsic to a psychic impulse which might be called the recovery of the soul — an evolutionary impulse arising from the very heart of humanity and perhaps even from the heart of the Cosmos. I mean recovery in two senses: first, the sense of something that was ailing, diminished or neglected being restored to health; secondly, the sense of something of great value being recovered.

The influence of the Feminine is responsible for the growth of the Environmental Movement; for the determination of women in every culture to free themselves from their long oppression and encourage their increased participation in society; for the interest in the so-called non-rational; for many new approaches to healing both psyche and body. It is reflected in the mounting revulsion for our weapons of mass destruction; in compassion for the helpless victims of our addiction to war; in the engagement of hundreds of thousands of people in the work of helping both the planet and the victims of oppression. These different channels of influence are creating new perspectives on life, new ways of connection that bring together body, soul, mind and spirit. All this is being accelerated by the connections between people facilitated by the Internet and by online organizations like Avaaz which now has many millions of subscribers.

The recovery of the Feminine invites a reorientation of consciousness: a receptivity not only to the events occurring in the external world but to the long-ignored voice of the Soul. The activation of the Feminine is helping us to relate to the deep cosmic source of our psychic life and draw up the living waters from those depths. This enormous shift challenges every aspect of our beliefs. It immeasurably deepens and broadens our perspective on our presence on this planet. It gives deeper meaning to our lives. It is changing everything.

It may be that the new epoch we are entering will see the birth of a very different image of God or Spirit, a new understanding of the instinctive intelligence within the processes and patterns of nature, and how the unseen or inner dimension of reality influences and interacts with this physical dimension. This new understanding may help us to recover an authentic spirituality that takes us beyond religious and secular beliefs into a new sense of relationship with a sacred Earth and an ensouled Cosmos. From our work on *The Myth of the Goddess* and its last chapter that Jules and I called 'the Sacred Marriage', I know that this emerging phase in the story of our species could herald an evolutionary advance as spirit and nature are reunited and humanity enters into a conscious relationship and partnership with life, seeking to serve it with insight, compassion and wisdom.

The Signs of a Change of Consciousness

In his late work, *Mysterium Coniunctionis*, Jung wrote that the "ultimate fate of every dogma is that it gradually becomes soulless. Life wants to create new forms, and therefore, when a dogma loses its vitality, it must perforce activate the archetype that has always helped man to express the mystery of the soul".[2] In the 1950's few people outside the Jungian community in Zurich would have connected a change of consciousness with a focus on the Feminine and a recognition of the feminine aspect of the divine. The first indication of this change came with the discovery in 1945 of the Gnostic texts hidden for nearly two millennia in earthenware jars at Nag Hammadi, in Egypt. As scholars began to translate and comment on these texts, it became apparent that certain Gnostic groups had worshipped God as both Mother and Father. Elaine Pagels' ground-breaking book, *The Gnostic Gospels* (1980) brought these discoveries to a wider public. Her book was the precursor of a flood of books on the Goddess, of which *The Myth of the Goddess* was one. This was one avenue through which the sacred image of the Feminine was restored to modern culture.

A second avenue was opened by the Papal Bull of Pius XII (1950), which, in response to a petition from millions of Catholics, officially declared the Virgin Mary to be "Assumed into Heaven, Body and Soul". An Encyclical of 1954 named her as Queen of Heaven, thereby restoring to her the cosmic dimension held by the Goddess in the great civilizations of the Bronze Age. The new Decree affirmed that, symbolically, Mary as Bride was united with her Son in the heavenly bridal chamber and that, as Sophia (Wisdom), she was united with the godhead.

With these two Decrees, the longing of the Catholic people, beginning over a thousand years earlier, to have an image of the divine mother — a Queen of Heaven — in the godhead, was answered. Some forty years later, in 1997, a further petition was presented to the Pope asking that Mary be declared co-redemptrix with Christ. Although he died before this later petition was assembled, Jung knew that the two Papal Decrees reflected the fact that something of great significance was happening in the collective psyche and saw them as the single most significant religious act since the Reformation. Mythologically speaking, the feminine archetype, including both body and soul and personified by the Virgin Mary, was being raised to the level of parity with the masculine one of spirit, heralding a 'sacred marriage' of the two great archetypal principles that would soon begin to find expression in the collective soul of humanity. The feminine dimension of the divine, so long denied recognition in a civilization dominated by the masculine archetype, would be included in the godhead and restored to the position it held in the pre-patriarchal world. Nature and spirit, long sundered in human consciousness, would be reunited; the long and disastrous polarization between them would come to an end.

Jung believed that this symbolic event, prefigured in the Renaissance in the many exquisite paintings of the Coronation of the Virgin, pointed to the reunion of spirit and nature and, within ourselves, the reunion of the dissociated conscious mind with the matrix of the psyche — the long-neglected instinctual soul. Familiar with the mythological history which had led to this moment, he saw this archetypal reunion as a new image of the sacred marriage, the ancient Bronze Age ritual which once celebrated the union of heaven and earth. He also saw it as a herald of the great event awaited in the Jewish mystical tradition of Kabbalah: the wedding of the two long-separated aspects of the godhead — the Holy One and His Shekinah (described in Chapter Three).

But it is not only the two papal Decrees that signified a change of consciousness in the relationship between the two archetypal principles. People have been surprised by the popularity of Dan Brown's *The Da Vinci Code* and the earlier *Holy Blood, Holy Grail*, co-authored by Michael Baigent, Richard Leigh and Henry Lincoln. The focus of both these books was the relationship between Jesus and Mary Magdalene. Together with many other books about her, they have brought Mary Magdalene out of her long obscurity, acknowledging her as the first among the apostles of Jesus as well as his close companion, possibly even his wife (See page 179 for *The Gospel of the Beloved Companion*).

From a Jungian perspective, the phenomenal sales of these books about Mary Magdalene reflect the power of a returning archetype and the unconscious longing for the union of the masculine and feminine principles at the highest level — reflected in the close and loving relationship between Jesus and Mary Magdalene. The 'child' born of their relationship signifies, in an archetypal sense, not the fruit of the blood-line of Jesus but the birth of a new level of consciousness in the whole of humanity.

The Triggers for a Global Awakening of the Anima Mundi or World Soul

Looking back over the last seventy years, there were other events which contributed to this change of consciousness. In 1945, one of these was the shocking revelation of human barbarism in the discovery of Auschwitz. Another was the discovery of nuclear fission, the making of the atomic bomb and the obliteration of Hiroshima and Nagasaki. These events separated the past from the future and made it clear that something had to change in human consciousness. We now had the god-like power to destroy ourselves but not the god-like intelligence to prevent ourselves doing so.

Then we were made aware of a different kind of threat. The biologist Rachel Carson was the first to sound the alarm in 1962 with her book *Silent Spring*. She drew attention to the interdependence of the human, animal and plant orders of life and the danger of contaminating air, soil and ocean with the dangerous chemicals (DDT) that were at that time being widely and indiscriminately used to control insects. With this book, the Environmental Movement was born. In it she challenged the scientific myth of the control of nature, born, she said, of the Neanderthal age of biology and philosophy when it was supposed that nature existed for the convenience of man. "It is our alarming misfortune," she wrote, "that so primitive a science has armed itself with the most terrible weapons, and that in turning them against the insects it has also turned them against the earth."[3] The furious anger and misogynistic contempt she provoked in the chemical companies who attacked her as "more poisonous than the pesticides she condemned", revealed both the abyss of human ignorance about the interrelated systems of life on the planet and also the power of entrenched attitudes to resist any change. Tragically, she died of cancer after the publication of her book. But long before her death she drew attention to the dangers of human interference with the balance of nature. In the preface to the 1961 edition of *The Sea Around Us*, first published in 1950, she warned of the effects of disposing of nuclear residues in the sea:

> In unlocking the secrets of the atom, modern man has found himself confronted with a frightening problem — what to do with the most dangerous materials that have ever existed in all the earth's history, the by-products of atomic fission. The stark problem that faces him is whether he can dispose of these lethal substances without rendering the earth uninhabitable.[4]

Silent Spring initiated the birth of a different attitude towards nature. Under its influence, the idea began to come into being that we could not continue to act as if we were the masters of the planet. It began to dawn on us that the kingdom of nature is a seamless robe. We are part of this robe, clothed with it, nourished and protected by it yet, at the same time, because of the unique development of consciousness in our species, we are the only aspect of life that can become aware of the marvel of the planetary organism in which all our lives are embedded. We therefore have a responsibility towards it; a responsibility to safeguard and protect it.

The Awakening of a Sense of Relationship with the Earth

Perhaps the most significant event for this awakening was the first view of the Earth appearing above the rim of the moon ('Earthrise'), taken during the second manned mission to the moon (Apollo 8 1968). Then the astronauts' landing on the moon in July 1969 (Apollo 11) gave us the breath-taking view of the Earth seen from space. 500 million people watched the Apollo landing and listened to Neil Armstrong's famous words. The technological feat of putting man on the moon was awe-inspiring in itself. But the very sight of the Earth seen from this distance was the catalyst that changed our relationship with it. For the first time we became visually aware of the exquisite beauty and fragility of our planet and knew it was our home in the vastness of the Cosmos. It seemed so beautiful, so precious and so vulnerable. Love of our blue planet awoke in our hearts. The words of Gene Cernan, the last astronaut to leave the moon on NASA's final mission (Apollo 17), convey the marvel of his experience for the whole of humanity: "I stood in the blue darkness and looked in awe at the earth from the lunar surface. What I saw was too beautiful to grasp — there was too much logic, too much purpose. It was too beautiful to have happened by accident."

In the space of a few hours, our planetary eyes expanded to become cosmic eyes. In those few hours the sense of expansion was extraordinary, as our relationship with the Cosmos and our perception of ourselves was transformed. The fact that it was the moon that was being explored — age-old symbol of the Great Mother, the Feminine and the soul — was in itself significant. But it was the sight of our planet from the moon that lifted us beyond national and regional allegiances and opened our awareness to cosmic consciousness and a sense of belonging to the Cosmos.

The mythologist Joseph Campbell gave expression to something that many of us felt: "We are at this moment," he said, "participating in one of the very greatest leaps of the human spirit to a knowledge not only of outside nature but also of our own deep inward mystery — the greatest ever."[5] He asked what the emerging myth of our time would be and answered his question by saying that it would be a mythology of the unified Earth as one harmonious being.

On a later journey back from the moon, the astronaut Edgar Mitchell, founder of the Institute of Noetic Sciences, realized that his distant view of the Earth was a glimpse of divinity. "Gazing through 240,000 miles of space towards the stars and the planet from which I had come, I suddenly experienced the Universe as intelligent, loving, harmonious."

What I experienced during that three-day trip home was nothing short of an overwhelming sense of the universal connectedness. I actually felt what has been described as an ecstasy of unity. It occurred to me that the molecules of my body and the molecules of the spacecraft itself were manufactured long ago in the furnace of one of the ancient stars that burned in the heavens about me… the awe-inspiring beauty of the cosmos suddenly overcame me. While still aware of the separateness of my existence, my mind was flooded with an intuitive knowing that everything is interconnected—that this magnificent universe is a harmonious, directed, purposeful whole. And that we humans, both as individuals and as a species, are an integral part of the ongoing process of creation.[6]

Books followed that were written from a totally different perspective and set the agenda for a transformation of our attitude to the Earth: in 1972 Barbara Ward's *Only One Earth: The Care and Maintenance of a Small Planet* was published and, in 1979, a second book called *Progress for a Small Planet* in which she laid out a plan for the care of the biosphere and another to address the problem of global poverty. In 1975, Schumacher's phenomenally influential *Small is Beautiful* was published. In 1972, Donella and Dennis Meadows' *Limits to Growth* addressed the threat to the Earth from over-population. In the early 80's Fritjof Capra's two books *The Tao of Physics* and *The Turning Point* focused on the need for a transformation of our attitude towards nature and matter, grounding this in his knowledge of the science of quantum physics which revealed life to be an indissoluble tissue of relationships and the observer an inseparable part of what he was observing. The very title of the second book was a significant pointer to a change of consciousness.

In that decade, we became alarmed by the threat of a Nuclear Winter which could throw us back to the beginning of evolution, contaminating soil and water with the residue of nuclear bombs a hundred times more powerful than those used on Hiroshima. Yet Einstein's prophetic warning was ignored: "The unleashing of the power of the atom bomb has changed everything except our mode of thinking, and thus we head toward unparalleled catastrophes."[7] Few governments consciously acknowledged the enormity of what they were willing to inflict on a helpless civilian population in order to ensure the survival of their particular nation. Each nuclear state was prepared to annihilate millions of innocent people and pollute the earth for generations in an exchange of nuclear missiles. For the decades of the Cold War the tension between competing empires and ideologies powered the escalation of military technology and, as this developed on each side, it was extended to the Star Wars programme and the race for military control in space as well as on earth. Arguing that the bomb would act as a deterrent, those promoting the arms race did not acknowledge that in an exchange of nuclear missiles, there would, as Jonathan Schell commented in his book, *The Fate of the Earth* (1982), be no victor and no vanquished: both would be extinguished along with hundreds of millions of helpless civilians. "The question now before the human species is whether life or death will prevail on the earth.... No generation before ours has held the life and death of its species in its hands.... In our present-day world, in the councils where the decisions are made, there is no one to speak for man and for the Earth, although both are threatened with annihilation."[8]

The Nuclear Disarmament Movement, which grew into CND, was founded and grew rapidly. Many people, including myself, began to think in planetary terms, rather than national ones, understanding that we had to transcend old habits, old patterns of behaviour if we were to survive as a species and protect the Earth. One example of this was the movement initiated in England in 1981 by Ann Pettitt, which grew into the protest of the Greenham Common women against the American Cruise and Pershing Missiles. They called themselves "Women for Life on Earth" because, they said, "These weapons go on killing silently and invisibly through generations as yet unborn."[9]

Increasing disillusionment with political and religious leaders and institutions was part of this awakening, together with the growing realization that each individual carried a responsibility, however humble, for challenging the dominant ethos of the culture — a responsibility highlighted by Jung's prophetic words: "The world today hangs by a thin thread and that thread is the psyche of man.... It is not the reality of the hydrogen bomb that we need to fear, but what man will do with it."[10]

These books and many others in recent years have made it clear that the fate of our species is inseparably bound up with the planetary biosphere, echoing the perception of Chief Seattle that whatever we do to the Earth, we do to ourselves. James Lovelock's book on the inter-relationship of all the Earth's systems and his naming the biosphere Gaia after the Greek Goddess of Earth restored to the world the ancient image of the Earth as Goddess and Mother.

Thomas Berry in his books *The Dream of the Earth* (1990) and *Evening Thoughts* (2006) insisted, in uncompromising language, that we wake up to what, in our fantasy of progress, we are inflicting on the Earth and its living systems:

> Just now our modern world, with its scientific technologies, its industrial processes, and its commercial establishments, functions with amazing arrogance in its attitude toward the natural world. The human is seen as the supreme reality. Every other being is available for exploitation.... The difficulty at present is not only that the individual nations see themselves and their own well-being as the ultimate referent as regards reality and value, but also that the human tends to establish a discontinuity between itself and the natural world. In this manner the nonhuman world is reduced to being objects to be

used by humans for their own purposes, rather than functioning as participants
in a single integral community of existence. Not only is the human community
out of alignment with the functioning of the planet, but also the human
community has become a predator draining the life of its host....[11]

The Environmental or Ecological Movement grew from the recognition of the
threat to the biosphere from the industrial and chemical pollution of air, water and
soil. Friends of the Earth was founded in 1972. Greenpeace followed. Fifty years
have seen the foundations laid for a transformation of our relationship with the
planet and the emergence of many groups of individuals who are committed to
trying to counteract the effects of human ignorance and greed. These form a new
planetary entity, no longer national in character but one which is held together by
shared values and a shared commitment to implementing them. Paul Hawken's
book, *Blessed Unrest* (2007), collates the many facets of this new movement and
mentions the fact that as a result of his research over fifteen years, he has identified
what may be the largest social movement in human history. This movement
comprises a million or more grassroots groups working to help the planet and to
improve the lives of the oppressed and destitute and those, like the indigenous
forest peoples of the world, whose survival is threatened by the predatory greed
of the trans-national companies. Thirty-eight organizations now exist to protect
the Amazon region alone and ever more strenuous efforts are being made to save
the Indonesian and Malaysian rainforests from being cut down to supply cardboard
for toys or to use the cleared ground to grow crops for biofuels or, in the case of
the Amazonian forest, grazing for cattle to satisfy the voracious demand for beef.

In this new worldwide collaboration on behalf of people, on behalf of the
ecosystem of the planet, the foundations have been laid for the development of a
contemporary image of man and woman as Custodians of Life — custodians
because the care of the planet is increasingly felt by many to be a sacred trust. All
this has arisen out of the activation of what might be called soul or heart values
— the desire to care for life and for our home in the Cosmos. It is these values
which are at the core of the emerging Feminine and are increasingly challenging
the long-established values of power, control and exploitation which still drive
the political and corporate agendas of the world. We are becoming more concerned
to protect the delicate ecological balance of the planet, more aware that we are
inviting our own destruction through our continued aggression towards each other
and our blind exploitation of the planet's dwindling resources. Quite apart from
this, the rapid growth of obesity with its attendant diseases on the one hand and
increasing hunger and deprivation on the other, as well as the trillions of dollars
wasted on weapons and wars, and the enormous debts now carried by many

governments, are being recognized as unsustainable.

The naturalist and biologist Sir David Attenborough has pointed out in his many television programmes the effects of what we have unwittingly done and are still doing to the millions of species on the planet and asks whether we are to be the cause of the sixth great extinction. He has warned us that never before has there been a challenge which involved the whole of humanity and that all the environmental problems we face become harder — and ultimately impossible — to solve with ever more people. At the end of the last programme of his series Frozen Planet (2011), he urges us to take heed of what we have seen:

> The poles, North and South, may seem very remote. But what is happening here is likely to have a greater effect upon us than any other aspect of global warming. If the Arctic sea ice continues to disappear, it will drive up the planet's temperature more quickly, and the melting ice sheets could contribute to a sea level rise of a metre, enough to threaten the homes of millions of people around the world's coasts by the end of the century. We've seen that the animals are already adapting to these changes. But can we respond to what is happening now to the frozen planet?

The Arctic ice sheet acts like a protective lid that regulates the Earth's temperature, keeping the climate stable. If it melts altogether, there is no protection from the effects of global warming. With regard to its extent, in just one year between 2006 and 2007, 1.5 million square kilometres of ice were lost in the Arctic Circle. In 2012 alone more than 600,000 square kilometres have melted. About 4 million square kilometres of ice are left. As early as 2020, there may be no ice left in summer. All the 'Great Powers' can think of doing is to compete with each other to lay claim to the oil and gas reserves to which the melting ice has given them access.[12]

It has now been ascertained that the gases created by scientists to replace CFC's which were causing the decrease of the Earth's ozone layer, have had an unexpected and devastating side-effect: they have increased global warming by 20%. Yet they have not received the urgent attention they merit. Powerful interests are resisting banning the hydrofluorocarbons (HFC) and perfluorocarbons (PFC) which are contributing to global warming (Sunday Times 16/9/2012).

James Lovelock has described the catastrophic effects of our technological culture on the planetary biosphere and has warned that during this century six billion of us could be wiped out by the effects of global warming. Both he and Sir David Attenborough have shown how life on this planet is an interconnected web of which we are a part and which we can no longer exploit for our sole benefit. The aerial views of the planet seen from space show us beyond a shadow of a doubt the effects of over-population and our industrial expansion on the land, the oceans and the atmosphere.

As the most powerful nations and corporations of the world compete for control of ever-diminishing water, oil, land for crops, and minerals, none of them is reflecting on the effects that an increasing scarcity of commodities will have on the growing population of the planet or the effect of that growing population on its diminishing resources and the planetary environment. Jonathan Porritt writes in the autumn 2012 edition of Resurgence magazine that "We are already using 50% more resources than the Earth can sustainably provide, and unless we change course very fast indeed, even two planet Earths will not be enough to meet our burgeoning economic demands (on a business-as-usual basis) by 2030."

The temperature of the oceans is changing and affecting the plankton on which multitudes of fish feed. The ocean is 30% more acidic than it was in pre-industrial times. We already know we are driving many species of fish to extinction but are incapable of imposing the necessary limits for the stock to replenish itself. Shockingly, huge amounts of fish are thrown away dead because they 'exceed the quota'.

We can now see the shrinking glaciers of the Himalaya, the Karakorum, the high Andes, and the Alps, the melting Arctic and Antarctic ice, the diminishing rainforests, the huge area of plastic detritus floating in the Pacific. The glaciers of Central Asia feed the great rivers — the Ganges, the Indus and the Brahmaputra — on which hundreds of millions of people and animals depend for their survival.

Today we are facing a choice and the greatest challenge humanity has ever faced — a crisis that our industrialized culture and our ever-burgeoning numbers have brought into being and of which governments as a whole are still only vaguely conscious and reluctant to address. James Lovelock gives us the un-welcome information that it is the breath of 7 billion of us and our dependent animals that is responsible for 23% of all greenhouse emissions — more than ten times the emissions of all air travel. In 1820 the population of the world was 1 billion. In 2018 it reached 7.7 billion. By 2050 it is estimated to reach 10.5 billion at present growth rates. Living in an ever more crowded world, young people may not realize that the world population has trebled since 1945, yet there is no concerted attempt by Christian, Muslim, Hindu or secular societies to suggest limiting families to two children so that parents replace themselves but do not leave a legacy of multiple descendents.

Since 1945 we have been faced with the growing danger from four new threats which were unimaginable sixty years ago.

- Firstly, climate change and its attendant problems.

- Secondly, the over-population of the planet which is already leading to armed struggles for increasingly scarce food and water. By 2025 three billion people will be short of water (estimate www.populationmatters.org). The problem is already acute in the Middle East where so much water has been taken from the headwaters of the river Jordan that the river has become a stream. Climate change has reduced rainfall and left aquifers depleted. There is simply not enough water to support the huge numbers of people which, in some places, have doubled in thirty years. Famine affects tens of millions of people in Somalia where constant fighting between a weak government and Islamist militants makes any long term solution to the food problem impossible.

- Thirdly, the renewed threat of war and the massive loss of life and contamination of the planet that would result from the deliberate or inadvertent use of our weapons of mass destruction.

- Fourthly, the decreasing amount of land available to grow food because it is being appropriated to raise crops for biofuels. Large companies in the West, backed by African governments, have designated huge areas of land in African countries for growing crops for biofuels, often seizing the land from already impoverished people without any form of compensation and paying them miserable wages for their work on palm oil plantations
(report: Friends of the Earth 2012).

If the temperature of the planet should rise by 2°C, it will make parts of the planet uninhabitable and drive billions to seek ever-diminishing supplies of food and water. China in 2011 has had five years of drought which has affected its rice and wheat crops. Russia had a severe drought which destroyed the wheat crop in 2010. The United States had the most severe drought in living memory in 2012, affecting both the wheat and maize crops. Parts of Europe have also suffered from drought in some areas and torrential rainfall in others, both of which affect crops. Huge fires devastate eastern Australia. All of these diminish the quantity and raise the cost of food. Yet still governments pursue their national agendas and fail to think with a global sense of urgency about all these issues. With survival instincts now registering on high alert, many people are challenging the whole power-driven ethos of modern culture with its rampant consumerism and emphasis on perpetual growth and are searching for ways to halt the apparent headlong impulsion of our species and its unconscious political leaders towards catastrophe.

The Healing Power of the Feminine

As long ago as Bronze Age Sumer and Egypt, records detailed the charitable impulses to care for the orphaned, the widowed and the sick. Today, apart from the thousands of charities and NGO's which have come into being to assist the millions in need of help, there is increasing pressure on governments to act ethically and with the welfare of the planet in mind. Thanks to television, we have a far greater awareness of the suffering of people all over the world. We participate through witnessing and empathizing with the suffering of people remote from ourselves. Wherever the call to compassion goes out, there is the voice of the heart, the voice of the Feminine.

The focus of the Feminine is on the values that have been obscured, marginalized or incompletely developed during the solar age. These values can never be recovered by force or even by strident demand. They can only manifest as human consciousness changes and facilitates their emergence. One example of the emergence of these values is the establishment of the International Court in The Hague, designed to try men and women who have been deemed to have committed crimes against humanity. Rape has now been designated a war crime. Leaders can no longer claim that the atrocities and acts of genocide they commit are in defence of their national interests.

Because we are now, through television and the internet, witness to the immense suffering in the world, we carry the grief of millions in our hearts — grief that so many helpless people are still the victims of conflict and oppression, autocratic rulers, drugs and trafficking, hunger and deprivation. Worldwide, we can collectively register outrage over the torture and murder of the thirteen-year-old Syrian boy Hamza al-Khatib, the threat to Sakineh Mohammadi Ashtiani of being stoned to death in Iran or a courageous fourteen-year old Pakistani girl, Malala Yousafzai, being shot in the face by the Taliban because she dared to speak up for women's education. In their treatment of women, certain Muslim societies today can be compared to Europe at the height of the witch trials, when women lived in fear of being denounced, tortured and burnt at the stake. Our collective responses to these atrocities reflect moral progress in the world soul. A shocking report by the UN some ten years ago showed that the 22 members of the Arab League, with a total population of 280 million people (65 million of whom are illiterate), have a lamentable shortage of the three essentials for growth and well being: freedom, education and women's rights. This report helped to light the fuse that led to the explosion of the Arab Spring in North Africa in 2011 (*The Times* 29/7/11).

A response to the Feminine asks that war and the creation of weapons of destruction are relinquished just as racism and conquests in the name of God or any other ideology need to be relinquished. If we can abandon our addiction to weapons and war, directing the trillions saved to feeding, educating and caring for the children of the world, the result will be an infinitely better world and the possibility of our own survival as a species. We need urgently to challenge the arcane warrior ethos of governments which demands continual preparation for war, selling arms for profit and bringing devastating new weapons into being.

As a new cultural impulse, the Feminine is putting us in touch with the deep sources of our psychic life, drawing up from these depths the living waters which nourish and sustain the soul. It is creating a new kind of planetary morality, assisted by the Internet and people on different continents drawn together by shared values and a common cause. It is encouraging people to overcome patterns of subservience established for millennia, helping them to throw off their bondage to oppressive autocratic leaders and establish democratic governments which serve their hopes for a better life. It is freeing women from centuries of oppression, enforced silence and virtual slavery.

The Emerging Power of Woman

The image of woman has been through a radical transformation during the twentieth century which continues in this new millennium. The Suffragette Movement broke the spell of the belief that men were the superior sex and opened the door to women in general to have access to education and to careers that had long been denied them. The First and Second World Wars and the arrival of contraception accelerated women's emergence into society after centuries of seclusion and oppression. A radical cultural revolution was initiated, shaking social attitudes to their foundations. The relationship between man and woman has been profoundly altered as women have emerged into the wider life of society hitherto dominated by men, taking up careers in medicine, science, law, politics and international affairs that were previously barred to them. The recent 2012 Olympics in London have been an extraordinary event for women when, for the first time, all countries which participated in them included women in their teams and they have triumphed in many sports formerly only open to men. But their new role in society is by no means complete or effective, particularly in the Islamic world but also in the West.

At the end of the Second World War, at the end of an essay on *Women in Europe*, part of a larger book called *Civilization in Transition*, Jung noted that it was the task of women to bring together what man had sundered and ended the chapter with the words, "God himself cannot flourish if man's soul is starved. The feminine psyche responds to this hunger, for it is the function of Eros to unite what Logos has sundered. The woman of today is faced with a tremendous cultural task — perhaps it will be the dawn of a new era."[13]

What then is woman's tremendous cultural task? It is surely nothing less than to free herself from oppression, persecution and marginalization so that her voice can act as an advocate for a new and better kind of civilization. UN Resolution 1325, passed in 2000, reaffirmed that women must be included in all aspects of peacemaking and peace-building discussions. The fact that this resolution has been effectively ignored humiliates women and shames men. The words of Michelle Bachelet, Executive Director of UN Women 2011, reminded the world that "Women's strength, women's industry, women's wisdom are humankind's greatest untapped resource."

Educated and articulate women on every continent are awakening to a new role as advocates of justice for their gender and also for the emerging soul values which have been so neglected and are so desperately needed. In many different parts of the world, individual women are speaking out with immense courage against oppression — of themselves and others. Women like Aung San Suu Kyi in Burma, for years a prisoner in her own house and recently freed (2012), and Shirin Ebadi in Iran, once a judge in Teheran, now in exile, are challenging the cruel and oppressive regimes that wish to silence their voice and the voice of free-dom. In these regimes, as Shirin Ebadi has said, women know that the victory of women's rights is the beginning of democracy.

The answer to the question "What do women really want?", asked by Freud early in the last century, is that women want themselves and their societies to live in freedom from fear, from hunger and destitution, from war and oppression. The world needs to hear the voice of women from every nation. Education and con-traception have transformed the lives of millions of women yet countless millions of others, through destitution, prejudice or tribal custom, have no access to either. These live in abject poverty, victims of the brutality and neglect of men, used as sexual objects and (in Africa in particular) infected with AIDS by their husbands and partners. They struggle to keep themselves and their children alive from day to day, are forced into prostitution through poverty, paid miserable wages that barely sustain them and their children and are unable to express their distress or find witnesses who will speak up for them. Contraception, which should be the right of every woman, is denied to them by religious prejudice and social custom.

Women in Afghanistan and Pakistan, for example, risk imprisonment, torture and death for speaking out against the oppression they endure in their misogynistic cultures where they are condemned by tribal custom to a diminished life of servitude and suffering. Women in India are still being burnt alive for their failure to supply a dowry (estimate 25,000 annually). Women widowed by war suffer poverty, neglect and misery. Thousands of women in Syria are being raped and their children kidnapped, tortured and murdered as part of their government's attempt to stifle dissent. Even in Egypt, where they participated in its revolution, highly educated women are not so far included in the drafting of new political institutions and there is a danger in the newly liberated Islamic countries that the old habits of repression will be re-established.

In so-called advanced societies with a high standard of living, domestic violence still blights the lives of women and their children. The plight of all these suffering women and their children is unacceptable in a world where communications are increasingly easy, where the pitiable condition of women and their children can be seen on television, where wealth and medical expertise exist which could alleviate the suffering of so many.

Woman's own awakening is part of the recovery of the Feminine. It is as if a momentous birth is taking place in the collective psyche of woman. This birth may be experienced as something that is difficult and even dangerous, as well as something exciting and transformative. The planet needs women to challenge the current established political ways and deplorable struggles for power, and awaken the human community to a higher destiny and a different goal. It needs women to come out of the dark: to emerge into the light; to become visible and audible; to take the initiative in creating the change they long for.

Aung San Suu Kyi, in her opening keynote address to the Fourth UN World Conference on Women in Beijing in 1995, made a memorable statement on the contribution women can make to a different world, a truly enlightened and balanced civilization:

> For millennia women have dedicated themselves almost exclusively to the task of nurturing, protecting and caring for the young and the old, striving for the conditions of peace that favour life as a whole. To this can be added the fact that, to the best of my knowledge, no war was ever started by women. But it is women and children who have always suffered most in situations of conflict. Now that we are gaining control of the primary historical role imposed on us of sustaining life in the context of the home and family, it is time to apply in the arena of the world the wisdom and experience thus gained in activities of peace over so many thousands of years. The education and empowerment of women throughout the world cannot fail to result in a more caring, tolerant, just and peaceful life for all.

As woman gives birth to herself, to her unique individuality, to the emerging awareness of her value as woman (not an imitation of man), the Feminine and the values that belong to it will also emerge in the consciousness of humanity. Woman, whose essential nature is to respond to suffering and need, is experiencing herself as a vessel of transformation in which a new global consciousness is being born. If we are to create a world that is not threatened — possibly even destroyed — by the ongoing power struggles between men, women need to be proportionately represented in national and international government and on every organization and committee set up to address injustice, persecution and human suffering.

Matthew Arnold, the philosopher and poet, declared that if ever there would be a time when women would come together purely and simply for the benefit of mankind, it would be a power such as the world has never known. The Sufi sage, Hazrat Inayat Khan said that he could see as clear as daylight that the hour was coming when women would lead humanity to a higher evolution. In 2009, the Dalai Lama astounded his audience at a conference in Vancouver by saying that the world would be saved by Western woman.

There is a saying by a great Hasidic saint, the Baal Shem Tov, which goes: "When the moon shall shine as bright as the sun, the Messiah will come." Woman through her struggle to articulate the highest values of the feminine principle will begin to make the moon shine so that it can balance the solar brightness of our present consciousness. In recognizing her depression, her suffering, her longing to outgrow the subservience and powerlessness of her past and present experience, in recognizing and supporting her deepest values and longings, she may accomplish something truly heroic and extraordinary for life and the planet, something that humanity in centuries to come will celebrate. For this reason, nothing is of more importance than woman's rescue of herself.

The Awakening of the Soul

The resurgence of the Feminine and the awakening of the Soul are focused on the feeling values that have been incompletely developed, marginalized or obscured during the patriarchal solar era, partly owing to the suppression of woman's voice that has been one of the characteristics of that age. These values can only emerge as human consciousness changes and allows them to emerge. The recovery of the Feminine may be the key to the transformation of our world culture from regression into mass uniformity, banality and brutality into something longed for and extraordinary.

This powerful evolutionary impulse, reconnecting us to our deepest instincts for relationship with each other and with the life of the planet, is working a profound alchemy beneath the surface of our culture. Women and men are participating in a process of transformation that is manifesting as a new planetary consciousness, a new cultural impulse whose emphasis is on the growing recognition of the inter-connection and interdependence of all aspects of life. The arrogant celebration of 'man's conquest of nature' is being replaced by the realization that if we are to survive we need to respect and cherish the planetary life on which our lives depend. While, on the surface, the culture is focused on the superficial concerns propagated by the media, beneath it a new evolutionary and planetary imperative is being prepared by millions of concerned individuals. These new values are embedded in the Earth Charter which offers an agenda for conscious and responsible action on behalf of the planet.[14] They have also been beautifully expressed by the Prince of Wales, who has done so much to protect the equatorial forests of the world, in a paper he wrote some years ago called *A Time to Heal*:

> As I have grown older I have gradually come to realize that my entire life so far has been motivated by a desire to heal: to heal the dismembered landscape and the poisoned soil; the cruelly shattered townscape, where harmony has been replaced by cacophony; to heal the divisions between intuitive and rational thought, between mind, body and soul, so that the temple of our humanity can once again be lit by a sacred flame; to level the monstrous artificial barrier erected between Tradition and Modernity and, above all, to heal the mortally wounded soul that, alone, can give us warning of the folly of playing God and of believing that knowledge on its own is a substitute for wisdom.[15]

Woman's age-old instinct to nurture and sustain life and man's instinct to protect and defend it, are being extended to embrace the life of the Earth. A planet which has taken over 4.5 billion years to evolve an organ of consciousness through which life can come to know itself may be under threat; our own survival is uncertain. Before too long, we may not be able to alter the course of events we have unwit-tingly set in motion. Yet, in response to the extreme peril of this situation, we are beginning to recover the forgotten lunar consciousness of a feeling of relationship with a sacred Earth and a sacred Cosmos. We are drawing together in closer relationship with each other, working towards the goal of rescuing this planet and the lives of future generations from our unconscious and predatory habits of behaviour. The resurgence of the Feminine and the recovery of the Soul are reflected in these different initiatives:

A growing sense of responsibility towards the planet.
A recognition of the inter-connectedness of life.
A conscious effort to heal the soul/mind/body split
A growth of insight into where we are still controlled by unconscious complexes

The emergence of a different quality of relationship between men and women.
A growing awareness of the suffering and needs of children
An awareness that we need to treat all species with respect and compassion

There are four great questions that challenge us now:

1. How do we recover our lost sense of being part of something totally sacred?

2. How do we develop respect and compassion for the life of the Earth in all its forms?

3. How do we find ways of meeting the deepest needs of the human heart for love, relatedness and connection?

4. How do we relinquish the beliefs and patterns of behaviour that have been so damaging to both soul and body as well as to the planet?

There are immense opportunities in this time of transformation but also immense dangers, for the very transforming power of the Feminine activates deep fear of change and evokes the response of reactionary forces which seek to re-assert or maintain control over people's lives. We tread a path which is on the knife-edge between the conscious integration of a new vision on the one hand and social disintegration and regression into barbarism — perhaps the virtual annihilation of our species — on the other. At the beginning of a new millennium, we are participating in the birth of a new era, one with radically different aims and values from those of the solar era. Mythologically speaking, this new era invites the marriage of lunar and solar consciousness and the birth of the 'child' of a new kind of consciousness arising in the soul of humanity that would be the fruit of this union and the true 'saviour' of our species. It is a tremendously exciting, challenging and creative time to be alive.

Notes:

1. Bache, Christopher (2000) *Dark Night, Early Dawn*,
   State University of New York Press, p. 220
2. Jung, C.G. CW14 (1963) trs. R.F.C. Hull, Routledge & Kegan Paul Ltd., par. 488
3. Carson, Rachel (1963) *Silent Spring*, Hamish Hamilton Ltd., London, p. 6
4. Carson (1950) *The Sea Around Us*, OUP, preface
5. Campbell, Joseph (1988) *The Power of Myth*, Doubleday, New York, p. xviii
6. Mitchell, Edgar (1996) astronaut and founder of the Institute of Noetic Sciences.
   The Way of the Explorer, Putnam, New York, pp. 3-4
7. Einstein, Albert (2000) *The Expanded Quotable Einstein*, collected and edited by
   Alice Calaprice, The Hebrew University of Jerusalem and Princeton University Press,
   Princeton, New Jersey, p. 184.
8. Schell, Jonathan (1982) *The Fate of the Earth*, Pan books Ltd., London, pp.113, 116 & 188.
9. Pettitt, Ann (2006) *Walking to Greenham*, Honno Press, UK
10. *Conversations with Carl Jung* (1964) (based on four filmed interviews), Richard Evans,
    Van Nostrand, Princeton
11. Berry, Thomas (2006) *Evening Thoughts*, Sierra Club Books, San Francisco,
    pp. 21 & 82-83
12. Wadhams, Peter (2016) *A Farewell to Ice: A Report from the Arctic*, OUP – an iceberg
    the size of France (Totten Glacier) has broken away from Antartica (March 2018), with a
    large proportion of it floating on the water and increasingly eroded by contact with it. If
    this enormous iceberg were to melt completely it would have the effect of raising the level
    of the oceans by three metres, threatening the cities and communities situated close to the
    shore.
13. Jung, C.G. CW10 (1964) trs. R.F.C. Hull, Routledge & Kegan Paul Ltd., par. 275
14. The Earth Charter was initiated in Rio and subsequently expanded and developed.
    www.earthcharterinaction.org
15. The concluding paragraph from *A Time to Heal* by HRH The Prince of Wales,
    first published in issue 5, The Temenos Academy Review, London, Autumn 2002.

This message was received long ago in the messages I mentioned at the beginning of this book. I record it here as it applies as much to our times as to those when it was received during the Second World War.

A PRAYER OF THE HOLY MOTHER

Gather My tears in your hands
Bathe your eyes in their sweetness,
For in My tears lies no bitter salt.
Rather like honey, or like dew will you feel them
As you take them to your face and heart.
They are the tears of womanhood,
Shed for the cruelty and blindness of man,
They are the tears of motherhood
Shed for the useless death of her sons.
Each time I see cruelty, greed or senseless destruction,
I shed these tears,
Hoping that they will melt the harshness
And the greed of man.

I weep when I see the gifts of Life
So shamelessly laid to waste,
O let My tears blind those
Who want to shed their brothers' blood,
Soothe those who are wounded in the battle,
Melt the heart of Cain, ever ready to murder Abel.

O listen to My voice,
And let the gentle sound of pity cling
To your devoted hearts.
These I will impregnate
With the gentleness of My healing powers
That I hereby bestow on your hands
If you will give your voice
To the service of My cause.

Chapter Eleven

JUNG AND THE REDISCOVERY OF THE SOUL

Only those who will risk going too far can possibly find out how far one can go.

— T.S. Eliot

Our psyche is set up in accord with the structure of the universe, and what happens in the macrocosm likewise happens in the infinitesimal and most subjective reaches of the psyche.

— C. G. Jung, *Memories, Dreams, Reflections*

I have included a chapter on Jung in this book because, in the last century, he was the primary influence on the recovery of the Feminine and the forgotten dimension of the Soul. His influence has been far-reaching and profound although many people may not be aware of how his discoveries have affected our culture.

One of the great themes of ancient myth is the hero's journey into the under- world, his encounter there with a fearsome adversary and his return to the world of everyday life, bringing with him a priceless treasure. With this treasure, he is able to regenerate his culture, heal the sick, free the people from the spell cast on them by demonic powers and release the waters of life so that fertility is restored to the Wasteland. The theme of the hero's journey, so brilliantly defined by the great mythologist, Joseph Campbell and the historian of culture, Mircea Eliade, has its mythic roots in the nightly and monthly journey of the sun and moon into darkness and their return to illumine our world. It is a timeless theme of life, death and regeneration and the essential relationship between the light and the dark, this world and another invisible world, the known and the unknown. Descending to us from Egypt, Mesopotamia and Greece this theme underlies all mythologies which suggest that we have become separated from our home in the divine world and are, therefore, exiled, fallen, lost or asleep. It tells of the need to embark on a quest, to enter the "wilderness" of the unexplored depths of ourselves in order to recover our connection with that world, thereby bringing about our awakening, transformation and return to the Source.

Jung was one of the cultural heroes who made the shamanic journey into the underworld of the soul and returned with a treasure that has enriched our culture. His greatest longing and his life-long task, as he saw it, was to build a bridge between the reality we see and know with our physical senses and another unseen reality. In the field of astronomy, Copernicus and Kepler transformed the medieval worldview by displacing the earth from its position at the centre of the solar system. Jung did the same for the modern psyche, displacing the conscious mind or ego from its central position by introducing the concept of a deeper matrix of consciousness to which the ego is related as child to mother and out of which, in evolutionary terms, it has emerged.

He reconnected the solar consciousness of the rational mind with the lunar consciousness of the instinctual soul, so healing the dissociation in the psyche and restoring to Western culture in a modern context the shamanic way of knowing that has been increasingly lost over some 4000 years. More specifically, it could be said that he opened the door to the right hemisphere of the brain and to the intelligence of the heart, both of which have been closed off during the course of the scientific revolution of the last 400 years, leading ultimately to the denial of the existence of the soul. As a potential carrier of consciousness for the whole culture, he had to engage with its need to recover the connection to what he called the spirit of the depths. He knew that ignorance of the tremendous power of the archetypes which lie beyond the range of the limited conscious mind puts us at risk of being taken over by them, falling into fanaticism and the dissolution of our humanity — something that we can increasingly see happening in our world at the beginning of this new millennium.

Like many titans of innovative thought who are ahead of their time, he has been contemptuously dismissed by many as a charlatan and a mystic and to a large extent ignored, notably by members of his own profession of psychiatry. But Jung rediscovered the wider meaning of the word 'Soul', extending and deepening the understanding of it for the whole culture, and rescuing it from the obscurity and neglect into which it had fallen for centuries. In his writings and his practice, soul becomes not so much something that belongs to us as something to which we belong — a vast and unexplored dimension of reality. He knew that our greatest need was for connection with the transcendent, not through belief and faith, but through opening our minds to the existence of that unrecognized dimension which is the ground of our familiar world. He asked again the great soul questions: What is life? What is God? What is the origin of evil? What is the purpose of our lives on this planet and how can we fulfil it?

Jung felt that Christianity had become transfixed in its belief system and needed to be regenerated by a deeper understanding of its great myth, interpreted as a metaphor of the soul's life in this dimension of reality. Belief had not helped Christians or, indeed, believers of other traditions, to fathom the deeper evolutionary intention of the spirit which he defined as the progressive awakening to awareness of the divinity carried within the human soul. In a late interview with Sir Laurens van der Post, he said, "My work has proved that the pattern of God exists in every man." However, he wrote,

> We are still looking back to the Pentecostal events instead of looking forward to the goal the spirit is leading us to. Therefore mankind is wholly unprepared for the things to come. Man is compelled by divine forces to go forward to increasing consciousness and cognition, developing further and further away from his religious background because he does not understand it any more. His religious leaders and teachers are still hypnotized by the beginnings of a then new aeon of consciousness instead of understanding them and their implications. What was once called the "Holy Ghost" is an impelling force, creating wider consciousness and responsibility and thus enriched cognition. The real history of the world seems to be the progressive incarnation of the deity.[1]

I believe that Jung can be placed among the great astronauts of the soul who have opened our awareness to the existence of another dimension of reality and given us a deeper insight into the unrealized potential of our nature. But he was also a scientist who developed a methodology to connect us with the dimension of the soul and he drew up a map to guide us. The terms introvert and extravert were coined by him as were the concepts of the *anima* and the *animus* — the contra-sexual elements in men and women. As a prophet, he foresaw the dangers for humanity in the decades ahead and felt that only a greater insight into our nature could help us to avoid destroying ourselves and much of the planet through the blind hubris of our ego and our addiction to the demonic power of our weapons:

> Our intellect has created a new world that dominates nature and has populated it with monstrous machines…. Man is bound to follow the adventurous promptings of his scientific and inventive mind and to admire himself for his splendid achievements. At the same time, his genius shows the uncanny tendency to invent things that become more and more dangerous, because they represent better and better means for wholesale suicide.[2]

How did Jung gain his insight into the existence of the soul? In the Prologue to his autobiography *Memories, Dreams, Reflections*, Jung says: "In the end the only events in my life worth telling are those when the imperishable world irrupted into this transitory one. That is why I speak chiefly of inner experiences, among which I include my dreams and visions. These form the *prima materia* of my scientific work. They were the fiery magma out of which the stone that had to be worked was crystallised."[3]

What were these inner experiences? Jung parted from Freud in 1912 when he was thirty-seven. During the next seven years from 1913–19 when he was trying to develop his own orientation to the treatment of his patients, he deliberately withdrew from his designated position as Freud's successor and turned towards his inner world, setting aside time to respond to and record a near-overwhelming irruption of visions, dreams and fantasies. He called this period his *Nekyia* — a Greek word which describes a descent into the underworld. It is important to note that this experience took place just before and during the First World War, whose catastrophic effects he had foreseen in a series of dreams and visions he had during the autumn of 1913 and the spring of 1914. The idea of war did not occur to him at all, and so he drew the conclusion that he must be threatened by a psychosis. But as events culminated in the outbreak of war in August 1914, he began to understand the meaning of these visions and dreams and to take the unconscious seriously as an unrecognized dimension of reality in which all humanity participates.

The shaman or visionary has to translate the images and words of an unseen world into the language and understanding of his time. His conscious mind, struggling to contain the overwhelming power and numinosity of the experience, will interpret it according to the level of his own understanding and the needs of the age in which he or she lives. Jung had to undergo the original shamanic experience in order to recover the knowledge that was missing in the culture of his day and then discover how to communicate that knowledge in a way that people could comprehend. He took great care to try and understand every single image, every item of his psychic inventory, and to classify them scientifically — so far as this was possible — and to embody his insights in his daily life, for he realized that this was an ethical obligation of the conscious mind towards the unconscious.[4]

Some have seen the experience of these years as a psychotic episode and have labelled Jung schizophrenic; others, including myself, see it as a shamanic initiation into the direct experience of a deeper level of reality. There are two dangers attendant on this kind of experience. One is the danger of insanity, of being overwhelmed by the material because the conscious ego is not strong enough to contain it and assimilate its meaning. The other is the danger of becoming identified with the material, inflated by it, taking it to be absolute, literal truth and setting oneself up as a messiah proclaiming it in the manner of those individuals who have led their credulous followers to a suicidal death or who anticipate the imminent end of the world and the 'Rapture' of the chosen.

Prior to 1945 and the discovery of the fifty-two Gnostic texts at Nag Hammadi in Egypt, there were very few texts that had survived destruction when the Gnostic sects were repressed and their books outlawed or destroyed by order of the Emperors Constantine and Theodosius during the course of the fourth century AD. But by 1912 Jung knew of these few surviving Gnostic texts and was familiar with the work of the German scholars who had studied them. This enabled him to grasp the significance of the images, fantasies and dreams that presented themselves to him during these seven years. He would have known that he was writing in the Gnostic tradition of listening to the voice of the soul and that what he was experiencing was similar to what the Gnostics had recorded of their visionary and auditory experiences. But — and this is crucially important — he also knew that he had to grow into the meaning of what he had heard. As a psychiatrist, he had to interpret this raw material and embody it in a form that people could understand, that could become the basis of a contemporary understanding of the need for a relationship between the two separated aspects of the psyche — the conscious mind and the deeper dimension of the soul that he called the unconscious.

Jung recorded his experience in over 1000 handwritten pages and illustrations, many of which he later bound together in a magnificent volume that he called *The Red Book* (finally published in 2009), which opens with a page written in fourteenth century German script.[5] Through these beautifully worked pages, we can follow Jung's quest for the lost dimension of the soul: how it is rescued from neglect and obscurity; how its life is given meaningful expression in meticulously painted images and words; how it becomes a living reality for him rather than a theoretical abstraction. These moving words record his realization that the soul is *an independent living entity or dimension of reality*, something whose immense range we cannot grasp, whose voice is "the Spirit of the Depths":

> I have returned, I am once again there — I am with you — after long years of wandering. I have come again to you…. But one thing you must know, one thing I have learnt, that one must live this life. This life is the way… the way to the incomprehensible, which we call divine…. I found the right way, it led me to you, to my soul.
>
> Then I was still utterly engrossed in the spirit of the times and thought differently of the human soul. I thought and spoke much about the soul; I knew many learned words about the soul; I judged it and made a scientific object of it. I did

not consider that the soul cannot be the object of my judgement; much more are my judgment and knowledge the object of my soul.

Therefore the spirit of the depths pressed me to speak to my Soul, to call upon it as a living and independent being whose re-discovery means good fortune for me. I had to become aware that I had lost my soul, or rather that I had lost myself from my soul, for many years.

The spirit of the depths sees the soul as an independent, living being, and therewith contradicts the spirit of the times for whom the soul is something dependent on the person, which lets itself be ordered and judged, that is a thing whose range we can grasp. Before the spirit of the depths this thought is presumption and arrogance. Therefore the joy of my re-discovery was a humble one…. Without the soul there is no way out of this time.[6]

In the course of listening to the voice of the spirit of the depths, Jung encountered a winged figure whom he called Philemon, the being who became his guide to the strange world of the Soul, rather as Virgil was guide to Dante. Philemon taught Jung that this unrecognized dimension was *as real as the physical world* and that it sought to gain the attention of the conscious mind. Because this idea is so unfamiliar to us, it is something that is extraordinarily difficult for the modern mind to comprehend.

Jung found it ironical that he, a psychiatrist, should encounter at almost every step of his experiment the same psychic material which is typical of psychosis. "This," he says, "is the fund of unconscious images which fatally confuse the mental patient. But it is also the matrix of a mythopoeic imagination which has vanished from our rational age. Though such imagination is present everywhere, it is both tabooed and dreaded."[7] Near the end of his life, he wrote:

It has taken me virtually forty-five years to distil within the vessel of my scientific work the things I experienced and wrote down at that time... The years when I was pursuing my inner images were the most important in my life — in them everything essential was decided. It all began then; the later details are only supplements and clarifications of the material that burst forth from the unconscious, and at first swamped me. It was the *prima materia* for a lifetime's work.[8]

The Concept of the Unconscious

Jung's great contribution to an expanded understanding of our nature is that our psychic life has, as it were, two poles. Beyond the conscious mind lies a vast unexplored hinterland — the unconscious — or the root and rhizome of the soul as he called it, whose existence is, even now, not acknowledged by either religion or science.

Jung named the aspect of the unconscious that is closest to us and relates to our individual experience of life the *personal unconscious* — those feelings and tendencies which may have been repressed due to parental and cultural conditioning, religious indoctrination, social and tribal custom as well as parental complexes and sibling rivalry. In this part of the unconscious that is closest to consciousness may be found feelings of fear, guilt, anxiety, unacknowledged rage which have their origin in early traumatic experience. But it also holds the creative potential — the ideas, longings and creative gifts — which could not be given expression because they were not helped to develop or because there was no cultural container to receive and develop them. Many people grow up utterly unaware of how complexes in the personal unconscious may direct and constrain them — perhaps stemming from a rigid internalized structure of control and repression — parental or religious — which may have been passed down in their family or culture for generations or, as is the case today in our secular culture, from the total absence of parental care in childhood and the consequent lack of boundaries and support of any kind.

The personal unconscious is embedded or nested like a smaller field within the greater transpersonal field of the *collective unconscious*. Consciousness rests like a lily-pad on this greater substratum of our psychic life which has a "collective, universal, and impersonal nature which is identical in all individuals." Jung described the collective unconscious as

> the mighty deposit of ancestral experience accumulated over millions of years, the echo of prehistoric happenings to which each century adds an infinitesimally small amount of variation and differentiation. Because the collective unconscious is, in the last analysis, a deposit of world-processes embedded in the structure of the brain and the sympathetic nervous system, it constitutes in its totality a sort of timeless and eternal world-image which counterbalances our conscious momentary picture of the world. It means nothing less than another world, a mirror-world if you will. But unlike a mirror-image, the unconscious image possesses an energy peculiar to itself, independent of consciousness. By virtue of this energy it can produce powerful effects which do not appear on the surface but influence us all the more powerfully from within. These influences remain invisible to anyone who fails to subject his momentary picture of the world to adequate criticism and who therefore remains hidden from himself. That the world has an inside as well as an outside, that it is not only outwardly visible but acts upon us in a timeless present, from the deepest and apparently most subjective recesses of the psyche — this I hold to be an

insight which, even though it be ancient wisdom, deserves to be evaluated as a
new factor in building a weltanschaung [worldview].[9]

Elsewhere he called it the two-million-year-old man or woman in whose house
we live but whose acquaintance we have not yet made. The collective unconscious
is like a vast memory field — a kind of psychic DNA — which holds the experience of all that has transpired since the beginning of our evolution as a species on
this planet. But more than this, it embraces the whole of what other species have
experienced — the total species and planetary memory and, above all, the basic
instinctive patterns which give rise to physical forms as well as to specific patterns
of behaviour common to all people on the planet. All of us are influenced by the
largely unknown dynamics of this unacknowledged part of our total psyche —
the basic archetypal patterns which, he said, are as fixed and immutable as the
flight patterns of birds or the migratory routes of animals. We bring these patterns
with us when we are born, part of our personal psychic DNA. Because of this
immemorial experience, the collective unconscious is, as he said, "the source of
all sorts of evils and also the matrix of all divine experience and, paradoxical as
it may sound — it has brought forth and brings forth consciousness."[10]

One of the most important aspects of his work was his understanding of dreams
as a means of reconnecting the conscious ego with this deeper dimension of the
unconscious: "The dream", he wrote, "is a little hidden door in the innermost and
most secret recesses of the soul, opening into that cosmic night which was soul
long before there was any ego-consciousness, and which will remain soul no
matter how far our ego-consciousness extends…. All consciousness separates;
but in dreams we put on the likeness of that more universal, truer, more eternal
man dwelling in the darkness of primordial night."[11] As his understanding of
his own dreams deepened, Jung realized that the development of the ego and
conscious mind was a staggering evolutionary achievement. A dream showed him
the importance of consciousness per se:

> It was night in some unknown place, and I was making slow and painful head-
> way against a mighty wind. Dense fog was flying along everywhere. I had my
> hands cupped around a tiny light which threatened to go out at any moment.
> Everything depended on my keeping this little light alive… This little light was
> my consciousness, the only light I have. My own understanding is the sole
> treasure I possess, and the greatest. Though infinitely small and fragile in
> comparison with the powers of darkness, it is still a light, my only light.[12]

While travelling in Africa, and gazing down over the immense plains spread out
before him where herds of animals were grazing and moving as they had for

countless thousands of years, Jung realized, in a moment of sudden illumination, that without the existence of human consciousness, all that he saw that had existed from time immemorial would have had no witness to its existence. Without our consciousness, there would have been no one to perceive the world, reflect upon it and interact intelligently with it. Recognizing this and looking for a myth for our time, Jung found it in the fact that, through the coming into being of consciousness, or the conscious self-reflective mind, man has become

> indispensable for the completion of creation, a second creator of the world, who alone has given to the world its objective existence — without which, unheard, unseen, silently eating, giving birth, dying, heads nodding through hundreds of millions of years, it would have gone on in the profoundest night of non-being down to its unknown end. Human consciousness created objective existence and meaning, and man found his indispensable place in the great process of being.[13]

"As far as we can discern," he observed, "the sole purpose of human existence is to kindle a light in the darkness of mere being. It may even be assumed that just as the unconscious affects us, so the increase in our consciousness affects the unconscious."[14] Our individual lives, apparently so unimportant, may, in ways that we do not yet understand, affect the life of the Cosmos and the unfolding of its evolutionary intention on this planet. That is perhaps why he felt that "the psyche is the greatest of all cosmic wonders and the *sine qua non* of the world as an object."

The Loss of a Living Myth

But, as described in Chapter Six, the emergence of the conscious ego tore us out of nature and a purely instinctive way of responding to life. Its coming into existence involved a great loss, the loss of the state of unconscious participation in the life around us, the loss of a different kind and quality of consciousness and the instinctive sense of belonging to a greater whole. In his last book, *Man and His Symbols*, Jung summarized this loss and it is worth quoting at length because it is so important:

> As scientific understanding has grown, so our world has become dehumanized. Man feels himself isolated in the cosmos, because he is no longer involved in nature and has lost his emotional "unconscious identity" with natural phenomena. These have slowly lost their symbolic implications.... No voices now speak to man from stones, plants, and animals, nor does he speak to them

believing they can hear. His contact with nature has gone, and with it has gone
the profound emotional energy that his symbolic connection supplied. This
enormous loss is compensated for by the symbols of our dreams. They bring
up our original nature — its instincts and peculiar thinking. Unfortunately,
however, they express their contents in the language of nature, which is strange
and incomprehensible to us. It therefore confronts us with the task of translating
it into the rational words and concepts of modern speech, which has liberated
itself... from its mystical participation with the things it describes.[15]

In a passage Jung wrote in his commentary on the Chinese text *The Secret of the Golden Flower* he describes how, as consciousness gains more and more auton-omy and independence from the deeper matrix of the instinct, the whole super-structure of consciousness becomes disengaged from the age-old instinctive base or ground out of which it has developed. "Consciousness thus torn from its roots... possesses a Promethean freedom but it also partakes of the nature of a godless *hybris*."[16] This unconscious split creates conflict between the two aspects of the psyche which finds its way into the many conflicts that are acted out in our rela-tionships as well as in the wider arena of the world. Yet what confronts us as an implacable enemy may be a convoluted expression of the dissociated instinct that we, in our conviction that the rational mind should be our sole guide and the ruler of our actions, have ignored.

Jung realized that the problems of our time are rooted not only in the grip that the mechanistic philosophy of scientific materialism has on our culture, but above all in the loss of a living myth which would give meaning to our lives. He saw that the dissociation of the conscious ego from what he called the primordial or instinctual soul presented a growing and unperceived danger to humanity. The more we emphasized reason and the supremacy of the rational mind, the greater the danger that instinct — whose power we have failed to acknowledge or under-stand — would drive, possess, delude and overwhelm us and the more we would fall victim to secular and religious ideologies and utopian goals which could ultimately lead us to destroy ourselves. The paramount goal we need to focus on is reconnecting our conscious mind with the deeper dimension of the soul.

In relation to what is still a potential within us to be developed, the conscious mind is in what could be called a pre-conscious state, characterized by uncon-scious identifications and projections of every kind that derive from various personal complexes and long-established collective beliefs. Moreover, it is still subject to the immense power of the instinctual drives of the older brain system which will be described in Chapters Twelve and Thirteen. This unconsciousness is reflected in the difficulties and conflicts in our relationships with each other, whether within a nation or as nation states, and in the fact that we repeat the same patterns of behaviour without any apparent ability to prevent ourselves doing so or even any awareness of what we are doing. Yet, with insight, we can begin to change these patterns and combat the evils we bring into being by tracing them to their source in our present incomplete concept of reality.

The Danger of an Inflated Ego

Jung hoped that if awareness of the fact that there are two poles or dimensions of consciousness could spread through our culture this would mitigate the dangers of a further inflation of the modern ego or 'rational' mind, which has set up a phobic defence against anything which threatens the hegemony of its current level of understanding. Jung developed this theme in *Man and His Symbols* where he writes:

> Modern man does not understand how much his "rationalism" (which has destroyed his capacity to respond to numinous symbols and ideas) has put him at the mercy of the psychic "underworld". He has freed himself from "superstition" (or so he believes), but in the process he has lost his spiritual values to a positively dangerous degree. His moral and spiritual tradition has disintegrated, and he is now paying the price for this break-up in worldwide disorientation and dissociation…. We have stripped all things of their mystery and numinosity; nothing is holy any longer.[17]

Nowhere is this *hubris* of the conscious mind more apparent and more dangerous than in the sphere of politics and religion. And no one was more aware of the dangers of this state of inflation than Jung when he wrote: "We are threatened with universal genocide if we cannot work out the way of salvation by a symbolic death."[18] By this, he meant the death or sacrifice of the omnipotent stance of the conscious mind or ego. On the eve of the outbreak of the First World War, as he recounts in *Memories, Dreams, Reflections*, Jung had a vivid dream which showed him the necessity of consciously making this sacrifice himself:

> I was with an unknown, brown-skinned man… in a lonely, rocky mountain landscape. It was before dawn; the eastern sky was already bright, and the stars fading. Then I heard Siegfried's horn sounding over the mountains and I knew that we had to kill him… On a chariot made of the bones of the dead he drove at a furious speed down the precipitous slopes. When he turned a corner, we shot at him, and he plunged down, struck dead… Filled with disgust and remorse for having destroyed something so great and beautiful, I turned to flee, impelled by the fear that the murder might be discovered. But a tremendous downfall of rain began, and I knew that it would wipe out all traces of the dead.[19]

Reflecting on the dream, Jung understood that it highlighted a problem that was being played out in the world. He realized that he had to sacrifice his own unconscious identification with the solar hero personified by the figure of Siegfried, and the inflated attitude that seeks power and supremacy over others. He understood that when we (either an individual or a nation) do not become aware of the existence of two aspects of consciousness — both the known and the unknown — we may project an unconscious power drive onto an opponent and embark upon a crusade to eliminate that enemy. As long as the evil is always 'out there' the world will be "torn into opposing ideologies; walls, psychic and material, will be built to separate enemies."

> An inflated consciousness is always egocentric and conscious of nothing but its own presence. It is incapable of learning from the past, incapable of understanding contemporary events, and incapable of drawing right conclusions about the future... It inevitably dooms itself to calamities that must strike it dead. Paradoxically enough, inflation is a regression of consciousness into unconsciousness. This always happens when consciousness takes too many unconscious contents upon itself and loses the faculty of discrimination, the *sine qua non* of all consciousness.[20]

Alchemy and the Individuation Process

One of Jung's greatest legacies was his insight into the mythological symbolism of alchemy, whose importance was conveyed to him in two dreams, recounted in *Memories, Dreams, Reflections*. Most people, when alchemy is mentioned, think of men working in laboratories, trying to turn base metal into gold, but Jung understood that for many alchemists this image was a metaphor for a process of soul-transformation and that when they spoke of the 'philosophical gold' they were not referring to what they called the common gold but to the true gold of the spirit which could, through repeated 'distillations', 'washings' and 'cleansings', be freed from the dross that had accrued to it in the course of human evolution.

For many decades Jung was engaged in extensive researches into the myths of the ancient world, as well as the Christian myth and the lesser-known myth of alchemy. He realized that these different myths arise out of the deep stratum of the soul that holds the collective memories of our evolutionary experience and are elaborated and developed over long periods of time. They demonstrate the basic archetypal patterns and dynamics carried in the individual and collective soul and thus give us a vital key to understanding human needs and human potential. The unconscious mythic content may be projected onto the figure of an extraordinary individual who, because of the power of the projection, takes on the mantle of an archetypal saviour, redeemer or teacher which enormously increases the power of the myth and the numinosity of the individual around whom it has constellated.

Because these great stories are not understood as metaphors of psychic processes, but are taken literally, whole cultures may worship a saviour figure for millennia, not realizing that this figure personifies an unrecognized content of their own soul. Because they fail to connect their myth with that inner, unknown content, they may fall into literalism, defending 'their' revelation against those of others or they may splinter into many sects which are antagonistic to each other. This applies as much to 'Jungians' as to any other group.

Jung thought that the interpretation of mythic imagery as a metaphor of the soul's life could help to awaken the modern mind to awareness of its deeper archetypal ground. He felt that the imagery of certain myths, including the Christian one, portrays both the inner landscape and the spiritual task of the soul and describes the archetypal powers which can heal, enlighten, regenerate and guide. Modern consciousness was, he felt, cut off from its roots, impoverished because of its ignorance of the undiscovered treasure-house of the soul. At the end of one of his earlier books, *Modern Man in Search of a Soul*, he wrote:

> The living spirit grows and even outgrows its earlier forms of expression; it freely chooses the men and women in whom it lives and who proclaim it. This living spirit is eternally renewed and pursues its goal in manifold and inconceivable ways throughout the history of mankind. Measured against it, the names and forms which men have given it mean little enough; they are only the changing leaves and blossoms on the stem of the eternal tree.[21]

Like the great teachers of Kabbalah, with whose tradition he was familiar, and certain of the alchemists, Jung knew that the evolution of life on this planet follows a very slow gradient of emergence from the organic life of nature. The whole of humanity suffers because the increase of consciousness is so slow and arduous. He realized that the alchemical images he found in the texts he studied were similar to those in the dreams of his patients and that they referred to a process of transformation taking place within the collective soul of humanity as well as in the soul of the individual. His task, as he saw it, was to help people participate consciously in this evolutionary process; to set their search for meaning, their suffering and the unfolding of their lives and relationships in this wider context:

> Only after I had familiarized myself with alchemy did I realize that the unconscious is a process, and that the psyche is transformed or developed by the

relationship of the ego to the contents of the unconscious. In individual cases that transformation can be read from dreams and fantasies. In collective life it has left its deposit principally in the various religious systems and their chang-ing symbols. Through the study of these collective transformation processes and through understanding of alchemical symbolism, I arrived at the central concept of my psychology: the process of individuation.[22]

Jung's concept of the process of individuation was to extend or expand the field of our awareness so that we are able to relate, to some extent at least, to the complex reality of the deeper dimension of the soul. Working to create a relationship with this mysterious entity over many years is like an extended meditation which connects us not only to the life of nature but to the inner life or soul of the Cosmos.

In his later writings, soul becomes not something that belongs to us but some-thing in whose greater life we unknowingly participate.

> If the human soul is anything, it must be of unimaginable complexity and diversity.... I can only gaze with wonder and awe at the depths and heights of our psychic nature. Its non-spatial universe conceals an untold abundance of images which have accumulated over millions of years of living development and become fixed in the organism. My consciousness is like an eye that penetrates to the most distant spaces, yet it is the psychic non-ego that fills them with non-spatial images. And these images are not pale shadows, but tremendously powerful psychic factors.... Besides this picture I would like to place the spectacle of the starry heavens at night, for the only equivalent of the universe within is the universe without; and just as I reach this world through the medium of the body, so I reach that world through the medium of the psyche.[23]

Jung knew that the modern psyche was in a state of suffering and alienation because the conscious ego knew nothing of this deeper ground and, therefore, could not grow to its full potential, its full stature, through the creation of a relationship with it, nor could the conscious mind or ego protect itself from being possessed or taken over by archetypal elements, having no experience in how to recognize, relate to or integrate them — a situation that is one of the most dangerous features of our time. He defined sickness or neurosis as a state of incompleteness, and health as a state of wholeness brought about through the reconnection of the conscious mind or ego with the unconscious through paying attention to dreams, synchronistic events and engaging in a dialogue with the spirit of the depths. Just as a child develops the ability to read and explore, thereby gaining access to an immense field of information relating to the physical world, so he thought we could gain experience of the dimension of the soul that lies beyond the threshold of the conscious mind.

The conscious mind can listen, interpret, assess, and apply what is discovered through that experience. It can also challenge or disagree with the content of what is brought to its attention. But if it does not accept the existence of such a dimension, it can also block access to it through ridicule, denial or overt repression. If the imagination is allowed no access to what lies beyond the current parameters of the rational left-hemispheric mind, it is likely to degenerate into destructive, even pathological, fantasies and behaviour. If we seek proof of the sickness of the modern psyche, we need look no further than the constant celebration of violence on our television screens, the growing arsenal of our weapons and the fundamentalist and polarized stance of so many who claim allegiance to a specific religion and promote their agenda in terms of a battle between good and evil.

From the alchemists, Jung took the idea of the *unus mundus*, a unifying cosmic ground in which both matter and psyche participate and whose connecting substratum gives rise to synchronicities as well as to miraculous healings, visionary experiences and sudden illuminations. In his *Seven Sermons to the Dead* (included in *The Red Book*) the Gnostic teacher Basilides describes this primary ground of being as the *Pleroma*, the root of all, present within all yet beyond all — a boundless, indefinable and totally transcendent dimension of reality which nevertheless permeates our world in the way that sunlight permeates air.[24] There is no clearer description of the cosmic dimension of the soul.

Just before he died Jung said to a friend: "I am practically alone. There are a few who understand this and that, but almost nobody sees the whole.... I have failed in my foremost task: to open people's eyes to the fact that man has a soul and that there is a buried treasure in the field and that our religion and philosophy are in a lamentable state...."[25] But he did not fail. The seeds sown by him are beginning to bear fruit, not only in the branch of psychology which has taken his name but in the culture as a whole. He asked the basic question:

> Is man related to something infinite or not? That is the telling question of his life. Only if we know that the thing which truly matters is the infinite can we avoid fixing our interest upon futilities, and upon all kinds of goals which are not of real importance.... The more a man lays stress on false possessions, and the less sensitivity he has for what is essential, the less satisfying is his life. He feels limited because he has limited aims, and the result is envy and jealousy.... In the final analysis, we count for something only because of the essential we embody, and if we do not embody that, life is wasted.[26]

Jung believed that the wider dimension of soul included the two polarities of matter and spirit, the finite and the infinite. But these were not separate as we had been taught but were two poles of an underlying spectrum of reality which interact with each other. He knew that the power of Christianity to hold society together was waning and that we needed a radically different image of God: one that did not split nature and matter from spirit. "It was only quite late that we realized (or rather, are beginning to realize), that God is Reality itself and therefore — last but not least — man. This realization is a millennial process."[27] With these two sentences he offers us a different image of God and a radically different image of ourselves — neither of which have yet been considered by our culture. Through the discoveries he made and his application of them in his practice and in his books, he was able to say near the end of his life in the famous BBC interview with John Freeman in 1959: "I don't need to believe... I know, I know." He also warned: "The only real danger that exists is man himself" and "Man cannot stand a meaningless life." He begged us to become more aware of the psyche so that we could understand the events of our time more intelligently, because, as he realized,

> It is becoming ever more obvious that it is not famine, not earthquakes, not microbes, not cancer but man himself who is man's greatest danger to man, for the simple reason that there is no adequate protection against psychic epidemics, which are infinitely more devastating than the worst of natural catastrophes. The supreme danger which threatens individuals as well as whole nations is a *psychic danger*. Reason has proved itself completely powerless, precisely because its arguments have an effect only on the conscious mind and not on the unconscious. The greatest danger of all comes from the masses, in whom the effects of the unconscious pile up cumulatively and the reasonableness of the conscious mind is stifled.... It is therefore in the highest degree desirable that a knowledge of psychology should spread so that men can understand the source of the supreme dangers that threaten them. Not by arming to the teeth, each for itself, can the nations defend themselves in the long run from the frightful catastrophes of modern war. The heaping up of arms is itself a call to war. Rather they must recognize those psychic conditions under which the unconscious bursts the dykes of consciousness and overwhelms it.[28]

The Emphasis on the Feminine

In the last chapter, I suggested that the word 'Feminine' stands for a totally different perspective on reality and for the feeling values which reflect, support and confirm that different perspective. The constellation or activation of the feminine archetype in our very masculine culture was to a great extent due to Jung, who saw the urgent need to bring balance to the psyche and the culture. His emphasis on the feminine concept of soul (as opposed to spirit) was the most important aspect of this need for balance. His emphasis on the deep unconscious as the feminine matrix which gives birth to the conscious ego as its 'son' was another important aspect of this emphasis on the Feminine but he extended this emphasis to include woman's important role in the re-balancing of the culture when he said, "The woman of today is faced with a tremendous cultural task — perhaps it will be the dawn of a new era."[29] Jung foresaw that as woman had access to education, financial independence and a wider role in society, developing and giving expression to the masculine qualities of her soul, she would find the words and the channel of expression to articulate what is of supreme importance to her and the strength to insist that her voice is heard. Equally, he foresaw that as man, who is more focused on logic alone and deeply suspicious of anything 'psychic' and 'unconscious', becomes aware of his *anima* — represented in his dreams by a feminine figure — and the feeling values carried in his soul, he would play a more conscious, balanced and enlightened role in the world.

> Unlike objective discussion and the verification of facts, a human relationship leads into the world of the psyche, into that intermediate realm between sense and spirit, which contains something of both and yet forfeits nothing of its own unique character. Into this territory a man must venture if he wishes to meet woman half way. Circumstances have forced her to acquire a number of masculine traits, so that she shall not remain caught in an antiquated, purely instinctual femininity, lost and alone in the world of men. So, too, man will be forced to develop his feminine side, to open his eyes to the psyche and to Eros. It is a task he cannot avoid...[30]

The Self

The word 'unconscious' might suggest that it is something inferior to consciousness whereas the true situation is the reverse. The conscious mind is unconscious of something that is infinitely greater than itself — the invisible psychic aspect of the cosmic and planetary matrix out of which it has evolved. This redefinition aligns Jung's discoveries with the far older tradition of the cosmic dimension of the soul that developed from Egyptian, Platonic, Gnostic and Kabbalistic roots and is concealed within the medieval idea of the Holy Grail. In India, Vedic teaching describes seven realms or planes of reality which can become accessible to human consciousness as our insight deepens. Kabbalah offers a similar multi-dimensional view of interconnected planes, fields or levels of reality. Jung was familiar with both of these traditions.

This greater consciousness or greater dimension of the soul has a focus or centre of consciousness within it, functioning there as an autonomous intelligence — a dynamic, structuring, ordering and integrating principle that Jung called the Self. In his view, this deeper intelligence (even when unrecognized) initiates and oversees the alchemy of the transformation of consciousness — whether in the individual or in our species as a whole — whereby the centre of gravity gradually shifts from the personal to the transpersonal or, to put it another way, where the conscious personality or ego grows and expands through aligning itself with the unseen ground of life. The creation of this relationship over the span of a life is the quintessence of the process of individuation.

In the Abrahamic religions the image of the Self has been carried by the image of God and, in Christianity, by the part-divine, part-human figure of Christ — images defined as being outside or beyond ourselves. The mystics bear witness to the fact that there can be a direct experience of the numinous ground of reality. Today, in a secular culture such as our own, the conscious ego has long ago banished visionary experience and any dimension of reality other than this physical world. There is, therefore, no possibility of dialogue and relationship with an interior Presence; dreams, messages, warnings and synchronistic events go unnoticed or ignored. My own visionary dream of the figure of a woman reaching from earth to heaven can be understood as an image of the Self. Her message to me was to develop and expand my consciousness, to centre the wheel in my abdomen as hers was centred. Had I not been in analysis at the time, I would not have known how to relate to that experience and might have either ignored it, thought I was mad or developed an inflated view of my own importance rather than seeking to integrate its message over many years. Nor would I have understood that my vision personified the macrocosm — the vast hidden matrix of the Soul of the Cosmos in which, as microcosm, my own life was embedded and which it was called upon to serve.

An encounter with the Self can be at once terrifying and life-transforming. One cannot communicate the experience to someone who has never had such an experience any more than one can communicate the feeling of being in love or the near-death experience to someone who has not had that experience. One may describe it, but it is almost impossible to convey its numinosity. The Self might be thought of as the archetype of wholeness, and its intention is to restore wholeness to the human psyche that has been so fragmented — even through means which may at first appear to be destructive. The process of individuation is an enormous cultural task, made more difficult in a culture that shows no inclination to acknowledge the need for it. Anyone who enters the lonely path of individuation, through whatever door, is drawn to respond to the suffering of the world. Working at this deep level for many years creates a bridge between two dimensions of reality. Through this work we are connected more deeply not only to the life of this planet but to the invisible dimension of the Cosmos. Marriage might best describe this relationship.

The general ignorance of the existence of the cosmic dimension of soul and our lack of relationship with it goes far to answer the question of why the suffering of humanity — despite a phenomenal improvement in our health, longevity and standard of living, at least in some of the industrialized nations — is so difficult to eradicate. This ignorance also sheds light on why people, despite their religious beliefs and often because of them, continue to behave in such unconscious, brutal and destructive ways that injure or destroy their own lives as well as those of others. So much of this cruelty springs from deep psychic wounds — many of them culturally imposed — of which people are unaware and which, therefore, remain inaccessible to healing. Religious indoctrination, such as the belief in original sin, a punishing, judgemental God, or the inferiority and dangerous sexuality of women, may inflict such wounds, many of them originating centuries ago but still carried in the memory field of the collective unconscious.

In the midst of their suffering, millions have cried out, "Why does God allow these things to happen? Why can't He intervene to help us?" But Jung knew that God cannot prevent human suffering any more than He can prevent human cruelty, avarice and greed. Only insight into our own nature and its power both to create and destroy can change our deeply ingrained habits of aggression and therefore our suffering. As he comments: "Individuation does not only mean that man has become truly human as distinct from animal, but that he is to become partially divine as well. That means practically that he becomes adult, responsible for his existence, knowing that he does not only depend on God but that God also depends on man."[31]

Jung's recognition of our huge potential, both for good and for evil, opened for us a new avenue for self-transformation, no longer through belief but through insight into our own nature. He wrote these prophetic words in the same letter:

> We have become participants of the divine life and we have to assume a new responsibility, viz. the continuation of the divine self-realization, which expresses itself in the task of individuation…. The responsible living and ful-filling of the divine love in us will be our form of worship of, and commerce with, God. His goodness means grace and light and his dark side the terrible temptation of power. Man has already received so much knowledge that he can destroy his own planet. Let us hope that God's good spirit will guide him in his decisions, because it will depend on man's decision whether God's creation will continue.[32]

Of the Self, Jung wrote, "Even the enlightened person remains what he is, and is never more than his own limited ego before the One who dwells within him, whose form has no knowable boundaries, who encompasses him on all sides, fathomless as the abysms of the earth and vast as the sky."[33]

The Shadow

Jung's understanding of the shadow is one of the most important aspects of his work and will be explored in the next chapter. He was deeply aware of the need for us to become aware of the unconscious drive for power and dominance and the obsessive need for control that affects so much of the way governments conduct themselves in the world and their relationships with other nations as well as the people they govern. This drive is reflected in unconscious habits of behaviour which perpetuate war, oppression, and suffering. He repeatedly spoke of our power to destroy not only our species but to create widespread devastation on the planet. One of his closest colleagues, Marie Louise von Franz, said in the film *Matter of Heart* that towards the end of his life Jung had a vision of enormous stretches of the Earth devastated, and another just before he died of which he said, "Thank God, it wasn't the whole planet." At the end of *The Undiscovered Self*, he wrote:

> A mood of world destruction and world renewal has set its mark on our age. This mood makes itself felt everywhere, politically, socially and philosophically. Coming generations will have to take account of this momentous transformation if humanity is not to destroy itself through the might of its own technology and science. As at the beginning of the Christian Era, so again today we are faced with the problem of the general moral backwardness of our species which has failed to keep pace with our scientific, technical and social progress. So much is at stake and so much depends on the psychological constitution of modern man. Is he capable of resisting the temptation to use his power for the purpose of staging a world conflagration? Is he conscious of the path he is treading and what the conclusions are that must be drawn from the present world situation and his own psychic situation? Does he know that he is on the point of losing the life-preserving myth of the inner man which Christianity has treasured up for him? Does he realize what lies in store should this catastrophe ever befall him? Is he even capable of realizing that this would in fact be a catastrophe? And finally, does the individual know that he [or she] is the make-weight that tips the scales... that infinitesimal unit on whom a world depends, and in whom, if we read the meaning of the Christian message aright, even God seeks his goal?[34]

In one of his last books, *Answer to Job*, he wrote: "Everything now depends on man: immense power of destruction is given into his hand and the question is whether he can resist the will to use it, and can temper his will with the spirit of love and wisdom."[35] What Jung offered was not a new belief system but a spirituality grounded in self-knowledge — particularly awareness of the shadow, so freeing ourselves from possession by it. This, he felt, could lead to a greater sense of ethical responsibility towards life in all its aspects, seen and unseen. He knew that we did not have much time in which to accomplish this momentous task because he saw the dangers of the god-like power that had been put into our hands through the development of our weapons, our unprecedented scientific and technological discoveries and our ignorance of how the conscious mind can be possessed by the power drive of the unconscious shadow.

Jung repeatedly drew attention to the fact that the fate of the planet depends on the individual, on our capacity to create a relationship with our soul, to become aware of and to value that part of ourselves we know least — our deepest feelings and instincts which are the root of our creative imagination. This instinctual dimension of ourselves, so dissociated from consciousness, so little explored and understood, is the matrix of our creative life, and is immeasurably older and sometimes wiser than the more recently developed aspect of ourselves we call our rational mind. But it also holds the predatory habits of behaviour inherited from our mammalian and reptilian past. Becoming aware of this dimension and the immense range of relationships and experience it embraces constitutes an evolutionary advance. For, until we learn how to relate to it, how to integrate it with our more familiar, focused ability to think, we remain immature, living on the surface of life, falling prey to events which we bring into being because we are unaware of the habits that compel us to repeat the mistakes of the past. We are then easily manipulated by political and religious leaders who think in terms of accruing power to their own particular group or ideology, rather than in terms of what truly benefits the people they are meant to serve and the wider needs of the planet itself.

Jung revived and recovered the lost dimension of the soul for our culture. He knew from his own shamanic encounter with this dimension that the conventional view of a personal soul was too limited to be able to hold his experience. From his first moving description of his encounter with this deeper dimension of reality, as recorded in *The Red Book*, until his realization, after years of observation, that there must be what he called a *psychoid* dimension of reality which underlay both psyche and matter, by which both are permeated and in which both participate — so giving rise to his concept of synchronicity — the whole focus of his work from 1913 until his death in 1960 was on the recovery of the soul.

In a letter to Miguel Serrano, written shortly before he died, Jung gave us hope for the future, reminding us that what seems of supreme importance to one's own life path may ultimately have value for the world as well:

> ...In each aeon there are at least a few individuals who understand what man's real task consists of, and keep its tradition for future generations and a time when insight has reached a deeper and more general level. First the way of a few will be changed and in a few generations there will be more... whoever is capable of such insight, no matter how isolated he is, should be aware of the law of synchronicity. As the old Chinese saying goes: "The right man sitting in his house and thinking the right thought will be heard 100 miles away.... Thus an old alchemist gave the following consolation to one of his disciples: "No matter how isolated you are and how lonely you feel, if you do your work truly and conscientiously, unknown friends will come and seek you."[36]

In answer to the question "What can I do"? Jung said, "Become what you have always been, namely, the wholeness we have lost in the midst of our civilized, conscious existence, a wholeness which we always were without knowing it."[37]

Notes:

1. Jung, C. G. (1976) *Letters 2* 1951-1961, ed. Gerhard Adler, Letter to Rev. Morton Kelsey, p. 436
2. (1964) *Man and His Symbols*, Aldus Books Ltd., London, p. 101
3. (1963) *Memories Dreams, Reflections* (MDR), Collins and Routledge & Kegan Paul Ltd., London, p. 18
4. ibid, p. 184
5. (2009) *The Red Book, Liber Novus*, edited and introduced by Sonu Shamdasani, W.W. Norton & Co, New York & London
6. Extract from *The Red Book, Liber Novus*, pp. 231-2. I have used the translation in Aniela Jaffé's book (1989), *From the Life and Work of C. G. Jung*, trs. by R.F.C. Hull and Murray Stein, Daimon Verlag, pp. 171-2
7. MDR, p. 181
8. ibid, p. 191
9. CW8 (1960) *The Structure and Dynamics of the Psyche*, par. 729
10. CW18 (1977) *The Symbolic Life*, par. 1586
11. CW10 (1964) *Civilization in Transition* par. 304
12. MDR, p. 93
13. MDR, pp. 240-1
14. MDR, p. 301
15. *Man and His Symbols*, p. 95
16. (1931) *The Secret of the Golden Flower*, translated and explained by Richard Wilhelm, with introduction and European commentary by C.G. Jung, p.85

17. *Man and his Symbols*, p. 94

18. CW18, par. 1661

19. MDR, pp. 173-4. This is also found in *The Red Book*, p. 241

20. CW12 (1953) *Psychology and Alchemy*, par. 563

21. (1933) *Modern Man in Search of a Soul*, Routledge & Kegan Paul Ltd., London, final paragraph

22. MDR, p. 200

23. *Man and his Symbols*, p. 103

24. *The Seven Sermons to the Dead* was originally privately published in 1925, then by Random House 1961 and in England by Vincent Stuart and John M. Watkins 1967. The reference to the *Pleroma* is in the section of the Red Book *Scrutinies*, page 347

25. From an unpublished letter written by Jung in 1960, quoted by Dr. Gerhard Adler in *Dynamics of the Self*, Coventure, London 1979, p. 92

26. MDR, p. 300

27. CW11 (1958) *Psychology and Religion: West and East*, par. 631

28. CW18, par. 1358

29. CW10, par. 275

30. ibid, p. 125

31. *Letters 2*, p. 316, letter to Elined Kotschnig

32. ibid, p. 316

33. *Answer to Job* in CW11, last paragraph 758

34. *The Undiscovered Self* in CW10, par. 585-587

35. *Answer to Job* in CW11, par. 745

36. Letter to Miguel Serrano, 1960 in *Letters 2*, p. 595

37. CW10, par. 722

For further reading I would recommend Jung's autobiography, *Memories, Dreams, Reflections* and *Man and His Symbols*. Also a beautifully illustrated book written by Claire Dunne called *Carl Jung: Wounded Healer of the Soul*. She has captured the quintessence of his legacy in both word and image.

In 2018 Peter Kingsley published a profound study of Jung's work and legacy called *Catafalque: Carl Jung and the End of Humanity*. In it he argues that none of Jung's contemporaries other than the great Sufi scholar Henry Corbin really understood the profundity of Jung's thought and the fact that Jung was a prophet.

Morning Landscape
Robin Baring 1978

Chapter Twelve

THE SHADOW: THE DRAGON
AND THE PRIMORDIAL SOUL

One does not become enlightened by imagining figures of light, but by making the darkness conscious.

— C.G. Jung

This chapter and the next are devoted to exploring our propensity for violence and cruelty. They are difficult chapters to write because it is far easier to detect these patterns in other people than to recognize them in our own behaviour towards our partners, children, or colleagues, or to see how, as nations, we justify actions and policies which add to the sum of human suffering rather than diminishing it. Yet, shining the light of consciousness on this opaque aspect of our nature may be one of the most challenging tasks facing us in this new millennium. It is beginning to dawn on us at this perilous moment that moving to a new level of consciousness is not an optional extra but an imperative if we are to survive as a species and safeguard the life of the planet.

Jung used the word 'shadow' in two senses: in a general sense, to describe the unrecognized dimension of the soul; secondly, in a personal sense, to describe certain unconscious patterns of behaviour which may affect us and others in negative ways, as well as personal complexes, experiences and unlived or diminished potential which exist below the threshold of our conscious awareness and which may, with insight and recall, become accessible. Over the course of our lifetime, we learn to identify ourselves with our conscious mind and with a specific image we hold of ourselves. We are not taught to be aware of the shadow aspect of our psyche nor how to relate to it. We are not told that consciousness has emerged over many millennia from the matrix of nature and that we are still bound to the latter by certain primordial habits. Through the unconscious shadow we are connected to deeper levels of the collective unconscious where the behaviour patterns of our species are stored in a kind of memory database, ready to be activated when they are called forth by events. Many elements go to make up the personal shadow aspect of ourselves: parental and educational influence, religious beliefs, tribal loyalties, long-forgotten traumas experienced in our childhood or the past of our national or ethnic group, various complexes of which we are not aware. But deeper than all of these are the largely unconscious instincts which derive from earlier phases of our evolution.

As suggested in Chapters Nine and Eleven, for all our remarkable intellectual and technological achievements, we are still, as a species, in a relatively unconscious or pre-conscious state, still liable to be taken over by an aspect of our nature that we know very little about. It may be difficult to grasp the fact that when survival and territorial instincts are aroused they can make us behave in ways that contradict the civilized image we hold of ourselves. We justify our actions, saying that they are necessary for our personal or national survival, yet we do not see how they may, in the long term, militate against our best interests, engender evil and bring horrendous suffering into being.

Two hundred and fifty years ago, the French philosopher Jean-Jacques Rousseau began his book *The Social Contract* (1762) with the words, "Man is born free and everywhere he is in chains." Today, as we witness the shocking violence in many parts of the world, the stockpiling of weapons and the arms sales that can wreak atrocious suffering on civilians, the oppressive regimes controlled by authoritarian despots who torture and murder thousands and keep millions in subjection, and our blind rapacity in relation to the Earth's resources, it is obvious that we are still in bondage to certain deeply engrained beliefs and habits that drive our political, economic and religious agendas. So many of our grandiose plans for a better future rest on the unstable foundation of the separate self and its alienation from the ground of the soul — a separation which ensures that we unwittingly repeat the patterns of the past.

The Dragon as an Image of Primordial Fear

I remember a dream I had just after I had decided to publish *The Birds Who Flew Beyond Time* against the advice of a close friend. She was frightened that I might incur a *fatwah* for using a revered Islamic text to create a modern story for children. I told her that I had taken the decision to go ahead with publication. That night I dreamt that an enormous dinosaur was ravaging the countryside, devouring hundreds of people every day. The ground was flat and treeless. There was nowhere to hide, no protection from its devouring jaws. The terror I experienced in the dream was greater than that engendered by any event in my life. I realized that this dragon-dinosaur was an image of primordial fear carried deep in my psyche, a graphic image of everything that has aroused terror since the beginning of our evolution as humans and, before that, as animals on this planet. The root of this terror is the experience of death at the hands of a creature or event of overwhelming power. Since this is something we, as a species, have experienced, both in relation to animal and human predators as well as natural disasters like earthquakes, volcanic eruptions and tsunamis, it is hardly surprising that fear and the instinctive response to it are so deeply imprinted on our cellular memory and so difficult to resist. No wonder so many myths celebrate the hero who has the courage to face and overcome the dragon of fear.

The dragon personifies the immense power of instinct. Instinct can never be conquered and subdued because it is the creative power of life itself but certain aspects of it can be transformed as we become more conscious of their power over us. The more the fragile conscious ego lost the original sense of participation in a sacred earth and a sacred cosmos, the more we became disconnected from our own deepest instincts. As this process developed, and as the human population increased and created ever-larger settlements, cities and tribal groups, the danger of our being possessed and driven by the will to power of the instinct was augmented as we began to see other people, other groups, other religions, as enemies whom we had to conquer and subjugate, or as an evil we had to eradicate. Whole cultures fell under the spell of this pathology. Christianity and Islam adopted the ethos of conquest for the greater glory of God with terrible sacrifice of human life. The increasing dissociation between the conscious mind and the realm of what Jung called our primordial soul gave rise to the multiple fragmentations, fears and projections that are at the root of many of the problems that we face today.

The dragon of myth and fairy tale is an eloquent image, not only of fear but of some of our oldest instincts which respond to fear and which can arouse fear in others. They may appear in our dreams, not only as a dinosaur but as other animals such as a mammoth, rhinoceros, wild boar, sabre-tooth tiger and lion, representing not only things we may be frightened of but powerful instincts within ourselves that may frighten or threaten others. We bring these primordial instincts with us when we are born, as part of our psycho-physical DNA. We carry them because we have evolved out of nature, with nature's power both to create and destroy. These instincts are activated, programmed and reinforced in each generation by our experience of family, school and our encounter with the wider world and the values, beliefs and models of behaviour we absorb in different cultures as we grow up.

In the event of war or tribal conflicts, these instincts and their emotional manifestations can burst through the fragile container of civilization we have painstakingly constructed and run amok, destroying all in their path, much as the dragon of myth does. This pattern has gone on for millennia without our gaining much understanding of what happens when these archaic instincts take us over, or of being able to anticipate and prevent this happening. Potentially, we have access to the priceless treasure the dragon guards — the possibility of freeing ourselves from the unconscious programming of countless millions of years, transmuting these primordial habits into the creative energy needed to throw off our bondage to them so that Rousseau's famous sentence need no longer apply.

Throughout the solar era the myth of the battle between hero and dragon was framed in terms of the battle of light against darkness and good against evil, with the belief that good would ultimately triumph over evil. Within the psyche, darkness was unconsciously identified with the fear of slipping back into the 'state of nature'. Yet regressing into a state of nature is precisely what we do when we fall under the power of these atavistic habits of behaviour. With the psychological insight now available to us, we can perhaps realize that the battle is not so much with enemies in the world as with these primordial habits that cause us to regress into unconsciousness and repeat the behaviour patterns of the past.

The real locus of the battle of light against darkness is the conscious mind and the immense effort of consciousness required to become aware of the moral quality of our own behaviour, to assess whether it is conducive to bringing good or evil into being. Secondly, it is to become aware of the tendency to project evil onto others while failing to recognize the same propensity for evil in ourselves. The image of the fight with the dragon can be re-framed in relation to this dragon lurking in our shadow rather than solely to the specific threats we encounter in the outer world.

Primordial Instincts: Predator and Prey

In our human species immensely powerful instincts are carried through into the field of human relationships from the older reptilian and mammalian brain systems: survival instincts, territorial instincts, sexual instincts and the millions-of-years-old programming of predator and prey. Because these archaic instincts function at a deeply unconscious level we, who see ourselves as the summit of creation, may nevertheless be influenced, even controlled by habits formed during pre-human or early human phases of evolution. Fear of becoming prey can swiftly transform us into predators.

Fairy tale and myth have given us many images of the destructive power of our instincts: the dragons emerging from their caves to ravage the countryside and destroy everything in their path, demanding live sacrifices as their daily food; the Gorgon turning all who saw her to stone. The transfixing power of the predatory aspect of instinct has been drawn for our day by Tolkien in *The Lord of the Rings* as the loathsome spider, Shelob, whom Frodo had to overcome in a desperate fight. These images symbolize pre-human instincts which, still overwhelmingly powerful in relation to our fragile conscious selves, can draw us back into self-destructive patterns of behaviour, or into behaviour towards others which transfixes them with terror. Then, in a state of psychic inflation we lose our humanity, our capacity for relationship, empathy and compassion and the priceless attainment of the differentiation of consciousness from autonomous unconscious processes. We revert to becoming ruthless predators, destroyers of the lives of others who become our prey.

Because we have lived in identification with the tribal, national or religious group for so many millennia, and because we have so little understanding of how the collective psyche works, it is extraordinarily difficult for an individual to stand against these archaic drives, to resist being swept away by the emotion (whether fear, anger or hatred) that can spread like a forest fire through the dry tinder of the group and can transform itself, as tension mounts, into the pathology of a mass psychosis. Then, millions of individuals (the vast majority males) willingly, even eagerly, embrace war and will acclaim a leader whose declared aim is the defeat or annihilation of an enemy. Killing then becomes a patriotic virtue; even a religious duty.

There is a strange saying of Jesus in the Gnostic Gospel of Thomas, "Blessed is the lion which becomes man when consumed by man; and cursed is the man whom the lion consumes and the lion becomes man." (*logion* 7) His words point on the one hand to the danger of the unconscious instinct of the predator 'taking over' or 'possessing' the conscious mind and, on the other, to the benefit that accrues to the man who is able to integrate the strength and fearlessness of the lion without succumbing to its power to kill.

Observations about the biological relationship between human beings and animals are unpopular because they conflict with idea of free will and self-determination. There has been even more resistance to accepting the idea that we may still be controlled by instincts that belong to our primate ancestors and even to the dinosaurs. However, it seems obvious that the predator/prey pattern is a genetic behavioural habit laid down in many species over hundreds of millions of years. We carry this habit in our own biological inheritance and are conditioned to act and react as predator (attacker) and to take avoiding action lest we become the prey (victim) of someone else.

In our species-memory are imprinted the behaviour patterns of all creatures who were predators and all creatures who were prey or food for them. Our own species has been prey to certain animals and predator to many others and it is the imprinting of our species-memory with this age-old experience that is our greatest problem. If we can become aware of how this pattern of behaviour can take us over when we feel threatened or when ethical and moral values that could set parameters for our behaviour are insufficiently developed or have collapsed, we may be able to resist succumbing to its power. One of the most perplexing aspects of our unconsciousness is the fact that religious leaders, who should have upheld these values, have frequently betrayed them — even to the present time — by succumbing to the predator/prey pattern of behaviour themselves.

With the development of the neo-cortex and the frontal lobes of the brain, the evolutionary development of our ability to reflect on our actions separated us from nature as well as from our primordial instincts, putting a space, so to speak, between the immediate response to an instinctive need (for food or to ward off a perceived threat) and the action that, in animal species, follows on from it. The sparrow-hawk does not pause to reflect before it falls on the blackbird, nor does the lion hesitate to attack another lion that is invading its territory. We, however, have developed the ability to reflect when we are confronted with a threat, to allow ourselves time to decide how to respond. Consciousness gives us the power to discriminate between two courses of action. When chased by a bull, we don't stop to reflect; when faced with an enemy or a threatening situation, we may have a measure of choice about how to respond.

As described in Chapter Six (The Solar Era), being powerful in relation to others — killing others and seizing their territory or their possessions — became a way not only of increasing one's power but of eliminating the anxiety arising from a fear of future threats and even, ultimately, from the threat of death itself. The desire for omnipotent power became a habit; something to be achieved through conquest, territorial expansion and extending control over resources such as gold, oil and minerals, as well as accumulating arms to anticipate future threats. This habit controls our political relationships today: we see the most powerful nations competing with each other for control of resources, to acquire the most lethal weapon/s. It is this archaic habit, incorporated into long-established government policy, that is one of our greatest problems.

The drive to conquer, to embark on pre-emptive wars, to develop and stockpile weapons, to extend the range of control over others is embedded in instinctive patterns of response to any threat — real or anticipated — to personal or group survival. The male, being physically stronger and programmed to focus on the hunt has, for millennia, acted as protector of the tribal group and the territory marked out as belonging to the group. But, at the same time, he has been programmed to act as predator towards any group or individual perceived as a threat; these become, perforce, his legitimate prey. In a situation of danger, the instinctive impulse of the male is to protect the tribal group to which he belongs by attacking the threat, whatever it may be, by defensive or offensive means — even to the extent of anticipating a danger that might happen in the future. This behavioural pattern has been carried through to our times in the Bush Doctrine which states that, in the interests of self-protection, America has the right to launch a pre-emptive military strike (on Iran, for example) and the ongoing right to use colossal sums gathered from the tax revenues of its citizens on preparing for war. One-third of the world's resources today are spent on the development and stock-piling of weapons.

The Origin of Evil

Evil has its origin in this deeply unconscious predator-prey pattern of behaviour. I think that, in relation to the harm we are capable of inflicting on other human beings, *evil may be defined as the act of inflicting terror, suffering, humiliation, torture or death on an individual or group of individuals*, ranging in kind from the murder of a child to the atrocities currently taking place in Syria to the viciously cruel attacks on others on Facebook and Twitter. One of the most difficult things to recognize is that each one of us is capable of acting in a hateful, cruel or evil way, or of being complicit in these ways of behaving, whether as an individual or as the member of a government, institution, corporate body or nation. These traits may emerge when we feel threatened and may cause us to act collectively in ways that, in the context of our individual lives, we would find unacceptable. We may remember the massacre of 8000 Muslim men and boys at Srebrenica ordered by the Serb Commander Ratco Mladic — the worst atrocity to take place on European soil since the Second World War. The fact that thousands of Serbs rallied to support him as a war hero when he was apprehended in 2011 and extradited to stand trial for war crimes in The Hague shows how difficult it is to change collective habits of behaviour when tribal loyalty is involved. What the world recognized as an atrocity was seen by the Serbs as a noble defence of their nation. The fact that an International Court of Justice now exists to try those who commit such crimes against humanity is evidence of collective progress in moral awareness. But this progress requires perpetual vigilance lest we slip back into old unconscious habits.

Three Experiments

In the twentieth century three experiments revealed how easy it is to persuade people to inflict pain on others: The Asch Conformity Experiment (1951), the Milgram Experiment (1963) and the Stanford Prison Experiment (1971). The first showed that by our unconscious desire to conform to the expectations of the group, we could deny the evidence of our own eyes. The Milgram Experiment, which invited students to inflict incremental electrical pain on people in another room by remote control, revealed that when authority figures told them to proceed with the experiment, people could subject others to potentially lethal electric shocks, going against their own instinctive revulsion. (The 'victims' were actually actors and the shocks not real.) Obeying orders without reflecting on what they were doing, they lost the capacity for empathy with their victims, the instinctive ability to know when to stop inflicting pain. They went on increasing the intensity of the electric shocks until the person supervising the experiment put a stop to it.

The third experiment (Stanford Prison) showed that ordinary well-meaning people could be transformed into either cruel tyrants or cowering victims in response to the situations in which they found themselves. Student volunteers were divided into two groups: prisoners and guards. Very quickly the guards became ever more vicious abusers and the prisoners cowering helpless wrecks. The fact that they all knew the situation was entirely artificial did not stop the descent into barbarity.

All three experiments are highly relevant to understanding how we can be drawn into acceptance of a situation of institutionalized evil, such as the horror of the Holocaust or the mass exterminations of Stalin or the murder of unarmed civilians ordered by autocratic regimes, most recently in Syria. Obeying orders is one of the principal ways in which this can happen. In the experiments mentioned above, none of the participants who acted out the cruel behaviour demanded of them by their 'superiors' was intrinsically evil but all became capable of this behaviour when the 'system' demanded their compliance. In all three of the above experiments, some individuals did resist the opportunity to hurt or terrify others. Some, horrified, did protest. One such observer (Christina Maslach) even brought the Stanford Prison Experiment to an early close, insisting that it be reduced from the planned two weeks to six days.

Philip Zimbardo, who originally masterminded this experiment and later married Christina Maslach, has written a book called *The Lucifer Effect: How Good People Turn Evil*. He cites examples, including the above experiments, to show that we can easily be corrupted by situations where we are encouraged to demonize others or treat them as our prey, causing us to behave in predatory and barbarous ways and to lose the ability to recognize that we have lost our humanity. As a footnote to this brief exploration of how evil develops, in his recently published memoir, *Decision Points* (2010), George W. Bush has defended the use of 'water-boarding' as a method of torture, saying that it saved lives and that he would not hesitate to use it again. The public condemnation of these practices shows that we are well aware of the danger of condoning them, yet many people, particularly those in a position of power, cannot resist falling into them if they are under orders to obey or if they believe the end justifies the means. Others are able to resist the call to obey orders, as in the example of Egypt (2011) where soldiers refused to fire on civilians.

The Danger of Corporate Thinking

Membership of a national, religious or corporate body tends to draw the individual's allegiance to that body as the *primary moral directive*. This may lead to situations where loyalty to the corporate body overrides the capacity for empathic, ethical behaviour, and respect for the individual as well as for people in general.

The Canadian philosopher, John Ralston Saul, in his book *The Unconscious Civilization*, describes the danger of this way of thinking, which is rooted in the long-term behaviour of religious institutions as well as in the instinctive pattern of group bonding.[1] It has spread throughout modern society into many of our institutions including those of government, the banking system, the media, international corporations and, above all, the military. (To give one example: at the time of writing five biotechnology firms own the vast majority of all seeds worldwide, controlling which seeds — including many that are genetically modi-fied — are available to farmers.) This corporate allegiance is also found in the drive to extend control over markets and commodities, ignoring the suffering and poverty of the people working to extract these valuable resources that benefit giant corporations and corrupt governments but never themselves. Commercial rivalry is exacerbated by economic and political rivalry between the most powerful nations. In a different context, it may be found in the corporate allegiance of any public body, such as the police, unions, banks, local councils, social workers, health and safety executives etc. Any such body may lapse into authoritarian behaviour, exhibiting a lack of empathy with the unfortunate people who happen to fall under its control or are sacrificed to its bureaucratic agendas. George Orwell in his novel *Nineteen Eighty-Four* brilliantly described the helplessness of citizens when confronted with the power of the corporate state and its insidious methods of surveillance and control. The shocking treatment of the people of the Chagos islands, mentioned in Chapters Six and Ten, is a prime example of this mentality but there are others, where the individual has no redress or appeal against the power of the state, even in so-called democratic countries.

An Example of the Corporate Mentality

One of the most revealing examples of the dangers of corporate mentality has been described by Carol Cohn, a woman teacher who, with 47 other teachers, spent the summer months of 1984 in an enclosed environment with a group of "defence intellectuals".[2] Because it is so relevant to an understanding of the shadow, I have extracted the main features of her article at some length. There is no clearer example than this paper of the danger of unbalanced left-hemispheric thinking; the kind of thinking brilliantly explored and described by the psychiatrist Iain McGilchrist in *The Master and His Emissary: The Divided Brain and the Making of the Western World* whose thesis was explored in Chapter Nine.[3]

The remit of the group Carol Cohn joined was to teach a course on nuclear weapons, nuclear strategic doctrine and arms control and to explain and defend the strategy which justifies nuclear weapons as a deterrent. What most shocked Carol Cohn as she listened to the men passionately discussing nuclear war and weaponry, was the abstraction from reality of their thinking — the arcane language, the total absence of any sense of empathy, revulsion or moral outrage in the scenarios they were contemplating and discussing. She was also struck by the euphemistic language used by these experts, for example their referring to the deaths that would result from the use of nuclear weapons as 'collateral damage' — a term used by Donald Rumsfeld during the Iraq War. Other terms used were 'escalation dominance', 'pre-emptive strikes', 'sub-holocaust engage-ments'. She also found that the sexual imagery used in the descriptions of the effects of these weapons was striking and shocking, yet the men themselves seemed unaware of the implications of the language they were using: deep penetration, holes, craters, the orgasmic effect of an explosion, a country 'losing its virginity' when it developed the bomb. As she listened and learned their special terminology until she too felt herself to be an 'insider', she saw that the entire nuclear bomb project had become associated with the male power to give birth. Like Oppenheimer's original bomb, all future bombs were described as the nuclear scientists' and atomic strategists' 'babies'. The conclusion she drew was that language and imagery that domesticates and describes these weapons in human terms distances those speaking about them from emotional affect and makes it possible for them to blank out their horrific power to destroy human lives, pulverize human bodies; "*The entire history of the bomb project seems permeated with imagery that confounds man's overwhelming technological power to destroy nature with the power to create — imagery that inverts men's destruction and asserts in its place the power to create new life and a new world.*" (Italics mine) Even the first atomic bomb test was called Trinity — the unity of the triune male forces of Creation. The progenitors of this atrocity were a new male priesthood, a new Brotherhood possessed by the desire for technological mastery. The language they used, she writes, precluded the intrusion of values, of empathic concern, even of the word 'peace'.

Carol Cohn found that she became indoctrinated into the language and way of thinking of this priesthood, eventually becoming inured to the effects of the weapons they were discussing. Like them, she too became removed from reality, coming to think that only the pre-eminence of the weapons and the 'strategy' mattered — intent like them on achieving the technological and political goal with no sense of responsibility for its effects. Fortunately, she retained enough objective insight to observe what was happening to her. Her paper is a devastating critique of the dangers of corporate or institutionalized thinking and can be applied to the banking industry and to powerful corporations as well as to all departments of government.

The Eichmann Syndrome

In situations where people are told to inflict torture or suffering on others by a higher authority, they can easily become desensitized and even immune to others' symptoms of suffering or terror. This pattern of behaviour can be related to what might be called the 'Eichmann Syndrome' whereby people can be brainwashed into abysmally barbaric behaviour by being trained to obey orders without question. Eichmann wrote in his memoirs, "From my childhood, obedience was something I could not get out of my system… It was unthinkable that I would not follow orders." In such people, sadism can easily become the approved norm of behaviour. The capacity to reflect on the moral content of their actions is cancelled out by the belief that the cause they are serving is just, and obedience to orders essential to safeguard their leader, their cause or their own life. When enough of such individuals with psychopathic tendencies serve a leader who gives orders to liquidate, torture or terrorize (as with the massacre at Srebrenica, the Gaddafi regime in Libya, the persecutory regime in Syria, the Taliban in Afghanistan, al-Qaeda and the Islamist groups in African states), the predatory collective shadow takes over and thousands may fall under its spell, obeying their leaders without question, accepting as normal what is in fact pathological behaviour. It can be applied to understanding how governments behave in war, how they justify arms purchases and sales and how whole nations can be brainwashed into accepting a course of action that is morally indefensible because a political leader declares that national defence requires it. Evil does not necessarily arise from 'evil' people: any one of us can be inducted into amoral or sadistic behaviour if we are part of a system or control group which enforces, justifies or rewards behaviour that humiliates, injures, tortures or murders others.

Regimes which inculcate terror and sadistic practices tend to attract individuals to carry out their orders who may have psychopathic tendencies. Documentaries have shown how some of the surviving guards and commandants who supervised the gulags in the former Soviet Union, the liquidation of millions in China or the extermination camps in Cambodia showed no remorse for what they had done. The same applies to the atrocities perpetrated by the Japanese army on the inhabitants of the Chinese city of Ping Fan in 1932–45 where scientists and doctors were ordered to find ways of transforming deadly bacteria into biological weapons. People were deliberately infected with bacteria and those showing signs of illness were taken away and rendered unconscious in order to take samples of the infected blood from their bodies. They were then killed. Thousands died in this way. This programme surpassed in scale, extent, and duration that of Nazi doctors in German-occupied Europe. Blindly obeying the orders of their commanders, all involved were apparently unable to resist the evil of what they were doing, very possibly because of the fear of being executed themselves. None of the Japanese scientists and doctors at Ping Fan was ever brought to trial, apparently because of a deal done with the USA whereby Japan would hand over all its information on biological weapons in return for not being tried for war crimes in this domain.

Intimidation is an ongoing feature of authoritarian regimes such as those of Saudi-Arabia, Iran, Egypt, Russia, Syria and Turkey which use torture, imprisonment and execution or assassination to instil fear in their populations. In these situations where orders are obeyed out of fear of being liquidated oneself or out of respect for a regime or its leader, the lives of civilians will be sacrificed without guilt or regret. Yet, the torture of a single human being should call forth a cry of protest from every one of us. The atrocious torture and murder of a 13-year old boy, Hamza al-Khatib by government forces in Syria in May 2011 did call forth a horrified protest from the world as well as from the Syrian people.

Primo Levi, one of the few survivors of Auschwitz, urges us in his last book, *The Damned and the Saved*, not to forget the horrors man has inflicted on defenceless people: "It is neither easy nor agreeable to dredge this abyss of viciousness, and yet I think it must be done, because what could be perpetrated yesterday could be attempted again tomorrow, could overwhelm us and our children. One is tempted to turn away with a grimace and close one's mind: this is a temptation one must resist."[4] He asks us to bear our capacity for evil constantly in mind because the opportunity for it to take hold is always a latent possibility in any society.

The Totalitarian Regime

Political or religious regimes whose aim is to extend their totalitarian power draw individuals into positions where they are given carte blanche to be as cruel and sadistic as they like because they are the servants of a regime which eliminates anyone who challenges its legitimacy or anyone who is designated expendable for ideological or political reasons. The main characteristic of the individuals who assist such a regime to maintain its power is their incapacity to feel any empathy for their victim; on the contrary, to take pleasure in their victim's terror and pain. The archaic pattern of the predator takes control of the psyche. Men regress into boasting of their prowess in torture and murder. One current example is the persecutory regime in Iran which, with the means of control exercised by the Revolutionary Guards, uses imprisonment, torture and anal rape as well as summary execution (hanging from a crane) as a method of terrorizing the population. A similar oppressive regime maintaining itself in power by intimidation and a ruthless secret police force existed in Egypt for thirty years under the rule of Hosni Mubarak and in Libya under Colonel Gaddafi for forty-two years. For political reasons, the West chose to support both these regimes and supplied them with weapons and funds, while fully aware of the atrocities they were perpetrating. None of the money donated went to the people of these countries, only to the military arm of their governments.

Paradoxically, the survival instincts which may justify the infliction of suffering and death on others also have the power to overthrow tyranny when roused in millions of oppressed people who have faced the 'dragon' and overcome the paralysing power of fear. We witnessed this happening with the demolition of the Berlin Wall, in Romania with the removal of the Ceauşescu, and in Serbia with the removal of Milošević. Now it seems to be happening in the Arab world with the attempt of the people to free themselves from their autocratic leaders.

Malignant Aggression

In his *Anatomy of Human Destructiveness,* the psychologist Erich Fromm uses the term malignant aggression or necrophilia (the fascination with death) to describe the tendency to sadism and cruelty in deeply traumatized individuals. Fromm defines sadism as the passion to have absolute and unrestricted control over a living being, whether animal, child, man, or woman. To force someone to endure pain or humiliation without being able to defend himself is one of the manifestations of absolute control. The sadistic act, Fromm says, "is the transformation of impotence into omnipotence."[5] I would add: the transformation of the impotence of the child into the omnipotence of the adult. Sadism is the ultimate expression of an imagination rendered malignant by trauma and bonded to a nervous system perpetually on high alert against attack.

The original situation where the child was forced through fear to obey a parent or other adult implicitly, to endure the pain and terror inflicted on him or her or to witness the torture or murder of a beloved parent or other individual may be inflicted on a future victim. There are many examples of this in the cruelty, sexual abuse and murder inflicted on small children by sadistic adults. But there are also examples of predatory and sadistic cruelty in the bullying that is rife in schools and the workplace, in the treatment of the elderly in hospitals and retirement homes, of children in the care of social workers, and cases (in the UK) where the individual has no redress against a miscarriage of justice, as when the courts enforce the separation of children from their parents at the behest of social workers, with no right of appeal by either parents or children.

With regard to tyrannies and oppressive regimes, beneath the aggressive persona of the tyrant there may be hidden the deeply traumatized childhood victim of an earlier situation. Studies of the childhoods and rise to absolute power of Hitler, Stalin, Saddam Hussein, Ceauşescu and Milošević and his wife support this conclusion. Alice Miller's books, particularly *Thou Shalt not be Aware: Society's Betrayal of the Child*, have shown how brutal childhood experiences may create brutal adults, particularly in a state system that encourages cruelty and brutality as a method of establishing absolute power and control over its citizens.[6] In the psyche of the individual who is taken over by the tendencies of the predator, there is no intercessor between the conscious will and the unconscious shadow that drives it. The ruthless exercise of power becomes essential to survival because the surrender of power means becoming vulnerable once again to pain and terror — the equivalent of death.

Sadism and Violence as 'Entertainment'

There are thousands of people on this planet who are engaged in acts of torture and destroying the lives of others. There are also thousands who are creating and marketing films and videos which display sadistic scenes of torture and murder. These images of violence are held to be harmless but they have a brutalizing and desensitizing influence on the fragile psyche of children as well as on that of adults. By the time an American child is eighteen, it will have seen two hundred thousand acts of violence and forty thousand murders on television. There is no doubt that watching scenes of violence over many years conditions individuals and society as a whole to view violence as acceptable, even heroic. Constant exposure to scenes of violence or participating in violent computer games weakens the capacity for empathy so that when children encounter cruelty or bullying in their environment, they may not respond empathically to the victim but may side with the aggressor. The sadistic cruelty of children texting images of the violence they have inflicted on some unfortunate victim is the obvious outcome of this conditioning; so is the gang violence that leads to the tragic murder of many young men.

What does all this violence reveal about the childhoods of the people engaged in promoting and showing these toxic images, the activation of primordial instincts and the buried pain and fear they are projecting into sadistic scenes reconstituted from their shadow? Quentin Tarantino, described as Hollywood's 'Shakespeare of Violence', has opened the gates to images of malignant aggression in the flood of torture and violence porn now incorporated into many videos and films. He and his cohorts, Robert Rodriguez and Eli Roth justify the creation and sale of these videos and films in the name of 'freedom of expression', no doubt enjoying the vast wealth accruing to them. "I want nudity," proclaims Roth. "I want sex and violence mixed together. What's wrong with that? We're in a really violent wave, and I hope it never ends."[7] But what these men are really doing is creating vicarious visual terrorism, presenting images which fuse extreme violence and sexual excitement and eroding social taboos which might inhibit attacks on women, children and defenceless victims. They are promoting the idea that revolting scenes of torture, savagery and murder can give rise to a desirable orgiastic experience. They are really asking the people who push up the ratings of their films and video, including millions of adolescents, to become complicit in acts of horrific violence, thereby reducing their ability to resist being drawn into sadistic acts when seeking peer approval (gangs) or obeying orders given them to people to whom they have granted authority, abnegating their own humanity in the process. It is hardly surprising that the murder of their classmates or members of the public by psychopathic individuals who are drawn into the net of malignant aggression by the viewing of these scenes of violence is becoming a regular feature of life in America or that some two million young offenders are in prison there.

There is now a large body of evidence indicating that these films and videos have harmful effects on young people but the 'rights' and 'freedom' of the people who continue to make these films is fiercely defended. There is an ongoing refusal to accept the fact that violent video games corrupt and desensitize both children and adults. Censorship is not the issue here: the real issue is the creation and protection of a civilized society.

"A heavy diet of media violence has a tendency to increase chronic levels of hostility and to lead people to interpret the world around them as a more hostile and dangerous place," states Joanne Cantor of the University of Wisconson-Madison, an internationally recognized expert on children and the mass media.[8] If children have a dysfunctional or toxic family life and are imprinted with images of violence, they will develop violent responses to life and other people, either in self-defence or in an unconscious impulse to avenge the suffering they themselves have experienced. In the effort to avoid becoming the prey of others, they may be drawn into situations where they enact the role of the predator towards someone else — perhaps a child — as victim. We should not forget the three experiments mentioned above which showed how quickly people can regress into both predator and victim. Recent cases of shocking cruelty meted out to children by other children, some as young as eight or nine, bear this out. During the trial of these children (Edlington case UK 2010), the fact has repeatedly emerged that, in the toxic atmosphere of their homes, they were fed a diet of violent videos, as well as being the helpless witnesses of the continual violent abuse of their mother by their father.

The Shadow of Religion: Atrocities Committed in the Name of God

Wherever immense power is concentrated in the hands of a few individuals or an institution, there will inevitably be shadow; the greater the power, the greater the shadow. Apart from the patterns of behaviour described above, there are three main areas involving possession by the will to power of the shadow which invite our attention: religion, politics and science. The shadow in religion can be recognized in the desire of a religious leader or institution to draw vast sections, if not the whole of humanity into one belief system named as superior and the sole purveyor of truth. Religious institutions do not acknowledge their archaic shadow, reflected in their need for power and control over those who belong to their particular faith and their repudiation of the value of other faiths. The power-driven shadow may, for example, be reflected in the insistence that certain passages of Scripture must be obeyed to the letter because these passages (written down millennia ago) are believed to reflect the will of God and must never be altered or modified. All this has nothing to do with spirituality: it is the very antithesis of spirituality. Archaic tribal custom and prejudice lurk beneath the cloak of religious teaching and the literal interpretation of religious texts, particularly in relation to patriarchal attitudes regarding the control of women's lives and bodies.

We see today how unspeakable atrocities are perpetrated by people who claim that the elimination of an enemy or the suppression of certain ways of behaving is a religious duty. Faith can be used as a tool of oppression because people have for centuries been programmed to accept the conquest of territory and the elimination of enemies in the name of Yahweh, God, Christ or Allah and have been trained unthinkingly to obey the dictates of their spiritual leaders. The power of the patriarchal father still holds immense influence over the immature or pre-conscious psyche. When one religion is pitted against another, or even one group within the same religion against another, predatory instincts may be aroused as people are exhorted to kill their 'brothers' with a barbarity too sickening to detail, as in the quagmire of Iraq and Afghanistan, and the brutally repressive regime in Syria where the Alawite minority controls the Sunni majority.

The Shadow of Politics: The Pervasive Tentacles of Militarism

The shadow in the political sphere is most easily observed in the military-industrial complex of the most powerful nations. Since this is not a subject I would normally have any knowledge of, I have been greatly helped by two books, the first detailing the power and extent of the military empire of the United States and offering a critique of the militarism that threatens to destroy that nation from within: *The Sorrows of Empire: Militarism, Secrecy, and the End of the Republic* by Chalmers Johnson (2004). The second is Vijay Mehta's survey of the nature and ramifications of worldwide militarism in *The Economics of Killing: How the West Fuels War and Poverty in the Developing World* (2012). Mehta's book offers a comprehensive and detailed analysis of the military-industrial complex which, like the tentacles of an octopus, has come to spread over much of the world. He explains how it is supported and perpetuated by the most powerful nations on the planet in order to increase their own power and how it also acts to impoverish nations in the developing world. Their sale of arms to regimes which use these same arms against their own people is one of the deplorable features of this system. Syria, for example buys up to $1 billion of armaments from Russia annually (*The Times* 18/8/12). Iran has supplied $5 million in military aid to Syria in the course of six months during 2012 (*The Times* 4/10/12). In 2017 India was the largest importer of arms, closely followed by Saudi-Arabia, China and the United Arab Emirates (report SIPRI - Stockholm International Peace Research Institute). India's proposed military upgrade is estimated to cost $100 billion over the next ten years.[9]

The world currently (2018) spends $1,686 billion on militarization whereas just $30 billion would end starvation worldwide, and $11 billion would provide clean water for every person on the planet. Few people outside governments are aware of the nature, extent and dangers of this complex and nothing illustrates its power better than the priority given to it by governments. Mehta's book is a timely wake-up call to concerned citizens who wish to see a better, more equitable world come into being, no longer controlled by a system ostensibly designed for defence, yet which acts like a spreading cancer on the body of the planet.

In his farewell address to the nation in January 1961, President Eisenhower gave this stark warning to the people of America:

> In the counsels of Government, we must guard against the acquisition of unwarranted influence, whether sought or unsought, by the Military Industrial Complex. The potential for the disastrous rise of misplaced power exists, and will persist. We must never let the weight of this combination endanger our liberties or democratic processes. We should take nothing for granted. Only an alert and knowledgeable citizenry can compel the proper meshing of the huge industrial and military machinery of defense with our peaceful methods and goals so that security and liberty may prosper together.

Eisenhower's warning, far from being taken to heart, has been ignored by subsequent governments which spend ever greater sums to feed the insatiable demands of the military and the powerful and wealthy industries that supply it. Some of the facts relating to this will be included in this section but will also be mentioned in the next chapter.

SIPRI reports that global military spending for 2017 was $1.7 trillion and that the United States has enormously increased its military spending since 2011, estimated to reach nearly $900 billion in 2018-2019.[10] The estimated military spending for the United States in 2018 was $886 billion (Trump's budget for the fiscal year October 2018-2019, submitted to Congress February 2018) The example of the United States has been followed by other nations — China, Japan, India, Pakistan, the United Kingdom, France, Israel, Russia, Iran and Saudi Arabia among them — many of whom are adding to their own arsenal of weapons and, at the same time, selling armaments and combat aircraft to other governments, often with corrupt and oppressive leaders. These nations form a global military elite whose dark shadow is reflected in the escalation of the arms race and the impoverishment and suffering of the billions whose needs are neglected. In addition, Mehta writes, "More than 36.4 million people in more than 120 countries have been affected by militarism. Refugees, migrants, internally displaced persons and stateless people flee from fighting or are forcibly driven out of their own countries as a result of internal disputes."[11]

This information is now becoming more widely available to the public through the Internet and such research institutes as SIPRI. In Mehta's view, "It is collective activity that offers the best hope for ending the military-industrial trading relations that have kept half the world in a state of war, misery and starvation. It is public unity that will divert tax revenues from the pockets of military companies into the human and economic development that provides lasting security."[12] It would be interesting to know how much of the aid given annually by Western nations to Indian, Pakistani and African governments is actually used to lift people out of poverty rather than spent on purchasing weapons and combat aircraft from the donor nations or lining the pockets of government officials.

As people become more aware through researching details on the Internet of this whole duplicitous scenario, they will slowly gain the power to dismantle it. In the light of the astounding discoveries of science (Chapter Fourteen) and the fact that every one of our actions affects the whole cosmic order, I think we can see why militarism is the corrupt and corrupting residue of an outworn view of reality even though we can understand why it has come into being and why it believes it has to perpetuate itself.

The same shadow drive for dominance and omnipotent control, facilitated through military power, contaminates all those utopian ideologies which claim to bring lasting benefits to humanity regardless of the violent and repressive means used to attain them. John Gray has shown in his book *Black Mass: Apocalyptic Religion and the Death of Utopia* how the utopian secular ideologies that caused such massive suffering in the last century were deeply tied in to Christian millennial beliefs — derived from the Book of Revelation — of an anticipated new world order that would be ushered in by cataclysmic destruction. He also shows how George W. Bush's concept of defeating the 'axis of evil' belongs to the same millennial mythology.[13] In pursuit of an utopian ideal, military aggression was tacitly accepted and justified in order to overthrow an old order and establish a new one — all in the name of democracy.

The Hubris Syndrome

This phrase, taken from a book of that title published in England in 2007 and again in 2012 by Dr. David Owen, who became Foreign Secretary under a former Labour Government, is a character trait that is often found in leaders, particularly leaders or corporate groups involved in military ventures or who have sudden access to immense power.

David Owen's book gives a clear definition of the pathology of leaders who display traits of grandiosity and psychic inflation — a *hubris* or god-almightiness — and heightens the need for awareness of how easily leaders of nations can persuade individuals as well as whole peoples to perpetrate and accept as 'normal' and 'patriotic' acts of immature folly as well as extreme barbarism.

The biggest danger in the sphere of both politics and religion comes from the mythic inflation of leaders — their unconscious identification with the archetypal role of the hero or saviour or, in the case of someone with a strong religious belief, the role of being the vehicle of God or some new utopian ideology. Leaders may believe they are being guided by God or Allah in the moral task of getting rid of an opponent whom they name as evil. They unconsciously fall into grandiosity and omnipotence and their speeches take on a demagogic, even a messianic tone.

In the view of David Owen, both Tony Blair and George W. Bush began to show symptoms of grandiosity after 2001, as if they had been chosen to fulfil a divinely ordained historical role in the confrontation with the 'axis of evil'. Blair dispensed with the advice of his cabinet and didn't even inform its members of his decision to take the nation into war. He disregarded the warnings of senior military and civil service advisors and began to exhibit symptoms of inflation — over-confidence, a tendency to simplify and a defensive, messianic tone. "Blair," Owen writes, "with no Parliamentary scrutiny, was to change the whole basis of Cabinet government as it related to foreign and defence matters…. This was not modernisation but hubristic vandalism, for which, as Prime Minister, Blair alone bears responsibility."[14]

In the United States, George W. Bush and his advisors enormously increased the power of the office of President as Commander-in-Chief as well as the Executive branch of government, suspending many of the constitutional rights of the American people and reducing complex issues to the single phrase "Those who are not with us are against us." The catastrophic effects of the invasion of Iraq and Afghanistan are detailed in a devastating critique of the Bush government by a highly respected academic, David Ray Griffin, entitled *Bush and Cheney – How they Ruined America and the World* (Olive Branch Press 2017). The consequences of the Iraq war include an estimated 2.3 million Iraqi deaths, 4,500

American deaths and hundreds of thousands of serious injuries, not to mention the disastrous effects of depleted uranium and the deformed babies resulting from its military use. The economic cost had reached $4 trillion by 2014 and the political fall-out, including the existence of Isil is now visible for all to see. His book also meticulously deconstructs the official explanation of the events of 9/11 and shows that the world has been consistently lied to about 9/11 and the American invasions in the Middle East. The hubristic stance of the United States is reflected in its belief that it has the right to intervene (and overthrow regimes) wherever it sees fit.

The recently published memoirs of Kofi Annan (2012), *Interventions — a Life in War and Peace* show that he believed Tony Blair could have prevented the invasion of Iraq if he had withdrawn his support for President Bush. America would then have been faced with the necessity of embarking on war alone. At the very least this would have given the President and his advisors pause for thought — time to reflect more on what they were doing and the huge risks involved.

David Owen concludes his book with the words, "It may be that the hubristic syndrome never has a medical cure or even a proven medical causation, but it is becoming ever clearer that, as much as or even more than conventional illness, it is a great menace to the quality of leadership and the proper government of our world."[15]

Wherever the words good and evil are mentioned in the context of preparations for war, we should be instantly alert for shadow projections, alert for the beginnings of a religious or political crusade and the call to eradicate evil. As Tzvetan Todorov warns us in his book *Hope and Memory: Reflections on the Twentieth Century*, "Projects aiming to eradicate evil so as to usher in a reign of universal good are best left alone."[16] Even if we cannot leave them alone, we should take care to proceed with the utmost caution and maintain a constant vigilance for our own shadow motives in taking a course of action to eradicate evil.

The Shadow of Science: Grandiosity and Omnipotence

The shadow in the sphere of science can be seen in a Promethean tendency to grandiosity and omnipotence and the belief that the aim of science is not so much a quest for an understanding of how nature works but the 'conquest of nature'. Scientists describe science as a methodology but science can easily fall under the control of the power drive of the shadow and morph itself into an ideology or belief system. Like other political ideologies, it may demand a free hand to do whatever it wants in the name of scientific progress: nothing and no one must be allowed to impede that progress (as with the genetic engineering of crops). It may proclaim with dogmatic certainty that it is the sole purveyor of the truth. It may attack as heretical any new scientific hypothesis, any therapeutic approach to healing or belief that it chooses to reject — such as the practice of homeopathy or acupuncture — thereby imposing a kind of rational 'Final Solution' which aims to eliminate whatever it designates as non-rational or unscientific.

An illustration of the unconscious power-seeking drive of the shadow was reflected in the events following the creation of the atomic bomb. Robert Oppenheimer, brilliant theoretical physicist and director of the Manhattan Project which developed the atom bomb, was appalled when the bomb was dropped on Hiroshima and Nagasaki; yet he was drawn into the train of events which led to this atrocity by his fascination with the technology of the bomb and being unable to intervene in the political process once the bomb had been tested: "It is my judgment in these things that when you see something technically sweet you go ahead and do it and you argue about what to do about it only when you have had your technical success. That's the way it was with the atomic bomb."[17] In Todorov's view, even if the crime is less grave than the elimination of the Jews by the Nazi regime, the moral guilt of those who killed in the name of democracy is greater.[18] When the scientist's shadow drive for technical success is drawn into the wake of the power-seeking shadow of governments in time of war or involved in the military-industrial complex, events are set in motion which may culminate in catastrophe, as with the bombs dropped on Hiroshima and Nagasaki and the hydrogen bombs detonated over islands in the Pacific, or in the accumulation of vast stores of chemical and biological weapons in the Soviet Union during the Cold War — an insidious story which will be explored in the next chapter.[19]

Harnessing science to serve a government's agenda for defence is considered praiseworthy and legitimate. Many scientists work for governments and the military. But science that is co-opted to serve the military arm of government can be taken over by the shadow when it develops weapons that have become a danger to humanity as well as capable of devastating vast areas of the planet. We need to challenge the ideology of scientific progress and ascertain where it is in thrall to the power-driven tendencies of governments and corporate bodies and where, in relation to what has been explored above, it may act to engender and promote evil.

Recognizing the Shadow

In today's world, the shadow is becoming easier to see, not only in the behaviour of our enemies but in our own. Things are being brought to light about the conduct of government that people had no idea of, such as the dubious justification for the wars with Iraq and Afghanistan, lying and corruption in high places and the general tendency to obfuscation, manipulation and 'spin' of politicians. People can see that the escalating sale of arms to unstable and persecutory regimes is morally corrupt because however much it increases the GNP of a nation, it fosters the conditions that promote war, destitution and the suffering of unarmed civilians. When nations engage in this trade, they are complicit at one remove in causing the suffering that follows. Financial scandals such as the Enron fiasco and the lack of responsibility of major banks in their duplicity, corporate greed and relentless pursuit of wealth have been revealed for all to see. The sexual abuse of children by the Catholic clergy as well as deeply held prejudices against women and homosexuals in Christianity and Islam are coming to light. All this is a revelation of the shadow.

Uncovering the shadow aspect of religious, political and scientific agendas is of great value if it can help to free us from bondage to unconscious habits of behaviour that lead to the suffering of others. But there is a massive amount still to do if we are to become more aware of how easily we can be manipulated by the shadow behaviour of governments, religions and science. If we are to become capable of resisting the drive for omnipotence in any of these fields, we have to be aware of our own shadow and where it may lead us into compliance with or acceptance of shadow tendencies in all three domains. At the same time we have carefully to distinguish between negative projections and the reality of evil in the form of a mass psychosis (such as the threat offered by Hitler to the whole of Europe) that may confront us in a specific situation. We need also to be aware of how easily a mass psychosis can develop in vast numbers of people. It is only by developing a greater power of discrimination that we can gain the power and the insight to deal with evil by recognizing it in ourselves as well as naming it in others.

Redeeming the Shadow of the Solar Era

Lord Rees, the Astronomer Royal, says in a book called *Our Final Century*, published in 2003, that we have a 50-50 chance of surviving this current century:

> Our choices and actions could ensure the perpetual future of life (not just on Earth, but perhaps far beyond it, too). Or in contrast, through malign intent, or through misadventure, twenty-first century technology could jeopardise life's potential, foreclosing its human and posthuman future. What happens here on Earth, in this century, could conceivably make the difference between a near

eternity filled with ever more complex and subtle forms of life and one filled with nothing but base matter.[20]

The principal dangers he cites are terrorism, the impact of climate change, the misuse of nano-technology, nuclear, chemical and biological weapons as well as the dangers presented by nature such as the catastrophic devastation that would be caused by asteroid impact and the eruption of calderas. To these, I would add the danger of nuclear reactors.

March 11th, 2018, is the seventh anniversary of the Fukushima nuclear disaster. Since that time between 300 and 400 metric tonnes of irradiated water has been flowing into the Pacific from the fourth reactor every twenty-four hours, contaminating the fish, algae and the birds who feed on the fish, and ultimately affecting humans. Contaminated fish have been found off the coast of Alaska and the west coast of America. The government of Japan has admitted that the process of removing the irradiated cores from the three other crippled reactors will take at least forty years. Other scientific studies estimate up to 80 years. The flow of radioactive wind and air as well as the contaminated sea-water are affecting North America and there is at present no way of preventing this. According to a report by the French Institute for Radiological Protection and Nuclear Safety, the initial breakdown caused "the largest single contribution of radionuclides to the marine environment ever observed".

Many of the human-induced threats arise from our survival instincts as well as our addiction to long-established patterns of territorial expansion and the accumulation and extension of power in different fields. This new century asks us to take on the mammoth task of recognizing the habits of behaviour which have been justified for millennia as necessary and right from the perspective of achieving national, territorial or religious supremacy. We need to move from a national to a planetary perspective and this can only be done by an increase in the number of individuals who hold this perspective. We have the innate intelligence and capacity to change but we do not have much time in which to accomplish this momentous transformation of consciousness.

One single example offers hope: As part of the catalogue of his unspeakable crimes, Saddam Hussein drained the marshes around Basra, building huge ramparts to block the annual inundation by the Euphrates River in order to drive out the people who for millennia had inhabited this area from their homes. The whole area was transformed into a desert where nothing grew and no one could live. A remarkable man visited this area as a child and was enchanted by its peace and primordial beauty and the profusion of birds that inhabited it. He vowed that one day he would return to restore the marshes to their former state. Exiled to

America to escape Saddam's purges, with Saddam's death he was able to return to Iraq and devote himself to restoring the marshes. By making channels in the great ramparts thrown up on the orders of Saddam Hussein, he freed the water to flow again into this whole region, and by so doing, enabled it to regenerate itself. A few years and much hard work have brought him the reward of seeing the reeds growing again, millions of birds flocking to this region, and the people able to return to their ancestral homes and rebuild their reed houses. All this was accomplished through the cherished childhood memory, vision and determination of a single individual (BBC 2, 2011).

The paramount moral challenge of the nineteenth century was slavery.[21] In the twentieth century, it was totalitarianism and the revelation of the holocausts of people sacrificed to the lethal will of psychopathic dictators. In this century, the primary challenge is climate change. Secondly, there is the continued challenge offered by oppressive regimes and the dwindling resources of food and water caused by population increase. A third moral challenge is the appalling oppression of women — the rapes, murders, trafficking and domestic violence they endure — which inevitably affects the well being of their children. Rape as a weapon of war is a method of control and humiliation as despicable as slavery and should be declared a war crime and a crime against humanity, with governments and military leaders being held to account for permitting and encouraging it.[22] A fourth challenge is the need to eliminate all weapons of mass destruction from the face of the Earth so that the planet is no longer polluted by their presence.

Jung's insight into the nature of the shadow is one of his greatest legacies to us. But, as he wryly commented, "One does not become enlightened by imagining figures of light, but by making the darkness conscious."[23] Making the darkness conscious involves sacrificing the mindset that would continue in the same tracks as before, ignoring the evils that our shadow behaviour brings into being. Our survival as a species may depend on our ability to accomplish this Herculean task by recognizing the genesis of evil at its source in ourselves.

What we could do to transform this situation

❧ We could help the children and adults of the world to become more aware of shadow projections and shadow behaviour, drawing their attention to the dangers of political and religious indoctrination and the practice of demonizing and dehumanizing others, calling them names like 'dogs', 'pigs', 'vermin', 'scum' or 'kaffirs'.

❧ We could set boundaries in schools, businesses and institutions, such as hospitals and care homes, for bullying and sadistic behaviour that will not be tolerated.

❧ We could extend awareness that the roots of pathological behaviour in adults may lie in childhood suffering and self-hatred, much of it caused by inadequate education and poor parenting. Condemnation changes nothing but hardens the resistance to change. Understanding that the aggressor was once a former victim can become the first stage of healing and transforming a destructive pattern of behaviour. This does not mean that crime is condoned but that punishment is not seen as the only solution.

❧ At a national level, we could learn to recognize the shadow in the portrayal of brutal and sadistic behaviour on television, videos and films and acknowledge that these constant images of male violence have a brutalizing and desensitizing influence on the fragile psyche of children as well as adults. There is no question that watching violence over many years conditions an individual and a society to view violence as an acceptable, even an admirable and heroic way of behaving.

❧ At an international level, we could learn to recognize and name the shadow of giant corporations that are seeking ever greater control over the resources of the Earth, such as a monopoly of plant seeds, which should be the common heritage of every inhabitant of the planet. The moral irresponsibility of the industrialized nations towards the non-industrialized ones may not be recognised as evil but it gives rise to evil and great suffering. Evil can take many forms and predatory patterns of behaviour can be concealed in the profit-taking of giant corporations, in competition that destroys rivals, in seeking lucrative investment returns that may bankrupt a nation and deprive helpless populations of their means of survival.

Notes:

1. Saul, John Ralston (1995) *The Unconscious Civilization*, House of Anansi Press, Canada, and (1998) Penguin Books Ltd., London
2. Cohn, Carol (1987) *Sex and Death in the Rational World of Defense Intellectuals*, Signs, Journal of Women in Culture and Society, University of Chicago Press
3. McGilchrist, Iain (2009) *The Master and His Emissary, The Divided Brain and the Making of the Western World*, Yale University Press
4. Levi, Primo (1988) *The Damned and the Saved*, Abacus Books, London
5. Fromm, Erich (1977) *The Anatomy of Human Destructiveness*, Penguin Books Ltd., p. 386
6. Miller, Alice (1985) *Thou Shalt Not Be Aware: Society's Betrayal of the Child*, Pluto Press, London
7. quoted in an article on ultraviolent sadism by Christopher Goodwin, Are You Sitting Comfortably? *Sunday Times* Magazine, 2009
8. ibid
9. Mehta, Vijay (2012) *The Economics of Killing: How the West fuels War and Poverty in the Developing World*, Pluto Press, London, p. 33.
   This book contains a most helpful Appendix listing the names of Global Peace Organizations in different countries
10. from Mehta's article on *The Arms Trade* in Resurgence Magazine, autumn 2012
11. ibid
12. *The Economics of Killing*, p. 164
13. Gray, John (2007) *Black Mass: Apocalyptic Religion and the Death of Utopia*, Penguin Books Ltd., London, p.192
14. Owen, David (2007) *The Hubris Syndrome*, p. 31, Methuen Publishing Ltd., London
15. ibid, p.134
16. Todorov, Tzvetan (2003) *Hope and Memory, Reflections on the Twentieth Century*, Princeton University Press, p. 71
17. quoted by Todorov, p. 234 from J. Glover, *Humanity* (Cape 1999). See also Kai Bird and Martin J. Sherwin, *American Prometheus, The Triumph and Tragedy of J. Robert Oppenheimer*, Alfred Knopf, New York, 2005
18. Todorov, p. 237
19. Hoffman, David (2009) *The Dead Hand: Reagan, Gorbachov and the Untold Story of the Cold War Arms Race*, Doubleday, New York and Icon Books, London, 2011
20. Rees, Sir Martin (Lord Rees) (2003) *Our Final Century*, William Heinemann Ltd., London
21. Hochschild, Adam (2009) *Bury the Chains*, Macmillan, London
22. In October 2012, the British Foreign Secretary, William Hague, said Britain "would lead a global effort to end the culture of impunity that surrounds this monstrous crime."
23. Jung, C.G. CW13 (1967) *Alchemical Studies*, par. 335

Saint George and the Dragon

Gustav Moreau 1890

Reproduced here with the kind permission of the National Gallery, London

Chapter Thirteen

WAR AS A RAPE OF THE SOUL

What greater pain could mortals have than this: to see their children dead before their eyes.

— Euripides

When many people are being killed,
They should be mourned in heartfelt sorrow.
That is why a victory must be observed like a funeral.

— *Tao Teh Ching,* 31, Trans. Gia-Fu Feng and Jane English

The divine and the demonic are very close together; only a thin line separates them. We who are indeed capable of divinity are also capable of the demonic. And the deepest of all demonic activity is the use of our divine imaginations to invent destruction.

— Matthew Fox, *Original Blessing*

This thing of darkness I acknowledge mine...

— Prospero in *The Tempest*

The destruction of the life of another human being and, in a wider sense, the life of the planet and the species it sustains, becomes easier to accept when the sense of the sacred is lost, when people no longer feel they are living within a Sacred Order and when the values of the 'real world' prevail over the values of another order of reality, values which religions have tried and failed to establish.

What is the effect of war on the soul? From the perspective of the cosmic dimension of soul and the different values related to humanity's responsibility towards the Earth described in Chapter Ten, war de-humanizes us and corrupts us in our very soul; it is a crime against the Sacred Order of life. War inflicts a terrible wound on the soul, a wound that can never heal because of the legacy of the traumas and memories it leaves behind, not only with the living but with the dead.

At the beginning of her book, *A Small Corner of Hell: Dispatches from Chechnya*, Anna Politkovskaya, the Russian journalist assassinated outside her home in Moscow in 2006 for speaking out against the atrocities she witnessed in Chechnya, quotes a passage from an early book written by Tolstoy. I have included it in this chapter in memory of her courage in exposing the horrors of war and also in memory of Tolstoy and his hatred of war:

> All nature seemed filled with peace-giving power and beauty. Is there not room enough for men to live in peace in this magnificent world, under this infinite starry sky? How is it that wrath, vengeance, or the lust to kill their fellow men can persist in the soul of man in the midst of this entrancing Nature? Everything evil in the heart of man ought, one would think, to vanish in contact with Nature, in which beauty and goodness find their most direct expression.
>
> War? What an incomprehensible phenomenon! When reason asks itself, is it just? Is it necessary? An internal voice always answers no. Only the permanence of this unnatural phenomenon makes it natural, and only the instinct for self preservation makes it just.[1]

Chapter Six described how, during the four thousand years of the solar era, war became endemic until, in the last century, the most demonic weapon ever devised by man was used against civilians in the bombing of Hiroshima and Nagasaki. The philosopher John Gray accurately observes in his book, *Straw Dogs*, that "as science and technology have advanced, so has proficiency in killing. As the hope for a better world has grown, so has mass murder."

In July1955, Albert Einstein, Bertrand Russell, Joseph Rotblat (who left the Manhattan Project when he saw where it was leading) and eight others signed a Manifesto warning of the dire consequences of nuclear war, urging complete global disarmament. This statement, known as the *Russell-Einstein Manifesto*, was Einstein's final public act and he died shortly after signing it. The immediate trigger for this Manifesto was the testing by the United States in 1954 of a hydrogen bomb at the Bikini Atoll in the Pacific Ocean, a bomb that was 1,300 times more powerful than the Hiroshima bomb. It produced enormous amounts of highly dangerous fall-out which still to this day are causing birth defects in infants born in the Marshall Islands over 120 kilometres from Bikini. Such infants, known as 'jelly-fish babies', are born with no bones and with transparent skin. They die within a day or two.

In this Manifesto the signatories urged people to remember their humanity and forget the rest: "We have to learn to think in a new way. We have to learn to ask ourselves, not what steps can be taken to give military victory to whatever group we prefer, for there no longer are such steps; the question we have to ask ourselves is: what steps can be taken to prevent a military contest of which the issue must be disastrous to all parties?"

War encourages and justifies the propensity for cruelty latent in each one of us. It desensitizes those of us who are in a position to kill others and unleashes our innate capacity for barbarism. To begin with, we may hesitate to kill others, restrained by an instinctive empathy. But the ability to kill soon develops into the pride — even the enjoyment of the skill of killing and the ability, whether as nations or individuals, to commit unspeakable crimes. The very first result of the bombing of Hiroshima was to encourage other states to develop the same weapon so they would be on an equal footing with the power of the nuclear state; proliferation has led to further proliferation in a kind of escalating sibling rivalry. It is not difficult to see that these agents of mass death do not protect us from war but inexorably draw us towards their ultimate use. Relinquishing these weapons is the most challenging task for our species to accomplish because it goes against all our conditioning and our deepest survival instincts. In addition to these, it goes against an immensely powerful solar mythology that holds us in a kind of collective spell, convincing us that we have continually to prepare for war and that, once embarked on war, we must achieve victory.

The Solar Era and the Warrior Ethos

During the four thousand years of the solar era war has been a constant presence, glorified as the noblest activity for man. Victory and the spoils of war were the coveted treasure to be won in battle, courage in the face of death the supreme virtue.

America and the Christian West as well as the State of Israel and the entire Muslim world are still under the polarizing spell of solar mythology which dramatizes the battle between Good and Evil. The forcible conversion and defeat of others by the sword, the bomb and now the unmanned, remotely guided missile, is more than a memory; it is an ever-present reality. War has for centuries consistently been encouraged, defended and promoted by patriarchal cultures; the Old Testament proclaims a war-like God, determined to vanquish his enemies; Christianity and Islam have both been warrior civilizations. If there is one book which illustrates this pattern of war embedded in all three patriarchal cultures, it is the blood-soaked history of Jerusalem, brilliantly explored by Simon Sebag Montefiore in *Jerusalem: The Biography* (2011).

Yet now, this ancient warrior ethos that is so deeply imprinted on the male psyche is being called into question as many individuals realize that, because of their devastating effect on the fabric of civilization, let alone the planet, the sacrificial rituals of war can no longer be an option for us. Law and order have come into being to restrain the dangerous propensities of our nature within civilized society. War demolishes that restraint and gives us permission to justify acts of the utmost barbarity as long as they are inflicted on an enemy.

War invites the release of a colossal amount of instinctive energy that may have no outlet in the more contained precinct of everyday life. It may develop skills that people did not know they had; give them access to emotions they have never experienced. With survival instincts on highest alert, war makes people feel intensely alive, released to act in savage ways that are unacceptable in a situation where peace and order prevail. War draws men together in a deep and lasting bond of brotherhood, and a nation together in a shared will to protect itself against a perceived threat. War arouses, excites, ennobles, fascinates but it also degrades and corrupts. Like sleepwalkers, under the spell of solar myth and the archetypal battle of Good against Evil, we enter into it, unaware that we are held in thrall to a pattern of behaviour that has the power to ensnare us in its web. Yet, one positive sign today is that people are becoming disillusioned with the rhetoric of war and resistant to their governments' efforts to engage in it. Government justification of war sounds increasingly hollow in the light of the horrific weapons we have developed, the colossal expense of war, the heavy civilian casualties, the anguish of bereaved parents, and the injuries, both physical and mental, that the survivors of combat will carry for the rest of their lives. War can never be anything other than a tragedy, as the Chinese Taoist sages perceived so long ago.

No one doubts the heroism of the young soldier who sacrifices his or her life for their country. What is increasingly doubted is the wisdom of political leaders who call for that sacrifice when the situation does not justify it, who dispense with the precious lives of young men and women and those of helpless civilians as if they were crumbs to be swept from a table. The presentation of war as a necessity is increasingly being challenged by people who believe that war sows the seeds of further conflict and encourages the potential use of nuclear, biological and chemical weapons, not necessarily by a nation but by a deranged individual who has gained access to one of these weapons or the means of manufacturing one and will not hesitate to use it. As a species, we are responsible for bringing these weapons into being and, as a species, we can choose to put an end to them because their very existence pollutes the Earth.

Generation after generation, people have accepted the call to sacrifice their sons in war and have endured the immense suffering caused by war as an inescapable fact of life. Imagining God to be all-powerful and on the side of 'Good' they have asked God to intervene to protect them and bring them victory, to stand by their side. Yet, it is we who carry within our nature the god-like capacity for creation and destruction, for bringing good and evil into the world. The burden of responsibility to change our fate therefore lies with us, not with God. With the help of the psychological insight gained over the last hundred years, we can now address the fundamental causes of human aggression and understand why certain patterns of behaviour are re-enacted over and over again — even before our eyes today.

Weapons, defence and war have traditionally been and still are the concern of men. Women have not, until the end of the last century, participated as combatants in war. They have suffered unspeakably, have lost their own lives and the lives of husbands, fathers and sons in war and have had to endure the largely undocumented rape of themselves and their daughters, but in the past their voice has been inaudible. Yet war is as much woman's concern as man's. If the destructive power of our weapons continues to escalate, then with the power of these weapons and our moral immaturity we risk destroying not only civilization and our own species, but much viable life on this planet. Today, women are adding their voices to those of men who can see that war leads nowhere and who are appalled by the irresponsible behaviour of leaders who take their countries into it — leaders whose immaturity and ignorance of the deeper archetypal and mythic issues involved may render them ill-equipped to assume such awesome responsibility.

In his *Gulag Archipelago* Alexander Solzhenitsyn warns us to bear in mind our own contribution to evil, commenting that it is not so easy to separate evil from ourselves and blame it on our enemy: "If only it were all so simple!" he writes, "If only there were evil people somewhere insidiously committing evil deeds, and it were necessary to separate them from the rest of us and destroy them. But the line dividing good and evil cuts through the heart of every human being. And who is willing to destroy a piece of his own heart?"

The Ongoing Addiction to War

The unconscious addiction to war remains an ever-present threat, summarized in the words of Colin Gray, Professor of International Politics and Strategic Studies at the University of Reading. In *Another Bloody Century*, he takes it for granted that there will be war in the future for the simple reason that there has been war in the past:

> War and warfare will always be with us: war is a permanent feature of the human condition.... Efforts to control, limit and regulate war, and therefore warfare, by international political, legal, and normative-ethical measures and

attitudes are well worth pursuing. However, the benefits from such endeavours
will always be fragile, vulnerable to overturn by the commands of perceived
belligerent necessity.[2]

The idea that war is part of the natural order of life is open to question since there
is little evidence for the existence of warrior cultures prior to the rise of the
powerful city-states in the Middle East ca. 3500 BC. There is, for example, no
evidence of war and weapons in the Civilization of Old Europe (6500–3500 BC),
nor in the extraordinary settlement of Çatal Hüyük in Anatolia (Turkey) during
the same period. There is evidence (although not in these two cultures) of human
sacrifice but not the massive collective sacrifice of war. The survival instinct is
certainly one of the factors in the history of war but the warrior ethos is something
that was highly developed during the solar era and has become a habit, an addiction.
What needs to be challenged is the deeply engrained belief in the inevitability,
necessity and benefits of war, reflected in the words of the German Field Marshal,
Helmuth Graf von Moltke who, in 1880, wrote: "Eternal peace is a dream, and
not even a pleasant one. War is a part of God's world order. War develops man's
noblest virtues, which otherwise would slumber and die out: courage, self-denial,
devotion to duty, and willingness to make sacrifices. A man never forgets his
experiences in war. They increase his capability for all time to come."[3]

His words were echoed a hundred years later, on the anniversary of the Prophet
Mohammed's birthday, by the Ayatollah Khomeini in 1983: "War is a blessing
for the world and for all nations. It is God who incites men to fight and to kill....
The wars the Prophet led against the infidels were a blessing for all humanity....A
religion without war is an incomplete religion."[4] This is not the conscious mind
speaking but a mind that has been possessed by the primordial instinct of the
predator. Because he was the spiritual leader of Iran, his words had the power to
activate shadow projections in millions of his followers, inciting collective hatred
of the despised 'infidel' that was carried forward in the next generation by Osama
bin Laden and Isil. In the Middle Ages, similar beliefs were being disseminated
in Europe: the call to rescue the Holy Land was proclaimed by Christian popes to
be the will of God, activating exactly the same kind of negative projection onto
Muslims and leading to the massacre, in the Fourth Crusade, of the entire population
of Constantinople. It was in this era that there arose the idea of the 'Just War', building on foundations believed to have been laid by St. Augustine in the fifth century
and defined by Thomas Aquinas (1225–1274).

The twentieth century was one of monstrous slaughter — "without question,"
as the historian Niall Ferguson writes, "the bloodiest century in history, far more
violent in relative as well as absolute terms than any previous era. Significantly

larger percentages of the world's population were killed in the two world wars that dominated the century than had been killed in any previous conflict of comparable geopolitical magnitude."[5] Tens of millions were traumatized by the loss of their parents, children and families, by terror, horror, starvation and suffering. These wounds do not die with those who have suffered them. They live on in the memory fields of the collective unconscious of our species. No one has detailed the indescribable suffering of civilians in war more comprehensively than Max Hastings in his harrowing and moving book, *All Hell Let Loose: The World at War 1939–1945*. (2011).

At the end of the Nuremberg Trials (October 1946), a lawyer commented: "This trial has shown that no nations can engage in aggressive war any longer." At that time, as at the end of the Second World War, we thought we had fought the war to end all wars, had nobly halted the tide of persecution and suffering; had saved Christian civilization from barbarism. Sixty years later, we have become embroiled in another major war (Iraq and Afghanistan), this time with very dubious justification, drawing the West into confrontation with the whole Muslim world. At the dawn of a new millennium, we stand on the edge of an abyss, witnesses to further conflict, further atrocities. *We have not learned to think in a new way.*

The Archaic Roots of War

The last chapter explained how the instinctive reflexes of the reptilian and mammalian brain, formed over millions of years, can easily 'take over' the far more recently developed neo-cortical levels of the brain. These unconscious survival and territorial instincts, deeply embedded in the autonomic nervous system, may control us in any situation which arouses fear. Once they are aroused, they can drive us to actions that our rational mind, in another context, would deplore. Then, if the situation demands it, politicians who have never experienced the horror of war will call for the sacrifice of young men and women and these will courageously and patriotically respond to the call of their leader/s to offer their lives in sacrifice and to sacrifice other men and, if necessary, women and children, in order to ensure the survival of the group to which they belong.

These instinctive drives are intrinsic to the training of the armed forces in any nation-state: the training to obey orders without question and to strive for victory at all costs. Superimposed on this primordial behaviour pattern, there is the male fear of losing face, of backing down from confrontation, of being shamed and humiliated in the eyes of other men or nations and there is also the sense of honour involved in securing victory rather than suffering the ignominy of defeat. The 'primal' male in any given group is watched obsessively by other males for any sign of weakness or incompetence, any flaw which might reveal him to be a weak or vacillating leader in time of war. Any such weakness or flaw is vigorously exposed and attacked, for the strength of the leader is identified with the survival of the group. The mass of the people, when survival instincts are aroused in them by their leaders, will support a belligerent response to attack.

Nuclear Weapons and Weapons of Mass Destruction

In January 2018, The Bulletin of the Atomic Scientists announced that they had moved the hands of the Doomsday Clock to two minutes to mid-night. A few days before this announcement was made a statement by General Sir Nick Carter appeared in *The Times* in the United Kingdom: "Our ability to pre-empt or respond to threats will be eroded if we don't keep up with our adversaries." This statement encapsulates the mind-set that drives the Military-Industrial Complex in the nuclear nations and its interminable preparation for and anticipation of a future war. It could ultimately lead to one of these nations, whether deliberately or inadvertently, unleashing on the world the unimaginable catastrophe of a nuclear war.

Many decades ago General Eisenhower warned America about the unwarranted power of the Military-Industrial Complex (see Chapter Twelve). Today, the entire planet is held hostage to this Complex whose lethal tentacles control the nine nuclear nations as well as those nations and corporations engaged in the lucrative arms trade. This Complex is one of the major causes of war and the persistence of war. Here is Eisenhower's comment on war in general, given on April 16th, 1953 to The American Society of Newspaper Editors:

> Every gun that is made, every warship launched, every rocket fired signifies, in the final sense, a theft from those who hunger and are not fed, those who are cold and are not clothed. The world in arms is not spending money alone. It is spending the sweat of its laborers, the genius of its scientists, the hopes of its children.... This is not a way of life at all, in any true sense. Under the cloud of threatening war, it is humanity hanging from a cross of iron.

Most of the planet's inhabitants, even those who are highly educated and working in governments and organizations like the United Nations have very little awareness of what the immediate and long-term effects of an exchange of nuclear weapons would be in terms of the millions of civilian deaths and the rapid and irreversible deterioration of the planetary environment in the "nuclear winter" that would follow such an exchange.

Weapons that were unimaginable a hundred years ago, operated by remote control thousands of miles distant from their target, can now obliterate the lives of millions of helpless civilians and devastate vast swathes of the Earth's surface, effectively sending survivors back to the Stone Age. In the last 60 years, nations have armed themselves with truly cosmic forces of destruction without any apparent awareness of the enormous evil they have unleashed. Matthew Fox spoke truly when he wrote in his book, *Original Blessing*, that the deepest of all demonic activity is the use of our divine imaginations to invent destruction.

The splitting of the atom was the most monumental scientific project of the twentieth century, delivering, as a post-war news announcement proclaimed, limitless power into the hands of man. The application of this discovery to the dark alchemy of nuclear weaponry has been a constant presence since the bomb was first used as a weapon in 1945 in the obliteration of Hiroshima and Nagasaki. This was an act of inconceivable aggression against civilians, of whom 75,000 died immediately from the bomb itself and as many again within two weeks from radiation sickness. The bomb that fell on Nagasaki destroyed, apart from the city itself, eighteen schools and universities with thousands of students inside them.

This act reflects the dualistic thinking which arose from the split between spirit and nature during the solar era. Our growing capacity to dissociate thinking from feeling, mind from soul led us to that fateful moment and to the sequence of decisions and events which have followed on from it. Exulting in the triumph of wresting from nature the new-found power of atomic energy to serve the degenerate aims of man, and knowing nothing of the chain of ideas that had led to the kind of thinking that could encourage political leaders to embark on this course of action, people could not comprehend what an act of sacrilege had been committed against nature, matter and the sacred order of life.

Only the ego-inflation of the solar age could have led to this act of *hubris*. The horrifying effects on human beings and the utter destruction of cities were written off as the inevitable price of war and the need to defeat an enemy. In 2018, with the United States, Saudi-Arabia and Israel worried by the possibility of Iran becoming a nuclear power and by the paranoid regime of North Korea brandishing its weapons, the inevitable consequences of that act of *hubris* are clearly apparent, since it has drawn other nations to follow the example of the United States. The genie is out of the bottle and no threats will get it back in again.

Nuclear weapons and other weapons of mass destruction are the culmination of the shadow aspect of the solar age and its glorification of war and weaponry. Their invention and use reflect a consciousness which sees matter divorced from spirit and, unbelievably, takes pride in the fact that man now has the power to transform matter into a force of pure destruction. The words of Robert Oppenheimer — the Prometheus who brought us the atom bomb — warned us of the dangers of attempting to master matter. Speaking to an audience of the American Philosophical Society, he said, "We have made a thing, a most terrible weapon that has altered abruptly and profoundly the nature of the world... a thing that by all the standards of the world we grew up in is an evil thing. And by so doing...we have raised again the question of whether science is good for man."[6]

Thanks to the remarkable research carried out by David Hoffman and presented in his book *The Dead Hand: Reagan, Gorbachov and the Untold Story of the Cold War Arms Race*, we now know that by 1982, "the combined [nuclear] strategic arsenals of the two superpowers held the explosive power of approximately 1 million Hiroshimas."[7] Even this was not enough for the Soviet regime. Its leaders drew up plans for a system that would guarantee a retaliatory strike, "a fully automatic system, known as the Dead Hand, in which a computer alone would issue the order to launch."[8] While nuclear weapons were the overwhelming threat of the epoch, Hoffman writes that another lethal weapon of mass murder was being grown in flasks and fermenters:

> From 1975 to 1991, the Soviet Union covertly built the largest biological weapons program in the world. Soviet scientists experimented with genetic engineering to create pathogens that could cause unstoppable diseases. If the orders came, Soviet factory directors were ready to produce bacteria by the ton that could sicken and kill millions of people.[9]

Although in 1975 a treaty (The Biological and Toxin Weapons Convention) came into force, signed by more than seventy nations, including the United States and the Soviet Union, which banned the development and production of biological weapons and the means of delivering them, the Soviet Union continued covertly to expand its biological weapons programme (called Biopreparat) under the cover of a civilian enterprise. "The Soviet program grew and grew into a dark underside of the arms race."[10] Gorbachov was unable to confront the power of the military priesthood which controlled the development of biological weapons.

Chemical weapons were also manufactured and stockpiled as part of this programme and concealed in industrial and agricultural compounds. Incredibly, this programme to develop a new generation of even more deadly chemical weapons was secretly pursued by the military *without knowledge of the Soviet government*, thereby betraying the genuine assurances given to the West by Gorbachov and Yeltsin that this programme had been halted.[11] By the end of the cold war, the United States had amassed 31,000 thousand tons of chemical agents and the Soviet Union 40,000 tons. Great Britain as it was known then, had also stockpiled them.[12]

The residue of Russia's biological warfare programme (during the Cold War) remains an ever-present danger, even greater since the dissolution of the Soviet Union, when some of the huge stocks of biological and chemical weapons stored in Kazakhstan were accessible to impoverished Russian scientists who set up a highly lucrative black market selling nerve gas to Syria and other lethal toxins and materials to Iran. Syria has the largest stockpile of chemical weapons in the Middle East and has not hesitated to use them against its own citizens. Israel is now threatened by the stores of mustard gas, sarin and cyanide gas which have apparently been incorporated into artillery shells, chemical bombs and war-heads for Scud missiles. Syria's cooperation with Hezbollah makes the danger of these weapons being used against Israel a very real one and its government issued its citizens with gas masks as a precaution (August 2012).

In Chapter 22 of his book, Hoffman writes, "Years had gone by since the Soviet collapse, yet pathogens in flasks, unguarded fissile materials, idle weapons scientists and marooned defense factories were still being discovered for the first time in the late 1990's"[13] These weapons that are the residual legacy of the Cold War are still with us today. They are, as he rightly says, the Dead Hand of our time, "a lethal machine that haunts the globe long after the demise of the men who created it".[14]

We owe a great debt to David Hoffman for detailing these facts. I have reported some of them here because I have been so shocked by them and because they show the still unrecognized dangers of corporate military thinking that were so clearly described in Carol Cohn's paper in Chapter Twelve. Now there is a whole new generation of what are called tactical nuclear weapons. They are much smaller than earlier nuclear bombs and when detonated they look like ordinary explosions.

The Nuclear Arsenals

Instead of drawing back in horror from the evil it had unleashed, America and then the Soviet Union embarked on an arms race that has led, step by step, to the current existence of nine nuclear nations and some 16,000 nuclear weapons, with the greater part of these situated in the United States and Russia. Russia has 8,000, the US 7,100, France 300, China 250, the UK 215, Pakistan 120, India 110, Israel 80 and North Korea 10. (Federation of Atomic Scientists 2018) These are enough to incinerate the entire population of the planet several times over. Thousands of these are kept on permanent "hair-trigger" alert. Some 180 B-61 hydrogen bombs, are located on European soil: in Belgium, Germany, Italy and the Netherlands as well as the United Kingdom with its Trident submarines. The US base at Inçirlik, in Turkey — a country that joined NATO in 1952 — holds about 50 hydrogen bombs. All these bombs have been placed in these countries principally to deter a Russian attack. The danger of the launch of one of these weapons in error is a constant possibility and would precipitate a genocidal catastrophe. It only needs one inadvertent mistake, one mis-reading of a computer (as nearly happened in the Soviet Union in 1983), one terrorist attack to unleash unimaginable horror and devastation on the world. Eric Schlosser's book, *Command and Control* (2013) recounts the desperate struggle of a handful of men to prevent the explosion of a ballistic missile carrying the most powerful nuclear warhead ever built by the United States. Governments promising to protect and defend their populations by holding these weapons do no such thing. Instead, they put them at risk of total annihilation by inviting a retaliatory strike in the event of a decision to launch a pre-emptive attack or an accidental release of a nuclear bomb.

At the present time (2018), around 1800 US and Russian warheads are on high alert, able to be launched within about 45 minutes or less of the warning of an attack.[15] They can travel in the stratosphere at a speed of 1000 miles every four minutes and are undetectable save by electronic sensors. Heads of government and Chiefs of Staff have 10-15 minutes to decide if we are really under attack after receipt of electronic information that we are. American arsenals include nuclear weapons with a destructive power of 455,000 tons of high explosive (30 times the destructive power of the Hiroshima bomb). Some Russian weapons have a destructive power of more than twice this figure.[16] In the United Kingdom, each of the four Trident Missile submarines carries three hydrogen bombs in its 16 missiles, making 48 warheads in all, each one having around eight times the destructive power of the Hiroshima bomb. Each missile has a range of 7,500 miles. One Trident submarine can incinerate 40 million human beings.

It is not only the lethal power of the bombs themselves that is a danger to humanity, but the radioactive clouds released by them which could be active for thousands of years, condemning to death people hundreds or even thousands of miles distant from the actual explosion and affecting future generations. The Earth and its millions of species were exposed to the radiation of nuclear bombs set off in the Pacific between 1946 and 1963 before we were aware of the long-term effects of these bombs. In addition to the radiation emitted since 1945 through nuclear tests (over 2500), affecting the health of people living close to them (as with the Navajo in Nevada), there has been the radiation emitted by the Chernobyl (1986) and Fukushima (2011) disasters and the accidents at Windscale (1956) and Three Mile Island (1979). As a result of all these, the world has been increasingly bathed in radio-activity since 1945. We are now seeing a virtual epidemic of cancer in many parts of the world that cannot all be attributed to lifestyle or diet or genetic inheritance. In the 1950's one in nine people developed cancer. In the 1990's it was one in five. In the last few years it has been one in three and by 2020 it is estimated by WHO that it will be one in two.

Few people including the Generals who support and promote the idea of a future nuclear war between nations are aware of the effects of a "nuclear winter" which would be the result of a catastrophic nuclear war. The environmental consequences of a massive exchange of nuclear weapons have been treated in a number of studies by meteorologists and other experts from both East and West. They predict that a large-scale use of nuclear weapons would result in fire storms with very high winds and high temperatures (similar to what happened in the bombing of Hamburg and Dresden). The resulting smoke and dust would block out sunlight for a period of many months, at first only in the northern hemisphere, but later also in the southern hemisphere. Temperatures in many places would fall far below freezing and much of the Earth's plant life and vegetation would be destroyed. Animals and humans would die of starvation.[17]

For over fifty years the concentration on the development of nuclear weapons by the nine nuclear powers has brought into being the very situation that is most feared: the ability of a nation, group or deranged individual to destroy life on an apocalyptic scale. The President of the United States is followed at all times, 24 hours a day, by a military aide carrying a case holding the nuclear codes that he would use and be authorized to use in the event of a nuclear attack on the United States. The struggle of these nations for military supremacy and control has become a lethal pursuit of colossal excess and the devouring greed for power that reveals a state of possession of the conscious mind by primordial instincts.

What is truly alarming is that a single individual who has access to the technology of destruction — whether nuclear, biological or chemical — now has the power to destroy the lives of tens of millions because he believes that the use of these weapons in a pre-emptive strike against a designated enemy is justified or because he sees himself as the agent of God in eliminating his enemies from the world and instituting a new order. A nuclear missile gives no protection against a single phial of deadly pathogens or chemical toxins.

From the perspective of the values defined in Chapter Ten, the actual development as well as the proposed use of these weapons is a betrayal of these values and is, as stated at the beginning of this chapter, a crime against the sacred order of life itself. The genesis of this evil is to be found in the drive to accumulate arms, to stockpile ever more lethal weapons, as well as in the corporate mentality that holds us in bondage to instinctive survival habits of defence and attack that have been built into the human psyche for millennia.

There still appear to be millions of people who are proud of their nation's weapons and prowess in war, even making the ludicrous claim that God is on their side. Millions approve of their nation being powerful in relation to others. Military and commercial rivalry between powerful nations like America, Russia and China are accepted as 'normal'. The race to control the resources of the Arctic and the mineral wealth of Africa is the most recent example of this primitive mentality.

Fortunately, this pathology is not universal. In 1968 during the Cold War the Non-Proliferation Treaty (NPT) was drawn up and signed by 187 countries. It was an attempt to contain the growing nuclear threat and has now been in force as international law since 1970 and is convened every five years to pursue further negotiations towards total nuclear disarmament. In Article VI of the Treaty, the non-nuclear states declared that definite steps towards complete nuclear disarmament would be taken by all states as well as steps towards comprehensive control of conventional armaments. However, these steps have not been taken by all the nuclear states. Israel has still not acknowledged that it holds nuclear weapons. India and Pakistan have not signed the Treaty. North Korea, which originally signed, withdrew in 2003.

In an article published in June 2015, Professor John Scales Avery writes that "The principle of no-first-use of nuclear weapons has been an extremely important safeguard over the years, but it is violated by present NATO policy, which permits the first-use of nuclear weapons in a wide variety of circumstances. Article VI of the NPT requires states possessing nuclear weapons to get rid of them within a reasonable period of time. This article is violated by fact that NATO policy is guided by a Strategic Concept, which visualizes the continued use of nuclear weapons in the foreseeable future."[18] Currently NATO holds nuclear weapons in four European non-nuclear-weapon states: Germany, Belgium, Italy and the Netherlands, which contravenes Articles 1 and II of the NPT.

The persistent efforts of many concerned nations and individuals to eliminate nuclear weapons culminated on July 7th, 2017, in the adoption by the United Nations General Assembly of the Treaty on the Prohibition of Nuclear Weapons which was accepted by a majority of 122 to 1. This important Treaty was the result of the concerted efforts of ICAN or The International Campaign to Abolish Nuclear Weapons, founded in 2007 by the International Physicians for the Prevention of Nuclear War. The purpose of ICAN is to change the focus in the disarmament debate to the "humanitarian threat posed by nuclear weapons, drawing attention to their unique destructive capacity, their catastrophic health and environmental consequences, their indiscriminate targeting, the debilitating impact of a detonation on medical infrastructure and relief measures, and the long-lasting effects of radiation on the surrounding area." On December 10th, 2017, the efforts of ICAN were recognized by the award of the Nobel Peace Prize. The acceptance speech by ICAN's executive Director, Beatrice Fihn, is worth reading in its entirety. She ended it with these words: "We are campaigners from 486 organizations who are working to safeguard the future and we are representative of the moral majority: the billions of people who choose life over death, who together will see the end of nuclear weapons."

The Devil's Repertoire

Millions of other people long for release from this scenario of ongoing rivalry and conflict. Victor Gollancz, writing in 1958 in a book called *The Devil's Repertoire*, gave the ultimate condemnation of nuclear weapons. To drop a nuclear bomb, in any circumstances whatever, he said,

> ...would be the final iniquity, final in the sense that no more abominable iniquity is possibly conceivable by the mind of man: sheer, unqualified evil. For what else would it be than the ultimate rejection of spirit, a total abandonment, by the men who did it, of any last vestige of sympathy with their fellow-creatures, and the conversion of their own beings as a matter of deliberate choice, into instruments for the unspeakable torture of millions upon millions?[19]

I was appalled when I heard that India had developed the nuclear bomb because it suggested to me that she, like the nations of the Christian West, had turned her back on her great spiritual heritage. The demands of a nation's perceived survival needs can override an ancient lineage of spiritual values. What, incredibly, is celebrated by politicians as a great good is in fact a great evil. Arundhati Roy asks in her book, *The Algebra of Infinite Justice*, whether the Indian people have any understanding of the monstrous implications of what was decided in their name and asks, "Who the hell is the Prime Minister to decide whose finger will be on the nuclear button that could turn everything we love — our earth, our skies, our mountains, our plains, our rivers, our cities and villages — to ash in an instant?"

> Is it possible for people who cannot write their own names to understand even the basic, elementary facts about the nature of nuclear weapons?... Has anybody bothered to explain to them about thermal blasts, radioactive fallout and the nuclear winter? Are there even words in their language to describe the concepts of enriched uranium, fissile material and critical mass? Or has their language become obsolete? Are they trapped in a time capsule, watching the

world pass by, unable to understand or communicate with it because their
language never took into account the horrors that the human race would dream
up? Do they not matter at all?[20]

In the same chapter, "The End of Imagination", she writes:

It is such supreme folly to believe that nuclear weapons are deadly only if
they're used. The fact that they exist at all, their very presence in our lives, will
wreak more havoc than we can begin to fathom. Nuclear weapons pervade our
thinking. Control our behaviour. Administer our societies. Inform our dreams.
They bury themselves like meat hooks deep in the base of our brains.... The
nuclear bomb is the most anti-democratic, anti-national, anti-human, outright
evil thing that man has ever made. Through it, man now has the power to
destroy God's creation.[21]

Man as Predator

The latest weapon is the guided missile or unmanned drone, named by the United
States as 'the most precise weapon in the history of warfare' and now used
extensively by it in its war against the Taliban and al-Qaeda in Afghanistan and
Waziristan and in Syria against Isil (Islamic State of Iraq and the Levant). Despite
official denials, it has been responsible for many civilian casualties. It will not be
long before other countries develop and use these lethal weapons, discharged by
remote control by operatives thousands of miles from their target — operatives
who will feel no guilt for the lives they will extinguish with technological
precision by focusing on their target. The hapless victims of these unmanned
executions — whether militant, civilian or child — are known in the military
jargon associated with these attacks as 'bug-splats'. The men who control and
launch these weapons no doubt consider themselves to be Christians. It is a pity
the so-called Christian West has no concept of karma.

The Pentagon announced in 2015 that it plans to spend $1 trillion over the next
30 years on a new generation of nuclear bombs, bombers, missiles and
submarines, including a dozen submarines carrying more than 1,000 warheads.
Russia has revealed plans for a new kind of weapon — a hydrogen bomb torpedo
that can traverse 6,000 miles of ocean just as a missile would in the sky. On
impact, the bomb would create a "radioactive tsunami" designed to annihilate
millions along a country's coast. All this lethal planning is still not viewed as a
pathology and a symptom of insanity but is considered perfectly acceptable by
the United States and its allies in the interests of defence. Would the Buddha have
viewed this as 'right livelihood'?

The Arms Trade: A Shadow World

Arms sales are another aspect of the drive for military supremacy. The arms trade is dangerous, corrupting and amoral. In 2017 the United States had the highest number of arms sales, followed by Russia, China, France, Germany, the United Kingdom and Spain. The main exporters of arms in that year were the United States, Russia, Germany, France, China, the United Kingdom and Israel (SIPRI). Sales of arms have consistently been made to autocratic regimes in North Africa, the Middle East and sub-Saharan Africa where abuse of human rights is known to have taken place and is still ongoing. Arms sales by the United Kingdom to Saudi-Arabia continue to escalate. This is not something to be proud of but, on the contrary, is a cause for deep shame and condemnation.

The fact that governments engage in this lucrative arms trade, disowning any responsibility for ultimately killing and wounding civilians in other countries who may rise up against their oppressive ruling elite, is a further example of the pathology of war. Governments exhibit the same psychopathology as individuals: paranoia, projection, denial, splitting, delusional certainty but all this is screened out because arms sales are deemed essential in the context of 'defence', contributing to the GDP of a nation or providing employment. How is it possible to call ourselves human and participate in the invention and manufacture of all these weapons let alone their sale and use? How have we fallen into such a demonic misuse of our great creative powers, a self-inflicted rape of our soul?

To summarize: the conviction that it is justifiable to murder others in defence of one's own group or territory (with God co-opted to support that group) has evolved out of the belief systems and territorial tribal habits of the past. The efforts of the greatest spiritual teachers of all religious traditions have attempted to free us from our enslavement to these primordial habits, defining the values that we should aspire to follow. But their fundamental message — that life is sacred and, at the deepest level, one and indivisible — has consistently been ignored. They would view the invention of our weapons of destruction in the interests of self-defence or maintaining the 'balance of power' and our proposed use of them to destroy the lives of innocent people in order to save our own lives as morally inconceivable.

As long ago as 1948 General Omar Bradley summed up in a speech the moral immaturity of the Christian West: "We have grasped the mystery of the atom and rejected the Sermon on the Mount. Ours is a world of nuclear giants and ethical infants. We know more about war than we know about peace, more about killing than we know about living." He also said, "If we continue to develop our weaponry without wisdom or prudence, our servant may prove to be our executioner."

The Cost of War

Governments pour incredible sums of money into the maintenance and renewal of weapons. Wars generate huge profits for a few individuals and corporate bodies. But the actual financial cost of war and the weapons required to wage it or to be dedicated to defence falls on the general population whose work generates the taxes that are used to pay for them. The accumulation of arms is a burden on every country that indulges in it because it wastes colossal sums that could otherwise be spent on raising the standard of living of those least able to help themselves. One example is the huge final cost of renewing the Trident Missile system in the United Kingdom that currently does not have this amount of money to spend.

Global military expenditure in 2017 amounted to $1.7 trillion (SIPRI).[22] The military spending budget submitted by President Trump to Congress for the year 2018-9 was nearly $900 billion. The estimated cost to it for the wars in Iraq and Afghanistan is estimated to reach $2.4 trillion by 2017 although the actual cost is thought to be twice that after taking into account payments to the families of the bereaved and the ongoing care of wounded veterans. There is also the huge cost of maintaining military bases in over one hundred different countries. In 2018 the US Department of Defense Inspector-General and the Defense Finance & Accounting Service report revealed that the Pentagon could not account for $21 trillion of taxpayer funding (Changemaker Media and Global Research 2018). Although mandated by federal law to conduct regular financial audits, the Pentagon, over some twenty years, has never complied with that law or accounted for the trillions of dollars of tax payers' money it has spent. The insanity of all this is reflected in the fact that two-fifths of the Earth's population live on less than $2 a day and a billion are hungry. Imagine the difference that could be made to the destitute and hungry people of the world if the obscene sums spent on wars, arms, military bases and budgets were instead directed to the worldwide distribution of food, healthcare and education.

Demonizing the Enemy: the Manipulation of Shadow Projections

In any conflict, an essential aspect of mobilizing collective opinion to justify the regression to predatory or pathological behaviour is the demonizing or dehuman-izing of the enemy and the presentation of the conflict as a simplistic one between victory and defeat, good and evil, right and wrong, thereby effectively polarizing two groups or nations and transforming them into enemies. Strategic lying to promote national interests has long been part of the repertoire of political leaders and fear-mongering is part and parcel of this repertoire. But it is precisely in these situations that we risk falling under the polarizing spell of solar mythology and into a state of possession by the unconscious shadow. Totalitarianism follows on from the process of demonizing another group — naming one group as 'good' and the other as 'evil'. The 'good' group may be trying to hold down another within a nation, as in modern Syria, or it may be trying to control another nation that presents a threat to it, as in India or Pakistan, or it may be preparing against a future threat, as with the perceived threat posed by Russia to the West. Then the belief is promoted: if our group or nation is to win, the other must be defeated, eliminated. If our cause is identified with good, the other must be evil and is, therefore, deserving of defeat, however great the sacrifice — ours and theirs. There is no third way. Barbaric acts are justified on both sides as a necessary means to victory. Few governments mention or mourn the loss of life on the enemy side, only those lost on 'our' side. In four thousand years little has changed. In a situation of conflict where survival instincts are aroused, the leader of a nation or primal male is expected to don the garb of the warrior and win the battle for supremacy.

Jung developed his ideas about the danger of the archetypal power of the shadow to overwhelm civilization in his essays on events in Germany (*Collected Works*, vol. 10) There he analyzed how negative projections onto others can develop and spread like a virus until they can contaminate a whole group or nation, causing it to fall into a psychosis, as they did in Nazi Germany or in Maoist China and, more recently, in the world-dominating ambitions of Isil. One of Jung's most important realizations was that when we project evil onto others, particularly when we feel threatened, we may lose the possibility of insight and the ability to deal with evil, becoming very easily contaminated by it ourselves:

> We know today that in the unconscious of every individual there are instinctive propensities or psychic systems charged with considerable tension. When they are helped in one way or another to break through into consciousness, and the latter has no opportunity to intercept them in higher forms, they sweep everything before them like a torrent and turn men into creatures for whom the word "beast" is still too good a name. They can then only be called "devils". To evoke such phenomena in the masses all that is needed is a few possessed persons, or only one. If this unconscious disposition should happen to be one which is common to the great majority of the nation, then a single one of these complex-ridden individuals, who at the same time sets himself up as a megaphone, is enough to precipitate a catastrophe.[23]

The most recent and obvious example of shadow projections was the invasion of Iraq by the United States and Britain, ostensibly to eliminate the threat of WMD developed by the oppressive regime of Saddam Hussein but in reality, in the view of Mohamed ElBaradei, winner of the Nobel Prize for Peace in 2005 and author of *The Age of Deception: Nuclear Diplomacy in Treacherous Times*, to "change the geopolitical landscape of the Middle East by establishing Iraq as an oasis of democracy."[24]

Apart from the number of Allied soldiers killed or maimed in this war, the number of Iraqi deaths is estimated at 2.3 million.[25] In addition, it created hundreds of thousands of seriously injured people, including maimed and traumatized children who witnessed and suffered unimaginable horror. It displaced between 4 and 7 million people, many of whom became refugees. It left behind a shattered economy and a weak and divided state torn by rival factions. In his detailed analysis of the events leading up to the invasion of Iraq, Mohamed ElBaradei comments:

> Ultimately, the story of the Iraq War may come down to a series of hard-hitting questions. If the community of nations seeks to live by the rule of law, then what steps should be taken when violations of international law result in massive civilian casualties? Who should be held accountable when military action has been taken in contravention of the law as codified in the UN Charter; or worse still, when military action is found to have been based on faulty information, the deliberately selective treatment of information, or the promulgation of misinformation?[26]

As the compulsion of the West to embark on wars to establish democracy in Iraq, Afghanistan and other countries in order to protect itself from future attack illustrates, we are in no sense free, rationally directed people but are still in thrall to ancient habits. John Gray acidly comments in his book *Black Mass: Apocalyptic Religion and the Death of Utopia*, "The attempt to remake the international system has had effects similar to previous Utopias.... Preserving the hard-won restraints of civilization is less exciting than throwing them away in order to realize impossible dreams. Barbarism has a certain charm, particularly when it comes clothed in virtue."[27]

As long as we make no effort to gain an insight into this monumentally dangerous aspect of our shadow behaviour, we will be drawn into repeating old patterns. During the Cold War, Jung commented that humanity was split into two apparently irreconcilable halves: "The psychological rule says that when an inner situation is not made conscious, it happens outside, as fate. That is to say, when the individual remains undivided and does not become conscious of his inner opposite [his shadow], the world must perforce act out the conflict and be torn into opposing halves." [28]

For those who are not familiar with Jung's ideas and the implications of ignoring the shadow, we can nevertheless see that his words are as relevant today as they were when the Berlin Wall which divided Germany was built, or when the Iron Curtain was drawn between the Soviet Union and the West during the Cold War. Today we have the ongoing 'War on Terror', the concrete wall built to separate Israel from the Palestinian Territories and the frontier, bristling with armed men, between North and South Korea. We have the lethal hatred between the Sunni and Shi'a in Islam and the attempts of Islamists to destroy the cultural and artistic heritage of Muslim countries in Iraq (Mosul)and Syria (Palmyra) as well as that of tribal groups in Africa (Mali). We imagine that if only 'they' can be eliminated the world will be a better and safer place, yet when that particular hydra head is cut off, two more appear in its place; the problem of evil is an ongoing and cumulative one. Jung's comment here is helpful: "Since it is universally believed that man is merely what his consciousness knows of itself, he regards himself as harmless and so adds stupidity to iniquity. He does not deny that terrible things have happened and still go on happening, but it is always "the others" who do them."[29]

The danger of such a situation is that these age-old habits do not encourage dialogue with the enemy. Paranoid projections fly back and forth and escalate until each combatant demonizes his enemy. The fear and hatred intrinsic to current conflicts activates memories of older conflicts, even those going back over a thousand years. When atrocities are committed on both sides, the reflexive impulse to avenge them makes it almost impossible to contain the survival instincts that are aroused.

Wherever there is a strong polarization of opposites, there is a situation which attracts shadow projections and the demonizing of others. The scapegoat or demonized individual or enemy group — often named as dogs, pigs or vermin — carries shadow projections coming from millions of others and relieves us of the responsibility of looking at our own shadow to see where we may have contributed to creating this enemy. Demonizing or dehumanizing an enemy, encouraged by politicians and the media as well as by fanatical religious leaders, can lead to the situation where the collective mind is flooded with shadow projections. But we can be encouraged by the fact that these shadow motives are being brought to light because there is now a growing number of people in many countries ready to challenge their governments' policies even if they cannot yet prevent them from being implemented. There are now many organizations such as Amnesty International, Human Rights Watch and the Internet organization Avaaz (www.avaaz.com) which are devoted to shedding light on situations constellated by shadow behaviour in governments and corporations.

Sam Keen, in *Faces of the Enemy*, gives a brilliant analysis of the way propaganda works and how collective shadow projections are manipulated by governments and the media. Healing begins, he says, "when we cease playing the blame game, when we stop assigning responsibility for war to some mysterious external agency and dare to become conscious of our violent ways."[30] He puts his finger on one of our greatest problems, one that has been highlighted by the wars in Afghanistan and Iraq:

> The most terrible of all the moral paradoxes, the Gordian knot that must be unraveled if history is to continue, is that we create evil out of our highest ideals and most noble aspirations. We so need to be heroic, to be on the side of God, to eliminate evil, to clean up the world, to be victorious over death, that we visit destruction and death on all who stand in the way of our heroic historical destiny.[31]

Political leaders carry and unconsciously act out the collective shadow of the past, perpetuating it in the present. Millions collude with their projections because they look to a leader for security when they are told they are in danger and survival instincts are aroused. Government and media propaganda compounds both the fear and the illusion of safety. To withdraw these projections and see clearly what the shadow is doing counteracts its power, freeing us from being possessed by it. We have enough consciousness to make this choice, to shed light on our own darkness. This involves dissociating ourselves as individuals from the rhetoric of patriotic or religious beliefs that, far from eliminating evil, engender it. Patriotism and religious conformity have long been promoted as the supreme virtues but now we urgently need to look beyond these to a more inclusive morality which invites awareness of the needs of the whole human community as well as the planetary environment. In Jung's highly significant words: "The immunity of the nation depends entirely upon the existence of a leading minority immune to the evil and capable of combating the powerful suggestive effect of seemingly possible wish-fulfilments. If the leader is not absolutely immune, he will inevitably fall a victim to his own will-to-power."[32]

Mark Gerzon, in a brilliantly argued book, *Leading Through Conflict*, shows that the demonizing of the 'other' is one of the main roots of evil:

> Holocaust and Genocide never, repeat never, happen without lies about an evil "Other". A single human being may hurt, or even kill, another human being. But in order to kill a hundred, a thousand, and certainly hundreds of thousands, the victims must be turned into something sub- or non-human. Demagogues are often twisted geniuses when it comes to the brutal craft of dehumanisation. They are brilliant at portraying those who fall outside the boundaries of "us"

as less than human. The demagogue never simply leads group A without systematically demonizing and often destroying group B. He justifies his fixation on "the enemy" with all sorts of sophisticated rationales, including self-defense. But what marks the Demagogue is that his leadership actually depends on, and is energized by, the existence of a hated Other.[33]

Wherever negative projections and the demonizing of others are encouraged to proliferate and take root, the archetypal power of solar myth can become active, take possession of millions of people and lead to acts of unspeakable barbarism. Political leaders have long known that deflecting people's attention from domestic problems onto an outside threat can work wonders for strengthening their power or supporting their decision to embark on a war — even, as with President Assad in Syria, a civil war with their own people. The mass of the people, when roused to survival mode by its leader/s, will accept and even call for a belligerent attack. Goering was well aware of this when he cynically observed:

> Naturally the common people don't want war, neither in Russia, nor in England, nor for that matter in Germany. That is understood. But, after all, it is the leaders of the country who determine the policy, and it is always a simple matter to drag the people along, whether it is a democracy, or a fascist dictatorship, or a parliament, or a communist dictatorship. Voice or no voice, the people can always be brought to the bidding of the leaders. That is easy. All you have to do is tell them they are being attacked, and denounce the pacifists for lack of patriotism and exposing the country to danger. It works the same in any country.[34]

The Crimes of War: Effects on the Environment and the Planet

One of the crimes of war that is rarely commented on is the devastation of the landscape as well as the destruction of a culture and its precious buildings, libraries and museums. Those who engaged in the ferocious battle for Aleppo destroyed the priceless heritage not only of their nation but of all humanity.

The devastation of the environment by invasion and bombing is one aspect of war. But there are other effects such as the long-term effects of weapons like depleted uranium on the soil as well as on human beings and animals. The distinguished biologist, the late Dr. Rosalie Bertell, in her book, *Planet Earth, the Latest Weapon of War*, comments,

> Wars result in immediate deaths and destruction, but the environmental conse-
> quences can last hundreds, often thousands of years. And it is not just war itself

that undermines our life support system, but also the research and development, military exercises and general preparation for battle that are carried out on a daily basis in most parts of the world. The majority of this pre-war activity takes place without the benefit of civilian scrutiny and therefore we are unaware of some of what is being done to our environment in the name of 'security'.[35]

She also warns of a new generation of weapons that are designed to interfere with the Earth's electro-magnetic atmosphere or penetrate deep below its surface into its magnetic field. Projects such as HAARP (High-frequency Active Auroral Research Programme) — whose first stage in Alaska was completed in 1995 — are designed to use the ionosphere, which envelops the earth, to reflect beams of ultra-high energy to destroy targets across the globe. Such weapons, she says, are capable of interfering with the dynamic equilibrium of the earth's support systems and life forms, of which we are one.[36] "When HAARP is completed, it will be able to warm specific areas of the ionosphere until they produce a curved-shape lens capable of redirecting significant amounts of electromagnetic energy. These reflected electromagnetic beams may be in the microwave or ultraviolet range and could be used as a weapon either to incinerate a forest or oil reserve or to selectively kill living things."[37]

Few of us can even begin to comprehend the danger to ourselves and to all humanity which attends the development of this kind of weapon. According to her research, interference with the ionosphere and the manipulation of electro-magnetic waves may result in the creation of unusually violent storms as well as earthquakes and volcanic eruptions. The people of the world are not aware of the existence of these 'initiatives' or the colossal sums of their money spent by governments on developing them. What is at present missing and urgently needed is the implementation of the Earth Charter and a global initiative for the protection of the planetary environment and all the species it sustains.

War and the Soul

There are not many books on the effects of war on the soul. One of the most profound has been written by the Jungian analyst, Edward Tick, who has devoted his life to treating traumatized veterans of war, in particular the Vietnam War. In his book, *War and the Soul: Healing our Nation's Veterans from Post-Traumatic Stress Disorder*, he writes that veterans can be haunted for years by reliving in nightmares the original terrifying experiences they underwent: "They may see themselves killing again, or friends and enemies dying again. They may have waking visions of dead friends, enemies, or both. They may also, in retrospect, feel moral anguish that the people they killed did not deserve to die."[38] They may have nightmares, insomnia, frightening mood swings and surges of anger in response to something that to others would be innocuous. They may have to endure living their young lives without the limbs that have been amputated, without sight if they have been blinded, without the capacity to develop into the full potential of what they might have been. All this gives rise to intolerable anguish and suffering both for veterans and their families which can endure for years. Sometimes these symptoms do not manifest for many years after the original traumatic experience:

> Though hostilities cease and life moves on, and though loved ones yearn for their healing, veterans often remain drenched in the imagery and emotion of war for decades and sometimes for their entire lives. For these survivors, every vital human characteristic that we attribute to the soul may be fundamentally reshaped. These traits include how we perceive; how our minds are organized and function; how we love and relate; what we believe, expect, and value; what we feel and refuse to feel; and what we judge as good or evil, right or wrong. Though the affliction that today we call post-traumatic stress disorder has had many names over the centuries, it is always the result of the way war invades, wounds and transforms our spirit.[39]

As he explores the effects of war on the soul and explains the reasons why post-traumatic stress disorder (PTSD) is so difficult to treat, he writes, "...the traumatic impact of war and violence inflicts wounds so deep we need to address them with extraordinary attention, resources and methods. Conventional methods of medical and psychological functioning and therapeutics are not adequate to explain or treat such wounds. Veterans and their afflictions try to tell us so."[40] Dr. Tick explains why these symptoms of unbearable stress are to be expected in survivors of trauma:

> War devastates not only our physical being but our very soul — for the entire culture as well as for the individual. In war, chaos overwhelms compassion, violence replaces cooperation, instinct replaces rationality, gut dominates mind. When drenched in these conditions, the soul is disfigured and can become lost for life. What is called soul loss is an extreme psycho-spiritual condition beyond what psychologists commonly call dissociation. It is far more than psychic numbing or separation of mind from body. It is a removal of the center of experience from the living body without completely snapping the connection. In the presence of overwhelming life-threatening violence, the soul — the true self — flees. The center of experience shifts; the body takes the impact of the trauma but does not register it as deeply as before. With body and soul separated, a person is trapped in a limbo where past and present intermingle without differentiation or continuity. Nothing feels right until body and soul rejoin.[41]

Psychotherapists know that the victim of trauma is dawn to repeat the traumatizing pattern in ongoing life situations. I think this insight could be applied to the life of humanity as a whole. The memories of conflict and the suffering engendered through past conflicts do not go away with the coming of new generations. They are held in the collective unconscious of the species, ready to be activated when specific 'triggers' call forth the same response. Tick concludes that as long as we remain unaware of the unconscious elements that drive us, we will not be able to release ourselves from their power over us. We will continue to be possessed by what James Hillman described as "the terrible love of war" in his book of that name until we become conscious of how easily it can take us over and are able to resist its powerful spell. We might then develop strategies to contain it so that it can no longer destroy our soul.

The Way Forward

The mass of humanity unconsciously follows the dual tracks of tribal or social custom and religious belief that were established centuries, even millennia ago. Conformity is safer. To resist the call to war is to be branded unpatriotic and invites shame and ridicule. Yet, the maturation and even the survival of humanity as a whole depend on courageous individuals opening new pathways for the species to follow. No pattern of behaviour is more resistant to change than the survival instincts that are triggered by fear. It is these instincts, together with the intoxicating effect of power in leaders manipulating these fears, and the pressure exerted by the Military-Industrial Complex in nations aiming for world domination that lead to war.

Only by bringing these deeply buried instincts into our conscious awareness can we hope to attain a *transcendent* perspective that could eventually lift us out of the tragic compulsion to repeat the patterns of the past. At the present time, this transcendent perspective is carried by organizations such as the United Nations, the International Court of Justice and by governments and individuals intervening to mediate between disaffected parties. But the United Nations, as recent events in relation to Syria have revealed (2018), has been rendered impotent to prevent the massacre of civilians or bring food and medical aid to them because Russia and China blocked the resolution of the Security Council to intervene. As the head of the United Nations General Assembly commented as long ago as March 2012, the Security Council is not fit for purpose.

There are a few million individuals who are thinking transnationally, in terms of the wellbeing of all peoples and the life-system of the entire planet. They are working to bring a new kind of civilization into being — a planetary civilization (but not a planetary government) that would truly honour the wellbeing of all people and all species of life on earth. The hope for the future lies with those individuals who have the courage to speak up against the whole ethos of war, who shame nations which promote this ideology, who develop existing methods of conflict resolution and hold politicians to account for embarking on a course of action which can only lead to further enmity and conflict — even to unforeseen catastrophe. Cyber War threatens us with a whole new area of conflict and the ability of one nation to paralyze another by closing down its electronic systems.

From the perspective of this book, the discoveries emerging from quantum physics suggest that the belief that we can achieve a position of dominance in relation to nature, life or each other is, ultimately, an illusion: each of us is an expression of a vast sea or holographic field of consciousness — as yet barely recognized by us. As quantum physics reveals, we are all connected to each other, part of a universal living web of life. We are, literally, 'our brother's keeper'.[42]

The belief that modern states can continue indefinitely to act as if they were autonomous units, competing with each other to gain control of the Earth's resources or, purportedly in the interests of self-defence, to acquire the power to destroy life on a colossal scale is not only the most insidious of illusions but an unrecognized pathology. Militarism itself is a pathogen that could wipe us out. In destroying others, or even imagining and rehearsing the destruction of others through the invention and development of ever more terrible weapons, we are, in effect inviting our own destruction and injuring all humanity, not to mention the planet. In seeking reconciliation and the wellbeing of others, resisting, even in the midst of conflict, the instinct to retaliate, we are contributing to our own wellbeing and ensuring that of future generations. Each individual who holds this perspective assists the process of humanity as a whole awakening to and acting from these utterly different values.

In 2002, I received this dream from a colleague in America, sent to her by one of her clients who had the dream shortly after 9/11:

> I am back in the army, assigned once again in my old role as a sharpshooter. I have all my equipment, and I am methodically putting it together, preparing to shoot my target, who is some distance away. Finally, I get the telescopic sight attached to the gun and trained on my target so that I can actually see who it is. And, to my great surprise, it is my brother, (who in real life is in another branch of the service). I am shocked and stopped in my tracks — I can't continue.

If only we could take the message of this dream to our hearts, something might begin to change in the pattern of aggression and war that is so deeply embedded in our psyche. War that is embarked on to serve a nationalistic need for aggrandizement needs to be viewed as a psychotic episode in the national psyche, a betrayal of the soul, where the fragile layer of rational consciousness is overwhelmed by the irrational depths of the unconscious shadow and co-opted into serving its atavistic aims. It is a pathology that is to be deplored and avoided if at all possible, rather than presented as an opportunity to win victory over a designated enemy or to act as the world's policeman. Jung's warning to us is relevant here:

> The supreme danger which threatens individuals as well as whole nations is a psychic danger. Reason has proved itself completely powerless, precisely because its arguments have an effect only on the conscious mind and not on the unconscious. The greatest danger of all comes from the masses, in whom the effects of the unconscious pile up cumulatively and the reasonableness of the conscious mind is stifled.... It is therefore in the highest degree desirable that a knowledge of psychology should spread so that men can understand the source of the supreme dangers that threaten them. Not by arming to the teeth, each for itself, can the nations defend themselves in the long run from the frightful catastrophes of modern war. The heaping up of arms is itself a call to war. Rather they must recognize those psychic conditions under which the unconscious bursts the dykes of consciousness and overwhelms it.[43]

When the survival instincts and the solar mythology which lie at the root of this ancient pathology are recognized and the unconscious control they exercise over us is acknowledged and addressed, we will find a way to relinquish our addiction to war and the depravity and devastation it engenders. There will be an end to this pattern when a different calibre of leader comes forward, a leader capable of articulating values which draw the highest spiritual response rather than the atavistic one from the people he or she represents. This would be a leader who offers a transcendent planetary perspective on the issues involved, who would serve the needs, acknowledge the wounds and allay the fears of *both* peoples in the conflict situation rather than polarizing them in ever more lethal conflict. Such leaders will emerge as we relinquish the illusion that our own security as a nation, or even the world's security, can be bought at the price of the sacrifice of the lives of others, as we recognize that such a belief, although still tenaciously held by many, must ultimately become obsolete. Things will only begin to change when we can acknowledge that the darkness we project onto others may be our own.

Postscript: It is possible that people caught up in a conflict are influenced by those who have died atrocious deaths and are still bound to this earthly dimension by the terror, grief, hatred and anguish in which they died. A number of individuals trained in spirit release are engaged in helping these traumatized souls but this practice could be extended if there were a greater understanding that the 'dead' may need release from the trauma of their deaths.

In writing the section on nuclear weapons in this chapter I am enormously indebted to a book written by Professor John Scales Avery called *Nuclear Weapons: An Absolute Evil.* It has given me what I needed to know and what I had no immediate access to — the details of everything pertaining to nuclear weapons, the history of their development and the effects of their use. It gives the complete picture of how, in developing these demonic weapons, we have lost our humanity and how, by ridding the planet of them, we could regain it.

Professor Avery's book can be purchased at:
http://www.lulu.com/home and http://www.fredsakademiet.dk/library/nuclear.pdf

LAMENT FOR THE TRAGEDY OF WAR

Although written in 1999, this poem is dedicated to all those who are suffering in the ongoing conflicts that are disturbing the life of the planet: to the refugees fleeing their devastated homes and living in camps; to the 3,000 Yazidi women who have endured the agony of rape and slavery; to the thousands of young men whose precious lives are being cut short; to the children who are suffering the trauma of witnessing the atrocities of war. (Appendix 1, page 539).

Notes:

1. Politkovskaya, Anna (2003) *A Small Corner of Hell: Dispatches from Chechnya,* University of Chicago Press
2. Gray, Colin (2005) *Another Bloody Century,* Weidenfeld & Nicolson, p. 24-5
3. quoted by Colin Gray, p. 35
4. Keen, Sam (1986) *Faces of the Enemy,* Harper & Row, San Francisco, p. 30
5. Ferguson, Niall (2006) *The War of the World,* Allen Lane, London
6. Bird, Kai and Sherwin, Martin J. (2005) *American Prometheus, The Triumph and Tragedy of J. Robert Oppenheimer,* Alfred Knopf, New York, p. 323
7. Hoffman, David E. (2009) *The Dead Hand: Reagan, Gorbachov and the Untold Story of the Cold War Arms Race,* Icon Books Ltd., London (2011), p. 23 (Doubleday, New York 2009)
8. ibid, p. 23
9. ibid, p. 14
10. ibid, p. 20
11. ibid, pp. 418-421
12. ibid, p. 309

324

13. Hoffman, p. 472 and Chapter 22, *passim*
14. ibid, p. 24
15. www.fas.org/programs/ssp/nukes/nuclearweapons/nukestatus
16. Blackaby Paper No 8, "Nuclear Weapons Abolition: an idea whose time has come."
17. Avery, John Scales (2017), Nuclear Weapons: An Absolute Evil, p. 87
    http://www.fredsakademiet.dk/library/nuclear.pdf
18. Avery, John Scales, article in www.dissidentvoice.org, June 2015
19. Gollancz, Victor (1958) *The Devil's Repertoire,* Gollancz, London
20. Roy, Arundhati (2002) *The Algebra of Infinite Justice*, HarperCollins (Flamingo)
    London, pp. 35 and 36-7
21. ibid, pp. 11 and 37
22. For annual military spending by each country see SIPRI (Stockholm International Peace
    Research Institute)
23. Jung, C. G. CW18 (1977) *The Symbolic Life*, par. 1374
24. ElBaradei, Mohamed (2011) *The Age of Deception: Nuclear Diplomacy in Treacherous
    Times*, Bloomsbury Books Ltd., London, p. 87
25. Griffin, David Ray (2017) Bush and Cheney – How They ruined America and the World,
    Olive Branch Press, Interlink Books US
26. ElBaradei, p. 85
27. Gray, John (2007) *Black Mass: Apocalyptic Religion and the Death of Utopia*,
    Allen Lane, London, p. 192
28. Jung, C. G. CW9 (1959) Part 11, *Aion*, par. 126
29. Jung, C. G. CW10 (1964) *The Undiscovered Self*, par. 572
30. Keen, Sam (1986) *Faces of the Enemy*, Harper & Row, San Francisco, p. 91
31. ibid, p. 30
32. Jung, C. G. CW18 *The Symbolic Life*, par. 1400
33. Gerzon, Mark (2006) *Leading Through Conflict*, Harvard Business School Press, p. 23
34. Gilbert, G.M. (1961) *Nuremberg Diary*, Signet, New York, pp. 255-6
35. Bertell, Rosalie (2000) *Planet Earth, the Latest Weapon of War*,
    The Women's Press, London, p. 2
36. ibid, pp.117-131
37. ibid, p.124
38. Tick, Edward (2005) *War and the Soul: Healing Our Nation's Veterans from
    Post-Traumatic Disorder*, Quest Books, Wheaton, Ill., p.138
39. ibid, p.1
40. ibid, p. 2
41. ibid, p.16
42. see Levy, Paul (2018) *The Quantum Revelation*, Select Books, New York
    Varan,Valerie (2015) *Living in a Quantum Reality*, Turning Stone Press, San Antonio, Texas
43. Jung, C.G. CW18, *The Symbolic Life*, para. 1358

Part Five

A New Vision of Reality

Wood engraving
from Flammarion's book *L'Atmosphere: météorologie populaire* of 1888
(created in the style of a 16th century woodcut)

Chapter Fourteen

A METAPHYSICAL REVOLUTION: SCIENCE AND A CONSCIOUS UNIVERSE

The intuitive mind is a sacred gift. The rational mind is a faithful servant. We have created a society that honours the servant and has forgotten the gift.

— Albert Einstein

In modern scientific man, evolution is becoming conscious of itself.

— Julian Huxley[1]

Science cannot solve the ultimate mystery of nature. And that is because, in the last analysis, we ourselves are part of nature and therefore part of the mystery that we are trying to solve.

— Max Planck

Life is ceaseless discovery.

— Pierre Teilhard de Chardin, *The Future of Man*[2]

S cience has given us a fantastic new story: the story of the evolution of the universe and the story of ourselves as witnessing and participating in an unfolding cosmic drama. The discoveries made by the Hubble telescope, as well as the discovery that the universe came into being 13.7 billion years ago, have utterly transformed our perspective on the evolution of cosmic and planetary life and our own origins. Edwin Hubble (1889–1953) has been compared to a new Copernicus and the famous telescope he developed has revealed a universe that is not only incredibly vast and incredibly strange — even terrifying in its immensity — but also breathtakingly beautiful, as if painted by a cosmic artist of unparalleled genius. The view of our planet from the moon, the ever-expanding dimensions of the universe, the ongoing complexity of the sub-atomic world and the story of the biological evolution of life on this planet may all be called revelations: it is almost as if the cosmos is speaking to us, telling us the story of how it came into being, how we came into being. And it is speaking to us through its own creation: human consciousness.

The powerful archetype of the quest lies behind science's drive to discover the secrets of sub-atomic matter and the astonishing complexity of the workings of the brain revealed by neuroscience. It is the instigator of the Apollo Mission to the moon and the breathtaking exploration of the depths of cosmic space. But, as Einstein said, "Behind the tireless efforts of an investigator there lurks a stronger, more mysterious drive: it is existence and reality that one wishes to comprehend."[3] A great scientist like Einstein or Hubble may be compared to the visionary or seer who sees beyond the boundaries of the known. He or she will be drawn to make discoveries that will take us out of Plato's cave where we have spent millennia watching the play of shadows on the walls instead of seeing clearly the extraordinary nature of the reality in which all our lives are embedded.

The discoveries of science have given us a cosmology as radically different from the Copernican and Newtonian ones as these were from the Ptolomaic one. We know that the sixteenth century discovery that the earth moved around the sun had a profound impact on the hierarchical structure of society: as well as promoting a feeling of disorientation, it gave rise to a tremendous sense of freedom as the medieval view of reality ceded ground to a new vision. So it is today in the surging creativity of our times that attends the deconstruction of an old paradigm and the birth of a new one.

Who would not marvel at the power of the human mind to explore these mysteries and the inventive genius which has led to the creation of those essential aids of exploration, the telescope and the microscope? Who would not be as excited as the physicists at Cern who, in July 2012, announced that they had found the Holy Grail of physics — the elusive Higgs boson or 'God particle'? Scientists claim that this could be the most significant discovery about the universe since Einstein's discovery of Relativity in 1905 — perhaps one of the most important discoveries of all time. It gives scientists the missing cornerstone of the Standard Model of the universe and an almost complete picture of the subatomic world. Further research into its nature could lead to further major discoveries and to an understanding of the mystery of dark matter. It may prove that the apparent vacuum of space is an omnipresent field which surrounds the whole universe and permeates every part of it and it would help to explain how mass is created and even perhaps why it exists. Without the holding power of this field, or something like it, these particles would weigh nothing at all and hurtle around at the speed of light. There would be no atoms as we know them; no stars or planets; no human beings like ourselves. Its discovery opens up a vast new field of scientific inquiry.

Science and technology have also transformed every aspect of our lives. What was it like to live without electricity, heat, rapid transportation by rail, car and plane, without telephone, computers, mobiles and all the aids to domestic life? What was it like to live in fear of fatal diseases like smallpox, leprosy, diphtheria, cholera and polio when there was no hope of a cure? Thanks to the revolution in medicine, energy, computer technology and transport as well as the fields of research more specifically associated with science, our length of life, our standard of living and our opportunities for communication with each other have been totally transformed from those that existed a century ago. New technologies, such as nuclear fusion, fuel-less cars, and solar energy applied to heating whole cities are being developed which may eventually diminish our dependence on fossil fuels and counteract the acceleration of global warming. Mobile phones and the Internet connect people all over the world to each other. All this has happened and is happening with breath-taking speed, allowing hardly any time to assimilate the effects of this radical transformation of our lives.

Reductionist Science or Scientism

Science as it is defined today does, however, present one huge problem: the material world is the only one it recognizes. Reductionist science or scientism rests on the belief that the matter it explores and manipulates is inanimate and dead, without consciousness. It has concluded that the universe itself has no inner dimension; no intelligence; no soul. We are the only aspect of life to have the inner dimension of reflective self-aware consciousness. The scientists who promote this reductionist or materialist belief system reject the idea of God, the soul and life beyond death. Astrophysicist Bernard Haisch, comments in his book, *The God Theory*:

> In a vicious cycle of exclusion, modern science, the champion of objective inquiry, excludes the esoteric as an object susceptible of investigation. In doing so, science has abrogated its responsibility to uncover objective truth and succumbed to a dogmatism of its own.... To claim that investigation of the physical world rules out inquiry into anything spiritual is both irrational and dogmatic. To reject evidence simply on the grounds that it cannot yet be measured with instruments in a laboratory is contrary to the scientific spirit of inquiry. It is time to move beyond this fundamentalist science model.[4]

A recent book by Rupert Sheldrake called *The Science Delusion* (2012) challenges the ten basic dogmas of science and shows how the sciences are constricted by assumptions originating in the nineteenth century that have hardened into dogmas and a belief system "whose central assumption is that everything is essentially material or physical, even minds. Many scientists are unaware that materialism is an assumption: they simply think of it as science or the scientific view of reality, or the scientific worldview."[5]

The danger of this situation is that when the one-eyed consciousness of the left-hemispheric rational mind is promoted as the only faculty which can define the nature of reality, it possesses, as Jung pointed out, "a Promethean freedom but also partakes of a godless hybris."[6]

The Birth of a New Paradigm

During the years when I was working as a Jungian analyst, I joined an organization called The Scientific and Medical Network. Through this, over some twenty years, I was able to attend conferences where distinguished scientists were invited to speak. I became more and more interested in science and gradually became aware that we are living in the midst of an astounding scientific revolution. With a sense of growing excitement, I realized that we are moving from the outworn Newtonian view of the universe as a perfectly ordered and precise mechanism to one that recognizes that, at the deepest level, it is alive, conscious and the eternally present ground of our own consciousness. For years I kept this illuminating passage written by the physicist Paul Davies in the Sunday Telegraph Magazine in July 1983 because I felt it reflected something of great importance:

> To study the new physics is to embark on a journey of wonderment and paradox, in which subject and object, mind and matter, force and field become intertwined.... We are moving towards an understanding in which matter, force, order and creation are unified into a single descriptive scheme. To me the laws of the universe, from quarks to quasars, dovetail together so felicitously that the impression that there is something behind it all is overwhelming.

The new paradigm which is emerging suggests that we are not the random creation of a mechanical, mindless universe as scientific reductionism proclaims: we participate in the life of a living and intelligent universe that appears to orchestrate its evolutionary unfolding from within its own cosmic, planetary and biological processes. We cannot separate ourselves from what we are observing. Again, in the words of Paul Davies, "The Universe is not a collection of objects, but is an inseparable web of vibrating energy patterns in which no one component has

reality independently from the entirety. Included in the entirety is the observer."
As I followed the details of this revolution over the last twenty years or so, it
seemed as if something as immovable as the Berlin Wall was crumbling, as the
long-established reductionist theory of science began to yield to an emerging
paradigm which restores the missing metaphysical dimension to the astounding
discoveries of science. Referring back to Pitirim Sorokin's theory explored in
Chapter Nine, I wondered whether a new Ideational culture is coming into being
as the certainties of the long-established Sensate culture weaken.

Consciousness as the Ground of Reality

In a secular culture that has been profoundly influenced by scientific reductionism,
described above and upheld by the majority of scientists worldwide, there is no
awareness, as there was in earlier cultures, of the existence of a dimension of
reality which might be compared to the starry night sky — a hidden dimension
which can only reveal its presence when the sun's bright radiance is dimmed. Just
as it dawned on the early Portuguese explorers that the world was not flat but
round, so the realization is dawning that the universe may not consist of dead,
insentient matter but is conscious in every part of itself, down to the minute
particles within the atom.

Einstein said that we cannot solve a problem from the level of consciousness
that created it. We have to create the new context in which the solution to a problem
can appear. The new context to which the formidable discoveries of science may
be aligned is the idea that consciousness rather than matter is the ground of reality
and the creative force that has brought the universe into being. Like the prince in
the fairy tale of the Sleeping Beauty, this idea is opening a way through the hedge
of thorns thrown up by centuries of entrenched beliefs, whether religious or
scientific. It has the power to awaken our soul, nurture our imagination, and arouse
in us a deeper capacity for relationship with each other and our planetary home.
Like the giant UFO in the film *Close Encounters of the Third Kind*, it seems that
an immense, invisible field of consciousness is making itself known to us, asking
to be recognized by us. The realization that we participate in a dimension of reality
that is the source and ground of our own consciousness may eventually shatter
the belief that material reality is all there is: that we exist on a randomly created
planet in a lifeless, purposeless universe and that there is no life beyond death.

It is perhaps appropriate that this new understanding should emerge from
science, since science, far more than religion, has given us the story of how and
when our universe, our planet and our species came into being. It is extraordinary

to realize that the new discoveries in science are leading to the recovery of the invisible ground of the cosmos that was known to shamanic cultures as well as to the Western esoteric traditions of Kabbalah and the contemplative traditions of Vedanta, Buddhism, Taoism and Sufism. *The Tibetan Book of the Great Liberation* states that matter is derived from mind, not mind from matter.

It is the discovery of the quantum vacuum that is changing our view of reality. It seems that we may be immersed in a sea or field or web of energy that is co-extensive with the immensity of the visible universe and the most minute particles of matter. This invisible web connects every one of us to each other and to every aspect of life in the cosmos. Just as we are now discovering that consciousness is distributed through every cell of our body, so we are discovering that it may be present in every photon or particle of light throughout the universe. This discovery tells us that we are literally bathed in a sea of light, invisible to us, yet permeating every cell of our being. This emerging vision is described by Christopher Bache, who, in a striking passage from his book, *Dark Night, Early Dawn,* describes his own experience:

> I saw humanity climbing out of a valley and just ahead, on the other side of the mountain peak and beyond our present sight, was a brilliant, sun-drenched world that was about to break over us. The time frame was enormous. After millions of years of struggle and ascent, we were poised on the brink of a sunrise that would forever change the conditions of life on this planet. All current structures would quickly become irrelevant.... I saw that evolution was indeed no accident but a creative act of supreme brilliance and that humanity was being taken across a threshold that would change it forever.[7]

> Just when Western culture had convinced itself that the entire universe was a machine, that it moves with a machine's precision and a machine's blindness, the ability to experience the inner life of the universe is being given back to us.... The entire human endeavor has been emptied of existential purpose and significance because it has been judged to be a product of blind chance. When one gains access to the inner experience of the universe, however, one learns that, far from being an accident, our conscious presence here is the result of a supreme and heroic effort. Far from living our lives unnoticed in a distant corner of an insentient universe, we are everywhere surrounded by orders of intelligence beyond reckoning.[8]

What Bache's experiences revealed to him is that the entire universe, seen and unseen is, in his words, "a unified organism of extraordinary design reflecting a massive Creative Intelligence." All this was once known and has long been forgotten. Despite the firewall set up by reductionist science, it is being recovered now and is leading to the recognition that the cosmos and all that we call Nature are ensouled and sustained by the unimaginable Intelligence that Bache calls Sacred Mind.

Just as we have the capacity to imagine, to think and to feel — an 'inside' play of consciousness and emotions within our physical organism — so the universe has an 'inside' to its visible form: an Intelligence, a Creative Mind, a Soul. Matter seems so solid, so obviously organized into distinct, separate forms. But what, in essence, is matter? The physicist Max Planck (1858–1947) who was the first scientist (in 1900) to name the 'quanta' of Quantum Theory, observed:

> As a man who has devoted his whole life to the most clear headed science, to the study of matter, I can tell, as a result of my research about the atoms, this much: There is no matter as such. All matter originates and exists only by virtue of a force which brings the particles of an atom to vibration and holds the most minute solar system of the atom together.... We must assume behind this force, the existence of a conscious and intelligent Mind. This Mind is the matrix of all matter.[9]

Our view of matter will undergo a transformation as new discoveries are made. But we need to know how the reductionist view came into being and why science came to reject spirit and to regard nature as inanimate.

Science and the 'Mastery' of Nature

Until the time of Copernicus (1473–1543), Kepler (1571–1630) and Galileo (1564–1642), science believed it was working in harmony with the laws of the cosmos and had no conflict with religion. The universe was regarded as a sentient organism governed by those laws. Newton still worked within this paradigm. But after the Catholic Church's condemnation of Galileo, science began to draw away from religion. Four hundred years ago there was a rupture between science and the metaphysical legacy of the medieval world. The astonishing discovery of Copernicus and Kepler that the earth orbited the sun deeply disturbed the 'Establishment' and accelerated this rupture. Copernicus's work *De Revolutionibus Orbium Cælestium* was banned by the Catholic Church in 1616 because it was said to be pseudoscientific. It was only taken off the index in 1820 when the Church accepted that it was proven and deemed to be scientific. In fact, Copernicus did not originate the heliocentric worldview. Aristarchus, known as 'the Greek Copernicus' envisioned a heliocentric view of the planets, but his view was rejected by Aristotle, the Alexandrian mathematicians and the astronomer Ptolemy, who favoured a geocentric perspective. It was the Ptolemaic model that still prevailed at the time of Copernicus. Kepler (who has never been given the recognition due to him) refined and developed Copernicus's theory. Kepler realized that in order to produce a true heliocentric model in which the earth is treated just like the other five planets known at his time he would need to calculate the earth's orbit. He did this by imagining that he was standing on Mars, viewing earth from there — an act of imagination that Einstein said was 'true genius'. Kepler's seminal scientific works were *New Astronomy* (1609) and *The Harmony of the World* (1619). His *New Astronomy* laid down the foundations of modern astronomy but *The Harmony of the World* was his *magnum opus*, integrating geometry, music, poetry, architecture, and astronomy into a glorious synthesis. Galileo did not trouble to read these but Newton did, describing in his *Principia* how Kepler's three laws of planetary motion could be incorporated in his (Newton's) inverse-square law of universal gravitation.[10] As a result of these major discoveries by four brilliant men, there was a fundamental shift of focus from religion to science, from faith to knowledge, from confinement within a rigid, controlling orthodoxy to release into the passionate exploration of the material world.

However, as science drew away from the oppressive control of religion and turned to the observation of nature, it was a nature that increasingly came to be regarded as a soul-less mechanism and as something completely separate from both man and the cosmos. The philosopher Joseph Milne, in a profound and illuminating book, *Metaphysics and the Cosmic Order*, offers a perceptive analysis of how science became an ideology — a belief system — regarding nature as something to be mastered, manipulated and controlled for the benefit of man. He places the onus for the change in our attitude to nature — as something separate and distinct from the Cosmic Order — on the writings of the philosopher, scientist and statesman, Francis Bacon (1561–1626) who declared that the object of knowledge was the control of nature and that nature, in itself, had no purpose. "It is this new orientation towards nature," Milne observes, "that marks the birth of the modern age, not the rise of the sciences as such." And, he continues, "At a single stroke human nature is alienated from the cosmos. With this alienation, the conception of human knowing shifts from participation in the being of things to the mastery of the will over things.... The quest for knowledge moves from the contemplation of reality, as an end in itself, to subjecting the resources of nature to human mastery and control."[11]

It may be that science retained, perhaps unconsciously, some of the basic precepts that had long been held by religion. Foremost among these was the idea derived from the Book of Genesis and deeply imprinted on the Christian psyche, that God had given man dominion over the Earth and its species.

Henceforth, the path that science took did not view nature, other species and human beings as ensouled and belonging to a Sacred Order but increasingly separated matter from spirit, thereby widening the split already long established by religion. Ultimately, it would reject spirit and soul altogether because it could find no evidence of either in the fields of its exploration: the idea of God was deemed irrelevant; the concept of soul an outgrown superstition. It concluded that the universe had come into being by chance and that consciousness, emerging out of matter, was a product of the neurology and biochemistry of the physical brain — a conclusion it has presented as irrefutable fact.

Science, like religion, was influenced by solar mythology and the idea of a great battle between light and darkness. It came to see the advance of science in terms of a battle between reason and superstition and between the rational and the non-rational or irrational. The subliminal influence of this ideology has led science into a position of tremendous hubris in relation to nature and matter, believing that the apparent omnipotence and uniqueness of the human mind gives man the right to master and control nature. It does not view man within the larger context of nature but sets man above nature. Since the invention of the atomic bomb, science has reached a position of immense power, similar to the power the Church once held. It has become so inflated by its discoveries that it cannot see that its attitude to nature and matter is gravely detrimental to the integrity and well-being of the whole planetary organism. In the terminology of psychology, science can exhibit the same symptoms of grandiosity and omnipotence as the military-industrial system described in the last two chapters.

In many television programmes on science, we hear the constant theme of how the amazing discoveries of science will lead to a further 'mastery' of nature. In 2008, I happened to hear Professor Brian Cox, one of the most brilliant particle physicists in the United Kingdom, communicating his excitement over the imminent activation of the Large Hadron Collider (Cern, Geneva). Because his words shocked me, I wrote them down: "We are looking for ever more sophisticated ways of torturing matter," he said, echoing the words of Francis Bacon who said that nature would be "bound into service, hounded in her wanderings, put on the rack and tortured for her secrets".

If matter is inanimate or 'dead', then torture can be applied to it because it has no intrinsic value and no apparent capacity to feel or to be aware of what is done to it, yet the choice of the word 'torture' is revealing, suggesting an awareness in the observer that matter is sentient. Why do we have to 'smash' elements of matter together in order to find the Higgs boson particle? Why do we design a laser that can 'tear apart' the fabric of space in order to reveal the secrets of dark matter? The aggressive language used to describe these technological initiatives derives from the deeply held conviction that man's role in relation to nature and matter is to master and control it, if necessary with violence.

It follows naturally from this that science's attitude to nature is reflected in the use of animals in laboratory experiments designed to test drugs for their safety in treating disease in humans. It used to be thought that animals were biological machines that could not feel pain in the way that humans do. Animals have been treated as a kind of subject race: their suffering, if acknowledged at all, is regarded as necessary to the outcome of the research. The morality of our attitude to animals — mainly primates, dogs, rabbits and mice — sent in their millions to laboratories, has gone almost unchallenged except by animal rights activists. These animals have no rights which might protect them from our abuse of them. It is apparent that we regard ourselves as the superior species, justified in causing suffering to other species if it serves the purpose of prolonging or enhancing our own lives.

However, on July 7th, 2012, at the Francis Crick Memorial Conference in Cambridge, and in the presence of Stephen Hawking, the scientists present signed The Cambridge Declaration on Consciousness in Non-Human Animals which announced their conclusion that consciousness was present in animals:

> The absence of a neocortex does not appear to preclude an organism from experiencing affective states. Convergent evidence indicates that non-human animals have the neuroanatomical, neurochemical, and neurophysiological substrates of conscious states along with the capacity to exhibit intentional behaviours. Consequently, the weight of evidence indicates that humans are not unique in possessing the neurological substrates that generate consciousness. Nonhuman animals, including all mammals and birds, and many other creatures, including octopuses, also possess these neurological substrates.

The distinguished primatologist Jane Goodall believes that the practice of using animals for laboratory experiments is no longer morally and ethically acceptable. To support this, she refers to the research of Andrew Knight and his recent book *The Costs and Benefits of Animal Experiments* in which he concludes that "it is clear that animal research is a highly inefficient means of attempting to advance human healthcare — particularly in the light of the very high costs associated with such research in public finances and animal lives" (*The Times* 17/3/12).

The Rational Mind and the Banishing of Soul

The scientific observer has become so detached from what he is observing that he has lost the instinctive awareness that he might be part of a living, intelligent cosmic and planetary organism and that his role should be more in the nature of a servant than a master. Because of the obsessive focus on the way the left-hemispheric rational mind perceives reality, empathic feeling — a vital part of our wholeness — has been deliberately and rigidly excluded from scientific methodology. One could say that reductionist science has banished the Feminine and the soul or *anima* — the carrier of feeling — from its research. Karl Stern's words in his book *The Flight from Woman* are worth recalling: "If man's relationship to Nature is nothing but that of technological victory, it amounts to a loveless union of man and Nature, a rape, and this will end in perdition."[12]

In a highly relevant and clarifying passage, Professor Ravi Ravindra, Professor Emeritus (formerly Professor in the three Departments of Physics, Comparative Religion and International Development Studies) at Dalhousie University in Halifax, Nova Scotia, comments on science's attitude to nature in his book, *Science and the Sacred: Eternal Wisdom in a Changing World*:

> The otherness of nature is an essential presupposition of the scientific attitude, which sees the universe as hostile or at least indifferent — not intentionally but mechanically — to human purposes and aspirations. Therefore nature needs to be fought and conquered. This view is what allows humans to exploit nature. The more advanced a society is scientifically and technologically, the more pronounced is the exploitation of nature in it. Modern technology is essentially of a piece with modern science in its fundamental procedures and attitudes... Utilizing natural resources for the fulfilment of legitimate human needs has shifted to exploiting nature for gratification of unbridled desires. This shift — clearly in the United States and increasingly elsewhere — is made possible by the increased capabilities of science and technology. It is made easy by the attitude, common to science and technology, of regarding nature as an enemy to be vanquished.[13]

He comments further on the devaluation of feeling in our culture:

> The tragedy is that popular awe of science has led to the devaluation of the function of feeling as a means of arriving at any aspect of the truth, and as a consequence the quality of feeling in our culture has declined to the level of the infantile or brutal. The mistaken conviction that those limited aspects of reality that are accessible to science constitute the whole has become so deeply ingrained in us that it maintains its tenacious hold even against reason itself, which proposes to us that the most complete view of reality possible for human beings must be that which includes the perceptions of all the faculties, and all the faculties perfected to the highest possible degree.[14]

Professor Ravindra's comments reflect the situation described by Iain McGilchrist, in his book, *The Master and His Emissary: The Divided Brain and the Making of the Western World*, described in Chapter Nine, where the left hemisphere of the brain now exercises too much control over the right: we have been confined without being aware of it within a left-hemispheric view of reality, within the limited vision of a one-eyed consciousness. We have mistaken the emissary for the master. Einstein's insight is relevant here: "The intuitive mind is a sacred gift. The rational mind is a faithful servant. We have created a society that honours the servant and has forgotten the gift."

In his comprehensive overview of the evolution of consciousness described in *Cosmos and Psyche, Intimations of a New World View*, Richard Tarnas, Professor of Philosophy at the California Institute for Integral Studies, presents us with a looming question of our time that science does not address:

> What is the ultimate impact of cosmological disenchantment on a civilization? What does it do to the human self, year after year, century after century, to experience existence as a conscious purposeful being in an unconscious purposeless universe? What is the price of a collective belief in absolute cosmic indifference? What are the consequences of this unprecedented cosmological context for the human experiment, indeed for the entire planet?[15]

A different approach to the universe is defined in the same book, quoted here and slightly abridged with his permission:

> Imagine that you are the universe — not the disenchanted mechanistic soulless void of conventional modern cosmology, but rather a deep-souled, subtly mysterious cosmos of great spiritual beauty and creative intelligence. Imagine then that you are being approached by two different epistemologies — two suitors, as it were, who seek to know you. To whom would you respond and to whom reveal your deepest secrets? Would you respond to the one who approached you as if he thought you were essentially lacking in intelligence or purpose, as though you had no interior dimension to speak of, who saw you as fundamentally inferior to himself, who treated you as though your existence were only of value to him if he could develop and exploit your resources to satisfy his own needs and whose motivation for knowing you was driven by a desire for increased mastery of you?
>
> Or would you, the cosmos, open yourself most deeply to that suitor who seeks to know you not that he might better exploit you but rather to unite with you and thereby bring forth something new, a creative synthesis emerging from both of your depths. He seeks to liberate that which has been hidden by the separation between knower and known. His ultimate goal is not increased mastery and control but rather a more richly responsive and empowered participation in a co-creative unfolding of new realities. His act of knowledge is essentially an act of love and intelligence combined, of wonder as well as

discernment, of opening to a process of mutual discovery. To whom would you
be more likely to reveal your deepest truths?[16]

Tarnas follows his story with an appeal to us to re-enchant the cosmos, to see it
with new eyes. He does not ask us to cast aside the methodology of science —
the capacity for proving hypotheses by experiment that has been developed with
such prodigious effort — but to honour and develop ways of knowing which are
worthy of the grandeur, depth and complexity of the cosmos, to integrate the
imagination, the moral and spiritual intuition, the revelatory experience and
subjective empathic approach that have so far been rigorously excluded from
scientific methodology. Above all, he asks us to withdraw our hidden anthro-
pocentric projection of soul-lessness onto the cosmos which is the end-result of
the dissociated ego's will to power over the cosmic and planetary matrix out of
which it has evolved. We need to develop ways of knowing which integrate the
wisdom of ancient spiritual traditions with the emerging scientific discoveries,
which can open our eyes to the existence of the invisible dimensions of the
cosmos which surround us and interact with our world. We have to move beyond
the limitations of our understanding which are the end result of the long-standing
dissociation within our psyche between the conscious ego and the instinctual soul,
whose origins were explored in Chapters Five and Six and whose effects were
summarized in Chapter Nine.

The Paradigm Shift: Consciousness as the Ground of Reality

What Tarnas asks for is actually taking place. A new cosmology is being born, a
new vision of our profound relationship with a conscious, intelligent universe.
There is an emerging consensus among certain physicists, astro-physicists and
cosmologists that consciousness and not matter is the primary ground of reality.
This is the basic premise of the paradigm shift that is taking place in our time.
Instead of seeing the universe as a conglomeration of parts functioning as a kind
of gigantic machine, they are seeing it as a unified and living organism, the unseen
and seen aspects of it functioning as a unified whole. They are formulating a
revolutionary concept of a creative and conscious universe, viewing consciousness
as primary and the manifest universe as the creation of cosmic consciousness.

Bernard Haisch comments in his book *The God Theory*: "The challenge for
science is going to be to free the tools, experiments, observations and logic of the
scientific method from the shackles of a reductionist-materialist ideology which
cannot tolerate the concept of a real consciousness and especially any conscious-

ness that would be primary over matter."[17]

Amit Goswami, Professor of Physics at Ohio State University, in his book *The Self-aware Universe*, states unequivocally that "Consciousness is the ground of all being, and quantum physics makes this as clear as daylight."[18] In a later book called *The Visionary Window*, which builds a bridge between quantum physics and the insights of Vedantic philosophy, he says:

> Positing consciousness as the ground of being calls forth a paradigm shift from a materialist science to a science based on the primacy of consciousness... Such a science leads to a true reconciliation with spiritual traditions, because it does not ask spirituality to be based on science but asks science to be based on the notion of eternal spirit... Spiritual metaphysics is never in question. Instead, the focus is on cosmology — how the world of phenomena comes about.[19]

In this, Goswami was echoing the thoughts of the brilliant physicist, Wolfgang Pauli, discoverer of the neutrino. In a lecture he gave in 1955, he stressed the importance of reconciling the rational stance of Western science with the mystical approach of the Eastern traditions in order to achieve a better balance for both the scientist and science. In this, Pauli was undoubtedly influenced by the many conversations he had with Jung and his realization, after considerable analysis, that he was exhibiting symptoms of imbalance in his life because he was so completely focused on his intellect that he had neglected to connect with his anima.[20]

Other physicists and cosmologists are reaching the same conclusion: the universe may not be dead, insentient matter as mainstream science currently holds, but may be conscious and intelligent in ways that are, at present, far beyond our capacity to comprehend. The extraordinary discoveries made over the last hundred years challenge what science has programmed us to believe: that, as a unique species, we are separate from all other species and from our planetary and cosmological environment. Quantum physics shows us that we can no longer separate ourselves as observers from what we are observing.

The Standard Model of the universe says that it started with the Big Bang some 13.7 billion years ago, that it rapidly inflated and then cooled sufficiently to allow the building blocks of matter to form, ultimately bringing into being the billions of galaxies we now know exist, but this is still a hypothesis. We only see 4% (some say 5%) of the known universe. What is concealed in the remaining 96%? Contrary to what was originally thought, there is no such thing as empty space between the 2 trillion galaxies of the observable universe. Instead, so-called 'empty space' is full of something called dark matter (comprising 23% of the universe) and dark energy (comprising 73%). The latter is causing the universe continually to expand while the former acts like a gravitational field, holding the gigantic web of the galaxies in the same relation to each other without allowing the expansion of the space between them. Dark matter emits no light at all and is therefore totally invisible to scientific instruments. Scientists say they are on the verge of discovering more about it since the discovery of the Higgs boson particle. There are currently 24 types of particle in the known universe. The particles of dark matter, as yet undiscovered, are different from these and pass through solid objects, including our bodies. No one knows how many of these there are and how many may be discovered.

In January 2012, astronomers announced that they think dark matter may have helped to form the entire cosmos. During the last five years, they have created a detailed map of the distribution of dark matter throughout the universe and it seems that galaxies and the trillions of stars that comprise them may be held together only by the enormous gravitational pull generated by this mysterious 'substance'. It appears that galaxies may be linked together by a vast cosmic 'spider's web'. This recalls the long discarded idea of the aether as a foam-like substance that expanded like a flexible mesh or net as the universe expanded. Galaxies that are visible are possibly surrounded by a 'halo' of dark matter whose concentration is greatest at the centre of the galaxy. It is thought that dark matter within the Milky Way is preventing the sun from hurtling out of the galaxy and into deep space (*Sunday Times* 8/1/12).

Another newly discovered factor that cosmologists call 'dark flow' makes whole clusters of galaxies move in an inexplicable way. Cosmologists think that this may indicate the existence of another universe beyond ours that is affecting the movement of our galaxies. This suggests to them that our universe may be part of a multiverse, a hypothesis put forward by Lord Rees, the Astronomer Royal some time ago. When cosmologists discover what dark matter, dark energy and dark flow are and how they affect the observable universe, the current Standard Model may need to be amended in the light of a new theory. As I complete this book (August 2012), a Horizon programme (BBC 2) mentions that the latest discovery from cosmologists in America is that the universe is apparently infinite: its circumference cannot be calculated because it is still expanding and, even more incredibly, it may be one of an infinite number of universes. The mind simply cannot assimilate these astounding facts.

What is being recovered at a new level of understanding is a development of the cosmology that once existed in shamanic and later Bronze Age cultures and was brought to a remarkable level of description in the voluminous legacy of Plotinus and in the cosmology of Kabbalah and Vedanta. These cosmologies recognized the existence and the interaction of many planes, levels or dimensions of reality held within an all-pervasive, connecting web of life. We are re-discovering this living web as the ground of our own consciousness.

The Quantum Vacuum

There are three vital components which have contributed to the emergence of this new cosmology: The first is the discovery of the quantum vacuum or quantum plenum as it is more accurately described. The second is the discovery of the principle of nonlocality and the recognition that all particles of matter are 'entangled' with each other. At the quantum level of reality, we are all connected. The third component is the concept of the universe as a hologram.

With the discovery of the quantum field (plenum) underlying our space-time reality, we find the idea returning after a 4000 year absence, of a cosmic womb, out of which all that we call reality and all that we are arises and to which it may return, similar to the out-breathing and in-breathing of the great cosmic cycles posited long ago by the Vedic sages of India. The quantum field is the source ground of the visible universe which holds the recorded information of every thing that has been, is and will be in the future. It is like a gigantic memory field holding other fields within it which eventually manifest as the 'forms' of life on this planet.

Quantum theory 'took off' in the 1920's, developing on the foundations laid by a paper published by Max Planck who, in 1900, formulated the concept of 'quanta' or bundles of energy that were later understood to manifest in space-time as both wave and particle. It utterly changed our concept of reality. I will take the description of the quantum vacuum (also called the zero-point field) from the astro-physicist Bernard Haisch since it is explained in words that a non-scientist can understand:

> The laws of quantum mechanics posit the sea of the zero-point field as a state of both paradox and possibility — a seething sea of particle pairs, energy fluctuations, and force perturbations popping in and out of existence... It may represent an unlimited source of energy available everywhere, and perhaps even a way to modify gravity and inertia. The quantum vacuum is, therefore, in reality a plenum... The fact that the zero-point field is the lowest energy state makes it unobservable... It acts as a kind of blinding light that precludes our perceiving it through contrast. Since it is everywhere, inside and outside of us, permeating every atom in our bodies, we are effectively blind to its presence.[21]

Bernard Haisch suggests that the deep connection between physics and metaphysics

> lies in the fact that the electromagnetic quantum vacuum is a form of light. It is an underlying sea of energy, predicted by the Heisenberg Uncertainty Principle, that permeates every tiny volume of space, from the emptiest intergalactic void to the depths of the Earth, the Sun, or our own bodies. In this sense, our world of matter is like the visible foam atop a very deep ocean of light.[22]

The mysterious light of the quantum plenum may be the creative ground of reality and the ground of everything we are and all that we perceive. Time does not exist in this limitless field of light-energy because by its very nature it is timeless. The information encoded in it is communicated instantaneously in every part of the universe. Through it, every single creature as well as every single aspect of creation is indissolubly connected with every other.

I can't help making the connection between the light of the quantum plenum and the tradition of Kabbalah, where light is said to emanate from the cosmic 'womb' of being through all the worlds or dimensions it brings into being until it creates our familiar world of physical reality. This light, not comparable to the light of the sun, is the unseen ground of the phenomenal world. Kabbalah sees our souls as the 'sparks' of this ineffable ground of light.

The all-important Heisenberg Uncertainty Principle states that the electro-magnetic field in the quantum plenum is in a perpetual state of oscillation or fluctuation. These constant vibrations create a sea of light which translates into enormous energy — the light that flows through the "matter" of the whole manifest universe, including our own physical form and may, in ways we don't yet understand, bring matter into being and sustain its existence. All possibilities are contained in it and any possibility can emerge from it. The implications of this are enormous because they mean that we could change our way of thinking, choosing not to follow old dualistic patterns.

The distinguished physicist David Bohm (1917–1992), Professor of Theoretical Physics at Birkbeck College, London, was the first scientist to describe the interaction of the quantum field with our visible world. In a book he published in 1980 called *Wholeness and the Implicate Order*, he defined the primary dimension of reality as the Implicate Order, the multi-dimensional, underlying source-ground of all life that he described as a limitless sea of energy and light. What we perceive with our senses as empty cosmic space is actually the plenum, the ground of all existence, including ourselves. He named our three-dimensional world the Explicate Order and hypothesized that it was enfolded into the invisible source-ground of the Implicate Order.[23] He saw the universe in both its aspects or Orders, as a single undivided whole and said that matter was nothing other than frozen light. "The entire universe of matter as we generally observe it is to be treated as a comparatively small pattern of excitation" on this invisible sea of light and energy.[24]

Bohm's hypothesis of the Implicate Order takes us back to the shamanic understanding of the underlying presence of the unseen Otherworld (Chapter Five). His image of the quantum plenum as an ocean or sea of energy recalls the ancient imagery of the Great Mother, origin of all (Chapter Four), and his idea of a unifying cosmic order recalls the *unus mundus* of the alchemists (Chapters Eleven and Eighteen). I find it absolutely fascinating that long-discarded ideas are being re-animated in the birth of this new paradigm of reality, formulated in the scientific language of modern cosmologists and physicists.

Bohm noted that in early civilizations man's view of reality was essentially one of wholeness rather than fragmentation and that this view still survives in the Eastern traditions, particularly that of India. He believed that the fragmentation of our world into different nations, ethnic groups, professions, arts, and sciences, which separates people and things into categories disconnected from each other, has its origin in the kind of thinking (even the subject-object structure of our language) which analyses and describes things as being inherently separate and distinct from each other, like parts of a machine. Hence, as he observed in the introduction to his book:

> Science itself is demanding a new, non-fragmentary world view, in the sense that the present approach of analysis of the world into independently existing parts does not work very well in modern physics. It is shown that, both in relativity theory and quantum theory, notions implying the undivided wholeness of the universe would provide a much more orderly way of considering the general nature of reality.[25]

> A centrally relevant change in descriptive order required in the quantum theory is the dropping of the notion of analysis of the world into relatively autonomous parts, separately existent but in interaction. Rather, the primary emphasis is now on the undivided wholeness, in which the observing instrument is not separable from what is observed.[26]

He warned of the dangers of our fragmented way of thinking and asked us to examine the actual way we are trained or conditioned to think. "What is primarily needed", he said, "is a growing realization of the extremely great danger of going on with a fragmentary process of thought. Such a realization would give the inquiry into how thought actually operates that sense of urgency and energy required to meet the true magnitude of the difficulties with which fragmentation is now confronting us."[27] It is precisely the causes and effects of this fragmentation that Iain McGilchrist addresses in his great contribution, *The Master and His Emissary: the Divided Brain and the Making of the Western World*. It is a pity they never met for they would have had much to share with each other.

It is interesting that Bohm saw the birth of the universe in very different imagery from the Standard 'Big Bang' theory, describing it more in the nature of a sudden wave pulse arising out of the fathomless ocean of cosmic energy. "This pulse would explode outward and break up into smaller ripples that spread yet further outward to constitute our 'expanding universe'. The latter would have its 'space' enfolded within it as a special distinguished explicate and manifest order."[28]

He wrote these moving words for the memorial service of Malcolm Sagenkahn, one of his classmates at university. The same words, which summarize his view of reality, were read out at his own funeral:

> In considering the relationship between the finite and the infinite, we are led to observe that the whole field of the finite is inherently limited, in that it has no independent existence. It has the appearance of independent existence, but that appearance is merely the result of an abstraction of our thought. We can see this dependent nature of the finite from the fact that every finite thing is transient.
>
> Our ordinary view holds that the field of the finite is all that there is. But if the finite has no true independent existence, it cannot be all that is. We are in this way led to propose that the true ground of all being is the infinite, the unlimited; and that the infinite includes and contains the finite. In this view, the finite, in its transient nature, can only be understood as held suspended, as it were, beyond time and space, within the infinite.
>
> The field of the finite is all that we can see, hear, touch, remember, and describe. This field is basically that which is manifest, or tangible. The essential quality of the infinite, by contrast, is its subtlety, its intangibility. This quality is conveyed in the word spirit, whose root meaning is "wind, or breath". This suggests an invisible but pervasive energy, to which the manifest world of the finite responds. This energy, or spirit, infuses all living beings, and without it any organism must fall apart into its constituent elements. That which is truly alive in the living being is this energy of spirit, and this is never born and never dies.[29]

The Discovery of Nonlocality

In 1982, a French physicist called Alain Aspect and his collaborators proved that when an atom emits two quanta of light, called photons, these can, at vast distances from each other and without exchanging any signals with each other, affect each other instantaneously at a speed faster than the speed of light. These photons were said to be 'entangled' with each other and this remarkable discovery gave rise to the theory of nonlocality. It was a crucially significant discovery because it pointed to the existence of a field or dimension of reality beyond that of our time and space which was the medium in which the photons were connecting or communicating with each other. It also suggested that this indicated the essential oneness or inseparability of all aspects of life. This discovery, described colloquially as 'the butterfly effect' and confirmed by later experiments in 1997, opened up the possibility of reconnecting science with the contemplative traditions of different cultures which have always recognized the existence of a transcendent level of reality as well as the existence of many levels or dimensions included or enfolded in that reality. However, because very few scientists are familiar with these traditions, the connection between physics and these ancient cosmologies may not be made. One scientist who has made this connection — Amit Goswami — realized from Alain Aspect's discovery that there is a downward movement of causation from a dimension beyond time and space as well as an upward movement from matter, and that everything begins with cosmic consciousness. Forces that are beyond or outside the dimensions of space and time can affect elements that are inside them.

The result of his reflections was the realization that if consciousness is accepted as the ground of being, the paradoxes that have baffled quantum physicists for decades could be resolved. Just as Aristotle realized so long ago, as described in Chapter Five, we could begin to see that cosmic consciousness (Spirit or Mind) is profoundly engaged in the whole process that we call evolution. It offers a tremendous panorama of interconnection and evolutionary intention in a Cosmic Grand Design, with ourselves increasingly participating in this unfolding design as our own understanding develops and as we make new discoveries. Goswami's book, *The Self-Aware Universe: How Consciousness Creates the Material World* (1993), and his later books grew out of these insights.

In their recent book *CosMos: A Co-creator's Guide to the Whole-World*, cosmologist Dr. Jude Currivan and systems analyst Dr. Ervin Laszlo summarize how our understanding has been changed by these extraordinary discoveries:

During the last thirty years, such phenomena as telepathy, clairvoyance, precognition, the power of meditation and prayer, and the ability by thought alone to affect the outcome of apparently random events have come under increasing scientific scrutiny. The hundreds of thousands of experiments throughout this time have accumulated a huge database, showing that the evidence for nonlocal awareness and influence is now overwhelming.[30]

A Holographic Universe

David Bohm was the first scientist to recognize that the universe was designed on the principle of a hologram and this idea is now being revisited and developed by other scientists. Jude Currivan and Ervin Laszlo explore the emerging vision of an informed cosmos "that is wholly integrated and coherent. Where, despite the communication between apparently separate events within space-time being limited by the speed of light — the deeper reality is enduring and quasi-instantly interconnected."[31] They describe the new understanding that is changing our view of reality, and manifesting in all fields of scientific endeavour: the understanding that the universe is designed as a holographic template and there is a Field of cosmic intelligence beyond our time and space that underlies, permeates and gives rise not only to physical reality but to all that we may discover to be reality. "The latest discoveries across all scientific disciplines are revealing a radical new vision of the nature of the physical world as being imbued with and in-formed by a holographic field; thus, it is innately inter-related, coherent and harmonic at *all* scales of existence."[32]

> It appears that all that we term "physical reality" is ultimately harmonically and holographically ordered. We cannot exclude ourselves from the holographic and coherent nature of the universe. Even when we believe we're making choices that are independent of others, we still find that those choices become part of collective patterns that are part of the coherent whole-world. As the ancient sages would say, we are the many expressed by the One — and we are the One that is expressed by the many. We are creation and we are co-creators.[33]

It seems as if, through the infinitesimal spark of cosmic light that is our human consciousness, the universe is revealing itself to our astounded gaze and what it is revealing is that the creation of the universe could not have been a random happening. As they comment:

> The exquisite harmony of these cosmic relationships includes the fundamental ratios between the electrical and nuclear forces that bind atoms and molecules

and the vastly weaker force of gravity. Their precisely balanced energies and the exact yet varied nature of their interrelationships, from the moment our universe was born, have enabled the formation and interaction of chemical elements; the birth of stars, galaxies, and planets; and the evolution of biological organisms and ecologies. Without their incredible level of finely tuned precision from the very beginning of space-time, the complex universe we experience could not exist.[34]

Even more mind-blowing is the hypothesis that the physical universe's continued expansion carries with it an inbuilt template of information that apparently existed from its very beginning, or possibly even before its beginning, prior to the existence of the quantum plenum. This cosmic informational template holds within it the design of the process of expansion and development of the universe as a coherent unified entity, yet it also facilitates the emergence of all kinds of possibilities as it expands.

Morphic Fields

Rupert Sheldrake's hypothesis of morphic fields belongs to what is being discovered about the universe as a holographic field of information, holding within itself the potential unfolding of a stupendous evolutionary design. As he describes them, morphic fields are multiple fields of information, nested within each other, which create and sustain the biological patterns which give plants, animals and humans their form and their instinctive behaviour patterns, sustaining these through thousands, even millions of years, yet adding to them as new skills are learned. These skills then become available, through morphic resonance, to all members of that particular species. As Sheldrake explains in his latest book, *The Science Delusion*,

> My own hypothesis is that the formation of habits depends on a process called morphic resonance. Similar patterns of activity resonate across time and space with subsequent patterns. This hypothesis applies to all self-organising systems... All draw upon a collective memory and in turn contribute to it... Self-organising systems including molecules, cells, tissues, organs, organisms, societies and minds are made up of nested hierarchies or holarchies of holons or morphic units. At each level the whole is more than the sum of the parts, and these parts themselves are wholes made up of parts. The wholeness of each level depends on an organising field, called a morphic field. This field is within and around the system it organises, and is a vibratory pattern of activity that interacts with electromagnetic and quantum fields of the system.[35]

Through morphic resonance, humans, animals and plants are connected with their predecessors. Each individual both draws upon and contributes to the collective memory of the species. Animals and plants inherit the habits of their species and of their breed. The same applies to humans.... An extended understanding of heredity changes the way we think of ourselves, the influence of our predecessors, and our effects on generations yet unborn.[36]

Like the evolutionary biologist, Elisabet Sahtouris, in her book *EarthDance*, Sheldrake does not see life as a ruthless battle for survival as suggested by Richard Dawkins in his book *The Selfish Gene*, but rather as a cooperative enterprise unfolding over billions of years with ever-increasing complexity. Evolution, he says, "may be the result of an interplay between habits and creativity. New forms and patterns of organisation appear spontaneously, and are subject to natural selection. Those that survive are likely to appear again as new habits build up, and through repetition they become increasingly habitual."[37]

Sheldrake's theory of morphic fields resonates with Jung's idea of the collective unconscious as well as with the Indian concept of the Akashic records — the vast memory fields which carry the imprint of all past planetary and human experience. Sheldrake believes his theory of morphic resonance might work either through the transfer of information from the Implicate to the Explicate Orders posited by David Bohm or else through the quantum-vacuum field, the mediator of all quantum and electromagnetic processes. He says that his hypothesis "is eminently testable and evidence from many fields of enquiry already supports it." [38]

The Harmonic Patterns of the Cosmos

Pythagoras, who spent long years of study with the Egyptian and the Babylonian astronomers, formulated the principles of sacred geometry which he believed reflected the innate harmonic order underlying the visible forms of the cosmos and knew that mathematics was the key to understanding this harmonic order. With the advent of computer technology, we are now beginning to discover the inherent harmony of the basic geometric patterns that underlie the complex systems of the universe.

Following Benoit Mandelbrot's discovery in 1975 of the exquisite patterns that he named 'fractals', which were found to replicate themselves from the smallest to the largest scale, these are being recognized as the basic patterns, the fundamental structures, whether in cabbages, coastlines or galaxies — even social systems and financial dynamics — that underlie the appearance of the entire manifest world. They reveal a profoundly harmonic, ordered and unified universe hidden beneath the apparent chaos and differentiation of multiple complex systems.

In a holographic quantum universe, everything is connected to everything else in what is virtually a stupendous intelligent field of information and a unifying web of life. This returning concept of wholeness or unity is, at a new level of the spiral of evolution, a rediscovery of the shamanic lunar participatory awareness of the unified nature of all cosmic and planetary life. It facilitates a union of the two kinds of consciousness that have for so long been separated in us, the consciousness of the rational mind and that of the instinctual soul, the masculine and feminine aspects of our being. It invites us to become more aware of connections, to move beyond concepts of cause and effect and external causation into a universe of relationships, interdependence and essential unity in the seething creative energy in which all our lives are embedded.

Because, at the quantum level, we are all connected to each other, when thousands of us begin to change our understanding of reality, millions are affected. The more conscious and connected we become, the more we can generate inspiration and ideas flowing to us from this deep ground of the cosmos. Humanity and cosmos become a co-creating partnership. This may still be far removed from the position of most scientists, yet the fact that even a few individual scientists are reflecting upon this idea goes far towards bringing together metaphysics and physics in a radically new cosmology — unifying life, consciousness and cosmos.

The Dangers of Science

Returning to the world of our everyday experience, science has brought us extraordinary discoveries as well as many material benefits and, for a small proportion of the whole of humanity, higher standards of living. Yet science, when it falls into the hubristic stance of seeing itself standing above nature has, as suggested in Chapter Twelve, the tendency to slip into the language of an ideology rather than the methodology it claims to be. Certain scientists claim that, thanks to the current information revolution and the development of nanotechnology, we will soon be able to 'programme matter to order', changing the actual structural patterns of matter and creating synthetic genes that could fulfil our every whim, giving us 'mastery' of life and of matter. In its positive aspect, this new technology could be applied to creating minute machines which deliver drugs to different parts of the body, or creating organs to replace damaged or failing organs, so prolonging our lives. But it could equally be used to develop new weapons systems which could infiltrate those of other nations and destroy them or enable them to destroy us. We learn that nanoparticles have been inserted into tennis rackets and that they could be used to cure certain diseases like cancer. Food manufacturers are considering inserting them in foods but will we be told in advance that strawberries, for example, will contain nanoparticles to enhance their colour and taste or prolong their shelf life? And will the scientists who develop this technology be fully informed of the effects it might have on the immune system of the body, possibly affecting the lives of our children and grandchildren? This new science could bring us the possibility of untold benefits but also an even greater capacity to interfere with or subvert the basic structures and processes of life.

Commenting on the new science of nanotechnology, Lord Rees, in the Epilogue of his book *Our Final Century*, questions whether we are morally capable of discriminating between the undoubted benefits and the unforeseen risks that might be engendered by our technology: "The obverse of technology's immense prospects is an escalating variety of potential disasters, not just from malevolent intent but from innocent inadvertence as well... The benefits opened up by biotechnology are manifest, but they must be balanced against the accompanying hazards and ethical constraints. Robotics or nanotechnology will also involve trade-offs: they could have disastrous or even uncontrollable consequences when misapplied."[39]

The public learn about these scientific 'advances' after they have taken place. We didn't know much about the genetic engineering of plants and seeds until we heard of Monsanto's attempts to prevent farmers in India from using the seeds generated by their own crops, replacing them with 'terminator' seeds that could not regenerate. Hundreds of thousands of farmers have committed suicide as a result of this because they could not afford the cost of buying new seeds every year and because the seeds they were forced to purchase often failed to produce crops. Vandana Shiva, Director of the International College for Sustainable Living at Dehra Dun in India, has repeatedly drawn attention to the suffering inflicted on Indian farmers as a result of this shocking practice and has challenged the encroaching power of Monsanto. She has also started a worldwide movement to ensure that seeds cannot be patented by these giant corporations, five of which already control 75% of the world's commercial seed supply. She has inspired many movements which are now emerging to prevent the multi-national corporations gaining greater control of the world's food supply, to prevent the commercialisation of genetically engineered crops for animal and human consumption and to preserve the right of people to protect biodiversity and oppose the patenting of any life forms. These are the heritage of all humanity and should not be appropriated for commercial use by any corporation, however powerful.[40]

In the field of nuclear science, we have now discovered that thorium instead of the far more dangerous uranium could have been the fuel used in nuclear reactors and that a design for a thorium reactor existed after the Second World War but, under pressure from the military, was rejected by the US government in favour of a uranium one. Uranium was chosen because plutonium, its residual by-product, could be used in nuclear weapons. Only since the Fukushima disaster has this fact emerged into the public domain.[41]

There seems to be no forum in which people could participate in a debate on whether these 'advances' should take place or these decisions be taken. Too much hangs on the dubious moral maturity of the scientific 'experts', corporate bodies and governments who take these decisions on behalf of a nation, or even humanity as a whole. The 'public'— that amorphous mass of voice-less and choice-less individuals who are manipulated by the 'spin' of governments and scientific experts — has no effective say in hugely important decisions which affect the lives of every one of us as well as those of future generations.

It is in the domain of technology that the amoral ethos which drives science is most clearly revealed. Why should there be a need for ethical concerns when humanity is so obviously the beneficiary of technological advance? And who better to preside over that advance than scientific 'experts'? Professor Ravindra's comment is cautionary:

> The metaphysics of modern science has built right into it the axiom that the state of being of the scientists is irrelevant to the science they produce. Whether one is good or bad, fearful, hateful or kind is beside the point in determining one's qualities as a scientist. (We should keep in mind that a majority of all scientists and technologists in the world actually work for the military or for the war machine in one form or another). The assumption that the level of a person's consciousness or moral preparation is irrelevant to the quality of science that the person does is built into the procedures of science.[42]

Bill Joy, some years ago co-founder and Chief Scientist of Sun Micro-systems and formerly Co-Chair of the Presidential Commission on the Future of IT Research, asks us to become more alert to the dangers of the direction in which we are moving. We have, he says, become used to scientific breakthroughs but have not recognized that the three new technologies of robotics, genetic engineering and nanotechnology are different from the ones that preceded them in that all three have the capacity to amplify through self-replication. Self-replication in these new technologies runs a much greater risk of substantial damage in the physical world — even the destruction of the biosphere on which all life depends: "A bomb is blown up only once, but one altered gene can become many, and quickly get out of control."[43]

In his article Bill Joy quotes Eric Drexler who explained in his book, *Engines of Creation*:

> Plants with "leaves" no more efficient than today's solar cells could out-compete real plants, crowding the biosphere with an inedible foliage. Tough omnivorous "bacteria" could out-compete real bacteria; they could spread like pollen in the wind, replicating swiftly and reducing the biosphere to dust in a matter of days. Dangerous replicators could easily be rapidly spreading, too tough and small to stop. We have trouble enough controlling viruses and fruit flies. We cannot afford these kinds of accidents with self-replicating assemblers.

These new technologies do not require large facilities and rare materials like uranium as is the case with nuclear weapons. It will suffice for a few people to have knowledge of them for them to be able to apply it to whatever ends they envisage — including the creation of new weapons of mass destruction.

In a few decades we will be able to build computers much more powerful than the ones we use today and this computing power could be fused with the advances in the physical sciences and radical developments in the field of genetics. We would then have access to unimaginable power to transform our environment and ourselves, redesigning the world according to our view of what it could and should be in terms of what brings our own species the greatest advantage through directing and, if necessary, changing nature's processes. But whose Utopian vision would this be and who would hold the whole of humanity and possibly millions of other species hostage to it? Bill Joy concludes:

> If we could agree, as a species, what we wanted, where we were headed and why, then we could make our future much less dangerous — then we might understand what we could and should relinquish. If the course of humanity could be determined by our collective values, ethics and morals, and if we had gained more collective wisdom over the past few thousand years, then a dialogue to this end would be practical, and the incredible powers that we are about to unleash would not be nearly so troubling.[44]

An Ethical Direction for Science

To define an ethical direction for science, we need to recover the missing values grounded in the metaphysical insights of the great spiritual traditions which stress our essential unity and our responsibility to care for each other. Integral to these values is the need to protect the interconnected systems or organisms of planetary life. In a secular society, there is no consensus as to what fundamental ethical values should guide us. The lure of financial profit drives many scientific endeavours, particularly those involving the application of new drugs but also new weapons and new technologies such as robotics and nano-technology.

In his book *Ancient Wisdom, Modern World: Ethics for a New Millennium*, published in 1999, his Holiness the Dalai Lama asks us to become aware of the motivation that influences what we do. He urges us to take as our ethical guide our latent capacity for empathy and compassion for others — the desire to increase and enhance their happiness and decrease their suffering. By imagining what might add to the happiness and decrease the suffering of *all* beings, not just those belonging to our national or ethnic group, we can develop this ethical capacity. His suggestion recalls the words of the message quoted in Chapter One: Every act of a human being must be judged against the question: Does it offend Nature? Does it offend God? Does it injure Life?

To adopt these values as an ethical guide, science would have to alter its current assumption that the universe it observes is without consciousness. If the whole universe is assumed to be made up of dead matter in purposeless motion — no more than an agglomeration of parts and functions — then it is difficult to regard it as a Sacred Order or Entity, with its own in-built intelligence and evolutionary intention, and it is very difficult to adopt an ethical attitude towards it, giving consideration to what might be helpful or harmful to it. If the cosmos is assumed to be without consciousness, meaning or purpose, then we, as the only conscious elements in a dead universe, are deprived of any deep meaning to our lives or any sense of responsibility other than that related to our own needs. We will continue to exploit the resources of the planet for the benefit of our species alone until such time as we wake up from our dream of power over nature and call a halt to our amoral and unconscious behaviour.

Trish Pfeiffer, co-editor, with the late Professor John Mack, of *Mind Before Matter: Visions of a New Science of Consciousness*, sums up the essence of a different approach to reality in the Prologue to their book:

🌟 What would a world be like based on a mindset that understood that all is One and interconnected?

🌟 How soon could the knowledge that we live in a participatory world initiate change in our thinking about war, and our desecration of the planet?

🌟 Would a world aware of the primacy of consciousness be akin to the world as seen by some of the Indigenous Peoples?

⚹ Would we then see the cosmos as a living presence; and the whole universe, and all of nature, as intelligent?

⚹ Would we discover that the physical laws of the universe were 'habits', evolving rather than immutable?

⚹ Would we begin to sense other realities and other dimensions?

⚹ When we realize that time and space are not fundamental dimensions underlying reality, would it change forever our ideas about death?

⚹ Would we strive for unconditional love?

⚹ How would human relationships, social justice, poverty, science, medicine, politics, the government, and the military be reframed according to consciousness-primary perspectives?[45]

We are perhaps the first to have a clear picture of our species' devastating impact on the biodiversity of the planet. Two Reports in October 2018 gave the world a clear warning of the ecological crisis threatening the planet and showed that massive changes would have to be made if irreversible damage to it was to be prevented. The Report by the IPCC warned that there are only a dozen years for global warming to be kept to a maximum of 1.5C, beyond which even half a degree would significantly worsen the risks of drought, floods, extreme heat and poverty for hundreds of millions of people as well as the life of the planet as a whole. Carbon pollution would have to be cut by 45% by 2030 and come down to zero by 2050.

An equally serious Report from the World Wildlife Fund showed that since 1970 60% of the Earth's animal species have been wiped out. Vital rain forests in the Amazon and Indonesia have been cut down and replaced by vast soya bean and palm oil plantations. The ice sheets in the Arctic and the Antarctic are melting four times faster than had been assumed. Another unnoticed danger is the disappearance of insects and the serious implications for food supplies and biodiversity. Without insects, food webs collapse and ecosystem services fail, threatening the existence of all other species, including humans. Yet it is humans who are responsible for the "insect apocalypse". Safeguarding both human and animal life on this planet requires ending and ultimately reversing human population growth.

Sir David Attenborough has shown us that all the Earth's seas from Greenland to the Antarctic have been polluted by plastic which has endangered the life of millions of birds and sea-creatures and has even entered the human chain. Speaking in Davos in January 2019, he said: "It is difficult to overstate the climate change crisis. We are now so numerous, so powerful, so all pervasive, the mechanisms we have for destruction are so wholesale and so frightening that we can exterminate whole ecosystems without even noticing it. There has never been a time when people have been more out of touch with the natural world than they are today. We have now to be really aware of the dangers of what we are doing."

The primary factor driving these dire statistics is our growing human population and the food, water and fossil fuels extracted from the Earth to sustain it. These reports together with a study from the Proceedings of the National Academy of Sciences presented in Davos in January 2019 shows that we have barely twelve years in which to act to avoid the effects of catastrophic climate change.

Notes:

1. from the foreword to the first English translation of Pierre Teilhard de Chardin's *The Phenomenon of Man*, (1959) William Collins & Co., Ltd., London
2. Teilhard de Chardin, Pierre (1959) *The Future of Man*, William Collins & Co., Ltd., London, p. 75
3. Einstein, Albert (1954) *Ideas and Opinions*, Crown Publishers, New York
4. Haisch, Bernard (2006) *The God Theory*, Weiser Books, San Francisco, pp. 146 & 151-2
5. Sheldrake, Rupert (2012) *The Science Delusion*, Coronet, London, pp. 7-8
6. *The Secret of the Golden Flower*, translated and explained by Richard Wilhelm, with introduction and European commentary by C.G. Jung, p. 85
7. Bache, Christopher (2000) *Dark Night, Early Dawn*, State University of New York Press, pp. 220-221
8. ibid, p. 4
9. Planck, Max, Quoted in John Davidson, *The Secret of the Creative Vacuum*, 1989, p. 128
10. I am indebted for the material on Kepler to Paul Hague, who is completing a book called *Wholeness: The Union of All Opposites*, and also for his observation that the scientific revolution was initiated by four remarkable men. Kepler is often left out.
11. Milne, Joseph (2008) *Metaphysics and the Cosmic Order*, Temenos Academy, London, pp. 23, 25
12. Stern, Karl (1985) *The Flight from Woman*, Paragon House, St. Paul, Minnesota, p. 269
13. Ravindra, Ravi (2002) *Science and the Sacred: Eternal Wisdom in a Changing World*, Quest Books, Wheaton, Illinois, pp. 50-51
14. ibid, p. 147
15. Tarnas, Richard (2006) *Cosmos and Psyche: Intimations of a New World View*, Viking Penguin, New York, p. 33
16. ibid, p. 39
17. Haisch, p. 67
18. Goswami, Amit (1995) *The Self-aware Universe: How Consciousness Creates the Material World*. Tarcher/Putnam, New York.
19. Goswami, (2001) *The Visionary Window*, Quest Books, Wheaton, Ill., p. 16
20. Miller, Arthur I. (2009) 137: *Jung, Pauli, and the Pursuit of a Scientific Obsession*, W.W. Norton & Co., New York & London, p. 230.

21. Haisch, p. 71
22. Haisch (2007) from his chapter in *Mind Before Matter: Visions of a New Science of Consciousness*, O Books, Ropley, UK
23. Bohm, David (1980) *Wholeness and the Implicate Order*, Routledge & Kegan Paul, London, p. 192
24. ibid, p. 192
25. ibid, xi
26. ibid, p. 135
27. ibid, p. 19
28. ibid, p. 192
29. address by David Bohm, from the last page of *Infinite Potential: The Life and Times of David Bohm*, by F. David Peat 1997
30. Laszlo, Ervin and Currivan, Jude (2008) *CosMos: A Co-creator's Guide to the Whole-World*, Hay House, New York & London, p. 84
31. ibid, p. 53
32. ibid, p. 19
33. ibid, p. 36
34. ibid, p. 20
35. Sheldrake, pp. 99-100
36. ibid, p. 185
37. ibid, p. 108
38. ibid, p. 101
39. Rees, Martin (Lord Rees) (2003) *Our Final Century*, William Heinemann, London
40. www.vandanashiva.org
41. Horizon Programme BBC2 with biologist Professor Jim Al-Khalili, September 2011. At the Shanghai Institute of Nuclear and Applied Physics the Chinese are concentrating on the development of thorium nuclear power that would be clean, cheap and safe. Thorium reactors would produce far less toxic waste that those fuelled by uranium. More over, they would not be vulnerable to dangerous implosion like the Fukushima reactors and they could burn up the current stockpiles of the waste left over from uranium reactors. Thorium reactors could apparently be small, lodged below ground, powering whole cities. If the Chinese can develop these reactors, the world will follow and we will need less oil, coal and gas (Ambrose Evans-Pritchard in *The Telegraph* January 2013).
42. Ravindra, p. 39
43. Joy, Bill, excerpt from an article in *Resurgence Magazine*, issue no. 208 September/ October 2001: Forfeiting the Future: Powerful new technologies threaten life on Earth and raise moral issues. See the full article at http://www.annebaring.com/anbar11_new-vis05_science.htm#ethicalscience
44. ibid
45. Pfeiffer, Trish and Mack, John E. MD, editors (2007) *Mind Before Matter: Visions of a New Science of Consciousness*, O Books, Ropley, Hampshire, United Kingdom

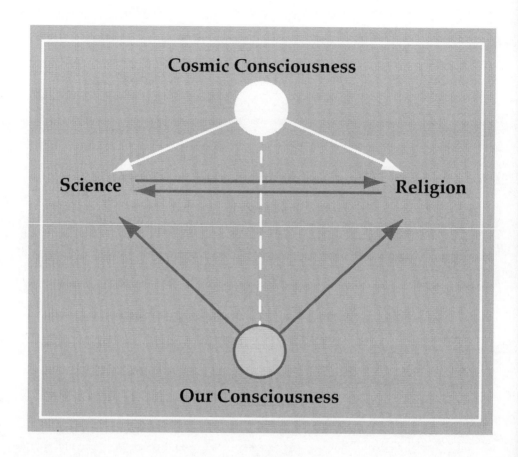

Diagram of Consciousness
adapted from the Author's diagram

Chapter Fifteen

THE SOUL OF THE COSMOS

You could not discover the limits of the soul, even if you travelled by every path in order to do so; so profound is its meaning.

— Heraclitus

I feel more and more every day, as my imagination strengthens, that I do not live in this world alone but in a thousand worlds.

— John Keats Letter 18th October, 1818

The moment when physics touches on the 'untrodden, untreadable regions' and when psychology has at the same time to admit that there are other forms of psychic life besides the acquisitions of personal consciousness... then the intermediate realm of subtle bodies comes to life again, and the physical and the psychic are once more blended in an indissoluble unity....We have come very near to this turning point today.

— C. G. Jung *Psychology and Alchemy,* ¶ 394

There is an exquisite tapestry in the Musée de Cluny in Paris, where a woman stands in the doorway of a tent, flanked by a lion and a unicorn. The artist who designed this fifteenth century masterpiece, discovered in a remote chateau in the Auvergne, placed them in a russet landscape filled with fruit trees, animals, birds and flowers. The series of six tapestries called "La Dame à La Licorne", which includes this exceptional one, is said to represent the five senses. However, to me they represent far more than this. In medieval iconography, the lion symbolized the body and the unicorn the spirit. Here, both are held, so to speak, in the field of the soul, personified by the beautiful woman who stands at the door of a tent emblazoned with fleur de lys. A young girl offers her a casket filled with jewels. Above the entrance of the tent are inscribed the words "Mon Seul Désir". Two posts or lances on either side of her are painted with crescent moons and display a banner with three crescent moons on them. They may represent a coat of arms but they are also the age-old symbol of the Feminine. It seems to me that this beautiful woman could represent the soul as the essential and long obscured link between body and spirit.

The soul has been described in languages other than English with feminine nouns. The Oxford Dictionary describes the soul as an entity distinct from the body, as the spiritual aspect of man in contrast to the physical aspect, as the seat of the emotions and feelings and as the aspect of our nature which survives physical death. Metaphysically, it was regarded as the vital, sensitive, or rational principle in plants, animals, or human beings. But millennia ago it was regarded as the animating principle of the world, the invisible containing Reality which underlies and permeates all form — the *Anima Mundi*.

The current concept of the soul in modern reductionist science is revealed in the title of a debate (October 30th, 2011) called "Battle of Ideas" and subtitled, "Is there a ghost in the machine?" The description of the subject of the debate began with this paragraph:

> The spirit, spark or personality — the concept of a soul, self or mind distinct from our physical shell — has long been a cornerstone of our understanding of what it means to be human, in both religious and secular spheres. Increasingly, however, scientific fields such as neuroscience, genetics, epigenetics and psychology continue to provide ever more intricate explanations for human functioning that are rooted in the tangible and the biological. There is a widespread expectation that aspects of our lives that currently elude understanding will eventually yield to scientific explication, given sufficient time and research.

Jung's comment is perhaps appropriate here: "The general under-valuation of the human soul is so great that neither the great religions nor the philosophies nor scientific rationalism have been willing to look at it twice."[1]

What has been lost in descriptions of the soul is the Platonic understanding that the Cosmos has a soul and that this cosmic soul is the origin or ground of our own individual soul — our own consciousness — and our connection with the deeper levels of the Cosmos; our individual soul is an inseparable part of the Soul of the Cosmos. To understand the Soul as an invisible cosmic reality, we need to broaden our concept of it to embrace the inner or unseen life of the universe and, following what was explained in the last chapter, recognize that it is alive, conscious and the eternal ground of our own consciousness.

The reason the soul has been thought of as feminine is, I believe, because the idea of the soul evolved out of the image of the Great Mother — the matrix of being — whose cosmic womb was the source of all life. One of the most important ideas derived from the image of the Great Mother, described in the preface to *The Myth of the Goddess* and in Chapter Four of this book, was that "life was instinctively experienced as an organic, living and sacred whole, where everything was woven together in one cosmic web and all orders of life were related, because all shared in the sanctity of the original source."

The Neolithic image of the Great Mother was transmitted to the Great Goddesses of the Bronze Age — specifically in Egypt, to the Goddesses Isis and Hathor, as described in Chapter Four. In Greece, it eventually gave rise to Plato's definition of the Soul of the Cosmos (*Psuche tou Kosmou*) and to the eloquent image of *Zoë*, the universal soul, and *bios*, the individual soul: the tiny, pulsing atom of our consciousness hung like a bead on the great necklace of being. Later, the idea of Soul as a cosmic reality was defined in the extensive cosmology of Plotinus and his idea of the *Anima Mundi* or Soul of the World. A similar concept can be found in the Shekinah of Kabbalah described in Chapter Three. Familiarity with the ancient cosmology surrounding the image of the Great Mother and later Great Goddesses as well as the Shekinah helped me to understand what the idea of 'Soul' once signified and what it could signify again.

Heraclitus was surely right. Even though we travel by every path to discover the limits of the Soul, we could never fathom its depths. For the depths of the Soul are the depths of the Cosmos itself and the multitude of invisible worlds about which, with our limited perception, we know virtually nothing.

When I was gathering sayings for *The Mystic Vision*, I came across a book called *The Story of My Heart* by Richard Jefferies (1848–1887), who lived in the Dorset countryside in the late nineteenth century. To me, there has never been a more beautiful or eloquent hymn to the Soul which, at the same time, is a hymn to the beauty and marvel of the Earth. I was amazed and moved to discover these words in his diary: "There is an Entity, a Soul-Entity, as yet unrecognised... It is in addition to the existence of the soul; in addition to immortality; and beyond the idea of the deity... There is an immense ocean over which the mind can sail, upon which the vessel of thought has not yet been launched. There is so much beyond all that has ever yet been imagined."[2]   In another passage, he expressed his longing for relationship with this Soul-Entity:

> I was utterly alone with the sun and the earth. Lying down on the grass, I spoke in my soul to the earth, the sun, the air, and the distant sea far beyond sight. I thought of the earth's firmness — I felt it bear me up; through the grassy couch there came an influence as if I could feel the great earth speaking to me... Touching the crumble of earth, the blade of grass, the thyme flower, breathing the earth-encircling air, thinking of the sea and the sky, holding out my hand

> for the sunbeams to touch it, prone on the sward in token of deep reverence, thus I prayed that I might reach to the unutterable existence infinitely higher than deity.[3]

His words convey two concepts of soul: the first being the personal one, traditionally thought of as feminine, which is the spiritual core of our being — that aspect of ourselves which is our conduit to an unseen spiritual reality and that is believed to survive the death of our body. But there is also the wider cosmic one that Jefferies calls a Soul-Entity and compares to an immense ocean. This wider concept of Soul embraces the life of the Cosmos and its billions of galaxies as well as the life of our planet and every stone, plant and creature on it. It is this older concept of Soul, the hidden source and ground of all life, which has been overlooked, forgotten or dismissed by our culture.

Jefferies was yearning for something that people once felt they belonged to, in whose invisible life they lived. Over the millennia of the solar era, this instinctive feeling of belonging to an entity beyond the community of tribe or nation, something experienced as numinous, immeasurable and all-embracing, filled with daemonic agents of the divine, was gradually lost and with it the sense of participation in a web of life which connected every single creature and element of life to every other. The great contemplatives of Kabbalah named this web the Tree of Life.

Without my vision of the Cosmic Woman and my discovery of Kabbalah, I would never have come to *know* that the soul is not in us: we are in the Soul. Many years after that visionary dream, another one helped me to understand the intimate connection between our world and the greater world of Soul:

> I dreamed that I came to a place where there was a large flat stone on the ground with a kind of fence or barrier extending horizontally from it on both sides. Lying on top of the stone was something that I had to bend down to see properly. It was a beautifully worked red enamel and gold buckle, whose two 'ends' fitted together precisely. In appearance it was like the exquisite enamelled buckles found in the Sutton Hoo burial chamber and now in the British Museum. As I looked up, I saw a different landscape extending beyond the fence and far into the distance in front of me. I realized that the buckle in the dream was giving me an image of how two realities fit together to form a whole. I was standing in one reality but could see clearly into another that was similar to the one familiar to me but infinitely more beautiful and extraordinary.

The Net of Indra

In India and China, there has long been an exquisite image of the cosmic web of life, known as the Net of Indra, king of the gods in the Vedic pantheon. This jewel, diamond or pearl-studded Net — delicate as a silken spider's web — was said to be suspended over Indra's palace on Mount Meru, the Holy Mountain and *axis mundi* of Vedic cosmology that I had found represented everywhere in temple sculpture on my journeys through India, Cambodia and Indonesia. The Buddha himself once described the cosmos as a "web of golden threads joining myriad many-faceted jewels, each reflecting the multihued light of all the others."[4] The jewels or pearls represent the souls of animate beings and each jewel holds a boundless universe of images and experiences, since all souls carry a fathomless past and are connected to each other through the Net.

The image of Indra's Net led me ultimately — near the end of writing this book — to a Buddhist text called the *Avatamsaka Sutra* or Flower Ornament Scripture, and to Hua-Yen Buddhism, regarded by Chinese and Japanese scholars as the highest form of Buddhism. Legend says that the teaching given within it was spoken by the Buddha when he was in the state of samadhi at the time of his enlightenment. Francis Cook in his book *Hua-yen Buddhism* (1977) gives us this description of Indra's Net:

> Far away in the heavenly abode of the great god Indra, there is a wonderful net which has been hung by some cunning artificer in such a manner that it stretches out indefinitely in all directions... the artificer has hung a single glittering jewel in each "eye" of the net, and since the net itself is infinite in dimension, the jewels are infinite in number. There hang the jewels, glittering like stars of the first magnitude, a wonderful sight to behold. If we arbitrarily select one of these jewels for inspection and look closely at it, we will discover that in its polished surface there are reflected all the other jewels in the net, infinite in number. Not only that, but each of the jewels reflected in this one jewel is also reflecting all the other jewels, so that there is an infinite reflecting process occurring.[5]

The *Avatamsaka Sutra* was originally written in Sanskrit, then translated into Chinese between the sixth and eighth centuries, where it formed the basis of a Chinese Buddhist School called *Hua-yen* or Flower Ornament School, incorporating elements of both Mahayana Buddhism and Taoism. In an outstanding work of scholarship and years of dedication, Thomas Cleary has translated all thirty-nine books of the *Sutra* into English and these were published with an introduction by him in 1993.

The whole extraordinary text of the *Avatamsaka Sutra*, the quintessence of centuries of Buddhist contemplation and meditation, might be said to describe the nature and significance of the Net of Indra. Its essential message is that all of existence, both seen and unseen, is an indissoluble unity. Nothing can exist separately from anything else. All aspects of life are interdependent and each interacts with the others in a state of continual flux, change and creativity.

The great Buddhist scholar, D.T. Suzuki, considered the *Avatamsaka Sutra* to be

> the consummation of Buddhist thought, Buddhist sentiment, and Buddhist experience. To my mind, no religious literature in the world can ever approach the grandeur of conception, the depth of feeling, and the gigantic scale of composition, as attained by this sutra.... Abstract truths are so concretely, so symbolically represented here that one will finally come to a realization of the truth that even in a particle of dust the whole universe is seen reflected — not this visible universe only, but a vast system of universes, conceivable by the highest minds only.[6]

Whereas in the Western tradition the concept of the visible universe was predicated on the idea of a primal cause or a Creator God bringing it into being, in this text the universe has no beginning and no end, no creator or hierarchical order but is seen as an immeasurable living 'entity' or cosmic web of relationships existing in a kind of unified field, with each aspect integral to and affecting every other. It describes a universe beyond our time-and-space world: one undoubtedly seen in meditation. All life is perceived as an organic whole, just as it was conceived in the lunar goddess cultures and is conceived in indigenous cultures today. All lives and elements of life are eternally and inseparably interwoven with all others, participating in mutual relationship with all others, dependent upon that jewelled or pearl-studded Net of relationships that are ceaselessly changing, ceaselessly coming into being. Everything we do in our lives affects this unimaginable Web, whether for good or for ill.

The Net of Indra may be aligned with the concept of the universe as a hologram where every tiny part reflects or contains an image of the whole — a concept put forward by the physicist David Bohm in his book *Wholeness and the Implicate Order*, described in the last chapter. Today we are discovering this network of relationships in James Lovelock's concept of Gaia as a vast living organism where each part is dependent upon every other part for its survival. What is to prevent us widening his discovery to include the whole universe? In the opening paragraph of his book Francis Cook says that Western man may be on the brink of an entirely new understanding of the nature of existence.[7] Although this Buddhist view of reality may seem unfamiliar to us, it is becoming more familiar as science discovers the interconnected nature of all aspects of life and how one single electron is connected to all others no matter how great the distance between them.

Science has looked at things in isolation, as separate units, but now it is discovering that life is a web of interdependent elements, where something as unremarkable as a bear eating salmon and discarding its remains in the Canadian forest can nourish the life of the trees growing there and the animals feeding on the vegetation on the forest floor. If one element is damaged or destroyed, the whole web is affected. Therefore, it is incumbent on us as individuals to take care of and cherish every aspect of life, aware that the least of our actions, whether in relation to our immediate families, to society as a whole or to the great web of life in nature, has an effect on the whole. As Cook observes in the concluding paragraph of his book, speaking from the Hua-yen perspective, "I am in some sense boundless, my being encompassing the farthest limits of the universe, touching and moving every atom in existence…. The interfusion, the sharing of destiny, is as infinite in scope as the reflections in the jewels of Indra's Net… It is not just that "we are all in it" together. We all *are* it, rising or falling as one living body."[8]

The Legacy of Plato and Plotinus

Returning to the Western metaphysical tradition, no description of the cosmic dimension of Soul can disregard the immensely influential legacy of two of the greatest philosophers of the Greek world: Plato (429–347 BC) and Plotinus (AD 205–270), a philosopher who was born in Hellenistic Egypt and later moved to Rome, where he had a wide circle of students. We are fortunate that one of his students, Porphyry, edited the huge body of his teachings known as the *Enneads* that formed the basis of what came to be known as Neoplatonism. Through the influence of Plato and Plotinus the idea of a Cosmic Soul and a World Soul was transmitted down the centuries by individuals who valued the Platonic ideas and their insights, and is coming to life again today. Their enduring influence is manifest in the words of the Sufi Sheik Llewellyn Vaughan-Lee in his book, *The Return of the Feminine and the World Soul*: "The World Soul is not just a psychological or philosophical concept. It is a living spiritual substance within us and around us. Just as the individual soul pervades the whole human being — our body, thoughts, and feelings — the nature of the World Soul is that it is present within everything. It pervades all of creation and is a unifying principle within the world."[9]

Plotinus, who developed and clarified Plato's cosmology, said that we were within a reality that is also within us. "All things depend on each other; everything breathes together." His concept of the totally transcendent One as the divine ground of being, emanating through the levels and dimensions of cosmic life in the way the sun radiates light, until the world of matter comes into being, is remarkably similar to the cosmology of Kabbalah. As in that tradition, the individual human soul is the expression or emanation of the divine ground of the Cosmic or World Soul and carries divinity within its very nature.

In the twelfth century, the works of Plato became accessible in France through the translations of Arab philosophers and gave rise to the marvel of the Gothic Cathedrals. Soul comes to life in the medieval quest for the Holy Grail — image of the boundless realm of the eternal pouring forth its light and love for the nourishment of humanity. Later, in fifteenth century Italy, with the translation of the works of Plato by the Florentine philosopher Marsilio Ficino, the idea of a Cosmic or World Soul and the quintessential divinity of man were revived. Within a small but influential circle of individuals, nature was again perceived as ensouled and this released a tremendous creative energy in one small part of Europe. Yet these ideas could not take root and flourish. The young Pico della Mirandola gave his great *Oration on the Dignity of Man* but was murdered before he could accomplish the dream he shared with Marsilio Ficino of bringing together the teaching of Kabbalah with that of Christianity. A little over a century later, Giordano Bruno, one of the most innovative and creative philosophers of his time, was sent to the stake in Rome in 1600 for declaring that nature was ensouled, that the World Soul illumined the universe and that there were other solar systems inhabited by living beings.

Even in the midst of the turbulence of the seventeenth century, the presence of Soul as the unseen ground of this material world still shines through the words of the visionary poet, Thomas Traherne (1637–1674) in his *Centuries of Meditations*: "The world is a mirror of infinite beauty, yet no man sees it. It is a Temple of majesty, yet no man regards it. It is a region of Light and Peace, did not men disquiet it. It is the Paradise of God."

> The corn was orient and immortal wheat, which never should be reaped, nor was ever sown. I thought it had stood from everlasting to everlasting. The dust and stones of the street were as precious as gold. The gates were at first the end of the world, the green trees when I saw them first through one of the gates transported and ravished me; their sweetness and unusual beauty made my heart to leap, and almost mad with ecstasy, they were such strange and wonderful things....
>
> You will never enjoy the World aright, till the sea itself floweth in your Veins, till you are Clothed with the Heavens, and Crowned with the Stars and perceive yourself to be the Sole Heir of the whole World: and more... because Men are

in it who are every one Sole Heirs, as well as you…. Till your Spirit fills the
whole World, and the Stars are your jewels.

After the turmoil and terrible slaughter of the religious wars of the seventeenth
century, Soul comes to life again in the work of the great poets of the Romantic
Movement: Wordsworth, Keats, Shelley, Coleridge, and later, Tennyson, Goethe
and the German poets of the nineteenth century who reconnected their culture to
nature and the imagination. Blake could see that "Everything that lives is Holy".
But their vision fades before the tremendous social, economic and technological
changes wrought by the Industrial and Scientific Revolutions.

Earlier chapters have explored the difference between lunar and solar culture
and shown how the perception of the Cosmos as a living being was lost during
the solar era, and how our self-aware rational mind gradually became dissociated
from the deeper instinctive ground out of which it had developed. They have
shown how, through the great meta-narrative of the Fall of Man, nature and this
world became desacralized and woman and all that was related to the Feminine
deeply wounded because of their association with nature — a nature that was split
off from spirit and seen as part of a fallen world.

From the fourth century, the powerful influence of St. Augustine and his
profoundly pessimistic Doctrine of Original Sin severed humanity from the
ground of Soul by imposing on the Christian community the belief that this world
was fundamentally flawed and man contaminated by sin and separated from God
— from which state only those who were predestined would be rescued by the
grace of God. Although there were many other factors contributing to the loss of
the wider concept of Soul, for many centuries this Christian doctrine drastically
undermined the older lunar participatory experience of life and, in my view, led
ultimately to the current philosophy of scientific reductionism and the loneliness
and alienation of man in an apparently inanimate and indifferent universe.

Soul as the Fathomless Sea of Being

From my dreams and from Jung's invaluable discoveries I know that the sea is
one of the primary images of the Soul — that mysterious sea so difficult to find,
so incomprehensible to the mind conditioned to believe that there is only material
reality. Perhaps that is why the *I Ching*, or Chinese Book of Oracles, enjoins us
to "cross the Great Waters".

No one has ever referred to the sea as 'he'. The sea has always been associated
with the feminine principle and with the image of a goddess — with Kwan Yin

in China and the Virgin Mary in the Christian West and long before these with Nammu, the Sumerian goddess of the primordial abyss. For millennia sailors invoked their protection when they set out in their frail vessels across the dark immensity of the sea. But transpose the image of the sea to the measureless sea of Cosmic Soul. And imagine the small vessel of our individual consciousness sailing on the surface of an infinite sea of light which is continually surging, dancing, flowing into being.

Imagine that we could see through the physical forms, including our own bodies which we experience as opaque and solid, and were able to see myriad patterns of energy interacting with each other and connecting us with the subtle worlds of the Soul. Imagine shining filaments of light (invisible to us) flowing through the starry galaxies of space as well as through our bodies and the forms of the animals, plants, trees and the landscape we see around us. We experience ourselves as separate entities, but if the whole universe is one integrated, living organism, one symphony of cosmic sound, then we are part of that whole. How did we ever come to believe that the universe and matter are inanimate and dead?

This cosmic web of life is an inconceivably complex, multi-levelled network of dimensions nested within dimensions, with information continually being exchanged between these dimensions — perhaps comparable to the way we now exchange information through websites and e-mails — at the molecular level, at the level of our own telepathic communication with each other, at the level of planetary life, and at the level of galaxies and perhaps any number of parallel universes of which, as yet, we know nothing. In this invisible Soul of the universe is encoded the experience of all orders of life over billions of years as we measure time. We participate as creators in the unfolding of our own lives in this fathomless unfolding evolutionary process but the potential for limitless creation is also there and we participate in that ongoing process of creation. We may inhabit one of these worlds or dimensions after our death when our physical body has been discarded.

What we call our consciousness is infinite, yet paradoxically as small as the lens through which we try to fathom that immeasurable greatness. How recent a development is our present consciousness in comparison with the age of the universe, even with the age of our planet; how difficult then for us to encompass the meaning of the Soul. If we were to ask ourselves the question put long ago by the great Indian sage Sri Ramana: "Who am I?" The answer would be "I am the Soul of the Cosmos discovering itself through its own creation."

In our modern culture, we are usually so completely absorbed in what the Taoists called the 'ten thousand things' that it may never occur to us that the longing we may experience to set out on journeys, to sail across seas or explore foreign lands might reflect the Soul's own longing to be explored, to reveal to us in the words of an Old Testament prophet "the treasures of darkness and the hidden riches of secret places" (Isaiah 45:3). The Soul may be calling to us but we may unknowingly ignore the foundation on which the whole edifice of life rests.

Reconnecting with the Soul

There is a voice, that of myth, fairy tale and legend and, also, of mystic vision, which points inwards, leading us, if we will allow it, into the neglected dimension of our inner life, our soul, which in turn connects us to the greater Soul of the Cosmos. In its simplest terms, the Soul is the secret, hidden dimension that is the goal of the hero's quest in myth and legend. It is the ultimate destination of all exploration: the unknown, mysterious, fabulous land. The way to it lies through the mysterious gates of horn so celebrated in the ancient world — the gates that guarded the threshold to the mysteries of the Goddess. In the language of mythology and fairy tale, it has been named the kingdom of faerie, the realm of the gods. In the language of visionary revelation, it is the Kingdom of Heaven, the Kingdom of God, the sacred ground of all cosmic reality. The Sufis know it as *alam al-mittal* or what the great Sufi scholar Henri Corbin described as the 'imaginal' world (*mundus imaginalis*): a world that is as real, alive and present as our world.[10] It is the ground or source of everything we are, everything we perceive. It is our true home in the Cosmos to which we return after our sojourn on earth. If the Soul is all this, it is not surprising that it transcends our present level of consciousness, that we cannot comprehend it after a few hours or years of search and study. Yet, paradoxically, we are both that which seeks to comprehend and the object of our comprehension. We are both part and whole.

What connects us to the invisible ground of the Soul? It is the quest for meaning, experienced differently in each individual life, which drives our longing to discover, create, explore, know and understand. But above all, it is our capacity to imagine, to make intuitive associations, to bring things together that have been fragmented and are felt to belong together. It is through our capacity to feel and to imagine that we are most closely connected to the Soul of Nature and the Cosmos. It is developing the ability to see with the eye of the heart — often spoken of by poets and artists — that makes the connection with a reality initially beyond the reach of the mind, acting like a plug connecting us to the socket of that deeper reality.

People sometimes dream of being in a house with rooms they had no idea existed, or find themselves going through a door into an unknown part of it. The

Soul can be thought of as a stranger in whose house we live but whom we have never met. This stranger has been the witness of everything experienced since the beginning of our evolution as well as holding everything that is still latent as an unrealized potential. This greater Consciousness to which our own consciousness belongs — though still unaware of its parentage — is the basic energy of life which creates, destroys and perpetually transforms itself. Its 'cosmic imagination' has brought forth the universe, the galaxies, our planet, the evolutionary process on the planet that has ultimately given us physical form and the self-aware creativity, intelligence and imagination which have transformed the physical and cultural conditions of our life on Earth.

The idea of meeting this stranger may seem faintly ridiculous at first, even somewhat alarming. The Soul speaks an unfamiliar language, like the language of hieroglyphs, whose symbols have to be painstakingly learned before we can understand their meaning. As the ability develops to become aware of what it is trying to communicate, to sense its presence and divine its intention and guidance, it begins to come alive. A dialogue develops; synchronicities occur which were not previously noticed.

Understanding the symbolic imagery of dreams can help to build this relationship. But there are also the insights that have become available to us through the painstaking work of pioneers who have opened up for us this unexplored dimension. Jung developed the method that he called Active Imagination to enter into dialogue with the soul. Meditation can help to give us access to the underlying ground that is obscured by the continual stream of concerns and anxieties which may distract us from awareness of its presence. Silence and contemplation are essential if we are to create the space for listening in our over-busy lives. I remember that the Maharishi said that meditation is like being dipped into a vat filled with golden dye. Eventually, after many dippings, we begin to take on a rich golden hue. What one individual experiences and understands affects the whole. As he suggested, and as Rupert Sheldrake's hypothesis of morphic fields would seem to confirm, once a critical mass is reached, there can be a shift in collective consciousness, a collective awakening.

Sacred Places

The idea that our world rests on the ground of an invisible 'Other' survived in the visionary and mystical traditions of the solar age which kept alive the lunar idea of the divinity of nature and the co-inherence of matter and spirit. It also survived in some of the close-knit indigenous communities of the world where the traditions which respected the sacredness of Earth and Cosmos and the methods of opening a connection with the inner dimension were passed from generation to generation — even to the present day. All over the world pilgrimages are still made to places held sacred for millennia because they act as portals which connect the two worlds. In Europe, the churches and shrines sacred to the Black Madonna, whose very blackness evokes the Mysteries of the Great Mother, of Nature and of Soul, still mark these as places of communion between this world and the invisible world. Many healings have been recorded in these places which continue to this day.

One of the places in Europe sacred to the Virgin, and long before her to an older Druidic Goddess, is Chartres Cathedral. Chartres has now been cleaned, so that within and without, it now gleams with the beautiful pale ivory stone used in its original construction. As you enter the cathedral, you may, as I do each time I visit it, find tears welling unbidden into your eyes in response to its extraordinary impact. Soul and body respond to the subtle harmony created by the sacred geometry which surrounds you, incorporated into every stone, arch and pillar. The very purpose of Chartres is to draw the pilgrim treading its stone-flagged floor from the visible to the invisible world, helping him to see through the veil of matter to the divine ground. The two towers of Chartres represent the sun and the moon and also, most interestingly, the solar and lunar, male and female principles of both Alchemy and Kabbalah. Their union is reflected in the central 'column' of the nave with the altar at the place of the heart in the human body.

The central line of the nave may also be understood to represent eternity and the two transepts the world of time. The high altar marks the place where they intersect. The labyrinth laid out on the floor of the cathedral symbolizes the pathway through life in this world as a conscious preparation for life in the eternal world, whose presence is indicated by the great rose window on the western façade. When the shape of the rose window is laid over the labyrinth it matches its dimensions exactly, emphasizing the relationship between them. The labyrinth itself acts like a vortex, drawing the pilgrim into the core of itself, causing him to lose his habitual orientation as he follows the multiple turns and folds of the path to the central six-petalled white rose, whose dimensions exactly match the rosette at the centre of the rose window which holds the figure of Christ.

William Anderson, in his wonderful book *The Rise of the Gothic*, observes that

> The sudden appearance in the years 1135 – 1150 of a group of men capable of transforming the artistic landscape of Europe was not fortuitous. It happened because these men had as an ideal a new conception of Man to make manifest, a new understanding of their own natures, and a new insight into the springs of art and science. The splendour of Gothic art and architecture derives from the

magnanimity of soul of its makers. That was the source of their imaginative grasp of the possibilities of the new technology and of the quality of life revitalized that shines from their work.[11]

The new image of man which is the work of the Gothic masters presents man as an individual endowed with free will, who is seen as God and His angels look upon him and is set within a framework of apparently abstract shapes of portals, arches, niches and vaults that nevertheless symbolize aspects of the laws and forms of the universe. The Christian concept of the worth of the individual soul, a concept with which the Gospels and the Pauline Epistles are instinct, only achieved its first full expression eleven hundred years after the death of Christ, in the column statues of St. Denis and Chartres…. They helped to excise the shame in men's souls at their being men; they spoke, without words, of peace of mind and rationality, and they gave new intensity to the doctrine of the Incarnation through the radiance of the spirit proclaimed by the stone from which they were carved.[12]

The whole cathedral, with its nine portals and its original plan of nine towers was designed to incorporate the nine celestial hierarchies defined by Dionysius the Areopagite, a Syrian monk of the fifth century, who wrote under the name of a much earlier man, also named Dionysius, who was converted to Christianity by St. Paul when he visited Athens, and is said to have written down the visionary experiences of St. Paul. The works of the fifth century Dionysius, who wrote extensively about the "Divine Darkness of God", were brought from Byzantium to France at the request of the French King, Charles the Bald, a grandson of Charlemagne. They were translated during the ninth century at the Abbey of Saint Denis in Paris by the renowned scholar and Neoplatonist monk, John Scotus Eriugena (810–877) who wrote an authentic commentary on the writings of Dionysius and whose other major work will be considered in Chapter Seventeen. These writings had an enormous influence on the builders of the Gothic cathedrals.

Chartres was built to offer the pilgrim entering its doors the experience of the 'Divine Darkness' of God illumined by the light flowing from those nine celestial hierarchies and filtered through the exquisite sapphire and ruby radiance of the stained glass windows.[13] As Dionysius himself described so beautifully in a letter to a woman called Dorothy the Deacon, "The Divine Dark is the inaccessible Light in which God is said to dwell. Into this dark — invisible because of its surpassing brightness and unsearchable because of the abundance of its super natural torrents of light — all enter who are deemed worthy to know and see God: and by the very fact of not seeing or knowing, are truly in Him who is above all sight and knowledge."[14]

How, you wonder, was such a marvel as Chartres ever created? How were the enlightened individuals brought together and the skills developed which could design the form, carve, lift and arrange such enormous amounts of stone in such sublime harmony and proportion? How did they come to incorporate the three great innovations which gave to Chartres its revolutionary structure: the pointed arch, the flying buttress and the ribbed vault? How could flimsy wooden scaffolding hold the tremendous weight of the stones that had to be hauled into place with ropes that could fray and break under the pressure — stones that fitted together with incredible precision and very little mortar?

Chartres was built as a temple for the Queen of Heaven. The rose itself was a symbol of Divine Wisdom and the whole cathedral with its three rose windows was a hymn to Mary as the Throne of Wisdom and Queen of Heaven:

> It was Abbot Suger who helped to develop the iconographical scheme of the Tree of Jesse culminating in the Virgin and her Son that was to lead to the triumphal portrayal of Mary as the Queen of Heaven in so many cathedrals and churches. Through the association with her of so many ancient images of the moon, the stars, the Milky Way, she came to possess a cosmic significance, seen most clearly in the great rose windows of France, as though she were the womb of the universe containing Christ the sunchild.[15]

The nameless men who designed Chartres, who called themselves "Masters of the Compasses", gave the twelfth century culture of France and Europe a new image of Man as radiant with divinity, the more so as he was able to bring such marvels into being. In exalting the image of the Virgin and making her the focus of their creation, they rescued the Feminine from the contempt into which it had fallen and they redeemed nature from its association with sin, releasing it into a glorious affirmation of its beauty in fruit, flower and foliage, presided over by the Green Man. Chartres is a phenomenal testament to the creative power of the human imagination when it is directed towards bringing something into being that connects this time-bound world with the eternal one. It is the honouring of this connection that creates civilization.

A most interesting book on Chartres by Gordon Strachan describes how there is evidence from the correspondence of notable scholars in the eleventh century that they didn't know how to solve very simple geometrical problems. By the thirteenth century, however, they did. This advance in learning, he concludes, could only have come from Islam during the twelfth century through the cultural contacts with Toledo and Cordoba in Spain and from the Crusades and the conquest of Jerusalem in 1099. The historical evidence, he suggests, shows that it was only through contact with the then highly developed civilization of Islam that the full works of Plato, Aristotle and Euclid were rediscovered and that it was the translation of these, disseminated mainly through the schools of Paris and Chartres, which initiated a cultural renaissance in northern France. The rise of Gothic architecture, was, he concludes, the most spectacular result of this.[16]

The master masons of Chartres were inspired and also instructed by the philosophy and sacred geometry taught at the Platonic School at Chartres that was founded in the eleventh century by a remarkable bishop called Fulbert and renowned all over Europe as a centre of learning. For scholars like Fulbert and Abbot Suger, inspired by the writings of Plato, it was the unseen realm of the metaphysical that was the real world and the material world, marvellous as it was, the shadow or copy of the divine one.[17]

Strachan believes that there is also evidence of the strong influence of Islam and the skills of Muslim workmen in Chartres and it is possible that a group of workmen returned from Jerusalem with the Crusaders and spent many years in France.[18] What is evident from the overall plan of Chartres and the sublime elements of its construction is that its builders — architects, sculptors, artists and designers — may have drawn their inspiration from learning how to enter into the world of the Soul, seeing in their imagination the prototype of what they wished to bring into being in the town that had been a sacred site for millennia.

The Rose as a Symbol of the Soul

The origins of the sacredness of the rose may be traced to the beautiful eight-year orbital pattern made by the planet Venus. It was from ancient times associated with the Great Goddesses of the ancient world: Isis, Aphrodite, Cybele, Venus and, later, the Virgin Mary and the rosary. In medieval Europe, the rose and the enclosed garden became a symbol of the soul as well as a place for lovers to meet. But more than that, it was the symbol of the greater Soul of the Cosmos in which the human soul was contained. The rose is also one of the oldest symbols of the Wisdom Tradition and of Wisdom herself radiating love to our world from the divine ground. Like the thousand-petalled lotus or the jewel in the heart of the lotus of the Eastern traditions, the rose came to symbolize the awakened soul, united with the divine ground, as in Dante's great vision of the white rose of the Empyrean. The rosary was sometimes called 'the rose garden' and Mary herself was spoken of as 'The Garden' (of Paradise) and also as the 'Rose without a Thorn' or the 'Peerless Rose'.[19] Mary was known in the Middle Ages — the time of the building of Chartres — as the *Rosa Mystica*. To find the shape of the rose so emphasized in the three great rose windows of Chartres and other Gothic cathedrals suggests that the symbolism of the rose held great significance for its builders. I knew none of this when I was haunted long ago by the words of a poem by Walter de la Mare, "O no man knows through what wild centuries roves back the rose".

The Garden as a Metaphor of the Soul

People often use the word 'soul' when they speak of a piece of music they love: a marvellous building like Chartres; a beautiful garden or a beloved person. Soul is a specific quality or radiance that people recognize as touching their heart. Anyone who has worked in a garden and seen the response of nature to his efforts, perhaps over many years of labour, will have felt the presence of soul in every leaf and flower. From earliest recorded times in every great civilization, in Egypt, in Persia and India, in China, in Roman times and in medieval and Renaissance Europe, people have created gardens as sanctuaries for the purpose of contemplation and communion, and for repose, enjoyment and delight. The rose garden in twelfth century Europe as well as in Sufi mysticism became a replica of Paradise, and the fountain or well at the centre, a symbol of the water of life flowing from the divine world. It is difficult to say when the garden became a metaphor for the soul and a sacred space for connection with the unseen world, but it is certainly found in the mystical streams of Christianity, Islam, Judaism and Taoism. In the tradition of Kabbalah, the Shekinah is often addressed as 'the Garden', and the wedding of the two aspects of the godhead — the Holy One and His Beloved — takes place in a garden of pomegranates, symbol of the innermost chamber of the soul.

From earliest times we have paintings of gardens and even (as in Egypt and Persia) of gardeners working in them. The gardens of Moorish Spain in the ninth century, in towns like Cordoba, Granada and Seville, were renowned for their beauty and tranquillity, as were the later gardens of Italy and those of Persia and Moghul India. Further to the East, there were the temple gardens of China and Japan. But the monasteries of Europe, such as that of Monte Cassino in Italy, also fostered the art of creating gardens as sanctuaries for prayer and contemplation as well as cultivating fruit and vegetables to feed the monastic community, and these had a fountain, well or tree at the centre, perhaps a residual memory from earlier shamanic cultures of the sacred space acting as a portal between the two worlds. Herb gardens were cultivated in these monasteries and the monks became skilled at using their fragrant essences to heal many illnesses. Gardens were always places which attracted birds as well as the bees gathering the nectar of flowers and plants to transform into honey. Here, a life of contemplation could flourish like the plants and the birds, protected from the turmoil and violence of the world. We may recall the words of Rumi:

> *When the rose is gone and the rose-garden fallen to ruin,*
> *Where will you seek the scent of the rose?*

The Many Dimensions of Reality and the Great Chain of Being

The ancient Wisdom Traditions tell us that we and our world are woven into a cosmic tapestry whose threads connect us not only with many dimensions of reality but with multitudes of beings inhabiting those dimensions. Beyond the present confines of our sight a limitless field of consciousness interacts with our own. They tell us that a great nested chain of being extends from the ineffable light source of the divine ground to our world, the densest level of physical manifestation. In the New Testament, Jesus may be referring to this multiplicity of dimensions when he says, "In My Father's House there are many mansions" (John 14.2). The deepest ground of reality which contains all other dimensions was known to the Gnostics in the early years of the Christian era as the *Pleroma*, the root of all, present within all yet beyond all — a boundless, indefinable, transcendent dimension which nevertheless permeates our world in the way that sunlight permeates air.

It may be helpful to imagine the whole universe as an unimaginably fine web of life holding three levels or planes of reality in relationship with each other, two of which are invisible to us and none of which is separate from the others.

- The plane of Eternal Spirit, the ground of pure Light beyond all form
- The intermediate plane of the many subtle realms of Soul connecting matter and spirit
- The plane of Earth and the visible material universe.

The first two realms of Spirit and Soul are filled with multiple concentric belts, spheres or zones of matter far finer than the composition of our world and varying in vibratory frequency. These planes are not separate from each other or from the plane of material reality. They interpenetrate each other but we cannot see the finer levels with our 'ordinary' vision nor, so far, with our scientific instruments although, in their encounter with dark matter and the Higgs boson field, they may be touching on them. They could be described as multiple nested fields of different grades of consciousness and different vibrational intensities held within a unifying Field, Ground or Web of Light. These spheres interact with our world and can influence us here in ways of which we are not aware. The worlds or spheres which make up this immeasurable realm of 'Soul' surround every planet in the solar system and possibly many of the galaxies. They may be part of other universes which interact with ours.

As will be explained in Chapter Nineteen, countless billions of souls inhabit these invisible spheres or zones of reality. We may wonder why none of this is known to our world. The answer is that it has been known to different metaphysical traditions and is described in the mass of evidence that now exists coming from 'the other side' but humanity as a whole has remained largely ignorant of it and will remain so until such time as the existence of these unseen dimensions of reality becomes more widely known, possibly through the discoveries of science but also through people's own experiences.

From the beginning of recorded history, and no doubt long before that, the greatest poets, shamans and visionaries, as well as artists, musicians and mystics of all cultures have connected us to this deep ground of Soul. They have connected the seen to the unseen, the time-bound world to the eternal, the waking mind to the dreaming soul. We know from the writings of the Sufi mystics that they have entered this intermediate world of psychic reality and have described it as a plane of reality similar to our world down to the finest detail but of a greater intensity of beauty, colour and exquisite form. It is composed of matter, but etherealised matter, without the density of the matter of our world. They called it "Celestial Earth" and they recognized our terrestrial world as a manifestation of this unseen world of Soul, seeing its beauty and majesty reflected in the deep forests of the earth, the snow-capped mountains, the depth and vast expanse of the sea, the dazzling immensity of the star-strewn night sky. From century to century, as links in a great golden chain, they kept alive the reality of the Soul's existence and the true values of the Soul — the values that honour and celebrate the wonder, sacredness and awesome mystery of life.

Whether we look at the ancient cosmologies of Egypt, India, Persia, China or Tibet or the tradition of Kabbalah, we find a description of subtle worlds or dimensions of reality beyond this material world and of beings inhabiting those worlds. Angels and archangels abound in the Old and New Testaments and adorn the great cathedrals of Europe. Kabbalists taught that there are four separate worlds that interpenetrate and interact with each other; each governed by archangelic and angelic beings and each a portal to a multitude of other worlds or dimensions. We find the nine celestial hierarchies known to the mystical Christian tradition, through the writings of the monk Dionysius, sculpted on the south porch of Chartres Cathedral above the seated figure of Christ, but unless a guide points them out we might not register their presence or understand their significance.

In the sixteenth century, the kabbalist Joseph Cordovero named thirteen gates to higher consciousness. In India for millennia the practice of Kundalini Yoga offered a method of enabling our limited consciousness to evolve to higher or deeper levels of perception and the experience of invisible worlds. Mahayana Buddhism teaches that there are three interpenetrating realities: this material world, a subtle intermediary soul world and finally, the formless world of pure spirit named the Clear Light of the Void. All these traditions teach that contemplation and specific exercises prepare us for the encounter with these transcendent realities. In the intermediate world of Soul are held all the memories of human experience — memories which may be said to correspond with the collective unconscious of Jung and the World of Formation (Yetzirah) of Kabbalah.

These memories are known to Hindu cosmology as the Akashic records — Akasha being the name of the limitless field in which they are held. The fact that our consciousness can be expanded to awareness of vast planetary and cosmic memory fields has been proven through the methods of holotropic breathing developed and recorded through thousands of sessions by the psychiatrist Stanislav Grof.[20] These transcendent worlds or dimensions of consciousness become accessible through subjective experiences which are not yet accepted by science yet this does not mean they do not exist. They are not so much 'places' as we might imagine them; rather they are 'states of being'. The Metaphysical Traditions confirm that we are living within subtle fields of reality which are imperceptible to our 'normal' level of consciousness and the instruments so far devised by science.

Cosmic Soul and Science

As the last chapter has shown, we are experiencing a profound paradigm shift as we move from seeing the universe as a lifeless machine to seeing it as a unified and living organism in whose life we participate as co-creators with it. Duane Elgin describes the paradigm shift in these words:

> Our actual identity or experience of who we are is vastly bigger than we thought — we are moving from a strictly personal consciousness to a conscious appreciation of ourselves as integral to the cosmos…. In this new paradigm, our sense of identity takes on a paradoxical and mysterious quality: We are both observer and observed, knower and that which is known. We are each completely unique yet completely connected with the entire universe…. Awakening to the miraculous nature of our identity as simultaneously unique and interconnected with a living universe can help us overcome the species-arrogance and sense of separation that threaten our future.[21]

Concepts like David Bohm's Implicate Order and his understanding of the universe as a "sea of being" and as an undivided whole, reanimate ancient ideas of the Cosmos as a great web of life, in which no part can be seen as intrinsically separate from any other. With Rupert Sheldrake's hypothesis of morphic fields, we are offered an understanding of how all the forms of our world come into being. There is also the mystery of dark matter and the Higgs boson field mentioned in the last chapter. Deno Kazanis, author of *The Reintegration of Science and Spirituality*, believes that scientists may actually be stumbling upon the subtle energy bodies that mystics have spoken of for millennia:

> Our ability to see, touch, taste, smell, and hear the world is really only due to atoms' electric charge. And because objects on the atomic level interact through electric forces, if there's no such force present, then objects can literally pass right through each other.... What intrigues me is that dark matter, being invisible and not able to produce light or any type of electromagnetic waves, means that this is a substance that is not composed of any electric charge... Its presence is determined by its gravity, which is an enormous amount, yet the material itself is totally invisible. So it occurred to me that when the mystics were talking about subtle bodies interpenetrating with our visible body, the only way that could be possible would be if these bodies were made up of something other than charged matter. And dark matter would fit that category quite well.

It seems that there have been many names for this unseen ground. Light is the primary image which connects the worlds of science and metaphysics. Science would be enormously assisted in all that it is discovering if it were aware of and could accept the validity of the metaphysical traditions. It could bring things together that have been separated for centuries through a failure to recognize the essential relationship of spirit and matter.

The Eye of the Heart: The Soul's Organ of Perception

As long as science tries to locate the soul in the physical brain and approaches the soul as an object to be observed through the instruments created by the mind, it will not be able to understand the soul either in the personal sense or in the wider cosmic aspect to which Heraclitus was referring. It will not understand the source of revelatory experience. Nor will it be able to answer the metaphysical questions which have preoccupied the greatest intellects of previous ages: questions of who we are, why we are here and what our relationship to the Cosmos might be. An understanding of the soul can only be recovered through what has been called the eye of the heart.

The heart is the soul's organ of perception. It has its own kind of consciousness, its own deeply instinctive way of knowing, just as the mind has its own way of knowing. It acts as a kind of umbilical cord connecting us to all life on this planet and to the greater life of the Cosmos. The heart is the source of our creative imagination, born of our instinct for relationship with that life. The heart generates our quests, our hopes and longings and will ultimately reunite us with the source from which we have come. Without the heart, without the instinct to imagine, to feel, to hope and to love, life is meaningless, sterile, dead. When we are in touch with our deepest instincts, feelings and intuitions it comes alive, it vibrates, it sings. Music, poetry, beauty, close loving relationships, inspiring ideas, magnificent, thrilling achievements like those of the Olympic athletes — all these nourish the heart and each of them is as essential to the soul in this dimension as food is to the body. What part of the body do you touch when someone asks "Where is the seat of your feeling?" Most people instinctively touch the area of their heart.

What exactly is the eye of the heart? I have found the clearest description of it in three books written by an Episcopalian priest called Cynthia Bourgeault. In them she explains the essential teaching of the Christian Wisdom Tradition about the transformation of consciousness. The eye of the heart, as she describes it, *is an organ of spiritual perception.* Learning how to develop this organ can help us to move into the different understanding of reality, the different worldview that I have attempted to describe in earlier chapters where I speak of a Sacred Order.

As the eye of the heart develops, so we become aware of the presence of the invisible dimension and discover how to align our consciousness with it as with an invisible partner, acting in this world from a sense of connection and attunement with that Other without in any way diminishing the importance and validity of experience in this world. The eye of the heart, as Cynthia Bourgeault describes it, is a "vibrant resonant field, that functions like a homing beacon between the realms; and when it is strong and clear, it creates a synchronous resonance between them".[22]

> The ancient Wisdom Traditions all saw that the physical world we take for our empirical, time-and-space-bound reality is encompassed in another: a coherent and powerful world of divine purpose always surrounding and interpenetrating it. This other, more subtle world is invisible to the senses, and to the mind it appears to be pure speculation. But if the eye of the heart is awake and clear, it can receive, radiate and reflect that divine Reality.[23]

We can learn to focus our consciousness on the eye of the heart as the door to the soul, and imagine two lines meeting there: the vertical line of eternity and the horizontal line of this world of time. As we learn how to develop the eye of the heart, we begin to live through a different focus, so that we become increasingly in touch with that deeper level of reality. Bringing the dissociated surface mind into harmony and balance with the deeper ground of the soul could change our beliefs, our lives and our culture. A beautiful quotation from the twelfth century reminds us of the importance of focusing on that point where the worlds of time and eternity meet, the point that is the meeting place of our soul with the eternal ground: "All that is moved is subject to time, but it is from eternity that all contained in the vastness of time is born and into eternity that it is to be resolved."[24]

It has long been known that we have undeveloped faculties that are beyond the reach of the rational mind — even that there are large areas of the physical brain that are not used. As Jung discovered and as many followers of Kabbalah, Vedanta and Sufism have known for centuries, the power of the imagination and proven methods of connection can be used to create a bridge to the unseen worlds. As Bourgeault describes it: "When... the vibrational field of a particular human heart comes into spontaneous resonance with the divine heart itself, then finite and infinite become a single, continuous wavelength, and authentic communion becomes possible. Bridging the created and uncreated realms within a human being, it is both a realm in itself and the means by which this realm makes itself known."[25]

The great Flemish mystic, Jan van Ruysbroeck put it in these words: "Unity is this: that a man feel himself to be gathered together with all his powers in the unity of his heart. Unity brings inward peace and restfulness of heart. Unity of heart is a bond which draws together body and soul, heart and senses, and all the outward and inward powers and encloses them in the union of love."[26]

As the relationship between our individual soul and the eternal ground of life grows stronger, so we become more aware of its voice, its presence and its subtle guidance. A deepening relationship with this ground can become the inner fabric and focus of our lives. It is an alchemy that we can weave into being with our attention, developing insight through our longing for understanding and relationship with it. If this path into the depth of ourselves is gently followed, we no longer live life unconsciously, responding blindly to events as they happen. We remain in touch with the invisible and receive increasing guidance from it, even as we interact with the visible.

Whoever ventures into the deepest realm of the Soul, will discover, as T.S. Eliot did, that "the end of all our exploring will be to arrive where we started and know the place for the first time".[27] She will know that each line of poetry that has stirred the reeds of longing, each image of beauty and fragment of what was felt to be truth has served to reveal, little by little, a Presence that has taken humanity countless millennia to discover, yet has always been there, awaiting the moment of recognition. The measure of commitment that is asked of us by the Soul in return for her gift of wisdom and guidance may be only gradually revealed, but the inscription on the lead casket chosen by Bassanio, in the hope of winning the hand of Portia, says it all:

Who chooseth me must give and hazard all he hath.[28]

The Greater Self, Presence and Guide

Every spiritual tradition speaks of the spirit guide, the hidden presence, the daemon, the angelic messenger, the revelatory voice. The tradition of the spirit guide is very ancient and originates with shamanic cultures. As we become more aware of that deeper reality within us and around us, it is more able to make us aware that we are not alone, as the wonderful story of Tobias and the Archangel Raphael in the *Apocrypha* illustrates. In that story, Tobias did not recognize the true nature of his companion until the end of his journey when Raphael revealed himself to him and to his father — whose sight he had just restored — saying, "I am Raphael, one of the seven holy angels which present the prayers of the saints, and which go in and out before the glory of the Holy One" (Tobit 12:15). There are many synchronicities in our lives, many messages from the realm of spirit that go unnoticed until our focus changes and we begin to attune our consciousness to it.

In Christianity, there has always been a strong tradition of guidance and protection from angels. One has only to look at the great angels portrayed in the medieval sculptures or stained glass of Gothic cathedrals and the paintings of the early Renaissance to see how alive this tradition still was for the people of Europe at that time. It has been lost to our culture because we have banished the radiant emissaries of the divine ground. So we might concur with Rilke in the second of his *Duino Elegies*, when he exclaims, "Oh where are the days of Tobias, when one supremely shining stood on the simple threshold, a little disguised for the journey, no longer terrifying...."

The teaching of the spirit guide is equally strong in Islamic culture, particularly in Sufism where the world of the Soul was a known reality. Henri Corbin, the great scholar of Sufism, writes that

> Some souls have learned everything from invisible guides, known only to them-selves.... The ancient sages... taught that for each individual soul, or perhaps a number of souls with the same nature and affinity, there is a being of the spiritual world, who, throughout their existence, adopts a special solicitude and

tenderness toward that soul or group of souls; it is he who initiates them into knowledge, protects, guides, defends, comforts them.[29]

My own life experience has taught me that we can receive help, inspiration and guidance from the cosmic ground that has brought our consciousness into being over aeons of time and holds all of us in its embrace. Although there are periods of intense darkness and depression that the alchemists called the '*nigredo*', and Christian mystics the Dark Night of the Soul, with the patient work of establishing a connection and in moments of sudden insight and illumination, we can experience the presence of that ground and develop the ability to listen to its guidance. What is it in us that urges us to grow beyond ourselves? Who is it who knows the end when we can only see the beginning, the form of the oak when we only see the acorn? What helps us when it seems no help is to be found? Is this all our own doing? Or are we within a Consciousness, a Presence, greater than our own limited consciousness, which is slowly, laboriously, awakening us to awareness of itself?

The poet Yeats speaks of this Presence in his autobiography, *The Trembling of the Veil*: "I know that revelation is from the self, but from that age-long memoried self, that shapes the elaborate shell of the mollusc and the child in the womb, and that teaches the birds to make their nest; and I know that genius is a crisis that joins that buried self for certain moments to our trivial daily mind."

All spiritual traditions have recorded the words of the great teachers of humanity whose teaching comes to them from that source-ground. In Christianity, the connection with this ground is mediated by the figures of Jesus and the Virgin Mary; in Buddhism by the great avatars of the Buddha and the goddess Tara; in Hinduism by Krishna; in Taoism by Lao Tzu and the enlightened Taoist sages; and in Islam by Mohammed, its greatest Sufi mystics and the figure of al Khidr, known as 'The Green One'. The divine ground itself has variously been described as the Tao, as Brahman, as God or Allah, as the Void, as the Holy One and His Shekinah. This divine ground is within us as well as all around us. We need to create a sanctuary within ourselves where we can listen to its guidance and receive its help.

Two thousand years ago, at the beginning of the Piscean Age, Jesus, as a fully awakened man, an emissary from the higher spheres of the Cosmos, taught his disciples the path of inner transformation — how to awaken the eye of the heart and to live through that awakened eye by building a bridge, moment by moment, day by day, between the visible and invisible worlds. But Christianity lost that teaching and became an institution which emphasized belief and belonging to the Church as the way to God rather than the transformation of consciousness and awakening to the presence of a living transcendent reality. As Cynthia Bourgeault says, "Like a river bank that is eroded when a river changes its course, so the Christian Wisdom tradition about awakening the eye of the heart and the transformation of consciousness was steadily eroded and finally washed away."[30] The distinction Christianity drew between the Divine Creator and fallen creation, deeply injured both God and man.

Jesus opened our awareness to our divinity and the change of consciousness that accompanies the creation of a relationship with that hidden ground. Why did he ask us to love one another and to be reconciled with our enemies? Was it because, as an emissary of the Divine Ground, he understood the sacred nature of the whole manifest order? Why did he say, "Ye are gods, sons of the Most High, all of you" (John 10:34) unless he knew that all of us have the potential of bringing forth the divinity latent within us through a direct and growing relationship with the source-ground that he called 'The Father'? Why, in the enigmatic saying in the Gnostic Gospel of Thomas (*logion* 77) did he say, "Cleave the wood and I am there; lift up a stone and you will find Me there" if not to point to the fact that nature and matter rest on the ground of spirit; that in their essence, they are spirit?

The revelation that he brought and that his disciples at first found so hard to comprehend was of opening the heart to awareness of the unity and divinity of life, and therefore, to love and compassion for all. Jesus himself lived his life from the values and wisdom intrinsic to that perception of reality. This astonishing revelation, this seeing truly into the hidden reality behind the forms of life, living in full awareness of and connection with it while in this earthly dimension, is the pearl of great price, the treasure in the field, the grain of mustard seed which, tiny at the beginning when it is first planted in the soil of the soul, can grow into a mighty tree, hung with the fruit of insight, wisdom and compassion.[31] The beautiful words recorded in the Gnostic Acts of John spoken by Jesus on the eve of his Passion often come back to me and I have silently spoken them to myself in moments of doubt or depression:

> *I am a lamp to you who behold Me;*
> *I am a mirror to you who perceive Me;*
> *I am a door to you who knock at Me;*
> *I am a way to you a wayfarer.*
> *You have me for a bed; rest then upon Me.*[32]

There are many passages in *The Mystic Vision* which bear witness to the guidance or presence of the divine ground but I particularly love these words of Bede Griffiths:

Each man must discover this Centre in himself, this Ground of his being, this

Law of his life. It is hidden in the depths of every soul, waiting to be discovered. It is the treasure hidden in a field, the pearl of great price. It is the one thing which is necessary, which can satisfy all our desires and answer all our needs. But it is hidden now under deep layers of habit and convention. The world builds up a great protective barrier round it.[33]

Sri Aurobindo, the great Indian teacher of the last century, speaks of the process of awakening to the presence and guidance of the soul in these words:

As the crust of our outer nature cracks, as the walls of inner separation break down, the inner light gets through, the inner fire burns in the heart, the substance of the nature and stuff of consciousness refines to a greater subtlety and purity and the deeper psychic experiences become possible in this subtler, purer, finer substance; the soul begins to unveil itself, the psychic personality reaches its full stature. The soul then manifests itself as the central being which upholds mind and life and body.... It takes up its greater function as the guide and ruler of our nature.[34]

The growing relationship with the eternal ground can change the quality of our lives, giving them a deeper resonance, a different focus. Relationship with the soul brings us into closer relationship with the whole of life. Anxiety and depression, for which we seek treatment through so many drugs and therapies, diminish. Through this transformation, so gradual and subtle that it is almost imperceptible, our perception of the world is transformed.

A different and more profound meaning to life comes into being. If we realize we are living within a Sacred Order, we find a more profound context for relationships and for changing our habits of behaviour, both as individuals and as nations and societies, which can help us to resolve many challenging problems in our lives and in the wider world.

Ultimately, what in the beginning was perceived as separate — inner and outer; myself and other; human and divine — begins to fuse and become a unity: one life, one consciousness, one unified whole. It used to be thought that we could not become 'spiritual' without sacrificing the life of the body, embracing a celibate life. The idea of celibacy as the way to the spirit was a fundamental error, derived from the split between mind and body which was so deeply imprinted by the polarizing beliefs of the solar age. The body is to be loved and cherished because it is the vehicle of the soul in this dimension of reality.

Each person can find his or her path with the help of others who have gone before, or through connecting with people who are teaching methods of awakening. Deep soul friendships can be formed. One of the greatest rewards is finding friends through the mysterious connecting and attracting power of the soul, now wonderfully facilitated by the Internet. Remarkable activist organizations like Avaaz (www.avaaz.com) are gathering tens of millions of people to speak with one voice to bring into being a different world ruled by different values. They are creating something at a planetary level similar to the cosmic Net of Indra. I found this beautiful passage in the introduction by Christopher Bamford to a book by Alice Howell called *The Dove in the Stone*:

> There is a path of love and knowledge to which the West is heir. Once on this path, the pilgrim is no longer alone, but in a visionary company of "friends of God".... This prophetic religion of Sophia, forever moved by love and beauty, is a living transmission and a perpetual renaissance; it has no formal church or earthly institution, but is revealed only in the hearts and minds of human beings. Of the spirit, it is present whenever two or three are gathered together in the service of the ensouling of the world — of the return of the soul to God by way of the soul's return to her true self.[35]

We are awakening to awareness that we and the phenomenal world are woven into a cosmic tapestry whose threads connect us not only with each other at the deepest level but with the divine ground of life. Beyond our present time-bound sight a limitless field of consciousness interacts with our own, asking to be recognized by us, embraced by us. The realization that we participate in a multi-dimensional reality that is the source and ground of our own being may eventually shatter the belief that this material reality is all there is; that we exist on a tiny planet in a lifeless universe and that there is no life beyond death. It may be that the Soul of the Cosmos has waited aeons for us to reach the point where more than a handful of individuals could awaken to awareness of the ground that animates and supports the whole of our existence. As we begin to relate to the intelligent Spirit that informs the whole, we begin to align ourselves with that greater life, like a planet orbiting the sun.

In 1841, the American philosopher Ralph Waldo Emerson wrote these beautiful words which are a fitting end to this chapter:

> We live in succession, in division, in parts, in particles. Meantime within man is the soul of the whole; the wise silence; the universal beauty, to which every part and particle is equally related, the eternal ONE. And this deep power in which we exist and whose beatitude is all accessible to us, is not only self-sufficing and perfect in every hour, but the act of seeing and the thing seen, the seer and the spectacle, the subject and the object, are one. We see the world piece by piece, as the sun, the moon, the animal, the tree; but the whole, of which these are shining parts, is the soul.[36]

Notes:

1. Jung, C.G. (1964) *Man and His Symbols*, p. 102
2. Jefferies, Richard (1947) *The Story of My Heart*, Constable & Co. Ltd., London, p. 46-7
3. Jefferies, pp. 20-21
4. Laszlo, Ervin & Currivan, Jude (2008) *CosMos, A Co-creator's Guide to the Whole-World*, p. 50
5. Crook, Francis H. (1977) *Hua-yen Buddhism: The Jewel Net of Indra*, Pennsylvania State University, p. 2
6. Suzuki, Daisetz Teitaro (1930) *Studies in the Lankavarara Sutra*, Google Books, p. 95
7. Crook, p. 9
8. ibid, p. 122
9. Vaughan-Lee, Llewellyn (2010) *The Return of the Feminine and the World Soul* The Golden Sufi Press, California
10. See his great work *Creative Imagination in the Sufism of Ibn Arabi*, Bollingen, Princeton, 1969
11. Anderson, William (1995) *The Rise of the Gothic*, Huchinson Ltd., London, p. 83
12. ibid, p. 85
13. Strachan, Gordon (2003) *Chartres: Sacred Geometry, Sacred Space*, Floris Books, Edinburgh
14. Critchlow, Keith (2003) *Chartres Cathedral: A Sacred Geometry*, DVD, Jansen Media
15. Anderson, p. 131
16. Strachan, pp. 16-17
17. ibid, p. 38
18. ibid, pp. 28-32
19. There are two wonderful and rare books about the rose and the rose garden: Eithne Wilkins, *The Rose Garden Game*, Gollancz, London, 1969. And Seonaid Robertson, *Rose Garden and Labyrinth – a Study in Art Education*, Routledge and Kegan Paul, London,1963.
20. Grof, Stanislav with Bennett, Hal Zina (1993) *The Holotropic Mind: Three levels of Human Consciousness and How They Shape Our Lives*, HarperCollins, New York
21. Elgin, Duane (2007) from his chapter in *Mind Before Matter: Visions of New Science of Consciousness*, O Books, Ropley, UK
22. Bourgeault (2010) *The Meaning of Mary Magdalene*, Shambhala Publications Inc., Boston, p. 51
23. Bourgeault, *The Wisdom Way of Knowing*, p. 35
24. Sylvester, Bernardus *Cosmographia*, in Anderson, The Rise of the Gothic, p. 23
25. Bourgeault, *The Meaning of Mary Magdalene*, p. 61
26. Ruysbroeck, Jan van *The Adornment of the Spiritual Marriage*
27. T.S. Eliot, *Four Quartets*
28. *The Merchant of Venice*
29. Abu'l Barahat, in Henri Corbin, *Creative imagination in the Sufism of Ibn Arabi*, p. 34
30. Bourgeault, *The Wisdom Way of Knowing*, p. 20
31. To grasp the depth, breadth and beauty of the Aramaic language Jesus spoke, I would recommend the books of Neil Douglas-Klotz, among them *Prayers of the Cosmos: Meditations on the Aramaic Words of Jesus*.

32. Mead, G.R.S. (1906 & 1931) *The Gnostic Acts of John in Fragments of a Faith Forgotten*, p. 431
33. Griffiths, Dom Bede (1976) *Return to the Centre*, Collins, St. James's Place, London and Templegate, Springfield, Ill. 1977
34. Aurobindo, Sri (1990) *The Life Divine*, Lotus Light Publications, Wilmot, WI.
35. Bamford, Christopher (1988) from the Foreword to Alice O. Howell's *The Dove in the Stone*, Quest Books, Wheaton, Ohio
36. Emerson, Ralph Waldo (1841) *The Over-soul*, Ninth Essay

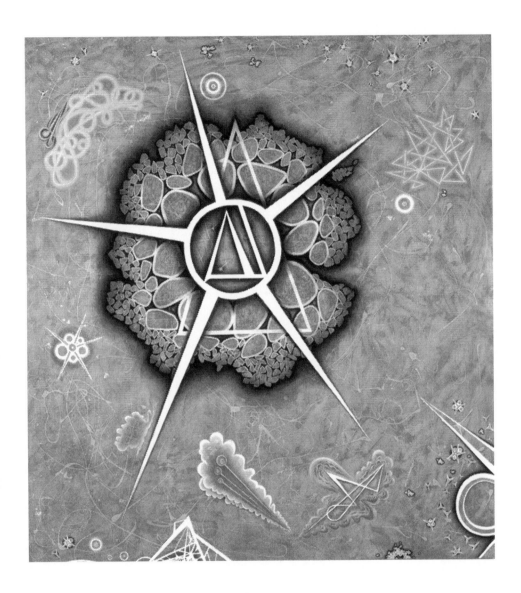

Cosmos
Robin Baring 1980

Chapter Sixteen

INSTINCT AND THE BODY
AS A MANIFESTATION OF THE SOUL

Man has no Body distinct from his Soul for that call'd Body is a portion of Soul discern'd by the five Senses, the chief inlets of Soul in this age.

— William Blake, from *The Marriage of Heaven and Hell*

People say that what we are seeking is a meaning for life.... I think that what we're seeking is an experience of being alive, so that our life experiences on the purely physical plane will have resonances within our innermost being and reality, so that we actually feel the rapture of being alive.

— Joseph Campbell, *The Power of Myth*

The soul is not in the body; the body is in the soul.

— Meister Eckhart

I have always liked the story of Androcles and the Lion because it illustrates so clearly how healing the wounds the instinct carries brings rich rewards in the arena of life:

Androcles was a Roman slave who had been taken to North Africa. He tried to escape to the coast and return to Rome. He knew that if he were caught he would be killed, so he waited until the nights were dark and moonless before creeping out of his master's house and stealing through the town into the open country. He hurried as fast as he could but when day broke he found that instead of reaching the sea coast, as he had hoped, he was in a desert. Seeing a cave in the side of some cliffs, he crept into it, lay down and very soon fell asleep. He was awakened by a terrible roaring and to his horror, saw a huge lion standing at the entrance to the cave. Androcles had been sleeping in the lion's den. There was no escape. The great lion barred the way.

Androcles waited for the lion to spring on him and kill him but it did not move. Instead, it moaned and licked one of its paws that seemed to be bleeding. Seeing that the animal was in great pain, Androcles forgot his terror and came forward. The lion held up its paw, as if asking for help. Androcles then saw that a great thorn had become embedded in the paw which had cut it and made it swell. He drew the thorn out with a quick movement. Relieved of pain, the grateful lion licked its paw, then limped out of the cave, and in a few minutes returned with a dead rabbit, which it laid at Androcles's feet. When Androcles had managed to light a fire and cooked and eaten the rabbit, the lion led him to a spring of fresh water gushing out of the earth.

For three years, man and lion lived in the cave, but at last Androcles began to crave the society of his fellow men. He left the cave but was soon caught by some soldiers and sent as a fugitive slave to Rome. There he was condemned to be killed by wild beasts in the Colosseum on the first public holiday.

A vast multitude of spectators came to see the sight, including the Emperor. Androcles was pushed into the great open space and a lance was thrust into his hand. With this, he was told, he was to defend himself against the powerful lion which had been kept for days without food to make it savage and fierce. Androcles trembled when the ravenous lion sprang out of its cage with a terrible roar, and the lance shook in his grasp as the great beast came bounding up to him. But instead of knocking him to the ground with a blow of its paw, it began to lick his hands. Androcles saw to his amazement that it was the same lion with which he had lived in the wilderness. He patted it and, leaning on its head, he cried. All the spectators marvelled at the strange scene and the Emperor sent for Androcles, asking him for an explanation. He was so delighted with the story that he made Androcles a free man.

Androcles had two encounters with the lion: the first was in the wilderness, the lion's domain; the second in the Roman arena, symbolically the arena of life. There are, even in this children's tale, undertones of heroic myth telling the story of the man who makes the journey into the wilderness of his soul, there to be reconciled with the instinctual powers symbolized by the lion, whose wound he heals. He makes the return journey into the world where, in the challenging arena of life, instead of having his life destroyed by the wounded and enraged animal, he has its support and friendship. To make friends with the lion and take the thorn out of its paw is to receive the protection and guidance of the instinctual powers of the soul.

Many people pass their lives in a state of slavery to misery, illness and depression, or to circumstances they loathe and feel imprisoned by, or in a state of hatred and resentment against something or someone they feel has injured them. These powerful emotions are symbolized by the wounded lion with the great thorn in its paw. If the thorn is not removed, it is likely that the lion will become dangerous. The lives of countless people are affected, even destroyed, by the enraged and wounded lion that is condemned to roam the wilderness beyond our conscious awareness. People can pose a threat to others, particularly children, because of their power to hurt and destroy them. Countless atrocities are committed by the enraged lion within us. We have, so to speak, been sleeping in the lion's den, like Androcles. The different forms of addiction prevalent in our culture are symptoms of an inability to relate to the instinct, a lack of understanding as to what its needs are and why, when these are not attended to, it can drive us into destructive life patterns.

If there is nothing to help us develop insight into this foundation of our lives, there is no way in which its voice can reach us. Nor can we be enriched and developed by a relationship with something that is infinitely more powerful than our conscious mind. Cut off from our instincts, we become impoverished and diminished. A vital part of us has no means of gaining our attention except through breakdown, addiction and disruptive or violent patterns of behaviour.

An extraordinary photograph, published in the newspapers on January 13th, 2007, showed a lion reaching through the bars of its cage to embrace a woman, giving her what looked like a passionate kiss on the lips. Its two paws were tenderly wrapped around her neck, its eyes were shut and it looked, for all the world, as if it were in a state of bliss. The woman, Ana Julia Torres, is a teacher who lives in Columbia. She had rescued this African lion, called Jupiter, from a circus where it had been mistreated and nursed him back to health. Ten years ago she began to rehabilitate abused animals and now has a centre housing eight hundred lions as well as a variety of other animals. There was something intensely moving about the warmth and tenderness of the lion's spontaneous embrace and the trust in this woman who dared to invite and welcome it, stroking the lion's thick rough mane as if it were an enormous dog. It was so perfect an image of the relationship we might have with our instinct, if only we knew how to embrace it and allow it to embrace us, to love it, as in the story of Beauty and the Beast, where the fearsome beast is transformed, through Beauty's love, into a prince.

The Split between Mind and Body

In our fascination with our mind, we have not paid nearly enough attention to the importance of instinct in our lives. As the conscious mind has gained more and more autonomy and independence from the deeper matrix of instinct out of which it has evolved, the whole super-structure of consciousness has become detached from the age-old base or ground out of which it developed, rather like an iceberg breaking away from the landmass to which it belonged. This unconscious split creates great tension between the two separated aspects of the soul which finds its way into many conflicts that are acted out in our personal lives as well as in the wider arena of the world.

During the four thousand years of the solar era, as explained in Chapter Six, everything became fragmented as we lost the sense of living within a Sacred Order. As this process developed, so spirit and nature, soul and body came to be separated: our conscious mind became separated from its instinctive foundation, becoming not only fearful but also repressive of it. In splitting nature from spirit, separating body from soul, and contaminating the instincts with guilt and fear, a vital part of our nature was injured; a great wrong was done to the body and the instincts associated with it. In nearly all religious and philosophical teaching of the solar age, the body was presented as the main impediment to spirituality, something to be treated with revulsion and contempt. A deep suspicion of feeling and emotion was built into the education of the ruling class from Greek times onwards. In Christianity, the mortification of the flesh was a habit dear to saints and ascetics.

Unconsciously influenced by this way of thinking, I used to think of the soul as the 'spiritual' aspect of myself and tended to look down on the body as something inferior to spirit and to mind. It did not occur to me that the body could be the vehicle of the soul in this material dimension of reality, that it could actually be contained within the field of the soul. It may be that, because death and the decomposition of the body seem so final, it is difficult to conceive of the physical body, subject to decay, as an intrinsic aspect of the soul. Yet, as Meister Eckhart observed, "The soul is not in the body; the body is in the soul".

With the waning of the influence of religion the focus of modern culture has now swung from spirit to body and we have become obsessed with sexuality and the body, particularly the body of woman that, in our consumer society, is subjected to every kind of modification to make it more sexually attractive in order to accord with the image of woman propagated by the media. But this brings no real relationship with the body, no love of it, no real care and respect for it or awareness of its signals of distress. It suggests an alienation from instinct and an unconscious state of possession by it.

The distinction that conditions our thinking between what is spirit or spiritual and what is matter or material has influenced not only the attitudes which still govern religion and science but the way we treat our own body and the bodies of other people. Many people treat the body as a much abused servant, doing the will of its 'master', the mind. Changing this habit and beginning to see the body and matter in general as part of the Sacred Order of life invites a fundamental rethink of current attitudes to the body. A more inclusive understanding of the soul which incorporates the body as the vehicle of living or incarnating on this planet may seem strange. Yet, in its widest definition I think it is essential to understand that the soul includes, at one end of the spectrum, the body we all inhabit and, at the other, the life of the universe, including its 'body' — the matter that science is exploring. Quantum Physics is discovering how these are related to each other through one unifying, underlying ground.

Instinct as a Cosmic Power

The dream that I described in Chapter Two, where I stood at the edge of a deep gorge and saw, rising out of it, an enormous cobra-like serpent with its seven hoods spread out in a great semi-circular fan, shocked me into awareness of the importance of instinct. It was a truly electrifying apparition that aroused awe, dread and wonder in me in equal measure. In Jungian terms, its message to me was that it personified something unknown that I needed to be aware of, that I was forcefully made aware of in a manner I would never forget. In mythological terms, it was a manifestation of the fearsome serpent or dragon that guards the treasure. Without actually seeing this archetypal serpent rising out of the gorge, I don't think I would ever have come to understand instinct as something so powerfully and overwhelmingly numinous — something that is at the very root of life and the medium through which we are all connected to each other and to the life of the planet and, beyond that, to the life of the Cosmos. Even more than this, I gradually became aware that this gigantic serpent personified the instinctive intelligence active within every aspect of life, active within all species and the whole evolutionary process on this planet, leading ultimately to the development of consciousness in our species. I now believe it represents the profound instinctive intelligence of the heart that has been overlooked in the fascination with the mind and the brain.

The Myth of the Fall in the Book of Genesis describes our separation from nature and the divine world. As this myth tells us, the serpent as an image of instinct was deeply implicated in the role it played in the drama of the Garden of Eden, tempting Eve to take the apple from the Tree of Knowledge. Long before this however, it was the primary symbol associated with the Great Mother and her power to regenerate life. In this influential myth it was vilified, punished by God and condemned to bite man's heel and to be bruised and crushed by him. Unsurprisingly, in the Christian tradition, the serpent came to be viewed as a symbol of evil, even of the devil. The instincts in general, but particularly the sexual instinct, associated with the deceptive role of the serpent, came to be regarded with the deepest suspicion, fear and revulsion.

Western myths of the solar era where the hero battles with a serpent or dragon portray man in a new dominant role towards nature. Following the theme of this mythology, it was believed that the body and its 'animal' instincts had to be controlled and subjugated by the mind — a concept which derives from the Genesis myth as well as from the chain of ideas descending from Plato and later philosophers who regarded the body and its passions as inferior to the mind, needing to be mastered and controlled by it. What was physical or instinctive became identified with what was feminine: darkness and chaos were associated with the feminine and seen as antithetical and threatening to the light and order of the masculine. Matter, darkness, chaos, evil and female were equated with each other and the body and its instincts were identified with these.[1] The rationality of the mind was contrasted with the irrationality of the body and its passions. It is extremely difficult to change the imprinting of these beliefs on the collective soul of a civilization, particularly when the mythology that is at the root of them is deeply embedded in religious teaching. But it is essential to do so because the wholeness of our nature and the wholeness of spirit and soul have been injured by them.

An altogether different attitude to the instinct is found in the East where the serpent and the dragon (in China) are ubiquitous as a symbol of life's eternal power to create, destroy and regenerate itself. In my journeys through the Far East, I found the serpent most strongly represented in the magnificent temples of Angkor in Cambodia and in countless temple sculptures throughout India and south-east Asia. The Buddha is often shown seated on the coils of a gigantic serpent whose seven cobra heads fan out behind him to form a protective canopy. To have the serpent as guardian and guide rather than adversary means that the immensely powerful energy of the instinct — unconscious in us in its primordial state — has been raised to a fully enlightened state of consciousness, the state that has been realized by the greatest spiritual teachers of humanity.

This potential awakening of human consciousness was, in ancient Indian spiritual teaching, named the Path of the Serpent or, in Sanskrit, *Nagayãna*. This path, which is known to be at least four thousand years old, describes the journey of the serpent goddess *Kundalini,* the divine creative power of the universe — also known as the Serpent Fire — from the lowest *chakra* at the base of the spine to the highest *chakra* at the top of the head. Here the twin serpents representing the lunar and solar aspects of the life energy (the *Ida* and *Pingala*) unite in blissful union in the central channel — the *Sushumna* — and flower in the crown of the thousand-petalled lotus. This is truly the inner expression of the sacred marriage: its effects are manifest in a transformation of the personality. The dormant power of Consciousness to know itself in its innate divinity awakens and manifests as the fullest expression of what, in essence, it is and we are. The Sanskrit term for the awakening of Kundalini is *Shaktipat* which also means 'the bestowal of grace'. Shakti Kundalini is the power of grace, transformation and revelation. Whatever name we give it, *Kundalini* is the instinctive power of our own innate and unrecognized divinity guiding us home to the source from which we have come. It is an act of love on the part of the divine that releases the dormant potential of the instinct residing in an unconscious state within our innermost nature.[2] The long and arduous journey of consciousness from root to crown signifies its transformation from an unconscious state to the highest expression of wisdom, insight and compassion. The body, in the eastern traditions, is the container, the vessel, the locus of this process of transformation and the repository of hidden wisdom.

The fact that our consciousness is capable of awakening to cosmic consciousness has been known and attested to for millennia in the East. In the West we can find it most clearly described in the alchemical tradition (see Chapter Eighteen) and in the esoteric teaching of Kabbalah. It is also described in the experience of mystics and in Dante's masterpiece, *The Divine Comedy*, which reveals Dante's own transformation and awakening as he is guided by Beatrice — image of his soul — into the higher realms of consciousness and his ultimate vision of the celestial rose and the "love that moves the sun and the other stars".

Our consciousness, as Jung described it, is like a plant that lives on its rhizome. Its true life is invisible, hidden in the rhizome. And that rhizome is the vast realm of instinct which, as I now understand it, is the ultimate source of the wisdom we need to guide us in our journey of awakening on this planet.

The largely unconscious drives and habits of behaviour that we call instinct are a fundamental aspect of the soul's life. Instinct is not 'lower' than or inferior to consciousness; it *is* consciousness — ultimately an expression of Cosmic Consciousness. It is a mighty cosmic power which organizes the holographic patterning of life forms, the infinite fractal proliferation of itself through countless 'fields' or levels. It cannot be separated from Cosmic Soul as I have described this in the last chapter, nor can it be separated from the deep ground of Spirit. In its different varieties of expression, it is the creative fire which gives form and meaning to our life. We slowly climb the ladder of insight and understanding of this power that lives in us and through us in every cell of our being.

The whole structure of our conscious mind rests on the foundation of instinct; has developed over countless millennia out of instinct. Instinct is the original root of our feelings, our imagination, our intuition, our rational mind. It is instinct which connects us to the great web of life of this planet and beyond that, of the universe. If we reject this vital dimension of our being, we cut ourselves off from the web of life to which we belong. The greater the dissociation within our nature, the greater is the distress and disharmony in ourselves and the greater the risk that we will destroy ourselves by attacking and killing each other.

    ❧ Instinct is the origin of our emotions and of our deepest feelings and longings — of our joy and delight in life as well as our grief and loneliness, our hope and fear.

    ❧ It gives rise to the feeling that something is right or wrong, helpful or harmful, which can grow into what we call conscience and the ability to make conscious choices and exercise some measure of free will. As we become more conscious it can become our guide.

    ❧ It is the origin of our desire to create, explore and discover; and to protect, preserve and prolong life both in ourselves and others.

    ❧ It is the power which, like the force of gravity, draws us into empathic relationships and connection with others, with nature, with the cosmos.

    ❧ It is the source of our attraction to beauty, harmony, order.

    ❧ It is the origin of our desire to improve the conditions of our lives, to heal the wounds that we and our species carry, to understand who we are and where we are going.

    ❧ Above all, it is the source of our creative imagination and our creative power.

It seems that a multi-layered cosmic field organizes every life system, from the great galaxies of space to all species of life including our own. The functioning of the instinctive life of nature with all its miraculous interacting and coordinating systems is ordered on this plane of reality by invisible fields which give every species their specific form and the patterns or habits of behaviour that we name instincts. As described in Chapter Fourteen, the work of Rupert Sheldrake, particularly the latest version of *A New Science of Life* (2009) and *The Science Delusion* (2012) offers the clearest explanation of these multi-levelled morphic fields. He sees the universe as an evolving system of habits that can, on this planet, mutate into new habits as we learn new skills and develop new understanding:

> Through morphic resonance, animals and plants are connected with their predecessors. Each individual both draws upon and contributes to the collective memory of the species. Animals and plants inherit the habits of their species and of their breed. The same applies to humans. An extended understanding of heredity changes the way we think of ourselves, the influence of our predecessors, and our effects on generations yet unborn.[3]

It may seem strange to think of instinct as the primary source of our imagination but re-ordering the different categories of our experience — reconnecting the imagination with instinct as the dynamic creativity of cosmic life — draws things together that have long been separated. Imagination is that aspect or expression of instinct that communicates most readily through images, in the way Einstein saw himself riding a sunbeam to the edge of the universe and returning towards the sun — an image that led him to his Theory of Relativity.

Yeats described the imagination as a sympathy with all living beings, recalling the lost sense of *participation mystique* of shamanic cultures. Coleridge understood it as the very ground of our consciousness, of our capacity to feel, to think and create: "The primary imagination I hold to be the living power and prime agent of all human perception, a repetition in the finite mind of the eternal act of creation in the infinite I AM."[4] Imagination is a vitally important faculty of our being because it acts as a bridge relating us to all that currently lies beyond our limited consciousness. And that bridge is itself an expression of instinct.

Instinct can sometimes drive us along a life path which it has chosen for us, not necessarily one we would have chosen for ourselves. The Greeks recognized its irresistible power and called it the *daemon*. They gave the different aspects of it the names of gods and goddesses, recognizing that they could be 'taken over' by one or another of them when they fell in love or were driven to embark on war. Because instinct is the power of life itself, it can both create and destroy. It is the source of the greatest danger to us, as described in Chapters Twelve and Thirteen and also, paradoxically, the greatest wisdom as the image of the dragon guarding the treasure suggests. It can possess and delude as well as heal, guide and enlighten. Above all, perhaps, it is the power that impels us to seek the meaning of our lives, a meaning that is specific and unique to each one of us.

Viktor Frankl observed in his profoundly moving book, *Man's Search for Meaning*, that "Man's search for meaning is the primary motivation in his life."[5] As I write this I think of the remarkable life of Marie Colvin, war correspondent for the *Sunday Times*, who was killed by Syrian shell fire in February 2012 in the city of Homs. She discovered the meaning of her life in her passionate desire to bring to the awareness of the public the suffering inflicted on civilians by oppression and war. Her immense courage in pursuit of what she saw as her life's purpose led her to her tragic death but not before she had informed the world of the horrors inflicted on the people of Syria by its government. She was someone who was truly alive.

The Heart

To respond to the quest for meaning in our individual lives, to find the pathway of connection to our deepest instincts, we need to listen to our heart, to feel its presence within us, to recognize its voice. The lion in the story of Androcles is an ancient symbol of the heart and the instinctual ground of our soul. It stands for the heart's strength and courage, its intelligence, resilience and boldness, its fierce passion and compassion. As described in the last chapter, the heart is the soul's organ of perception and plays a far greater role in our lives than we realize. The heart is the key to understanding how the instinct works, how powerful and all-pervasive and amazing it is. It is through the electro-magnetic energy field of the heart that we have access to a wider energy field that connects us to each other and the greater field of the planetary organism. So, as you read this, take a moment to connect with your heart as if you were encountering it for the first time with full awareness of its importance.

There have been discoveries in the field of neurocardiology that do not reach the general public and are, in the words of Joseph Chilton Pearce, far more awesome than the discovery of nonlocality in quantum physics. He noted that Rudolf Steiner observed over a century ago that the greatest discovery of 20th century science would be that the heart is not a pump but vastly more, and that we need to allow the heart to teach us to think in a new way.[6]

The heart is not only a pump circulating blood around the body. Speaking in purely physiological terms, the heart is now known to be another 'brain': an organ that is a centre of intelligence and consciousness as important, if not more important, than the brain that we associate with our mind. It is now thought that the heart is the main organ in the body that coordinates the functioning of the autonomic nervous system, the immune system and the endocrine system and that the heart communicates continuously with the brain. As summarized by the Institute of HeartMath in Boulder Creek, California, "The heart communicates with the brain in four ways: neurologically, (through the transmission of nerve impulses), biochemically (via hormones and neurotransmitters), biophysically (through pulse waves) and energetically (through the interactions of their electro-magnetic fields)."[7] Cardiologists call this whole system the 'heart brain'. These four different transmitters of information function below the awareness of the conscious mind, yet continually interact with the brain, exchanging information with it and profoundly affecting the way we think, feel and behave from moment to moment. It is now known that there is a continuous highway of neural communication between the older limbic emotional brain, the heart and the two hemispheres of the neo-cortical brain but that the "neural connections from the emotional to the cognitive centres is greater than the number going the other way."[8] The heart responds instantaneously to the signals coming from the older 'emotional' brain and passes them via its own intrinsic nervous system to the neo-cortical brain. It apparently plays a role in the control of cardiac function independently of the autonomic nervous system. Without this 'personal' nervous system, which is vital for its stability and efficiency, the heart cannot operate properly. It has also been discovered to be a hormonal gland, releasing a hormone which has an effect on the kidneys, the adrenal glands and certain regions of the brain.

Exploring the connection between the heart, the older instinctive emotional (limbic) brain, and the newer neo-cortical one that we usually refer to as our mind, can help us to understand, in terms of brain chemistry and neuronal connections, why the heart is so important, why the instincts and emotions are so powerful, why they can have both a positive or negative effect on us and why it takes a great deal of insight and attention to become aware of how and where they are influencing our lives, sometimes in creative ways that bring us great happiness and sometimes in ways that drive us to inflict harm on others as well as on ourselves.

If the heart, conduit of our deepest instincts, emotions and feelings, carries wounds, these, like blocked arteries, can restrict the flow of energy through the soul's circulatory system, leading to the impairment of mental and physical health. The body remembers everything that has happened to it and many therapies are focused on helping to recover these buried memories so that the nervous system can be released from the memory of the traumas it has experienced.

The Institute of HeartMath has discovered that making a conscious connection with the heart can initiate changes in deeply imprinted patterns in the nervous system and improve mental coherence. It has developed methods of improving the coherence (ordered, harmonious function) of the heart rhythm which in turn affects both the older emotional brain and the neo-cortical one. These can improve sight, hearing, mental clarity and the ability to relate to others:

> The heart produces by far the body's most powerful rhythmic electromagnetic field, which can be detected several feet away by sensitive instruments. Research shows our heart's field changes distinctly as we experience different emotions. It is registered in people's brains around us and apparently is capable of affecting cells, water and DNA studied in vitro. Growing evidence also suggests energetic interactions involving the heart may underlie intuition and important aspects of human consciousness.[9]

The psychiatrist Dr. David Servan-Schreiber, who is familiar with the discoveries made by the Institute of HeartMath, comments in his book *Healing Without Freud or Prozac* that heart and brain can either cooperate or compete for the control of our thoughts and our way of behaving: when they work together, we feel a sense of harmony, calm and well-being; when they are in conflict, we can feel agitated, anxious, depressed and unhappy.[10] With practice, we can learn to become aware of these fluctuations in mood and take steps to help ourselves regain a state of harmony and balance.

Here are some of the known facts about the heart drawn from the website of the Institute of HeartMath (www.heartmath.org) and from an interview with Joseph Chilton Pearce:

☙   The heart is the most powerful generator of electromagnetic energy in the body, with the largest rhythmic electromagnetic field of any of the body's organs. The electro-magnetic field of the heart envelops every cell of the body.

☙   The electrical field of the heart is about 60 times greater in amplitude than the electrical activity generated by the brain and the magnetic field produced by the heart is more than 100 times greater in strength than the field generated by the brain, and can be detected a number of feet away from the body (12–25 feet) in all directions.

☙   The heart is connected to all the vital organs of the body and maintains the balance of these for the optimal functioning of the entire body-heart-mind organism.

☙   Sixty to sixty-five percent of all the cells in the heart are neural cells which function in the same way as brain cells, but monitor and maintain control of the entire mind/brain/body organism and the direct unmediated connections between the heart and the older 'emotional' brain as well as the neo-cortical one.

☙   The heart is the coordinating centre of the major endocrine glandular structure of the body, which produces the hormones that profoundly affect the operations of body, brain, and mind and coordinate the functioning of the other systems in the body, including the immune system.

What is fascinating, Joseph Chilton Pearce says, is that it has been found that the heart produces two and a half watts of electrical energy at each pulsation, creating an electromagnetic field that is like a hologram of the electromagnetic field around the earth:

> The electromagnetic field of the heart produces, holographically, the same field as the one produced by the earth and solar system. Now, physicists are beginning to look at the electro-magnetic auras as, simply, the organization of energy in the universe. All these are operating holographically — that is, at the smallest, unbelievably tiny level between the dendrites at the synapse, the body, the earth, and on outward. All are operating holographically and selectively.[11]

Just placing our hand over the area of our heart changes the brain waves. The heart as well as the brain produces a balancing hormone, oxytocin — the bonding hormone — which can and should be activated at the beginning of our lives by a loving and nurturing relationship with our mothers. We seek it and rediscover it in a close relationship with our partner. Frustration, anxiety and fear make the heart rate jagged and rapid and this has an effect on the whole nervous system. Loving, stroking, caressing the body can make it calm and rhythmic.[12]

The Institute of HeartMath has found that as individuals learn how to sustain heart-focused states of appreciation or love, the brain's electrical activity comes into coordination or coherence with the heart rhythms. Changing the emotions can alter brain activity. "The brain's alpha wave activity is synchronized to the cardiac cycle. During states of high heart rhythm coherence, alpha wave synchronization to the heart's activity significantly increases."[13]

All of this is of interest to anyone working in the field of healing and psychotherapy. It may be that when therapists become aware of the presence of a 'field' between themselves and their client, it is the electro-magnetic field of the heart. Their attitude to their client, whether caring and heart-centred, or perfunctory and distant, may affect the heart of the client and the electro-magnetic field between and around them, enhancing or negating their power to heal:

> Our data indicate that one person's heart signal can affect another's brainwaves, and that heart-brain synchronization can occur between two people when they interact. Finally, it appears that as individuals increase psychophysiological coherence, they become more sensitive to the subtle electromagnetic signals communicated by those around them. Taken together, these results suggest that cardioelectromagnetic communication may be a little-known source of information exchange between people, and that this exchange is influenced by our emotions.[14]

There is a method called Quick Coherence, which is explained on the HeartMath website www.heartmath.org whereby one can intentionally alter one's emotional state through focusing on the heart and doing specific exercises which can change a negative into a positive feeling state, rendering the heart's rhythm more coherent and influencing the clarity of one's thoughts and intuitions and cognitive performance in general. I have found it extremely helpful in my own life and, with the permission of the Institute of HeartMath, offer a practice for connecting with and altering the rhythm of the heart in three stages and a further one for consolidating this practice. These are an excellent alternative to meditation — a form of meditation in itself:

Quick Coherence Technique:

1. **Heart Focus**: Focus your attention on the area of your heart, placing your left hand on the centre of your chest.
2. **Heart-Focused Breathing**: Imagine your breath is flowing in and out of that area, breathing slowly and gently in through your heart (to a count of five or six) and slowly and easily out through your heart (to the same count). Continue to breathe in and out in this way until your breathing feels smooth and balanced and has found a natural inner rhythm that feels good to you.
3. **Heart Feeling**: Continue to breathe through the area of your heart. As you do so, recall a positive image or feeling, a time or place where you felt happy and at peace with yourself, when you were doing something you enjoyed or felt love or compassion for a special person or animal, or aspect of nature, something that can bring a smile to your face as you recall it. Once you have connected with this feeling, sustain it while you continue to practice your Heart Focus, Heart-Focused Breathing and Heart Feeling.

Heart Lock-In Technique: Hold the feeling of genuine love or care for someone or something in your life. Send this feeling of love and care towards yourself, extending it to the boundaries of the electro-magnetic field that surrounds your body, then expand it to flow outwards towards others and to the wider world in the form of waves of energy. If you experience uncomfortable, anxious feelings, send love and compassion to those feelings. Befriending a negative feeling and sending compassion to it can release or dissolve the blockage. These exercises will gradually strengthen your conscious connection to your heart, build up resilience and the ability to be aware of subtle changes in its rhythm.[15]

The Bodymind Organism

There is another aspect to understanding our body and the importance of the emotions which can be related to everything that the HeartMath Institute has discovered about the importance of the heart. Some decades ago, the biologist

Candace Pert wanted to answer the question: How can emotions transform the body, either creating disease or healing it, maintaining health or undermining it? She discovered that our emotions are the crucial link between mind and body and that specific chemicals called neuropeptides are related to specific emotional states and further, that these neuropeptides are found to be active all over the body, including the older limbic brain, the neo-cortex, the stomach and the intestines. Realizing that peptides are the universal biochemical language of the emotions, she called them "molecules of emotion" — the title of her extraordinary book, one of the most interesting I have ever read.

This was a ground-breaking discovery because she realized that neuropeptides are the connecting factor between the emotions and physiological processes. Each specific peptide (chemical) mediates a specific emotional state. We can no longer speak of such a thing as objective, rational thought because thought is inextricably involved with emotion. She found that neuropeptides connect the brain, the hormonal system and the immune system, acting as messengers between them and able to alter or modify both mood and behaviour. She realized that every change in the physiological state is accompanied by an instantaneous change in the emotional state and every change in the emotional state is accompanied by an instantaneous change in the physiological one. This led her to understand that it is a mistake to think in terms of two separate categories of 'mind' and 'body' because these form a single organism that she called 'Bodymind' and saw as "an amazing field of interacting information which travels everywhere instantaneously".[16] She realized that we can no longer view the body as a machine but as an incredibly efficient information network with inbuilt intelligence and that this intelligence is not only to be found in the brain but in cells in every part of the body. The implications of her discoveries are huge and are a key to understanding the origins of disease and how to heal it.

> Wherever there are receptors there is memory, so some of our old patterns and our old subconscious ways of doing things are really located within the body. Trauma can be stored not just in little parts of our brain but deeply within our body, which may explain some of the very powerful aspects of the various kinds of body work…psychological interventions in cancer, visualisation for other diseases can change the immune system, can truly change physical measurements. It's very profound. I believe that there needs to be more research and that people need to pay very close attention to it. It does seem foreign. However it must have seemed very foreign and shocking when we heard that the earth revolved around the sun. It's really of that magnitude.[17]

Birth and the Importance of the Mother–Child Bond

The importance of the heart and the way specific neuro-peptides mediate specific emotional states goes far to explain why the heart-bond between mother and child is so significant. It may be that the electro-magnetic field of the mother's heart affects the minute field of the baby's heart.

The life of the body begins with our conception and birth into the world. Our understanding of the formation and development of the embryo and foetus in the womb and the birth of a child has been enormously expanded by seeing this process described in books and on television. Medicine and science between them have revealed to us more and more of the miraculous growth of the foetus in the womb.[18] In addition, the pioneering work of two remarkable men, Michel Odent and Frederick Leboyer, has emphasized the importance of the heart and the positive or negative impact on children's instincts and emotions of the way they are brought into the world. In their approach to birth, water takes on the utmost importance, both for the mother prior and during birth and for the baby after birth. Odent, in his book, *Water and Sexuality*, shows how important the connection with water is for humans generally and how even a woman's seeing a water bath in the delivery room can hasten and facilitate the delivery of her child.

Water-births as initiated by Michel Odent in his hospital at Pithiviers in France and introduced in hospitals the world over, offer mothers an unusual and calming experience, allowing them to enter into what he calls the primal adaptive process — where instincts and emotions are, as it were, fused with each other and where the momentous change taking place in both mother and baby can be allowed to unfold as the instinctive responses of the older primordial brain direct it. We need, Odent says, a new word added to our vocabulary which embraces both emotion and instinct and which does not set up an artificial barrier between them.[19]

Leboyer's graphic description of the acute pain, terror and distress that the newly born baby can experience if insensitively handled, held upside down by the feet, slapped on the buttocks, its eyes blinded by bright lights, its ears assaulted by loud voices, is deeply disturbing, the more so when this unconscious brutality is contrasted with the sensitive and gentle way a baby can be welcomed into a darkened, hushed atmosphere where there are no loud voices, bright lights or cold surfaces to terrify it. In his book, *Birth Without Violence*, he writes: "We should be crying tears of shame, crying for our own blindness. The same blindness that made us think women had to suffer simply because we didn't know any better. Happily we no longer believe in the old saying: 'in pain shall ye give birth'. Isn't it time to do for the child what we've been trying to do for the mother?"[20] He demonstrated that babies are incredibly sensitive and vulnerable: they can feel far more intensely than adults; they are conscious, sentient beings in the womb and at birth. Incredibly, not so long ago, babies (and animals) were thought to be incapable of feeling because they had not developed a conscious sense of self. Fortunately, these old attitudes are changing.

Leboyer advocated that the umbilical cord should not be cut immediately after birth, allowing the baby to adjust to the new experience of breathing through the cord as well as through the lungs until the cord stops beating, indicating that the lungs were ready to take over and that the cord could be cut. Immersing a baby in water after having placed him for a while on his mother's warm body, gives him again the feeling of being weightless, as in the womb, and this can soothe and calm him. Leboyer takes his insight into the effects of a traumatic birth further, connecting it with the aggressive patterns of behaviour in later life that re-enact it; the pain and terror we experienced at birth is inflicted on others decades later in the acts of violence and terrorism that ravage the world: "The memory of birth and the terror that accompanies it remains in each one of us. But since it is so loaded with fear and pain, it lies dormant and totally repressed, like a dreadful secret at the bottom of our unconscious.... How few of us are aware of how much unconscious fear there is in our lives! All this fear linked with the horror which is birth.... It is as if the fear of death, the dark shadow that casts its gloom over our whole lives, is nothing but the unconscious memory of... the fear we felt when we were born."[21] In this, he is supported by the research of Stanislav Grof, as explained in his book *Beyond the Brain: Birth, Death and Transcendence in Psychotherapy* which brilliantly details the three stages of the perinatal experience and how they affect our lives.

Although the sensitive approach of these men to the birth of the child may not be fully realized in every hospital where currently there are not nearly enough midwives to care for mothers through the different stages of labour, nevertheless their ideas have had a profound influence on the way infants are handled when they emerge from the womb, making that emergence less of a traumatizing ordeal. There is a new emphasis on gentleness and on the primary need of the infant to bond with the mother's body immediately after birth.

If their suggestions are followed, the infant's feeling of intense bliss after the trauma of expulsion from the womb is transmitted to the heart from the older instinctive limbic brain. The infant can experience these feelings of bliss in the womb prior to birth and in the first few moments of being reconnected with the mother after birth, in close sensory contact with her touch, her voice, her smell and her facial expression, and these sensory experiences continue throughout infancy. This original visceral experience can lay the foundation of later feelings of trust in life, the capacity for empathy and love, and the ability to feel joy, ecstasy and delight. It is in the first minutes, hours, days and months of an infant's life that the heart and the nervous system can be programmed to a fulfilled and happy life or, conversely, to an anxiety-laden, difficult and even tragic one. Abandonment by the mother or her inability to love her child, are two of the greatest traumas an infant or small child can experience. Early adoption by loving foster parents can go far to diminish the effects of the grief and profound distress the infant feels. The current delays in the adoption process are disastrous for the instinctive needs of an infant who has been taken away from his mother and has no one to bond with.

We now know that the foetus in the womb registers everything the mother is experiencing: her happiness and delight in her growing baby or her fear and anxiety. We know that the development of the nervous system, the heart and the developing cognitive functions of the brain can be positively or negatively affected by her serene or stressed state. We know the foetus can be affected by the quality of the mother's nutrition or lack of it, as well as by alcohol, smoking and drugs and also by tension and violence in the parental relationship. We know it is sensitive to music, loud noise and the quality of the environment the mother is experiencing.

We are born with 100 billion neurons in our brain connected by 50 trillion synapses (this number may change as we learn more and also more about the neurons in the heart). From three to ten months a culling takes place with the loss of 50,000 connections between brain cells every second; cells that are not used during this time die. Every cell has several branchings off it called dendrons. The more the cells are used the more connecting dendrons develop. They develop complexity and increase by use. The mother's empathic response to her infant in its early months and years is vital to the development of these dendrons. Care and bonding with the mother or primary carer help the cells and dendrons to become active during the crucially important first ten months. If care and love are absent or deficient, they will not be activated.[22]

The first three years of life are the most important for the future emotional and mental development of the child. Until the age of three to five years, the neural connections between the older limbic brain, the heart and the frontal lobes of the neo-cortical brain are not fully established. Until then, we live through the reflexes of the limbic brain and through purely instinctual (unconscious) behaviour, assimilating sounds, sights and encounters with people and our environment at a phenomenal rate. If there is insufficient verbal and sensory stimulus in these years, we will not be able to develop to the optimum level of which we are capable at birth. Our natural instinct is to reach out to people and respond to them, to explore through the senses everything that surrounds us. Between three and five years the neo-cortical level of the brain and the frontal lobes become activated and we begin to develop a sense of self and to differentiate between ourselves and our environment. The memories associated with the older brain during the earliest years gradually become 'unconscious'. Yet these earliest memories, imprinted on the older brain and held in the limbic brain and the heart's memory field, have immense power to influence our lives and our behaviour. A wound to the instinct in these early years can affect our lives in negative ways to the end of our days unless and until we become aware of them.

Study after study has shown that emotional and physical abuse of the mother-to-be affects the neuronal circuits (nervous system) of the child she is carrying and that the abandonment, neglect or abuse of the infant and small child can alter the balance of its neural chemistry and programme it to depression or to violent and criminal behaviour later on. It has been found that the brain and nervous system of children traumatized by their experiences in a dysfunctional home exhibit the same patterns of functioning as those of war veterans suffering from PTSD.[23] When constant anxiety and distress are experienced in infancy, the adrenal glands produce a high level of the stress hormone cortisol and this upsets or disturbs the optimal formation and equilibrium of the autonomic nervous system, the endocrine and immune systems, as well as interfering with the neural connections between the heart, the two hemispheres of the brain and the frontal lobes. The higher brain centres may be unable to develop due to the stress of constant anxiety. The heart, as explained above, is the primal organ of the whole bodymind organism. When the heart is deeply distressed and cannot function in an optimal way this affects the hormonal, immune and autonomic nervous systems and all the other organs of the body. Children who have been subjected to a chronically abusive environment grow up to be hyper-vigilant of other people's moods and body language as a protective measure. They sense changes in mood or a subtle inflexion in the voice or body language long before others do. This hyper-vigilance affects every system in the body, programming it to live in a state of constant arousal and anxiety.

Damage to the heart and the nervous system can endure throughout our lives with no way of healing it if we are not aware of it. We need to ask whether the rise in violent crime as well as the bullying and aggressive behaviour that is increasingly apparent in our culture at all levels does not in part originate in foetal and infant distress, contributing to the later disorientation and distress of the adolescent in a brutal and uncaring environment and therefore to the arousal of the most aggressive survival instincts and the curtailment of the neo-cortical skills of emotional intelligence and the ability to contain and manage anger.

The increasing tendency to put infants and toddlers into nursery school at a very early age may have a negative effect on their emotional development because they are deprived of the unique emotional bonding experience with the mother. On the other hand, if the mother is incapable of bonding with her child, indifferent to or abusive of it — either from innate inadequacy or suffering from post-natal depression — nursery school may be a better alternative to a dysfunctional home environment. It has been noted recently that many small children enter nursery and primary school unable to speak or to interact with other children or adults because they have had hardly any personal interaction with their mothers at home, most probably because they are placed for hours in front of the television or because they are simply left to cry alone or are cowed into silence by physical abuse.

Memories of happiness and delight or of terror, abandonment, anxiety and grief which are imprinted on the field of the heart and limbic brain in earliest infancy and early childhood — even in the womb — remain imprinted on them throughout our lives and can affect the frontal lobes of the brain as these develop, whether positively or negatively. With the development of the frontal lobes comes the ability to reflect, to reason, to apply knowledge gained to specific goals but also to develop the ideas conveyed by the imagination, to make intuitive connections between apparently unrelated things and ideas. But if the heart and the whole instinctual system connected with it are traumatized and deflected from a normal path of growth by the intense anxiety and fear aroused by neglect, abandonment or abuse, this capacity for harmonious and balanced interaction between the heart, the nervous system and the brain will be impaired. Nothing, therefore, in relation to the well-being and creativity of a whole society, is more important than the care of the mother and child and the way a child is treated both at home and at school in its early years. This applies to all societies, however rich or poor.

The Neglect of Instinctive Needs

In most modern areas of the world, millions of us live in hideous over-crowded cities: there are over 400 cities with populations greater than a million. We are no longer closely in touch, as our ancestors were, with the Earth and the star-strewn night sky. This in itself does violence to our heart and our instincts. Children, through fear that they might be kidnapped or harmed by paedophiles, are not encouraged to play out of doors, to explore, take risks and discover their power to survive. They sit for hours watching television, their computer screens or mobile phones. Millions of adults are dependent upon work which does not satisfy them and from which there is no escape. Millions have no work, possibly for as long as three generations, and live on state benefits. With the doubling and tripling of the world population over the last fifty years, this situation has been made incomparably worse because, even with a flourishing economy, there can never be enough employment for all the growing numbers who are seeking it, particularly for the young. Political leaders are slow to comprehend that the planet's resources are limited and there cannot be perpetual increase — of the world population, economic growth or jobs.

The breakdown of families which is, in part, an effect of this alienation from the instinct, contributes to patterns of behaviour which reflect its distress and disorientation. There is nothing in secular society to give a foundation for values which respect the needs of the instinct. Boys without a male role model provided by a caring father turn to gangs to give them security, structure and status. Girls follow the role models offered to them by media 'celebrities', forcing a premature development of sexual awareness, and adapt their feminine nature to the masculine ethos and goals of the culture. An exaggerated focus on sexuality distorts the need for love and trust in relationships. Men and women come to view each other in terms of immediate gratification, to be discarded if their partner fails to meet their requirements. Children, the precious repository of our future, become the unhappy victims of the serial relationships of their parents, and targets not only for paedophiles but for commercial exploitation and online cyber bullying. The appalling treatment and neglect of children taken into care has just come to light in the United Kingdom. Mothers may be too stressed and exhausted by the combined demands of full-time work and running a home to attend to their children's emotional needs and to the relationship with their partners. The current benefits system in the UK which has encouraged young women to become mothers without the desire or the need to find a supportive and caring partner has led to the situation where one in three children (3.8 million) in the UK now live without a father. Fifty thousand births are registered annually without the father's name on the birth certificate. This situation might be ameliorated if adolescents were helped to understand the responsibilities of parenthood and why a child's need for the loving care of both parents is paramount.

The most important factor in the education of children in kindergarten and primary school is to nourish the imagination with activities that put them in touch with nature and help to connect them with their instincts. Exploring the woods and learning about birds and animals, learning how to grow vegetables; painting, dancing, singing, carpentry, cooking and learning to play a musical instrument as thousands of children in the poorest cities of Venezuela are doing, would go far to help children acquire confidence and balance and, above all, to *enjoy* learning.

Too much emphasis on exam-focused left-hemispheric learning without the balancing focus on activities which nurture the imagination and involve the coordination of eye, heart and hand can cripple the instincts and the heart. By providing children with the conditions in which they can develop and express their natural instinct to enjoy what they are learning or by failing to notice the boredom and discouragement inflicted on them by bad teachers and inadequate, perfunctory education, we can profoundly affect their future. The best teachers know all this and can inspire and encourage a child to discover his or her creative path in life. The worst, like the worst parents, can crush and destroy a child's soul. The distress children feel — distress caused not only by inadequate education and bullying in schools but by parental quarrelling and separation — is often expressed in physical symptoms such as abdominal pain. When they are very young they can only articulate what they are feeling through physical symptoms. Such distress leaves traumas embedded in the nervous system. As these young people grow to adulthood, many turn to drugs or alcohol or fall into depression and a kind of paralysis, not knowing how to deal with their distress as they are driven from day to day by a sense of failure because of their inability to attain the goals and material benefits which our competitive culture urges on them.

Governments try to deal with the symptoms of this distress, manifested not only in crime but in diseases such as cancer and diabetes as well as depression and mental illness and the obesity that affects one third of the population in the UK. Over 67 million anti-depressants were prescribed in 2016, many of them to adolescents. A recent survey from the Institute of Clinical Psychology and Psychotherapy in Dresden (2011) reports that 30 million people in 30 European countries suffer from depression and that more than a third of the populations in these countries suffer from mental disorders, with only a quarter of these receiving help.[24] World wide, there seems to be an epidemic of anti-depressant use, with the United States as the highest user. But the billions spent on health do not address and therefore cannot alleviate the underlying problem of the quality of care infants and young children receive in an over-crowded and dysfunctional society. Because the superficial values which dominate the media do not address our real needs and because their very superficiality cuts us off from connection to our deepest ground, they draw us into addictive patterns which can destroy lives, health and relationships. The tragic fate of the gifted singer Amy Winehouse is one example of this.

Reconnecting with the Body

The body experiences life through the five senses. Taking the time to become acutely aware of sensory experience is a form of meditation. It puts us in touch with the body and the rhythm of our breathing and our heart. It helps us to slow down, to become aware of everything around us that is communicating its presence to us. We don't think of the past or the future: we are in the present. Breathing more freely helps us to let go of the need to do anything. Taking time to lie on our back on the ground or the floor for a few minutes during the day, or perhaps in our bed when we wake up in the morning, gives us time to listen to our breathing; to be in touch with our earthly home; to reconnect with our instinctual soul.

As children, we once had this connection to the body. We had it unconsciously, instinctively. We moved freely, joyously, without thinking what we were doing, expressing every thought and feeling in physical movement. We loved running, jumping, exploring, shouting to each other, feeling the soft rain or the warm sun on our skin, in touch with the aliveness of the earth, the plants and the trees, stroking the softness of an animal's fur, feeling the rapture of being alive. As we grow up and are taught to conform to the expectations of parents, teachers and society in general, we lose that instinctive physicality and spontaneous emotional freedom of early childhood. As we learn to conform, our breathing becomes more constricted and parts of our body — usually our spine and our neck — become more tense. This process gradually develops into the rigidity of adulthood, where we sit, stand and move in a certain habitual way. It also explains why almost any form of bodywork involving breathing and/or muscle relaxation can release emotion and energy that have been suppressed and locked into the body, sometimes for as long as thirty or forty years. Fortunately, many healing methods exist today for releasing this tension and re-discovering our ability to feel connected to our body. In the words of a man who learned a method of deep massage from the Kahuna shamans of Hawaii and teaches a method of reconnection with the body: "The more fully physically present we become the more we are aware of subtle flows of energy in our body. We begin to sense that the body is a conduit between heaven and earth, which is perhaps its deepest purpose and function."[25]

If we can rediscover this connection to our bodies, perhaps remembering a time long ago when we did feel that connection — when swimming or ski-ing, walking in the woods, by the sea or breathing in the astonishing clear air of mountains — we gain a deep experience of being 'at home' in ourselves: an aliveness, and a sense of safety, security, happiness and well-being. This feeling communicates itself to other people, who feel safe in our presence and more in touch with their own bodies. Often people find that their best ideas come to them when they are walking, swimming, lying in the bath or feeling the water of the shower cascading down their bodies. Water seems to activate the imagination.

Although we may not immediately recover the sense of connection with the Earth and the Cosmos that shamanic peoples had and still have, we can begin to open our senses to that awareness. A beautiful passage from the Irish *Carmina Gadelica* reminds us of the relationship with nature that we have lost and could recover:

> The old people had runes which they sang to the spirits dwelling in the sea and in the mountain, in the wind and in the whirlwind, in the lightning and in the thunder, in the sea and in the moon and in the stars of heaven.[26]

Singing reminds me of the remarkable hidden powers of the body discovered in the art of Mongolian overtone chanting and introduced in many workshops all over the world by Jill Purce. It is a thrilling experience to find that we can make these wonderful sounds — even people who have never been able to sing. This is a shamanic art and it is now available to anyone who chooses to learn it. It would be wonderful if all children could be taught Mongolian chanting in schools, giving them a common bond, a shared skill and the excitement of discovering the wondrous sound their bodies can make.[27]

Healing the Heart

As the relationship with the ground of life changes, so do we change in our relationships to partner, child or parent; our understanding of life and other people deepens and expands. Over the course of many years of attending to the voice of our heart, the base metal of a personality which was unaware of the numinous ground on which it rests or the source of the light which gives it life is transformed into gold as it learns how to engage with this ground as with an invisible partner and friend. Aspects of our psychic life which may, in our unconsciousness, have controlled our lives and our relationships are slowly transformed as our relationship with this deep instinctive ground of our soul grows and develops.

Following the guidance of the heart may lead us in unexpected directions in our lives. Instinct carries within it the active intelligence, the intention and the power to transform these unconscious patterns so that humanity can reach its evolutionary goal of a mature, transformed and integrated consciousness. This instinctual soul, focused through the heart and connected to the greater cosmic web of life, is the tap root of our imagination and our creativity.

The Main Initiatives which could assist the Well-Being of the Child

   Teaching children the clinical facts of sexual intercourse through using a book like Nillson's *A Child Is Born* instead of a banana and a condom might instil a sense of wonder and respect for sexuality, conception and childbirth instead of approaching these in a mechanistic way.

   Teaching adolescents and parents-to-be the importance of good nutrition for both parents *before* the conception of their child as well as during its growth in the womb is essential. This should be recognized as part of the preparation for parenthood and doesn't receive nearly enough attention. Plenty of protein, fresh fruit and vegetables are vitally important. Abstaining from alcohol, drugs and anti-depressants is also important. It is also vital that both parents take an omega-3 fish oil supplement or eat fish because our diet lacks fish. It is as important as taking a folic acid supplement to prevent spina bifida.

   Increasing the number of midwives so that mothers could receive really good supportive care during pregnancy and childbirth would help to counter the fear of childbirth and the suffering and fear of mothers left too long unattended. The process of birth has become perfunctory, uncaring and mechanical because of the chronic lack of midwives. This need for care extends to more training in recognizing and treating postnatal depression which can be greatly helped by taking omega-3 supplements and receiving hormonal treatment as a possible alternative to anti-depressants.

   Educating children and adolescents to take responsibility for their future sexual relationships, teaching them about responsible parenthood and the physical and emotional needs of their child should be part of the school curriculum. One of the facts that could be imparted to them is that the excessive consumption of alcohol (binge-drinking) in their teens and twenties harms the immune system not only of their children but also their grandchildren.

As we begin to pay attention to our inner life, it becomes apparent that there is an intelligence in its depths that is infinitely superior to our conscious ego or personality. In relation to this greater intelligence, the surface personality is like a tiny planet compared to the size and power of a supernova.

If these initiatives were implemented, an enormous amount of mental and physical illness could be avoided and the billions expended on healthcare reduced. If young men and women were told these basic facts about parenthood during their adolescence and, in addition, shown the damaging effect that drinking to excess and taking drugs have on the immune system of their children — and even their grandchildren — leading to physical and mental illness, much suffering and disease could be prevented. They would become more aware of the responsibility of becoming a parent. They might take more care in choosing a partner who would be a good mother or father to their children and more care of their health before embarking on parenthood.

Notes:

1. see Hillman, James (1972) *The Myth of Analysis: Three Essays in Archetypal Psychology*, Part Three: On Psychological Femininity, Northwestern University Press
2. see *Kundalini Rising*, Sounds True Publications, Boulder, Colorado, 2009. I am indebted to Lawrence Edwards Ph.D. for the insights given here.
3. Sheldrake, *The Science Delusion*, p. 185
4. Coleridge, Samuel Taylor, *Biographia Literaria*, p. 167
5. Frankl, Viktor (2004) *Man's Search for Meaning*, Rider, London, p. 105
6. Pearce, Joseph Chilton (1992) *Evolution's End*, HarperCollins, San Francisco and notes from an interview on the Internet
7. Institute of HeartMath website www.heartmath.org
8. ibid
9. ibid
10. Servan-Shreiber, David (2004) *Healing Without Freud or Prozac*, Pan Macmillan, London, p. 36
11. Interview with Joseph Chilton Pearce on the Internet
12. HeartMath website
13. ibid
14. ibid
15. ibid
16. Pert, Candace (1998) *Molecules of Emotion*, Simon and Schuster Ltd., London
17. ibid
18. See Nilsson, Lennart and Hamberger, Lars (1994 & 2010) *A Child is Born*, Doubleday. An essential and fascinating book that will interest both parents and children and should be used in every school as an introduction to sexuality and parenthood.
19. Odent, Michel (1990) *Water and Sexuality*, Arkana, London, pp. 106–9
20. Leboyer, Frederick (1995) *Birth Without Violence*, trs. Yvonne Fitzgerald, Mandarin Paperbacks, p.19
21. Leboyer, pp.131,134
22. See Gerhardt, Sue (2004) *Why Love Matters: How Affection Shapes a Baby's Brain*, Brunner-Routledge, London
23. Camila Batmanghelidjh in *The Times* 24/12/11
24. report in the Scientific and Medical Network Review Winter 2011
25. Janni, Nicolas, Co-founder and Director of Strategic Partnerships and Olivier Mythodrama. www.oliviermythodrama.com
26. Freeman, Mara (2001) *Carmina Gadelica* from *Kindling the Celtic Spirit*, HarperSanFrancisco
27. Purce, Jill, Mongolian Overtone Chanting workshops. www.healingvoice.com

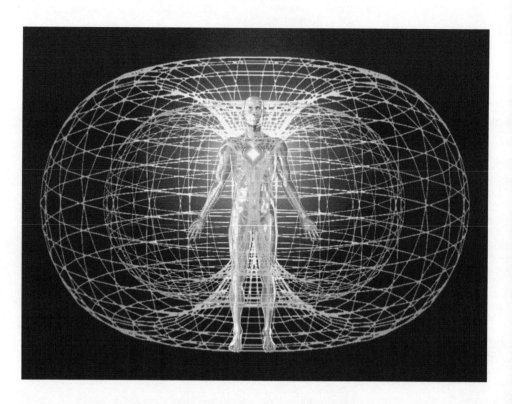

Heartmath electro-magnetic field

With grateful thanks to the Institute of Heartmath, Boulder Creek, California.

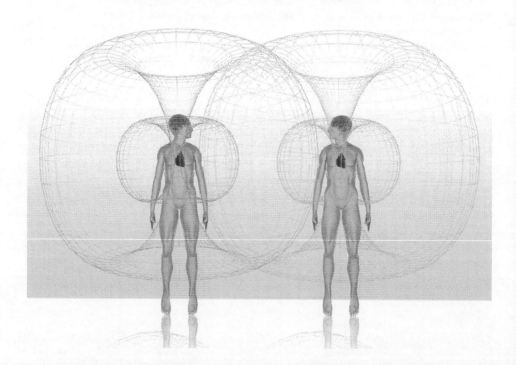

Chapter Seventeen

New Wine in New Bottles:
A New Image of God

Neither do men put new wine into old bottles; else the bottles break, and the wine runneth out, and the bottles perish: but they put new wine into new bottles and both are preserved.

— Matth. 9:17; Mark 2:22; Luke 5:37,38

The human world of today has not grown cold but is ardently searching for a God proportionate to the new dimensions of a Universe whose appearance has completely revolutionised the scale of our faculty of worship.

— Pierre Teilhard de Chardin, *The Future of Man*

If it be true, that Spirit is involved in Matter and apparent Nature is secret God, then the manifestation of the divine in himself and the realization of God within and without are the highest and most legitimate aim possible to man on earth.

— Sri Aurobindo, *The Life Divine*

There is nothing I want to find out and long to know with greater urgency than this. Can I find God, whom I can almost grasp with my own hands in looking at the universe, also in myself?

— Johannes Kepler

From the first stirrings of conscious awareness, we have sought relationship with the Cosmos. This is perhaps our deepest instinct. Gazing in wonder at the stars, naming the constellations, minutely charting the rising and setting of the moon and the sun, imagining a divine intelligence that has created the beauty and marvel of the Earth, and longing to communicate with that intelligence, we have created many sacred images to draw us closer to the mystery.

We now know that over a time-span of many millennia, the image of deity changed from the primordial Great Mother of the Palaeolithic and Neolithic eras to the many goddesses and gods of the Bronze Age and finally, in the three patriarchal religions of the solar era, to the image of a single Father God, although, in the East, the older polytheistic pantheon with all its rich mythology survives to this day. Throughout this time, whatever the religion or the culture, the sacred image gave us a vertical axis, an Archimedean point beyond ourselves, keeping us in touch with a Source or Ground or Mystery instinctively felt to exist.

I think we can understand that, as our conscious mind slowly evolved out of the matrix of instinct, the sacred image and the mythologies which grew up around it were like an umbilical cord holding us in touch with the foundation of life. But, as we moved into the solar era and the monotheistic transcendent god-image of the three patriarchal religions, the older shamanic relationship with the Earth and a living Cosmos was gradually lost and with it the idea that the whole of nature was sacred, infused with divinity, ensouled.

Today we live in an extraordinarily challenging time when we face greater dangers but also greater opportunities than we have had in the whole course of our evolution on this planet. Many people feel that this century will be the ultimate test of our survival as a species. Not since the beginning of the Christian era has there been such a powerful impulse for transformation. On the one hand the image of deity that has presided over Christian civilization for two thousand years is dying and this process of the decay or waning of an archetype is affecting the whole world. On the other hand, beneath the surface concerns of our culture, we can see that a spiritual awakening on a planetary scale is taking place. This awakening is beginning to heal the great split in the patriarchal psyche between spirit and nature and the dissociation between thinking and feeling that lies at the core of scientific reductionism. It is being led by men and women who are bringing into being a new paradigm of reality and a spirituality arising from the need for direct connection with a transcendent dimension, a spirituality which recognizes and honours the interconnectedness, indivisibility and utter sacredness of life. Their vision is creating a powerful alchemy in the culture, slowly trans-forming our understanding from lead into gold.

Because of its fear of animism and its emphasis on a creator god transcendent to creation, Christianity lost the wider unifying dimension of Soul that had held spirit and matter together. It lost the vital sense of relationship and communion with an unseen reality that ensouled the great organism of the planet — its mountains, rivers, springs, trees, plants and animals. There has consequently arisen a dissociation between spirit and nature within Western civilization and within the human psyche, creating a deep wound that needs healing.

During the solar era, the literal interpretation of the Myth of the Fall and the doctrine of Original Sin cast a pall over our lives and led us to look upon the Earth as a fearsome place of punishment, suffering, toil and death. I think it was these two related beliefs that undermined the older participatory experience of life that Indigenous Peoples have retained to this day in certain parts of the world. The ramifications of these two beliefs are enormous. I have explored them in earlier chapters and leave the reader to reflect on them — relating them to the current political situation where all three Abrahamic religions and the peoples who have embraced them are embroiled in conflict in the area of the planet where, long ago, they originated.

The Christian meta-narrative, arising out of the matrix of Judaism, emphasized an image of God as a loving Father, concerned for the well being of each and every creature — even the humble sparrow. Christ himself became a new God-image — unifying divinity and humanity in his person and offering a template to humanity of what all men and women could become by discovering and manifesting the latent divinity within them through the creation of a direct relationship with that mysterious ground. Yet this great revelation which pointed to the further evolutionary potential of humanity — already highly developed in the Eastern religions — was deflected into a new religion in which Christ's sacrificial death was interpreted as being offered for the redemption of the sins of the world and, specifically, for Christians who had been baptized into the faith. The emphasis was on redemption through faith and belonging to a group with a superior revelation rather than on the transformation of consciousness. Redemption was only available to believers.

The New Story

We are moving from the story of a dead, insentient cosmos to a new story of a Cosmos that is vibrantly alive and the primary ground of our own consciousness. But more than this, we are moving towards a new concept of God and of our relationship with God which is a revelation as great as any we have ever had. We are moving from an image of God as a creator separate from creation to an image of spirit as the ineffable Intelligence *within* the process of cosmic and planetary evolution, with ourselves as participants in that process. An Eternal Consciousness participates in the life of this universe and we are a manifestation of that Consciousness just coming to awareness that we participate in its life, that we are co-creators with it, that we are, essentially, divine beings.

Four of the greatest sages of the last century, Sri Aurobindo, Carl Jung, Bede Griffiths and Pierre Teilhard de Chardin saw the inner history of the world as the progressive incarnation of spirit, lived through the evolving soul of the individual. Jung said that the 'Holy Spirit' was an impelling force, creating wider consciousness and responsibility and increased understanding. "It was only quite late that we realized (or rather, are beginning to realize), that God is Reality itself and therefore — last but not least — man."[1] With that single sentence, he offered us a radically different image of God and a radically different image of ourselves.

> We have become participants of the divine life and we have to assume a new responsibility. The responsible living and fulfilling of the divine love in us will be our form of worship of, and commerce with, God. His goodness means grace and light and his dark side the terrible temptation of power. Man has already received so much knowledge that he can destroy his own planet. Let us hope that God's good spirit will guide him in his decisions, because it will depend on man's decision whether God's creation will continue.[1]

Could we perhaps understand the story of the evolution of life on this planet as the story of the 'incarnation' of cosmic spirit in our time and space, the story of its long evolutionary journey through stages of greater and greater complexity and diversification and its awakening, through our own human consciousness, to awareness of itself? Seen in this way, the evolutionary unfolding of the universe becomes a divine drama, the drama of spirit incarnating in (from our perspective) the infinitely slow process of the forging of consciousness in the crucible of planetary life, and then being constrained within the limitations of that consciousness until it can reach the point of awakening and self-awareness. Cosmic consciousness, hidden from us by the filter of galactic and planetary evolution, cannot be recognized by us for what it is until our consciousness is sufficiently developed to become capable of recognizing it.

Meister Eckhart (1260–1327) put it like this: "The supreme purpose of God is birth. He will not be content until his Son is born in us. Neither will the soul be content until the Son is born of it." (Sermon 12) That 'Son' is the transformed consciousness of the individual and, ultimately — if we accept the evolutionary template offered by the four sages above — of all humanity.

The world is not a random assembly of parts but resonates with the imprint of a unifying and coherent intelligence. The physical universe is a kind of divine hologram that reflects in its tiniest parts the imprint of the higher unifying intelligence that created it. How we are treating planetary life, matter and each other becomes a matter of how we are treating God. To injure the Earth or to inflict pain and suffering on other human beings is to injure the Universal Consciousness and, since we are that Consciousness, to injure ourselves. Everything we do affects the whole. This is such a different conception of God and of ourselves that it takes some time to assimilate its implications.

The Waning of the Old Order

Three hundred and fifty years ago the Christian image of God was still the focus of Western civilization and no one could imagine life without belief in God. The highest vision of the different religions of what has been named the Axial Age (beginning ca.700-600 BC) was that we were in the world, yet not entirely of the world and could, through meditative and contemplative techniques, gain access to a transcendent dimension of reality that lay beyond the phenomenal world. In the Christian tradition, through prayer, we could ask God or Christ or the Virgin Mary to intercede in our lives. We could live a godly life, following the model of compassionate service offered by Christ. We could trust in the teaching of the Church that our sins had been redeemed by Christ's sacrificial death and that, at our death, we would be united with Christ in his kingdom.

Then came the Enlightenment of the eighteenth century and the gradual weakening of this great meta-narrative. The roots of this change go back to Kepler and Copernicus and their discovery that the earth moved round the sun, so displacing the belief that the earth was stationary and the fixed centre of the solar system. Their discovery, together with those of Galileo (1564–1642), shattered the long-established Ptolomaic system and the belief in an ordered Cosmos where the earth occupied the intermediate space between heaven above and hell below. They initiated the great age of science which developed over the subsequent four centuries.

Some time before Galileo, Luther's (1483–1546) radical suggestion that each individual could have a direct connection to God undermined the authority of the Catholic Church as sole intermediary between man and God. The impact of these events was profound and gave rise to centuries of religious conflict as their implications worked their way into the consciousness of the culture as whole. A further influence was Newton's (1643–1727) formidable discoveries and the development from these of the idea of a mechanistic, causally-determined 'clock-work' universe governed by immutable laws. The powerful influence of Descartes' (1596–1650) philosophy contributed to the growing fissure between religion and science and between mind and matter. Galileo, Copernicus, Kepler and Newton still saw their great discoveries as giving man insight into the mind of God and how the universe He created functioned. A universe without God was, to them, still unthinkable.

A later strand of influence came from the publication of Darwin's *Origin of Species* (1859) and his totally different rendering of the appearance of man on this planet from that set forth in the Book of Genesis. Just as Kepler and Copernicus's great discovery shattered the foundations of the medieval worldview, so Darwin's appeared to invalidate the Christian meta-narrative of the story of Creation and the Fall of Man and therefore, implicitly, the need for redemption by the sacrificial death of Christ. His theory seemed to undermine the need for the existence of God. Darwin's theory inaugurated a great age of discovery as scientists working in different fields began to explore the geological, biological and anthropological history of the planet. While science had begun to diverge from religion as a result of the persecution of Galileo, it gradually began to replace religion as the purveyor of new and exciting discoveries that could be tested and proven by scientific methods.

Yielding to the pressure of this secular philosophy, Christianity began to weaken. In 1867, Matthew Arnold in his great poem *Dover Beach* wrote of the "long withdrawing roar" of the tide of Christianity. Recognizing the impact of Darwin's theory of evolution, Nietzsche in his introduction to *Thus Spake Zarathustra*, asked the question: "Have you not heard that God is dead?" He was describing not so much the literal death of God as the decay of a belief system and an image of spirit that was worn out, because it was no longer numinous and therefore relevant to millions of people. Within a hundred years, the tide of faith had withdrawn so far that there was nothing to aspire to beyond the pursuit of the aims that now dominate modern secular culture, whose gods appear to be money, power and the rational mind. Within a few generations, the old certainties, weakened by all the influences outlined above, seemed, like Prospero's cloud-capped palaces, to have vanished into thin air as the image of a transcendent reality and our long relationship with it faded. Reason, it was claimed, would replace Faith. The rational mind of man would be the new god.

The combined influence of Darwin, Nietzsche, Freud and Marx in the late nineteenth century laid the foundation of a new secular meta-narrative: this material reality is the only one we need to recognize; there is no other reality, no transcendent dimension. There is no need to pray to God nor can there be the expectation of union with God or Christ after death because there is no God, no soul, and no kingdom of heaven: death brings the extinction of consciousness. In 1963 Sir Julian Huxley confirmed this belief: "Today," he wrote, "the God hypothesis has ceased to be scientifically tenable, has lost its explanatory value, and is becoming a burden to our thought. It no longer convinces or comforts, and its abandonment often brings a deep sense of relief."[2]

A huge vacuum was left by the weakening of the older meta-narrative and into this poured the secular ideologies which ravaged the world in the twentieth century. The Utopian ideologies of Communism and Hitler's vision of National Socialism seduced millions of individuals into succumbing to beliefs which brought enslavement and death to millions of others. The men who promoted them became inflated with a god-like omnipotence, as have contemporary leaders of whatever faith or none who have unconsciously identified themselves with the power of the missing archetype. Edward Edinger sums up the effects of this situation in his book, *The Creation of Consciousness: Jung's Myth for Modern Man*:

> The breakdown of a central myth is like the shattering of a vessel containing a precious essence; the fluid is spilled and drains away, soaked up by the surrounding undifferentiated matter. Meaning is lost. In its place, primitive and atavistic contents are reactivated. Differentiated values disappear and are replaced by the elemental motivations of power and pleasure, or else the individual is exposed to emptiness and despair.[3]

The Breakdown of the Old Meta-narrative

This was the general cultural atmosphere which, as a young woman, I found so perplexing and unsatisfying, having, through my travels in the East, encountered the idea that there was an enlightened state of mind or state of consciousness which could be accessed through contemplation, meditation and a gradual alignment with a transcendent order of being. There seemed to be nothing in the secular West that could bring me to this level of being, no path to follow other than that of conventional Christianity with its emphasis on belief, worship and charitable works or the path of science with its exclusive focus on the physical aspect of reality. The direct experience of the numinous was never mentioned in Sunday sermons. There was an emptiness; a longing for something that I sensed was missing at the heart of both religion and secular science; an answer to the perennial human questions: who are we and why are we here? What is the meaning of my existence? Why is life so full of evil and suffering? I became aware that thousands like myself were on a quest to answer these questions, to fill the vacuum left by the deconstruction of the old image of God and a weakening of the moral values that had guided Christian culture for centuries, however much these had been tarnished by the predatory emphasis on territorial conquest and the unbridled pursuit of wealth and power.

At that time (in the 1950's and 60's) millions of people including myself were turning away from Christianity because its beliefs no longer evoked a response in our soul. For many they were too literal, too remote from us, too male and paternal, too tied up with the inflexibility of dogma, too ignorant and intolerant of other traditions and convinced of the infallibility of their own. Seeking a direct relationship with spirit, people turned to shamanic traditions, to the writings of Aldous Huxley and to mystics like the Sufi poet Rumi. Many, as I did, travelled to the East to explore the teachings of Hinduism, Buddhism, Taoism and Zen Buddhism and study at the feet of Eastern teachers. Women went in search of what has long been missing in the patriarchal image of God — the feminine dimension of the divine and the feminine values which were becoming increasingly diminished in a culture intent on 'the survival of the fittest' and driven by a competitive ethos and a voracious consumerism.

In a predominantly secular culture, it has become fashionable to dismiss religious beliefs as the residue of primitive and outgrown superstition. While I have sympathy with the secularist position I am concerned that if we do away with God and a transcendent order, we are left with man's idea of what creation should be and man's dream of manipulating creation to serve his own interests and needs. Whatever the abuses of it by religions which have claimed to know the will of God, the transcendent image has given us a moral compass to forge the values which could protect humanity from the dangerous hubris — the 'god-almightiness'— of the secular dream as well as the undoubted distortions of the religious dream. These primary values are grounded in the service and protection of life: compassion, mercy, love, truth, justice and freedom.

An Outworn Image of God

Mythologically speaking, as the prevailing myth of our civilization wanes, dies and disappears into the underworld of the collective unconscious, it could be said that we are living through a lunar phase of death or darkness. As the historian of culture Thomas Berry comments, "We are in between stories. The old story, the account of how the world came to be and how we fit into it, is no longer effective. Yet we have not learned the new story."[4] In mythic terms, we are waiting for the rebirth of the moon and a new story which could unite the whole of humanity in a shared vision of reality.

During the phase of darkness, however, we are still living under the spell of the solar meta-narrative described in Chapters Six, Nine and Fourteen — the Promethean myth of progress and the mastery of nature through the power of our science and technology. This meta-narrative has no relationship with a transcendent dimension. The human mind is the supreme value. 'Progress' serves the perceived needs of our species alone. In its hubristic stance, this secular meta-narrative has banished the unknown, unexplored, transrational aspect of life and of our own nature. Yet, paradoxically, this secular meta-narrative has developed out of the belief enshrined in the Book of Genesis that God gave Adam dominion over the Earth.

The great mythologist, Joseph Campbell, writes in *The Inner Reaches of Outer Space* that from time to time the image of God has to die if it is not to become an idol. It has, he says, to become transparent to transcendence in order to be renewed.[5] The same theme is reflected in the image of the death of the Old King that is found in many alchemical treatises. In our time the Old King may be identified not only with an outworn image of God but outworn beliefs — part religious, part secular — which can no longer provide an adequate container for the soul of humanity. It may be that the image of God needs to evolve because something in the old image is missing or incomplete.

It may not be God who has died but rather the image we have projected onto Him, an image that was formulated by different priesthoods according to their level of understanding at a specific historical time. It may be that 'God' is longing for release from His imprisonment in the strait-jacket of our beliefs. Or, to use a gardening metaphor, 'God' has become pot-bound, constricted by the anthropomorphic, gender-biased, paternalistic image that was projected onto Him millennia ago. Like a conjurer demonstrating his skills, we have cut God in two and have utterly lost the sense of the divinity of nature. We have fixed the image of deity in the masculine gender, refusing until very recently to entertain the idea that the feminine aspect of spirit is essential to the completion and balance of the image of deity and to the balance of a civilization.

As Teilhard de Chardin suggested, we need to formulate a radically new image of God and a new cosmology that is related to the phenomenal discoveries of science which have revealed the stupendous dimensions of the universe. We also need an image of the sacred marriage that can reunify spirit and nature — the two aspects of life sundered by the beliefs that arose during the solar era. As Teilhard de Chardin pointed out, "Something seems to have gone wrong in the way God is represented to man. Man would seem to have no clear picture of the God he longs to worship."[6]

Jung foresaw this situation in his book, *Psychology and Religion: West and East*. He understood that Nietzsche's phrase "the Death of God" was not to be taken literally, any more than the doctrines of the Church about the Virgin Birth and the bodily Resurrection of Christ were to be taken literally, but described a profound transformation that was at work in the depths of the modern psyche. Addressing the need for the emergence of the Christian myth in a new form, and offering a new mythical and symbolic interpretation of Christ's death and resurrection, he wrote:

> The myth says he [Christ] was not to be found where his body was laid. "Body" means the outward, visible form, the erstwhile but ephemeral setting for the

highest value. The myth further says that the value rose again in a miraculous manner transformed. The three days' descent into hell during death describes the sinking of the vanished value into the unconscious, where, by conquering the power of darkness, it establishes a new order, and then rises up to heaven again, that is, attains supreme clarity of consciousness. The fact that only a few people see the Risen One means that no small difficulties stand in the way of finding and recognizing the transformed value.[7]

Once again, as in the early centuries of the Christian era, it seems as if new bottles are needed to hold the wine of a new revelation. As Jesus pointed out 2000 years ago, bottles become worn out and have to be replaced. But how do we create the vessel which can assimilate the wine of a new vision of reality and a different image of God? How do we relinquish the dogmatic beliefs and certainties which have, over the millennia of the patriarchal era, caused indescribable and quite unnecessary suffering and the sacrifice of countless millions of lives? I cannot answer these questions. But I do know that as the new wine comes into being, we have to hold the tension between the old and the new.

It must have been like this 2000 years ago when the disciples of Jesus tried to assimilate what he was telling them, something so utterly different from the belief-system and the brutal values that governed the world of their time. Those new teachings and those different values seem barely to have touched the consciousness that currently governs the world, however much political and religious leaders proclaim their allegiance to them. Millions claim to be Christians yet those same millions subvert the teaching of Christ about compassion and not shedding their brothers' blood. Christianity seems to have degenerated into feuding between its different branches over such issues as homosexuality and women priests.

Much of what was lost to Christianity during the early centuries of persecution has been recovered, including the important Gnostic texts discovered in 1945 at Nag Hammadi in Egypt.[8] But there is as yet no cultural vessel to receive this recovered material, no way in which it can be integrated or married with the orthodox religious traditions because these cling tenaciously and even fanatically to the literal interpretation of the 'old bottles', the revelatory texts written down millennia ago.

The level of consciousness so far attained by 'believers' does not seem strong enough to tolerate a change in the image of God; yet if the image of spirit does not change so that there is a marriage between the masculine and feminine archetypes, it seems doubtful that human consciousness can evolve further, either because it is in thrall to an unbalanced or incomplete image of God or to an atheism which repudiates the whole idea of God. We now know why the feminine dimension of the divine was repudiated by the three patriarchal religions but it does seem astonishing that they do not appear to question the concept or image of God they have inherited from the past. As Susanne Schaup points out in her book *Sophia, Aspects of the Divine Feminine:*

> The image of God in Western religion, including Judaism and Islam, is a masculine one, despite all protests to the contrary, and as such is a direct cause of the devaluation of the Feminine and feminine priorities in our culture...That which gives a culture legitimacy is, ultimately, its underlying concept of God. If this concept does not change, nothing can actually change… No scientific, ecological, or social paradigm shift can take effect, as long as the theological paradigm does not change along with it.[9]

Despite the efforts of many feminists to 'marry' a feminine image of deity with the masculine one and the worldwide change of consciousness that is gathering momentum with regard to our relationship with the planet, it is nevertheless a fact that the world is still ruled by a patriarchal mindset. The great nations of the world are still competing with each other for power and resources rather than coming together to serve the endangered planetary organism. There is as yet no political consensus about how to work together and how to formulate different values, although a movement in that direction is growing and becoming increasingly articulate.

It seems as if we are living through a tumultuous interregnum, made critically dangerous because of our immeasurably enhanced capacity to destroy each other and irreparably damage the fabric of life on this planet. While the "death of God" has been welcomed by a secular culture, this fact nevertheless creates in many people an unconscious anxiety and a deep fear of the void, and gives rise to a moral vacuum as well as to a defensive fundamentalist position in both religion and secular science. The Jihadist who believes that it is God's will that Islam should conquer the world may draw the power of his ideology from this fear, as may Christian Fundamentalists. The roots of the tendency to polarize lie deep in our solar past but they are strengthened whenever there is a situation which arouses uncertainty, anxiety and conflict.

The Conflict between the three Patriarchal Religions

It could be said that the dangerous political situation in the Middle East with Jerusalem at its heart is, at root, a conflict between three religious traditions, each of which believes itself to be the carrier of a special and unique revelation and each of which holds Jerusalem as its holy city. Any threat or challenge to the collective belief system is met by a furious, and at times hysterical, defence. The reason for this seems to be that, at the deepest level of the psyche, religious beliefs are tied in to survival instincts and also to possession of the land, held sacred for generations. A threat to a religion is a threat to the survival of that group and the deep and sacred bonding between members of that group and the land that God was believed to grant to that group millennia ago. Because these beliefs are so deeply held and because beneath them lies the terror of the meaninglessness of human existence, it is rarely possible to have a discussion about whether certain beliefs might need to be modified and even discarded in the light of a new understanding.

In the distant past, the Jewish belief that they were the Chosen People left other groups excluded and gave a Cain and Abel twist to relationships between different religions and ethnic groups. The Christians claimed that they too were 'chosen' to carry a revelation that was brought to them by the only Son of God and their religion was therefore, by implication, superior to others which it would ultimately supplant. This conviction led Christianity into an inflated evangelical position which led it to look down on other religious traditions and attempt to convert their believers to the 'true' path. What course was left to Islam other than to try and emulate the Christian example by propagating the spread of its religion by all possible means, attempting to supplant Christianity by sheer weight of numbers and force of arms? Psychologically speaking, this whole unconscious process set up a massive sibling rivalry between the three patriarchal 'brothers' wherever their specific revelations were interpreted in a literal and divisive way.

The old atavistic behavioural pattern of predator killing prey, already deeply embedded in tribal rivalries, was unconsciously incorporated into religions: human sacrifice in defence of a belief system or an ideology was sanctioned as something that was acceptable to God, something that God would approve of and support. The idea that a particular belief system was truer, more pleasing to God than others and offered a path to salvation denied to those following a different belief system was accepted and taught as part of a religious tradition, indoctrinating generations of children with this pernicious idea. Worse, the idea that anyone who was a threat to that tradition could be killed in order to preserve or promote the 'true' religion was woven into the fabric of the teaching and from there found its way into ideologies and relations between nations. The Christian Church was flawed from the fourth century by the exclusion of certain Gnostic texts that were deemed unacceptable by a group of very powerful individuals as well as by its incorporation into the powerful political institution of the Roman Empire. Its sacred mission was subverted by the means it adopted to maintain and extend its power.

The Abuse of God

The image of God we have inherited from the patriarchal religions portrays a transcendent God creating the Earth from a distance, distant and separate from the created world and ourselves. What was lost was the idea of the immanence of God — an idea that the Jewish philosopher Spinoza (1632–1677) was briefly to revive in the seventeenth century, suffering persecution by his Jewish community for daring to suggest it. This image of God became embedded in belief systems which fixed the godhead in the image of a male deity and rejected or failed to include both the feminine dimension of the divine and the idea that material creation, including the body, is a theophany — a showing forth or manifestation of a divine ground or source. How then could human life, human experience, be valued and honoured as something precious, something sacred, a vehicle of divinity? How could the life of the Earth and its species be respected?

The archetypal image we created widened the split within our own nature between the conscious mind and the matrix of instinct. The problem may not lie with God but how God has been used to serve our own agendas. Christians (to focus on one religion) have believed that God ratified their prejudices in their persecution of women, homosexuals, people of colour and people with a different belief system from their own, whether Jews, Muslims or the Indigenous People of different continents. They have claimed that the Christian revelation was superior to that of others, and have tried to convert people to the 'true' path to God, proclaiming that belief was the path to redemption and that outside the Church there was no salvation. For centuries they persecuted shamans, visionaries, prophets, mystics and all those who might have introduced a different experience of spirit. Meister Eckhart, one of Christianity's greatest mystics, who said "Outside of God there is nothing", would have been burnt at the stake if he had not fortunately died before the Church could implement a trial and a sentence of death. Giordano Bruno died at the stake for proclaiming that God was present in nature.

For all its extraordinary achievements in holding society together in a shared vision, the abuse of God and God's creatures has been a major flaw throughout the history of patriarchal religion. With the 'death' of God proclaimed by a secular culture, many of these old habits and beliefs are changing. Yet still we hear Christian 'believers' quarrelling among themselves over homosexuals and women priests. In the name of Islam, we see the ongoing persecution of women, as in Afghanistan and Pakistan and in Iran, an authoritarian and oppressive theocratic regime. We see the unresolved bloody enmity between the Shi'a and Sunni branches of Islam. In many of these instances of persecution, there is a conflation of ancient tribal custom and human prejudice with divine command.

What use is belief if it does not lead to a deepening of understanding and compassion? And what use is the continued worship of God's sacrificed Son if nothing fundamentally changes in our habits of behaviour? Would Christ have approved of weapons of mass destruction? Of Hiroshima? Of depleted uranium, cluster bombs, unmanned drones and the bombing of Baghdad?

The literalist reading of the Book of Revelation has led Evangelical Christians (no fewer than 40% of Americans) eagerly to anticipate the 'End Days' and Armageddon — the final battle which is to be the precursor of the 'Rapture' and Second Coming of Christ. Shi'a Muslims await the return of the Mahdi in the same expectation of a New World Order. Ultra-orthodox Jews await the Messiah. All ideologies which invoke the coming of a New Order after the elimination of an old one, and the recurrent millennial belief that a New Order will be ushered in by a final battle, have their ultimate origin in lunar mythology and the rebirth of the crescent moon after the 'banishment' of its dark phase. However, influenced by the polarizing legacy of solar mythology, expectations of the arrival of a New Order generally accept massive sacrifice in the final battle between the forces of light and darkness as a necessary preliminary to the establishment of the New Order. Born-again Christians believe that only the 'Chosen' will be saved in the Rapture, taken up to heaven from one moment to the next. The rest will perish.

When literalist beliefs take over the collective psyche, aroused in a credulous public by priests and prophets convinced of the authenticity of their message, they can override the highest values of religion and cast what can only be described as a spell on those who claim to believe in God. All this perversion has arisen from a mistaken concept of what Deity is — the worship of an idol rather than true insight into the nature of divinity.

Yet when read as metaphor rather than the literal Word of God, these prophecies about the end of the world and the coming of a Messiah and a New World Order could be understood as referring to the raising of the consciousness of the whole of humanity rather than predicting the appearance of a redeemer who will impose a New Order. Rabbi David Cooper, for example, writes in his book, *God is a Verb*, "Kabbalists say that we are rapidly approaching another major paradigm shift in awareness. It will be called messianic consciousness, and we will understand everything in an entirely new light."[10]

The Influence of the East

From the 1950's more and more people, disillusioned with Christianity, began to travel to the East in search of the wisdom enshrined in the teachings of Hinduism,

Buddhism, Zen Buddhism, Taoism, and Sufism — the mystical tradition of Islam. A priceless treasury of texts from the East began to flow to the West. From these they learned methods of meditation which could open a direct path of communion with a transcendent dimension of reality — a path to the experience of enlightenment. As I had done on my two journeys to the East, they encountered a radically different image of spirit as well as the concepts of karmic responsibility and reincarnation. They absorbed the idea that suffering arises from unconsciousness or ignorance of the fact that spirit is the ground of all life.

Each of these ancient traditions has contributed to the birth of a new consciousness in the West. Many texts became available in excellent translations for a new and interested audience. The celebrated poems of Rumi drew a cult following. Tsultrim Allione drew attention to extraordinary women in the Tibetan Buddhist tradition in her book *Women of Wisdom* (1984). Aldous Huxley's books opened the door to psychedelic experience and the recovery of the shamanic traditions of Indigenous People. Publishers sprang up who specialized in these books.

The invasion of Tibet by China in 1950 forced many Tibetan monks to flee to India, America and Europe. Some learned English and other languages, became renowned teachers, and wrote books which had a considerable impact on Western culture. Sogyal Rinpoche's book, *The Tibetan Book of Living and Dying*, for example, was widely read. They brought with them ancient methods of healing and meditation and offered different approaches to healing the sickness of body and soul. His Holiness the Dalai Lama is recognized by millions as the greatest spiritual leader in the world today.

California was for many years a focus for the development of these ideas, practices and contemplative methods of the East and a centre for the spiritual development of the individual; but Europe also benefited as Tibetan monks established temples and teaching centres in several countries, bringing Buddhism to many thousands of people looking for a different approach to spirituality. The Vietnamese monk Thich Nhat Hahn established a renowned centre at Plum Village in France. The Maharishi Mahesh Yogi attracted thousands to follow his method of Transcendental Meditation and established a centre in England.

People began to seek out new methods of healing such as acupuncture, aromatherapy, reflexology and Chinese herbalism, as well as Ayurvedic medicine and the already well-established approach of Homeopathy. Despite the sometimes virulent opposition of established medicine and science to these ancient methods of healing, thousands of men and women have now trained in them and millions are being treated by them. The focus of this approach to healing is on an empathic holistic attitude which treats body and mind as an organic whole. All these different influences began to have an impact on the vacuum left by the deconstruction of the image of God inherited from the patriarchal past.

The Cosmology of the East

In the religions of the East, we find a unifying approach — one that is much closer to the teaching of Kabbalah described in Chapter Three. Apart from that tradition, the Indian science of the soul is the oldest, wisest and most highly developed on the planet. For at least 5000 years, possibly longer, the great sages of India taught the underlying unity of all creation and never separated the visible and invisible dimensions of reality. In their view, the entire organism of the world we know as well as the organism of our individual human self are the expression, manifestation and dwelling place of spirit. Professor Ravindra tells us in his book *Science and the Sacred*:

> The one central insight into Truth to which all Indian wisdom points is the *oneness of all that exists*. This insight is not alien to other cultures; but in India all the great sages again and again return to it. In fact the realization of this truth is what defines the greatness of a person in India. Although the truth is easily stated as "All is one", the sages have also said that the realization of this truth in the core of one's being can take many lifetimes. And the realization of this truth is held to be the purpose of human existence. All art, philosophy and science, if they are true, reflect this vision and further its realization... During a period of at least four thousand years, the sages in India have repeatedly asserted the underlying unity of all that exists, including everything we call animate or inanimate, and have said that the cultivation of wisdom consists in the realization of this truth.[11]

The mystics of all the great cultures of which we have knowledge discovered that our consciousness can interact with the invisible ground of all life that they named Brahman, the Tao, or simply, the Void. Christian mystics spoke of the mystery of the Divine Darkness of God. Dionysius the Areopagite, living in the fifth century AD, wrote that "the most divine knowledge of God, that in which He is known through unknowing, according to the Union that transcends the mind, happens when the mind, turning away from all things, including itself, is united with the dazzling rays and there and then illuminated in the unsearchable depth of wisdom."[12] Over a thousand years later, an English poet, Thomas Vaughan (1622–1695), wrote these beautiful words: "There is in God — some say — a deep and dazzling darkness.... O for that night that I in Him might live, invisible and dim."

The Search for a Unified Vision:
Healing the Wound in the "Body" of God

Many years ago I had a dream that I was walking in a wilderness of rock and shale, a landscape similar to one above the tree line of the Alps. Suddenly I heard a faint voice crying, "Help me. Help me". I looked around but could see no one. The cry was repeated and seemed to come from the ground at my feet. I looked down and saw a tiny leather purse lying in the dust, almost hidden among rocks and boulders. I picked it up and opened it. Inside was a small stone and it was from this that the voice was coming. Does a stone have consciousness? I wondered. Can it communicate with me in words? "How can I help you?" I asked the stone, as it warmed to the touch of my hand. It gave me no answer but the urgency of its plea haunted me. I had to find out what needed help and how I could help.

Finally, I understood that what needed help was the consciousness that is buried in the deepest aspect of our psychic life as well as in the densest aspect of matter that, we are told, is 'dead' and has no consciousness — a lost aspect of spirit that has not been recognized as spirit; something that asks to be redeemed from a state of immolation created by our beliefs. The image of spirit inherited from the past may from time to time need to be discarded but the archetype of spirit will always be re-discovered in a new form, incorporating aspects of itself that may have been split off or excluded in the past by our too limited understanding. Years after this dream, when I was exploring the teaching of Kabbalah, I found this passage in a translation of a text written by the great sixteenth century kabbalist, Moses Cordovero, and realized that this was the definition of God that I had been searching for and could not find in Christianity:

> The essence of divinity is found in every single thing — nothing but it exists. Since it causes every thing to be, no thing can live by anything else. It enlivens them; its existence exists in each existent…. Do not attribute duality to God. Let God be solely God…. Do not say, "This is a stone and not God." God forbid! Rather, all existence is God, and the stone is a thing pervaded by divinity…. Nothing is devoid of its divinity. Everything is within it; it is within everything and outside of everything. There is nothing but it.[13]

These words seem to resonate not only with those of Meister Eckhart and many other mystics but also with the words of Jesus in the Gnostic Gospel of Thomas when he said that the Kingdom of God is spread out upon the Earth and men do not see it. The insight that divinity is present in every single atom of life is precisely what has been missing in our concept of God and it is this which has led to the split between spirit and nature and, ultimately, to that between religion and science as well as to our growing capacity to inflict destruction on each other and on planetary life.

Nature as a Theophany

Amazingly, in the ninth century there was a most beautiful and clear exposition of nature as the expression or theophany of spirit. This concept flourished in Celtic Christianity until this branch of Christianity was set aside (after the Synod of Whitby in AD 664) in favour of the Roman or Catholic version of Christianity. Yet it must have survived for it is found in the work of John Scotus Eriugena (810–877), a renowned Irish scholar and Neo-Platonist who lived at the royal court in France for many years and contributed, by his translation of the works of Dionysius the Areopagite, to the great cultural impetus which led to the building of the Gothic Cathedrals. He also wrote an extraordinary book called *Periphyseon* or *De Divisione Naturae*. I first came across this book many years ago when I was studying medieval history at Oxford and it made a deep impression on me at the time. But I did not realize its significance and its relevance for our times until recently, when I came across these electrifying words, communicated from teacher to pupil, which eradicate the split between creator and creation:

> We should not therefore understand God and creation as two different things, but as one and the same. For creation subsists in God, and God is created in creation in a remarkable and ineffable way, manifesting Himself and, though invisible, making Himself visible, and though incomprehensible, making Himself comprehensible, and though hidden, revealing Himself, and, though unknown, making himself known; though lacking form and species, endowing Himself with form and species; though superessential, making Himself essential... though creating everything, making Himself created in everything. The Maker of all, made in all, begins to be eternal and, though motionless, moves into everything and becomes all things in all things... Hence matter itself, from which, as we read He made the world, is from Him and in Him and He is in it insofar as it is understood to have being.[14]

How radically different is this view of God from the one currently set forth by the three major patriarchal religions; how satisfying it is and how close it is to the Eastern traditions. God is described as both Hidden Source and Manifest Process or Form, both transcendent and immanent, just as in the tradition of Kabbalah. Eriugena's book was condemned by the Church because it was thought to promote the idea of pantheism — that God was present in nature. Fortunately, his remarkable book survived although he himself is said to have been murdered by his own monks at Malmesbury Abbey when he returned to England, no doubt because of the heretical nature of his ideas.

New Wine in New Bottles: the New Spirituality

Over the past fifty years a gradual restoration of a sense of the sacred has been taking place beneath the surface of our culture, called forth by the multi-faceted crisis of our times. Now, through the awakening power of the environmental movement, as well as through the new discoveries of science, we are invited to enter a new era, where nature — the life of the Earth — and all the miraculous processes and patterns of life can once again be recognized as sacred as they once were in shamanic cultures.

This new movement that some name as "the Great Awakening" is beginning to heal the split between spirit and nature or the wound in the body of God which has so tragically flawed the three patriarchal religions and the whole solar era. However, because neither mainstream religion nor science are aware of the origin of this split and its influence on our attitudes and our behaviour, neither seems able adequately to engage in this process of awakening and address the immense challenges we face today. There is huge resistance to change because, instinctively, we perceive change as a threat to our survival: it is safer to stay with the known rather than forge a path into the unknown.

Something beyond either needs to come into being: a new meta-narrative, a new worldview. As in the medieval story of the Grail where Parsifal, after many trials, heals the wound of the Fisher King by asking the question, "What ails thee, Father?" Perhaps we need to ask this same question of our beliefs, our values and our culture.

Joseph Campbell recognized the need for a new myth when he wrote: "The old gods are dead or dying and people everywhere are searching, asking: What is the new mythology to be, the mythology of this unified earth as of one harmonious being?"[15] And he answered the question by saying that the new myth is that Earth is the country to which all people belong. He saw that this new myth of the Earth as our cosmic home could take us beyond the divisions and rivalries that veil our essential relationship to each other and our relationship to the planet and the wider Cosmos.

Thousands, if not millions of individuals today are searching not only for the unified field in science but for a unified vision of life — a unified vision of spirit, nature and humanity that could be in time to mitigate the catastrophic effects of our fragmented view of life. The birthing of this vision asks us to relinquish many cherished beliefs and requires a fundamental transformation of our values. Our knowledge about the world and the universe is accelerating geometrically. We are overwhelmed with information about every aspect of what we observe, yet we understand almost nothing about the mystery of why we are here and what the evolutionary role of our species on this planet might be.

Suppose the cosmic source we come from is attracting us back to itself, helping our consciousness to connect with it, to respond to its evolutionary intention. There is today a crying need for a new way of living and relating to each other and the Cosmos. It is brilliantly reflected in a poem written in 1945 by Christopher Fry in his play called *A Sleep of Prisoners*.

> *The human heart can go the length of God,*
> *Dark and cold we may be, but this*
> *Is no winter now. The frozen misery*
> *Of centuries breaks, cracks, begins to move;*
> *The thunder is the thunder of the floes,*
> *The thaw, the upstart Spring.*
> *Thank God our time is now when wrong*
> *Comes up to face us everywhere.*
> *Never to leave us till we take*
> *The longest stride of soul men ever took.*
> *Affairs are now soul size,*
> *The enterprise*
> *Is exploration into God.*
> *Where are you making for? It takes*
> *So many thousand years to wake*
> *But will you wake for pity's sake?*

The old idea that we are separate from God is breaking, cracking, beginning to move. A regenerative spring is urging us to take the longest stride of soul we have ever taken into the heart of God. The extraordinary discoveries about the size, complexity and incredible beauty of the universe are opening the door to a new cosmology, a new way of living and relating to each other and the planet. This dawning meta-narrative is bringing about a breakdown of old beliefs, old images of God and nature and our own human nature. It is challenging our political and economic structures, our enslavement to obsolete beliefs and atavistic habits of behaviour. It is awakening our heart, our soul, often through means which may appear bizarre or threatening. Sometimes, as people working in the field of psychotherapy know, there has to be a breakdown before there can be a breakthrough. The deconstruction of the old image of God may be one aspect of that necessary process. There is a risk that breakdown could precipitate regression to a more unconscious state where we could lose the priceless treasure of civilization. Everything depends upon whether we assist or resist the simultaneous process of death and rebirth that is taking place within us and our culture. It is a time of awesome responsibility.

The problem now is that the culture is in a dilemma. Part of it — particularly that part concerned with established institutions, whether religious or political — is still acting from the old solar paradigm of the separation of spirit and nature. It still thinks in terms of competition between nation states. It is still hypnotized by the idea of power and progress, intent on conquering and controlling nature and exploiting the resources of the planet for the financial gain of a few nations and corporations and for the benefit of the human species alone. It glorifies the technological achievements of science but neglects to address the poverty and suffering of billions of people and the disastrous effects of the burgeoning growth of the human population on the planetary organism. As, in 2018, the human population passes the 7.6 billion mark, it cannot see that a viable life is becoming increasingly impossible for those billions who already struggle merely to survive, without adequate food and water, let alone quality of life

Millions who are deeply troubled by these facts are rapidly learning to think in global terms, understanding that our species cannot be separated from the planetary biosphere. It realizes that nationalist power struggles are becoming increasingly obsolete and dangerous and that war is no longer an option for us. It regards our weapons and the colossal sums of money spent on them and on arms sales as something truly obscene. It sees population growth as one of the greatest threats to the survival of our species, as well as millions of other species and the well-being of the planet in general. The deep malaise in society may help us to grow beyond the current secular mind-set and beyond the religions of the past which carry so much dead wood, towards a new spirituality which unifies the two great archetypes of life in a sacred marriage of spirit and nature. This new spirituality, which incorporates the best aspect of the great spiritual traditions of the past, including the indigenous traditions, could open the door to a new understanding of our role in a mindblowing cosmic drama. Many people are discovering that the experience of spirit is utterly different from what they had accepted as 'truth' in the past. In these discoveries there is no division of God. There is nothing outside God. God, as Meister Eckhart realized, is all cosmic life.

Cosmic Consciousness

I remember how excited I was to discover this passage in Bede Griffiths' book, *Return to the Centre*:

> The evolution of matter from the beginning leads to the evolution of consciousness in man; it is the universe itself which becomes conscious in man…. It is the inner movement of the Spirit, immanent in nature, which brings about the evolution of matter and life into consciousness and the same Spirit at work in human consciousness, latent in every man, is always at work leading to divine life.[16]

His words, like Aurobindo's in his extraordinary book, *The Life Divine*, and Teilhard de Chardin's vision of humanity moving towards what he called the Omega Point, helped me to see that the evolution of life on this planet is like a plant, an organic growth, which has its roots in an unknown depth. Its flowering is a potential within us, something that we have still to experience, that only a few pioneers of consciousness have experienced. Again, it is something which is unfolding and evolving from within, over millions of years, as the potential form of an oak is contained within an acorn. We cannot know the final form until we have grown into it but we can begin to understand the process of evolution which has formed us and begin consciously to cooperate with it.

Precisely as these three greatest sages of the last century have suggested, spirit may have always been immanent or active in this dimension of reality, leading us to the ultimate revelation that answers Kepler's question at the beginning of this chapter and tells us that, in both our spiritual and physical substance, we are of the essence of divinity: everything we can see, perceive and reflect on, is of that essence. From the perspective of spirit, it has brought into being this material dimension of reality in order to extend the experience of itself — to come to know itself through all the facets of life it has created, including our species, which is the only one at present capable of consciously recognizing it.

Teilhard's understanding of the process of evolution, showing the rising tide of consciousness embedded in the life processes of the earth, is one of the most enthralling ideas of our time. But, he asks, will this universal Spirit of Evolution "flower in time to ensure that, arrived at the point of super-humanity, we avoid dehumanising ourselves?"[17] That is the question that confronts us at this perilous time.

Our consciousness is now poised at the threshold of the encounter with cosmic consciousness. The invisible field that relates us to galactic life resonates with the call to relationship with it and many people are responding to this call. There is a new perception of life pouring into the culture through many thousands of individuals: the perception of the universe as an organic, sacred and living whole, with ourselves as conscious participants in that living whole. We seem to be reaching the point where we can experience cosmic consciousness, cosmic mind or cosmic soul (I use these terms interchangeably) as the greater field or ground from which our consciousness derives and in which it participates. Could this new (yet very ancient) idea transform our relationships with each other as well as with the Earth and the vast entity of the Cosmos in whose life our lives participate?

Every mystical tradition says that at the core of our being we are one with the divine. We are one with the immensity we contemplate. Each teaches that the eye of the heart — the eye which perceives with gnosis or insight into the nature of reality — can only slowly open to awareness of this mystery. The ground has to be well prepared to hold the revelation of this vision and the preparation for it requires much time for contemplation as well as a growing respect and love for all aspects of life.

What seems to be happening now is that a new or perhaps very ancient understanding of spirit is dawning on us. Although it is not yet fully conscious, the realization that our brain acts both as a receiver and transmitter for a greater field beyond our 'normal' range of awareness is leading us to the point where we may be able to say, as Arjuna says to Krishna in the *Bhagavad Gita*: "Thou art the Knower within me and the One to be known. By Thee alone this universe is pervaded. Overjoyed am I to see what I have never seen before." (11:38, 45)

In the light of this different understanding, spirituality invites us to focus more on the experience of illumination and insight than on faith and belief, although belief may initially be a path which can lead to illumination. During the solar era, we have learned to think of spirit and matter as separate, but now we may be able to see that there is no essential separation between them: the seen and unseen dimensions of reality are aspects of the whole and are continually interacting with each other, flowing into each other.

We need an image of God which is related to these insights. Of all the challenges we have to face, this is one of the most difficult, because it means that we have to relinquish a structure of thought or meta-narrative by which we have lived for millennia.

The mystics of all the great cultures of the past discovered that our consciousness can interact with the invisible field or ground they named variously as God, Brahman, the Tao, or Light, Divine Darkness and the Void. In our normal state we cannot initiate or perceive this interaction, but this does not mean it does not exist.

The *Vedas*, the *Upanishads*, the *Bhagavad Gita*, the Jewish mystical tradition of Kabbalah, the Christian and Sufi mystics, all say that spirit can, ultimately, only be known or apprehended experientially, and that spirit is omnipresent, at once transcendent to and immanent within the forms of life. We are bathed in, permeated by spirit every moment of our existence, in every breath we take. In the light of this different understanding, spirituality invites us to focus more on the experience of illumination than on faith and belief. There is no better text to describe this fusion of the human and the divine than the *Bhagavad Gita*. Here is Krishna, speaking to Arjuna:

> *I am the one source of all: the evolution of all comes from me.*
> *I am beginningless, unborn, the Lord of all Worlds.*
> *I am the soul which dwells in the heart of all things.*
> *I am the beginning, the middle and the end of all that lives.*
> *I am the seed of all things that are:*
> *And no being that moves or moves not can ever be without me.*[18]

I don't think we can really understand ourselves unless we understand the history of the evolution of consciousness and begin to bring together the different branches of knowledge that have developed with such extraordinary rapidity during the last hundred or so years and have become separated from each other.

As we discover this incredible story, the realization is dawning that we are participating in a Cosmic Consciousness or Intelligence which is co-inherent with every particle of our being and every particle of matter. If we connect these ideas to God, then God or Spirit or Divine Mind is not something transcendent to ourselves. We are co-inherent with It, at the very heart of It. To co-inhere means to be together, to abide together.

This realization calls for a huge shift of awareness and a fundamental change in our values. If God or Spirit is not something separate from ourselves, something transcendent to nature and planetary life, but is the intelligence and energy of the life process itself, flaring forth at every instant in every region of this vast universe as well as in ourselves, then how we treat so-called 'inanimate' matter, planetary life and each other becomes a matter of how we are treating God. It transforms obedience to God's commands into love and respect for God's creation, including ourselves, our neighbour and, most importantly, our enemy.

It is clear to me from my study of visionary experience in many cultures that a visionary is aware of the reality of worlds and presences inaccessible to our 'normal' state of consciousness. I am absolutely certain through my own experience and my study of visionary experience that a wider, deeper consciousness than our own is trying to make itself known to us. It has been doing so for millennia. As long as this dimension of consciousness is denied existence and dissociated from our own, it will act in the manner of an unconscious autonomous complex, influencing us in all kinds of ways, some of them negative and destructive, until it finally attracts our attention. As long as we believe that consciousness begins and ends with the physical brain, we will never reach what we are capable of becoming — people who are in conscious communion with metaphysical reality.

In his book, *Cosmic Consciousness*, Richard Bucke describes the experiences of individuals who have had that opening to cosmic consciousness and sees these as forerunners of a more advanced race that is slowly coming into being. He himself had such an experience that changed his life and his understanding. Because this passage means so much to me and has helped me to change my own understanding, I would like to share it with readers who may not know of it:

> *I had spent the evening (in 1872 in England) in a great city, with two friends, reading and discussing Wordsworth, Shelley, Keats, Browning, and especially Whitman. We parted at midnight. I had a long drive in a hansom to my lodging. My mind, deeply under the influence of the ideas, images, and emotions called up by the reading and talk, was calm and peaceful. I was in a state of quiet, almost passive enjoyment, not actually thinking, but letting ideas, images, and emotions flow of themselves, as it were, through my mind. All at once, without warning of any kind, I found myself wrapped in a flame-colored cloud. For an instant I thought of fire, an immense conflagration somewhere close by in that great city; the next, I knew that the fire was within myself. Directly afterward there came upon me a sense of exultation, of immense joyousness accompanied or immediately followed by an intellectual illumination impossible to describe. Among other things, I did not merely come to believe, but I saw that the universe is not composed of dead matter, but is, on the contrary, a living Presence; I became conscious in myself of eternal life. It was not a conviction that I would have eternal life, but a consciousness that I possessed eternal life then; I saw that all men are immortal; that the cosmic order is such that without any peradventure all things work together for the good of each and all; that the foundation principle of the world, of all the worlds, is what we call love, and that the happiness of each and all is in the long run absolutely certain. The vision lasted a few seconds and was gone; but the memory of it and the sense of the reality of what it taught has remained during the quarter of a century which has since elapsed. I knew that what the vision showed was true. I had attained to a point of view from which I saw that it must be true. That view, that conviction, I may say that consciousness, has never, even during periods of the deepest depression, been lost.*[19]

To reunite with the ground from which we have come, so assisting the further evolution of Cosmic Consciousness, is one of the most exciting quests that I can imagine. To discover that spirit, so long projected onto a transcendent Creator, remote from our world, is the quintessential consciousness which is awaiting discovery both in nature and in ourselves is one of the greatest revelations it is possible to experience. The other revelation, no less overwhelming, is that we have the extraordinary responsibility of helping spirit to become conscious in ourselves. It may be that Cosmic Consciousness has waited aeons for us to reach the point where more than a handful of individuals could awaken to this revelation. To respond to what is happening at the deepest level, to enter a new phase of our evolutionary journey, we have to create the vessels to hold the new wine that is now pouring into our culture through the awakening consciousness of many thousands, even millions, of individuals.

Notes:

1. Jung, C.G. (1973) Letters 2, p. 312
2. quoted in the Observer, March 31st, 1963
3. Edinger, Edward (1984) *The Creation of Consciousness: Jung's Myth for Modern Man*, Inner City Books, Toronto, pp. 9-10
4. Berry, Thomas (1988) *The Dream of the Earth*, Sierra Club Books, San Francisco
5. Campbell, Joseph (1986) *The Inner Reaches of Outer Space*, Alfred van der Marck Editions, New York, p. 17
6. Teilhard de Chardin, Pierre (1959) *The Future of Man*, William Collins Sons & Co., Ltd., London, p. 272
7. Jung, C.G. (1963) *Memories, Dreams, Reflections*, Chapter Xl, Collins & Routledge edition, p. 300
8. Pagels, Elaine (1980) *The Gnostic Gospels*, George Weidenfeld and Nicolson Ltd., London
9. Schaup, Susanne (1997) *Sophia, Aspects of the Divine Feminine*, Nicolas-Hays Inc. Maine, p. xi
10. Cooper, Rabbi David (1997) *God is a Verb*, Riverhead Books, New York, p.1
11. Ravindra, Ravi, Prof. (2002) *Science and the Sacred*, Quest Books,Wheaton, Ill. p. 27
12. Louth, Andrew (1989) *Denys the Areopagite*, Morehouse–Barlow, London
13. Matt, Daniel (1995) *The Essential Kabbalah: The Heart of Jewish Mysticism*, HarperSanFrancisco, p. 24
14. Uhlfelder, Myra, and Potter, Jean A.(1976) *Periphyseon: On the Division of Nature*, Book III 678c. Bobbs-Merrill, Indianapolis, republished 2011 by Wipf & Stock Publishers, Eugene, Oregon, p. 197 in both editions.
15. Campbell (1968) *The Inner Reaches of Outer Space*
16. Griffiths, Dom Bede (1976) *Return to the Center*, Collins, St. James's Place, London and Templegate, Springfield, Ill. 1977, p. 31-32
17. Teilhard de Chardin, *The Future of Man*, p.141
18. The *Bhagavad Gita* 10:8, 3, 20, 39, translated by Juan Mascaró, Penguin Books, 1962
19. Bucke, Richard Maurice (1923) *Cosmic Consciousness* E.P. Dutton & Co., New York. His experience is described in William James's book, *The Varieties of Religious Experience* (1929), p. 399

A Landscape of Rebirth
Robin Baring 1975

Interlude II

THE WAY OF THE TAO

There is a very ancient spiritual tradition which offers a feminine balance to masculine solar consciousness, one of the few surviving cultural legacies which point to the deep intelligence of lunar culture. I was fortunate enough to have as a godfather a man who had lived for decades in China and I was able to spend many hours with him on my return from my journeys to the East. In his old age, he even looked like a Chinese sage and he taught me about Taoism, showing me many precious manuscripts and paintings he had brought back from his sojourn in China. He told me never to forget the wisdom of the Taoist sages, explaining that they had discovered how to develop the mind without losing touch with the soul and this is why an understanding of their philosophy — China's inestimable gift to humanity — was so important. In particular, he mentioned the genius of a poet of the T'ang dynasty called Wang Wei (701–761).

> *In the deep bamboo forest I sit alone*
> *Loudly I sing and tune my lute*
> *The forest is so thick that no one knows about it.*
> *Only the bright moon comes to shine upon me.*

Whereas the West imagined the creative ground of being as a transcendent Father, Taoism, more subtly and comprehensively than any other spiritual tradition, nurtured the quintessence of the Feminine as a Primordial Mother, keeping alive the ancient feeling of relationship with Nature as the manifest expression of this mysterious ground:

> *There was something formless yet complete*
> *That existed before heaven and earth;*
> *Without sound, without substances,*
> *Dependent on nothing, unchanging,*
> *All pervading, unfailing.*
> *One may think of it as the Mother of all things under heaven*
> *Its true name we do not know.* [1]

The elusive essence of Taoism is expressed in the *Tao Teh Ching*, the only known work of the great sage Lao Tzu (born ca. 604 BC) who, legend says, was persuaded to write down the eighty-one sayings by one of his disciples when, reaching the end of his life, he had embarked on his last journey to the mountains of the West. The word *Tao* means the fathomless Source, the One, the Deep. *Teh* is the way the *Tao* comes into being, growing organically like a plant from the deep ground or source of life, from within outwards. *Ching* is the slow, patient shaping of that process through the activity of a creative intelligence within nature that is expressed as the organic patterning within all instinctual life, a kind of cosmic DNA: "The *Tao* does nothing, yet nothing is left undone."

No group of people has understood the indivisibility of spirit and nature better than the Taoist sages of China. None has entered more deeply into the soul of nature and understood and respected the relationship between body, soul and spirit. Observation and contemplation over thousands of years brought them the insight that the body exists within the wider matrix of nature and nature within the wider soul of the cosmos. They understood that the boundless energy of the universe that they called *qi* flows through everything that exists. Through the flow of that energy everything is connected to everything else. Their insight might be summed up in the words of a modern teacher of *Qigong*: "I am within the universe and the universe is within me."

The origins of Taoism come from the shamanic practices and the oral traditions which were developed as long ago as the Neolithic era. Its earliest written expression was the Book of Changes or *I Ching*, a book of divination consisting of sixty-four oracles, thought to date to 3000–1200 BC and still consulted today. The tradition of Taoism was transmitted from master to pupil by a succession of shaman-sages, many of whom were sublime artists and poets.

From the source which is both everything and no-thing, and whose image is the circle, came heaven and earth, yang and yin — the male and female principles whose dynamic interaction brings into being the world we see and maintains it in balance. The *Tao* is both the source and the creative process of life that flows from it, imagined as a Mother who is the root of heaven and earth, beyond all yet within all, giving birth to all, containing all, nurturing all. The Way of *Tao* is to reconnect with the Mother source or ground, to be in it, like a bird in the air or a fish in the sea, in touch with it, while living in the midst of the myriad forms that the source takes in manifestation. It is to become aware of the presence of the *Tao* in everything, to discover and observe its rhythm and its dance, learning to trust it, no longer interfering with the flow of life by manipulating, directing, resisting, controlling. It is to develop a relationship with and intuitive awareness of a mystery which only gradually unveils itself.

Following the Way of *Tao* requires a turning towards the hidden within-ness of things, a receptivity to the unseen through contemplation of the seen in relationship with the unseen, enough time to reflect on what is inconceivable and indescribable, beyond the reach of mind or intellect, that can only be felt, intuited, experienced at ever deeper depth. Action taken from this position of balance and freedom will be aligned to the harmony of the *Tao* and will therefore embody its mysterious power and wisdom, enabling it to act in the world without attachment to action.

Enlightenment, according to Lao Tzu and Chuang Tzu, two of Taoism's greatest sages, uncovers unknown powers of the mind which lie beyond the threshold of normal consciousness. Sudden enlightenment breaks through the habitual structure of consciousness and opens the mind to the powers and insight held latent in the depths of the soul.

The Taoists never separated nature from spirit, consciously preserving the instinctive knowledge that although it manifests as a duality, life is One. No people observed Nature more passionately and minutely than these Chinese sages or reached so deeply into the hidden heart of life, describing the life and form of insects, animals, birds, flowers, trees, wind, water, planets and stars. They felt the continuous flow and flux of life as an underlying energy that was without beginning or end; that was, like water, never static, never still, never fixed in separate things or events, but always in a state of movement, a state of changing, becoming and relating.

They called the art of going with the flow of this energy *Wu Wei* — not-doing (*Wu* means not or non, *Wei* means doing, making, striving after goals), under-standing it as the art of relinquishing control, not trying to force or manipulate life but, through an act of conscious observation and connection, attuning them-selves to the underlying rhythm and ever-changing modes of its being. The Taoists would never have entertained the idea of targets or goals, other than the mastery of the medium — poetry or painting — through which they expressed their relationship with the *Tao*.

The stilling of the surface mind that is preoccupied with the 'ten thousand things' brings into being a deeper, more complete mind and a meditative state of consciousness and creative power that they named *Te* which enabled them not to interfere with life but, in their words, to "enter the forest without moving the grass; to enter the water without raising a ripple."

The mind of man searches outward all day
The further it reaches,
The more it opposes itself.

> *Only those who look inward*
> *Can censor their passions,*
> *And cease their thoughts.*
> *Being able to cease their thoughts,*
> *Their minds become tranquil.*
> *To tranquillize the mind is to nourish one's spirit.*
> *To nourish the spirit is to return to Nature.*[2]

They cherished the *Tao* with their brushstrokes, observing how it flowed into the patterns of cloud and mist between earth and mountain peak, or the changing rhythm of air currents and the eddying water of rivers and streams; the exquisite opening of plum blossom in spring; the rustling dance of bamboo and willow. They listened to the sounds that can only be heard in silence. They expressed their experience of the *Tao* in their paintings, their poetry, their temples, in remote mountain retreats and gardens and in their way of living which was essentially one of withdrawal from the world to a sanctuary in the heart of nature where they could live a simple, contemplative life, concentrating on perfecting their brush strokes in calligraphy and painting and their subtlety of expression in the art of poetry. Humility, reverence, patience, insight and wisdom were the qualities that they sought to cultivate.

> *Out of non-being, being is born;*
> *Out of silence, the writer produces a song.* [3]

The Taoist artist or poet intuitively reached into the secret essence of what he was observing, making himself one with it, then inviting it to speak through him, so releasing the dynamic harmony within it. He imposed nothing of himself on it but reflected the soul of what he was observing through the highly developed skills that he had cultivated over a lifetime of practice. Through the perfection of his art, he did not define or explain the *Tao* which, as Chuang Tzu said, cannot be conveyed either by words or by silence, but called it into being so that it could be experienced by the beholder. The *Tao* flows through the whole work as a Presence, at once transcendent in its mystery and immanent in its form. The distillation of what the Taoist sages discovered is bequeathed to us in the beauty and wisdom of their painting, poetry and philosophy, and in their profound understanding of the relationship between the observer and what is observed and the eternal ground that underlies and enfolds them.

In *A Treatise on Painting*, Chuang Huai writes:

> Only he who reaches Reality can follow Nature's spontaneity and be aware of
> the subtlety of things, and his mind will be absorbed by them. His brush will

secretly be in harmony with movement and quiescence and all forms will issue forth. Appearances and substance are caught in one motion as the life breath reverberates through them. He who is ignorant of Reality becomes a slave of passion and his nature will be distorted by externalities. He sinks into confusion and is disturbed by thoughts of gain or loss. He is nothing more than a prisoner of brush and ink. How can he speak of genuine works of Heaven and Earth?[4]

Whenever I look at one of the great Taoist paintings of the T'ang or Sung dynasties or read a Taoist poem, I find myself subtly permeated by them. They evoke a state of calm, helping me to let go of the things that normally distract the mind — the preoccupation with the ten thousand things that they called "dust". They relate me instantaneously to the source or ground which unites everything. There is one particular story that I love, recounted to Jung by Richard Wilhelm, who gave us the first English translation of the *I Ching*:

Once, not long ago, there was a great drought in a province of China. The situation was catastrophic. The land was utterly parched, and the crops were failing; many people were facing the prospect of starvation. Desperate, they tried to produce rainfall by performing all the religious rites they knew: the Catholics made processions, the Protestants made prayers, and the Chinese burned joss-sticks and shot off guns to frighten away the demons of the drought, but with no result. Finally the people decided to send for a renowned rainmaker who lived in a far distant province. After some days, a withered old man appeared. The only thing he asked for was a quiet little hut somewhere, and there he locked himself in for three days. On the fourth day the clouds gathered and the rain poured down. As a result, the town filled with rumours about the wonderful rainmaker and the people went to the hut of the rainmaker and asked him what he had done during the three days that had caused the rain to fall on the fourth. He said: "I come from another country where things are in order. Here they are out of order; they are not as they should be under the ordinance of heaven. Therefore the whole country was not in *Tao*, and I also was not in the natural order of things because I was in a disordered country. So I had to wait three days until I was back in *Tao* and then, naturally, the rain came."[5]

To let go of the need for striving and control, to rest in the quietness of mind and humility of heart that the Taoist sage embodies, is to live in a state of instinctive spontaneity that they named *Tzu Jan* — a being-in-the-moment that can only exist, as in earliest childhood, when the effort to adapt to collective values is unknown or of no importance. What exists is what is. There is no need to change it by imposing one's will or trying to manipulate circumstances. Change will come about by changing the quality of one's own being, by consciously re-connecting, moment by moment, with the presence of the Source, particularly in moments of confusion or stress. To feel what needs to be said without striving to say it, to speak from the heart in as few words as possible, to act when action is required, responding to the needs of the moment without attachment to the fruits of action, this was the essence of the Taoist vision. It is a response to life that is essentially gentle, balanced, dynamic and wise. It is still reflected today in the faces and demeanour of modern sages who live in the sacred mountains of China where, for centuries, retreats have been built as places of contemplation in a landscape of utter stillness and breathtaking beauty.

> *The wide pond expands like a mirror*
> *The heavenly light and cloud shadows play upon it.*
> *How does such clarity occur?*
> *It is because it contains the living stream*
> *from the fountain.*[6]

Notes:

1. *Tao Teh Ching*, trans. Arthur Waley
2. Tao Teh Ching 52, trs. Chang Chung-Yuan, from *Creativity and Taoism*, Wildwood House, London 1963
3. Lu Chi, from Wen Fu: *The Art of Writing* trans. Sam Hamill
4. Chuang Huai, *A Treatise on Painting*
5. from a story told to Jung by Richard Wilhelm who translated the *I Ching* or *Book of Changes*, published in 1951 by Routledge and Kegan Paul, London
6. Chu Si, from Chang Chung-Yuan, *Creativity and Taoism*

View of Lu Shan

by Chiang Ts'an, Sung Dynasty

Part Six

Stellar Consciousness

Transformation and Final Participation

The Alchemist following in the footsteps of Nature
Michael Maier, *Atalanta Fugiens*, 1618

Chapter Eighteen

THE GREAT WORK OF ALCHEMY:
THE PROCESS OF THE SOUL'S TRANSMUTATION

Imagination is the star in man: the celestial and super-celestial body.
— Ruland the Lexicographer

Hidden within man there exists such a heavenly and divine light which cannot be placed in man from without but must emerge from within.
— Zosimus of Panopolis

Join the male and the female and you will find what is sought.
— Maria Prophetessa

To all of us falls one heritage — Wisdom. All of us inherit of it equally. But one man makes the best of his heritage, and another does not; one buries it, lets it die, and passes over it; another draws profit from it — one more, one less. According to how we invest, use, and administer our heritage, we obtain much or little from it; and yet it belongs to all of us, and it is in all of us.
— Paracelsus

A lchemy flows beneath the surface of Western civilization like a river of gold, preserving its images and its insights for us so that we could one day understand our presence on this planet better than we do. Alchemy builds a rainbow bridge between the human and the divine, the seen and unseen dimensions of reality, between matter and spirit. The Cosmos calls to us to become aware that we participate in its life, that everything is sacred and connected: one life; one spirit. Alchemy responds to that call. It asks us to develop cosmic consciousness, to awaken the divine spark of our consciousness and reunite it with the invisible Soul of the Cosmos. It changes our perception of reality and answers the questions: "who are we?" and "why are we here?" It refines and transmutes the base metal of our understanding so that we — evolved from the very substance of the stars — can know that we participate in the mysterious ground of spirit while living in this physical dimension of reality.

The Royal Art

Alchemy has been called the Royal Art. What does this mean? It means that each one of us carries latent within his or her nature the royal value — the greater, finer, more complete or whole person we are capable of becoming. Alchemy is about the process of redeeming or giving birth to that royal value — the quintessence of our nature — assisting it to come to full consciousness and to bring us to wholeness or spiritual maturity. It is the process which transmutes the volatile matter of our being into finer and finer elements. It tells the story of the rescue of spirit buried or lost in the forms of its creation which needs our help to emerge from its place of exile. In entering the alchemical Great Work, we become the co-redeemers of spirit, working hand in hand with spirit to release, redeem and re-unite with the divine cosmic ground of our psychic life and all of nature. Alchemy is a process of revelation and transmutation. The aim of the alchemist was to rescue the 'living gold', the treasure of spirit buried in the underworld of his soul. Zosimus of Panopolis, living in Egypt in the third century AD, said, "I swear to you that if you do this work properly, you will one day have a river of flowing gold."

We are embedded in the world of spirit. Our physical bodies carry cosmic elements that have come from the stars. We are the living embodiment of spirit but we don't know this. Alchemy is about a slow and arduous process of attunement to this realization: arduous because the evolution of consciousness takes aeons of earth time and it is so difficult to recover and understand what has been lost over the centuries. Many deeply imprinted beliefs and habits impede this understanding and it is hard to dismantle the structures of belief that have been built up over millennia. European alchemy, the inheritor of Egyptian, Greek and Arab alchemy, is the Western tradition of inner psychic transmutation; like the tradition of Kabbalah in the West and Kundalini Yoga in the East, it assists the process of reuniting us with our source.

The Image of Gold

Gold is the image that comes to mind when alchemy is mentioned — gold or the mysterious philosopher's stone. This gold or stone was said to be not only a cure for all disease and sickness but was thought to represent the awakened subtle or spiritual body that would act as a vehicle for the soul in the worlds beyond this one. The gold or stone symbolizes the gift of wisdom, insight or gnosis and the power to heal human suffering as well as awareness of the presence of the subtle soul body. "There are two categories in this art, namely, seeing with the eye and understanding with the heart, and this is the hidden stone, which is fitly called a gift of God... And this divine stone is the heart and tincture of gold which the philosophers seek."[1]

The symbol of the alchemical gold was the circle. In many images and symbols which have their origin in Egypt, the alchemical quest describes the process which transmutes what we are into what we are capable of becoming; transmutes us from base metal into gold, bringing us from a state of ignorance and fragmentation into one of enlightenment and wholeness. It gradually opens our eyes to an incandescent vision of reality. It brings into being a deep state of communion between our consciousness and the invisible dimension of spirit. "Alchemy is not merely an art or science to teach metallic transmutation so much as a true and solid science that teaches how to know the centre of all things, which in the divine language is called the spirit of life."[2]

At the present time, the neglect of our inner life and our deepest instinctual needs has led to the situation where, as in the Grail legend, the territory of the soul is in the grip of a terrible drought. Few people understand any more what the landscape and the language of the soul are like; few can read the images that are like hieroglyphs whose key has been lost. An understanding of the basic concepts of alchemy can help us to reconnect with the soul and with the hidden ground of life. The alchemical images yield their secret to those who contemplate them.

The Need to Awaken

The evolution of human consciousness on this planet is a very slow gradient of ascent from unconsciousness to self-consciousness and, ultimately, to awakened consciousness. There are many setbacks and long periods of stagnation and incubation. The whole of humanity suffers because the increase of consciousness is so slow and the transformation needed to diminish human suffering and ignorance so difficult to implement. Now, it seems that because of the turmoil in the world and the harm to the planet caused by our unconscious behaviour, our evolution is being accelerated, taking us to a point where we have to make the choice between transformation and annihilation.

It is as if, during the last seventy years or so, we have been placed in an alchemical retort, forced to live through the fire of transformation, for the most part unconsciously. The more individuals who are able to awaken to this process of transformation and cooperate with it, the less suffering there will be for the whole body of humanity because, essentially, we are one life. Collectively, humanity in the last century and this one has been through a fiery *calcinatio*, an alchemical term for the first stage of the alchemical process. We have witnessed the images of incineration in the gas ovens of Auschwitz; the fire-bombing of Coventry, Hamburg and Dresden; the obliteration of Hiroshima and Nagasaki; death by napalm, depleted uranium and white phosphorus bombs; the horrific fiery collapse of the twin towers; the bombing of Baghdad and all the senseless acts using explosives to destroy lives. These events, combined with the suffering and destitution created by wars, by the sale of arms, by corruption, greed and fear urge all of us to do whatever we can to contribute to the process of awakening and transformation that is now engaging the whole of humanity.

Given the default position of governments which have to act on behalf of national interests, only individuals or groups of individuals can hope to make some contribution towards change. Yet, because the crisis we face is so grave, the very limitations and ineptitude of governments and the general chaos of the financial markets are accelerating the awakening of people all over the world. In relation to the lives of those whose desperate concern is survival, this inner work may seem irrelevant, even absurd, yet if change in the world situation is ever to come about, it can only come through an increase in the number of concerned and committed individuals engaging in the awakening and transformation of their own consciousness and giving expression to that transformation in some form of service to the world. This service may take the form of the struggle for freedom from oppressive regimes; it may seek to alleviate the hunger and deprivation in areas where starvation stalks the lives of millions; or the liberation of women from oppression and servitude to religious beliefs and social customs; or the protection of the planet from the failure of governments to take collective action on its behalf. Whatever form it takes, its inspiration will spring from an awakened and compassionate heart.

The Roots of Alchemy

Alchemy is at least 4000 years old and has deep roots in Egyptian, Babylonian and Greek, as well as Chinese, Indian and Persian civilizations. Some scholars think that the word alchemy comes from an Arabic word meaning "the preparation of silver and gold"; others that it means "black earth". The word 'alchemy', because it contains the prefix '*al*', suggests an Arab derivation, but the word '*chemeia*' points to a connection with the Egyptian word '*Khem*' which was a word used to describe Egypt, whose black earth was created by the annual inundations of the Nile. The great obelisks which stood gleaming in the courtyards of the Egyptian temples were once covered with electrum, which was an alloy of silver and gold. But certain Egyptians knew how to apply this science to the soul. They discovered how to make an alloy of its two basic elements: the solar gold of the masculine element and the lunar silver of the feminine one.

There have been men and women in every culture: in Egypt and Babylonia; in Persia, Tibet, India and China; in mountains and forests remote from the centres of civilization, who have transmitted their knowledge of ways of relating to the dimension of spirit — ancient ways that until recently were the closely guarded secret of a handful of initiates. There are two aspects to alchemy: one approach is through seeing the soul as the alchemical vessel of transformation; the other is the creation of physical gold. Alchemy is a science, both in the sense that it has a methodology and in the sense that it gives astonishing insights into the nature of matter and our own nature.

The work of alchemists in different cultures laid the foundations of modern science: chemistry, biology, physics on the one hand, and psychology on the other. They also developed the knowledge of how to distil the essence of plants for the purposes of healing — leading to the sciences of Homeopathy and Herbal Medicine. Much precious knowledge transmitted from earlier shamanic cultures was lost because so many transmitters of this knowledge were murdered by the religious fanaticism that has so regrettably prolonged the suffering of humanity. Even today, in our supposedly enlightened times, we can still see the deep suspicion of alternative therapies and herbal medicines and the ongoing attempts to disparage and eliminate them on the dubious suggestion that their efficacy cannot be proven by scientific methods and that they may even be dangerous.

In Europe, alchemy had its great age of flowering in the sixteenth and seventeenth centuries although there were well-known alchemists in earlier times and other places. Just as the city of Prague was the centre of European alchemy in the sixteenth and seventeenth centuries, so the thriving city of Alexandria was the centre of alchemy in Hellenistic times. Recently discovered manuscripts (Zosimus of Panopolis 3rd century AD) show that from earliest times alchemy was understood as the art of soul transmutation, not the literal transmutation of metals into gold. Hence the alchemical saying: "Our gold is not the common gold".

The origin of alchemy lies in the shamanic traditions of the lunar cultures which kept alive the vital connection between the visible and invisible worlds. There has always been a chain of teachers (known as the Golden Chain or *Catena Aurea*) who have transmitted this knowledge from generation to generation over thousands of years. Two great streams of alchemical knowledge, one flowing from ancient Egypt and Babylonia with their highly advanced knowledge of astronomy and mathematics, and the other from Arabia and Islamic Spain, came together in Europe in the late Middle Ages and Renaissance. There were some 4000 alchemists working in Europe between 1200 and 1650 and they created dozens of extraordinary and, in some cases, very beautiful alchemical texts.[3] Alchemy, like Kabbalah, was a visionary and contemplative tradition handed down from teacher to pupil and, indeed, many alchemists were kabbalists and vice versa. In attempting to understand alchemy, it is helpful to have some knowledge of Kabbalah. All were astrologers, for the Great Work required the knowledge of the alignment of the alchemical processes and the physical elements undergoing transmutation, with the position and relationship of certain planets. Among the most famous Egyptian alchemists, were the mythical figures of Hermes Trismegistus and Maria Prophetessa, a Jewess of Alexandria, from whose name comes the bain-marie or pan of water which, even today, is used by chefs to heat dishes gently in the oven or to keep them warm. Later, in Europe, there were great Jewish as well as Christian alchemists, among them the brilliant and controversial physician Paracelsus. We owe them an immense debt of gratitude and it is helpful to invoke their presence and ask them for assistance in understanding their writings. Here are the names of some of the alchemists who were part of this Golden Chain:

> Geber or Jabir — 8th century alchemist who lived at the Court of Harun al-Rashid in Baghdad; founder of Chemistry who had an immense influence on European alchemists.
> Rhazes, Rasis or Al-Razi (c.825–c.924), Persia
> Roger Bacon (1220–1292), England
> Albertus Magnus (1200–1280), Germany
> Arnold of Villanova (1235–1311), Spain
> Raymund Lull (1232–1316), Deia, Majorca
> Nicolas Flamel (1330–1413), Paris
> Basil Valentine – German, 17th century (this name may be an alias)
> Salomon Trismosin 16th century, author of an exquisite manuscript, the *Splendor Solis* — one of the treasures of the British Library
> Paracelsus (1493–1541), Swiss

Gerhard Dorn, (1530–1584), Belgian
Giordano Bruno (1548–1600), Italian (burnt at the stake in 1600)

We also owe a debt of gratitude to Jung, a modern alchemist, for without his rediscovery of alchemy much that he discovered might have remained unknown to the general public. Jung came to study alchemy through two dreams recounted in his autobiography, *Memories, Dreams, Reflections*. These prompted him to collect many books on alchemy and to make an inventory of all the images and descriptions in them. It could be said that through his understanding of alchemy he reconnected solar with lunar consciousness and the left hemisphere of the brain with the right hemisphere. He recovered the ancient shamanic way of knowing of the lunar era that the alchemists had managed to keep alive through centuries of persecution. He realized that the images of alchemy were similar to those in the dreams of his patients and that they described a process of inner psychic transformation which he named the individuation process.

Where Christianity taught that the Redeemer is outside us and that our redemption (as Christians) has been assured by Christ's sacrificial death, Jung realized that the secret science of alchemy taught that the alchemist can become the redeemer of the lost aspect of spirit hidden within himself and nature, working with spirit to accomplish this redemption. Alchemy gives great importance and significance to the individual since the divine drama of redemption is consummated in and through us, not accomplished on our behalf. It is an awesome and heroic task. Each one of us carries the mystery of the incarnation of spirit in this physical dimension of reality. In the rich library of alchemical images, we are looking at spirit's manifestation and transformation of itself as well as its desire for recognition and communication with us. Our human consciousness, our soul, is the vessel in which this mysterious transformation takes place. That is why Jung recognized that alchemy is a sacred rite, an *opus divinum*.

Jung realized that when the alchemists spoke of the "philosophical gold" they were referring to the true gold of the spirit which could, through repeated "distillations", "washings" and "cleansings", be freed from the dross that had accrued to it in the course of human evolution. From the alchemist Gerhard Dorn, Jung took the idea of the *unus mundus*, the unifying cosmic ground in which both matter and psyche participate and whose connecting substratum gives rise to synchronicities as well as to miraculous healings, visionary experiences and sudden illuminations. He said that alchemy had two aims: the rescue of the human soul and the salvation of the Cosmos. His last and most profound book on the alchemical Great Work is *Mysterium Coniunctionis*. After he had finished the first draft, he had an accident, followed by a serious illness and, sensing that he was on the threshold of death, had the great visions of the *coniunctio* which he describes in his autobiography, *Memories, Dreams, Reflections*.

An Alchemical Dream

I was first attracted to alchemy when I studied Medieval History at Oxford and with great excitement read about the alchemists of the Middle Ages. A striking visionary dream when I was twenty-eight and had just embarked on a Jungian analysis alerted me to a spiritual journey I was unconsciously (at that time) making. It was only many years later when I read Jung's writings on alchemy that I recognized its alchemical symbolism:

> *I am in a garden, walled and square with a central wall bisecting it through the middle. In one part of the garden is a beautiful blossoming apple or cherry tree. Beyond the garden the whole horizon of the world is ringed by burning cities. I am crawling on my stomach along the central wall which is ablaze with fire. As I crawl slowly and with great difficulty along the wall I look up towards another wall in front of me, forming a T-junction with the one I am on. Appearing over the top of this, as if standing on a ladder on the other side, there is a man wearing a strange hat that falls to one side. He is waiting for me to pass through the fire and come to meet him. As I inch my way along the wall towards him, I realize that he is the Gardener, the Keeper of the Garden.*

I am still assimilating the message of that dream and another later dream, described in the last chapter, where a stone spoke to me, saying, "Help me, help me". I discovered later that the hat worn by the Gardener of my dream was the Phrygian cap once worn by devotees of the goddess Cybele (Kybele), and later by the medieval alchemists. I came across a sculpture on the outside of Notre Dame in Paris of a man wearing this cap, illustrated in a book on alchemy by Fulcanelli called *Le Mystère des Cathédrales*. Only through my study of alchemy did I begin to sense the meaning of the 'Dream of the Water' which had haunted me for so many decades ever since those early channelled messages. Only in alchemy did I find the reference to the 'Divine Water' and understood that this 'water' was the invisible sea of being in which we are all immersed without being aware of it; immersed as Mechthild of Magdeburg (1210–c.1285) describes it in her book, *The Flowing Light of the Godhead*, "like a bird in the air, like a fish in the sea." Very gradually, over many years of wondering, I began to understand the 'Divine Water' as an image that mirrored the deep ground of the soul to the surface personality that is unaware of its existence. But I felt it was more than this: it was the longing of that deep ground to bring humanity to conscious aware-ness of the sacredness of life, of the unity and perfection of the cosmic order and our potential role in creating a conscious relationship with this Sacred Order. I began to understand alchemy as a shamanic method leading to a direct encounter with spirit.

As I learned more, I saw that alchemy throws a bridge between the seen and the unseen dimensions of life. One of the great maxims of the alchemists, following the words written on the Emerald Tablet, said to have been written by Hermes Trismegistus, was "As Above, so Below". Their aim was to assist the 'marriage' of two dimensions of reality: between the unseen reality of the highest order — the macrocosm — and the visible, manifest world as well as our own human organism — the microcosm. Squaring the circle by uniting these two dimensions of reality leads to the birth of the divine child — the awakened consciousness that is the treasure, the pearl of great price and the ultimate fruit of this union. So the alchemists said: "Whoever shall make the hidden manifest knoweth the whole work".

The Importance of Myth

Like the Rosetta Stone, the greatest myths contain a meaning which can be decoded from the symbolic imagery that conceals it and used as a key to a deeper understanding of life. In the evocative words of the great mythologist, Joseph Campbell, "Myth is the secret opening through which the inexhaustible energies of the cosmos pour into human cultural manifestation."[4] Certain myths have the power to heal and transform if their images are understood in relation to the soul. In symbolic images and allegorical stories they tell of the hidden workings of the spirit within the matrix of the soul.

They chronicle the evolution of human consciousness and the tremendous struggle for greater consciousness through search, suffering and heroic endeavour that the human story represents. Such myths can be applied as much to the life of an individual as to the life of a culture or to the whole evolutionary journey of humanity on this planet. They describe what has to be accomplished over and over again if humanity is to reach the goal that spirit intends. They tell the story of the quest for a deeper, more complete relationship with life that is described as the treasure — the supreme value. The treasure is not power, nor any kind of supremacy over any thing or any one. The treasure is an enlightened state of being or, in the more familiar language of the West, the wisdom, insight and compassion that are the fruits of a relationship with the hidden ground of life.

Certain myths flow beneath the surface of our lives like a mighty river, connecting our superficial awareness with its roots, ready always when we are ready, to well up like a perennial spring whenever we call upon our soul for help. In European civilization there was a wealth of ideas that had to go underground, since they could only escape persecution by being hidden in metaphor and allegory. Only now are they emerging, having been preserved for the day of their 'resurrection' by a strong mythological tradition expressed in alchemy on the one hand and in countless legends and stories such as the fairy tale of the Sleeping Beauty and the legend of the Holy Grail on the other.

The revelations transmitted by awakened individuals in all cultures later become embodied in religious institutions which gradually lose or exclude elements that are vital to our balance and well being. A tendency to crystallization, dogmatism and literalism may cause religions to become fixated in the past, unable to apply their great revelation to the human soul and contemporary events. In the case of the three patriarchal religions, there has been an excessive emphasis on the masculine principle, on theological dogma and an insistence on belief rather than the transformation of consciousness as the path to God. As Chapters Seven and Eight have shown, oppressive social customs became associated with specific beliefs.

Alchemy kept alive the shamanic participatory consciousness of the lunar era through some 4000 years (see Chapters Four and Five). The principal themes of alchemy descend from the great Bronze Age lunar myths of death and regeneration that were celebrated in Egypt, Sumer, Babylonia and Greece and were originally related to the annual death and regeneration of the life of the crops. The major themes of alchemy echo the major themes of these great lunar myths: in Sumer, the Descent of Inanna; in Egypt, Isis's search for the fragmented body of Osiris; In Babylonia, Ishtar's descent into the Underworld and her rescue of her son Tammuz, and in Greece, Demeter's search for her daughter Persephone. Certain themes found in these great lunar myths are related to the transformation of the consciousness in the alchemist. These themes are:

> The descent into the underworld and the return
> The struggle with a superhuman adversary
> The quest for a priceless treasure
> The rescue of a divine element lost in the underworld
> The theme of transformation
> The sacred marriage
> The birth of the divine child

In alchemy, the alchemist undertakes the redemption of his own soul and, simultaneously, of the *Anima Mundi* or hidden feminine aspect of spirit imprisoned in matter. Alchemy transposes the images and themes of ancient mythology — the rescue of the divine element lost in the underworld, the quest for the treasure and the image of the sacred marriage — to the human soul. It also incorporates the shamanic tradition of the initiatory death and rebirth involved in the process of becoming a shaman, which is what the alchemist, in effect, was. The alchemist made the descent into the underworld of his soul to recover the treasure buried in the 'matter' of his instinctual life in order to give birth to the new value or transformed consciousness. He became (with the help of divine grace) the redeemer of his soul, discovering the revelatory experience of the treasure. Men and women sometimes worked together as partners to bring into being the treasure of the alchemical gold as did Nicolas Flamel and his wife Perenelle in 14th century Paris, where, amazingly, their house still stands. The partner in the alchemical Work was called the "*soror mystica*" or "*frater mysticus*".

There is a fascinating story about Nicolas Flamel. One night he had a dream that an angel came to him. The angel held a book, the book of Abraham the Jew, and spoke these words to Flamel, "Look well at this book, Nicholas. At first you will understand nothing in it but one day you will see in it that which no other man will be able to see." Not long after having this dream a man came into Flamel's book shop carrying a book. Flamel recognized it as the same book the angel had held out to him. He purchased the book and for twenty-one years studied its mysterious twenty-one pages in search of the fundamental secrets of nature. He was one of the few alchemists who, with his wife Perenelle, was able to create the physical gold and with this he endowed many hospitals in Paris, some of which still exist today. He designed his own tomb and covered it with alchemical images. When it was opened years after his death, his body was not there.

The Quest for a Priceless Treasure

Alchemy was the secret tradition which taught that the priceless treasure spoken of in so many myths lies within our own human nature — unrecognized and neglected or, putting it the other way round, that we live unknowingly within the field of the treasure even though our existence in this physical dimension of reality seems so separate, so remote from it. Alchemy gives the treasure many beautiful names which resonate down the centuries: the Elixir of Life; the Philosopher's Stone; the Heavenly Balsam; the Flower of Immortality; the Divine Water; the Quintessential Gold.

The alchemical Great Work involves a descent into the underworld of the soul in order to recover the lost awareness that the life of nature, matter and the body is also a manifestation and embodiment of spirit — an insight reflected in the words of the great Indian teacher, Sri Aurobindo: "Hidden nature is secret God."[5] Alchemy today invites us to change our attitude to nature and matter and the way we exploit all aspects of planetary life for the exclusive benefit of our species. The Great Work of alchemy is about recovering the lost lunar sense of participatory awareness and applying it consciously to our relationship with nature. It is about reanimating the imaginative vision, the poetic sensibility and the heightened awareness or insight which connects us to the unseen ground of being. At the same time it is about growing into our unique individuality, differentiating ourselves from the deficient collective values that presently direct the political and religious life of society, without in any way seeing ourselves as superior to other people or forcing our views upon them.

The alchemist descended into the depths of his soul to undergo a death and rebirth, to transform his consciousness from base metal into gold, to recover the treasure buried in the matter of his instinctual life and to be reunited with the divine ground personified by Sophia, the feminine image of Divine Wisdom. In the vessel of his glass retort he attempted to transmute metals and chemical substances, but it was the images and dreams that came to him as he did this work which reflected what was taking place in the vessel of his own soul and alerted him to, then deepened his understanding of the process of psychic transformation that was taking place within him. The retort acted like a mirror that reflected the processes taking place within the vessel of his soul. He deduced from his observation of these processes that matter and spirit were mysteriously connected with each other.

The alchemists had first to bring the primordial life energy into consciousness within them, and then discover how to work with it to transform it and allow it to transform them. In the course of this process of attunement and transformation the centre of gravity within their psyche gradually shifted from the needs and desires of the ego-bound personality to a deeper focus created by a growing relationship with and awareness of spirit in all its manifestations. This process — which in some took many decades and in others was sudden and unexpected — opened the one who was transformed by it to values utterly different from those which govern the world: values associated with the mentality that the alchemists called the 'Old King'. As the process transformed their understanding, it awakened them to a new kind of relationship with matter, Earth and Cosmos. Ultimately, the soul gave birth to the enlightened consciousness that they named 'The Young King'. The alchemists stressed that the Work was to be done gently, patiently, allowing it to unfold. To try to achieve this state by force, greed or ambition was to risk inflation, madness and death.

The 'Young King' and the King Who Needs to Die

Alchemy gives us the image of a king who has to die in order that his son may
rule in his stead. Many startling alchemical images illustrate the processes which
bring about the 'death' of the Old King. Those of you who are familiar with the
Grail stories will remember the story of the aged king, who lies wounded in the
groin, waiting for the redeemer who will free the waters of the soul so that the
Wasteland he rules over may be restored to fertility. The texts of European
alchemy carried forward the imagery of this medieval story. In particular, there is
a beautiful text (Trismosin, *Splendor Solis*) that accompanies an equally
beautiful alchemical picture in the same manuscript which says: "The King's son
lies in the depths of the sea as though dead. But he lives and calls from the deep:
'Whosoever will free me from the waters and lead me to dry land, him will I
prosper with everlasting riches.'"[6]

  We can identify the Old King — the king who needs to die — with the deficient
values that currently control the so-called 'real' world: the values driven by the
will to power that have ruled the world throughout the solar era. He can also be
identified with our current perception of reality, where, in St. Paul's words, "we
see through a glass, darkly" (1Cor. 13:12). We can also identify the Old King with
an outworn image of spirit that needs to be relinquished in order for a new image
— the Young King — to emerge from the depths of the soul. As described in the
preceding chapter, just as from time to time we have to buy new clothes to replace
worn out ones, so an image of spirit or God which has long presided over a
civilization may need to die in order for a new image of spirit to come into
manifestation. The King's Son in the above text personifies the different values
generated by a deeper relationship with spirit, based on direct spiritual experience
rather than belief.

  Two thousand years ago, Jesus was the 'Young King' who brought potential
renewal to the culture of that time and the possibility of a transformation of the
values governing the 'real' world. Five hundred years before him, at the beginning
of what has been called the Axial Age, the Buddha did the same for his culture in
India. St. Francis was to do the same for 13th century Italy and, in my view, Jung
did the same for Western culture in the twentieth century. Yet still it seems that
we have the utmost difficulty in freeing ourselves from the power of the Old King
who, at the present time, seems more entrenched than ever.

  In relation to the collective soul of humanity, the whole world may fall under the spell of the values which characterize the Old King and remain under it for centuries, if not millennia. We may risk regression to an inferior psychic state if there is too great an inflexibility on the part of those who are the dominant element in a culture so that no change is allowed, no new element integrated with the deficient ruling system of values. The extreme example of this would be tyranny in the form of an inflexible political or religious dogma or the desire for world domination by one nation or one religious group. But this impulse to dominate arises when the conscious personality, symbolized by the Old King, is out of touch with the spirit of the depths. It is then possessed and driven by its shadow: the will to power of the unconscious instinct. Jung warned about the danger of the inflation of the modern mind, saying that "every increase in consciousness harbours the danger of inflation."

> An inflated consciousness is always egocentric and conscious of nothing but its own presence. It is incapable of learning from the past, incapable of understanding contemporary events, and incapable of drawing right conclusions about the future. It is hypnotized by itself and therefore cannot be argued with. It inevitably dooms itself to calamities that must strike it dead. Paradoxically enough, inflation is a regression of consciousness into unconsciousness. This always happens when consciousness takes too many unconscious contents upon itself and loses the faculty of discrimination, the *sine qua non* of all consciousness… the bigger the crowd the better the truth — and the greater the catastrophe.[7]

The Sacred Marriage

Four thousand years ago in the courtyards of the great temples on the banks of the Nile the Sacred Marriage of goddess and god was celebrated. The theme of the Sacred Marriage has come down to us in myth, in fairy tales like Cinderella and the Sleeping Beauty, and in the Biblical Song of Songs. Alchemy sets the supreme quest for the treasure in the context of a marriage between the solar and lunar aspects of the soul, the fiery gold of the masculine element and the volatile silver of the feminine one, a union between our mind and our soul, our head and our heart, between the solar King and the lunar Queen. This marriage also unites the invisible dimension of the subtle world of spirit with the material world of our experience, rendering the latter transparent to spirit. The Sacred Marriage is the age-old image of this mysterious double union. The alchemists called the consciousness that was the fruit of this inner marriage Stellar Consciousness — signifying that they had become reunited with the invisible cosmic ground that is the foundation of the phenomenal world.[8]

The alchemists said that in order for consciousness to be transformed from base metal into gold, both king and queen have to undergo a process of dissolution and transformation. The alchemists associated the king with the sun, with gold, sulphur and the colour red. The king today might be identified with the limited consciousness we associate with our rational mind which may be entirely bound to the perception of reality offered by our senses and is unaware of a deeper dimension of reality or a deeper dimension of the psyche. The king formulates many goals but these goals may be unrelated to anything pertaining to the realm of spirit.

The images they associated with the queen are the moon, silver, quicksilver (mercury) and the colour white. The rose, the lily, the dove and the swan were also associated with her. Her nature is described as volatile, liquid, watery and changeable. Related to the inner world of the psyche, the queen is our instinctual soul, whose focus is the heart. At the archetypal level, she represents the cosmic dimension of the *Anima Mundi*, the hidden soul of nature, the matrix of our creative energy and the womb of our imagination, which derives ultimately from the Soul of the Cosmos. Just as the awakened and transformed consciousness of the king is represented by the 'Young King', so the awakened and transformed consciousness of the queen is personified by the 'Young Queen'. Their union creates the child of the awakened, integrated consciousness symbolized by the alchemical gold and the other numinous images of the completion of the Great Work.

To awaken the consciousness personified by the king to the values associated with the wisdom of the soul, he has to undergo a symbolic death, vividly described by the shamanic initiation. He makes a descent into the watery realm of the soul, the realm of the emotions, feelings, instincts, that has never been associated with anything of value and that has been both feared and despised and has consequently remained largely dissociated from consciousness during the solar era and therefore undeveloped. He comes to know the queen intimately, becoming aware of his feelings not as something inferior to his rational mind, but as something like his own mother, something that he has been born from, emerged from, and can now unite with consciously as his bride — the feminine and royal counterpart of himself.

By descending into this dimension, overcoming his suspicion of and contempt for it, and surrendering his desire for control, the king develops respect for mysteries he was not aware of and does not yet understand. He develops insight; he develops wisdom; he develops humility and compassion. The queen as the personification of the soul is also transformed as the king enters into a conscious relationship with her. She is no longer forced to remain in a dissociated state. She is no longer in thrall to the deficient values and limited perception represented by the Old King; nor is she any longer bound by the powerful unconscious drives of blind instinct to which he also was bound. The values of the heart begin to be heard and strengthened. Feeling begins to function in a more conscious related way as both king and queen are transformed. As in the story of the Sleeping Beauty, the king discovers a new relationship with the queen as she becomes his beloved and bride. Where before there had been a hedge of thorns separating them, now king and queen are joined together in the bridal chamber of the soul. This alchemical union works a profound transmutation of both, resulting in the birth of the child of the new consciousness. Both have to undergo a process of fragmentation, dismemberment, reconstitution and regeneration described by the different stages of the alchemical Great Work. In relation to the man or woman of today, this process is essential for them both, since woman has been educated in the same way as man, has absorbed the same values and been imprinted with the same ideas and may give the highest value to the masculine principle and the rational mind, knowing nothing of the deeper dimension of the soul and the invisible dimension of reality.

In the kabbalistic tradition (and many alchemists were kabbalists) the union of the king and queen in their regenerated state signifies the meeting or union of the male and female branches of the Tree of Life in the heart centre of Tiphareth (Tifereth) in the central pillar, whose signature is Beauty and Harmony. There are some very beautiful alchemical images of the Hermaphrodite who symbolizes this union of Sol and Luna, King and Queen and these can be related to the imagery of union in Kabbalah. In one such image, to the left of the king and the right of the queen are two tree-like forms, each planted in a stone, one hung with red suns and the other with silver moons, representing the two 'pillars' or branches of the Tree of Life. The unified king and queen in the centre, whose feet also rest on two stones, symbolize the completion of the alchemical work in the union or *conjunctio* of the "two natures" of the king and the queen. Beneath their feet lies a dragon who symbolizes the *prima materia* of alchemy and also Mercurius, whose meaning will be explained below. Those who are familiar with *Kundalini Yoga* will be able to relate the two pillars or branches of the Tree of Life with the two 'channels' — the lunar *Ida* and the solar *Pingala* — which meet in the central channel of the *Sushumna* as the creative fire of the Goddess *Kundalini* makes her ascent from the base of the spine to her flowering in and above the head (Chapter Sixteen). So similar are these three traditions, that it seems possible that each discovered a similar method of transmuting consciousness through specific exercises, visualizations and meditative practices.

The Prima Materia

The *prima materia* is the foundation of the alchemical work, the raw material out of which the stone or the gold or divine elixir is produced. The alchemists said, "This matter lies before the eyes of all; everybody sees it, touches it, loves it, but knows it not. It is glorious and vile, precious and of small account, and is found everywhere…. To be brief, our Matter has as many names as there are things in the world; that is why the foolish know it not."[9] I have long wondered whether they could have meant that spirit is the *prima materia*, present within everything, seen by all, yet unrecognized because our consciousness is not capable of recognizing its presence within all the forms of life, having been taught for centuries that spirit is not present in nature or matter.

The alchemists said to look for the *prima materia* in what has been most despised. In the *prima materia* are all the elements that have been rejected and shut out of our conscious mind. Here are the deepest instincts, the deepest feelings, and the deepest capacity for relationship with life — above all, the elements that were associated with the despised or neglected Feminine and excluded from spirit: nature, matter, soul and body. The alchemists called the *prima materia* "black earth" or the dragon and sometimes even shit. When Paracelsus started his teaching at the University of Basel, he put a steaming pot of human excrement on the table and said, "This is what the work is about, this is life, this is God." The response of the horrified students was to pull him off the podium and chase him out of the classroom. He was probably lucky to escape with his life.

The Dragon

The dragon is the most eloquent and powerful image of the *prima materia*. As has been explained in Chapter Twelve, the dragon is an image of the immense and unrecognized power of instinct, which ultimately is the creative and destructive power of life itself — the power that lives in and through all of us in an untransformed or unconscious state. As with the eastern traditions, the art of the alchemist was to assist in bringing this apparently chaotic and overwhelming power to a fully awakened state, yet never to forget that he was its servant; never its master, using it for his own ends. The so-called Black Arts describe the work of someone who is in thrall to the dragon, serving his own desire for power or the desire for power of governments; a situation that could be related to the many scientists who have been working to develop weapons capable of destroying life. Paradoxically, the dragon presents the greatest danger to us and is also guardian of our greatest treasure — the gold that is the outcome of the alchemical Great Work.

Mercurius

Mercurius is one of the most enigmatic figures in alchemy and is sometimes shown in male and sometimes female form or, in the later stages of the alchemical process, as a hermaphrodite. The origin of Mercurius goes back to Hermes or the Egyptian Thoth, the guide of the soul in the underworld. Many alchemical images portray Mercurius holding a caduceus and its entwined serpents. The alchemists saw him/her (for Mercurius was often androgynous) as many different forms: as the *prima materia* — the primal matter that is to be transformed by spirit; as spirit itself; and as the guide, agent of transformation and the longed for treasure and goal of the alchemical work — the philosophical gold, elixir or stone. They recognized Mercurius as the living gold, the divine creative fire, the *lumen naturae* — the light of unseen spirit hidden within the forms of life, matter and each one of us. Some alchemists associated Mercurius with the Holy Spirit.

Perplexingly, Mercurius could take the form of a dragon, a lion, a wolf, a raven, a dove and a phoenix, and many other images including the hermaphrodite, depending on which stage of the alchemical process was being portrayed. During the process of transformation the dragon is slain, the lion has its paws cut off, the wolf is killed, as these symbolic images of the destructive or dangerous aspect of instinct — the will to power, lust, cruelty, greed — are transformed. What the alchemists seem to be saying is that Mercurius is everything because spirit is everything viewed at different stages of its own awakening and transformation within the soul of the alchemist. It is important to bear in mind that all these images were related to actual changes in the constitution of the minerals in the alchemical retort or vessel.

All over Europe, particularly in the great cathedrals, the image of the Green Man (Mercurius) gazes out at us from entrance arches, ceiling bosses, choir stalls, and carvings at the top of columns. All these marvellous images are the work of the master builders of the Middle Ages, many of whom were familiar with alchemy and its secrets. All these images proclaim: I am the *lumen naturae*, the light of nature, the ever-living presence of the creative spirit; spirit as light that is all around you, permeating all that you see and touch as matter. Another name for the *lumen naturae* was the *Anima Mundi*. The image of the Green Man goes back to Osiris, Attis and Tammuz, all gods of the Earth's regeneration.

As the alchemists watched the matter in their alchemical vessel transform before their eyes, matter came alive. They saw it undergo a transformation and they began to speak to it and to respond to the images it gave rise to through their imagination. The mystery drew them into the midst of itself. What scientists are discovering now rests on foundations they laid centuries ago. But the alchemists saw themselves as the servants, not the masters of the stone and they knew that the dangers involved in the Work were haste, arrogance and avarice. Listening to the scientists speaking of their excitement and wonder at the discovery of the Higgs boson particle, one can see them as modern alchemists, drawn to work together in the quest to penetrate the mysteries of the universe, astounded and moved by what they are discovering, yet aware of how much more there is to be discovered. But the humility of the alchemists may be missing.

Sophia or Divine Wisdom

The Feminine image of Divine Wisdom or the Holy Spirit is the presiding image of alchemy. The alchemists called themselves the Sons of Wisdom. Sometimes she is named *Anima Mundi*, sometimes Sophia, Sapientia or Lady Alchymeia. Alchemists who were kabbalists knew her as the Shekinah, the Bride of God — the divine ground of the phenomenal world. All these images point to the hidden wisdom of nature which the alchemists took as their guide although they also knew that their work was *contra naturam* — against nature — because it went against the attitudes and instinctual habits that were so hard to overcome. They saw themselves working with nature, assisting the release of spirit hidden within her forms.

But they knew that Divine Wisdom represented far more than what we call nature. We are connected with each other and with planetary and cosmic life through an immense and complex web of hidden relationships that scientists are only beginning to discover as they try to fathom the mystery of dark matter and the 95% of the universe that still eludes their understanding. This inner life of the Cosmos, as I have suggested in Chapters Four and Fifteen, is best described in metaphysical language by the idea of Cosmic Soul and by the image, in the Hindu and Buddhist tradition, of the unifying Net of Indra. The feminine archetype has always been associated with the Earth, with Nature and with Soul — not soul in a personal sense but soul as the unseen dimension of reality and the great connecting web of life.

For many thousands of years this cosmic matrix of relationships was personified by the image of the Great Mother and later by specific goddesses like Hathor and Isis in Egypt. Later it was carried by the image of Divine Wisdom and the Holy Spirit in the Old Testament, by the Shekinah of Kabbalah and by the Cosmic or World Soul of Plato and Plotinus; still later, in the Middle Ages, by the image of the Black Madonna and the Holy Grail: the mysterious vessel or stone described as the source of all abundance. For many centuries in a European culture that was deeply repressive of the Feminine, alchemy secretly carried the image of this disowned aspect of the Divine. Alchemists had visions of a cosmic woman and knew her to be a living force and divine presence, pouring out the waters of love and illumination on humanity. Perhaps this is why Dr. Marie–Louise von Franz says in her commentary on an alchemical text called the *Aurora Consurgens*, "Alchemy lays upon the man the task, and confers upon him the dignity, of rescuing the hidden, feminine aspect of God from imprisonment in matter by his opus, and of reuniting her with the manifest, masculine deity."[10] In memorable words in this text, Wisdom speaks to the alchemists, saying, "Understand ye sons of Wisdom, Protect me, and I will protect thee; give me my due that I may help thee."[11] One of the most powerful and profound statements of alchemy, this is a message for our own times when the instinctive desire to protect nature and serve the life of the planet is arising in so many of us.

The Aurora Consurgens

This is an extraordinary book that anyone wishing to understand more about alchemy would benefit from reading and would find fascinating. I have included some passages from the *Aurora* because they are deeply meaningful and very numinous for me and may, perhaps, resonate with others also. Not only are the words of the text exquisitely beautiful but the commentary by Dr. Marie–Louise von Franz is profound and illuminating. She says that "*Aurora* is one of the earliest medieval treatises in which we find the nascent idea that the alchemical opus involves an *inner experience* and that a numinous content, Wisdom (the *anima*), is the secret which the adept was looking for in the chemical substances."[12]

The author of this illuminating book that brings alchemy so vividly to life was believed by Dr. von Franz to be Thomas Aquinas, the great medieval theologian. In it a man speaks of a vision and a revelation he had just prior to his death, a revelation whose words were transcribed as he spoke them by the monks sitting with him. It is truly remarkable that this text has come through to us apparently uncensored. In the first chapter a mystical female figure is introduced, the personification of the *Sapientia Dei* or Wisdom of God: the same figure who appears in the biblical books of Proverbs, Ben Sirach and the Wisdom of Solomon and who represents the divine cosmic ground which gives life to all. It is she who suddenly manifests and speaks to the author of the *Aurora*. Dr. von Franz comments:

We can understand how shattered the author of *Aurora* must have been when Wisdom suddenly appeared to him in personal form. Doubtless he did not know before how real an archetypal figure like Wisdom is, and he had taken her merely as an abstract idea. For an intellectual it is a shattering experience when he discovers that what he was seeking… is not just an idea but is psychically real in a far deeper sense and can come upon him like a thunderclap…. He is saying that she is not merely an intellectual concept but is devastatingly real, actual and palpably present in matter."[13]

His experience describes the power and numinosity of the visionary experience of the *Anima Mundi* or Soul of the World. He heard words which invoked Solomon's description of Wisdom (Wisdom of Solomon 7:7, 10, 21-7, 29; 8:1-2):

She it is that Solomon chose to have instead of light, and above all beauty and health…. For all gold in her sight shall be esteemed as a little sand, and silver shall be counted as clay…. And her fruit is more precious than all the riches of this world, and all the things that are desired are not to be compared with her…. She is a tree of life to them that lay hold on her, and an unfailing light…. He who hath found this science, it shall be his rightful food for ever…. Such a one is as rich as he that hath a stone from which fire is struck, who can give fire to whom he will as much as he will and when he will without loss to himself.[14]

Wisdom spoke to him, saying:

Be turned to me with all your heart and do not cast me aside because I am black and swarthy, because the sun hath changed my colour and the waters have covered my face… because I stick fast in the mire of the deep and my substance is not disclosed. Wherefore out of the depths have I cried, and from the abyss of the earth with my voice to all you that pass by the way. Attend and see me, if any shall find one like unto me, I will give into his hand the morning star.[15]

and in words that resonate with those attributed to Jesus in the Gospels:

I am that land of holy promise, which floweth with milk and honey and bringeth forth sweetest fruit in due season; wherefore have all the philosophers commended me and sowed in me their gold and silver and incombustible grain. And unless that grain falling into me die, itself shall remain alone, but if it die, it bringeth forth threefold fruit: for the first it shall bring forth shall be good because it was sown in good earth, namely of pearls; the second likewise good because it was sown in better earth, namely of leaves (silver); the third shall bring forth a thousand-fold because it was sown in the best earth, namely of gold. For from the fruits of (this) grain is made the food of life, which cometh down from heaven. If any man shall eat of it, he shall live without hunger.[16]

I think this revelatory alchemical text lays the ground for what is emerging in human consciousness now: an awareness of the divinity of nature and matter, as well as our own divinity and our responsibility to protect the planet from our unthinking exploitation of its resources.

The Phases of the Work

Alchemy defines three and sometimes four phases of the Great Work, saying "This art is like an embryo and then the birth of a child." The process is circulatory and continuous and moves through the different phases over and over again, so what is defined as the *nigredo* or 'blackness' of the first phase may be experienced again by the alchemist in the context of the final phase, the *rubedo*.

The Seven Processes involved in the Alchemical Great Work are:

The rescue of the lost feminine aspect of spirit hidden within nature and ourselves
The process of transformation involved in this rescue
The death of the old consciousness symbolized by the old king and queen
The formation of the new consciousness symbolized by the young king and queen
The formation of the Hermaphrodite – the union of the two transformed elements
The integration of body, soul and spirit
The union with what the alchemists called the *unus mundus*, the divine cosmic ground

Stage 1: The First Phase of the Lesser Work
– The Creation of the White Stone –
known as the *Nigredo* or *Separatio* and ruled by the element Fire

The word *Nigredo* means 'blackness' — the blackness of the *prima materia* as well as the blackness of depression. The raven was the symbol of this stage where the alchemist undergoing the process of transformation found himself falling into what is described as a 'blackness blacker than black', a blackness which he saw reflected in the blackening of the matter in the alchemical retort and that could be said to correspond cosmically with the dark phase of the moon. The *nigredo* may also be associated with the many years of loneliness and isolation of someone who has been called to follow this inner path.

The alchemists also named this state the *unio naturalis* and the *massa confusa* as well as the black earth and the dragon — all terms which describe the semi-conscious state, the unconscious entanglement of different aspects of our psyche that is the inevitable result of our emergence from the matrix of nature. They saw the *Nigredo* as the state of blind suffering and ignorance before the dawning of awareness. It may be said to describe the state where we live from day to day, responding to events as they happen; where we believe we have control of our lives but are the victim of the complexes, imprinted ideas and beliefs, archaic drives, instinctual habits and values which control both the collective life of humanity and ourselves in our individual lives. In this state the spirit is not awake, not free, but is the prisoner or victim of all these things.

The alchemical processes associated with the *Nigredo* are *Putrefactio* (decay), *Calcinatio* (incineration, blackening, burning) and *Mortificatio* (dying or suffocation). Paracelsus, a sixteenth century alchemist and physician, said, "Putrefaction is of so great efficacy that it blots out the old nature and transmutes everything into another new nature, and bears another new fruit. All living things die in it, all dead things decay, and then all these dead things regain life."

The process of the *separatio* or differentiating between the elements of our nature is difficult, confusing and often frightening owing to the sense of losing control. In Jungian analysis, the *nigredo* or *separatio* brings one into direct contact with the shadow or unknown aspect of one's psyche. Our original sense of oneness is split into two and this can be experienced as a kind of dismemberment, often graphically illustrated in the alchemical texts. Yet, this work of differentiation and separation is the first stage of reuniting the conscious solar aspect of the psyche with the unknown and dissociated lunar aspect which includes the shadow and the whole realm of the soul. It brings us into direct contact with the power of the unknown archaic aspects of our psyche. The alchemist has first to separate out the different elements of body, soul and spirit and then reunite them in a new conscious union, based on the awareness that each is an essential aspect of spirit: that what was darkness — unknown and even terrifying — can be illumined by the light of consciousness entering into or descending into that darkness. Paradoxically, the discovery of the light is through a descent into darkness. So they followed the instructions of the Emerald Tablet of Hermes Trismegistus which said: "Thou shalt separate the earth from the fire, the subtle from the dense, gently, with great ingenuity." The word 'gently' was given special emphasis, contrasting with the violence, contempt and repression with which the body and the instincts had generally been treated.

The alchemists called themselves washerwomen and cooks and compared the process of transformation to being cooked, kneaded, washed, hardened, softened, raised, lowered, divided and, finally, united. "Study, meditate, sweat, work, wash, cook," they said. It is an impossible process to describe and the images may offer a better understanding than the words. One cannot delete something from the psyche as one deletes a sentence or paragraph on a computer. One can only gradually become aware of a hitherto unknown aspect of oneself and slowly deepen one's insight into the causes, power and persistence of unconscious habits of behaviour and projections, causes that originate not only in personal experience but in the whole religious and political inheritance of a civilization. This insight is part of the process of the dawning of a different kind of light within the darkness of what was previously unknown.

Jung stressed the vital importance of the ego in this work. The ego or conscious personality is the mediator between the conscious part of our psyche (the king) and the unknown part of it that he called the unconscious (the queen). Without its cooperation no transformation can take place. Trying to get rid of it creates resistance. As the new centre of consciousness comes into being, the ego is strengthened — not in the sense of imposing its will but in the sense of being strong enough not to be overpowered or inflated by the emerging elements of the unconscious. Jung's own experience, described in great detail in *The Red Book*, testifies to this need. The conscious ego or conscious mind has to learn to relate to this greater power rather than to deny its presence or suppress its voice and its attempts to communicate. Ultimately it becomes the servant of this greater power and surrenders to its guidance.

Today, and probably in the past, the call to enter the alchemical process may be initiated by trauma: the experience of profound and devastating loss where the foundation of our life seems to disintegrate. The ego or conscious personality can be assailed by a paralysing depression, a deep melancholia and lose all hope and will to live. These feelings may result from the loss of a parent, partner or child or from the loss of our marriage, our home, our health, our job or our money or from a betrayal of some kind — our life seemingly reduced to dust and ashes. If we can understand this traumatic event as a preparation for a new orientation in our life, even as the call of the buried spirit, this may be of some help; otherwise it may be experienced as blind, apparently pointless suffering: the infliction of a cruel, negative, incomprehensible fate. There may be a risk of suicide if there is no insight into what is happening. Writers and artists know that this descent into the paralysing darkness of depression can be a prelude to a new creative initiative but it feels as if, like Persephone, one has been snatched into the underworld and has been abandoned there. If one looks for a contemporary example of the *nigredo* on the world stage, the devastating tsunami that wiped out the coastal villages of Japan would provide it as does the collapse of the euro and the banking system, together with the unemployment and human suffering caused by them. This experience of disintegration and *mortificatio* can be the prelude to a new beginning, a new and hitherto unimagined creative initiative.

Stage 2. The Second Phase of the Lesser Work
– known as the *Albedo, Solutio* or *Purificatio* –

The two primary symbols of the phase of the *Albedo* are the dove of the Holy Spirit and the White Stone. This phase is presided over by the element Water and is about baptism and regeneration in the watery womb of the soul, awakening to the feminine principle and the neglected feeling values, opening the eye of the heart in the sense described in Chapter Fifteen. In this phase water and, specifically, water associated with the ethereal substance of the soul — the *aqua permanans* — is the agent of transformation: "This divine water makes the dead living and the living dead, it lightens the darkness and darkens the light."[17]

Other symbols describing this phase are the white rose and the lily, the pelican and the swan and, most importantly, the Young Queen. The moon is also a symbol of the *Albedo* for it shines in the darkness and presides over the mysteries of transformation that take place in the darkness, in a part of the psyche of which we are not aware at the beginning of the alchemical process. The rising moon signifies the dawning of insight, understanding and a developing relationship with spirit. The copious shedding of tears accompanies this stage as fixed habits, beliefs and powerful complexes are dissolved or melted down. It can indicate the opening of the heart in the first powerful experience of deep feeling.

The alchemists compared the *Albedo* to the gradual whitening of the early dawn sky after the darkness of night. In vivid imagery they describe the process of transforming the *prima materia* of the initial psychic state by repeated washings, cleansings, purifications, repeated immersions in water, and repeated submissions to the heating power of fire which together separate out and remove the rust or verdigris which had accrued to and hidden the gold of the spirit in the pre-conscious state. So there are images of the sun drowning in the mercurial fountain, the king sweating in a confined space or drowning and calling out for help. But in the deep waters of the soul, the king and queen are being brought together in what is known as the first *coniunctio*, described in many images. The imagination begins to be activated, new possibilities are born.

The phase of the *Albedo* describes the process of the soul beginning to become conscious of the hidden spirit whom the alchemists called Mercurius and whose secret presence oversees the Great Work of the process of transmutation. In this phase they began to work consciously with spirit, to serve it with trust and devotion yet also become aware of how they might be deceived or misled by its trickster-like qualities, which in essence are the trickster-like qualities of the shadow. Some Christian alchemists likened this phase to the Assumption of the Virgin. "Little by little and from day to day," wrote the sixteenth century Belgian alchemist Gerhard Dorn, "he will perceive with his mental eyes and with the greatest joy some sparks of divine illumination."

Stage 3. The Greater Work:
The Rubedo, Coniunctio and Multiplicatio
— the re-unification of body, soul and spirit —

The alchemists named the third and final phase of the alchemical process the Greater Work and the *Rubedo*. In some texts it is preceded by a phase called the *Citronitas* or yellowing phase. They likened the *Rubedo* to what the medieval alchemists and mystics called the 'Rising Dawn' (*Aurora*) or 'Golden Hour' (*Aurea Hora*) as a description of the soul's mystical union with God.[18] They also likened it to Resurrection and to the reddening of the sky as the sun begins to rise to the zenith, spreading its irradiating and warming rays over the earth. Red-gold is the colour of the *Rubedo* and the red rose and the red stone are symbols of the completion of the Greater Work.

The phase of the *Rubedo* involves the long and difficult work of fixing the new attitude so that it is stable and constant, not alternating between the old and new states and, above all, avoiding the danger of inflation. It may involve commitment to some creative work, bringing into manifestation insights and knowledge that have been learned, communicating these to the world or serving life in some way which reflects a deeper compassion and commitment. It can be compared to the physical processes of churning milk into butter, turning grapes into wine, wheat into bread, raw elements into cooked food. As my teacher, Barbara Somers, once unforgettably described it, "the jam begins to set".

This phase describes the awakening of the conscious personality to full awareness of spirit as guide and companion within the illumined soul, the conscious alignment with spirit, and the final union (*coniunctio*) of the two formerly estranged aspects of the psyche, the solar King and lunar Queen — in Jungian terms the conscious and the unconscious. There is no longer conflict and enmity between them, nor indeed the inflated claim of the conscious mind that it constitutes the totality of consciousness, ignoring the existence of the soul.

The *Rubedo* announces the full expansion or awakening of the heart, the incandescent flowering of the imagination that a sixteenth century alchemist called Martin Ruland, who was a pupil of Paracelsus, called the star in man: the celestial or super-celestial body. Body, soul and spirit are unified and transfigured in this experience of enlightenment and union; sometimes at the moment of death, as in the *Aurora* but also, I believe, in the startling enlightenment of the near-death experience which offers a glimpse of life beyond death. We grow through the *Nigredo* and *Albedo* phase of alchemy into the *Rubedo*. We cannot force entry into it by spiritual exercises or any formulation of goals. It may happen to us, as with the near-death experience, or we can grow into it through the expansion of the heart, the instinctive capacity to love, to give to others, to serve life through an awakened compassion. His Holiness the Dalai Lama would be a modern example of this capacity to give, to serve.

The *coniunctio* involves the whole process of psychic transformation as the union of the two aspects of the psyche proceeds through the different phases of alchemy that are repeated over and over again, in what the alchemists called the *circulatio*, relating this word to the rotation of the planets around the sun. The alchemical transformations the alchemist worked with were carried out during appropriate astrological transits, conforming to the understanding that the cosmic events in the 'Above' are reflected in the realm of the 'Below'. But in another sense, the *coniunctio* stands for the final awakening, the final union with the divine ground, now fully recognized, honoured and consciously present within the soul. The power to transform, to serve, to heal, comes from this source. The stone or elixir has the power to multiply (*multiplicatio*) as in the Miracle of the Loaves and the Fishes in the Gospels. The whole alchemical process is about the incarnation of spirit in the human soul and the long incubation or preparation needed for the soul to become capable of containing the tension, dangers and revelation of the gradual incarnation or awakening of spirit.

The final phase of alchemy is about becoming aware of and entering into the immortal "body of light"— the 'starry' or 'celestial' body that we may ultimately inhabit after our death. It is about the awakening of the heart, the flow of compassion towards all living things, and the union with the divine ground that the alchemists called the *unus mundus*. A primary symbol of the *Rubedo* is the phoenix, symbolizing life regenerated from the ashes of the old, unconscious life. The beautiful and evocative images of the treasure belong to this final stage: the Quintessential Gold; the Stone of the Wise; the Pearl of Great Price; the Golden Phoenix; the Elixir of Life; the Flower of Immortality; the Heavenly Balsam and the Divine Water, as well as the perfume of flowers, a flowering tree and the celestial blue colour. One text describes the stone (*lapis*) as a "light without shadow, a marvellous thing that makes a great golden fountain to gush forth from itself."[19]

Conclusion

So, to summarize, the alchemists wanted to free the quintessential gold of the spirit hidden within nature, to free the divine life impulse from the beliefs, fixed attitudes, instinctual habits and unconscious projections that veil it from us. Their aim was to help this mysterious spirit to become conscious in themselves so they could come to the full experience of its presence and guidance but in doing this, they knew that they were actually influencing and perhaps transforming in a positive sense (by refraining from harming it), the very nature of matter and therefore all life, since all things are connected. The gradual revelation of the treasure involved great loneliness, suffering and sacrifice on the one hand and illumination, wonder, and inexpressible joy on the other as the light of the unified consciousness dawned. "No one," wrote Gerhard Dorn, "may accomplish this work except through affliction, humility and love, for it is the gift of God to his humble servants."

As they watched the matter of their own psychic life transform in the mirror of the alchemical retort, the greatest and also the most humble of the alchemists experienced the immense mystery of what they were witnessing. They realized they were assisting spirit in the process of its own transformation, bringing itself to consciousness over aeons of earth time, reconnecting creation with its source. They had revealed to them, in a gradual process of illumination, the divinity of nature and all life processes; they saw that one divine spirit was at work in all forms of life as well as in their own human consciousness. They sought to bring to birth in themselves the hidden spirit that longed to be rescued from its buried state in nature and themselves. In accomplishing this double act of redemption they became the sons of Divine Wisdom, inheritors of the treasure, the true philosophical gold. As their understanding grew, they realized they were the ministers, not the masters of the stone, their lives illumined by the Wisdom of the Holy Spirit eternally pouring forth the water of life.

The three phases of the Great Work blend imperceptibly into each other and they are repeated over and over again in a process known as the *circulatio* as the three-fold union of body, soul and spirit proceeds. There is not one awakening, but many, not one illumination but many. As the darkness at the heart of our nature is entered, so the windows of the soul are opened and the light begins to shine: the light radiating from the *lumen naturae*; the light that is the hidden ground of all life, revealing what was previously unknown or shrouded in darkness. The image of the alchemical diagram of the squared circle points to the recognition of the incarnation of spirit in matter, the unification of the masculine and feminine principles and the *coniunctio* or indissoluble 'marriage' of the Above with the Below.

The late Father Bede Griffiths (1906–1993), one of the great sages of our time, tells of how he suffered a stroke, and thinking he was dying, prepared for death. But instead of death, he felt the need to surrender to the Mother, to the Feminine. He made that act of surrender and felt a wave of love overwhelm him, a wave so powerful that he didn't know whether he would be able to survive it. He realized that all of us carry this love within our being but are shut off from it because the mind gets in the way of it and creates the dualistic consciousness in which we live. Since that experience, he said he was able to live beyond the dualistic mind in the time that remained to him. He said this about the Great Work:

> The soul discovers its source of being in the Spirit, the mind is opened to this inner light, the will is energized by this inner power. The very substance of the soul is changed; it is made a 'partaker of the divine nature'. And this transformation affects not only the soul but also the body. The matter of the body — its actual particles — is transformed by the divine power and transfigured by the divine light — like the body of Christ at the resurrection.[20]

In becoming aware of our soul, in discovering how to relate to it, transform and be transformed by it, heal its wounds, listen to its guidance, receive illumination and insight from our dreams, we help to bring about the marriage between the King and the Queen and eventually, the sacred marriage of all humanity with the Divine Ground which is the principal theme of Alchemy, Kabbalah and Vedanta and is, I believe, the tremendous destiny of the human race. This unrecognized yet immanent Holy Spirit is the flow of life in our veins, the flux and flow of our thoughts, the primordial power of our instincts, the miracle of our bodily organism, the creative genius of our imagination. Anyone who has experienced the sheer ecstasy of serving life to the utmost of his or her ability will have touched the spirit and experienced its awesome power.

"One is the stone, one the vessel, one the procedure, and one the medicine." The process of transformation is unique for each one of us yet intrinsically the same for all. Alchemy gives us the blazing revelation of the divinity of life in the reunion of body, soul and spirit and calls us to the service of that life with whatever creative gifts it has bestowed on us.

What I have learned in the last fifty years is that alchemy is:

❀ A return journey to the unseen dimension of spirit with the help of spirit.

❀ A journey that can take each one of us as far as our longing can reach.

❀ A process that attunes our awareness to a hidden order of reality.

❀ A revelation that we are at all times and in all places living within the light of spirit. There is nothing beyond or outside spirit. There is only one life which is the life of the Cosmos and the life of each and all. Each one of us is a unique atom in the invisible life of the Whole.

❀ A discovery that there is no death for consciousness nor does the matter of the body really die. Our purpose on this planet is to discover this truth, and live this truth with every breath of life; to love and serve life as best we can by doing harm to no one and activating the flow of light and love in our lives.

The Alchemist's Prayer

Oh, most singular and unspeakable Presence, first and last in the universe, heighten the fury of my fire and burn away the dross of my being. Cleanse my soiled soul; bathe me in your awesome light. Set me free from my history and cut me loose from my boundaries. Unite me with the One Thing hidden in my life, wherein is my only strength. Fill me with your Presence, allow me to see through your Eye, grant me entry to your Mind, let me resonate with your Will. Make me transparent to your flame, and fashion me into a lens for your light only. Transmute me into an incorruptible Stone in your eternal service, like the golden light that surrounds you.[21]

Notes:

1. quoted in the *Aurora Consurgens* (1966) edited and with a commentary by Marie-Louise von Franz, Bollingen, New York and Routledge and Kegan Paul, London, p. 160, from a manuscript by Petrus Bonus.
2. Fabre, Pierre-Jean (1636) *Les Secrets Chymiques*, Paris
3. Adam McLean has spent many years taking immense trouble to assemble, translate and put many of these texts onto his website, together with hundreds of extraordinary images from the alchemical texts, many of them hitherto unknown. www.levity.com/alchemy More recently in the magnificent 'House of the Heads' in Amsterdam, Joost Ritman has donated his priceless collection of Alchemical and Hermetic books and manuscripts to the *Embassy of the Free Mind*, available to all. https://embassyofthefreemind.com/en/library
4. Campbell, Joseph (1968) *The Hero with a Thousand Faces*, p. 269
5. Aurobindo, Sri (1990) *The Life Divine*, p. 4
6. One of the priceless manuscripts in the British Library
7. CW12 (1953) *Psychology and Alchemy*, par. 559–563
8. see website www.alchemylab.com
9. Waite, A.E. (1953) *The Hermetic Museum*, London 1, 13
10. *Aurora Consurgens*, p. 242
11. from the *tractatus aureus*, quoted by Jung in par. 155 of CW12, *Psychology and Alchemy*. Compare the passage in Proverbs 4:6–8 "Forsake her not and she shall preserve thee; love her and she shall keep thee."
12. *Aurora Consurgens*, p. 186
13. ibid, p. 192
14. ibid, pp. 35 & 37. For comparison, see Proverbs 3: 13–18
15. ibid, p. 133
16. ibid, pp. 141 and 143
17. Jung, C.G. CW14 (1963) *Mysterium Coniunctionis*, par. 317
18. *Aurora Consurgens*, p. 205
19. ibid, p. 324, from the *Carmina Heliodori*
20. Griffiths, Dom Bede (1976) *Return to the Centre*, Collins, London, pp. 133-134
21. from website www.alchemylab.com

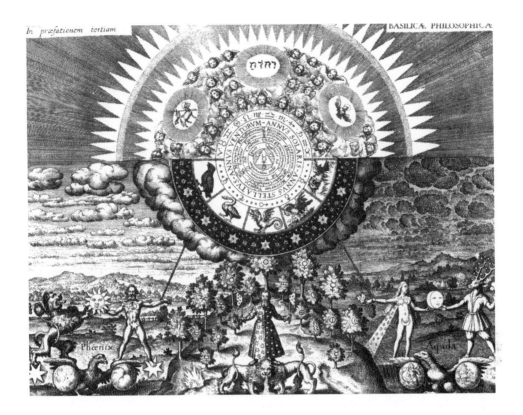

Completion of the Great Work
Engraved by Matthäus Merian ca. 1630

Above the Holy Trinity and the angels of Light influencing the zodiac. Below the Raven of the *Nigredo*, the Swan of the *Albedo*, the Dragon, the Pelican who symbolises the lunar mercury and the Phoenix who symbolises the solar sulphur. On the right is the figure of a stag-headed shaman holding a moon and the figure of Luna with a stream of stars flowing from her breast and a bunch of grapes held in her hand. Below them is an eagle with wings enfolding water and earth. On the left is the figure of Sol and a magnificent lion, together holding an image of the sun. Below them is a phoenix with wings enfolding fire and air. The central figure of the alchemist or kabbalist wearing a star-spangled robe, surrounded by the signs of the zodiac, stands on two lions with a single head. From their jaws flows a stream of living water. Sol and Luna are connected to the subtle body of the cosmos. This whole magnificent scene symbolises the indissoluble unity of the Golden Stone and the union of the alchemist with the *unus mundus*, the divine ground and also the union of the Above and the Below.

Three phases in the Evolution of Consciousness
adapted from the Author's original diagram

Chapter Nineteen

SEEING BEYOND THE VEIL:
THE SURVIVAL OF THE SOUL AND LIFE BEYOND DEATH

*For life is eternal and love is immortal and death is only an horizon,
and an horizon is nothing save the limit of our sight.*
— Anonymous

There is no death — only a change of worlds.
— Native American Chief

No book on the soul can be complete without a consideration of what happens to us when we die. It is truly astonishing that after millennia of human life on this planet and all the vast amount of knowledge that is now available to us, we still know virtually nothing about the most mysterious, frightening and challenging experience of our lives: our birth and our death. From what other dimension of reality do we come at our birth? And to what other dimension of reality do we go when we die? The answers to these questions, which Socrates addressed on the eve of his own death in the account given in Plato's *Phaedo*, seem clearer then than they are now, nearly two and a half thousand years later. Even more extraordinary is the fact that science, and our culture as a whole have, until very recently, ignored the existence of the large body of material gathered over the past hundred or so years by institutions devoted to recording non-ordinary experiences: near-death, after-death and out-of-the-body experiences (NDE, ADE and OBEs), as well as communications to the living from the 'dead'. Nor has science accepted as worthy of attention the shamanic experiences of visionaries and mystics of all cultures and times which have testified to the existence of other dimensions of reality and the possibility of communion with them. The belief of mainstream science that the death of the physical brain is the end of consciousness has created a kind of firewall, closing our minds to this evidence as well as to the growing evidence that consciousness is not limited to the human brain — thereby confining us to a prison of our own making. This reductionist belief is reflected in a statement by Stephen Hawking (reported in *The Guardian* 2011) "Brains are like computers. There is no heaven or afterlife for broken-down computers; that is a fairy story for people afraid of the dark."

In view of the fact that death has always been part of human experience and comes to us all, sooner or later, it seems strange that something of the greatest significance to everyone is given so little attention. However, as Jung pointed out in his autobiography,

> Critical rationalism has apparently eliminated, along with so many other mythic conceptions, the idea of life after death. This could only have happened because nowadays most people identify themselves almost exclusively with their consciousness, and imagine that they are only what they know about themselves. Yet anyone with even a smattering of psychology can see how limited this knowledge is... a great deal will yet be discovered which our present limited view would have ruled out as impossible.[1]

As long as science insists that the universe is 'dead', with no inner dimension, consciousness or soul and that the physical brain is the origin of consciousness, these beliefs will continue to cripple and constrict the human spirit and limit the horizon of our sight. As long as it continues to believe with Bertrand Russell that "No fire, no heroism, no intensity of thought and feeling, can preserve an individual life beyond the grave," it will continue to block the growth of human understanding and stifle the longing of the human heart. Christopher Bache comments on this situation in his book *Dark Night, Early Dawn*:

> Western thought has committed itself to a vision of reality that is based almost entirely on the daylight world of ordinary states of consciousness while systematically ignoring the knowledge that can be gained from the night-time sky of non-ordinary states…. Trapped within the horizon of the near-at-hand mind, our culture creates myths about the unreliability and irrelevance of non-ordinary states. Meanwhile, our social fragmentation continues to deepen, reflecting in part our inability to answer the most basic existential questions.[2]

This restricted view of reality has left an aching void in many people's lives that neither religious belief, nor scientific progress, nor improving the material circumstances of our lives can fill, although these are presented as offering all that is necessary to ameliorate the suffering of the human condition. What is missing is a sense of our relationship with an invisible dimension, knowledge of how this relationship can be cultivated, and how fear of death can ultimately be replaced by trust in our survival. There have been many great teachers who have pointed the way to a direct experience of reality but their message and their teachings have, for the most part, been misinterpreted or ignored.

The neglect of a vitally significant field of human experience has meant that the experiences and discoveries related to this field are considered to be irrelevant or worse, symptoms of deluded and 'superstitious' minds. We no longer have access to other levels or modes of consciousness because our 'rational' mind has, over the last four centuries, increasingly ridiculed, disparaged and repressed what it has been unable, so far, to accept, prove or comprehend. It has therefore cut us off from those deeper instinctive aspects of our nature that have the power to connect us with other dimensions of reality. Access to those deeper-dwelling faculties has been denied for centuries and has led to them becoming atrophied for want of use. From this metaphysical desolation — the denial and repression of these intuitive, creative and imaginative aspects of ourselves together with the sense that life is fundamentally meaningless — has come our secular belief system and a culture of escalating violence which now threatens us with the disintegration of civilization and, ultimately, with the possible extinction of our species.

William James' carefully chosen words, written a hundred years ago, seem more relevant than ever today:

> Our normal waking consciousness, rational consciousness as we call it, is but one special type of consciousness, whilst all about it, parted from it by the filmiest of screens, there lie potential forms of consciousness entirely different. We may go through life without suspecting their existence; but apply the requisite stimulus, and at a touch they are there in all their completeness, definite types of mentality which probably somewhere have their field of application and adaptation. No account of the universe in its totality can be final which leaves these other forms of consciousness quite disregarded.[3]

Our understanding of life and the interconnectedness of all aspects of it is now tragically deficient. Sogyal Rinpoche writes in *The Tibetan Book of Living and Dying*:

> All the greatest spiritual traditions of the world, including of course Christianity, have told us clearly that death is not the end. They have all handed down a vision of some sort of life to come, which infuses this life that we are leading now with sacred meaning. But despite their teachings, modern society is largely a spiritual desert where the majority imagine that this life is all that there is. Without any real or authentic faith in an afterlife, most people live lives deprived of any ultimate meaning.[4]

> I have come to realize that the disastrous effects of the denial of death go far beyond the individual: They affect the whole planet. Believing fundamentally that this life is the only one, modern people have developed no long-term vision. So there is nothing to restrain them from plundering the planet for their own immediate ends and from living in a selfish way that could prove fatal for the future…. Fear of death and ignorance of the afterlife are fuelling that destruction of our environment that is threatening all our lives.[5]

Suppose we knew beyond any possibility of doubt that we are immortal, that the finality of death is the greatest of our illusions. Suppose we knew that death is simply a change of worlds and that when we die we enter another dimension of reality, another state of being, without losing the consciousness we have in this one. The perspective on our lives would change if we knew that death is like a second birth — a birth into a world that is as real as this one, where we are reunited with family and close friends, and can explore, grow and use our creative gifts with a freedom that many of us do not have here. How would the way we live our lives in this world change if we knew that the journey beyond the death of the body leads us into a vastly expanded life in multiple dimensions or worlds beyond this one and that we inhabit a soul body after we have parted with our physical one?

We could awaken to awareness of something that was once instinctively known and has long been forgotten: an understanding that we participate in and are contained by the creative consciousness and loving intelligence of the universe. Whatever name we give this consciousness — God, Universal Mind or Intelligence, Cosmic Soul, Energy or Spirit — does not really matter. What matters is that we recognize the existence of a dimension of reality beyond the one we know and begin to enter into a relationship with it.

In all cultures, even our own modern secular one, the belief in immortality is deeply, instinctively present in the human soul. It may be that this belief has its far distant origins in the observation of the moon and its cyclical process of death and regeneration. The greatest myths from the ancient world — those of Sumer, Egypt and Greece, as well as the Christian myth of the death and resurrection of Jesus — all offer the lunar imagery of rebirth after the three days of darkness.

While working together on the last chapter of *The Myth of the Goddess*, Jules and I came across these deeply reflective words of the poet Rilke which enlarge the boundaries of our limited vision:

> Death is the side of life averted from us, unshone upon by us: we must try to achieve the greatest consciousness of our existence which is at home in both unbounded realms, inexhaustibly nourished from both… The true figure of life

extends through both: there is neither a here nor a beyond, but the great unity in which the beings that surpass us, the 'angels', are at home…. We of the here and now are not for a moment hedged in the time-world, nor confined within it… we are incessantly flowing over and over to those who preceded us….[6]

The Sudden Intrusion of Death

I know that for many people in their later years the inevitability of death weighs like a stone on their hearts, yet they cannot share their grief and apprehension with their children or friends because, even though death is an experience that awaits each one of us, it is still deeply threatening to talk about it. In a culture which believes that consciousness originates in the brain and that the death of the brain must inevitably bring about the extinction of consciousness, the subject of our survival beyond the death of the body rarely comes up for discussion. And so the deeper concerns of the heart are unable to find a channel of expression. Unsurprisingly, in view of this silence, the greatest sorrow, the greatest fear we can experience in our lives is the loss of a beloved parent, child or companion, believing either that he or she may be lost to us forever or that reunion with them is uncertain. Despite my trust in our survival and the certainty that this life is not my only one, the awareness of death evokes deep sorrow in me. Sooner or later I, like everyone else in the world, will experience the loss of a loved one and, eventually, my own death and the parting from my husband, daughter and grandson.

So many millions of people today lose their lives suddenly and prematurely, not only through terrorist bombs and war but through devastating diseases such as AIDS and cancer, as well as fatal accidents and unforeseen natural disasters like earthquakes and tsunamis. The brutal intrusion of the premature death of a loved one into people's lives, and the anguish of their deep grieving, creates a pressure to discover more about the fate of those so abruptly banished from this dimension. Many old people prolong their lives through fear of death and separation from those they love. If we knew more about what happens after death, it might lessen the pain of the loss of a loved one and encourage people to trust in their own survival and trust that those closest and dearest to them are not lost to them forever. This trust is particularly vital in the lives of children, whose grief at being abandoned by the death of a parent can develop later in life into uncontrollable rage or self-destructive patterns of behaviour.

In our Western society it is no longer part of the ritual of death to sit with the body or have relatives and friends come to say goodbye to the deceased and put flowers in the coffin. Children very rarely see the body of a grandparent or a parent and are shielded from the reality of what a dead body looks like. Many people are cremated rather than buried. That particular ceremony seems almost surreal because it ends abruptly after an allotted number of minutes in order to make room for the next group of mourners coming to say goodbye to a loved one. While there may be mention of eternal life, a return to God and similar time-honoured and reassuring ideas at a funeral or a cremation, people are given no idea of what the afterlife might be like, or what the passage from this life to another might entail, or of how to prepare for this experience.

Whether it is our own death or the death of someone close to us, we may be deeply distressed by the fact that when so much passion and effort, suffering and love have been expended in living, everything we have built up, everything we have loved and cherished in our own lives or in those we love, has to be relinquished, often without preparation. Moreover, all that rich experience is, so to speak, gone forever, vanishing without trace in a moment. Many people who have lost loved ones may be left with deep feelings of grief, guilt and anger as well as regret over 'unfinished business' with the departed that may affect them for the rest of their lives.

What do we take with us as we approach the threshold of death? Surely the quintessence of our being: the memories of what we have loved; the love of children and grandchildren to whom we have given life; the love of the friends we have cherished and who have cherished us; the creative work whose residue we leave behind us — part seen, part unseen — because no one can express the full range of his or her being nor can those closest to us know the extent of it. When my mother died, I instinctively put a rose into her coffin as a symbol of my love for her and the continuity of my relationship with her. Several years later I was amazed to hear a medium say that my mother had been very touched by my gesture of farewell. Her words did not really surprise me but confirmed what I already felt to be true: that our consciousness survives death.

Thanks to my early out-of-the-body experience, and the direction my life took in response to that and to the early messages received by my mother and her friends, I have gathered together over the years the testimony of many individuals who have spoken of their out-of-the-body experiences and how these have changed their lives and their attitude to death. The variety of human experience is so rich, extensive and fascinating that I feel it is essential to include this subjective experience in any consideration of what is of greatest value to us. And what could be of greater value than to know that consciousness survives the death of the body as well as to know what actually happens to us when we die? Although I have enormous respect for science as a methodology, I do not accept the reductionist belief that the brain is the origin of consciousness because it seems implausible in the light of what I and many others have experienced, the evidence that is now available about our survival and the testimony of visionaries, mystics and shamans of cultures past and present.

Effects of the Fear of Death

I wonder whether the violence that is so endemic in humanity could be born not only from the experience of calamitous loss but also from the unconscious fear of death and the anger arising from the fact that we know so little about the deeper purpose of our presence on this planet and believe that we have only one life to live. The fear of death and the desire to ensure our own survival has led us to kill others without the awareness that in doing so, we are injuring all life. What would be the point of celebrating the killing of others if we knew that our bodies were only a temporary casing for an immortal consciousness? What would be the point of the huge engine of destruction that centuries of warfare have brought into being with the aim of destroying the body? Would we not realize that all our efforts to conquer, control and kill others in order to protect our own tribal group or extend its power are a waste of resources, energy and precious life?

For centuries, Christians were taught to believe that death was a punishment introduced into the world through the sin of the Fall, and that Christ's redemptive death on the cross had broken the power of death and given us access to the kingdom of heaven — provided we were baptized as Christians. According to this doctrine, to rise again in a physical body (not a spiritual body) at the Day of Judgement, we needed to have been baptized into the Christian faith. Not to have been baptized condemned the non-believer and, until very recently in the Catholic religion, even the unbaptized infant, to limbo. The atheist, of course, believes that death is the final end. He has only this one life and nothing beyond it. What is there in our modern society that can prepare people for life beyond death?

Past Beliefs about the Survival of the Soul

For thousands of years shamanic cultures have known that there is a ladder of connection between this world and an unseen reality and that this reality sustains, permeates and interacts with our own. Even to the present day, they have maintained a connection with their ancestors. Wherever a strong lunar mythology existed, there was a belief in the immortality of the soul.

If we look back as far as Bronze Age Egypt, we find a highly developed and comprehensive cosmology and a detailed concept of the survival of the soul after death. This extraordinary civilization was as aware of the afterlife as of this life. People lived in awareness of the presence of the unseen world and the goddesses and gods who inhabited the starry cosmos and descended each day into their temples. Far from seeing death as extinction, the Egyptians saw death as a journey towards awakening to cosmic life and the invisible dimension of the cosmos that they called the *Dwat*. The *Book of the Dead* and many books about the Underworld are guides to entering ever more refined states of spiritual awareness in this invisible realm. When an Egyptian left his physical body, his *ba* (soul) might cling to the body, unable to free itself from identifying with his former life and he might therefore be bound to this earthly plane. But with the help of the gods he could find release from this state and move into a spiritual body called the *sah* or *sahu*. In its fully awakened state this spiritual body was represented by the *akh*, the "shining one" or "shining form", symbolized by the crested ibis. In this shining body, the *ba* soul could be carried to the higher cosmic planes associated with the sun and the stars. The Egyptians described this experience as "Coming forth into the Day".[7]

Likewise, in ancient Greece, the secret rituals of the Mysteries, celebrated at Eleusis and believed to have lasted for over a thousand years, gave initiates the certainty of immortality: "He who has seen the Mysteries will not taste death."

There are four other ancient cosmologies that speak of multiple hidden worlds and dimensions: the Vedic, the Sufi, the Tibetan and the Jewish mystical tradition of Kabbalah. As explained in earlier Chapters, Kabbalah recognizes four interconnected worlds or planes of existence, set out as a Tree of Life, each one containing many more worlds or dimensions, each one transmitting the light emanating from the divine source, eventually bringing our material world into manifestation. Everything in this world is the reflection of its prototype in the higher worlds of finer vibrations. Everything is sacred because it has emanated from and is contained within the divine ground. Hence the kabbalistic saying, which actually originates in Egypt: "As Above, so Below."

Within this tradition, as well as in Judaism, Christianity and Islam, and in Hinduism and Buddhism, there was (and still is) a belief in the existence of angels or spiritual beings who intervene to help and guide humanity. There was and still is a belief that the soul survives the death of the physical body. Strangely, however, with the exception of Tibetan Buddhism, there is no manual or guide on offer which might prepare us for what we will encounter in the extra-terrestrial worlds.

Long ago, in the eighth century, a great Buddhist Tantric master called Padmasambhava, who brought Buddhism to Tibet, gave out a teaching on the after-death experience to his closest disciples and the ruler of Tibet. At his request, the text of this teaching was to remain concealed in one of Tibet's sacred mountains, there to await the appointed time when it was appropriate that it should be found and made available to a wider world. A long era of persecution followed but, incredibly, in the fifteenth century, the text of Padmasambhava's teaching was found and news of it carried far and wide through the mountainous regions adjoining Tibet. Early in the last century, two great scholars, W.Y. Evans-Wentz and the Lama Anagarika Govinda, translated one chapter of it into English and this translation was first published in 1927 as *The Tibetan Book of the Dead*. The third edition of this translation was published in 1957 by Oxford University Press with a commentary by Jung. Now, for the first time, Penguin has published the entire text of twelve chapters or sections in a new translation called *The Tibetan Book of the Dead*, with an introduction and commentary by his Holiness the Dalai Lama (2005).

The greatest spiritual teachers have testified to the existence of this transcendent reality; have experienced the higher dimensions of it; may even have come as emissaries from them. Only by cleansing the doors of perception, as Blake advised us, can we become aware of the presence of these transcendent worlds. During the last quarter of the twentieth century, a growing number of people have become convinced through their own subjective experience and through reading the many books on the subject that consciousness continues beyond the death of the body. Those who have been unexpectedly precipitated into a near-death or out-of-the-body experience and returned to their bodies have found that it has given them a new perspective on life. They now live life in a different way, with less fear of death and a greater sense of responsibility for their actions.

Reincarnation

In a lunar culture, the idea that we have many lives, moving in and out of this physical dimension of reality, would have been thought of as perfectly natural, given the influence of the recurring cycles of the moon. I have long been convinced that we have many lives, fragments of which may return to us, some vividly and some as a faint memory — perhaps as a longing for a specific place or a strong attraction to someone who seems strangely familiar to us or, conversely, a fear or dislike of places or people we barely know. When I first went to India and came across the belief in reincarnation in both Hinduism and Buddhism, it never occurred to me to question it. I felt totally at home in these religions so different from my own. Because of the breadth and depth of their concept of divinity and the Oneness of life, the *Upanishads* and the *Bhagavad Gita* meant more to me than the Christian image of a remote God I had grown up with. I found myself drawn to study the life and teaching of the Buddha and the wonderful images of him that had spread from India all across Asia to China and Japan. They were so startlingly different from the images of the crucified Christ.

It seemed obvious to me that thousands of years of contemplation in traditions that were far older than Christianity needed to be respected and, moreover, the idea that we have many lives seemed so logical. One life was not long enough to encompass all aspects of the human condition, or to embrace all that was in me that wanted to live and experience, nor did it give me time to learn all I wanted to know and apply that knowledge to how I lived my own life, however it was to unfold. The idea of one life was claustrophobic and somehow outrageously limited. The idea that we are continually reborn into this material dimension until we are able to recover the knowledge of our divine origin and begin consciously to relate to that source or ground made perfect sense.

The teaching about the long-term karmic effects of my actions, carried over from life to life, made me more conscious of the need to act with greater awareness of how I was living and how I was treating other people. The concept of karma seemed more compassionate as an explanation of suffering and release from suffering than the concept of original sin (although its shadow aspect is reflected in the contempt with which people in India treat those belonging to the lowest caste, believing that their birth into this caste indicates misdemeanours in another life). There were so many questions that could never be answered if the framework were limited to one life. But if widened to embrace many lives, everything made more sense. There was more time to pause and reflect on things instead of packing every moment with frenetic activity, in case something was left out of my one and only life.

In a recent book, *Science and the Re-enchantment of the Cosmos* (2006), Dr. Ervin Laszlo sums up the many cultures and peoples who have believed in reincarnation:

> It has been an intrinsic part of myth, metaphysics, and philosophy for thousands of years. It is an essential element in Hinduism, Buddhism, Jainism, Sikhism, Zoroastrianism, Tibetan Vajrayana Buddhism, and Taoism. It is present in the belief systems of African tribes, of Native Americans and pre-Columbian cultures, of the Hawaiian kahunas, and of the Gauls and Druids. It was adopted by the Essenes, the Pharisees, the Karaites, and other Jewish tribes and groups; it remains an important element in the Kabbalah. In ancient Greece the Pythagorians and the Orphics subscribed to it. Plato spoke of "metempsychosis" (the transmigration of the psyche) in many of his famous dialogues — *Phaedo*,

Phaedrus, Republic, and *Timaeus* — Julius Caesar mentioned it as a doctrine held by the Celts and Roman historians noted that it was shared by the Germanic people.[8]

Reincarnation was once part of Christian doctrine until it was removed at the time of the Second Council of Constantinople in AD 553 (Fifth Ecumenical Council) when the Emperor Justinian anathematised the teachings of the great Christian teacher Origen about the pre-existence of the soul. Origen, (ca. AD 182–ca. 251) described by Saint Gregory as "the Prince of Christian learning in the third century," wrote: "Every soul comes into this world strengthened by the victories and weakened by the defeats of its previous life." It seems nothing less than tragic that the Emperor Justinian — who, with his wife Theodora facing him, stands clothed in magnificent robes in the apse of San Vitale in Ravenna — in AD 529 closed down the 1000-year-old Platonic Academy in Athens, driving out its last teacher, Damascius. Fortunately, he and his colleagues were invited by the King of Persia to teach in a great university near present day Basra, taking with them priceless manuscripts from the Academy which eventually, via Arab Spain, reached the Schools of Chartres and Paris in twelfth century France. (This extraordinary story is told in a book called *Europe's Debt to Persia from Ancient to Modern Times* by Minou Reeves). Through the decision of one powerful man, Christianity was deprived of a teaching that could have given it far greater depth and a more comprehensive perspective on life. Western civilization was impoverished for nearly six centuries by the loss of the legacy of Platonic and Neo-Platonic teaching with all its rich insight into the nature of the soul — a legacy that only became fully accessible in fifteenth century Italy when Cosmo dei Medici commissioned the philosopher Marsilio Ficino to translate the works of Plato.

Healing the Traumas of Past Lives

Past-life Regression is a recently developed approach to a deeper understanding of ourselves that confirms the fact that we each hold the experience and memory of many other lives. Using this method of regression, we can access buried memories which are held over from life to life in the wider field of the soul. We can, for example, re-live and heal the trauma of a terrible death in another life whose memory, held at the unconscious level of the psyche, affects our mental and physical health in this one, transmitting a legacy of constant anxiety and obsessive fear or guilt. Roger Woolger (d. 2011) was a Jungian analyst and a pioneer in this field. For the last two decades he worked to develop past-life regression, calling it "Deep Memory Process". As he writes in his most recent book, *Healing Your Past Lives* (2004), this method "offers a set of tools for delving into the deep recesses of your unconscious mind — what we call the soul — to discover where memories of past existence are stored, and bring them to light... They can open to you the transcendent reality of the soul."

The physical, emotional and mental memories and negative refrains from other lives can affect our present life, inhibiting our ability to respond to life's difficulties and challenges in a positive way. Severe depression in this life may stem from the memory of trauma carried through from another one. An individual may repeat the negative patterns of a previous life by being drawn to situations or people which may re-constellate the effects of the original trauma. As for healing this trauma, many people are involved in helping to release the souls of those still bound to this dimension by their suffering, particularly the souls of soldiers killed in war who may not realize that they have died or those who have met an atrocious death at the hands of others. One of the most effective ways of helping those we have lost is to imagine them bathed in light, healed and whole and free of pain and distress as clearly described in Sogyal Rinpoche's book. The pioneering work of Edith Fiore as explained in her book, *The Unquiet Dead*, is of particular note in this connection, as is the work of the Jungian analyst, Edward Tick, working with war veterans as well as the souls of the dead, described in his moving book, *War and the Soul* (see Chapter Thirteen). There is so much that is still to be discovered. What we perceive in this physical dimension of reality is only a fraction of the whole.

Major Sources of Documentation for Our Survival beyond Death

There is now an extensive amount of evidence for our survival beyond the death of the body as well as detailed studies of how the afterlife is envisaged in different religious traditions. Much of this evidence has been carefully examined by a number of distinguished people, among them scientists and lawyers, who were interested in ascertaining the facts about our survival. One of the most important testimonies comes from a book called *The Supreme Adventure* (1961 and 1974) by a scientist called Dr. Robert Crookall. He analysed a vast amount of material from every country and continent — from Brazil, from South Africa, from Tibet, from Europe, from India and from Australia — and found that all accounts were consistent.

There are at least seven main sources of evidence for our survival after death and these have been assembled on an outstanding and most informative website: www.victorzammit.com. Among these sources are:

1. Tens of thousands of OBEs and NDEs

2. Communications through high-level mediums from people who have died.

3. Direct experience through clairvoyance, clairaudience and deathbed visions.

4. The out-of-body experiences of shamans and remote viewers

5. The testimony of cardiologists including Dr. Pim van Lommel of the Netherlands, whose book, *Consciousness Beyond Life: the Science of the Near-Death Experience*, was published in English in 2010.

6. The holotropic states recorded by Stanislav Grof, M.D. and Hal Zina Bennett in *The Holotropic Mind* and by Christopher Bache who describes his revelatory experience of the inner nature of the universe in two books: *Dark Night, Early Dawn* (2000), and *LSD and the Mind of the Universe*: *Diamonds from Heaven* (2019).

7. Electronic voice phenomena (EVP) and instrumental trans-communication (ITC)

A Great Pioneer

The greatest modern pioneer in opening up the subject of life after death for Western culture as a whole was Dr. Elisabeth Kübler-Ross. Like the stunning impact of Rachel Carson's book *Silent Spring* in 1962, which opened our awareness to ecological concerns, the publication of her book *On Death and Dying* in 1969 tore away the opaque veil that had shrouded the subject of death.[9] Almost single-handedly, assisted by her strong personality as well as her extensive clinical experience as a doctor and psychiatrist, she broke the taboo on the subject of death and transformed attitudes towards death and the care of the dying. Her later books, particularly *On Life After Death* (1991), kept the subject before the eyes of the public and, thanks to the rapid dissemination of her ideas through the media as well as many workshops in different countries, led to many thousands, if not millions, having a greater trust in their own and their loved ones' survival after death.[10] Her writing also led for a time to far better care of the dying and respect for their needs — with many hospices for the dying being established.

Her experience of caring for her dying patients taught her that many of them had NDEs and OBEs which gave them trust in their survival beyond the death of their body. Increasingly fascinated by this subject, she and her team studied the records of the case-histories of over 20,000 people from all over the world and from every cultural and social background who had had an NDE and returned to life after being declared clinically dead.[11] Some had returned to life naturally and some through the rapidly developing skills of medical resuscitation. She compared the death of the physical body to the shedding of a worn-out casing or cocoon, releasing the "butterfly" of the soul into life in another dimension. These thousands of testimonies convinced her that there was no such thing as death — that it was an experience of transition to another state of consciousness "where you continue to perceive, to understand, to laugh, and to be able to grow."[12] It seemed to her that it was nothing short of a tragedy that so many millions of us are not aware of this. She realized that, after her many years of work as a psychiatrist with schizophrenic patients, and many more years of work caring for the dying, she needed most of all to communicate to people the fact that death was not the end of consciousness. "The dying experience is almost identical to the experience at birth. It is birth into a different existence which can be proven quite simply. For thousands of years you were made to "believe" in the things concerning the beyond. But for me it is no longer a matter of belief, but rather a matter of knowing."[13] Through the many years of her work, she, like others who followed her, was able precisely to define what happens as we move from this dimension into another.

She described how the first stage of the near-death experience begins with a feeling of serenity and calm, even feelings of joy and bliss. A person may become aware that he or she is leaving the body, floating above it and with the unfamiliar ability to move around in the room and look down on the body, often from the ceiling.

> As soon as your soul leaves the body, you will immediately realize that you can perceive everything that is happening at the place of dying, be it in a hospital room, at the site of an accident or wherever you left your body. You do not register these events with your earthly consciousness, but rather with a new awareness, even during the time your body has no blood pressure, no pulse, no breathing, and in some cases, no measurable brain waves.[14]

She found that people gave clear descriptions of what they saw happening to them during surgery, or cardiac resuscitation, or when being cut free from a car after an accident, even to such details as the license plate on the car that hit them. They could hear the words of the doctors and nurses working on their shattered bodies and could repeat these later to the astonished and often sceptical helpers. A special study of blind people that she conducted showed that they were able to see and remember the colours, jewellery, clothes and even the patterns on the clothes of the people engaged in resuscitating them.

In the second stage of the NDE, the 'dead' person who previously had been seriously injured, or perhaps blind or deaf in their earthly life, realizes that they are restored to perfect wholeness and health. Those formerly blind and deaf reported that during their NDE, they could see and hear. Even patients who had multiple sclerosis and were confined to a wheel-chair reported that during their NDE they were able to move again, even to dance and sing. A person might be fully aware that he or she had lost a limb in an accident, but in the NDE he or she sees that limb rejoined to the body. This experience would seem to reflect the words in *The Tibetan Book of the Dead*, "Even though you may have been blind, deaf or lame while you were alive, now your eyes see forms, your ears hear sounds and all your sense faculties are faultless, clear and complete."[15] While the Tibetan words refer to the person who has just died rather than to one who is undergoing a near-death experience, the similarity between them is striking.

Kübler-Ross found that children who were close to death moved in and out of an NDE state as the time of their death drew nearer. They said that a grandparent or other close relative on the other side had come to be with them and help them with the transition. As her work gathering the thousands of experiences of NDE's developed, she found that no one who had one of these experiences was any longer afraid of dying. Many indeed wanted to return to the out-of-the-body state where they experienced themselves as healed and whole. Since the care of dying children was her special concern, she sat with many who had been brought to hospital after car accidents. As she sat watching for the signs of serenity immediately preceding death, she found that a child might sometimes say that everything was all right and that their loved ones were waiting for them. In one example she shared, a child told her that her mother and brother were waiting for her — even though no one had told her that her mother and brother had been killed in the same accident.

Another striking case that Kübler-Ross mentions describes how a young American Indian woman died in the arms of a stranger shortly after a hit-and-run accident, asking him as she passed to give a message to her mother that she was happy because she was with her dad. The stranger was so moved by this experience that he drove seven hundred miles to see the woman's mother on an Indian reservation. There he was told that her husband, father of the victim, had died of a coronary one hour before his daughter's accident.[16] Many cases like this were reported where the dying person had not known of the prior death of another member of the family, yet was greeted by them.

The third stage of the NDE — which can sometimes anticipate the awareness of the physical body being separate from the observing consciousness — is the experience of moving very rapidly through a tunnel or cylinder-like funnel, often accompanied by a loud roaring noise as of a rushing wind, avalanche or waterfall. This is the experience that I myself had when I was eleven and I remember the loud roaring noise and the tunnel as being terrifying because I didn't know what was happening to me. Had I known then what I know now, it would have greatly diminished my fear. As they move through the tunnel (not everyone experiences an accompanying noise), many people describe seeing a light at the end of it which grows brighter as they advance through the tunnel until they find themselves bathed in its indescribably brilliant radiance. In 1480, the artist Hieronymus Bosch painted this exact scene as part of a larger painting, showing the deceased person being accompanied by an angel as he entered the tunnel and another being waiting for him at the far end of it.

Near the end of her book *On Life After Death*, Dr. Kübler-Ross describes her own experience of the light and love of the divine ground:

> It started with a very fast vibration, or pulsation, of my abdominal area which spread through my entire body and then to anything that my eyes could see — the ceiling, the wall, the floor, the furniture, the bed, the window, the horizons outside of my window, the trees, and eventually the whole planet earth. It was as if the whole planet was in a very high speed vibration, every molecule vibrated. At the same time, something that looked like a lotus flower bud appeared and opened into an incredible, beautiful, colorful flower. Behind the lotus flower appeared the light that my patients so often talk about. And as I approached this light through the open lotus flower, with a whirl in a deep, fast vibration, I gradually and slowly merged into this incredible unconditional love, into this light. I became one with it.[17]

Unconditional love often accompanies an NDE and she describes how, soon afterwards, as she went out of her house, she experienced "the greatest ecstasy of existence that human beings can ever experience on this physical plane. I was in total love and awe of all life around me. I was in love with every leaf, every cloud, every piece of grass, every living creature." There was, she says, "no questioning the validity of this experience, it was simply an awareness of a cosmic consciousness of life in every living thing, and of a love that can never ever be described in words."[18]

Elisabeth Kübler-Ross laid the foundation for a new approach to the experience of dying, one that is based on trust instead of fear and presents the invisible dimension of the Cosmos as loving and caring of those who are about to leave this dimension. There is a gentleness, a true feminine compassion, an empathy in her books that is something new. There is also the fierce passionate strength needed to bring her vision through into a culture which treats old people in retirement homes and people dying in hospital with shocking indifference, even outright cruelty and contempt.

Traditionally, women have been the ones who care for the dying just as they care for the new-born. However, in the past, all the pronouncements on the nature of death and the survival of the soul from whatever religious tradition have been formulated by men. Here, suddenly, is a woman's perspective on death, a woman's experience of the dying and trust in the survival of the soul. Her experiences as well as those of many others offer us an opportunity to create a new vision of reality and an enlightened approach to dying that could take humanity into a different understanding of both life and death. On the next to last page of *Death, the Final Stage of Growth*, she concludes, through her experience of working with the dying for many years, that "Death is the final stage of growth in life. Only the body dies. The self or spirit or whatever you may wish to label it, is eternal."

Near-Death Experiences and Cardiac Arrest

For some years, certain cardiologists have been recording the occurrence of NDEs in cardiac arrest, a state when the patient is confirmed as clinically dead — in a state of unconsciousness caused by lack of oxygen to the brain due to the cessation of circulation and/or breathing. Dr Pim van Lommel, a cardiologist working in the Netherlands, has recently published a book (2010) called *Consciousness Beyond Life: the Science of the Near-Death Experience*. He records and comments on the results of a study he set up to investigate this phenomenon in patients who had undergone cardiac arrest and whose experiences while in this 'unconscious state' were recorded under controlled conditions in a number of hospitals. He addressed the question, "How can an extremely lucid consciousness be experienced outside the body when the brain has momentarily stopped functioning during a period of clinical death?"[19]

The findings of the definitive study which answers this question caused an international sensation when it was published in *The Lancet* in 2001, and suggests that what has been variously named as mind, consciousness or soul exists as a separate entity from the physical brain and that an NDE cannot be attributed to imagination, psychosis, epilepsy or oxygen deprivation. "The experience of consciousness should be impossible during cardiac arrest. All measurable electrical activity in the brain has been extinguished and all bodily and brain-stem reflexes are gone. And yet, during this period of total dysfunction, some people experience a heightened and enhanced consciousness, known as an NDE."[20] His book should be read by every neuroscientist who is convinced that consciousness begins and ends with the physical brain. I find it one of the most interesting and comprehensive books I have ever read on the subject of the nature of consciousness and the survival of the soul.

Dr van Lommel quotes a passage from a book by the neurophysiologist John C. Eccles, *Evolution of the Brain, Creation of the Self*:

> I maintain that the human mystery is incredibly demeaned by scientific reductionism, with its claim in promissory materialism to account eventually for all of the spiritual world in terms of patterns of neuronal activity. This belief must be classed as a superstition.... We have to recognize that we are spiritual beings with souls existing in a spiritual world as well as material beings with bodies and brains existing in a material world.[21]

Dr van Lommel writes: "It is hard to avoid the conclusion that our endless consciousness preceded birth and will survive death independently of the body and in a nonlocal space where time and place play no role. According to the theory of nonlocal consciousness, there is no beginning and no end to our consciousness."[22] And he observes that:

> An NDE is both an existential crisis and an intense learning experience. People are transformed by the glimpse of a dimension where time and space play no role, where past and future can be viewed, where they feel complete and healed, and where infinite wisdom and unconditional love can be experienced. These transformations are primarily fuelled by the insight that love and compassion for oneself, others, and nature are essential. After an NDE, people realize that everything and everybody are connected, that every thought has an impact on oneself and others, and that our consciousness survives physical death. The realization that everything is nonlocally connected changes both scientific theories and our image of mankind and the world.[23]

His book summarizes what has been learned about different aspects of the near-death experience over the last decades of the twentieth century and the first decade of this one. He concludes his ground-breaking book with the words:

> It often takes an NDE to get people to think about the possibility of experiencing consciousness independently of the body and to realize that consciousness has probably always been and always will be, that everything and everybody are connected, that all of our thoughts will exist forever and have an impact on both ourselves and our surroundings, and that death as such does not exist. An NDE provides an opportunity to reconsider our relationship with ourselves, others, and nature, but only if we continue to ask open questions and abandon preconceptions.[24]

One of the most recent and interesting of these NDE experiences has been that recounted by Anita Moorjani. Living in Hong Kong, she had been taken to hospital in the last stages of cancer and was expected to die within hours. This is an extract of her experience that I first read on the Internet and is now described in her book, *Dying to be Me* (2012):

> I was drifting in and out of consciousness during this time, and I could feel my spirit actually leaving my body. I saw and heard the conversations between my husband and the doctors taking place outside my room, about 40 feet away down a hallway. Then I actually "crossed over" to another dimension, where I was engulfed in a total feeling of love. I also experienced with extreme clarity why I had the cancer, why I had come into this life in the first place, what role everyone in my family played in my life in the grand scheme of things, and generally how life works. The clarity and understanding I obtained in this state is almost indescribable. Words seem to limit the experience — I was at a place where I understood how much more there is than what we are able to conceive in our 3-dimensional world. I realized what a gift life was, and that I was surrounded by loving spiritual beings, who were always around me even when I did not know it.... The amount of love I felt was overwhelming. I saw the amazing possibilities we as humans are capable of achieving during a physical life. I found out that my purpose now would be to live "heaven on earth" using this new understanding, and also to share this knowledge with other people.

Anita found that to her, her family and her doctors' astonishment, her terminal cancer was completely healed within weeks. She compared her normal experience prior to her NDE with living in a darkened warehouse where she only had a torch to see what was on its shelves. Her NDE experience was like switching on a light where everything in the warehouse could be clearly seen for the first time. Her recently published book has switched on the light for many thousands of people by showing them how her experience changed her understanding of both life and death. In the course of her NDE she realized that we are all connected: "I realized that the entire universe is alive and infused with consciousness, encompassing all of life and nature. Everything belongs to an infinite Whole. I was intricately, inseparably enmeshed with all of life. We're all facets of that unity — we're all One, and each of us has an effect on the collective whole."[25] She tells us to remember our magnificence and never to doubt for a moment that we are surrounded by love and by loving beings.

There is a growing body of material documenting the recorded testimonies of tens of thousands of near-death and out-of-the-body experiences, as well as the evidence gathered through organizations such as the Alister Hardy Research Centre in Oxford, and the many videos available on YouTube. In one such video, a neurosurgeon called Dr Eben Alexander (2012) describes his experience of a transcendent dimension of reality while he was in a life-threatening coma caused by bacterial meningitis. The coma lasted for seven days and during this time CT scans of his brain showed no activity whatsoever in his neocortex. He had only a 2% chance of survival and the chance of returning to his 'normal' state was almost zero. Yet during this 'absence' he found himself in another dimension of reality: "What I saw and learned there has placed me quite literally in a new world: a world where we are much more than our brains and bodies, and where death is not the end of consciousness but rather a chapter in a vast, and incalculably positive, journey." He describes what he saw there in a book called *Proof of Heaven: A Neurosurgeon's Journey into the Afterlife* (2012). What is most striking about these experiences is their vivid, precise imagery and the intensity of the emotions generated by them, as well as their capacity to change people's perspective on their existence, giving them a sense that their lives hold a much deeper meaning and value.

There is now a sub-culture formed of thousands of people who have a hunger to know more about these experiences. This hunger would seem to reflect the soul's need for a deeper insight into the meaning of our lives and the creation of a relationship with other dimensions of reality and with loved ones who have left this world. Belief for these people is no longer enough: people want to know and they want to connect. Many thousands of people in indigenous cultures still routinely connect with their ancestors. They consider it perfectly natural and indeed necessary, to build ongoing relationships with them for the benefit of the particular group to which they belong and to align the life of their community with the deeper life of the invisible world. Here is one experience recounted to me by a woman who has practised shamanic visualization:

> I have been involved in a formal shamanic training for almost two years and as one of our exercises we journeyed to the moment following our death. I won't go into detail about all that I saw on the other side, but I will say that I came back with a radically different feeling about life on this earth. I did see something of what you describe, the idea that this world is embedded within a vast matrix of cosmic life. One image — metaphor — that I received was of myself standing in a still centre before rebirth while around me turned, like a great carousel, "entrances" to world after world, dimension after dimension, planet after planet. They were all there and could be accessed at the proper time. For all I know, the possibilities are infinite. During that meditation/vision I saw more clearly than I have ever seen that this is not a flawed, "inferior" world, as Christianity teaches. We already exist in paradise, if only we had eyes to see it — the beauty of this world is immense and dazzling. I realized that in all my best moments, especially in the natural world — near the ocean, on the

mountaintop among the redwoods, in the fields and woods of my childhood —
I have felt that oneness, that wholeness, that ecstasy of belonging, that sense of
immortality and the eternal, that understanding that all is well at the foundation
of the world. I recognized that feeling as I looked through the entrances that
led to the borders of all these worlds.[26]

Other Features of NDE's

Many testimonies describe a "being of light" who comes to meet them and who
is experienced as loving and embracing them — almost the quintessence of love
itself. This is a deeply emotional experience, the memory of which stays with
them on their return to their earthly life. Others are met by a close family relative,
already deceased or by a dear friend who welcomes and reassures them. Anita
Moorjani was met by her father and her best friend.

A further feature of the NDE is witnessing a life-review, experienced 'in a
flash' even though the review includes minute details of the experiences, relationships, thoughts and emotions of many years of earth life. People are made aware
of all the things they have said and done that have affected others in both a positive
and negative sense. Their experience suggests that every thought, every word we
utter, every act, is somehow recorded. Also the events that we experience here, as
it were in slow motion, are speeded up in that other dimension. Our capacity to
view these events and assimilate them is apparently accelerated there.

What is so interesting about this particular feature of the modern near-death
experience is that it reflects a similar experience in Egyptian times, which gave
the Egyptians the mythic image of Osiris as the Judge of the Dead and Weigher
of the Soul in the scales of the goddess Maat. *The Egyptian Book of the Dead*
shows the soul of the deceased passing through the Hall of Judgment to be
"weighed" before it passes on to the "Fields of Ra" or the starry world of
the *Dwat*.

To live one's life in the awareness that we not only survive death but that every
thought, every nuance of relationship, every act is recorded in a deeper dimension
of reality gives a far greater awareness of our responsibility for how we conduct
ourselves in our relationships with others and how far-reaching our words and
actions are in affecting the lives and well-being of others. If all our lives and
consciousness are connected, then this makes perfect sense.

Naturally, people who have been critically injured want to stay in this strange
new environment which is often described as being exquisitely beautiful.
However, if their destiny is to return to earth life, they come up against some kind
of barrier or they encounter someone, a deceased family member or perhaps a

being of light, who gives them reasons why they need to go back to care for their family or to complete their work on earth. The choice is left to them. They accept the need to return to their earth-life, although sometimes not without protest, and find themselves back in their physical body, not knowing quite how they returned to it.

Moving from One Dimension to Another

There are interesting descriptions in a book called *On Dreams and Death* by Jung's closest colleague, Marie-Louise von Franz, on what it feels like to pass from one dimension to another. She writes:

> All of the dreams of people who are facing death indicate the unconscious, that is, our instinct world, prepares consciousness not for a definite end but for a profound transformation and for a kind of continuation of the life process which, however, is unimaginable to everyday consciousness.

> The image of light appears more often than any other image in our quoted material. Jung has expressed the assumption that psychic reality might lie on a supraluminous level of frequency, that is, it could exceed the speed of light.[27]

One of the accounts she cites is that of a man who was thought to have been clinically dead for twenty-three minutes:

> I was moving very quickly toward a bright shining net which vibrated with a remarkable cold energy at the intersection points of its radiant strands. The net was like a lattice which I did not want to break through. For a brief moment my forward movement seemed to slow down, but then I was in the lattice. As I came in touch with it, the light flickering increased to such an intensity that it consumed and, at the same time, transformed me. I felt no pain. The feeling was neither agreeable nor disagreeable, but it filled me completely. From then on everything was different — this can be described only very incompletely. *The whole thing was like a transformer, an energy-transformer, which transported me into a formlessness beyond time and space.* I was not in another place —for spatial dimensions had been abolished — but rather in another state of being.[28]

She cites another observation: that of an architect named Stefan von Jankovich:

> One of the greatest discoveries I made during death...was the oscillation principle.... Since that time "God" represents, for me, a source of primal energy, inexhaustible and timeless, continually radiating energy, absorbing energy and constantly pulsating.... Different worlds are formed from different oscillations;

the frequencies determine the differences.... Therefore it is possible for different worlds to exist simultaneously in the same place, since the oscillations that do not correspond with each other also do not influence themselves.... Thus birth and death can be understood as events in which, from one oscillation frequency and therefore from one world, we come into another.[29]

Healing the Trauma of Bereavement

Many bereaved people have the experience of seeing their loved ones appearing to them or communicating with them in some way after their death. Others feel a very strong presence of that person in their lives, as if they were still close to them, even close enough to have a dialogue with them. They can feel the presence of the other even if they cannot see them with their physical eyes. Often, synchronicities are noticed. Sogyal Rinpoche gives a most helpful practice for sending rays of light and compassionate love to a loved one which can help them if they are in a state of fear and bewilderment after a traumatic death.

One of the most interesting recent initiatives with regard to assuaging the trauma of bereavement is explored in a book by Dr. Allan L. Botkin called *Induced After Death Communication* (2005). Using the EMDR technique (Eye Movement Desensitisation and Reprocessing), which has been used with great effectiveness in treating veterans with PTSD, he has developed a method of treating the trauma of bereavement by taking this method to a further stage which results in the actual manifestation of the individual who has died or been killed. The bereaved individual finds that he or she can see the 'dead' person and sometimes talk to him or her. At first hesitant to tell colleagues about this new development and its potential for healing the trauma of bereavement, Dr. Botkin found that his growing experience increased his trust and confidence in this method. He brings many case histories to show the effectiveness of this ground-breaking new method of treating bereavement and also refers to cases of veterans who have seen comrades killed or who have killed others in combat and carry deep guilt because of this. Being able to talk to these deceased men and realize that those whom they thought were dead are alive and well removes the enormous burden of grief and guilt they may have carried for years.

I wonder whether our world and the worlds or dimensions we cannot see exist as levels in the vast electro-magnetic vibrational field of the universe where each level is vibrating at a different rate. It appears that the world of the 'living dead' moves at a different vibratory rate than the physical matter of our world. Occasionally, in some way we don't yet understand, these different levels come close to or overlap with each other, or perhaps our field of consciousness expands so that we have a glimpse, a brief connection, before we are returned to our usual state. In a talk he gave on Angels, the artist the late Cecil Collins said, "Perhaps there are not two things, spirit and matter... but different degrees of one reality: different degrees of vibrations on a scale from the lower end of vibrations we call matter to the higher, the vibration and radiance of the world of light which is the world of angels. We see according to our place on the scale of vibrations."[30]

Summary of the Worlds or Dimensions beyond Ours

1. We are immortal and we retain our individuality after our death.

2. As described in Chapter Fifteen, there are literally millions of unseen worlds, planes or dimensions inhabited by countless numbers of souls but there appear to be three basic levels of reality: our physical world; an intermediate multi-dimensional soul world; and a level that is beyond description which represents what may be called the divine world. Some souls reincarnate into this material world. Others don't. There seems to be a possibility for souls to circulate between many of these different worlds or dimensions of reality.

3. There is no specific heaven or hell to which people can be consigned indefinitely but there are states of being which can be compared to these. There is always the possibility of help being given by more advanced souls to those who are in denser, more unconscious states and who have the choice of responding to the help that is offered.

4. It is not what we believe but how we live our lives here that draws us to the plane we will inhabit there. No saviour accomplishes our redemption for us. We save, redeem and heal ourselves through the care and service we give to others and to life because we have the innate capacity to do so and because we carry divinity within us, as part of the innate divinity of all life.

Underlying and permeating this plethora of worlds or dimensions is the light and love of the divine ground which emanates from the highest plane and animates and sustains all worlds, all levels of reality. The cosmic ground of being is described as an immeasurable ocean of light and love. Our world is permeated and sustained by this cosmic light and love but we cannot see it or feel it. We and everything on this planet are the embodiment, the creation of that light and love. Light in the higher worlds does not come from the sun but from this ineffable source of light. The closer the zones or spheres are to the source, the more radiant they are and the finer their vibrational frequency. The beauty of these higher, inner or finer zones is indescribable. A communication recorded in a most interesting book written by a lawyer, Edward C. Randall, first published in 1922 and republished in 2010, called *Frontiers of the Afterlife*, says:

> Our world is composed of matter as real and definite as your own, but that matter vibrates at a higher rate, consequently your undeveloped senses can have but little cognisance of it. And, your own sphere being composed of matter at a low rate of vibration, it is almost equally as difficult for us to manifest on your plane as it is for you to penetrate ours.... The principle of cooperation between the two planes is what we desire to establish, for this principle of cooperation is an essential condition for the development of the consciousness from your low and stagnant vibrations to those that are higher and healthier and more in keeping with the spirit's deepest longing, more in harmony with that process that is working for the ultimate and absolute destiny of the evolving spirit of man.[31]

Three Bodies

According to the many communications that have been received about the nature of our existence in this transcendent reality, each of us has several 'bodies' corresponding to the three orders of reality described above and in Chapter Fifteen: the physical plane of reality; the intermediate plane of the subtle forms of the soul-worlds and, finally, the plane of spirit, or pure light beyond form. Corresponding with these three orders of reality,

1. We have a physical body for this material world.

2. We have a soul-body or light-body composed of much finer particles than the physical body but resembling it exactly. At the point of death this soul-body emerges from the physical body and is connected to it by a silver cord. Death ensues when the silver cord is severed from the physical body. When we discard the physical body our soul-body comes into its own and we discover to our surprise that we are not dead but very much alive in a 'body' which has the same features as our old one but in a more youthful and healthy state. In this soul-body we can see and hear as before, only more intensely. We can communicate with others telepathically and have instantaneous access to the thoughts of others as well as to places or people whom we wish to see or communicate with. This soul-body can create form through thought and imagination alone, without the need for speech. To some extent we can visit other planes of that subtle reality but we cannot visit the highest realms of the spirit world for very long until our soul vibrations are attuned to the very fine

vibrations of that plane of reality.

3. Within the soul body, we have a spirit body or a sequence of bodies consist
ing of ever finer particles which correspond to the higher levels of the spirit
world. These are gradually unveiled or entered into as we draw closer and
closer to the light of the divine ground.

Those who don't realize they are dead or who cling to the memories and habits
of their earthly life may remain in the denser, darker regions known as the Shadow
Lands because of the harm they did to others or to themselves or because of fixed
beliefs imprinted during their earthly lives, or their inability to realize that they
have died and are in another dimension of reality. For anyone who is convinced
that death is the end of consciousness, it is a shock to realize that he or she is still
conscious and it takes time to adjust to this realization. Our culture encourages
addictions of all kinds and when they die, people may remain trapped in these.
But with help from those in higher spheres they can move towards the light. Still-
born children and children who died young are apparently cared for by loving
adults and are reunited with their parents when the time comes for them to make
the transition.

> When any individual, on earth, or here, omits doing something that he feels
> and knows he should do, the whole creation feels the loss. Whereas when we
> do something that adds grandeur and stature to life, the whole created universe
> gains from that action. It can make you shiver inside to know and appreciate
> how far-reaching a thought or deed or word of any person can be.[32]

This statement recalls the Net of Indra described in Chapter Fifteen. In relation to
the clarity of vision and freedom of movement that seem to characterize life in
the subtle dimensions of reality we, in this physical dimension are living a
diminished or restricted existence, enclosed like an oyster in its shell, as Plato put
it in his *Phaedrus*.

The Forms of Life in the Spirit World

The forms of the intermediate soul worlds and the higher spirit worlds are
prototypes of the forms of this world, only more beautiful and extraordinary, just
as Plato and the Sufi mystics have described them. In these worlds are mountains,
oceans, rivers and lakes; rocks, trees and flowers; animals, wonderful birds and
exquisite butterflies. Everything is as real and familiar to the inhabitants of these
worlds as the forms of this planet are to us. But there we don't need to eat, to earn

our living, to procreate. Nor do we need to defend ourselves against attack. We can move about freely in our soul or spirit bodies and so we don't need tarmac roads, cars, trains, aeroplanes. We don't need oil or electricity. We can communicate telepathically by thought alone so we don't need mobiles. Above all, we don't need money or banks because we can create the houses, furnishings and gardens we would like to live in with the imagination alone.

There is plenty to do in these worlds. We can continue with the pursuits that interested us in this world: cultivate gardens, create houses for ourselves, imagine, invent, explore, discover and generally develop ourselves as well as help those lost in denser, darker regions to move out of them. Here are houses, magnificent temples, great cities, schools, wonderful universities and libraries; places for scientists and astronomers to study the universe; for artists and craftsmen to create beauty; for writers to write; for teachers to teach; for musicians to play instruments. Beautiful music is one of the features most often commented on. Music can apparently create form. There are hospitals where people can rest and recover as they adjust to their new environment. New discoveries can be made which can be communicated to scientists on Earth if they will listen.

The Subtle Body

In 1919 G.R.S. Mead, translator of major works of Egyptian and Neo-Platonic philosophy and the then known Gnostic texts, published his *The Doctrine of the Subtle Body in Western Tradition*.[33] This revealed, as the introduction to a new edition published in 2005 says, that there is and always has been an esoteric tradition in the West, as well as in the East, concerning the "subtle body" of man. This would seem to correspond to what is generally referred to as the soul in the Christian tradition. But the concept of the soul as the subtle body we inhabit after death was never developed by Christian theology and offered to the culture as a whole, so the pre-existent teaching about the survival of consciousness after the death of the body derived from Egypt and, subsequently, from the Platonic School in Athens and the Neo-Platonism of Plotinus was virtually lost.

Mead writes of the subtle body: "Conjectures concerning it vary with every stage of culture and differ within every stage. But the underlying conception invariably holds its ground, and makes good its claim to be one of the most persistent persuasions of mankind in all ages and climes."[34] Even in 1919, he could write in words that are, unfortunately, as applicable to our day, nearly a hundred years later, as they were for his: "It is, however, the prevailing habit of the sceptical rationalism of the present day to dismiss summarily all such beliefs of antiquity as the baseless dreams of a pre-scientific age, and to dump them all indiscriminately into the midden of exploded superstitions. But this particular superstition, I venture to think, cannot be justly disposed of in so contemptuous a fashion."[35] Mead anticipated that physicists would one day discover the existence of subtle energy fields and would therefore be able to prove the existence of the subtle body, using their own methodology. I think they are on the verge of doing so today in their discovery of dark matter.

Many writers of earlier cultures speak variously of a "subtle" body, a "resurrection" body (St. Paul), a "celestial" body, a "shining" body, a "radiant" body, an "ethereal" or etheric body, an astral or "starry" body. In the sixteenth century, an alchemist who goes by the unforgettable name of Ruland the Lexicographer, identifies the faculty of the imagination itself with the subtle body when he writes "Imagination is the star in man; the celestial and super-celestial body." These different "bodies" or sheaths were believed by different cultures to exist within or to surround and enfold the physical body when it incarnates in this earthly dimension. When we discard the body, our subtle or "soul" body comes into its own and we discover to our surprise that we are not dead but still very much alive.

One of the most beautiful descriptions of the subtle body is to be found in *The Hymn of the Robe of Glory* or *Hymn of the Pearl* as it is also known. Believed to have been written by a Gnostic called Bardasanes, who lived in Edessa in the third century AD, and originally translated by Mead, it tells the story of the soul taking leave of her father and mother in the heavenly realms, her descent into mortality, her lapse into forgetfulness of her divine origin, her receiving a message from the divine realms, her awakening and seizure of a pearl from the jaws of a great dragon and her return to the source from which she came, where she is finally clothed in a "body of glory" and received into the Kingdom. The vibrant words of this short extract from the poem translated by Mead describe the soul clothed with the robe of glory or "body of light":

> *My bright embroidered robe,*
> *Which... with glorious colours;*
> *With gold and with beryls,*
> *And rubies and agates*
> *And sardonyxes varied in colour...*
> *And like the sapphire stone also were its manifold hues...*
> *It hastened that I might take it*
> *And me too my love urged on*
> *That I should run to meet it and receive it;*
> *And I stretched forth and received it,*

With the beauty of its colours I adorned myself
And in my royal robe of brilliant colours
I clothed myself therewith, and ascended
to the gate of salutation and homage....[36]

The Transition

These beautiful lines written by the sixteenth century English poet John Donne in his poem "Hymn to God, My God", awaken deep reflection on the moment of transition when we move from this dimension into another:

Since I am coming to that holy roome
Where, with thy Quire of Saints, for evermore
I shall be made thy music; as I come
I tune the instrument here at the door,
And what I must doe then, think here before.

How do we tune the instrument of our being to the music of the Cosmos? Even the act of reflecting on this gentle metaphor of communion or reunion may help to quieten the turmoil of our thoughts, bring to mind what is most important to us, how we might refine our being. Too often those who are dying may find themselves intensely alone and afraid at the moment when they are in the greatest need of comfort and support. If they have been wounded in battle or involved in a car accident, they may have been rushed to hospital and the Intensive Care Unit. Doctors and nurses may be busily engaged in trying to prolong the moments of their life when, sensing the approach of death, all they want is to be able to prepare for the moment of transition and have another kindly human being sitting by them, perhaps holding their hand.

In the final days, hours and minutes of our lives, we may experience strong feelings: fear and uncertainty about what is to come; regret about things we may have done or were not able to do; bitterness at the suffering we may have endured or caused; deep sadness that we were unable to do more, that our lives have been cut short; the longing to communicate all that we were unable to say to loved ones — above all, to express the love we felt and feel for them. It helps greatly if those feelings can be shared with someone who can spare the time to listen to us. Those who do quietly sit and listen, in empathic companionship, even when a person has lost consciousness, may become aware that just before the person dies, a deep feeling of peace and serenity pervades the room.

In *The Tibetan Book of Living and Dying*, Sogyal Rinpoche asks us to live our lives in awareness of this moment of death so that, when it comes, we are able to relinquish the pressing concerns of the personality and focus on reunion with the Source from which we have come. This Source, in the Tibetan tradition, as in others, is conceived of as a great light — the Clear Light of the Void. Whatever effort we can make in our last moments to free ourselves from the powerful emotions, regrets and concerns that may have ruled our lives, will ease our transition from one level of reality to another. With death approaching it is important, where possible, to resolve old problems of relationship with others: to let go of old angers, jealousies, resentments and fears; to be reconciled with people from whom we have become alienated; to speak lovingly and reassuringly to parents or children from whom we have become separated.

Summary of the Stages of the Transition

❁ There are feelings of peace, bliss, intense happiness; an awareness of no more pain

❁ Separation from the body — a sense of weightlessness — "like taking off a diving suit"

❁ Going through a tunnel — a rushing, roaring noise

❁ Seeing a bright light and feeling a magnetic pull towards it

❁ Someone coming to meet us: a close relative, or a being of light. Many testimonies describe a "being of light" who comes to meet them and who is experienced as loving and embracing — almost the quintessence of love itself. Others are met by a close family relative, or a dear friend already deceased who welcomes and reassures them

❁ The feeling of being embraced or surrounded by overwhelming, unconditional love

❁ Sometimes a life review

❁ Restoration to a perfect state of health — eyesight, hearing, limbs — even those who have had MS or who have been blind, deaf or paralysed.

> Then, as quietly as the dawn meets morning, the separation comes. Out of the housing of the flesh, the inner body emerges, and it is welcomed by those who have gone before. This is the second birth, so like the first, except that all the knowledge, individuality and spirituality gained in our earth life is retained,

and we live on in the fullness of our mentality and strength as before. Dissolution neither adds to nor subtracts from the sum total of our knowledge. The inner body in which we have functioned, we shall still function in for all eternity.[37]

Nothing is more important for our well-being than to know that when we die we move into another reality that is as real and vitally alive as this one. Consciousness does not die with the death of the body: consciousness is eternal.

A few years ago, a manuscript came into my hands called *The Miracle of Death*. I wrote a Foreword to it because I felt it could help many bereaved people to trust in the survival of their loved ones. Betty J. Kovács, the author, who lost first a son and then a husband in car accidents two-and-a-half years apart, describes how, out of a sustained meditative attention, there was born in her not only a deeper capacity for insight but the opening of her awareness "to a dimension so vast that I was stunned to realize how excruciatingly small a space I had been trained to live in and call reality." What she experienced as her awareness of this dimension expanded was the shattering of the myth of materialism which condemns so many to a meaningless life of "mediocrity, addiction, violence, indifference and fanaticism". The message of her book is one of hope and trust that we will be able to open ourselves to the experience of the mysteries of the Cosmos and weave these mysteries into our daily lives, and by so doing heal the deep fragmentation in our souls. On the last page of her book she writes, "As we reconnect, full circle, to the roots of our existence in the Mind of the universe… we experience the deep unity of birth and death and the radical creativity of both. We understand that "Death is as Divine as Life", because it is Life — because there is nothing *but* Life."[38]

Other Books giving a New Perspective on Death and Dying

One of the most comprehensive book on reincarnation is *Lifecycles and the Web of Life* by Christopher Bache (1994). Books on the Afterlife that I have found helpful are *The Afterlife Unveiled* by Stafford Betty (2011) and *Testimony of Light* by Helen Greaves (1977). I vividly remember the impact of Raymond Moody's two books, *Life after Life* (1975) and *Reflections on Life after Life* (1978) which, like Elisabeth Kübler Ross's books, aroused enormous interest in the possibility of life after death. In 1973 Robert Monroe founded the Monroe Institute America to study out-of-body experiences and wrote *Journeys Out of the Body*. The Monroe Institute offers seminars on the Afterlife, preparing people for transitioning. In 1980, Kenneth Ring, Professor of Psychology at the University of Connecticut, published his book, *Life at Death: A Scientific Investigation of the Near-Death Experience*, and followed this up with the founding of the International Association for Near-Death Studies, dedicated to the exploration of near-death experiences and encouraging their investigation at an international level. His later books, among them *Heading Towards Omega: In Search of the Meaning of the Near-Death Experience* (1984) and *Lessons from the Light* (2000), gave further detailed accounts of an experience that must have long been familiar to people in shamanic cultures but had, until very recently, not been discussed in our own. In 2005 the late Professor David Fontana published a book called *Is there an After-life?* Commenting on it, Dr. Peter Fenwick, who, with his wife, has recently published *The Art of Dying*, writes, "After reading it and assessing the evidence, there can no longer be any doubt that there is life after death." I would like to include here *The Final Frontier* by Julia Assante (2012) which covers the ground explored in this chapter in much more detail and presents a brilliant elucidation of three categories of evidence for the survival of consciousness after death: the science, the history, and the personal experience. I cannot recommend it more highly. Lastly, I would add a remarkable book by Annabel Chaplin called *Release into the Light* (2019), originally published in 1977.

It is not only possible and lawful, ... but an absolute duty on the part of mortals to ... keep up a loving intercourse with the loved ones who have gone before.

— W.T. Stead, preface to *After Death; or Letters from Julia* (1905)

Websites:

www.victorzammit.com

www.anitamoorjani.com

www.collegeofpsychicstudies.co.uk

www.mellen-thomas.com (An extraordinary account of an OBE – see appendix 2)

www.sagb.org.uk (The Spiritualist Association of Great Britain)

Notes:

1. Jung, C.G. (1963) *Memories, Dreams, Reflections*, p. 278
2. Bache, Christopher (2000) *Dark Night, Early Dawn: Steps to a Deep Ecology of Mind*, Suny Press, Albany, New York, p. 5
3. James, William (1929) *The Varieties of Religious Experience*, Longmans Green & Co., New York, p. 388
4. Sogyal Rinpoche (1992) *The Tibetan Book of Living and Dying*, Harper San Francisco, p.8
5. ibid, p. 8

6. *Letters of Rainer Maria Rilke* 1910-1924, trs. Jane Bannard Green and M.M. Heerter, New York, W.W. Norton & Co., New York, 1947, pp. 373-4)

7. Naydler, Jeremy (1996) *Temple of the Cosmos*, Inner Traditions, Vermont, pp. 207-210

8. Laszlo, Ervin (2006) *Science and the Reenchantment of the Cosmos*, Inner Traditions, Vermont, pp. 65-66

9. Kübler-Ross, Elisabeth (1975) *On Death and Dying*, Spectrum, US

10. Kübler-Ross (1991) *On Life After Death*, Celestial Arts, Berkeley, CA

11. ibid, p. 47

12. ibid, p. 30

13. ibid, p. 10

14. ibid, p. 11

15. *The Tibetan Book of the Dead*, quoted in a review of this book, *The Times*, October 15th, 2005

16. Kübler-Ross, *On Life After Death*, p. 55

17. ibid, p. 67

18. ibid, p. 68

19. van Lommel, Dr. Pim (2010) *Consciousness Beyond Life: The Science of the Near-Death Experience*, HarperCollins New York, p. 158

20. ibid, p. 193

21. ibid, p. 261. Sir John Eccles *Evolution of the Brain: Creation of the Self* (Routledge 1989), p. 241

22. ibid, p. 346

23. ibid, p. 347

24. ibid, p. 348

25. Moorjani, Anita (2012) *Dying to be Me*, Hay House, Inc, New York, p. 70

26. recounted to me by Joy Parker

27. von Franz, Marie-Louise (1986) *On Dreams and Death*, Shambhala Publications Inc, Boston, Mass., pp. 156 and 146

28. ibid, pp. 147-8

29. ibid, pp. 147-8

30. Collins, Cecil (2004) *Angels*, edited by Stella Astor, Fool's Press, London, p. 43

31. Randall, Edward C. (2010) *Frontiers of the Afterlife*, White Crow Books, UK, p. 66

32. Betty, Stafford (2011) *The Afterlife Unveiled* , O Books, UK, p. 94

33. Mead, G.R.S. (1919) *The Doctrine of the Subtle Body in Western Tradition*, John M. Watkins, London. Third edition Solos Press, Dorset, UK, 1995

34. ibid, p. 1

35. ibid, p. 1

36. Mead, G.R.S. (1906) from *Fragments of a Faith Forgotten*, John M. Watkins, London, pp. 406-414. Another beautiful translation and interesting commentary has been made by John Davidson in *The Robe of Glory, An Ancient Parable of the Soul*, Element Books, UK, 1992

37. Randall, p. 11

38. Kovács, Betty J. (2003) *The Miracle of Death*, The Kamlak Center, California

The Oracle
Cecil Collins 1940

Chapter Twenty

LIGHT AND LOVE AS THE PULSE OF THE COSMOS

The flute of the Infinite is played without ceasing, and its sound is love.
— Kabir

Love is the inner, the universal, the cosmic Self.
— Swami Muktananda

The heart is nothing but the sea of light... the place of the vision of God.
— Rumi, *the Mathnavi*

He who sees that the Lord of all is ever the same in all that is, immortal in the field of mortality — he sees the truth. And when a man sees that the God in himself is the same God in all that is, he hurts not himself by hurting others: then he goes indeed to the highest Path.
— *Bhagavad Gita* X111. 27-28

The day will come when, after harnessing the ether, the winds, the tides, gravitation, we shall harness for God the energies of love. And on that day for the second time in the history of the world, human beings will have discovered fire.
— Pierre Teilhard de Chardin, *Toward the Future*

This book has been written with love: love of life, love of the beauty, wonder and sacredness of the Earth and all its incredible species; love of humanity and the sublime expressions of its creative spirit and indomitable courage; love of my family and my close friends and love of the mystery of the Cosmos, both visible and invisible, whose life I serve. In the course of writing it and following the thread of my dreams, I have been able to answer the question "Who am I?", posed so long ago by Sri Ramana Maharshi, and to a small extent discover the nature of the Soul whose immense reach into unseen dimensions I had no idea of when I started out on my journey seventy years ago. My quest has been guided by the archetype of the Feminine which has held no place of honour in Western civilization, whether as Nature, Soul or Matter. I have taken as my mentors the great mystics of all traditions as well as Jung because he, more than anyone in the last century, recovered for us the neglected dimension of the soul. I have also, as far as I am able, tried to honour the discoveries of the great scientists, which are transforming our view of the universe, this planet and ourselves.

But although love and a passionate desire to fathom the reason for our presence on this planet and the causes of our suffering have informed all my writing, I have had only one experience in my life that I would describe as one of cosmic love. This experience, when I was sixty years old, is precious because it is not often in the course of a life that a glimpse of the eternal breaks through the cloud of our earth-bound consciousness. It felt like the sun coming out after a winter of darkness: a warm, enveloping feeling of intense and unconditional love which flowed through me like a river of gold towards every person I met, folding them in its embrace. It lasted for about ten days. It was as if a dam in my heart had burst and the water of love poured out into the world. I was simply the vehicle of that love. How, I wondered, could this ecstatic experience, which came and went without warning, change my understanding of life and my relationships with other people? How could I attune myself to this incandescent power within all of us which could transform the way we see and relate to each other and to the Earth, our planetary home?

We are the inheritors of an immensely rich spiritual tradition — from the Christian West, from India, Persia, the Middle East and elsewhere — which speaks of love as the pulse of the Cosmos and the secret pulse of our own being. The exquisite poetry of this tradition — which includes *The Divine Comedy*, the *Upanishads*, the poems of Rumi and Kabir, and the Song of Songs — speaks of the longing of the human heart for reconnection with its Source but also the longing of that Source for communion with ourselves. "I was a treasure longing to be known; that is why I created the world", says a *hadith* from the Koran.

The inner life of the Cosmos can only communicate through those individuals during the millennia of our human experience on this planet who have become receptive to its presence. We only know of the existence and nature of this cosmic ground of being through the men and women who have spoken of their experience of it: some have described it as Father, as Christ did; others as Mother, as the Taoists and the Indian sage Ramakrishna did. Some describe it as Cosmic Love; others as Creative Intelligence or Sacred Mind. Mystics know it as the Divine Ground of Being. People who have had a near-death experience describe it as both Light and Unconditional Love.

The writings of the world's greatest mystics and spiritual teachers as well as these personal testimonies affirm that light and love are the fundamental principles of the universe: the universe we see and marvel at is brought into being and sustained by light and love. We sail the fragile vessel of our consciousness on the surface of this fathomless sea of light and love not knowing that we are, in essence, what we seek. A master of the Tibetan Tantric path says, "The luminous awakened mind is always present; we have simply to recognize it." The secret intention of the life that lives us — the secret Dream of the Cosmos — is to bring us to the discovery that we belong to this divine ground, that we *are* it, even though we have no awareness of this. The temple of our body is created and sustained by this ground. When the body dies, our consciousness discovers its identity with this eternal ground. As the *Bhagavad Gita* tells us: "Thine own consciousness, shining, void and inseparable from the Great Body of Radiance, hath no birth, nor death, and is the immutable Light."[1]

All traditions say that, as Blake understood, the doors of our perception have to be cleansed before we can see and experience the full radiance of that ground. A passage from the *Zohar* says that when a man has been shut up in darkness for a long time, a tiny opening has to be made for him at first, and then another a little larger, and another larger still, until he can bear the full radiance of the Light. Then, the eye of the heart and the eye of the mind can be opened to the revelation that we are, in our essential being, eternally one with that light and love.

In the Indian Vedic texts, which may be the remnants of an oral tradition from a lost civilization buried beneath the waters of the Great Flood, we hear the answers to the questions arising from the heart of a people who lived long before us:

> There was not then what is nor what is not. There was no sky, and no heaven beyond the sky. What power was there? Where? Who was that power? Was there an abyss of fathomless waters? There was neither death nor immortality then. There were no signs of night or day. The ONE was breathing by its own power, in infinite peace. Only the ONE was: there was nothing beyond.... And in the ONE arose love: love the first seed of the soul. The truth of this the sages found in their hearts: seeking in their hearts with wisdom, the sages found that bond of union between Being and non-being...[2]

Later, in the *Upanishads*, Brahman — the supreme reality that is named in the *Vedas* as *Purusha* — is described as Truth and Love: Eternal Spirit both transcendent and immanent; dwelling beyond all and within all that we can know or apprehend. In part of the *Brihadaranyaka Upanishad* (fifth *Brahmana*) honey is used as a metaphor to describe how all things, all elements of creation, are contained within and sustained by the divine ground: "This Self is the honey of all beings, and all beings are the honey of this Self."[3]

While speaking of the *Upanishads*, I would like to mention the story of one of the great Sufi mystics, Prince Dara Shikuh (1615–1659), who is not well known in the West. He was the eldest son of the emperor Shah Jehan and his beloved wife Mumtaz Mahal (for whom he built the peerless Taj Mahal) — a poet, scholar and mystic who spent many years studying with two of the greatest Sufi sages of that time. While in Kashmir in 1640, he heard of the *Upanishads* and had fifty of them and other Sanscrit texts, including the *Bhagavad Gita*, translated into Persian.

Wanting to show the close relationship between Islam and these great Vedic texts, Prince Dara wrote a beautiful and profound treatise called *The Confluence of the Two Seas* (*Majma' al-bahrayn*), also known as *The Mingling of the Two Oceans*. In this great contribution to comparative religion, he attempted to show how Hinduism and Islam were of the same essence, transmitting the same teaching. In it he wrote:

> All that you see as other than God is one with God in essence though separate in name. When you transcend ordinary consciousness, you will realize that everything is God and it will inevitably follow that you will know yourself as you are in reality. You will no longer remain within the confines of the consciousness of 'I-and-you'. It is here that you will find the truth of unity.

In 1646, he wrote one of the most profound Sufi treatises called *The Compass of Truth* (*Risala-yi haqq-numa*), a detailed guide to the transcendent realms of the soul. But in 1658 in a brutal coup organized by his younger brother Aurangzeb and backed by the orthodox mullahs who disapproved of his treatises and accused him of apostasy, Prince Dara was captured and beheaded, with his head sent to his imprisoned and grief-stricken father. By this tragic blow of fate, he never became the rightful ruler of the Mughal Empire. He would perhaps have ruled India as a philosopher king, following the example of his grandfather, Akbar, who had united Hindus and Muslims under the principle of "universal peace". He might have been able to hold together the followers of the two great religions who have now split apart into two different nations, poised to strike each other with their nuclear weapons. From the time I travelled in India and heard the story of this remarkable Prince I have always felt drawn to him and for this reason have paid tribute to him here.[4]

Prince Dara would have understood the profound message of the *Bhagavad Gita* and the bond of love between the Divine Ground and the human soul that is enshrined in its peerless poetry. There, Krishna says to Arjuna "only through constant love can I be known and seen as I really am, and entered into."[5] and at the end, repeating his earlier instruction to follow the path of love, he says: "Fix your mind on Me, give thy heart's love to Me, consecrate all thy actions to My service, hold thine own self as nothing before Me. To Me then shalt thou come; truly I promise for thou art dear to Me."[6]

In the later Buddhist texts, we hear the Buddha's teaching about how to clear the mind of all that clouds the luminosity of the Clear Light of the Void so that we may become vehicles of the compassion that radiates like the sun from the source of life.

In the Christian tradition, we hear the voice of Christ in the Epistle of John: "God is love, and he that dwelleth in love dwelleth in God, and God in him" (1 John 4:16). And the great commandment he gave to his disciples on the eve of his Passion: "Love one another. As I have loved you that you also love one another." (John: 13: 34).

In the Gnostic *Gospel of Eve*, we hear the beautiful words which could be those of the Holy Spirit or, equally, those of the Shekinah of Kabbalah:

> I am thou and thou art I and wheresoever thou art, I am there;
> and I am sown (scattered) in all things, and from whencesoever thou willest,
> thou gatherest Me, but in gathering Me thou gatherest Thyself.[7]

Mystics of all traditions have spoken of their encounter with the cosmic love of the divine ground and none more beautifully than Julian of Norwich (1342–1416/19): "Thus I learned that love is our Lord's meaning. And I saw full surely in this and in everything else, that before God made us, he loved us. And that love was never ended nor ever shall be. And in this love he has performed all his actions; he has made all things profitable to us. And in this love our life is everlasting. In our making we had our beginning: but the love wherein he made us is without beginning.... And all this shall we see in God without end."[8]

The different traditions I have referred to, as well as modern testimonies to the existence of this deeper ground of consciousness and the many accounts of the near-death experience, tell us that love and light as the pulse of the cosmos flow to us in the creation and becoming of our own lives, holding this world of time in the embrace of the eternal. The words of the great Flemish Christian mystic, John of Ruysbroeck (1273–1381), offer the essence of this embrace:

> When love has carried us above all things we receive in peace the incompre-
> hensible Light, enfolding us and penetrating us. What is this Light, if it be not
> a contemplation of the Infinite, and an intuition of Eternity? We behold that
> which we are, and we are that which we behold; because our being, without
> losing anything of its own personality, is united with the Divine Truth.[9]

Truly with all these traditions, each of which connects us with the light and love of the divine ground, we have been offered a feast. Who has been preparing this feast if not Cosmic Intelligence, or the Holy Spirit, or Divine Mind working through centuries and millennia and the souls of countless individuals to awaken our slumbering consciousness to awareness of its radiant ground and our profound connection with each other.

"Truth", wrote Teilhard de Chardin near the end of his life "has to appear only once, in one single mind, for it to be impossible for anything ever to prevent it from spreading universally and setting everything ablaze."[10]

Perhaps we have reached the point in our evolution where a new truth, a new revelation of the whole of life as a divine unity could be born in our hearts — the realization that we are part of the divinity we have worshipped for millennia as something separate from ourselves and from the life of this world. There is no essential distinction between transcendent and immanent spirit. As the mystics have always told us, the distinction and the duality are in our incomplete perception of reality: the divine is what we are; we are eternally in the divine. This was long known to the alchemists — a vision of reality they called stellar consciousness, which reflected their astounding *experience* of the lost sense of the unity and divinity of all life.

How could we define the feeling of love? In my experience, it is associated with a feeling of bliss, an ecstatic joy, an upwelling of a feeling that exists prior to any conception of what that feeling might pertain to. It may well up suddenly and un-expectedly as we awaken from sleep and we may lie in bed immersed in it as we return from communion with a deeper ground to the focus of our daily lives. It may express itself as ecstatic emotional and sexual union with a beloved partner. It may be experienced as the love of a parent for a newborn child or a grandparent's delight in watching a beloved child grow in strength until he or she reaches matu-rity. Anyone who has created something wrought from the heart with love and pa-tience, will know it. A scientist or doctor who has discovered or invented something of immense value to humanity, such as the Salk vaccine for polio, may experience it. The athletes who, after years of dedication to their sport, achieve a medal in the Olympics, know it as tears of pride and joy well into their eyes. A verse from one of the *Upanishads* says, "And then he saw that Brahman was joy: for from joy all beings have come, by joy they all live, and unto joy they all return."[11]

How does this capacity for joy, for love, for ecstasy awaken in us? First of all it arises through the blissful experience of the infant's relationship with its mother. Look at the face of a newly born infant that has been delivered with all the care, attention and love shown by two outstanding physicians, Frederick Leboyer and Michel Odent, in their sensitive approach to childbirth. Watch how it responds instinctively to its mother's touch, feel, scent and loving gaze. As the child grows up, trust may be one of the fruits of this primary love and care: the mutual trust between child and parent that leads her to trust life, other people, herself.

Later, we know it through our own experience as the feeling that spontaneously arises in us when we suddenly feel an intense love for someone close to us, perhaps fused with anguish at the moment of saying goodbye to them at the moment of death. Or we may feel it as an intense attraction to a place or the memory of a place. During the course of our life joy may manifest through some kind of activity that attracts us and arouses our passionate interest; that draws us to develop a talent, a skill of some kind through which we can express our essential nature — basically our passion to create, to love. It manifests in our relationships, our ability to trust others and to give love to them and receive love from them, often sustained through the most difficult circumstances. It may come through the discovery that we can help others in some way, that we enjoy helping others — perhaps people we will never meet; that we can help in some tangible way to alleviate the suffering of the world. Intense love is found in the bond between warriors facing death on the battlefield, in the care of a parent or grandparent for a child. It may be discovered in the feeling that our heart is bursting with longing to stand with people who are suffering in the aftermath of a tsunami, earthquake, devastating drought or volcanic eruption, or bursting with grief for those who are facing terrible persecution, torture, imminent death — to alleviate their suffering in some tangible way.

Love may also arise in our heart when we can truly see something clearly for the first time with fresh eyes as when we saw our planet from the depths of space, as the astronaut Edgar Mitchell did when he wrote these words on his journey home from the moon: "Gazing through 240,000 miles of space towards the stars and the planet from which I had come, I suddenly experienced the Universe as intelligent, loving, harmonious. The presence of divinity became almost palpable, and I knew that life in the universe was not just an accident based on random processes."

Time is needed to reflect on and absorb all these and more aspects of love, time to become conscious of the power and intelligence of the energy that is living through us and in us, time to open the eye of the heart to awareness of its unconditional love. I am reminded of the story of Martha and Mary in the New Testament: Martha caught in the net of the preoccupations of everyday life; Mary sitting in stillness, listening to the symphony of a deeper reality.

If we trust the word of the mystics and those who have broken through our limited consciousness to the divine ground, love is the great holding, connecting power of the universe. It is so difficult for us to realize that our life is an expression of that love, that everything we are and do flows from that love: all our relationships, our creative endeavours, our hopes, our longings, our fears and failures — even the wounds inflicted by our cruelties and hatreds — exist within that vast ocean of love.

Teilhard de Chardin could help us here in the words that he wrote in his *Hymn of the Universe*:

> Humanity has been sleeping — and still sleeps — lulled within the narrowly confining joys of its little closed loves. In the depths of the human multitude there slumbers an immense spiritual power which will manifest itself only when we have learnt how to break through the dividing walls of our egoism and raise ourselves up to an entirely new perspective, so that habitually and in a practical fashion we fix our gaze on universal realities.[12]

And again in the words that he wrote in his essay *The Spirit of the Earth*, written in 1931, "Love is the most universal, the most tremendous, the most mysterious of the cosmic forces. Is it truly possible for humanity to continue to live and grow without asking itself how much truth and energy it is losing by neglecting its incredible powers of love?"[13]

What about our propensity for evil, for hatred and cruelty? I think these are born of fear and self-hatred; from the belief that we are not loved, not lovable; that we have been abandoned on this planet; that our lives have no meaning, value or purpose; that a death awaits us that will extinguish the memory of everything we have been, everything we have loved. They are born of the terrible wounds inflicted in childhood by neglect, abandonment, abysmal cruelty and the experience of unbearable pain or loss, the breaking of a child's trusting, loving heart. They are born from self-rejection, from ignorance of who and what we are and a distortion of our nature caused by past and present beliefs that live deep in our unconscious — unrecognized and untransformed. Children who have been rescued from unimaginable suffering inflicted by cruelty, horror or neglect can be healed by the loving attention of an adult. The Vietnamese monk Thich Nhat Hanh had this to say about love as the ability to contain anger and the desire for vengeance. After 9/11 he said, "If I were given the opportunity to be face to face with Osama bin Laden, the first thing I would do is listen. I would try to understand all of the suffering that had led him to violence… because such an act of violence is a desperate call for attention and for help."[14]

The love flowing to us from the Cosmos can act more effectively through us as our capacity to feel empathy for the suffering of others expands. Thich Nhat

Hanh exemplifies in his life and his teaching that empathic understanding which could bring about healing at the international level if we were able to embody it in our relations with others. Paul Hawken in his book *Blessed Unrest* has described the impulse to heal and to help arising in the millions of people who are engaged in countless initiatives to help others and to help the planet.

There are many old and new methods of healing that are being rediscovered and implemented. In relation to my own profession of psychotherapy, I treasure these words of a counsellor called Brian Thorne:

> There are moments in my work as a therapist when I feel outside time and space and cannot conceive that heaven itself could be more desirable. They are characterised for both my client and me by a sense of radical, unconditional unearned acceptance and by an empowerment within that makes us capable, however briefly, of loving the whole created order. In short, we have ourselves been swept up into the divine relationship…. For a moment, however fleeting, we are whole and holy, fully human and therefore the incarnation of the divine.

> I believe that we therapists have an opportunity… to affect the course of human history if we can but seize the moment. We are the guardians of knowledge given us by countless suffering individuals who seek our help…. It is not fanciful to see the counsellors and therapists of our day as the chief recipients of the collective pain and yearning of the age. This is a treasure beyond price; but its value lies in its capacity, if fully revealed and articulated, to give meaning to present distress and to provide hope and guidance for the future.[15]

Healing the wounded heart of humanity is about cherishing in every sense: cherishing our own lives as having infinite meaning and value; cherishing the time given to us in order to discover our true direction in life and who we truly are; cherishing the body which has been sacrificed for so long to our distorted image of spirituality; cherishing the lives of the people who have been given into our care; cherishing the planetary life which is the greater field of all our endeavours. Love calls us to caring, solicitude, insight, gentleness and understanding but also to strength, power, and intelligence used in the service of humanity and all species on the planet. It calls us to make conscious and contain the desire for power, control and dominance that are rooted in the opposite of love — in fear.

In her wonderful and inspiring book, *Songlines of the Soul: Pathways to a New Vision for a New Century*, Veronica Goodchild writes:

> In the breakdown of ordinary reality as we know it, a different kind of gnosis is occurring all around us. At the turn of the Aeon, it brings us a new kind of knowledge — revealed rather than rational knowledge — that wishes to make itself felt. This disclosure hints at the union of soul and life in a revelation of

love: our human love, and the love of the cosmos for us. Held within this larger perspective we come to know what not only the Ancients, the Mystics, the Gnostics, and the Alchemists once knew, but also what we know today through our dreams, visions, and anomalous experiences, which perhaps we have kept secret for too long, but which now cry out for each of us to add to the chorus that is singing the songlines of the soul.[16]

The Image of Light

Everything that I have written in this book seems to converge on the image of light, a light that is different from the light of the sun and comes from a supernal source, a light that is the unseen creative ground of our consciousness and the world of physical reality. So, in this last chapter, I would like to draw together images of light from three different sources: the light of the quantum vacuum discovered by science; the ineffable light described by mystical experience and by those who have gone beyond our usual way of seeing; and, finally, the description of an encounter with the light in an astonishing out-of-the-body experience.

The discoveries of quantum physics tell us that we are literally bathed in a cosmic sea of light, invisible to us, yet permeating and sustaining every cell of our being, every atom of matter. At the quantum level, all apparently separate aspects of life are connected in one invisible and indivisible whole. All life at the deepest level is essentially One. In the words of astro-physicist Bernard Haisch the deep connection between physics and metaphysics

> lies in the fact that the electromagnetic quantum vacuum is a form of light. It is an underlying sea of energy... that permeates every tiny volume of space, from the emptiest intergalactic void to the depths of the Earth, the Sun, or our own bodies. In this sense, our world of matter is like the visible foam atop a very deep ocean of light.[17]

The Metaphysical Descriptions of the Light

There are numerous metaphysical descriptions of the cosmic Light encountered in the near-death experience. The earliest is found in the *Upanishads* where Brahman is described as "the radiant light of all lights whose radiance illumines all creation."[18]

In the Christian tradition there is a remarkably consistent description in the first three Gospels of the Transfiguration of Jesus that was witnessed by three of the disciples, Peter, James and John (Matth. 17:2-9, Mark 9:2-9, Luke 9:28-36).

Jesus is described in the Gospel of Matthew with his face shining like the sun and his clothes as white as the light.

There is also another, less known description of the Transfiguration, recorded in a Gnostic manuscript called the *Pistis Sophia*, thought to date — although there is some dispute about this — from the first half of the third century AD. It was translated by G.R.S. Mead and first published in 1896 with a fully revised edition in 1921 and a reprint in 1947. In this extract from the manuscript, Jesus and his disciples — who are not named — were gathered together on a mountain, on the day of the full moon, shortly after dawn.

> *It came to pass… that there came forth behind him a great light-power shining most exceedingly, and there was no measure to the light conjoined with it. For it came out of the Light of lights… And that light-power came down over Jesus and surrounded him entirely, while he was seated removed from his disciples, and he had shone most exceedingly, and there was no measure for the light which was on him. And the disciples had not seen Jesus because of the great light in which he was, or which was about him; for their eyes were darkened because of the great light in which he was. But they saw only the light, which shot forth many light-rays. And the light-rays were not like one another, but the light was of divers kind, and it was of divers type, from below upwards, one ray more excellent than the other…, in one great immeasurable glory of light; It stretched from under the earth right up to heaven. And when the disciples saw that light, they fell into great fear and great agitation. It came to pass then, when that light-power had come down over Jesus, that it gradually surrounded him entirely. Then Jesus ascended or soared into the height, shining most exceedingly in an immeasurable light. And the disciples gazed after him and none of them spake until he had reached unto heaven; but they all kept in deep silence.*[19]

In our own time there is the remarkable testimony of Gopi Krishna who, in 1937, experienced a sudden and overwhelming ascent of *Kundalini* described in his book *Kundalini* that was published in 1967 with a commentary by the Jungian analyst James Hillman. In an interview published in a recent book called *Kundalini Rising* (2010) he says that the stage is being set for a movement from the outer world to the inner world of consciousness, that an unlived potential of human consciousness — a supersensory channel of cognition — is being activated and will, in time, manifest in our species. He believes that we may eventually be able to answer the question "How does Eternal Consciousness come to be embodied and then rise, step by step, through aeonian spans of time, to the realization of its own sovereignty?" and also the question of how this process unfolds in the organic evolution of the brain. Bearing witness to the fact that this supersensory channel of cognition has been opened in himself, he writes that at every moment of his life he lives in two worlds:

> One is the sensory world which we all share together.... My reactions to this
> world are the same as of other human beings. The other is an amazing super-
> sensory world.... I am always conscious of a luminous glow, not only in my
> interior but pervading the whole field of my vision during the hours of my
> wakefulness. I literally live in a world of light. It is as if a light were burning in
> my interior, filling me with a luster so beautiful and so ravishing that my
> attention is again and again drawn towards it.... I do not claim that I see God,
> but I am conscious of a Living Radiance both within and outside of myself. In
> other words I have gained a new power of perception that was not present
> before. The luminosity does not end with my waking time. It persists even in
> my dreams.... The enchanting light I perceive both internally and outside, is
> alive. It pulsates with life and intelligence. It is like an infinite Ocean of Aware-
> ness pervading my own small pool of consciousness within and the whole
> universe I perceive with my senses outside.... For me, the universe is alive: a
> stupendous Intelligence that I can sense but never fathom, looms behind every
> object and every event in the universe, silent, still, serene, and immovable like
> a mountain. It is a staggering spectacle.[20]

Thirdly, there is the moving testimony of Christopher Bache, author of *Dark Night, Early Dawn*, whose words I have quoted before: "I was brought to an encounter with a unified energy field underlying all physical existence. I was confronting an enormous field of blindingly bright, incredibly intense energy...This energy was the single energy that comprised all existence."[21] And he continues,

> The unified field underlying physical existence completely dissolved all
> boundaries. As I moved deeper into it, all borders fell away, all appearances of
> division were ultimately illusory. No boundaries between incarnations, between
> human beings, between species, even between matter and spirit. The world of
> individuated existence was not collapsing into an amorphous mass, as it might
> sound, but rather was revealing itself to be an exquisitely diversified manifes-
> tation of a single entity.

> Though these experiences were extraordinary in their own right, the most
> poignant aspect was not the discovered dimensions of the universe themselves
> but what my seeing and understanding them meant to the Consciousness I was
> with. It seemed so pleased to have someone to show Its work to. I felt that it
> had been waiting for billions of years for embodied consciousness to evolve to
> the point where we could at last begin to see, understand and appreciate what
> had been accomplished. I felt the loneliness of this Intelligence having created
> such a masterpiece and having no one to appreciate Its work, and I wept. I wept
> for Its isolation and in awe of the profound love which had accepted this
> isolation as part of a larger plan. Behind creation lies a Love of extraordinary

proportions, and all of existence is an expression of this love. The intelligence of the universe's design is equally matched by the depth of love that inspired it.[22]

Thousands of people who have had a near-death or an out-of-the-body experience have borne witness to the all-embracing light they see and the unconditional love they experience. One particular account of such an experience has moved and impressed me deeply. It is the out-of-the-body experience of a man called Mellen–Thomas Benedict, who described what happened to him during the hours after he had clinically died of cancer, later returning to life. He describes the journey he took into the Light and how the Light answered his questions and took him deeper and deeper into Itself. Because the description of his experience is so remarkable, so clearly expressed and so inspiring, I have, with his permission, included it as an appendix to this book in the hope that it will interest, inspire and help others. His experience offers a message of hope for humanity, delivered with a joy and clarity that is astonishing and authentic.

Epilogue

During the twenty years I have been writing this book on the Soul, my own consciousness has been changed by the process of writing it and by the facts and ideas I discovered while researching the different chapters. While I have been experiencing this change, a similar change has been taking place in the collective consciousness of humanity. Not only are long-established political, economic, financial and religious institutions in disarray, but the whole ethos of power and dominance that has driven Western civilization for some 4000 years is faltering in the face of the grave problems we face, many of which have been created by this ethos and cannot be resolved by continuing with the old responses. What is being born in the collapse and dissolution of the old mythologies — the old belief systems which have divided instead of uniting humanity — is the recognition that we do not live within a meaningless, dead universe but within a Sacred Cosmic Order and that we have a responsibility to attune ourselves to the service of that Order to the best of our ability.

We face a choice between continuing in the patterns of the past which may lead to our extinction or beginning to live and act from this radically different understanding of life and of ourselves. The immensity of the task facing us is daunting. Yet the indomitable courage and creativity of our species can rise to it, challenging the depravity, greed and malignancy that characterize the worst aspects of the old order. Since, at the quantum level, we are all connected, when thousands of us begin to change our consciousness, millions will be affected.

It could be said that the Incarnation did not end with the life of Christ: rather, it can be understood as a process unfolding through millennia in the lives of thousands, even millions, of individuals, many of whom are not affiliated to any religious tradition. The great images of the Christian myth, like the Annunciation, are archetypal realities that can come alive again in our time because an arduous process of birth is taking place in the collective soul of humanity.

We are awakening to what I have called the Dream of the Cosmos — the dream of an enlightened humanity engaging in a new role on this planet: a role that is in harmony with the evolutionary intention of the Cosmos and is no longer driven by the quest for power, conquest and control and the appropriation of the Earth's resources for the benefit of the few. As we begin consciously to align ourselves with this luminous ground of reality, our minds will serve the deepest longing of our heart, the deepest wisdom of our soul. We will know who we are and why we are here.

The passionate longing of the human heart has always been to press beyond the boundaries of the known, to break through the limitations of our understanding, to extend the horizon of our awareness. This is perhaps our most fundamental and essential freedom. Now, more than ever, we need to honour that longing and welcome those pioneers who can unveil new horizons, new possibilities of understanding our nature, our potential and our destiny. We need, in the words of T.S. Eliot in his great poem *Ash-Wednesday*, to "Redeem the time. Redeem the unread vision in the higher dream."

Notes:

1. Prem, Krishna (1958) *The Yoga of the Bhagavad Gita*, Watkins, London, p. xiii
2. The *Upanishads* (1965) trans. and introduction by Juan Mascaró, Penguin Books Ltd., London, *Rig Veda* x. 129, pp. 9-10
3. van Over, Raymond (editor) (1977) *Eastern Mysticism*, Volume One: The Near East and Asia, New American Library Inc., New York, p. 125
4. I have drawn on material from Juan Mascaró's translation of the *Upanishads*, p. 8 and also an article on Prince Dara Shikuh that was published in Elixir Magazine, Issue I on Interspirituality, Autumn 2005.
5. *Bhagavad Gita* 11.54.
6. *Bhagavad Gita* 18.65, trans. Krishna Prem, p. 186
   See also *The Bhagavad Gita,* trans. and introduction by Juan Mascaró, Penguin, London
7. Mead, G.R.S. (1939) *Fragments of a Faith Forgotten*, John M. Watkins, London, p. 439
8. Julian(a) of Norwich (1977) *Revelations of Divine Love*, trans. M. L. Del Mastro, Doubleday, New York
9. van Ruysbroeck, Jan (1916) *The Adornment of the Spiritual Marriage, The Book of Truth, The Sparkling Stone*, Dutton & Co. New York
10. Teilhard de Chardin, Pierre, last unpublished Essay, *Le Christique*
11. *The Upanishads*, translated by Juan Mascaró. *Taittiriya Upanishad*, p. 111
12. Teilhard de Chardin (1977) *Hymn of the Universe*, William Collins, Fount Paperbacks, London, p. 120
13. Teilhard de Chardin (1931) *The Spirit of the Earth*
14. Thich Nhat Hanh (newspaper report 2001)
15. Thorne, Brian (1998) *Person-Centred Counselling and Christian Spirituality*, Whurr Publishers, London. See also *The Mystical Power of Person-Centred Therapy: Hope Beyond Despair*, Whurr Publishers, London, 2002.
16. Goodchild, Veronica (2012) *Songlines of the Soul: Pathways to a New Vision for a New Century*, Nicolas-Hays Inc., Fort Worth, Florida
17. Haisch, Bernard (2007) from his chapter in *Mind Before Matter: Visions of a New Science of Consciousness*, O Books, Ropley, UK
18. *Mundaka Upanishad*, trans. Juan Mascaró, pp. 78-9
19. Mead, G.R.S. (1947) *Pistis Sophia*, John M. Watkins, London, pp. 3 & 4.
20. Interview with Gopi Krishna published in *Kundalini Rising*, (2009) Sounds True Inc., Boulder, CO., p. 295
21. Bache, Christopher (2000) *Dark Night, Early Dawn*, p. 67
22. ibid, p. 70

Appendix 1

LAMENT FOR THE TRAGEDY OF WAR
©Anne Baring

Although written in 1999, this poem is dedicated to all those who are suffering in the ongoing conflicts that are disturbing the life of the planet: to the refugees fleeing their devastated homes and living in camps; to the 3,000 Yazidi women who have endured the agony of rape and slavery; to the thousands of young men whose precious lives are being cut short; to the children who are suffering the trauma of witnessing the atrocities of war.

EASTER 1999

Listen to the Good News, they said...

Then, over the mountain pass,
deep in snow, we watched those who had lost all
except life stumble towards hope;
carrying infants, dragging children,
old people wrapped in plastic like loaves of bread,
so they could be pulled more easily
over the icy surface.
A woman tall and cragged as an oak
leads a line of survivors.
Some can walk no further
in the heavy snow and die where they fall.
A young girl holds her mother in her arms
as life ebbs from her body.

This time we saw the face of barbarism.
This time we saw them: people like us,
in clothes like ours, arriving in shock,
avoiding the mined land, trudging the last miles
along the rail track to the frontier;
faces contorted with grief.
Women, men, children weeping uncontrollably,
having lost everything save each other.

Day after day we saw a human flood
pouring across frontiers:
lines of wagons, carts, tractors, trailers,
a horse, a donkey; the old in wheelbarrows,

and people walking, walking, soaked in icy rain
through days and nights of anguish,
carrying the old and young so dear to them.

We saw bewildered people forced onto trains
trying to hold families together;
women giving birth alone,
driven trembling with their new-born
into the maw of that suffocating mass.

Helplessly we wept with them,
seared by their suffering, longing to help,
to put our arms around them, comfort, warm them;
but we could only send money, food, love
and hope that they would reach shelter
from that relentless rain.

There was no time to gather children
gone to play with friends, no time to warn others,
no time to feed the animals, milk the cows,
or say goodbye to the dear land, home for centuries.
There was no time to gather provisions for the journey:
milk for babies, food for toddlers,
shoes, nappies, warm clothing.
Women made knife-sharp choices
- what to carry, what to leave -
choices to make the difference between
life and death for those too young
to know what was happening.

Women who had seen husbands, sons, fathers
shot before their eyes,
kneeling, hands clasped behind heads,
knowing they had only seconds
to remember everything they loved,
to treasure the precious blood
that would soon, so soon seep into the ground.

Listen to the Good News, they said…
Can this be happening still?

This time we saw the face of barbarism.
Men obeying orders.
They took the young girls away
out of the cars, out of the trailers.

Everyone knew what would happen.
Girls too young to imagine
the coming thrusts tearing their soft skin,
the rank smell of masked men
crazed with blood lust,
and hatred for the innocent girl,
mother of tomorrow's enemy.
Some they shot, some returned to the convoy
hours or days after the rape.
How could they hope to find their families,
comfort for soul and body
in that mêlée of desperate humanity?

What solace could they find among people
for whom rape is defilement,
a shame to be hidden?
How could this further pain be endured
by those who had already known annihilation?

If I had seen my daughter taken,
her still fragile body shrinking with fear,
her eyes pleading for help I could not give,
my heart flayed by feeling,
my scream would sound through centuries.
Even now I hear it torn from my gut
for those young lives blighted
by the encounter with beasts.

Century after century men have tracked each other
through greening forests blessed with birdsong,
Intent on killing.
Could they see or hear the marvel?
Could they stop in wonder at the sound?

How does a man become a predator,
able to kill, rape, mutilate?
Surely it is time to ask.
Surely it is time to enquire.
Surely it is time to search for answers.
All this has happened so many times before
and will happen again.
Is it the old herd instinct
that binds together the men of a tribe?
Is it the territorial instinct
that attacks the stranger?

Is it the memory of the primordial clan
bonded together in the hunt?

Is it the warrior ethos passed from father to son?
Or the secret vengeance of mothers
who have lost their sons?
Is it the brutality endured by children
who grow up to brutalise others,
avenging impotence with omnipotence?
Or is it the hatred nurtured by priests who,
century by century, have called in God's
name for the extermination
of those they demonized, anathematized,
banished from the circle of God's love?

'Malignant Aggression' Fromm called it.
Malignant is a strong word, an appropriate word
for the kind of barbarism we have seen and heard.
Men are trained to obey orders reflexively,
without thinking.
Obedience to tribal leaders, military leaders,
religious leaders, has conditioned them
to obey the call to kill, fearing shame, rejection;
numbed to the pain of the other.

'To be a man I have to kill.
To be a patriot I have to kill.
I wear a mask to inspire terror
I wear a mask to hide from myself.
I do not know that I am mad.
My orders are to kill, rape, destroy:
My orders are to kill because
the others are a different race.
My orders are to kill because
the others profess a different belief.
My orders are to kill because the others
are the ancient enemy.
Killing is easy:
as easy as saying 'Good Morning'.'

What does it feel like to be this man?
Does he ever ask the question:
'What am I doing as I raise my gun
to murder my brother?
'What am I doing as I mutilate his body?

'What am I doing as I force my body
into the violently trembling body
of his wife or his daughter?
'What am I doing as I kick
the head of a decapitated man
around the yard of his home
while his children vomit?
'What am I doing as I shoot the young child
at his grandfather's knee?
'What am I doing as I slowly sever
the ear of my brother
and throw it to a dog to eat?
'What am I doing as I destroy his home?
'What am I doing as I rob him of all he has left?
'What am I doing as I tear him from all he holds dear?
'What am I doing as I allow hatred
to corrode my soul?'

'I cannot escape the guilt of what I have done.
I have obeyed orders: I have lost my soul.'

And what of the men who shrink from barbarity
yet must kill or be killed
for that is the law of the tribe?
And what of the conscripts,
who cannot endure the killing?
Deserters on trial for their lives,
they cannot forget the eyes
of those they murdered, pleading for life;
the rigid bodies of girls taken away to be raped;
homes burnt to bone, orphaned children
screaming for fathers, mothers;
the eyes of the dying, the eyes of those
who, like themselves, knew fear for the first time.

And what of the mothers who see the life
they have loved and nourished and
cherished through hours, days,
years of growth destroyed in a second
by a bullet, a knife, a bomb? For nothing.

Can this be happening still?

And in the camps thousands crowd together
in the mud, the faecal stench, struggling for

a patch of earth, a tent, water,
blankets to survive the freezing night.
Mothers searching, searching for a child
lost on the journey who sobs somewhere, alone.

Some children cannot speak
of what they have witnessed.
They draw pictures to tell the story of what
they have learned from us
who, despite saviours, religions,
belief in redemption, higher standards of living,
endlessly re-enact the habits of the past.
We have taught them hatred, cruelty, terror.

A father asks his son
what he will do when he meets the enemy.
The boy, loving his father, hesitates, uncertain...
He cannot imagine the answer expected.
"You will kill him."
That is the legacy of father to son
in a warrior culture:
the soul's innocence and trust
raped by indoctrination.

All this has happened so many times before.
Why is it happening still?

And the bombs rained down
night after night upon the 'enemy':
the 'intelligent' missiles
aimed to destroy the infrastructure
of the military machine, hurled from planes
painted with images of scythe-wielding death
and the word 'Apocalypse'.
How appropriate that word.
Missiles tipped with depleted uranium,
radioactive ceramic
designed to bring slow death years later;
Missiles targeting oil refineries
bridges, communications.
"You cannot have war without casualties."
Immaculate; objective; words
remote from the experience
of being in the path of a missile:
a lion leaping upon you, no time to prepare
for extinction.

We cannot yet see our shadow.
We cannot yet see that the continued invention
of ever more terrible weapons perpetuates war.
We cannot yet see
that the proliferation of demonic
agents of death ultimately invites
our own destruction.

The people of the world ache for deliverance
from belligerent, psychopathic leaders,
from servitude to the ancient belief
that there are only two alternatives:
power or powerlessness, victory, defeat.

And what of the dead?
Prisoners between dimensions
the dead ache for release
from the cycle of vengeance
so they do not have to return
to ancestral soil to repeat
the bloody pattern of sacrifice,
the hatred between peoples who,
could have been reconciled centuries ago,
but for their leaders, but for their priests,
but for their inability to renounce the evil
of killing the other who is also the brother.

Listen to the Good News, they said…

How foolish we are to believe
that we are redeemed.
Surely we must accomplish
our own redemption by renouncing the illusion
that some of us are closer to God than others.
Surely we must redeem Christ
from the crucifixion continually re-enacted
in the rape of our sister, the murder of our brother
before we speak of Redemption,
before we speak of the Good News,
before we, the dead, can hope for Resurrection.

Appendix 2

MELLEN-THOMAS BENEDICT

HIS EXPERIENCE IN HIS OWN WORDS

www.mellen-thomas.com
(reproduced with his permission)

Journey Through the Light and Back

After suffering from a terminal illness, in 1982 Mellen-Thomas 'died' and for an hour and a half he was monitored showing no vital signs. Miraculously he returned to his body with a complete remission of the disease.

While on the "other side" Mellen journeyed through several realms of consciousness and beyond the "light at the end of the tunnel". He was shown, in holographic detail, Earth's past and a beautiful vision of mankind's future for the next 400 years. He experienced the cosmology of our soul's connection to mother earth (Gaia), our role in the Universe, and was gifted with access to Universal Intelligence.

Since his near-death experience, Mellen-Thomas has maintained his direct access to Universal Intelligence, and returns to the light at will, enabling him to be a bridge between science and spirit. He has been involved in research programs and has developed new technologies for health and wellness. With humility, insight, and depth of feeling he shares his experience and insights.

He brings back with him a message of hope and inspiration for humanity, delivered with a joy and clarity that is refreshing. His depth of feeling and passion for life is a gift to be shared.

The Experience in his own words

In 1982 I died from terminal cancer. The condition I had was inoperable, and any kind of chemotherapy they could give me would just have made me more of a vegetable. I was given six to eight months to live. I had been an information freak in the 1970's, and I had become increasingly despondent over the nuclear crisis, the ecology crisis, and so forth. So, since I did not have a spiritual basis, I began to believe that nature had made a mistake, and that we were probably a cancerous organism on the planet. I saw no way that we could get out from all the problems we had created for ourselves and the planet. I perceived all humans as cancer, and that is what I got. That is what killed me. Be careful what your world view is. It can feed back on you, especially if it is a negative world view. I had a seriously negative one. That is what led me into my death. I tried all sorts of alternative healing methods, but nothing helped.

So I determined that this was really just between me and God. I had never really faced God before, or even dealt with God. I was not into any kind of spirituality at the time, but I began a journey into learning about spirituality and alternative healing. I set out to do all the reading I could and bone up on the subject, because I did not want to be surprised on the other side. So I started reading on various religions and philosophies. They were all very interesting, and gave hope that there was something on the other side.

On the other hand, as a self-employed stained-glass artist at the time, I had no medical insurance whatsoever. So my life savings went overnight in testing. Then I was facing the medical profession without any kind of insurance. I did not want to have my family dragged down financially, so I determined to handle this myself. There was not constant pain, but there were black-outs. I got so that I would not dare to drive, and eventually I ended up in hospice care. I had my own personal hospice caretaker. I was very blessed by this angel who went through the last part of this with me. I lasted about eighteen months. I did not want to take a lot of drugs, since I wanted to be as conscious as possible. Then I experienced such pain that I had nothing but pain in my consciousness, luckily only for a few days at a time.

The Light of God

I remember waking up one morning at home about 4:30 am, and I just knew that this was it. This was the day I was going to die. So I called a few friends and said goodbye. I woke up my hospice caretaker and told her. I had a private agreement with her that she would leave my dead body alone for six hours, since I had read that all kinds of interesting things happen when you die. I went back to sleep. The next thing I remember is the beginning of a typical near-death experience. Suddenly I was fully aware and I was standing up, but my body was in the bed. There was this darkness around me. Being out of my body was even more vivid than ordinary experience. It was so vivid that I could see every room in the house, I could see the top of the house, I could see around the house, I could see under the house.

There was this light shining. I turned toward the light. The light was very similar to what many other people have described in their near-death experiences. It was so magnificent. It is tangible; you can feel it. It is alluring; you want to go to it like you would want to go to your ideal mother's or father's arms. As I began to move toward the light, I knew intuitively that if I went to the light, I would be dead. So as I was moving toward the light I said, "Please wait a minute, just hold on a second here. I want to think about this; I would like to talk to you before I go."

To my surprise, the entire experience halted at that point. You are indeed in control of your near-death experience. You are not on a roller coaster ride. So my request was honored and I had some conversations with the light. The light kept changing into different figures, like Jesus, Buddha, Krishna, mandalas, archetypal images and signs. I asked the light, "What is going on here? Please, light, clarify yourself for me. I really want to know the reality of the situation."

I cannot really say the exact words, because it was sort of telepathy. The light responded. The information transferred to me was that your beliefs shape the kind of feedback you are getting before the light. If you were a Buddhist or Catholic or Fundamentalist, you get a feed-back loop of your own stuff. You have a chance to look at it and examine it, but most people do not.

As the light revealed itself to me, I became aware that what I was really seeing was our Higher Self matrix. The only thing I can tell you is that it turned into a matrix, a mandala of human souls, and what I saw was that what we call our Higher Self in each of us is a matrix. It's also a conduit to the Source; each one of us comes directly, as a direct experience from the Source. We all have a Higher Self, or an oversoul part of our being. It revealed itself to me in its truest energy form. The only way I can really describe it is that the being of the Higher Self is more like a conduit. It did not look like that, but it is a direct connection to the Source that each and every one of us has. We are directly connected to the Source.

So the light was showing me the Higher Self matrix. And it became very clear to me that all the Higher Selves are connected as one being, all humans are connected as one being, we are actually the same being, different aspects of the same being. It was not committed to one particular religion. So that is what was being fed back to me. And I saw this mandala of human souls. It was the most beautiful thing I have ever seen. I just went into it and, it was just overwhelming. It was like all the love you've ever wanted, and it was the kind of love that cures, heals, regenerates.

As I asked the light to keep explaining, I understood what the Higher Self matrix is. We have a grid around the planet where all the Higher Selves are connected. This is like a great company, a next subtle level of energy around us, the spirit level, you might say. Then, after a couple of minutes, I asked for more clarification. I really wanted to know what the universe is about, and I was ready to go at that time.

I said, "I am ready, take me." Then the light turned into the most beautiful thing that I have ever seen: a mandala of human souls on this planet. Now I came to this with my negative view of what has happened on the planet. So as I asked the light to keep clarifying for me, I saw in this magnificent mandala how beautiful we all are in our essence, our core. We are the most beautiful creations. The human soul, the human matrix that we all make together is absolutely fantastic, elegant, exotic, everything. I just cannot say enough about how it changed my opinion of human beings in that instant. I said, "Oh, God, I did not know how beautiful we are." At any level, high or low, in whatever shape you are in, you are the most beautiful creation, you are. I was astonished to find that there was no evil in any soul. I said, "How can this be?"

The answer was that no soul was inherently evil. The terrible things that happened to people might make them do evil things, but their souls were not evil. What all people seek, what sustains them, is love, the light told me. What distorts people is a lack of love.

The revelations coming from the light seemed to go on and on, then I asked the light, "Does this mean that humankind will be saved?"

Then, like a trumpet blast with a shower of spiraling lights, the Great Light spoke, saying, "Remember this and never forget; you save, redeem and heal yourself. You always have. You always will. You were created with the power to do so from before the beginning of the world."

In that instant I realized even more. I realized that WE HAVE ALREADY BEEN SAVED, and we saved ourselves because we were designed to self-correct like the rest of God's universe. This is what the second coming is about.

I thanked the light of God with all my heart. The best thing I could come up with was these simple words of total appreciation: "Oh dear God, dear Universe, dear Great Self, I love my life."

The light seemed to breathe me in even more deeply. It was as if the light was completely absorbing me. The love light is, to this day, indescribable. I entered into another realm, more profound than the last, and became aware of something more, much more. It was an enormous stream of light, vast and full, deep in the heart of life. I asked what this was. The light responded, "This is the RIVER OF LIFE. Drink of this manna water to your heart's content." So I did. I took one big drink and then another. To drink of life Itself! I was in ecstasy. Then the light said, "You have a desire." The light knew all about me, everything past, present and future. "Yes!" I whispered.

I asked to see the rest of the universe; beyond our solar system, beyond all human illusion. The light then told me that I could go with the Stream. I did, and was carried through the light at the end of the tunnel. I felt and heard a series of very soft sonic booms. What a rush!

Suddenly I seemed to be rocketing away from the planet on this stream of life. I saw the earth fly away. The solar system, in all its splendor, whizzed by and disappeared. At faster than light speed, I flew through the center of the galaxy, absorbing more knowledge as I went. I learned that this galaxy, and all of the universe, is bursting with many different varieties of LIFE. I saw many worlds. The good news is that we are not alone in this universe!

As I rode this stream of consciousness through the center of the galaxy, the stream was expanding in awesome fractal waves of energy. The super clusters of galaxies with all their ancient wisdom flew by. At first I thought I was going somewhere; actually travelling. But then I realized that, as the stream was expanding, my own consciousness was also expanding to take in everything in the universe! All creation passed by me. It was an unimaginable wonder! I truly was a wonder child; a babe in Wonderland!

It seemed as if all the creations in the universe soared by me and vanished in a speck of light. Almost immediately, a second light appeared. It came from all sides, and was so different; a light made up of more than every frequency in the universe. I felt and heard several velvety sonic booms again. My consciousness, or being, was expanding to interface with the entire holographic universe and more. As I passed into the second light, the awareness came to me that I had just transcended the truth. Those are the best words I have for it, but I will try to explain. As I passed into the second light, I expanded beyond the first light. I found myself in a profound stillness, beyond all silence. I could see or perceive FOREVER, beyond infinity. I was in the void. I was in pre-creation, before the Big Bang. I had crossed over the beginning of time - the first word - the first vibration. I was in the eye of creation. I felt as if I was touching the face of God. It was not a religious feeling. Simply I was at one with absolute life and consciousness.

When I say that I could see or perceive forever, I mean that I could experience all of creation generating itself. It was without beginning and without end. That's a mind-expanding thought, isn't it? Scientists perceive the Big Bang as a single event which created the universe. I saw that the Big Bang is only one of an infinite number of Big Bangs creating universes endlessly and simultaneously. The only images that even come close in human terms would be those created by supercomputers using fractal geometry equations.

The ancients knew of this. They said Godhead periodically created new universes by breathing out, and de-creating other universes by breathing in. These epochs were called yugas. Modern science called this the Big Bang. I was in absolute, pure consciousness. I could see or perceive all the Big Bangs or yugas creating and de-creating themselves. Instantly I entered into them all simultaneously. I saw that each and every little piece of creation has the power to create. It is very difficult to try to explain this. I am still speechless about this.

It took me years after I returned to assimilate any words at all for the void experience. I can tell you this now; the void is less than nothing, yet more than everything that is! The void is absolute zero; chaos forming all possibilities. It is absolute consciousness; much more than even universal intelligence.

Where is the void? I know. The void is inside and outside everything. You, right now even while you live, are always inside and outside the void simultaneously. You don't have to go anywhere or die to get there. The void is the vacuum or nothingness between all physical manifestations; the SPACE between atoms and their components. Modern science has begun to study this space between everything. They call it zero-point. Whenever they try to measure it, their instruments go off the scale, or to infinity, so to speak. They have no way, as of yet, to measure infinity accurately. There is more of the zero space in your own body and the universe than anything else!

What mystics call the void is not a void. It is so full of energy, a different kind of energy that has created everything that we are. Everything since the Big Bang is vibration, from the first word, which is the first vibration.

The Biblical "I am" really has a question mark after it "I am? What am I?" So creation is God exploring God's Self through every way imaginable, in an ongoing, infinite exploration through every one of us. Through every piece of hair on your head, through every leaf on every tree, through every atom, God is exploring God's Self, the great "I am". I began to see that everything that is, is the Self, literally, your Self, my Self. Everything is the great Self. That is why God knows even when a leaf falls. That is possible because wherever you are is the center of the universe. Wherever any atom is, that is the center of the universe. There is God in that, and God in the void.

As I was exploring the void and all the yugas or creations, I was completely out of time and space as we know it. In this expanded state, I discovered that creation is about absolute pure consciousness, or God, coming into the experience of life as we know it. The void itself is devoid of experience. It is pre-life, before the first vibration. Godhead is about more than life and death. Therefore there is even more than life and death to experience in the universe!

I was in the void and I was aware of everything that had ever been created. It was like I was looking out of God's eyes. I had become God. Suddenly I wasn't me anymore. The only thing I can say, I was looking out of God's eyes. And suddenly I knew why every atom was, and I could see everything.

The interesting point was that I went into the void, I came back with this understanding that God is not there. God is here. That's what it is all about. So this constant search of the human race to go out and find God ... God gave everything to us, everything is here - this is where it's at. And what we are into now is God's exploration of God through us. People are so busy trying to become God that they ought to realize that we are already God and God is becoming us. That's what it is really about.

When I realized this, I was finished with the void, and wanted to return to this creation, or yuga. It just seemed like the natural thing to do.

Then I suddenly came back through the second light, or the Big Bang, hearing several more velvet booms. I rode the stream of consciousness back through all of creation, and what a ride it was! The superclusters of galaxies came through me with even more insights. I passed through the center of our galaxy, which is a black hole. Black holes are the great processors or recyclers of the universe. Do you know what is on the other side of a black hole? We are; our galaxy; which has been reprocessed from another universe.

In its total energy configuration, the galaxy looked like a fantastic city of lights. All energy this side of the Big Bang is light. Every sub-atom, atom, star, planet, even consciousness itself is made of light and has a frequency and/or particle. Light is living stuff. Everything is made of light, even stones. So everything is alive. Everything is made from the light of God; everything is very intelligent.

The Light of Love

As I rode the stream on and on, I could eventually see a huge light coming. I knew it was the first light; the Higher Self light matrix of our solar system. Then the entire solar system appeared in the light, accompanied by one of those velvet booms.

I saw that the solar system we live in is our larger, local body. This is our local body and we are much bigger than we imagine. I saw that the solar system is our body. I am a part of this, and the earth is this great created being that we are, and we are the part of it that knows that it is. But we are only that part of it. We are not everything, but we are that part of it that knows that it is.

I could see all the energy that this solar system generates, and it is an incredible light show! I could hear the music of the spheres. Our solar system, as do all celestial bodies, generates a unique matrix of light, sound and vibratory energies. Advanced civilizations from other star systems can spot life as we know it in the universe by the vibratory or energy matrix imprint. It is child's play. The earth's wonder child (human beings) make an abundance of sound right now, like children playing in the backyard of the universe.

I rode the stream directly into the center of the light. I felt embraced by the light as it took me in with its breath again, followed by another soft sonic boom. I was in this great light of love with the stream of life flowing through me. I have to say again, it is the most loving, non-judgmental light. It is the ideal parent for this wonder child.

"What now?" I wondered.

The light explained to me that there is no death; we are immortal beings. We have already been alive forever! I realized that we are part of a natural living system that recycles itself endlessly. I was never told that I had to come back. I just knew that I would. It was only natural, from what I had seen.

I don't know how long I was with the light, in human time. But there came a moment when I realized that all my questions had been answered and my return was near. When I say that all my questions were answered on the other side, I mean to say just that. All my questions have been answered. Every human has a different life and set of questions to explore. Some of our questions are universal, but each of us is exploring this thing we call life in our own unique way. So is every other form of life, from mountains to every leaf on every tree.

And that is very important to the rest of us in this universe. Because it all contributes to the Big Picture, the fullness of life. We are literally God exploring God's Self in an infinite Dance of Life. Your uniqueness enhances all of life.

My Return to Earth

As I began my return to the life cycle, it never crossed my mind, nor was I told, that I would return to the same body. It just did not matter. I had complete trust in the light and the life process. As the stream merged with the great light, I asked never to forget the revelations and the feelings of what I had learned on the other side. There was a "Yes." It felt like a kiss to my soul.

Then I was taken back through the light into the vibratory realm again. The whole process reversed, with even more information being given to me. I came back home, and I was given lessons on the mechanics of reincarnation. I was given answers to all those little questions I had:

"How does this work? How does that work?" I knew that I would be reincarnated.

The earth is a great processor of energy, and individual consciousness evolves out of that into each one of us. I thought of myself as a human for the first time, and I was happy to be that. From what I have seen, I would be happy to be an atom in this universe. An atom. So to be the human part of God... this is the most fantastic blessing. It is a blessing beyond our wildest estimation of what blessing can be. For each and every one of us to be the human part of this experience is awesome, and magnificent. Each and every one of us, no matter where we are, screwed up or not, is a blessing to the planet, right where we are.

So I went through the reincarnation process expecting to be a baby somewhere. But I was given a lesson on how individual identity and consciousness evolve. So I reincarnated back into this body.

I was so surprised when I opened my eyes. I do not know why, because I understood it, but it was still such a surprise to be back in this body, back in my room with someone looking over me crying her eyes out. It was my hospice caretaker. She had given up an hour and a half after finding me dead. She was sure I was dead; all the signs of death were there – I was getting stiff. We do not know how long I was dead, but we do know that it was an hour and a half since I was found. She honored my wish to have my newly dead body left alone for a few hours as much as she could. We had an amplified stethoscope and many ways of checking out the vital functions of the body to see what was happening. She can verify that I really was dead. It was not a near-death experience. I experienced death itself for at least an hour and a half. She found me dead and checked the stethoscope, blood pressure and heart rate monitor for an hour and a half. Then I awakened and saw the light outside. I tried to get up to go to it, but I fell out of the bed. She heard a loud "clunk", ran in and found me on the floor.

When I recovered, I was very surprised and yet very awed about what had happened to me. At first all the memory of the trip that I have now was not there. I kept slipping out of this world and kept asking, "Am I alive?" This world seemed more like a dream than that one.

Within three days, I was feeling normal again, clearer, yet different than I had ever felt in my life. My memory of the journey came back later. I could see nothing wrong with any human being I had ever seen. Before that I was really judgmental. I thought a lot of people were really screwed up, in fact I thought that everybody was screwed up but me. But I got clear on all that.

About three months later a friend said I should get tested, so I went and got the scans and so forth. I really felt good, so I was afraid of getting bad news. I remember the doctor at the clinic looking at the before and after scans, saying, "Well, there is nothing here now."

I said, "Really, it must be a miracle?"

He said, "No, these things happen, they are called spontaneous remission." He acted very unimpressed. But here was a miracle, and I was impressed, even if no one else was.

The Lessons I Learned

The mystery of life has very little to do with intelligence. The universe is not an intellectual process at all. The intellect is helpful; it is brilliant, but right now that is all we process with, instead of our hearts and the wiser part of ourselves.

The center of the earth is this great transmuter of energy, just as you see in pictures of our earth's magnetic field. That's our cycle, pulling reincarnated souls back in and through it again. A sign that you are reaching human level is that you are beginning to evolve an individual consciousness. The animals have a group soul, and they reincarnate in group souls. A deer is pretty much going to be a deer forever. But just being born a human, whether deformed or genius, shows that you are on the path to developing an individual consciousness. That is in itself part of the group consciousness called humanity.

I saw that races are personality clusters. Nations like France, Germany and China each have their own personality. Cities have personalities, their local group souls that attract certain people. Families have group souls. Individual identity is evolving like branches of a fractal; the group soul explores in our individuality. The different questions that each of us has are very, very important. This is how Godhead is exploring God's Self - through you. So ask your questions, do your searching. You will find your Self and you will find God in that Self, because it is only the Self.

More than that, I began to see that each one of us humans are soul mates. We are part of the same soul fractaling out in many creative directions, but still the same. Now I look at every human being that I ever see, and I see a soul mate, my soul mate, the one I have always been looking for. Beyond that, the greatest soul mate that you will ever have is yourself. We are each both male and female. We experience this in the womb and we experience this in rein-carnation states. If you are looking for that ultimate soul mate outside of yourself, you may never find it; it is not there. Just as God is not "there." God is here. Don't look "out there" for God. Look here for God. Look through your Self. Start having the greatest love affair you ever had... with your Self. You will love everything out of that.

I had a descent into what you might call hell, and it was very surprising. I did not see Satan or evil. My descent into hell was a descent into each person's customized human misery, ignorance, and darkness of not-knowing. It seemed like a miserable eternity. But each of the millions of souls around me had a little star of light always available. But no one seemed to pay attention to it. They were so consumed with their own grief, trauma and misery. But, after what seemed an eternity, I started calling out to that light, like a child calling to a parent for help. Then the light opened up and formed a tunnel that came right to me and insulated me from all that fear and pain. That is what hell really is.

So what we are doing is learning to hold hands, to come together. The doors of hell are open now. We are going to link up, hold hands, and walk out of hell together.

The light came to me and turned into a huge golden angel. I said, "Are you the angel of death?"

It expressed to me that it was my oversoul, my Higher Self matrix, a super- ancient part of ourselves. Then I was taken to the light.

Soon our science will quantify spirit. Isn't that going to be wonderful? We are coming up with devices now that are sensitive to subtle energy or spirit energy. Physicists use these atomic colliders to smash atoms to see what they are made of. They have got it down to quarks and charm, and all that. Well, one day they are going to come down to the little thing that holds it all together, and they are going to have to call that... God. With atomic colliders they are not only seeing what is in here, but they are creating particles. Thank God most of them are short-lived milliseconds and nanoseconds. We are just beginning to understand that we are creating too, as we go along.

As I saw forever, I came to a realm in which there is a point where we pass all knowledge and begin creating the next fractal, the next level. We have that power to create as we explore. And that is God expanding itself through us.

Since my return I have experienced the light spontaneously, and I have learned how to get to that space almost any time in my meditation. Each one of you can do this. You do not have to die to do this. It is within your equipment; you are wired for it already.

The body is the most magnificent light being there is. The body is a universe of incredible light. Spirit is not pushing us to dissolve this body. That is not what is happening. Stop trying to become God; God is becoming you. Here...

I asked God, "What is the best religion on the planet? Which one is right?"

And Godhead said, with great love, "I don't care." That was incredible grace. What that meant was that we are the caring beings here.

The Ultimate Godhead of all the stars tells us, "It does not matter what religion you are." They come and they go, they change. Buddhism has not been here forever, Catholicism has not been here forever, and they are all about to become more enlightened. More light is coming into all systems now. There is going to be a reformation in spirituality that is going to be just as dramatic as the Protestant Reformation. There will be lots of people fighting about it, one religion against the next, believing that only they are right.

Everyone thinks they own God, the religions and philosophies, especially the religions, because they form big organizations around their philosophy. When Godhead said, "I don't care," I immediately understood that it is for us to care about. It is important, because we are caring beings. It matters to us and that is where it is important. What you have is the energy equation in spirituality. Ultimate Godhead does not care if you are Protestant, Buddhist, or whatever. It is all a blooming facet of the whole. I wish that all religions would realize it and let each other be. It is not the end of each religion, but we are talking about the same God. Live and let live. Each has a different view. And it all adds up to the Big Picture; it is all important.

I went over to the other side with a lot of fears about toxic waste, nuclear missiles, the population explosion, the rainforest. I came back loving every single problem. I love nuclear waste. I love the mushroom cloud; this is the holiest mandala that we have manifested to date, as an archetype. It, more than any religion or philosophy on earth, brought us together all of a sudden, to a new level of consciousness. Knowing that maybe we can blow up the planet fifty times, or 500 times, we finally realize that maybe we are all here together now. For a period they had to keep setting off more bombs to get it in to us. Then we started saying, "We do not need this any more."

Now we are actually in a safer world than we have ever been in, and it is going to get safer.

The clearing of the rain forest will slow down, and in fifty years there will be more trees on the planet than in a long time. If you are into ecology, go for it; you are that part of the system that is becoming aware. Go for it with all your might, but do not be depressed. It is part of a larger thing.

Earth is in the process of domesticating itself. It is never again going to be as wild a place as it once was. There will be great wild places, reserves where nature thrives. Gardening and reserves will be the thing in the future. Population increase is getting very close to the optimal range of energy to cause a shift in consciousness. That shift in consciousness will change politics, money, energy.

What happens when we dream? We are multi-dimensional beings. We can access that through lucid dreaming. In fact, this universe is God's dream. One of the things that I saw is that we humans are a speck on a planet that is a speck in a galaxy that is a speck. Those are giant systems out there, and we are in sort of an average system. But human beings are already legendary throughout the cosmos of consciousness. The little bitty human being of Earth/Gaia is legendary. One of the things that we are legendary for is dreaming. We are legendary dreamers. In fact, the whole cosmos has been looking for the meaning of life, the meaning of it all. And it was the little dreamer who came up with the best answer ever. We dreamed it up. So dreams are important.

After dying and coming back, I really respect life and death. In our DNA experiments we may have opened the door to a great secret. Soon we will be able to live as long as we want to live in this body. After living 150 years or so, there will be an intuitive soul sense that you will want to change channels. Living forever in one body is not as creative as reincarnation, as transferring energy in this fantastic vortex of energy that we are in. We are actually going to see the wisdom of life and death, and enjoy it.

As it is now, we have already been alive forever. This body that you are in, has been alive forever. It comes from an unending stream of life, going back to the Big Bang and beyond. This body gives life to the next life, in dense and subtle energy. This body has been alive forever already.

Bibliography

Abram, David (1996) *The Spell of the Sensuous*, Vintage Books, New York

Adler, Gerhard (1979) *Dynamics of the Self*, Coventure, London

Ali, Ayaan Hirsi (2010) *Nomad, From Islam to America: A Personal Journey through the Clash of Civilizations*, Simon and Schuster Ltd., London

Anderson, William (1985) *The Rise of the Gothic*, Huchinson Ltd., London

Anderson, William and Clive Hicks (1990) *Green Man, The Archetype of our Oneness with the Earth*, HarperCollins, London and San Francisco

Annan, Kofi (2012) *Interventions: A Life in War and Peace*, Allen Lane, London

Apuleius (1950) *The Golden Ass*, Penguin Books Ltd., London

Armstrong, Karen (1993) *The End of Silence, Women and the Priesthood*, Fourth Estate, London

Aurobindo, Sri (1990) *The Life Divine*, Lotus Light Publications, Wilmot, WI

Bache, Christopher (2000) *Dark Night, Early Dawn*, State University of New York Press

Baker, Ian A. (2000) *The Dalai Lama's Secret Temple*, Thames and Hudson, London

Barfield, Owen (1988) *Saving the Appearances, A Study in Idolatry*, Second Edition, the Wesleyan University Press, Middletown, Conn. USA.

Baring, Anne & Cashford, Jules (1993) *The Myth of the Goddess: Evolution of an Image*, Penguin Arkana, London

Bayley, Harold (1912) *The Lost Language of Symbolism*, Vol.1, Williams and Norgate, London

Berry, Thomas (1988) *The Dream of the Earth*, Sierra Club Books, San Francisco,
(2006) *Evening Thoughts*, Sierra Club Books, San Francisco

Bertell, Rosalie (2000) *Planet Earth, the Latest Weapon of War*, The Women's Press, London.

Betty, Stafford Ph.D. (2011) *The Afterlife Unveiled*, O Books, Ropley, UK

Bettenson, Henry Bettenson ed. & trs. (1970), *The Later Christian Fathers*, OUP

Bird, Kai and Sherwin, Martin J. (2005) *American Prometheus, The Triumph and Tragedy of J. Robert Oppenheimer*, Alfred Knopf, New York

Blake, William, letter to Thomas Butts, 22 November, 1802, *Complete Poetry and Prose*, ed. Geoffrey Keynes

Boethius (1969) *The Consolation of Philosophy*, trs. E.V. Watts, Penguin Books Ltd., London

Bohm, David (1980) *Wholeness and the Implicate Order*, Routledge & Kegan Paul Ltd., London,

Bolte Taylor, Jill PH.D (2008) *My Stroke of Insight*, Hodder and Stoughton Ltd., London

Bourgeault, Cynthia (2003) *The Wisdom Way of Knowing*, John Wiley & Sons, San Francisco
(2010) *The Meaning of Mary Magdalene*, Shambhala Publications Inc., Boston

Bucke, Maurice Richard (1923) *Cosmic Consciousness*, Dutton & Co., New York

Budge, E.A. Wallis (1969) *The Gods of the Egyptians*, Dover Publications, New York

Campbell, Joseph (1958-68) *The Masks of God*, Vol. 1-1V, Secker & Warburg, London
(1968) *The Hero with a Thousand Faces*, Princeton University Press
(1984) *The Way of the Animal Powers*, Times Books, London
(1986) *The Inner Reaches of Outer Space*, Alfred van der Marck Editions, New York
(1988) *The Power of Myth*, Doubleday, New York

Carson, Rachel (1950) *The Sea Around Us*, OUP
(1963) *Silent Spring*, Hamish Hamilton, London

Cashford, Jules (2003) *The Moon: Myth and Image*, Cassell Illustrated, London

Chauvet Cave, (1996) Thames and Hudson Ltd., London

Cohn, Carol (1987) *Sex and Death in the Rational World of Defense Intellectuals, Signs, Journal of Women in Culture and Society*, University of Chicago Press

Collins, Cecil (2004) *Angels*, edited by Stella Astor, Fool's Press, London

Cook, Francis H. (1977) *Hua-yen Buddhism: The Jewel Net of Indra*, Pennsylvania State University

Cooper, Rabbi David (1997) *God is a Verb*, Riverhead Books, New York

Corbin, Henri, (1969) *Creative Imagination in the Sufism of Ibn Arabi*, Bollingen Series XCI, Princeton University Press

Crick, Francis (1994) *The Astonishing Hypothesis*, Simon and Schuster, London

Davidson, John (1992) *The Robe of Glory*, An Ancient Parable of the Soul, Element Books, UK

Devereux, Paul (2010) *Sacred Geography: Deciphering Hidden Codes in the Landscape,* Octopus Publishing Group, London

Diköter, Frank (2011) *Mao's Great Famine*, Bloomsbury Books Ltd., London

Douglas-Klotz, Neil (1990) *Prayers of the Cosmos: Meditations on the Aramaic Words of Jesus*, HarperSanFrancisco

Dreams: Visions of the Night, Thames and Hudson, London (no date) ed. Jill Purce

Dunne, Claire (2000) *Carl Jung, Wounded Healer of the Soul*, Parabola Books, New York

Edinger, Edward (1984) *The Creation of Consciousness: Jung's Myth for Modern Man*, Inner City Books, Toronto

Edwards, Lawrence (2013) *Awakening Kundalini*, Sounds True Publications, Boulder, Colorado

Einstein, Albert (2000) *The Expanded Quotable Einstein*, collected and edited by Alice Calaprice, The Hebrew University of Jerusalem and Princeton University Press, Princeton, New Jersey

Einstein, Albert (1954) *Ideas and Opinions*, Crown Publishers, New York

Eisler, Riane (1988) *The Chalice and the Blade*, Harper & Row, San Francisco

ElBaradei, Mohamed (2011) *The Age of Deception*, Bloomsbury Books Ltd., London

Eliade, Mircea (1959) *The Sacred and the Profane*, Harcourt, Brace & World, Inc.

        (1964) *Shamanism; Archaic Techniques in Ecstasy*, Bollingen Foundation, Princeton

Eliot, T.S. (1969) *The Complete Poems and Plays of T.S. Eliot*, Faber & Faber Ltd., London

Eriugena, Joannes Scotus (1976) Uhlfelder, Myra, and Potter Jean A. *Periphyseon: On the Division of Nature*, Book III 678c. Bobbs-Merrill, Indianapolis, republished 2011 by Wipf & Stock Publishers, Eugene, Oregon

Feinstein, Andrew (2011) *The Shadow World: Inside the Global Arms Trade*, Hamish Hamilton, London

Ferguson, Niall (2006) *The War of the World*, Allen Lane, London

Fox, Matthew (1983) *Original Blessing*, Bear & Co. Santa Fe

Frankl, Viktor E. (2003) *Man's Search for Meaning*, Rider, London

Freeman Charles (2003) *The Closing of the Western Mind*, Pimlico, London

        (2008) *AD 381: Heretics, Pagans and the Christian State*, Pimlico, London

Freeman, Mara (2001) *Kindling the Celtic Spirit*, HarperSan Francisco,

French, Marilyn (2002) *From Eve to Dawn: A History of Women*, McArthur & Co., Toronto

Fromm, Erich (1977) *The Anatomy of Human Destructiveness*, Penguin Books Ltd., London

Gerhardt, Sue (2004) *Why Love Matters: How Affection Shapes a Baby's Brain*, Brunner-Routledge, London

Gerzon, Mark (2006) *Leading Through Conflict*, Harvard Business School Press

Gilbert, G.M. (1961) *Nuremberg Diary*, New York, Signet

Gimbutas, Marija (1974 &1982) *The Goddesses and Gods of Old Europe*, Thames & Hudson, London

        (1989) *The Language of the Goddess*, Harper & Row, San Francisco

Gollancz, Victor (1956) *The Devil's Repertoire*

Goodchild, Veronica (2012) *Songlines of the Soul, Pathways to a New Vision for a New Century*, Nicolas-Hays Inc., Fort Worth, Florida

Goswami, Amit (1995) *The Self-aware Universe: How Consciousness Creates the Material World.* Tarcher/Putnam, New York

        (2000) *The Visionary Window*, Quest Books, Wheaton, Ill.

Gray, Colin (2005) *Another Bloody Century*, Weidenfeld & Nicolson Ltd., London

Gray, John (2007) *Black Mass: Apocalyptic Religion and the Death of Utopia*, Penguin Books Ltd., London

Gray, William G. (1968) *The Ladder of Lights*, Helios Book Service Ltd., Cheltenham
Griffiths, Dom Bede (1976) *Return to the Centre*, Collins, St. James's Place, London and
    Templegate, Springfield, Ill. 1977
                        (1992) *A New Vision of Reality*, HarperCollins, London
Grof, Stanislav (1985) *Beyond the Brain*, State University of New York Press
                        (1993) Grof and Hal Z. Bennett, *The Holotropic Mind: Three levels of Human
    Consciousness and How They Shape Our Lives*, HarperCollins, New York
                        (1998) *The Cosmic Game*, State University of New York Press
                        (2001) *LSD Psychotherapy*, published by the Multidisciplinary Association for
    Psychedelic Studies, Sarasota, Florida, USA.
Gurmukh Kaur Khalsa (2009) *Kundalini Rising, Exploring the Energy of Awakening*,
    Sounds True Publications, Boulder, Colorado
Haisch, Bernard (2006) *The God Theory*, Weiser Books, San Francisco
Halevi, Z'ev ben Shimon (1986) *The Work of the Kabbalist*, Samuel Weiser Inc., Maine
Happold, F.C. (1963) *Mysticism, A Study and an Anthology*, Penguin Books Ltd., Harmondsworth
Harvey, Andrew (1983) *A Journey in Ladakh*, Jonathan Cape Ltd., London
                        (1991) *Hidden Journey*, Bloomsbury Publishing Co., Ltd., London
Hastings, Max (2011) *All Hell Let Loose: The World at War 1939–1945*, HarperPress, London
Hillman, James (1972) *The Myth of Analysis, Three Essays in Archetypal Psychology*, Part Three:
    On Psychological Femininity, Northwestern University Press
Hochschild, Adam (2009) *Bury the Chains*, Macmillan, London
Hoffman, David E. (2009) *The Dead Hand, Reagan, Gorbachov and the Untold Story of the Cold War
    Arms Race*, Doubleday, New York. Icon Books, London, 2011
Hoffman, Edward (1981) *The Way of Splendor: Jewish Mysticism and Modern Psychology*, Shambala,
    Boulder, Colorado
Holland, Jack (2006) *Misogyny, The World's Oldest Prejudice*, Constable and Robinson Ltd., London
Howell, Alice O. (1988) *The Dove in the Stone*, Quest Books, Wheaton, Ohio
Hubbard, Barbara Marx (2012) *Birth 2012: Humanity's Great Shift to the Age of Conscious Evolution*,
                        (2012) *Emergence: The Shift from Ego to Essence*, Shift Books, US
Jaffé, Aniela (1989) *From the Life and Work of C. G. Jung*, translated by R.F.C. Hull and Murray Stein,
    Daimon Verlag, Einsiedeln, Switzerland
James, William (1929) *The Varieties of Religious Experience*, Longmans, Green and Co. London
    & New York
Jefferies, Richard (1947) *The Story of My Heart*, Constable & Co. Ltd., London
Johnson, Chalmers (2004) *The Sorrows of Empire: Militarism, Secrecy and the End of the Republic*,
    Henry Holt & Company LLC, New York
Juliana of Norwich (1977) *Revelations of Divine Love*, trs. M. L. Del Mastro, Doubleday,New York
Jung, C.G. (1963) *Memories, Dreams, Reflections*, Collins and Routledge & Kegan Paul Ltd., London
Jung, C.G. *Collected Works*, trs. R.F.C. Hull, Routledge & Kegan Paul Ltd., London
                        (1931) *The Secret of the Golden Flower*, translated and explained by Richard Wilhelm, with
    introduction and European commentary by C.G. Jung. trs. Cary F. Baynes
                        (1933) *Modern Man in Search of a Soul*, trs. W.S. Dell & Cary F. Baynes
                        (1973 & 1976) *Letters*, Volumes 1 & 2, Routledge and Kegan Paul Ltd. London
                        (1964) *Conversations with Carl Jung* (based on four filmed interviews), Richard Evans, Van
    Nostrand, Princeton
                        (1964) *Man and His Symbols*, Aldus Books, London
                        (2009)*The Red Book, Liber Novus*, edited and introduced by Sonu Shamdasani,
    W.W. Norton & Co., New York & London
Keen, Sam (1986) *Faces of the Enemy*, Harper & Row, San Francisco
                        (1992) *Fire in the Belly: On Being A Man*, Bantam

King, Ursula (1989) *The Spirit of One Earth: Reflections on Teilhard de Chardin and Global Spirituality*, Paragon House, New York

Kingsley, Peter (1999) *In the Dark Places of Wisdom*, Golden Sufi Press, California

Korten, David (2009) *Mind Before Matter, Visions of a New Science of Consciousness*, ed. John Mack and Trish Pfeiffer, O Books, Winchester, Hampshire

Kovács, Betty J. (2003) *The Miracle of Death*, The Kamlak Center, California

Kübler-Ross, Elisabeth, (1991) *On Life After Death*, Celestial Arts, Berkeley, CA
                    (1975) *On Death and Dying*, Spectrum, US

Lamy, Lucy (1981) *Egyptian Mysteries*, Thames and Hudson, London

Laszlo, Ervin (2006) *Science and the Reenchantment of the Cosmos*, Inner Traditions, Vermont

Laszlo, Ervin and Currivan, Jude (2008) *CosMos: A Co-creator's Guide to the Whole-World* , Hay House, Inc., USA, UK

Lawrence, D.H. *Last Poems, The Complete Poems of D.H. Lawrence*, Vol 1, p. 17

Lawrence, D.H. (1931) *Apocalypse and Other Writings*, Cambridge University Press

Lawrence, D.H. (1993) *The Letters of* vol. VII. eds. Keith Sagar and James T. Boulton, CUP

Leboyer, Frederick 1995) *Birth Without Violence*, trs. Yvonne Fitzgerald, Mandarin Paperbacks, London

Levi, Primo (1988) *The Damned and the Saved*, Abacus Books, London

Levy, Gertrude (1968) *The Gate of Horn*, Faber & Faber Ltd., London

Louth, Andrew, (1989) *Denys the Areopagite*, Morehouse-Barlow, London

Lovelock, James (1991) *Healing Gaia*, Harmony Books, New York

McGilchrist, Iain (2009) *The Master and His Emissary, The Divided Brain and the Making of the Western World*, Yale University Press

McGilchrist, (2010) from his chapter in *A New Renaissance; Transforming Science, Spirit and Society*, ed. David Lorimer and Oliver Robinson, Floris Books Ltd., Edinburgh

MacLean, Paul (1990) *The Triune Brain in Evolution*, Plenum Press, New York,

Marshack, Alexander (1972) *The Roots of Civilization*, Weidenfeld & Nicolson, London

Mascaró, Juan   (1962) trs. and introduction to the *Bhagavad Gita*, Penguin Books, London
              (1965) The *Upanishads*, trs. and introduction, Penguin Books, London

Matt, Daniel (1995) *The Essential Kabbalah, The Heart of Jewish Mysticism*, HarperSanFrancisco

Mead, G.R.S.   (1906 & 1931) *Fragments of a Faith Forgotten*, John M. Watkins, London
              (1947) *Pistis Sophia*, John M. Watkins, London
              (1919) *The Doctrine of the Subtle Body in Western Tradition*, John M. Watkins, London
              (1995) Solos Press, Dorset, UK

Mehta, Vijay (2012) *The Economics of Killing: How the West fuels War and Poverty in the Developing World*, Pluto Press, London

Michell, John (1972) *City of Revelation: on the Proportions and Symbolic Numbers of the Cosmic Temple*, Garnstone Press, London

Miller, Alice (1985) *Thou Shalt Not Be Aware, Society's Betrayal of the Child*, Pluto Press, London

Miller, Arthur I. (2009) *137: Jung, Pauli, and the Pursuit of a Scientific Obsession*, W.W. Norton & Co., New York

Milne, Joseph (2008) *Metaphysics and the Cosmic Order*, Temenos Academy, London

Mitchell, Dr. Edgar (1996) *The Way of the Explorer*, Putnam, New York

Moorjani, Anita (2012) *Dying to be Me*, Hay House, Inc., New York

Nag Hammadi Library (1977) ed. James M. Robinson, E.J. Brill, Leiden

Narby, Jeremy (1998) *The Cosmic Serpent; DNA and the Origins of Knowledge*, Victor Gollancz, London

Naydler, Jeremy (2009) *The Future of the Ancient world: Essays on the History of Consciousness*,
              (1996) *Temple of the Cosmos: Ancient Egyptian Experience of the Sacred*, Inner Traditions, Rochester, Vermont

Neumann, Erich (1955) *The Great Mother, An Analysis of the Archetype*, Pantheon Books Inc., New York

Nilsson, Lennart and Hamberger, Lars (1994 & 2010) *A Child is Born*, Doubleday, London

Odent, Michel (1990) *Water and Sexuality*, Arkana, London

Owen, David (2007and 2012) *The Hubris Syndrome*, Methuen Publishing Ltd., London

Pagels, Elaine (1980) *The Gnostic Gospels*, Weidenfeld and Nicolson Ltd., London

Pearce, Joseph Chilton   (1992) *Evolution's End*, HarperCollins, San Francisco
                (2011) *The Death of Religion and the Rebirth of Spirit: A Return to the* *Intelligence of the Heart*, Inner Traditions, Vermont

Perera, Sylvia Brinton (1981) *Descent to the Goddess*, Inner City Books, Toronto

Pert, Candace (1998) *Molecules of Emotion*, Simon and Schuster Ltd., London

Petit, Ann (2006) *Walking to Greenham*, Honno UK

Pfeiffer, Trish and Mack, John E. MD, editors, (2007) *Mind Before Matter, Visions of a New Science of Consciousness*, O Books, Ropley, Hampshire, UK

Pizan, Christine de (1999) *The Book of the City of Ladies*, Penguin Books Ltd., London

Politkovskaya, Anna (2003) *A Small Corner of Hell, Dispatches from Chechnya*, University of Chicago Press

Prem, Krishna (1958) *The Yoga of the Bhagavat Gita*, John M. Watkins, London

Randall, Edward C. (2010) *Frontiers of the Afterlife*, White Crow Books, UK

Ranke-Heinemann, Uta (1990) *Eunuchs for Heaven*, English trs. André Deutsch Ltd., London

Ravindra, Ravi (2002) *Science and the Sacred: Eternal Wisdom in a Changing World*, Quest Books, Wheaton, Illinois

Rees, Sir Martin (1967) *Before the Beginning*, Simon & Schuster
                (1999) *Just Six Numbers, The Deep Forces that Shape the Universe*, Basic Books, London
                (2003) (Lord Rees) *Our Final Century*, William Heinemann, London

Rilke, Rainer Maria (1947) *Letters1910-1924*, trs. Jane Bannard Green and M.M. Heerter, W.W. Norton & Co., New York

Rinpoche, Sogyal (1992) *The Tibetan Book of Living and Dying*, HarperSanFrancisco

Roberts, Alison (1995 & 2000) *Hathor Rising, The Serpent Power of Ancient Egypt*, and *My Heart, My Mother*, Northgate Press, Devon

Robertson, Seonaid (1963) *Rose Garden and Labyrinth – a Study in Art Education*, Routledge and Kegan Paul Ltd., London

Roy, Arundhati (2002) *The Algebra of Infinite Justice*, HarperCollins (Flamingo) London.

Rudgley, Richard (1998) *Lost Civilisations of the Stone Age*, Arrow Books, London

Russell, Bertrand (1903) *The Free Man's Worship*

Sagar, Keith (2005) *Literature and the Crime Against Nature, from Homer to Hughes*, Chaucer Press, London

Sahtouris, Elisabet (2000) *EarthDance: Living Systems in Evolution*, iUniversity Press, Lincoln Nebraska.

Saul, John Ralston (1995&1998) *The Unconscious Civilization*, House of Anansi Press, Canada, and Penguin Books Ltd., London

St. Augustine, (1958) *The City of God*, Image Books,

Sanders N.K. (1960) *The Epic of Gilgamesh*, Penguin Books Ltd. London

Schaup, Susanne (1997) *Sophia, Aspects of the Divine Feminine*, Nicolas-Hays Inc. Maine

Schell, Jonathan (1982) *The Fate of the Earth*, Pan books Ltd., London

Scholem, Gershom (1954 &1961) *Major Trends in Jewish Mysticism*, Schocken Books Inc., New York

Sebag Montefiore, Simon (2011) *Jerusalem*, Simon and Schuster, New York & London

Servan-Shreiber, David (2004) *Healing Without Freud or Prozac*, Pan Macmillan Ltd., London

Sheldrake, Rupert (2012) *The Science Delusion*, Coronet, London

Sherrard, Philip (1987) *The Rape of Man and Nature*, Golgonooza Press, Ipswich, Suffolk

Shlain, Leonard (1998) *The Alphabet Versus the Goddess*, Viking, New York

Skafte, Dianne (1997) *When Oracles Speak*, Thorsons, London

Sorokin, Pitirim (1992) *The Crisis of Our Age*, Oneworld Publications Ltd., Oxford
Stern, Karl (1985) *The Flight from Woman*, Paragon House Publishers, St. Paul, Minnesota
Strachan, Gordon (2003) *Chartres: Sacred Geometry, Sacred Space*, Floris Books Ltd., Edinburgh,
Swimme, Brian (1996) *The Hidden Heart of the Cosmos*, Orbis Books, New York,
Tarnas, Richard (1991) *The Passion of the Western Mind*, Ballantine Books, New York
    (2006) *Cosmos and Psyche, Intimations of a New World View*, Viking, New York
Teilhard de Chardin, Pierre (1959) *The Phenomenon of Man*, William Collins & Co., Ltd., London
    (1959) *The Future of Man*, William Collins & Co., Ltd., London
    (1977) *Hymn of the Universe*, William Collins Ltd., Fount Paperbacks, London
    (1931) *The Spirit of the Earth*
Thorne, Brian (1998) *Person-Centred Counselling and Christian Spirituality*, Whurr Publishers Ltd.,
  London
Tick, Edward (2005) *War and the Soul, Healing Our Nation's Veterans from Post-Traumatic Disorder*,
  Quest Books, Wheaton, Ill.
Todorov, Tzvetan (2003) *Hope and Memory, Reflections on the Twentieth Century*,
  Princeton University Press
Torjesen, Karen Jo (1995) *When Women Were Priests*, HarperSanFrancisco
Trish Pfeiffer and John E. Mack MD, editors (2007) *Mind Before Matter, Visions of a New Science of
Consciousness*, O Books, Ropley, Hampshire, United Kingdom
Turner, Frederick (1983&1992), *Beyond Geography, The Western Spirit Against the Wilderness*, Rutgers
  University Press
Van Lommel, Dr. Pim (2010) *Consciousness Beyond Life; The Science of the Near-Death Experience*,
  HarperCollins New York
Van Over, Raymond (editor) (1977) *Eastern Mysticism*, Volume One: The Near-East and Asia, New
  American Library Inc., New York
Van Ruysbroeck, Jan (1916) *The Adornment of the Spiritual Marriage, The Book of Truth, The Sparkling
Stone*, Dutton & Co. New York
Vaughan-Lee, Llewellyn (2010) *The Return of the Feminine and the World Soul*,
  The Golden Sufi Press, California
Von Franz, Marie-Louise ed. (1966) *Aurora Consurgens*, Routledge & Kegan Paul, Ltd., London
    (1986) *On Dreams and Death*, Shambhala Publications Inc., Boston,
  Mass., Routledge and Kegan Paul Ltd., London
Waddell, Helen (1927, 1949) *The Wandering Scholars*, Constable & Co., London
Waite, A.E. (1953) *The Hermetic Museum*, London
Wilkins, Eithne (1969) *The Rose Garden Game*, Gollancz, London
Woolger, Roger (2004) *Healing Your Past Lives: Exploring the Many Lives of the Soul*,
  Sounds True, Inc., Boulder Colorado.
Zabkar, Louis V. (1989) *Hymns to Isis in Her Temple at Philae*, Published for Brandeis University Press
  by University Press of New England
Zilboorg, Gregory (1941&1967) *A History of Medical Psychology*, W.W. Norton & Company, New York

Grateful acknowledgement is made to the Institute of HeartMath, Boulder Creek, California, for permission to use the material on the heart and the diagram of the heart's electro-magnetic field in Chapter Sixteen.

Artemis of Ephesus, photograph courtesy Barnaby Rogerson.

A